AF798577

ASCENT®

CENTER FOR TECHNICAL KNOWLEDGE

AutoCAD® 2026 Essentials

Learning Guide

Mixed Units - Edition 1.0

ASCENT - Center for Technical Knowledge®
AutoCAD® 2026
Essentials

Mixed Units - Edition 1.0

Prepared and produced by:

ASCENT Center for Technical Knowledge
630 Peter Jefferson Parkway, Suite 175
Charlottesville, VA 22911

866-527-2368
www.ASCENTed.com

Lead Contributor: Renu Muthoo

ASCENT - Center for Technical Knowledge (a division of Rand Worldwide Inc.) is a leading developer of professional learning materials and knowledge products for engineering software applications. ASCENT specializes in designing targeted content that facilitates application-based learning with hands-on software experience. For over 25 years, ASCENT has helped users become more productive through tailored custom learning solutions.

We welcome any comments you may have regarding this guide, or any of our products. To contact us please email: feedback@ASCENTed.com.

AS-ACD2601-ESS1MU-SG // IS-ACD2601-ESS1MU-SG

Contents

Chapter 2: Basic Drawing and Editing Commands 2-1

Chapter 3: Projects: Creating a Simple Drawing 3-1

Chapter 4: Drawing Precision in AutoCAD 4-1

Chapter 17: Text 17-1

Chapter 18: Hatching 18-1

Preface

The *AutoCAD® 2026: Essentials* guide is designed for those using AutoCAD® 2026 with a Windows operating system. This guide is not designed for the AutoCAD for Mac software.

The objective of *AutoCAD 2026: Essentials* is to enable you to create, modify, and work with a 2D drawing in the AutoCAD software.

This guide covers the essential core topics for working with the AutoCAD software. The guide begins with learning the basic tools for creating and editing 2D drawings. It then continues to explore the tools used to annotate drawings by adding text, hatching, dimensions, and tables. More advanced tools, such as working with blocks and setting up layouts, are introduced to improve your efficiency with the software. Not every command or option is covered, because the intent is to show the essential tools and concepts.

Topics Covered

- Understanding the AutoCAD workspace and user interface
- Using basic drawing, editing, and viewing tools
- Organizing drawing objects on layers
- Using reusable symbols (blocks)
- Preparing a layout to be plotted
- Adding text, hatching, and dimensions

Prerequisites

- Access to the 2026.0 version of the software, to ensure compatibility with this guide. Future software updates that are released by Autodesk may include changes that are not reflected in this guide. The practices and files included with this guide are not compatible with prior versions (e.g., 2025).
- A working knowledge of basic design/drafting procedures and terminology.
- A working knowledge of your operating system.

Note on Software Setup

This guide assumes a standard installation of the software using the default preferences during installation.

Note on Learning Guide Content

ASCENT's learning guides are intended to teach the technical aspects of using the software and do not focus on professional design principles and standards. The practices aim to demonstrate the capabilities and flexibility of the software rather than following specific design codes or standards.

Lead Contributor: Renu Muthoo

Renu is a learning content developer for Autodesk products at ASCENT. She has over 25 years of experience working with Autodesk products and specializes in AutoCAD and design visualization software.

Holding a bachelor's degree in Computer Engineering, Renu began her career as an Instructional Designer, co-authoring 3ds Max and AutoCAD books. At ASCENT, she continues her passion for instructional design by developing off the shelf and custom courseware for AutoCAD, AutoCAD Toolsets (Electrical, Mechanical, Raster Design, and Plant 3D), Autodesk 3ds Max, and other software products. An Autodesk Certified Professional in AutoCAD, Renu also enjoys educating users by sharing her knowledge through webcasts and blogs.

Renu Muthoo has been the Lead Contributor for *AutoCAD: Essentials* since 2015.

In This Guide

The following highlights the key features of this guide.

Feature	Description
Practice Files	The Practice Files page includes a link to the practice files and instructions on how to download and install them. The practice files are required to complete the practices in this guide.
Chapters	A chapter consists of the following: Learning Objectives, Instructional Content, Practices, Chapter Review Questions, and Command Summary. • **Learning Objectives** define the skills you can acquire by learning the content provided in the chapter. • **Instructional Content**, which begins right after Learning Objectives, refers to the descriptive and procedural information related to various topics. Each main topic introduces a product feature, discusses various aspects of that feature, and provides step-by-step procedures on how to use that feature. Where relevant, examples, figures, helpful hints, and notes are provided. • **Practice** for a topic follows the instructional content. Practices enable you to use the software to perform a hands-on review of a topic. It is required that you download the practice files (using the link found on the Practice Files page) prior to starting the first practice. • **Chapter Review Questions**, located close to the end of a chapter, enable you to test your knowledge of the key concepts discussed in the chapter. • **Command Summary** concludes a chapter. It contains a list of the software commands that are used throughout the chapter and provides information on where the command can be found in the software.
Appendices	Appendices provide additional information to the main course content. It could be in the form of instructional content, practices, tables, projects, or skills assessment.

Practice Files

To download the practice files for this guide, use the following steps:

1. Type the URL *exactly as shown below* into the address bar of your Internet browser to access the Course File Download page.

   Note: If you are using the ebook, you do not have to type the URL. Instead, you can access the page by clicking the URL below.

   https://www.ascented.com/getfile/id/paphiniaPF

2. On the Course File Download page, click the **DOWNLOAD NOW** button, as shown below, to download the .ZIP file that contains the practice files.

3. Once the download is complete, unzip the file and extract its contents.

   The recommended practice files folder location is:
   C:\AutoCAD 2026 Essentials and Beyond the Basics Practice Files

   Note: It is recommended that you do not change the location of the practice files folder. Doing so may cause errors when completing the practices.

Stay Informed!
To receive information about upcoming events, promotional offers, and complimentary webcasts, visit:
www.ASCENTed.com/updates

Chapter 1

Getting Started with AutoCAD

In this chapter, you learn how to start the AutoCAD® software, become familiar with the basic layout of the AutoCAD screen, and learn how to access commands, use your pointing device, and understand the AutoCAD Cartesian workspace. You also learn how to open an existing drawing, view the drawing by zooming and panning, and save your work in the AutoCAD software.

Learning Objectives

- Launch the AutoCAD software and identify the features available at startup.
- Identify the basic layout and features of the AutoCAD user interface.
- Locate commands and launch them using various command interfaces.
- Locate points in the AutoCAD Cartesian workspace.
- Open, edit, and close existing drawings.
- Move around a drawing using the navigation options.
- Save drawings in various formats and set the automatic save option.

1.1 Starting the Software

The AutoCAD 2026 software runs on the most recent version of the Windows operating system.

Launch the AutoCAD 2026 software using the Windows desktop icon or the **Start** menu.

- Double-click on (AutoCAD 2026) on the desktop.
- If there is no shortcut on the desktop, click (Start) in the Task bar at the bottom of the screen and select **AutoCAD 2026>AutoCAD 2026**.
- When the AutoCAD software is launched, an initial Start window displays.

  Note: *When launching the software for the first time, you are prompted to migrate custom settings and files from the earlier releases of the software.*

Start Tab

When you launch the software or if you click in the *Start* tab while working in an active drawing, the initial Start window displays, as shown in Figure 1–1.

- By default, the *Start* tab is always available in the *File Tabs* bar (drawing tabs) as you create and open additional drawings.
- While working in a drawing, you can click the *Start* tab to display the initial Start window.
- You can use <Ctrl>+<Home> to jump from an active drawing to the *Start* tab.

Left Pane

- The left pane of the *Start* window provides you with drop-down lists containing options for creating new files from templates, new sheet sets, or opening existing and sample drawings. When you click on **New**, a blank drawing automatically opens based on the most recently used template. (Note that when you are using **New** for the very first time, the AutoCAD default template is used to create the new drawing.) Hover your cursor over the **New** button to display the template name that is used for creating the drawing.
- There are four headings in the left pane: **Recent**, **Autodesk Projects**, **Learning**, and **My Insights**, as shown in Figure 1–1. Clicking a heading opens relevant options and information in the right pane.
- A list of links is also provided to access online services such as **Online help, Customer support,** and **Community forums**, as shown in Figure 1–1.

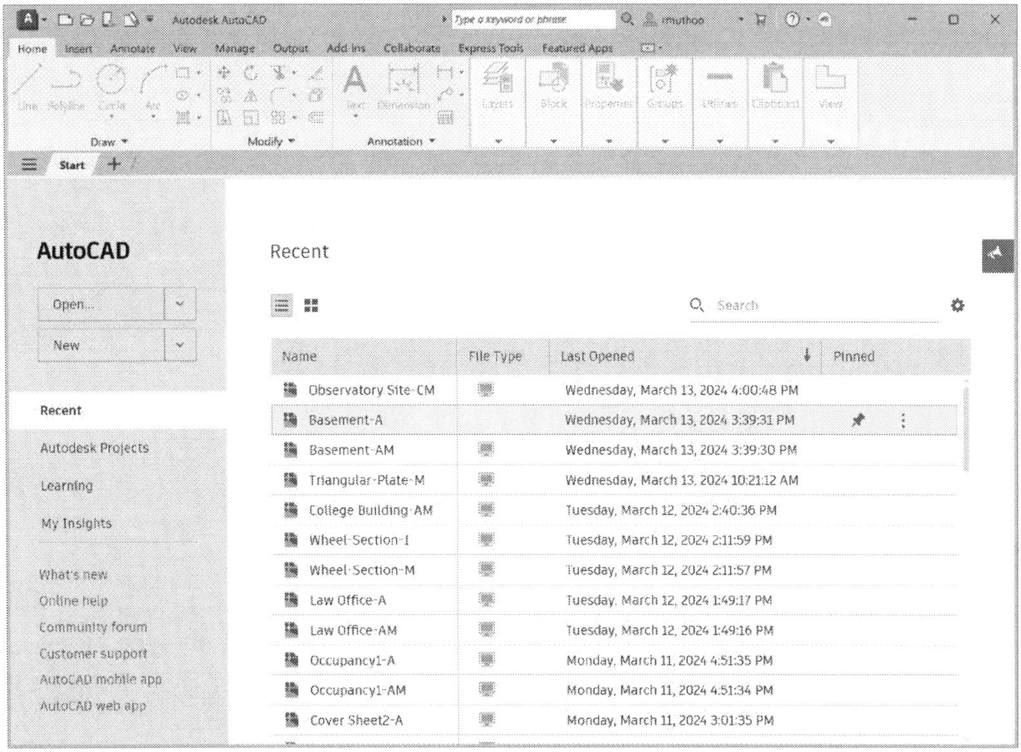

Figure 1–1

Right Pane

- When you click on **Recent** in the left pane, it displays a list of recently used files in the right pane, as shown in Figure 1–1. The recently opened drawings can be displayed in **List view** ( ) or **Grid view** ( ), by selecting their respective icons. You can open drawings directly from the *Recent* list. To easily find a drawing from the list of recently opened drawings, use the **Search** and **Sort** capabilities provided in the *Recent* area, as shown in Figure 1–2.

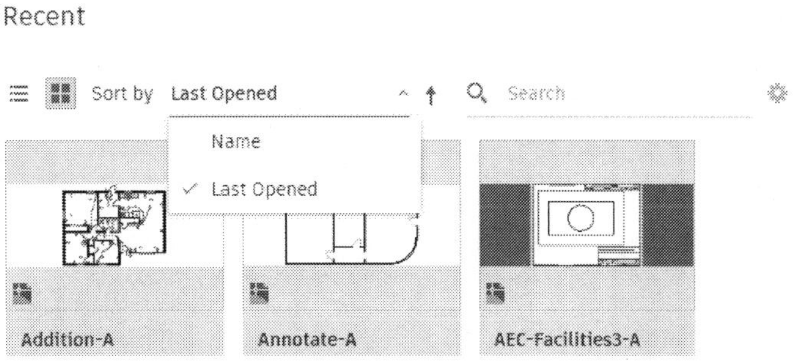

Figure 1–2

- In the *Recent* pane, clicking on the trumpet- icon ( ) opens the *Connect* area, which displays your Autodesk account sign in and provides you with the option of sending feedback to Autodesk, as shown in Figure 1–3.

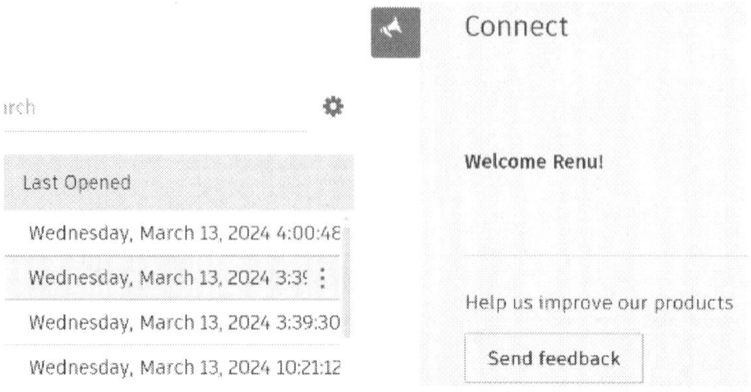

Figure 1–3

- **Autodesk Projects** enables you to access your connected drives, and then open and save files from your desktop to those connected drives. You are required to have the Autodesk Desktop Connector installed on your system for Autodesk Projects to work. The Desktop Connector is an integration service that connects your desktop folder with the Autodesk data management source.
- The **Learning** pane contains videos, tips, and online resources to help you learn about new features in the software and how to start using the software.
- The **My Insights** pane displays your personalized insights. These are based on your usage of your AutoCAD software.

1.2 User Interface

The interface includes the main components that are used to operate the AutoCAD software. By default, the display of the interface uses the **Dark** color theme. You can change it to the **Light** color theme by right-clicking anywhere in the drawing window to display a shortcut menu and then selecting **Options** to open the *Options* dialog box. In the *Display* tab, in the *Window Elements* area, expand the *Color theme* drop-down list and select **Light**, as shown in Figure 1–4, then click **OK** for the background color of the interface components to change to light. The light color scheme is used throughout this guide for printing clarity.

> ***Note:*** *You are required to have a drawing open to access the interface elements. Click* ***New*** *in the Start window to have a drawing open.*

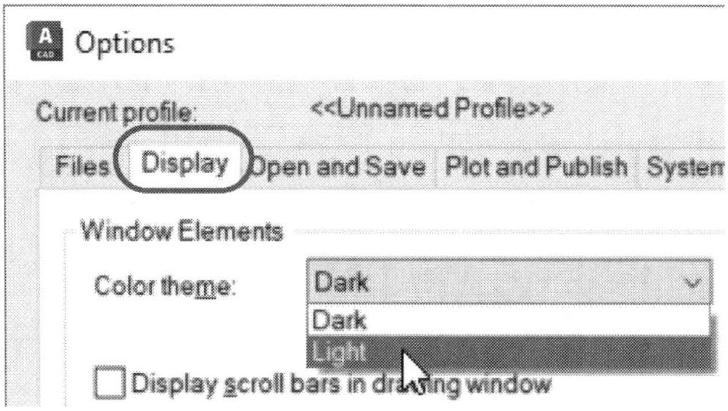

Figure 1–4

To change the drawing window color, in the *Options* dialog box>*Display* tab, click **Colors** and in the *Drawing Window Colors* dialog box, for *2D model space*, change the *Color* to **White**. Click **Apply & Close** in the *Drawing Window Colors* dialog box and click **OK** in the *Options* dialog box.

The software interface is shown in Figure 1–5. The drawing window color has been changed to white and the drawing grid display has been turned off for printing clarity.

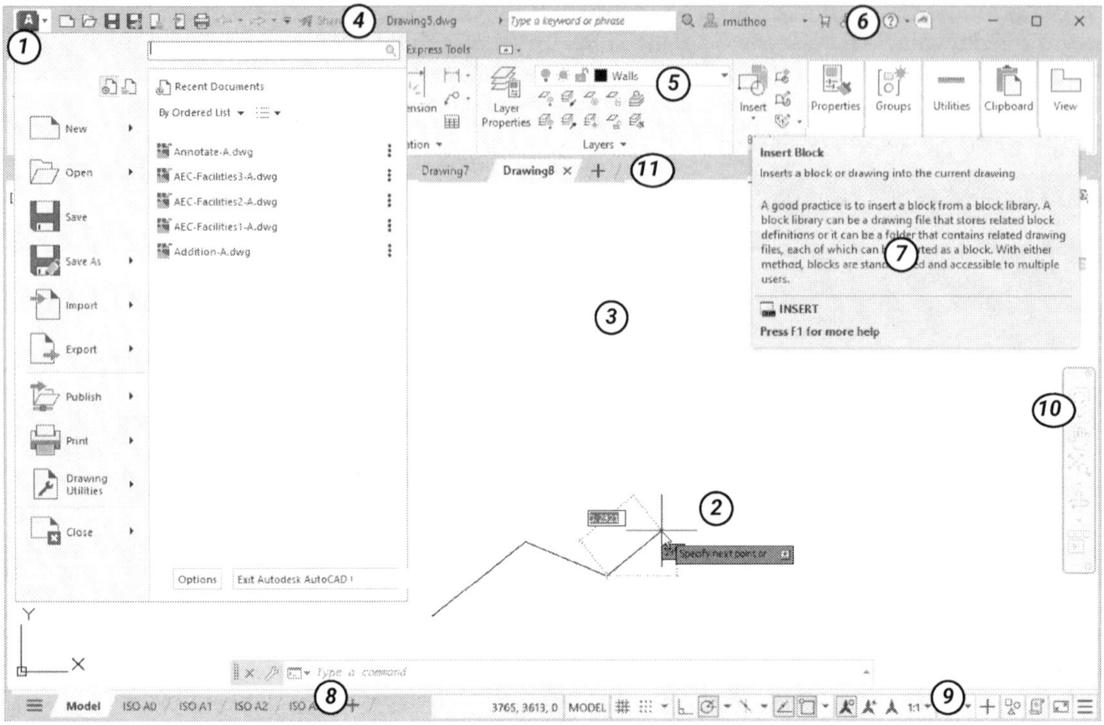

Figure 1–5

1. Application Menu

The *Application Menu* provides access to AutoCAD file commands, settings, and documents.

Click  (Application Menu) to expand the *Application Menu* and display its contents.

2. Crosshairs and Prompts

The *Crosshairs* indicate the current cursor location. As you draw, prompts display near the cursor to explain how to complete each command. It displays badges that provide additional information when you are working in a command. This can help you to successfully complete the command.

3. Drawing Window

The *Drawing Window* is the area of the screen in which the drawing displays. Near the lower left corner of the window a horizontal line labeled **X** and a vertical line labeled **Y** might be displayed. This is called the UCS icon and indicates the current drawing plane. Several drawing windows can remain open at the same time. They can be resized, minimized, and maximized.

- By default, the background of the drawing window is dark with a light gray grid. This can be changed in the *Options* dialog box>*Display* tab by clicking **Colors**.

4. Quick Access Toolbar

The *Quick Access Toolbar* provides access to commonly used commands, such as **New**, **Open**, and **Save**, as shown in Figure 1–6.

Figure 1–6

5. Ribbon

The ribbon contains the AutoCAD tools in a series of tabs and panels, as shown in Figure 1–7. Clicking on a tab displays a series of panels. The panels contain a variety of tools, which are grouped by function.

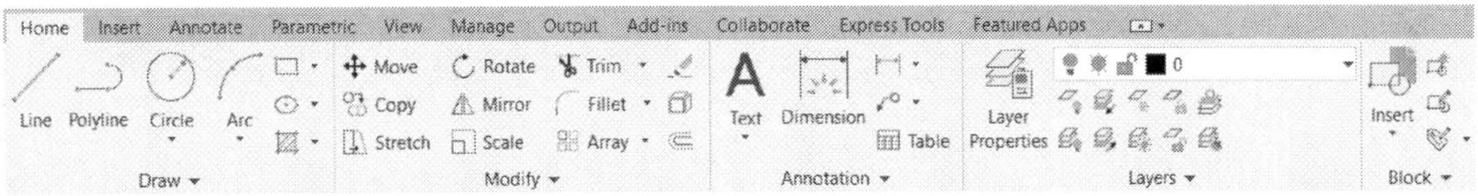

Figure 1–7

6. InfoCenter

The *InfoCenter* (shown in Figure 1–8) provides you with tools that enable you to quickly access the online Help system, stay connected with the online AutoCAD community, and access the Autodesk App Store. You are required to be signed into your Autodesk account to access various online services and sync your settings.

Figure 1–8

- Clicking  opens the initial help screen, which displays videos about new features and getting started with the software. The help screen also includes a heading called **Have You Tried**, which lists various topic links. Clicking on a link opens a help page that has more information about the listed feature. These topics include new features that you might not be aware of and other topics that are based on user feedback received by Autodesk.
- You can directly open the help information about a specific command by hovering your cursor over the command icon in the ribbon and then clicking <F1> on your keyboard.

- You can search for a specific help topic by entering a keyword and selecting from the list of available related documents. If you are in the Help window and want to locate a command icon in the ribbon, *Status Bar*, and the *Application Menu*, click **Find** next to the command's icon in the Help window, as shown in Figure 1–9. A red animated arrow displays in the interface identifying the location of the command, as shown in Figure 1–9.

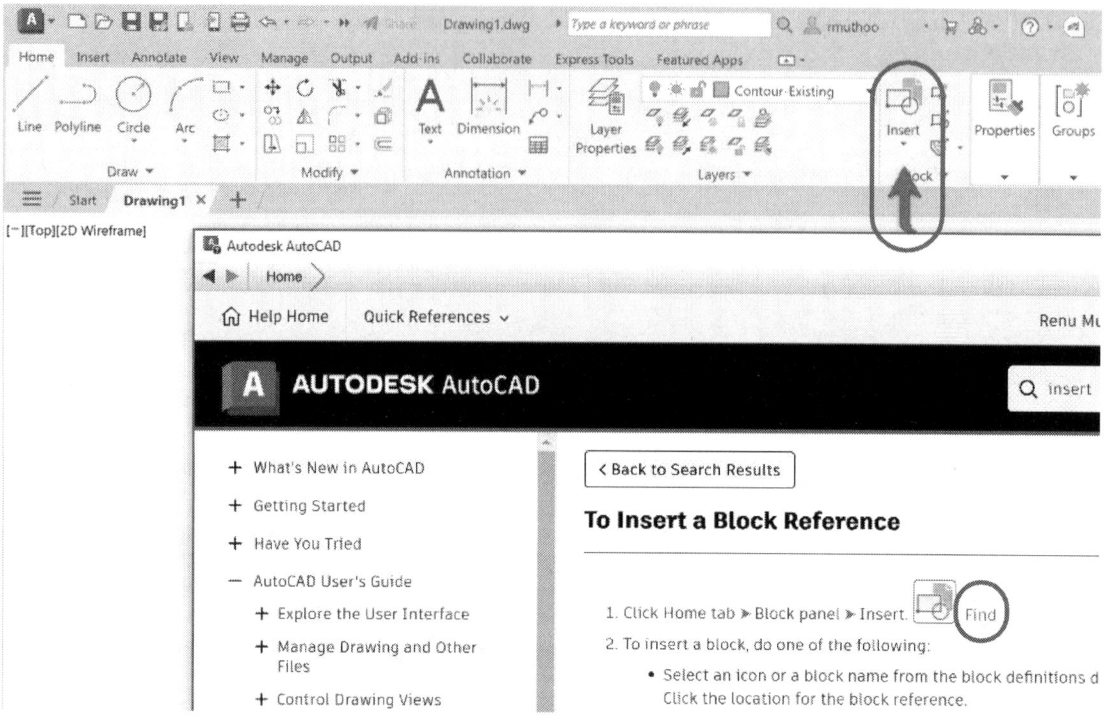

Figure 1–9

- In the Infocenter, use the (Autodesk Assistant) to find tailored support including finding solutions about the AutoCAD software questions, chat with AutoCAD support agents, request to be called back, and log a support case. Click (Autodesk Assistant) to open the Autodesk Assistant palette to ask a question related to the AutoCAD software, as shown on the left in Figure 1–10. It provides you with AI generated answers, as shown on the right in Figure 1–10.

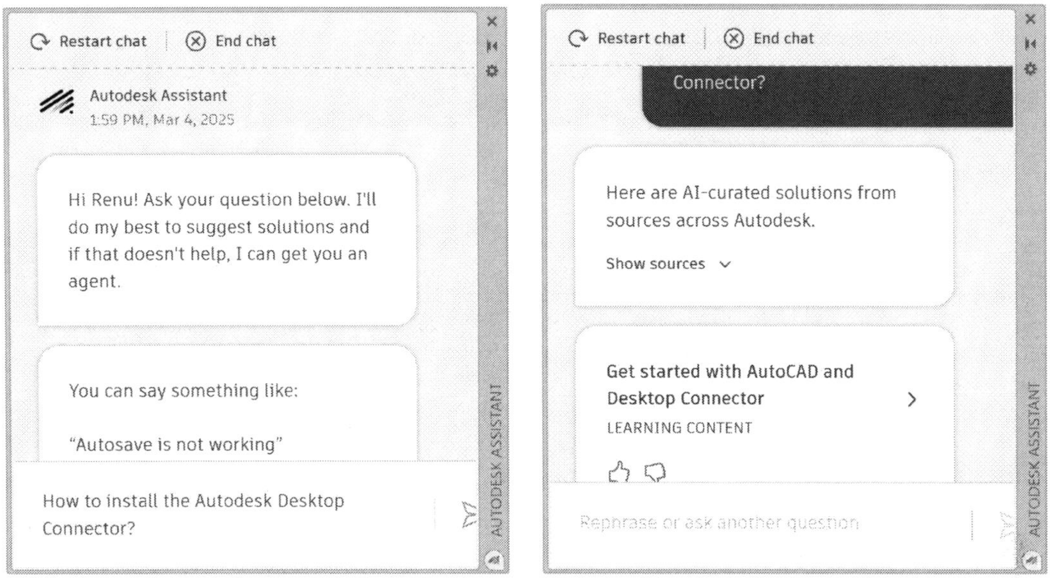

Figure 1–10

7. Tooltips

When you hover the cursor over a tool, a *Tooltip* displays the name of the tool and a short description. Continuing to hover the cursor on the tool displays an additional extended description, as shown in Figure 1–11. These tooltips provide information about tools, commands, and drawing objects. With the tooltip displayed, press <F1> to open the Help window and display the help information related to the tool.

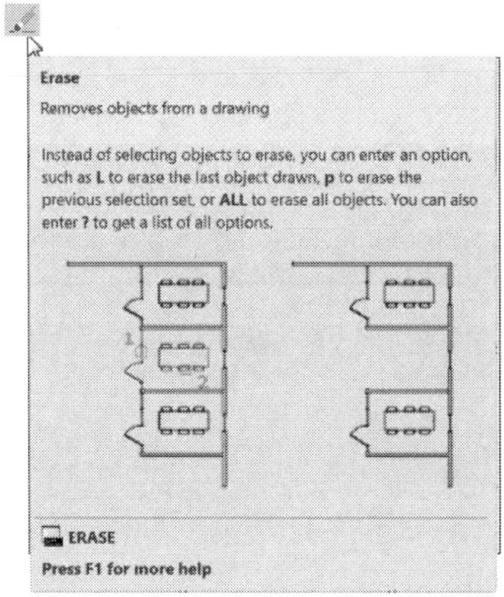

Figure 1–11

You can control the display of tooltips using the *Options* dialog box ((Application Menu)>**Options**), in the *Display* tab>*Window Elements* area. You can also set the delay to display the tooltip and the extended description, as shown in Figure 1–12.

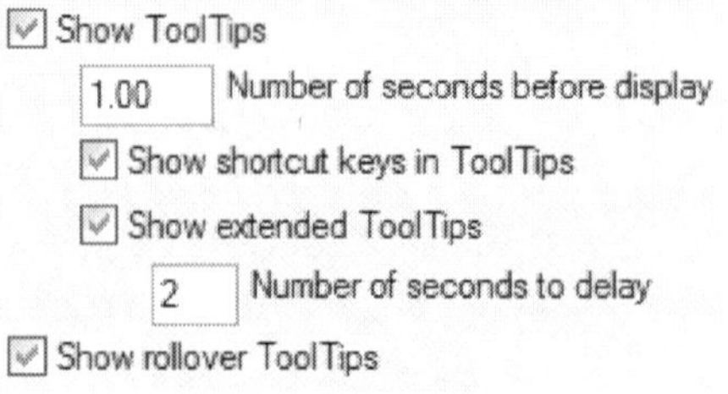

Figure 1–12

8. Command Line

Command prompts also display in the Command Line, which is by default, a text window located at the bottom of the screen, as shown in Figure 1–13. You can dock and undock the Command Line by clicking on the left edge and dragging it around. The command history has a gray background to distinguish it from the active command line.

Figure 1–13

9. Status Bar

The *Status Bar* enables you to change many of the AutoCAD software's drafting settings. All of the tools are located in the (Customization) list and their icons can be displayed or removed from the *Status Bar* by selecting them in the list. After displaying the tool icons in the Status Bar, you are required to toggle them on to take affect. The icons display with a blue background box when they are toggled on.

Along the left side of the *Status Bar* icons, the *Model* tab and one or more layout tabs display, as shown in Figure 1–14. If the *Model* and layout tabs are not displayed, set the **LAYOUTTAB** system variable to **1**. In the beginning of the layout tab bar is the (Layout tab menu) from where you can switch between layouts, create a layout, and publish layouts, etc.

Figure 1–14

10. Navigation Bar

The *Navigation Bar* enables you to access the various methods of moving around in the drawing, such as **Zoom** and **Pan**, as shown in Figure 1–15. If the *Navigation Bar* is not displayed, in the ribbon, go to the *View* tab>*Viewport Tools* panel and click (Navigation Bar).

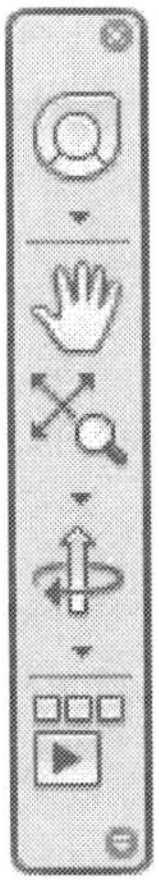

Figure 1–15

11. File Tabs

The drawing's *File* tabs (shown in Figure 1–16) are located near the top of the drawing window. They provide a quick way of switching between open drawings, creating new ones, opening, saving, or closing the required drawings. The (Files tab menu) and the *Start* tab persist in the *File Tabs* bar. Clicking (Files tab menu) displays a complete list of open files along with options to create, open, save, and close the drawing files. Clicking the *Start* tab displays the initial *Start* window.

Figure 1–16

1.3 Working with Commands

Most commands in the AutoCAD software are accessed using the ribbon. For example, to access the **Line** command in the ribbon, in the *Home* tab>*Draw* panel, click (Line), as shown in Figure 1–17. Several of the file commands are available in the *Quick Access Toolbar* or in the *Application Menu*. Some commands are available in the *Status Bar* or through shortcut menus. There are additional access methods, such as *Tool Palettes*. The names of all of the commands can also be typed in the Command Line or near the cursor in the drawing window (Dynamic Input).

Ribbon

The ribbon provides easy access to the tools, which are organized in tabs and panels. The tabs (*Home*, *Insert*, etc.) contain a series of panels (*Draw*, *Modify*, etc.) which contain the command tools, as shown in Figure 1–17. The tools are organized by function.

By default, the ribbon is docked at the top of the interface, as shown in a partial view in Figure 1–17.

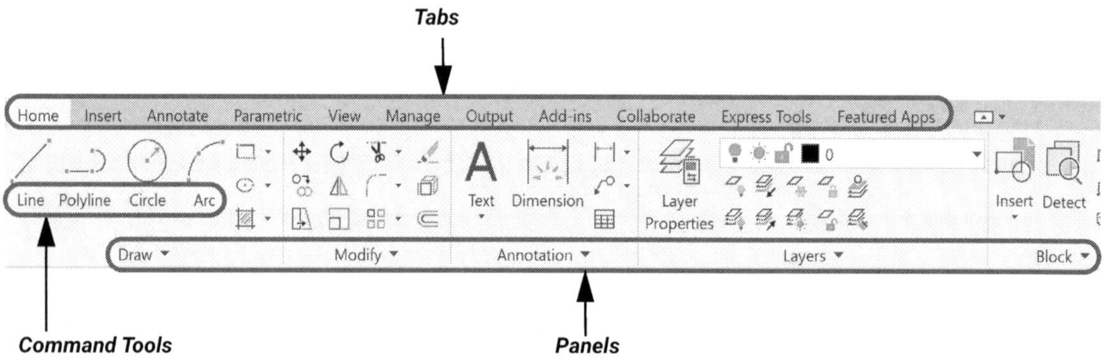

Figure 1–17

Some panels have a small downward arrow along the panel name which indicates that it has additional tools, apart from the ones displayed in the main panel. To view additional tools, click the panel title, which expands the panel. The expanded portion of a panel closes automatically when you move the cursor away, unless it is pinned, as shown in Figure 1–18.

- Click (Push Pin) to keep a panel open. The image changes to (Push Pin). Click it again to return the panel to its default setting.

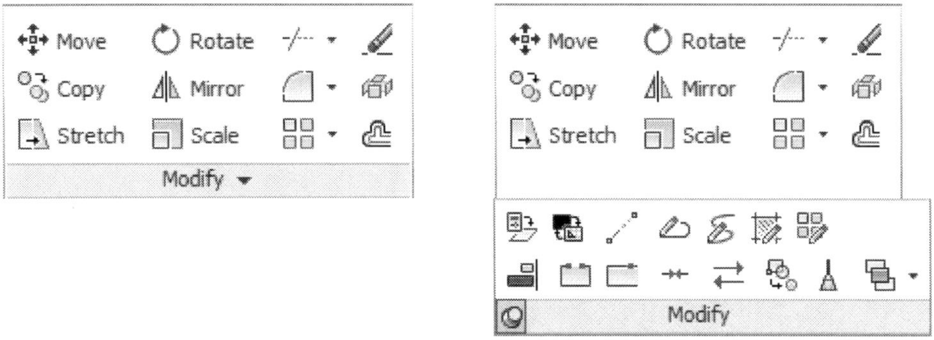

Figure 1–18

- The ribbon can float (as shown in Figure 1–19) and be docked to the side. To float the entire ribbon, right-click in the empty space at the end of the ribbon and select **Undock**. To dock it back, drag the ribbon by the title towards the top and when a horizontal rectangle place holder appears, drop it. It snaps back to its docked horizontal position.
- The ribbon palette can be hidden using **Auto-hide**. Only the title bar remains visible. If hidden, the ribbon displays when you hover the cursor over the title bar.
- Click on a panel tile to display the tools within that tile, as shown in Figure 1–19.

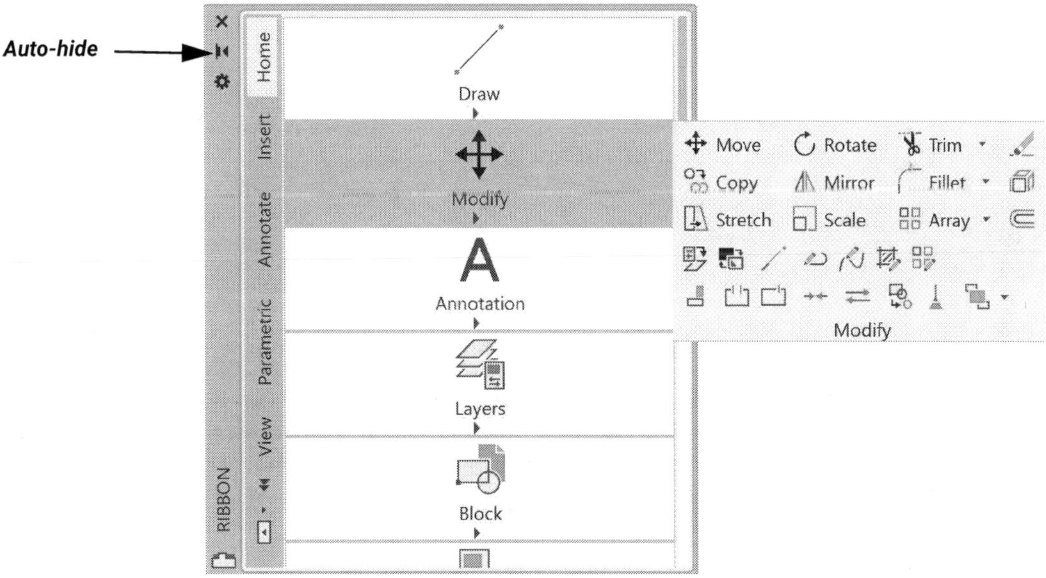

Figure 1–19

- Individual panels can also be floated in the drawing window, as shown in Figure 1–20. To float a panel, drag it by the title and drop it in the drawing window. To return it to the ribbon, drag and drop it onto the ribbon area. This method can also be used to rearrange the panels available in the ribbon.

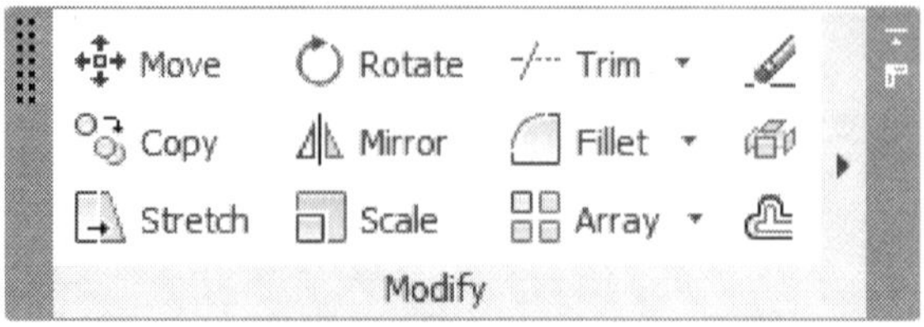

Figure 1–20

- Some tools have a small downward arrow indicating that a flyout is available. Click on the arrow to open the flyout which might contain additional options of the same command as shown on the left of Figure 1–21 or it might contain some other similar tools, as shown on the right of Figure 1–21.

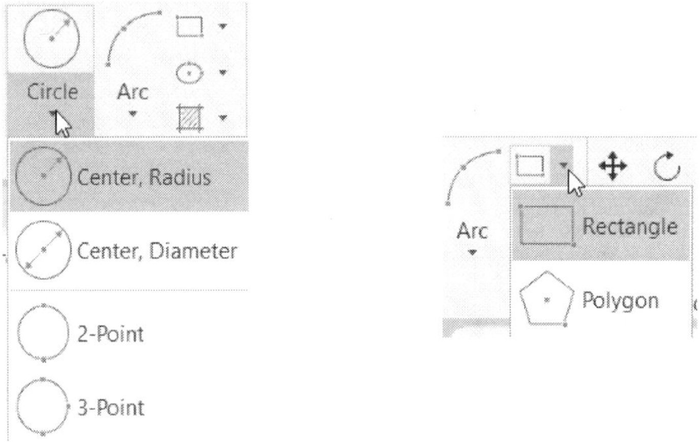

Figure 1–21

- Some tools include a gallery containing thumbnail previews of the available options, as shown in Figure 1–22. The display of these image previews can be controlled by the system variable **GALLERYVIEW** which is set as **1**, by default. To hide the thumbnail preview and display them as a list instead, set the value to **0**.

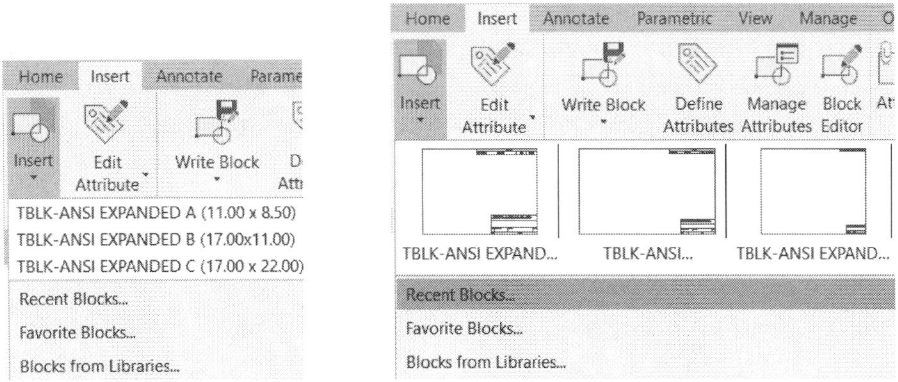

GALLERYVIEW=0 ***GALLERYVIEW=1***

Figure 1–22

Command Line and Dynamic Input Prompt

You can directly enter the name of a command in either the Command Line or in the Dynamic Input prompt. When the (Dynamic Input) is **On** (by default), and you start typing a command name, a command box displays near the crosshair with the letters you are typing, as shown in Figure 1–23. You can also specifically click inside the Command Line and then type the command name there, as shown in Figure 1–24. When the **Dynamic Input** option is **Off**, typing a command name automatically starts it in the Command Line.

- For both input methods, the **AutoComplete** option automatically completes the entry you are typing when you pause. It also supports mid-string search by displaying all of the commands that contain the word that you typed, as shown in Figure 1–24. You can then scroll through the list and select a command to start it.

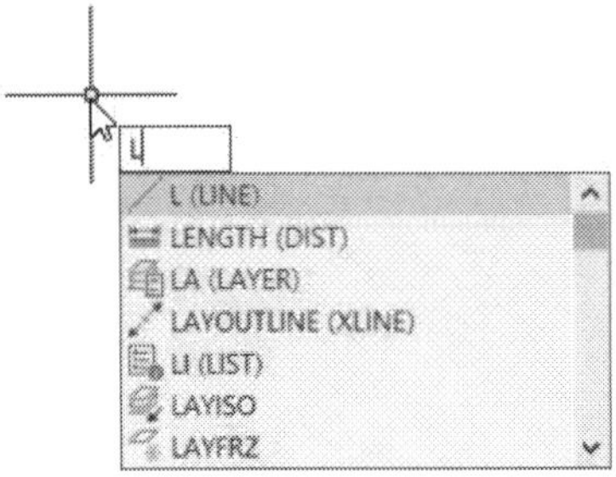

Figure 1–23

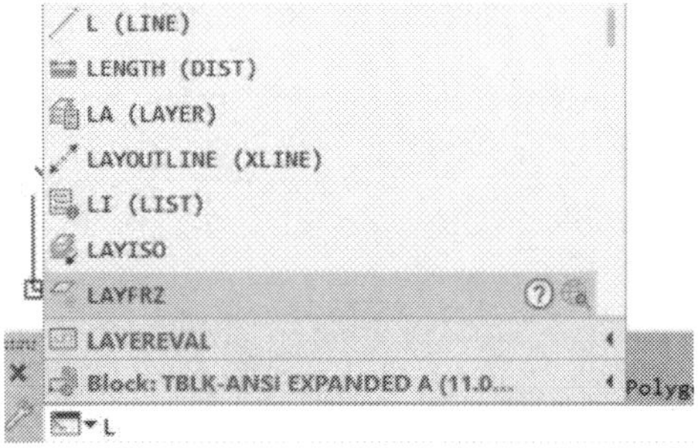

Figure 1–24

- The order in which commands are listed in the suggestion list adapts as you use the software.

- To set specific options for command input, including the **AutoComplete** feature, right-click on the Command Line, expand **Input Settings**, and select from the various options, such as the ability to search for system variables or to set the delay response time, as shown in Figure 1–25. You can also click  (Customize) to display the **Input Settings**.

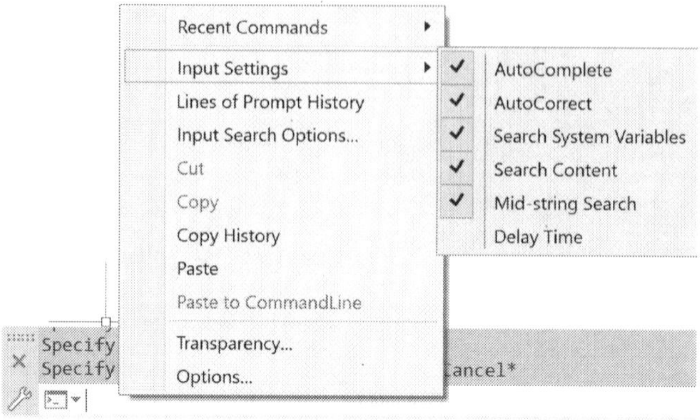

Figure 1–25

- As you work in the AutoCAD software, the software prompts you for the information that is required to complete each command. These prompts display in the Dynamic Input prompt and in the Command Line. It is important that you read the command prompts as you work, as shown in Figure 1–26.

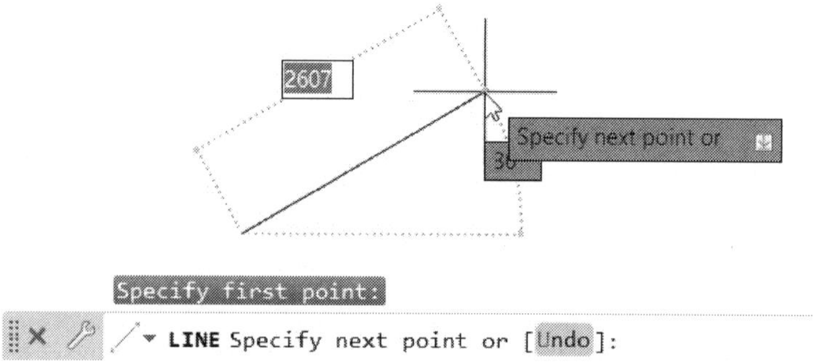

Figure 1–26

- If you press <Enter> when no command is active, it launches the command that you last used. It is a quick and easy way of repeating a command.
- If you need to stop a command, press <Esc> to cancel it. You might need to press <Esc> more than once.
- Depending on the Command Line being docked/undocked, pressing <F2> opens an AutoCAD Text Window or an expanded version of the Command Line, which contains a record of each command and prompt that has been used in the current drawing session.

- In the *Status Bar*, click (Customization) and select **Dynamic Input** in the list to display (Dynamic Input) in the *Status Bar*, as shown in Figure 1–27. Click to toggle the option on and off. The icons have a blue background when they are toggled on.

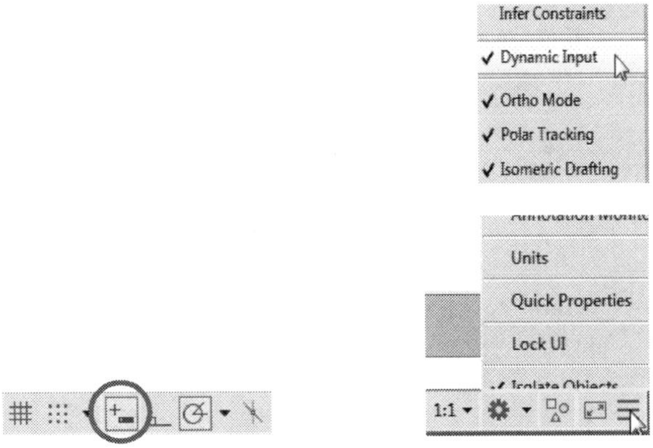

Figure 1–27

Selecting Command Options

If a command has options, you can specify it either in the Command Line, the Dynamic Input prompt, or the shortcut menu, as shown in Figure 1–28.

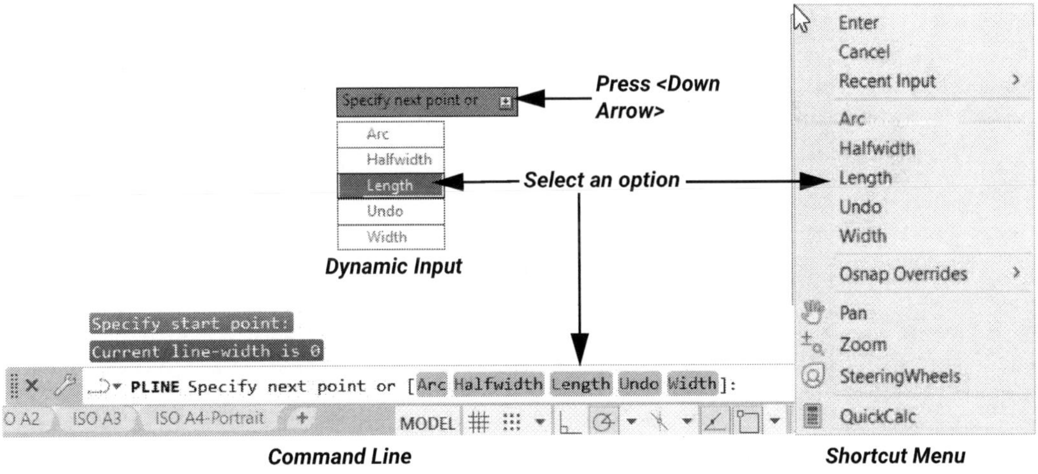

Figure 1–28

- In the Dynamic Input prompt, indicates that more options are available. Press <Down Arrow> to expand the list and select an option, as shown above in Figure 1–28.
- The shortcut menu opens when you right-click. It includes the same selections as dynamic input, and several standard options that display with every command.

- In the Command Line, the command name, its default prompt, and a list of options display. You can select the required option in the Command Line by clicking on it or by typing the option's capitalized letter(s) (displayed in blue) to activate it, as shown in Figure 1–29.

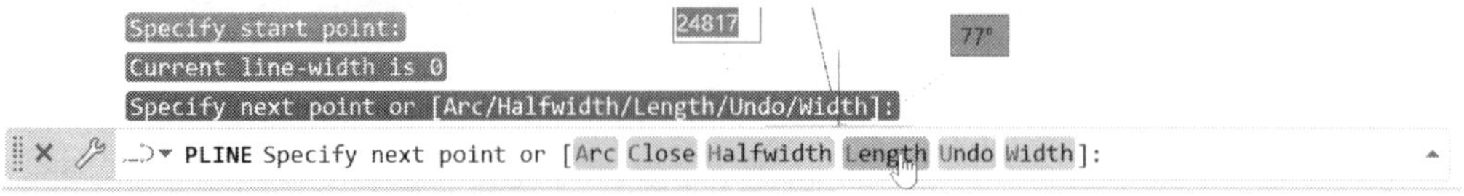

Figure 1–29

Application Menu

The *Application Menu* (shown in Figure 1–30), contains the file tools. It includes a search field in which you can type command names to locate them in the ribbon, *Quick Access Toolbar*, or *Application Menu*, and an area in which to browse for recent and open documents.

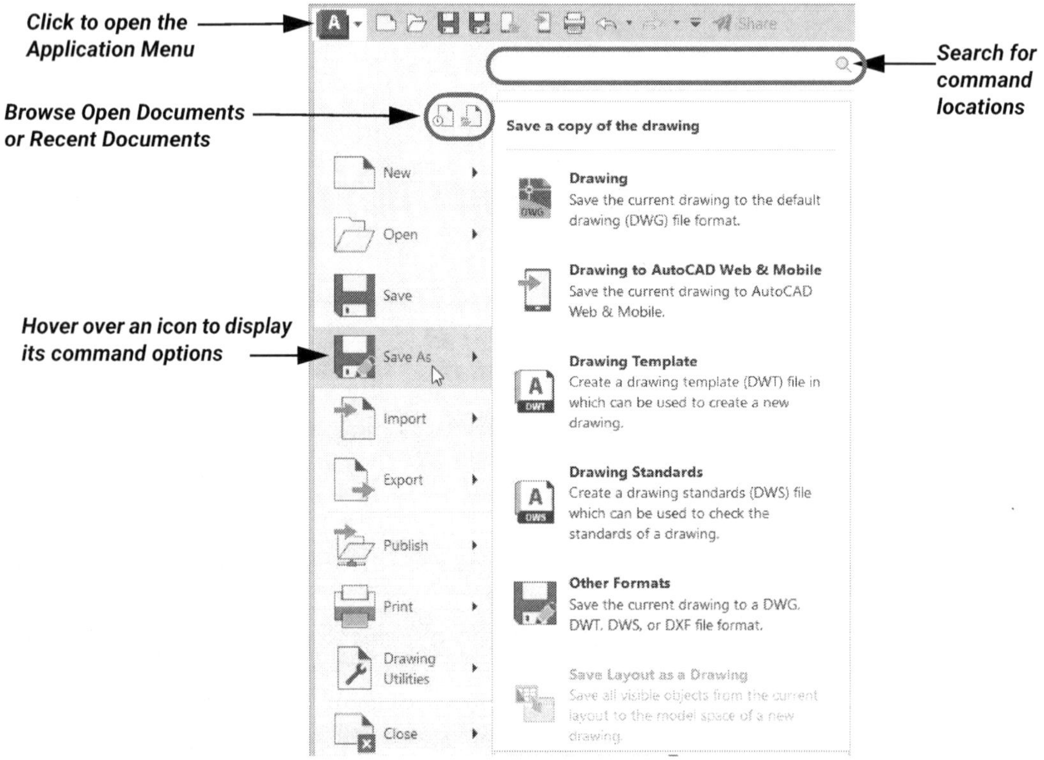

Figure 1–30

- Hover the cursor over a primary icon to display its options and select the required option. If you click the primary icon rather than the arrow, the default command starts.

- Click **Options** to open the *Options* dialog box and modify the default settings to customize how the AutoCAD software performs. For example, to change the color of the drawing window, click **Options**, select the *Display* tab in the *Options* dialog box, and click **Colors**. In the *Context* area, select **2d model space**, in the *Interface element* area, select **Uniform background**, and in the expanded *Color* drop-down list, select a color.
- Click **Exit Autodesk AutoCAD** to close the software.

How To: Find Command Access Locations

1. Click to expand the *Application Menu*.
2. In the *Search* field, start typing the name of a command. Tools related to the command name you are typing display in the *Application Menu*, as shown in Figure 1–31.
   - You do not have to type the full command name. As you start typing, the command options display.

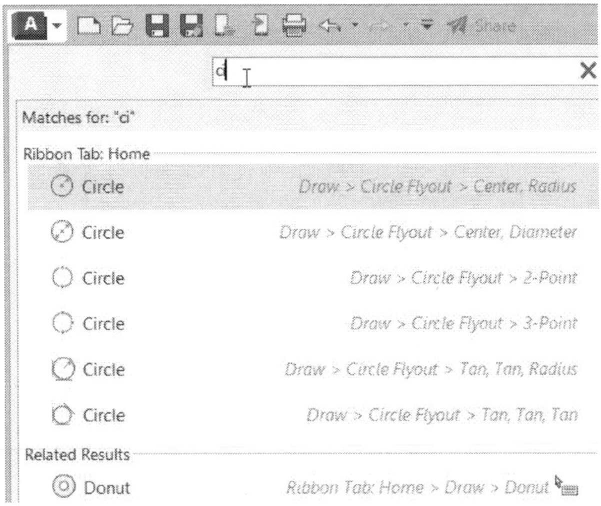

Figure 1–31

3. Select the command that you want to use.

How To: Select Drawings from the Application Menu

1. Click to expand the *Application Menu*.

2. Ensure that  (Recent Documents) is selected so that the list of recently opened documents displays, as shown in Figure 1–32.
   - You can also access **Recent Documents** in the *Start* tab, and they are displayed as List view or Grid view.

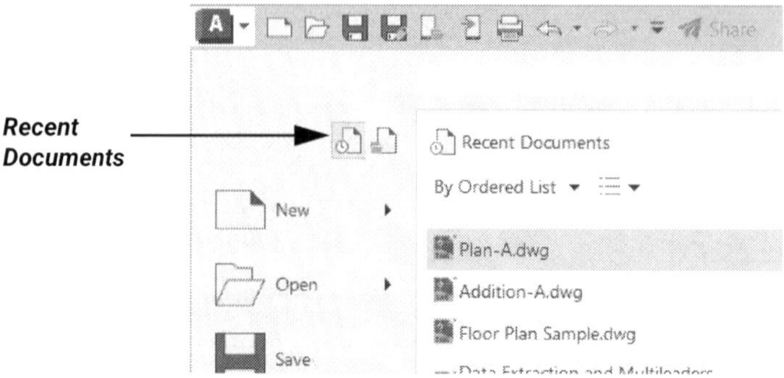

Figure 1–32

3. The default display option is **By Ordered List**. In the expanded drop-down list you can also select **By Access Date**, **By Size**, or **By Type** to change the display option. You can also change the size of the images, as shown in Figure 1–33.

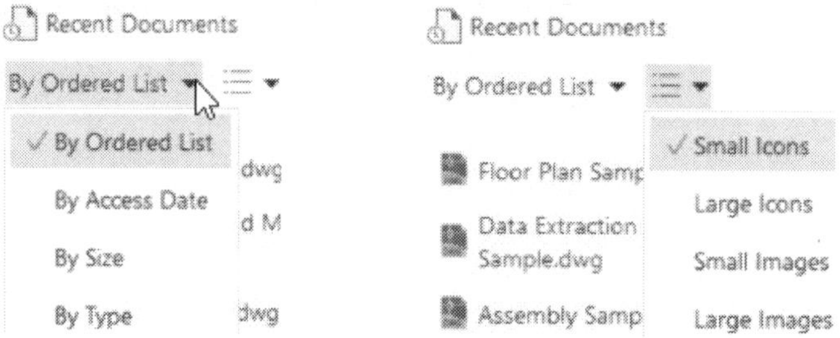

Figure 1–33

4. Click  (Open Documents) to display a list of open drawings, as shown in Figure 1–34.

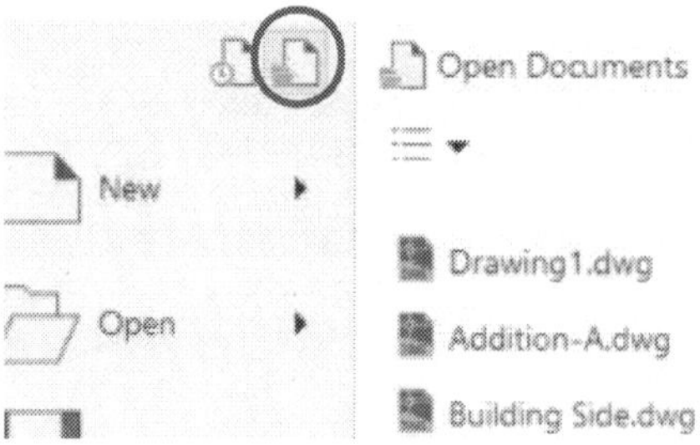

Figure 1–34

Quick Access Toolbar

The *Quick Access Toolbar* provides fast access to the common tools: **New**, **Open**, **Save**, **Save As**, **Open from Web & Mobile**, **Save to Web & Mobile**, **Plot**, **Undo**, **Redo**, and **Share**. You can customize it by adding and removing typical commands displayed in the list. Click (as shown in Figure 1–35) to expand the list and select from a list of typical commands. The commands with a checkmark are already displayed in the *Quick Access Toolbar*.

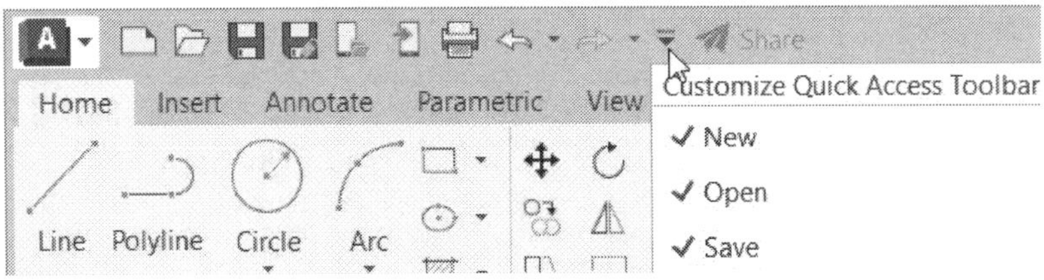

Figure 1–35

- When the *Start* tab is open, only **New**, **Open**, **Open from Web & Mobile**, and **Sheet Set Manager** display in the *Quick Access Toolbar*.

Hint: AutoCAD Web and Mobile

Included with the Autodesk Web & Mobile online account (subscription feature) is the option of opening ( ) and saving ( ) your drawing files to a remote location. Using your mobile device, you can view drawings and perform some light editing when you are in the field or at computer in a remote location. To use this option, you must be connected to the Internet and using a standard web browser.

Hint: AutoCAD Share

You can share your current drawing by using the (Share) command in the *Quick Access Toolbar*. It opens a dialog box where you can create a copy of the drawing for viewing only or for editing and saving it, as shown in Figure 1–36. Click on **Copy link** to create a link of the copy and send it. Anybody with the link can open the drawing in AutoCAD web app where they have to Sign in first. This copy of the drawing contains all the Xrefs, layers, blocks and properties.

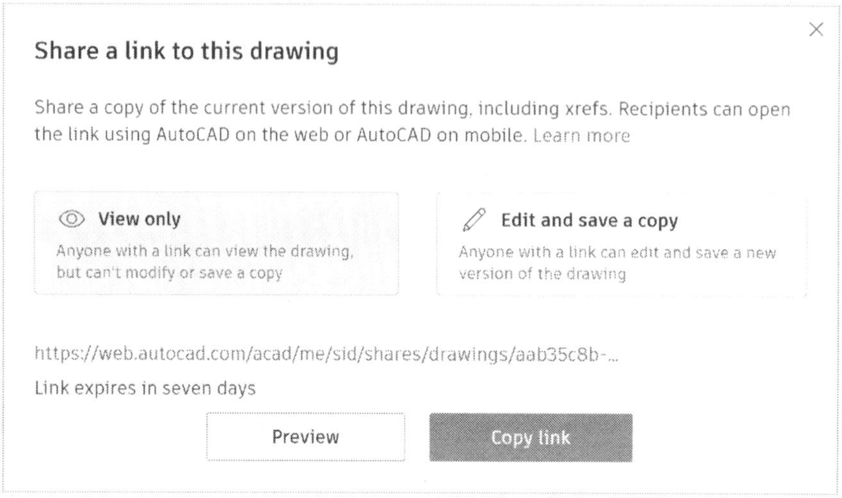

Figure 1–36

Additional Shortcut Menus

When you right-click, a menu usually displays next to the cursor, called a *shortcut menu*. The menu that displays depends on what you are doing in the AutoCAD software and where you right-click in the AutoCAD interface.

In the Quick Access Toolbar

When you right-click on the *Quick Access Toolbar*, a list of options displays, which enable you to customize or locate the *Quick Access Toolbar*, shown in Figure 1–37.

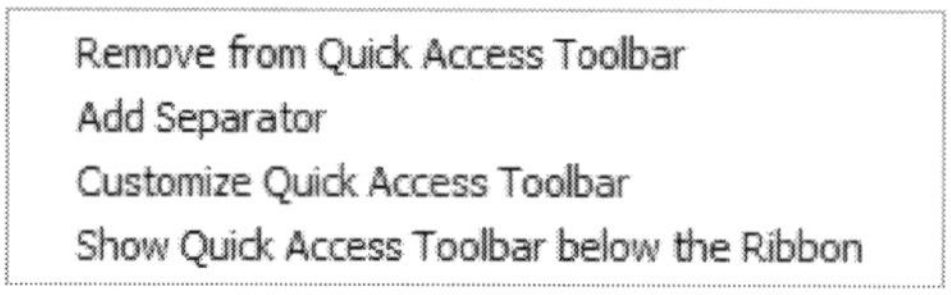

Figure 1–37

In the Ribbon

If you right-click on a tab or in an empty space in the ribbon, you can select which tabs or panels to display. You can also change the visibility and docking status of the ribbon. Right-clicking on a ribbon panel title only displays the tab and the panel options.The options that display in the shortcut menu are determined by where you click in the ribbon, as shown in Figure 1–38.

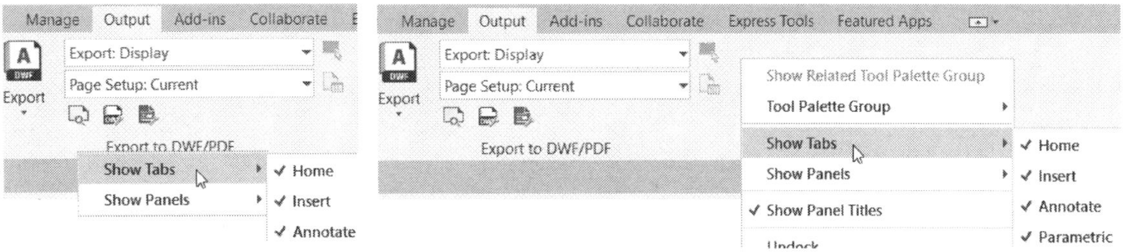

Ribbon shortcut menu when right-clicking on a panel title

Ribbon shortcut menu when right-clicking on the tabs or empty space in the ribbon

Figure 1–38

If you right-click on an icon in a panel, you can select the tabs and panels to be displayed in the ribbon. You can also add the icon to the *Quick Access Toolbar*, as shown in Figure 1–39.

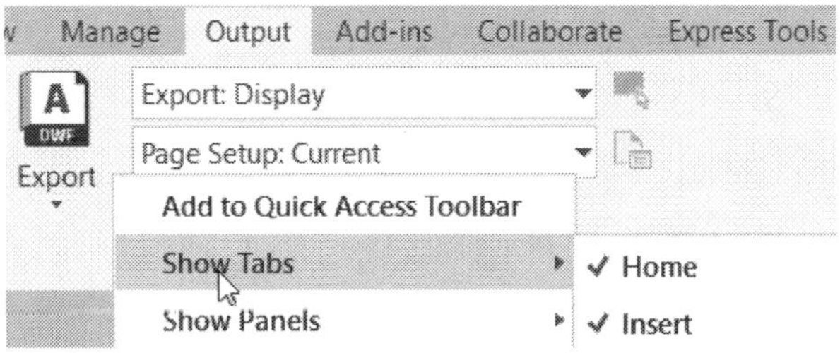

Figure 1–39

In the Command Line

When you right-click on the Command Line, you can select the various **Copy** and **Paste** commands, as shown in Figure 1–40. You can also access the **AutoComplete** options using the **Input Settings** selection. Using the *Options* dialog box, which can be accessed by selecting **Options...** in the shortcut menu, you can change many of the AutoCAD settings.

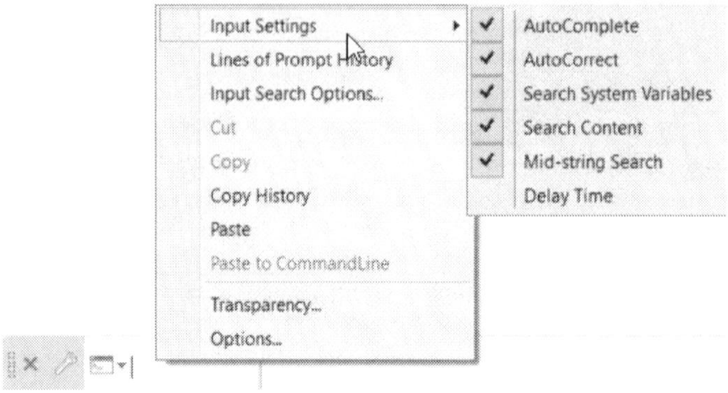

Figure 1–40

In the Drawing Window

When no command is active and you right-click in the drawing window, a shortcut menu opens, as shown in Figure 1–41. You have the option of repeating the previous command used or recently used commands (**Recent Input**), selecting **Zoom and Pan**, and the standard Windows clipboard functions. You can also access several other utilities or open the *Options* dialog box.

Figure 1–41

1.4 Cartesian Workspace

Locating Points

The AutoCAD software uses Cartesian (X,Y) coordinates to indicate locations in a drawing. Points are located by designating a horizontal (X) and vertical (Y) distance as measured from the origin (0,0), as shown in Figure 1–42. There is also a third coordinate (Z), which is only used in 3D drawings.

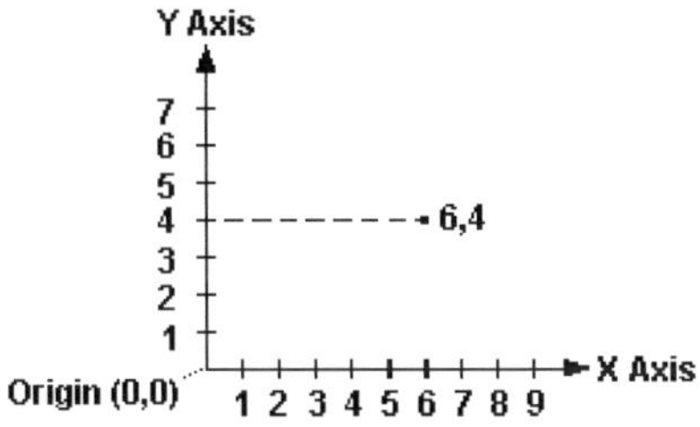

Figure 1–42

The current coordinate location of the cursor can be displayed in the *Status Bar*, as shown in Figure 1–43. By default, this display is toggled off. If you want to display the coordinates, click (Customization) in the *Status Bar* and select **Coordinates**.

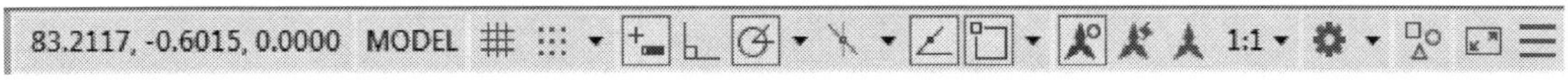

Figure 1–43

When you start a drawing command that requires you to select a point, the current coordinates also display near the crosshair in the Dynamic Input prompt (when **Dynamic Input** option is toggled **On**). For example, to draw a line, you must indicate where to begin and end the line. You can specify the point using one of two methods:

- Selecting a point on the screen with the cursor.
- Typing coordinates (when it is requesting point entry) in the form X,Y as shown in Figure 1–44. For example, the point (6,4) would be typed as **6,4**.

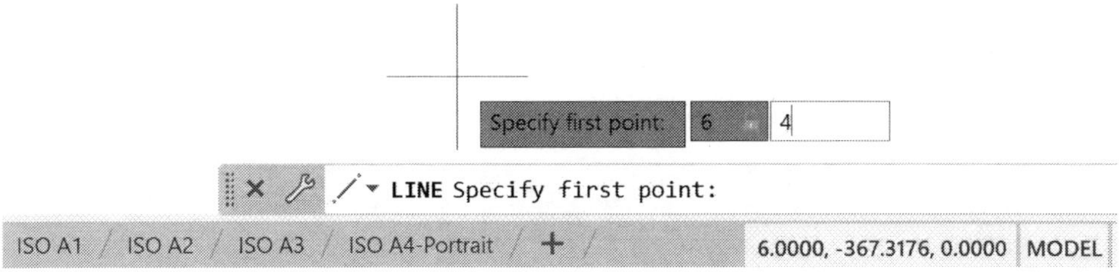

Figure 1–44

Measuring Angles

With the Cartesian coordinate system, you also need to understand how angles work in the AutoCAD software, as shown in Figure 1–45. This becomes important for coordinate entry, rotating objects, and working with arcs.

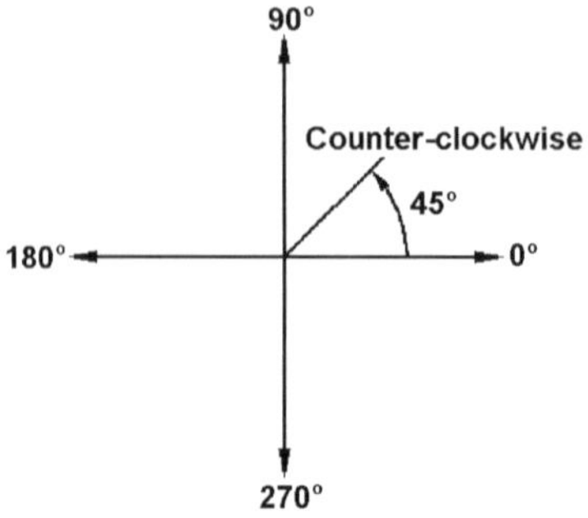

Figure 1–45

- By default, the AutoCAD software measures angles in a counter-clockwise direction relative to the positive X-axis.

Drawings Created at Full Scale

The AutoCAD Cartesian workspace is essentially unlimited in size. Whatever object you are creating, you typically draw it in the software at full scale, as shown in Figure 1–46. Whether you are drawing a building that is 100 x 200 meters or feet, a city that is 10 square kilometers or miles, or an IC chip that is 0.1" x 0.1", you always draw in the real units of the object. Your drawing area is as big as you need it to be. If needed, the entire solar system could be drawn at full scale in the software.

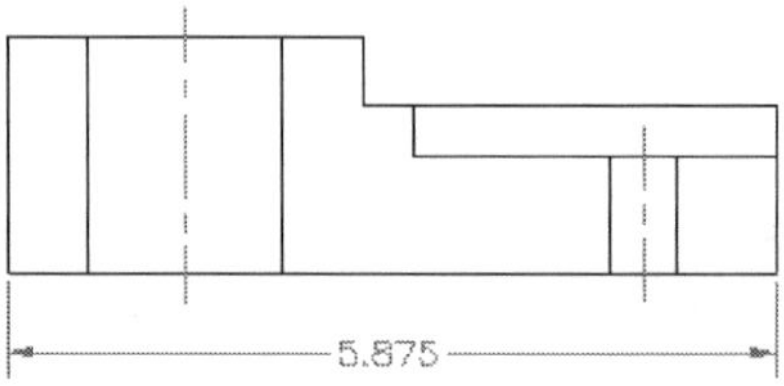

Figure 1–46

- Scaling the drawing only becomes necessary when the drawing is printed.

Hint: Drawing Accuracy

In addition to being potentially enormous, the AutoCAD drawing plane is also remarkably precise. Each point you enter in the software has an accuracy of at least 14 significant digits (e.g., 1.0000000000000).

1.5 Opening an Existing Drawing File

The **Open** command enables you to open and edit an existing drawing. This command opens the *Select File* dialog box, which is similar to the standard *Windows File* dialog box, as shown in Figure 1–47.

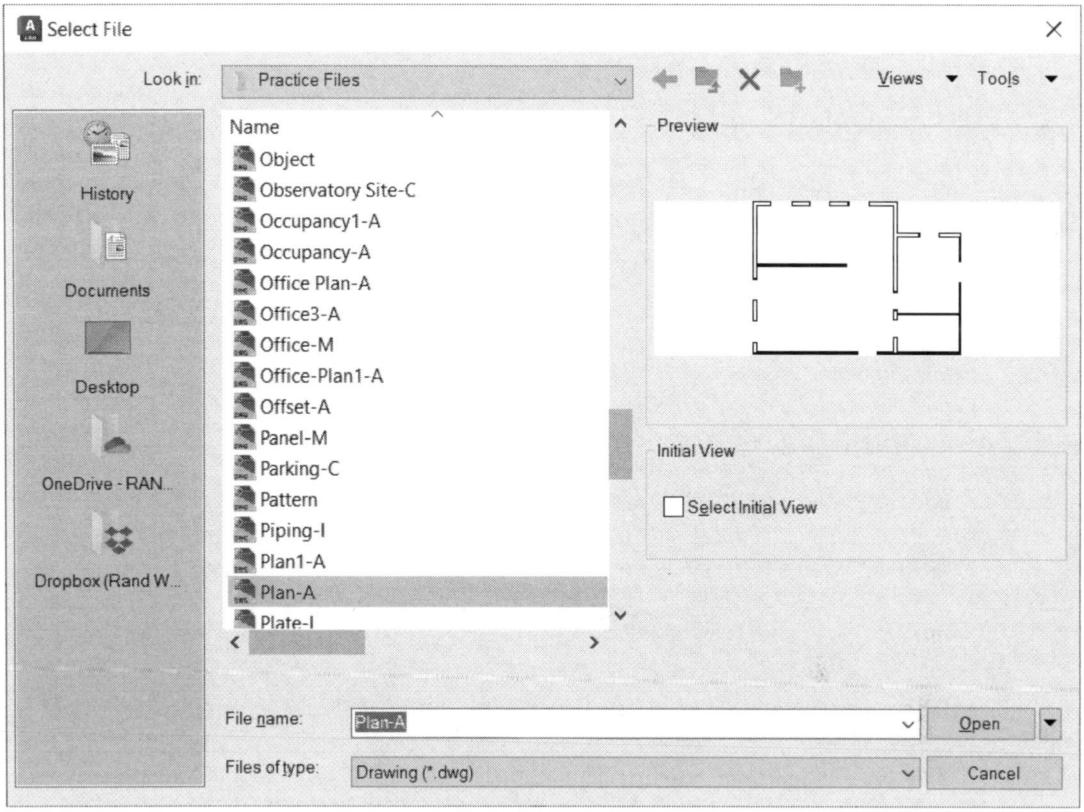

Figure 1–47

- You can access the **Open** command in the *Quick Access Toolbar*, in the *Application Menu* by clicking (Open), or by typing **Open** in the Command Line. You can also open the command from the initial *Start* window (*Start* tab>**Open**).
- Drawings that have recently been opened can be reopened quickly using **Recent Documents** in the *Application Menu* or from the *Recent* area of the initial *Start* window.
- In the *Recent* area of the *Start* tab, to easily locate drawings from the recently opened drawings, use the **Search** (in List or Grid view) and **Sort** (in Grid view) capabilities provided by the software.

How To: Open a Drawing

1. In the *Quick Access Toolbar*, click (Open).
2. In the *Select File* dialog box, locate the required file folder.
3. Select a drawing from the list. A preview displays on the right side of the dialog box.
4. Click **Open** or double-click on the drawing name.

File Location Options

	History: Displays shortcuts to recently opened drawings.
	Documents: Goes to the *My Documents* folder.
	Desktop: Displays the Windows Desktop and enables you to navigate to any folder. Select a file to display a preview.

Navigation and File Options

	Back to: Returns to the previous folder.
	Up one level: Moves up one level in the directory structure.
	Delete: Deletes the selected file(s).
	Create new folder: Creates a new folder in the current folder.
Views ▾	**Views:** Select the **List**, **Details**, or **Thumbnails** view for files, and toggle the Preview window on or off. If you have selected the details (Date, type, etc.) of the files to be displayed, the sort order of the columns is remembered by the AutoCAD software next time a file is opened.
Tools ▾	**Tools:** Locates files in the AutoCAD search path, adds FTP locations, adds folders to *Places*, or adds files to the *Favorites* folder.

- To make your most commonly used folders easier to access, you can select them individually in the *Look in:* drop-down list and then select **Tools>Add Current Folder to Places** to add them to the *File Location* drop-down list.

Multiple Drawings

You can have several drawings open at once. You can open them individually and have them open at the same time or open a several files together by using <Ctrl> or <Shift> and selecting them in the *Select File* dialog box. You can open multiple new drawings by clicking + (plus) in the *File Tabs* bar.

- All of the open drawings display as tabs in the *File Tabs* bar. The currently active drawing displays with a white background.
- The drawings that have been changed and not saved, display a * next to their name in the *File Tabs* bar, as shown for **Building Side*** in Figure 1–48.

Figure 1–48

You can switch between the drawings using any of the following methods:

- Pressing <Ctrl>+<Tab>.
- Selecting the required *File* tab (as shown on the left in Figure 1–49).
- Clicking (Files tab menu) to display a list of all currently open files and selecting the drawing file that you want to switch to.
- Clicking (Application Menu) and selecting a drawing under *Open Documents* (as shown on the right in Figure 1–49).

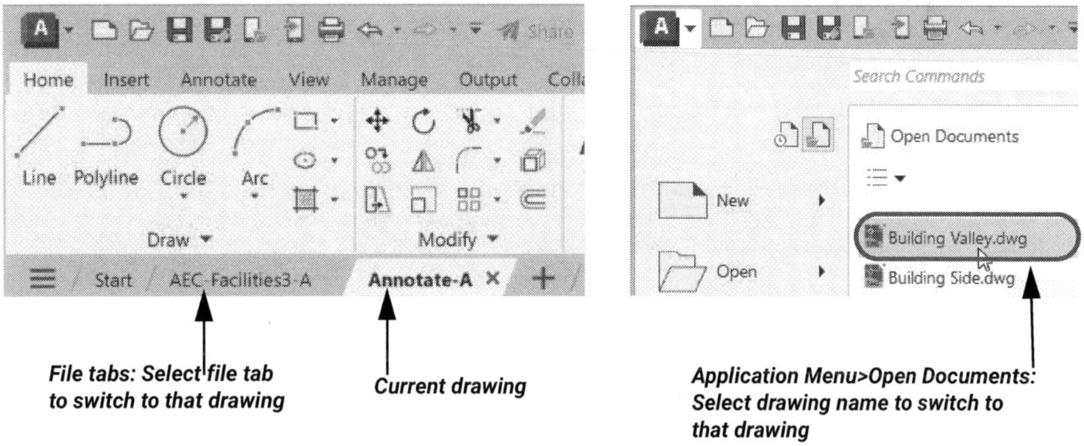

Figure 1–49

Closing Files

You can close a drawing file without leaving the software using any of the following methods:

- Clicking (Close) in the *Application Menu*.
- Clicking (Close) in the upper right corner of the drawing window.
- Clicking (Close) in the required *File* tab.

The software prompts you to save any changes if you have not yet saved the drawing before closing.

In the *Application Menu*, (Close) has two options:

- (Current Drawing), which closes the current drawing.
- (All Drawings), which closes all of the drawings together, leaving the *Start* tab open.

There are various Close options available from the *File Tabs* bar. Right-click on a tab to display a menu. While using any of the close options, the *Start* tab, along with the (Files tab menu) and remain persistent in the *File Tabs* bar. The options are:

- **Close All**: Closes all of the drawings and opens the initial *Start* window.
- **Close All Other Drawings:** Closes all of the drawings, except the drawing where the shortcut menu has been opened, and the *Start* tab. If not already active, this also makes the drawing the active one.
- Using the **CLOSEALLOTHER** command to close all of the drawings except the current drawing and the *Start* tab.
- With any Close option, the *Start* tab is not affected and remains persistent in the *File Tabs* bar.

When you close all of the drawings, the initial Start window is displayed and the *Quick Access Toolbar* becomes shorter and displays (New), (Open), (Open from Web & Mobile), and (Sheet Set Manager) only.

Practice 1a
Open a Drawing

Practice Objective

- Open and close existing drawings, and switch between open drawings.

In this practice, you will use the *Select File* dialog box to open two existing files and view them, as shown in Figure 1–50.

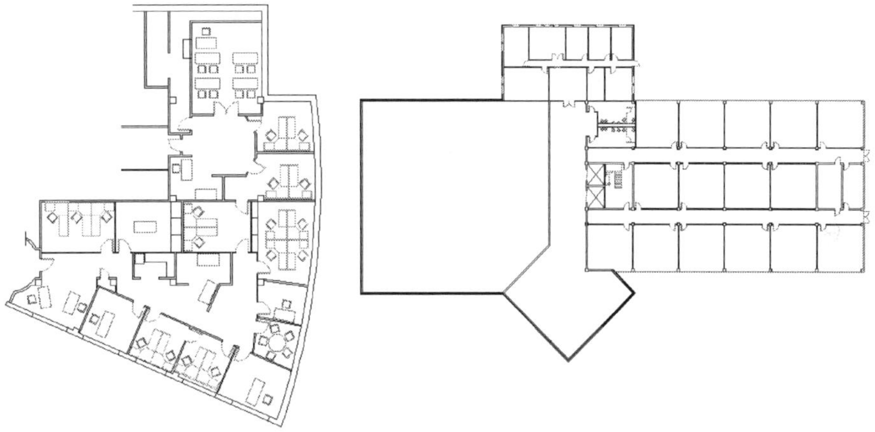

Figure 1–50

1. If the Autodesk AutoCAD software is not already open, select **Start>All Programs>AutoCAD 2026>AutoCAD 2026** or double-click on the **AutoCAD 2026** icon on the desktop.
2. In the *Quick Access Toolbar*, click (Open), or if you are in the *Start* tab initial window, select **Open files** in the *Open* drop-down list.
   - You can also click (Open) in the *Application Menu*.
3. In the *Select File* dialog box, navigate to and open the practice files folder. In the *Name* area, select **Building Rock.dwg** and click **Open**. The drawing is opened and displayed in the drawing window.
4. Start the **Open** command again. In the *Select File* dialog box, note that you are already in the practice files folder. In the *Name* area, select **Building Side.dwg** and click **Open**. This drawing is displayed in the drawing window.
   - After you navigate and open a drawing from the practice files folder once, the software remembers the path and opens the folder automatically.You are not required to navigate to the folder again.

5. In the *File Tabs* bar, in addition to (Files tab menu) and the *Start* tab, the names of both the drawing files display as tabs, as shown in Figure 1–51.

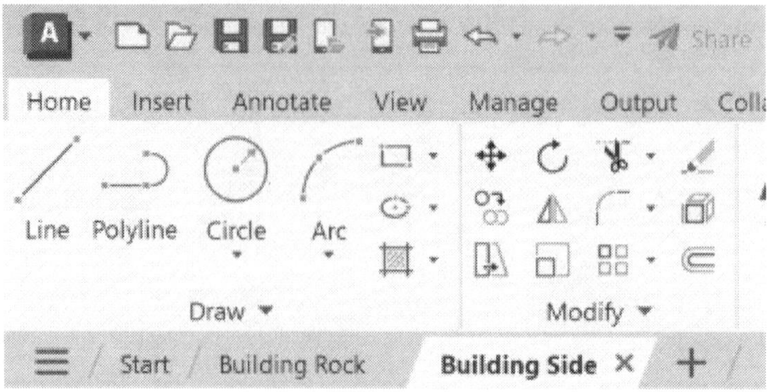

Figure 1–51

6. Click (Application Menu) and click (Open Documents). The two files that you have opened are listed, as shown in Figure 1–52.

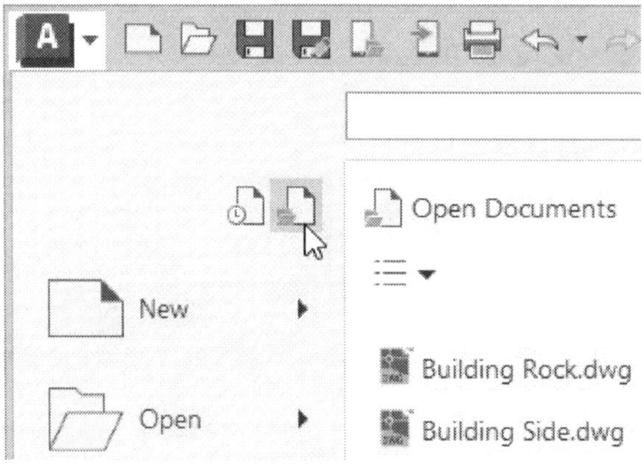

Figure 1–52

7. In the *Application Menu*, in the *Open Documents* list, select **Building Rock.dwg**. It becomes the active drawing.
8. In the *File Tabs* bar, select **Building Side**. It becomes the active drawing.
9. Press <Ctrl>+<Home>. The *Start* tab is active and the initial *Start* window displays.
10. In the *Start* window, in the left pane, select **Recent**, if required. Note that all the recently opened drawings are listed in the right pane.
11. In the *Recent* pane, click **Grid view** ( ) to display the images of the drawings. Click **List view** ( ) to display the list of drawings,

12. In the right *Recent* pane, select **Building Side** to make it active and open the drawing as well.
13. In the *File Tabs* bar, right-click in the *Building Side* tab and select **Close All**. If prompted to save changes, click **No**. This closes all of the open drawings and the initial Start window displays again.

End of practice

1.6 Viewing Your Drawing

Because AutoCAD drawings are drawn to full scale, it would be difficult to create them precisely on the computer screen without being able to move in and out around your work.

For example, if you are working on a map of the United States, you need to get closer to clearly display the roads in specific cities. If you are working on a house, you might want to focus on specific areas to be able to place doors precisely, as shown in Figure 1–53.

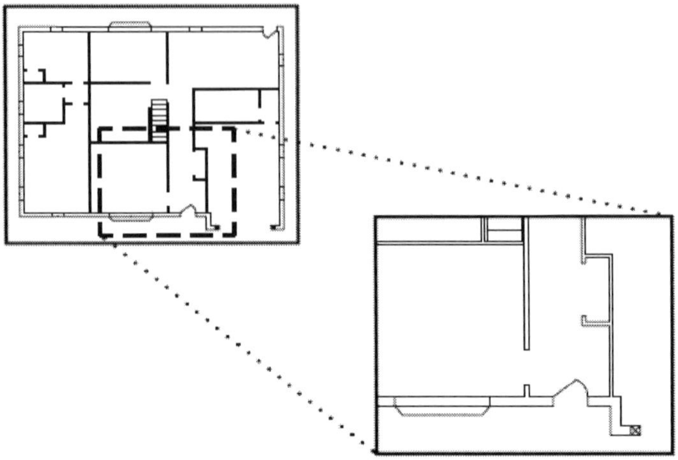

Figure 1–53

The **Zoom** and **Pan** commands enable you to specify which area of the drawing to display on the screen.

Wheel Mouse Zoom and Pan

The easiest way to zoom and pan is to use a wheel mouse.

- Roll the mouse wheel away from you to zoom in and roll the wheel toward you to zoom out. The AutoCAD software zooms in and out around the location of the cursor.
- Hold the wheel and move the cursor to pan. Note that a hand icon displays at the cursor location while panning.
- Double-click on the wheel to fit the entire drawing in the drawing window.
- Press <Ctrl> while you hold the wheel and move the mouse to use another mode of panning, called *joystick pan*.

Navigation Tools

The viewing and navigation tools are grouped together in the ViewCube and *Navigation Bar* (as shown in Figure 1–54), and are located along the top right corner of the drawing window. The display of both the *Navigation Bar* and ViewCube can be toggled on/off in the *View* tab/*Viewport Tools* panel.

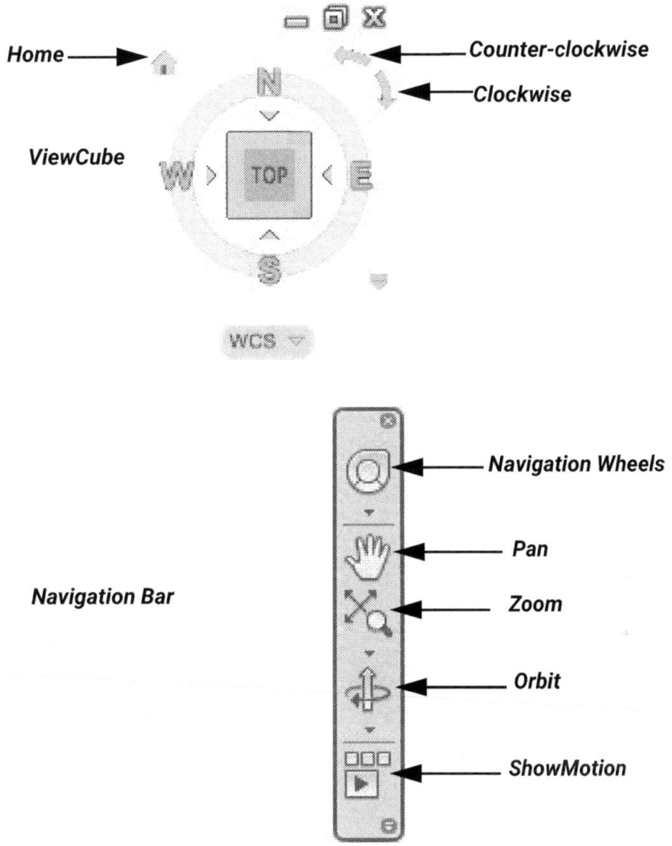

Figure 1–54

- The *Navigation Bar* provides a quick way of accessing the navigation tools such as **Pan** and **Zoom**. It displays in a very light gray until you hover the cursor over it. displayed below a tool indicates that it can be expanded and additional options can be selected. In Paper Space, fewer tools display because you can only use 2D viewing commands. The different options are shown in Figure 1–55.

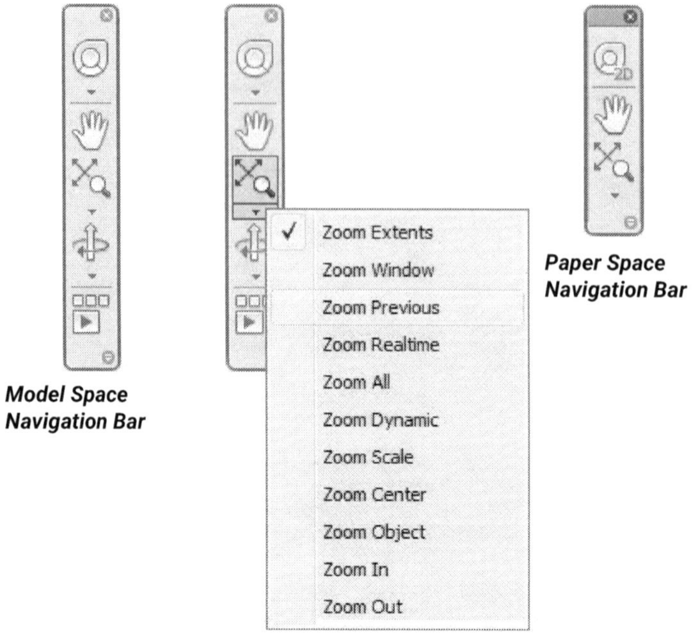

Figure 1–55

- Most of the ViewCube options are primarily used in 3D views. However, you can use the Clockwise and Counterclockwise controls to rotate the viewport in the 2D plane, as shown in Figure 1–56.

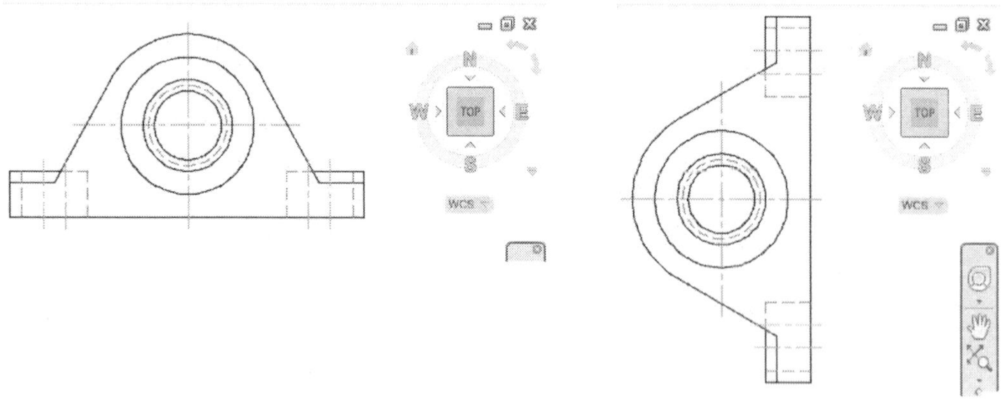

Figure 1–56

- Navigation Wheels provide access to groups of commonly used navigation tools. Depending on the wheel selected, you can access a small group of commands, such as **Zoom**, **Rewind**, and **Pan**, or a group with many more options. The Navigation Wheel displays at the cursor, enabling you to quickly select the navigation tools.
- **ShowMotion** is used when creating animations in 3D.

Pan and Zoom Commands

The **Realtime** commands are really two parts of one command. **Pan Realtime** enables you to shift the display without changing the current magnification. **Zoom Realtime** enables you to zoom in closer to the drawing or away from the drawing, displaying the results dynamically (in real time) while the command is used.

How To: Pan in Realtime

1. In the *Navigation Bar*, click (Pan). The crosshair changes to (Hand cursor).
   - You can also right-click in the drawing window and select **Pan**, or type **P** in the *Command Line*.
2. Position the cursor over the part of the drawing that you want to visually move to a different part of the screen. Hold the left mouse button and drag in the direction you want to go.
3. After you release the mouse button, you can pan again, or press <Esc> or <Enter> to complete the command.

- You can also pan using the scroll bars on the sides of the drawing.

How To: Zoom in Realtime

1. In the *Navigation Bar*, expand (Zoom) and select **Zoom Realtime**. The crosshair changes to (Magnifying glass).
   - You can also right-click in the drawing window and select **Zoom**, or type **Z** in the Command Line.
2. Hold the left mouse button and drag the cursor up to zoom in or down to zoom out.
3. After you release the mouse button, you can zoom again, or press <Esc> or <Enter> to complete the command.

- If you select a **Zoom** option in the *Navigation Bar*, the top level Zoom icon changes to the selected option.

Switching Between Zoom and Pan

In either **Zoom Realtime** or **Pan Realtime**, you can right-click in the drawing window to open a shortcut menu, as shown in Figure 1–57. Select an option and continue with the viewing operation.

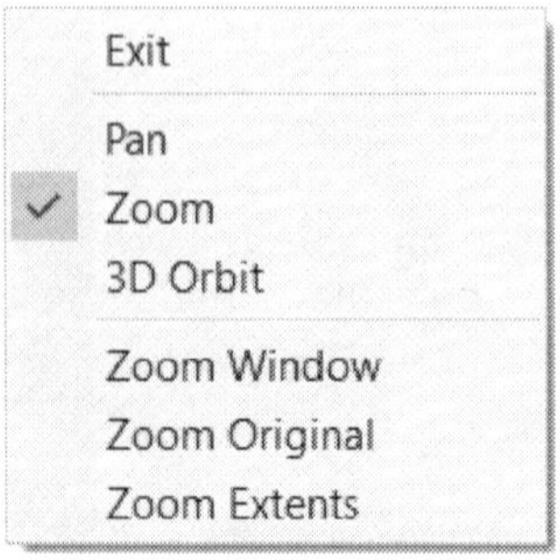

Figure 1–57

- **Zoom Window:** Requires you to hold the left mouse button while you drag a window.
- **Zoom Original:** Returns the display to the view that was current before the **Zoom/Pan Realtime** command was started.
- **Zoom Extents:** Fills the screen with all of the objects in the drawing.

Practice 1b
View a Drawing

Practice Objective

- Display parts of a drawing using the **Zoom** and **Pan** commands.

In this practice, you will use several options in the **Zoom** command and **Pan** to display parts of a large drawing, as shown in Figure 1–58.

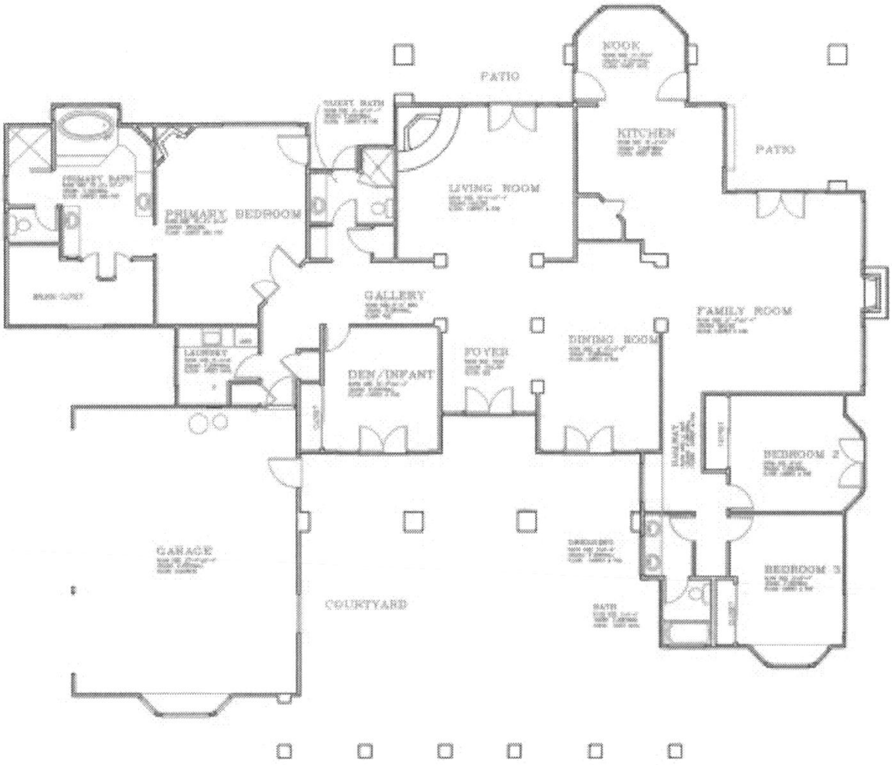

Figure 1–58

1. Open **Bighouse-A.dwg** from your practice files folder.
2. If you have a mouse wheel, scroll the wheel to zoom in and zoom out. Press the wheel and move the mouse to pan. Double-click on the mouse wheel to zoom to the extents of the drawing.
3. In the *Navigation Bar*, expand (Zoom) (click to display the **Zoom** menu) and select **Zoom Realtime**. Click, hold, and move the magnifying glass cursor to zoom in and out of the drawing.

4. Right-click and select **Pan**. Click, hold, and move the hand cursor to pan around the drawing.
5. Right-click and select **Exit**. Double-click on the mouse wheel to zoom to the extents of the drawing, or in the *Navigation Bar,* expand the **Zoom** menu and select **Zoom Extents**.
6. In the *Navigation Bar*, expand the **Zoom** menu and select **Zoom Window**. Select two corner points to create a window around the kitchen area, as shown in Figure 1–59. As soon as you click the second corner, you are zoomed in to the kitchen area.

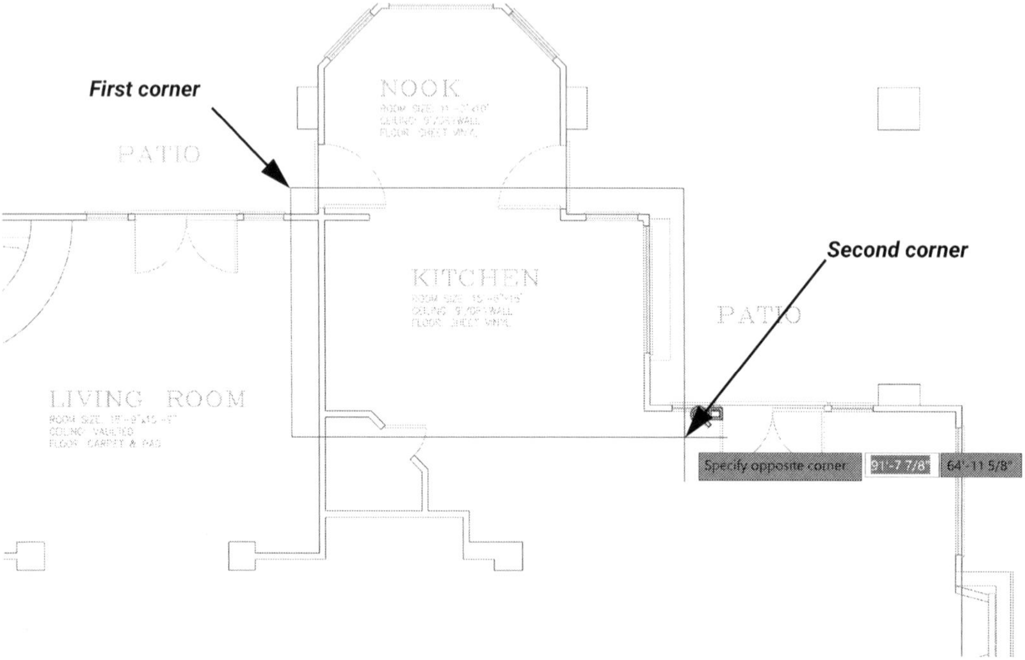

Figure 1–59

7. In the *Navigation Bar*, click (Pan). Pan leftwards from the kitchen to the Primary Bedroom (upper left corner).
8. Right-click and select **Zoom Extents**. Right-click again and select **Exit**.
9. In the *File Tabs* bar, click (Close) in the *Bighouse-A* tab to close the drawing. Click **No** to not save the changes.

End of practice

1.7 Saving Your Work

Saving your work is vitally important. You should save early and often to avoid losing and redrawing information. The drawings that have been changed and not saved, display a * next to their name in the *File Tabs* bar. To provide added security, you can create automatic saves to a backup file. You can also save your drawings so that they can be used in previous versions of the AutoCAD software that might not be compatible with the one you are using.

- The save commands only save to the current drive. Remember to regularly back up your work to another machine or other data storage.
- When you click (Save) in the *Quick Access Toolbar* or *Application Menu*, the drawing file you are working on is saved without prompting you for the name or location. This is called a *quick save*.
- You can also quick save by entering **qsave** in the Command Line or by pressing **<Ctrl>+<S>**.
- If you are working in a new drawing that has not been saved with a specific name, you are prompted for a name and location in the *Save Drawing As* dialog box.
- Clicking (Save As) in the *Quick Access Toolbar* or *Application Menu* (or typing **save**) opens the *Save Drawing As* dialog box where you can save the current drawing with another name and location.

Automatic Saves

While it is critical for you to save a drawing regularly as you are working on it, the AutoCAD software is also set up to save a drawing to a backup file every 10 minutes. These files can be used to recover work that might not have been saved. They have an SV$ extension.

- By default, the AutoCAD software also creates a backup copy of the file every time you save. It has a .BAK extension.
- Most of the times, automatic saves are performed incrementally. This is much faster than performing full saves, which can take a lot of time.

- You can modify the Automatic Save and backup features in the *Open and Save* tab of the *Options* dialog box (*Application Menu*>**Options** or by right-clicking in the empty space of the drawing area). You can also control the interval between saves. By default, the feature is toggled on with an interval of 10 minutes between saves and the **Create backup copy with each save** option is selected, as shown in Figure 1–60.

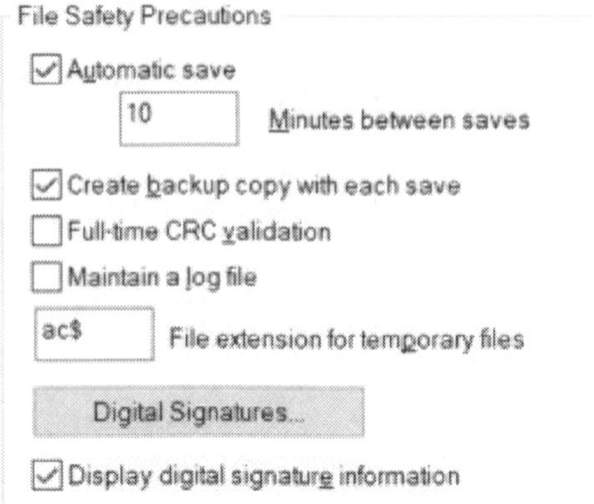

Figure 1–60

Saving in Various Formats

Using the **Save As** command, in *Files of type:*, you can select the version of the DWG file format so that the file can be opened with that version of the AutoCAD software, as shown in Figure 1–61.

- The latest AutoCAD software uses the **AutoCAD 2018 Drawing** file format to save the drawings. If you want to share a drawing with someone that has the AutoCAD 2017 software or an earlier version of the software, you need to save it in the previously used *AutoCAD 2013* file format.

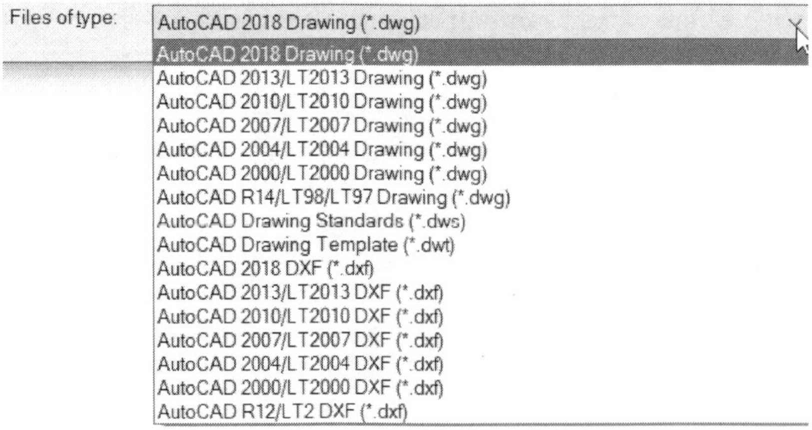

Figure 1–61

Practice 1c
Save a Drawing File

Practice Objectives

- Open and save a drawing.
- Modify the **Automatic save** option.

In this practice, you will open a drawing (as shown in Figure 1–62), save it, and modify the **Automatic save** option.

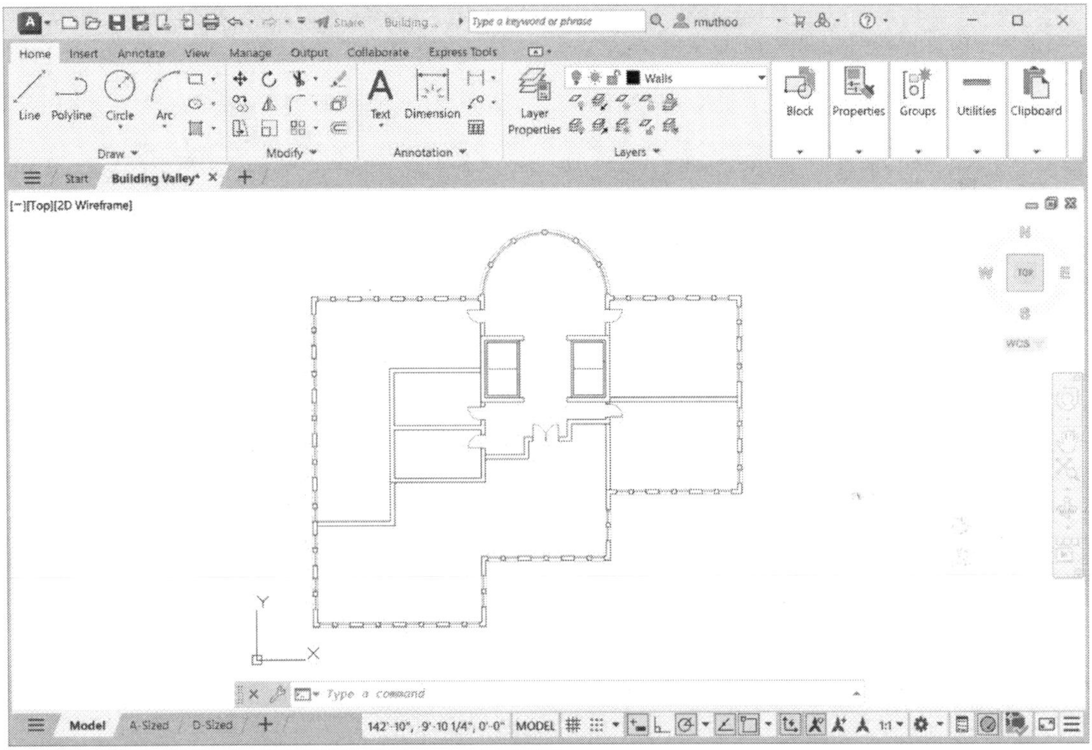

Figure 1–62

1. Open **Building Valley.dwg** from your practice files folder.
2. In the *Quick Access Toolbar*, click  (Save). The AutoCAD software performs a quick save.
3. In the *Application Menu*, click **Options**, or right-click anywhere in the drawing window and select **Options** to open the *Options* dialog box.

4. In the *Open and Save* tab, in the *File Safety Precautions* area, change the time for *Automatic save* to **15** minutes.
5. Click **OK** to close the *Options* dialog box. Note a * beside the **Building Valley** name in the *File Tabs* bar (as shown in the Figure 1–63), indicating that there are some unsaved changes to the drawing.

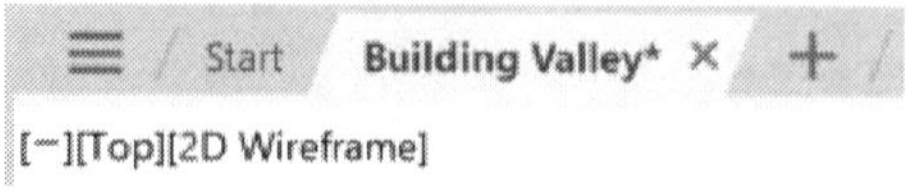

Figure 1–63

6. Save the drawing by clicking  (Save) in the *Quick Access Toolbar*. In the *File Tabs* bar, note that **Building Valley** does not have a * beside it anymore.
7. Close the drawing.

End of practice

Chapter Review Questions

1. What displays when you click the *Start* tab in the *File Tabs* bar?
   a. The recently opened drawings
   b. An expanded version of the Command Line
   c. The initial *Start* window
   d. The *Application Menu*

2. How do you cancel a command using the keyboard?
   a. Press <F2>
   b. Press <Esc>
   c. Press <Ctrl>
   d. Press <Delete>

3. What is the quickest way to repeat a command?
   a. Press <Esc>
   b. Press <F2>
   c. Press <Enter>
   d. Press <Ctrl>

4. To display a specific ribbon panel, you can right-click on the ribbon and select the required panel in the shortcut menu.
   a. True
   b. False

5. How are points specified in the AutoCAD Cartesian workspace?
   a. X value x Y value
   b. Y value, X value
   c. X value, Y value
   d. X value - Y value

6. How do you know if a file has not been saved after it is modified?
   a. Its tab displays a white background in the *File Tabs* bar.
   b. It displays a * next to its name in the *File Tabs* bar.
   c. Its tab is highlighted in blue in the *File Tabs* bar.
   d. Its tab always displays next to the *Start* tab in the *File Tabs* bar.

7. How can you switch between the current drawing, other open drawings, and the *Start* tab? (Select all that apply.)
   a. By pressing <Ctrl>+<Tab>.
   b. By pressing <Ctrl>+<Shift>.
   c. By right-clicking and selecting **Open** in the shortcut menu.
   d. By selecting the required drawing file tab in the *File Tabs* bar.

8. How do you fit the entire drawing in the drawing window?
   a. Double-click on the right mouse button.
   b. Hold <Ctrl> and scroll the mouse wheel.
   c. Double-click the mouse wheel.
   d. Hold the mouse wheel and move the cursor.

Command Summary

Button	Command	Location
	**N/A**	• **Application Menu**
	**Close**	• **Drawing Window** • **Application Menu** • **Command Prompt:** close
	**Close Current Drawing**	• **Application Menu** • Tabs bar shortcut menu
	**Close All Drawings**	• **Application Menu** • Tabs bar shortcut menu
NA	**Dynamic Input**	• **Status Bar:** expand Customization
Exit Autodesk AutoCAD	**Exit AutoCAD**	• **Application Menu**
	**Open**	• **Quick Access Toolbar** • **Application Menu** • **Command Prompt:** open, <Ctrl>+<O> • *Start* tab window>Open
	**Open Documents**	• **Application Menu**
	**Open from Web & Mobile**	• **Quick Access Toolbar** • **Application Menu>Open**
Options	**Options**	• **Application Menu** • **Shortcut Menu:** Options
	**Pan**	• **Navigation Bar** • **Shortcut Menu:** Pan • **Command Prompt:** pan or P
	**Recent Documents**	• **Application Menu**
	**Save**	• **Quick Access Toolbar** • **Application Menu** • **Command Prompt:** qsave, <Ctrl>+<S>
	**Save As**	• **Quick Access Toolbar** • **Application Menu** • **Command Prompt:** save

Button	Command	Location
	**Save to Web & Mobile**	• **Quick Access Toolbar** • **Application Menu>Save As**
	**Zoom Realtime**	• **Navigation Bar:** Zoom Realtime • **Shortcut Menu:** Zoom • **Command Prompt:** zoom or Z

Chapter 2

Basic Drawing and Editing Commands

In this chapter, you learn how to draw lines, rectangles, and circles, use Dynamic Input and Polar Tracking, erase objects, and use the Undo and Redo commands.

Learning Objectives

- Draw, edit, and close a line or series of lines.
- Remove objects from a drawing.
- Draw angles, rectangles, circles, and horizontal and vertical lines.
- Reverse the effects of the last command and return the drawing to its former state (before the last undo).

2.1 Drawing Lines

The most fundamental drawing element is the line. Almost any drawing contains line segments. The **Line** command enables you to add straight-line segments to the drawing as required, as shown in Figure 2–1. Each segment created with the command is a separate object.

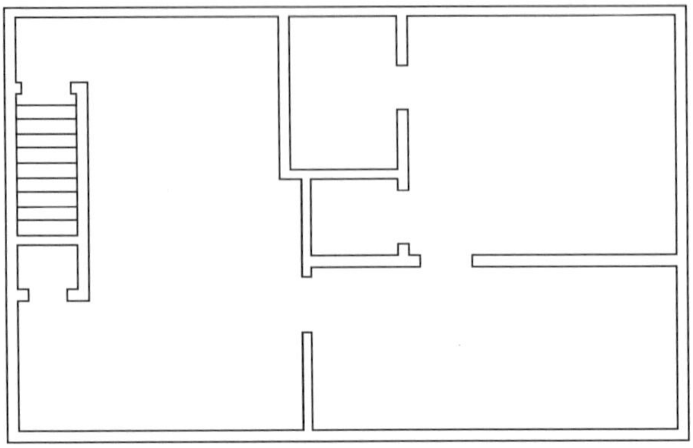

Figure 2–1

How To: Draw a Line

1. In the ribbon, in the *Home* tab>*Draw* panel, click (Line).
   - You can also type **L** or **line** in the Command prompt.
2. Select the first point.
3. Select the next point.
4. Continue to select points at the *Specify next point:* prompt to create a series of line segments as required or press <Enter> to complete the command.

Specifying Length and Angle

After you select the first point for the line and move the cursor, the AutoCAD® software displays its length and angle at the cursor location, if (Dynamic Input) is toggled on. The length value is highlighted, as shown in Figure 2–2. Enter the required length and press <Tab>, which highlights the angle value. Enter the required angle.

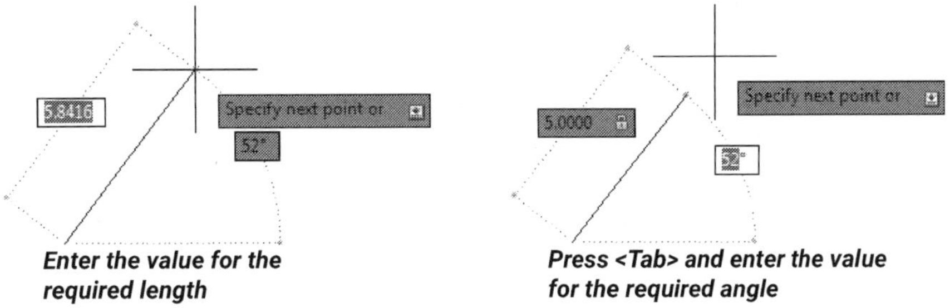

Figure 2–2

- The angle depends on the direction in which the cursor is moved. For example, 90° can be either straight up or straight down, depending on where the cursor is located. Move the cursor in the approximate direction first.
- Note that 0° is the positive X-direction (straight and to the right).
- In the *Status Bar*,  (Dynamic Input**)** must be toggled on for the length and angle to be displayed.

Line Command Options

At the *Specify next point:* prompt, press the <Down Arrow> to display the command options at the cursor prompt, as shown in Figure 2–3. Select an option or type the first letter (**C** or **U**) and press <Enter> to exit the command.

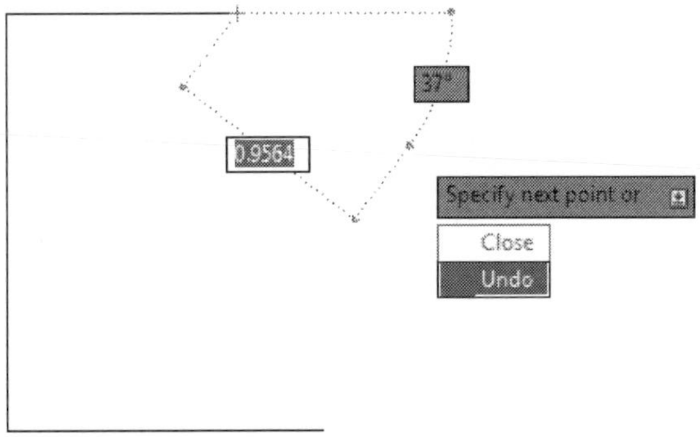

Figure 2–3

Close (C)	After two or more line segments are drawn, this option adds a final line segment between the first and last points entered.
Undo (U)	Removes the last segment drawn.

- You can also right-click at the *Specify next point:* prompt and select **Enter**, **Cancel**, **Close**, or **Undo**.

2.2 Erasing Objects

As with manual drafting, you often need to correct mistakes or make revisions in an AutoCAD drawing. You can erase objects by deleting them or by using the **Erase** command.

The easiest way is to select the objects and then press <Delete>. When you select an object, the object is highlighted and blue squares display, as shown in Figure 2–4. These are called *grips* and are very useful tools for modifying objects.

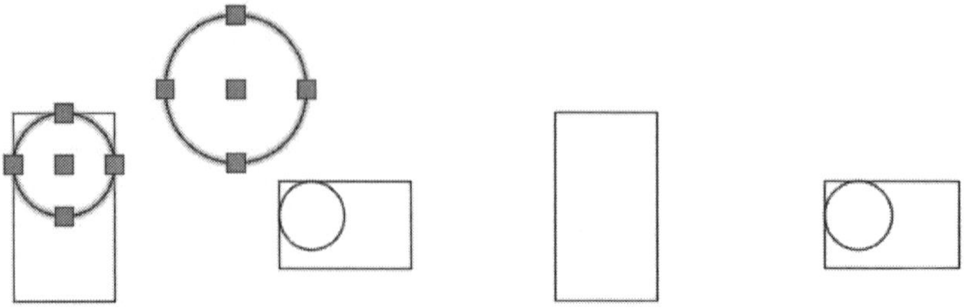

Figure 2–4

How To: Erase an Object Using the Erase Command

1. In the *Home* tab>*Modify* panel, click (Erase).
2. The *Select objects:* prompt displays. Hover the cursor (do not click) by positioning the small pick box directly over the object to be erased. As soon as it touches an object, the cursor displays as and turns the object gray, indicating the object before selection, as shown in Figure 2–5.

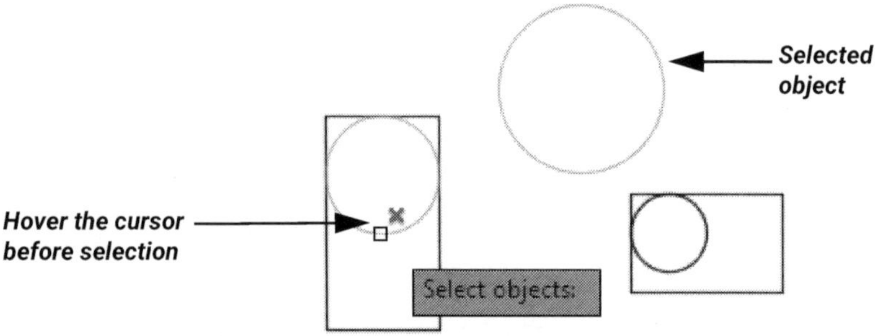

Figure 2–5

3. Click on the object to select it.
4. You can continue selecting additional objects to be erased.
5. Press <Enter> or right-click to erase the objects and complete the command.

2.3 Drawing Vertical and Horizontal Lines

Ortho Mode

Ortho Mode restricts the movement of the cursor to horizontal and vertical directions by forcing lines to use only 0°, 90°, and 180° angles.

To toggle Ortho Mode on or off, in the *Status Bar*, click (Ortho Mode), as shown in Figure 2–6. The keyboard shortcut for this command is <F8>.

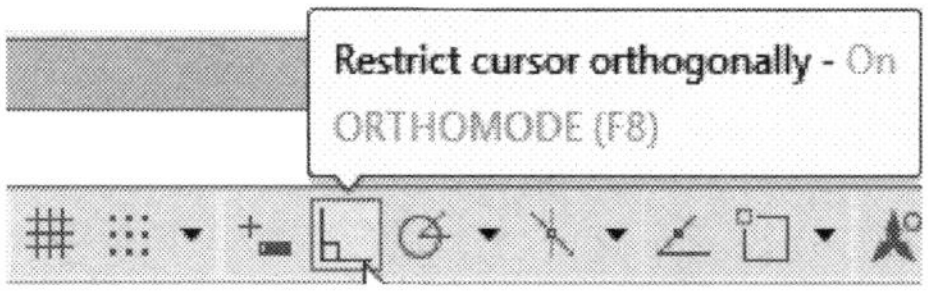

Figure 2–6

How To: Use Ortho Mode to Draw Vertical and Horizontal Lines

1. In the *Status Bar*, click (Ortho Mode) to toggle it on.
2. In the *Status Bar*, click (Dynamic Input) to toggle it on.

   Note: *The tools have a blue background when they are toggled on.*

3. In the *Home* tab>*Draw* panel, click (Line) to start the **Line** command.
4. At the *Specify first point:* prompt, select a starting point for the line.
5. At the *Specify next point:* prompt, move the crosshairs in the direction that you want the line to extend. Note that the line is restricted to either the horizontal or vertical direction, as shown in Figure 2–7.

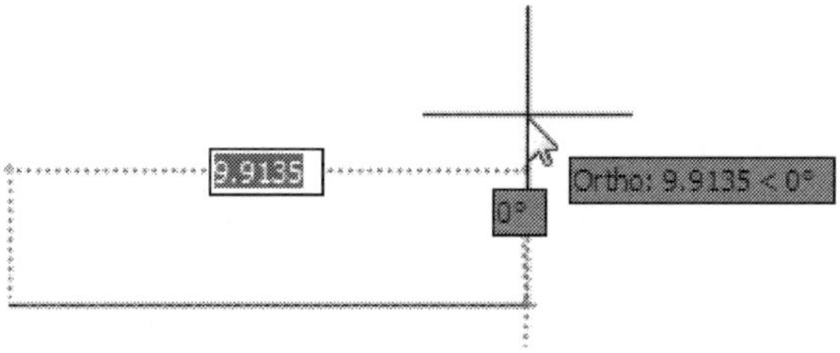

Figure 2–7

6. When the line displays in the required direction, enter a distance.
7. Press <Enter>. The line is drawn to the set length in the direction you selected.

8. Repeat Steps 4 to 7 for additional line segments, or press <Enter> to end the **Line** command.

Polar Tracking

Another way to draw horizontal and vertical straight lines is to use the **Polar Tracking** command. This command restricts the movement of the cursor to specified (preset) angles.

> ***Note:*** *While you can set any Polar angle, this topic uses only standard 90° increments to draw horizontal and vertical lines.*

- Polar Tracking makes it easy to work with preset angles as you draw. Rather than typing the angle, you move the cursor to find the tracking line (dotted line) and enter the distance.
- To toggle Polar Tracking on and off, click  (Polar Tracking) in the *Status Bar*, as shown in Figure 2–8. The keyboard shortcut for this command is <F10>.

Figure 2–8

- Between Polar Tracking and Ortho Mode, Polar Tracking is versatile, as it permits the use of other angles in addition to the 90° angles.
- Ortho Mode and Polar Tracking cannot be toggled on at the same time.

How To: Use Polar Tracking to Draw Vertical and Horizontal Lines

1. In the *Status Bar*, click the arrow in  (Polar Tracking) to display the angles list. Select **90,180,270,360**, as shown in Figure 2–9.

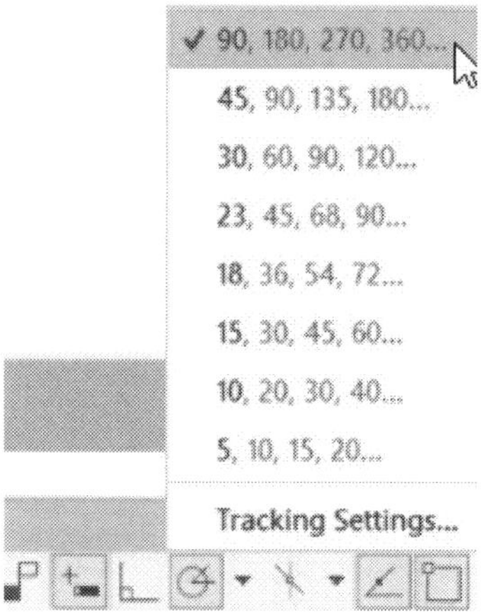

Figure 2–9

2. Click (Polar Tracking) or press <F10> to toggle it on, if required. The tool has a blue background when it is toggled on.
3. In the *Home* tab>*Draw* panel, click (Line) to start the **Line** command.
4. At the *Specify first point:* prompt, select a starting point for the line.
5. At the *Specify next point:* prompt, move the crosshairs in the direction in which you want the line to extend.
6. When the correct Polar Tracking line displays, enter a distance.
7. Press <Enter>. The line is drawn that length in the direction in which you pick.
8. Repeat for another line segment or press <Enter> to end the **Line** command.

- When the cursor approaches one of the polar angles, the dotted tracking line displays with a tooltip specifying *Polar:*, followed by the distance and angle from the last point (distance<angle), as shown in Figure 2–10.

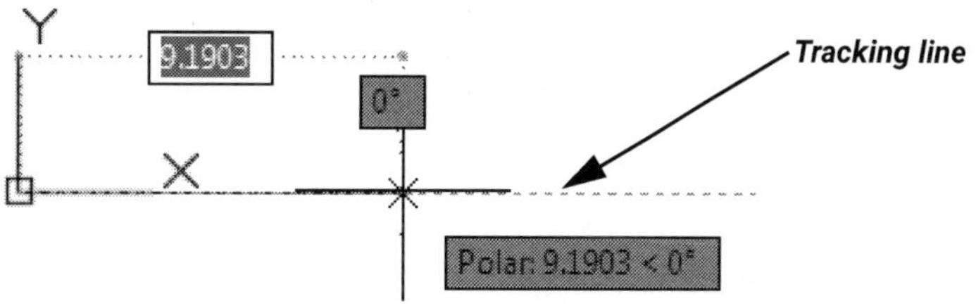

Figure 2–10

- You can use Polar Tracking with or without Dynamic Input.

2.4 Drawing Rectangles

Like lines, rectangles are fundamental building blocks in most drawings, as shown in Figure 2–11. A rectangle can be created from a series of lines or you can create it as a single object using the **Rectangle** command.

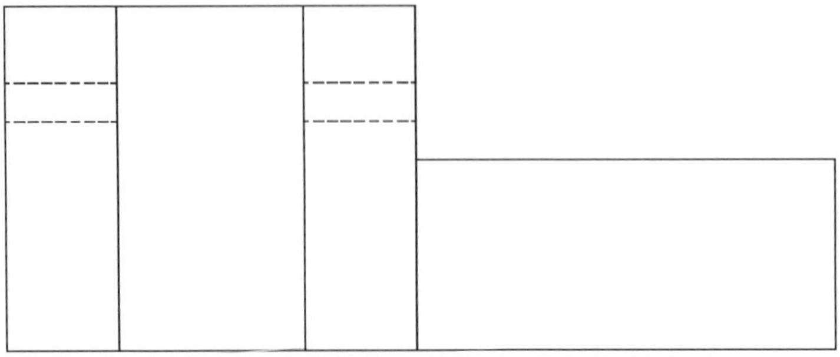

Figure 2–11

How To: Draw a Rectangle

1. In the *Home* tab>*Draw* panel, click (Rectangle).
2. Select the first corner of the rectangle.
3. Select the opposite diagonal corner of the box.

- You can also specify the exact length and width of a rectangle as you create it, using either:
  - **Dynamic Input:** At the *Specify other corner point:* prompt, enter a distance for the X axis (length) and Y axis (width), separated by a comma (e.g., **3,4**). The values (positive or negative) specify the direction in which the rectangle is created. Note that the (Dynamic Input) should be toggled **On** in the *Status Bar*.
  - **Command Line:** At the *Specify other corner point:* prompt, select the **Dimensions** option. At the *Specify length for rectangles* prompt, enter a distance for the length and press <Enter>. At the *Specify width for rectangles* prompt, enter a distance for the width and press <Enter>. A preview of the rectangle displays, which you can reposition using the cursor. Click in the direction in which you want the rectangle.
- The numbers you enter for the length and width are X,Y coordinates that are measured relative to the first corner of the rectangle.

2.5 Drawing Circles

The **Circle** command enables you to place circles in the drawing as stand-alone objects or as parts of a more complex construction, as shown in Figure 2–12.

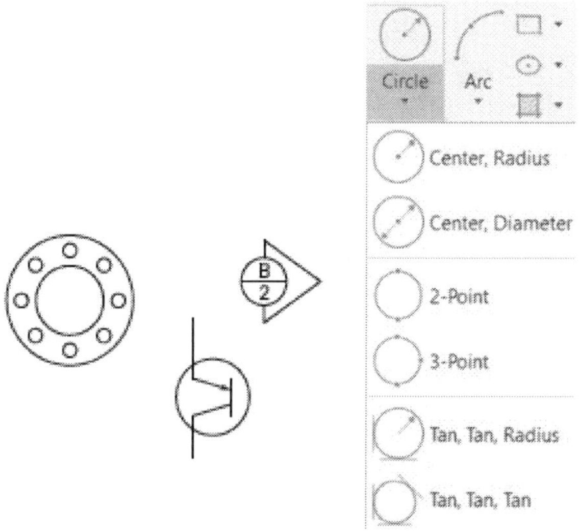

Figure 2–12

- In the *Home* tab>*Draw* panel, expand (Circle) to open the flyout (shown in Figure 2–12) to access the various options in the **Circle** command.

How To: Draw a Center, Radius Circle

1. In the *Home* tab>*Draw* panel, in the *Circle* flyout, click (Center, Radius).
2. Select the center point of the circle.
3. Specify the radius. The value can be entered or specified by selecting a point on the screen.

- The *Radius* is the distance from the center to the edge of the circle. The *Diameter* is the distance across the circle through the center point, as shown in Figure 2–13.

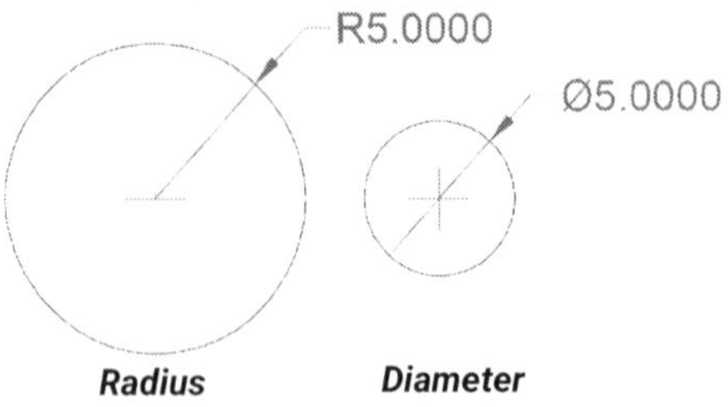

Figure 2–13

How To: Draw a Center, Diameter Circle

1. In the *Home* tab>*Draw* panel, expand the *Circle* flyout and click (Center, Diameter).
2. Select the center point of the circle.
3. Specify the diameter. The value can be entered or specified by selecting a point on the screen.

- If you need to add circles with the same radius or diameter, you can restart the **Circle** command, select the center point, and press <Enter> to use the default value for the radius or diameter. You can also select the value in the *Dynamic Input Prompt* drop-down list (press <Down Arrow>), as shown in Figure 2–14.

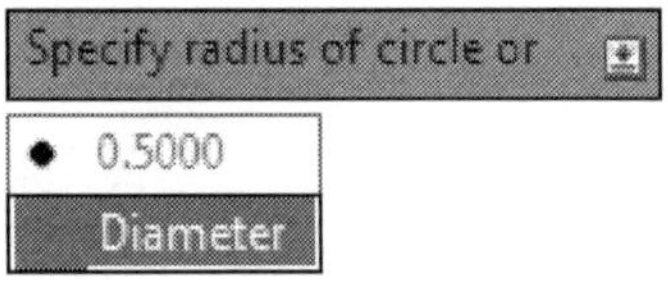

Figure 2–14

- The default value at the prompt is the same value as the last specified distance and is saved as the radius value. For example, if you specified a *Diameter* of **5.0**, the default value of the *Radius* is **2.5** the next time you start the command.
- You can type **D** for the **Diameter** option if you are using the typed command.

How To: Draw a 2-Point or 3-Point Circle

1. In the *Home* tab>*Draw* panel, expand the *Circle* flyout and click (2-Point) or (3-Point).
2. Select the two or three points that you want to use to draw the outside of the circle.

How To: Draw a Circle Tangent to Objects

A *tangent* is a point on a circle where another circle or object only touches it at one point, as shown in Figure 2–15. When you use these commands, an icon displays when you hover over a potential tangent point.

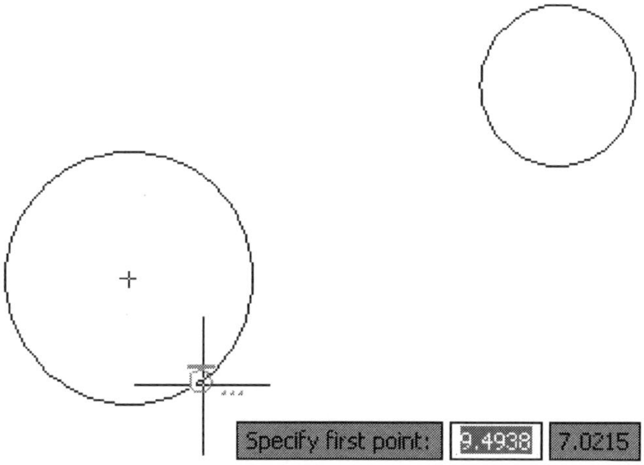

Figure 2–15

1. In the *Home* tab>*Draw* panel, expand the *Circle* flyout and click  (Tan, Tan, Radius).
2. Hover the cursor over an object to which a circle can be tangent and click when the icon displays in the correct location.
3. Hover the cursor over another object to which the circle can be tangent and click to set its location.
4. Enter a radius for the circle or select an additional tangent point for **Tan, Tan, Tan**.

- The  (Tan, Tan, Tan) option is only available in the *Draw* panel.
- If the radius is not big enough for the circle to be created in relationship to the tangent points, the circle is not created with a *Circle does not exist:* prompt displayed in the Command Line. This indicates that you need to use a larger radius.

2.6 Undo and Redo Actions

The **Undo** command reverses the effects of the last command. For example, if you draw a circle and then start the **Undo** command, the circle is undone and the drawing displays as it was before you started the **Circle** command. The **Redo** command returns your drawing to the state before the last undo. It is only available immediately after an undo.

- You can access the (Undo) and (Redo) commands in the *Quick Access Toolbar* or by right-clicking in the drawing window with no command active and selecting **Undo** or **Redo** in the shortcut menu.
- To undo or redo one command, click the respective icon.
- To undo or redo a series of commands, in the *Quick Access Toolbar*, expand the **Undo** or **Redo** command (as shown for the **Undo** command in Figure 2–16) and select the number of commands that you want to undo.

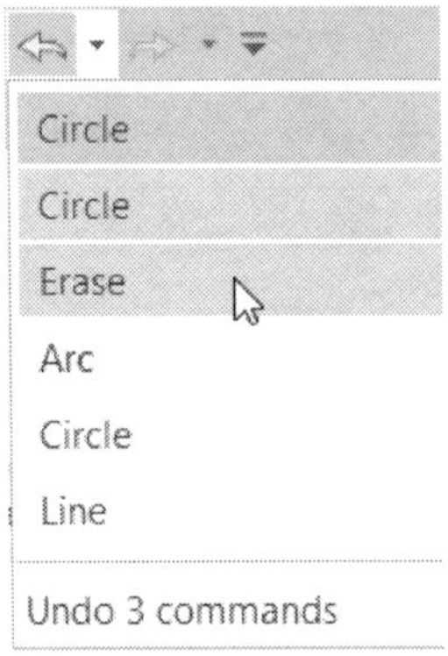

Figure 2–16

Practice 2a
Basic Drawing and Editing Commands

Practice Objectives

- Draw lines using **Dynamic Input**.
- Delete objects from a drawing using the **Erase** command.
- Draw horizontal and vertical lines using **Polar Tracking**.
- Draw rectangles and circles using various **Circle** command options.

In this practice, you will use drawing and editing commands. In Tasks 1 and 2, you will draw lines using **Dynamic Input** and then erase them, as shown on Figure 2–17.

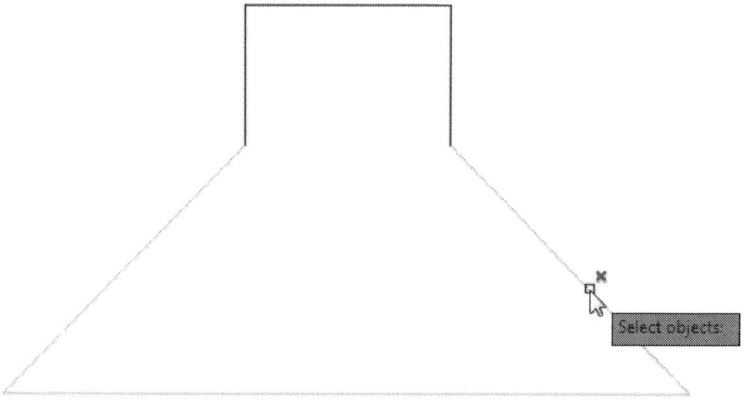

Figure 2–17

In Tasks 3 to 5, you will use **Polar Tracking** to draw an object. You will also draw rectangles and circles, as shown in Figure 2–18.

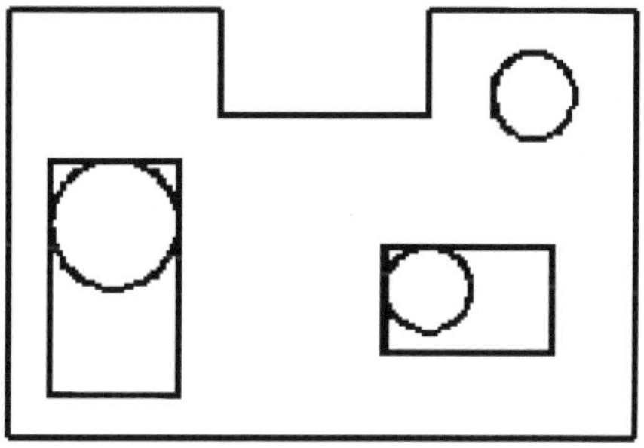

Figure 2–18

- Note that the dimensions are provided for drawing reference only.

Task 1: Draw lines with Dynamic Input.

In this task, you will draw lines using **Dynamic Input**, as shown in Figure 2–19.

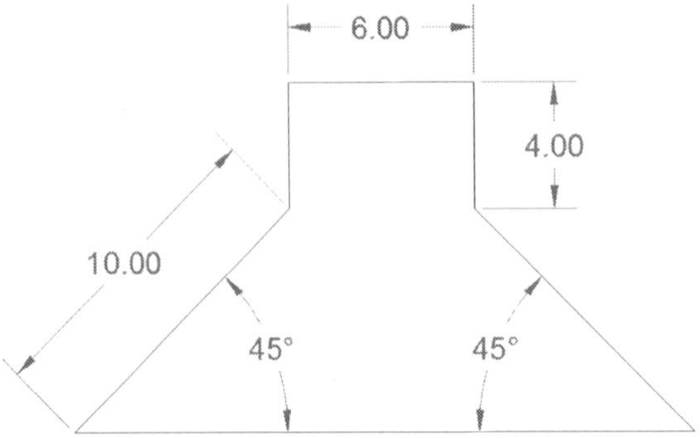

Figure 2–19

1. Open **Object.dwg** from your practice files folder. It is a blank drawing.
   - If grid lines display, click (Grid Mode) in the *Status Bar* to toggle it off. (The tool icon has no background color when it is toggled off.)
2. In the *Status Bar*, verify that (Dynamic Input) is toggled on.
   - If the (Dynamic Input) is not displayed in the *Status Bar*, click (Customization) and select **Dynamic Input** in the list to display it.
3. In the *Home* tab>*Draw* panel, click (Line).
4. At the crosshair, note the *Specify first point:* prompt and dynamic input boxes. Enter **5,5** which automatically enters in the dynamic input boxes (as shown in Figure 2–20) and press <Enter>.

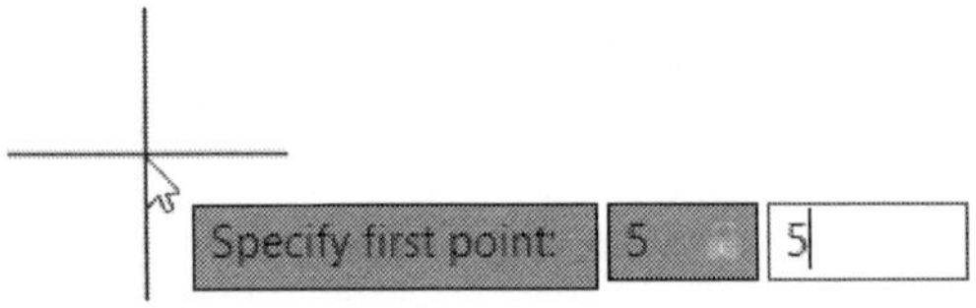

Figure 2–20

5. Move the crosshairs up and to the right from the first point, and enter **10** for the distance. Press <Tab>, enter **45** for the angle (as shown in Figure 2–21), and press <Enter>. The line is drawn with your cursor still attached to the end point of this line.

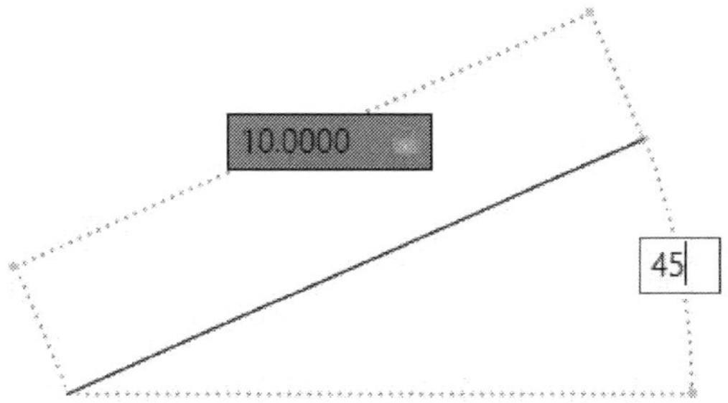

Figure 2–21

6. Move the crosshairs above the last point. Enter **4** for the distance, press <Tab>, enter **90** for the angle, and press <Enter>. This draws the next segment straight up.

   Note: *You can Pan while in an active command by pressing and holding the mouse wheel and then dragging the mouse. Release the mouse wheel and note that you are still in the **Line** command.*

7. Move the crosshairs to the right and draw the next segment **6 units** straight to the right (**0°**).
8. Move the crosshairs down and draw the next segment **4 units** straight down (**90°**).
9. Move the crosshairs down and draw the next segment **10 units** at **45°** down and to the right.
10. For the last segment across the bottom of the shape, press <Down Arrow> to display the command options. Select **Close** (as shown in Figure 2–22) to close the figure.

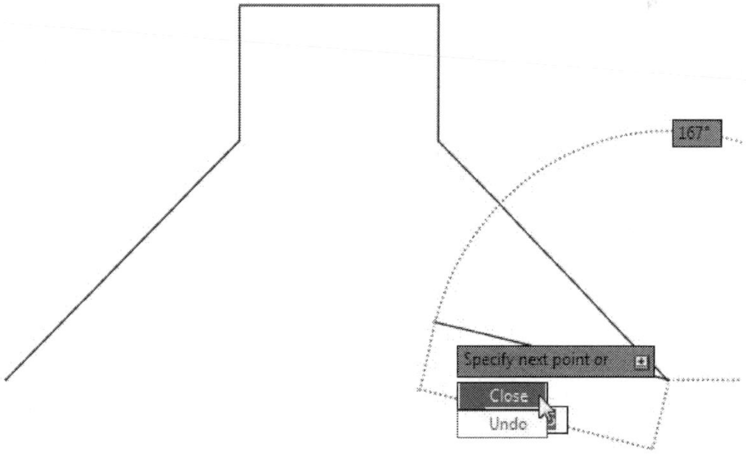

Figure 2–22

Task 2: Erase objects.

1. In the *Home* tab>*Modify* panel, click (Erase). Hover the cursor over any line segment. It turns light gray. Click on it to confirm selection. Similarly, select few other lines, which turn light gray indicating that they are selected for erasing, as shown in Figure 2–23. Press <Enter> to delete the selected lines together.

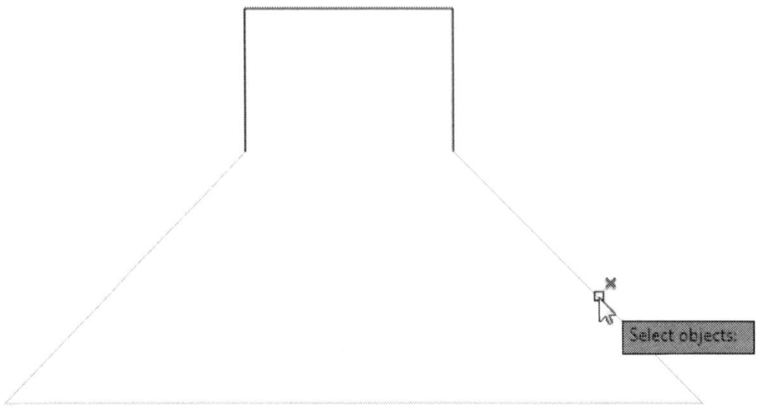

Figure 2–23

2. Without being in a command, select any remaining lines, which are highlighted with blue squares (grips). Press <Delete>. You have a blank drawing now.

Task 3: Use Polar Tracking.

In this task, you will use the **Line** command with Polar Tracking to draw horizontal and vertical lines, as shown in Figure 2–24.

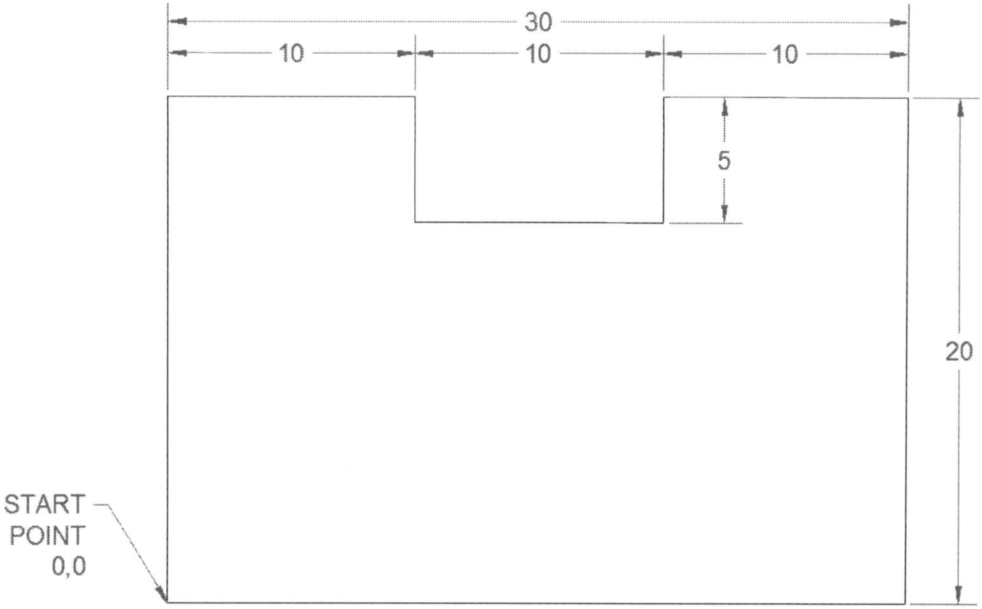

Figure 2–24

1. In the *Status Bar*, click the arrow in (Polar Tracking) to display the angles list. Select **90,180,270,360**, if required, as shown in Figure 2–25. Verify that this angle list is checked.

2. In the *Status Bar*, toggle on (Polar Tracking) if it is not already on, as shown in Figure 2–25.

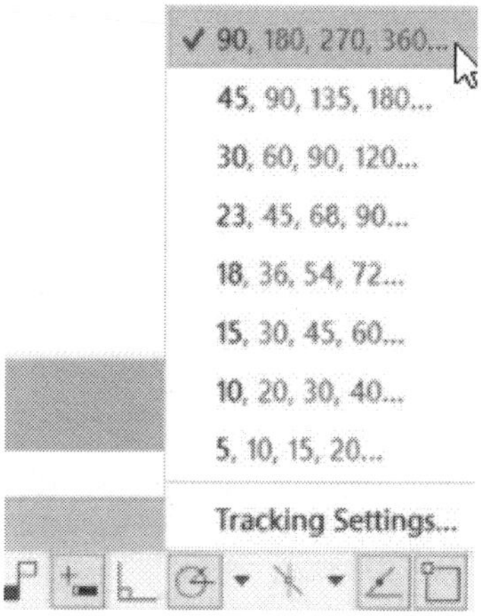

Figure 2–25

3. Start the **Line** command. At the *Specify first point:* prompt, enter **0,0**, and press <Enter>.

4. Move the crosshairs straight to the right from the start point (you might need to first pan down in the drawing). When the cursor feels restricted and the tracking line displays with *Polar: distance < 0* (as shown on the left in Figure 2–26), enter **30**. This automatically overwrites the value in the length edit box (as shown on the right in Figure 2–26). Press <Enter>.

   • Use the mouse wheel to zoom in/zoom out while in a command, as required.

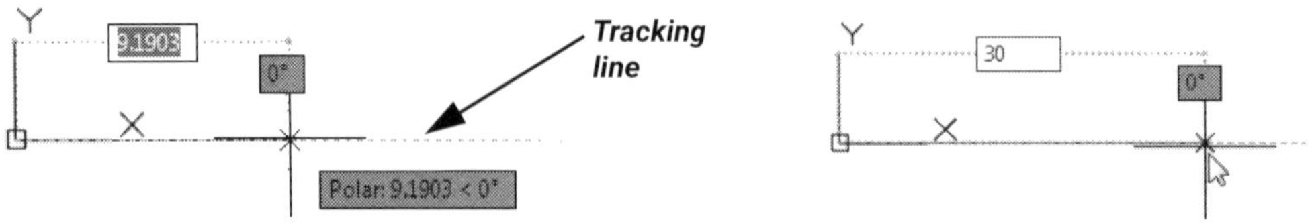

Figure 2–26

5. Move the crosshairs straight up from the new point. When the tracking line displays with *Polar: distance < 90*, enter **20** and press <Enter>.
6. Continue to draw the shape shown previously in Figure 2–24 by moving the crosshairs in multiples of 90° angles and typing the distance for each segment.
7. For the last segment, type **C** and press <Enter> to close the figure and exit the **Line** command.

Task 4: Draw rectangles.

In this task, you will draw rectangles and locate them precisely using coordinates and **Dynamic Input**, as shown in Figure 2–27. You will create them inside the shape created in Task 3.

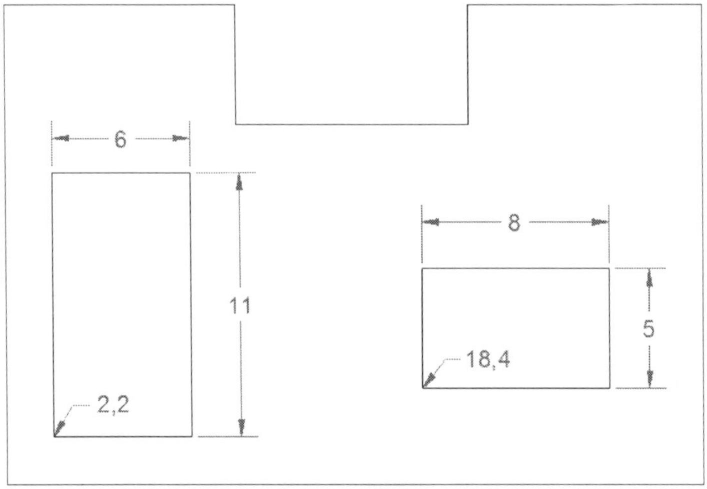

Figure 2–27

1. In the *Home* tab>*Draw* panel, click  (Rectangle).
2. For the first corner point, enter the coordinates **2,2** and press <Enter>.
3. For the other corner, move the cursor to the right and then enter **6,11**. Press <Enter> to create a **6 x 11** rectangle.
4. Draw a second rectangle that is **8 x 5**, with the first corner at point **18,4** as shown in Figure 2–27.
5. Save the drawing.

Task 5: Draw circles.

In this task, you will draw circles (as shown in Figure 2–28) using various circle creation options.

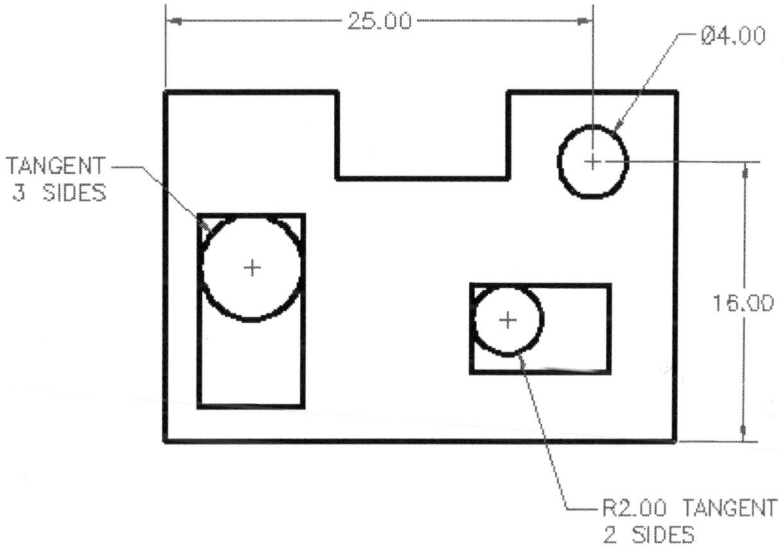

Figure 2–28

1. In the *Home* tab>*Draw* panel>*Circle* flyout, click  (Center, Diameter). To create the circle in the upper right corner, enter **25,16** to place the center point and enter **4** for the diameter.
2. To draw a circle inside the rectangle on the right side (8 x 5 rectangle), in the *Circle* flyout, click  (Tan, Tan, Radius). Select the top line of the rectangle as the first deferred tangent point and the left vertical line as the second tangent point. Press <Enter> to accept the default radius of **2**.

3. Draw a circle touching the three sides of the rectangle, shown on the left side using  (Tan, Tan, Tan).
4. Save and close the drawing.

End of practice

Chapter Review Questions

1. When using the **Line** command, how do you exit the command once you have finished drawing line segments?
   a. Click the left mouse button.
   b. Double-click.
   c. Press <Enter>.
   d. Type **Done** in the Command Line.

2. When drawing a line using the **Line** command, you can specify its length, but not its angle.
   a. True
   b. False

3. Which of the following statements are true for Polar Tracking and Ortho Mode? (Select all that apply.)
   a. With Polar Tracking on, a dotted tracking line displays when the cursor is at a specified angle location.
   b. Ortho Mode enables you to draw lines horizontally and vertically only.
   c. With Ortho Mode on, you can draw lines at specified preset angles.
   d.  (Ortho Mode) and  (Polar Tracking) can be used (toggled on) at the same time.

4. What is the best method to draw a perfectly horizontal line using the **Line** command?
   a. Drag the cursor horizontally until it looks horizontal.
   b. Toggle on Ortho Mode.
   c. Draw a line at any angle and then rotate it until it is horizontal.
   d. Follow the horizontal line of the grid.

5. How do you draw a rectangle using the **Rectangle** command?
   a. Draw individual lines and join them together to form a rectangle.
   b. Click and create three corners of the rectangle with the fourth corner being created automatically.
   c. Click to specify all the four corners of the rectangle.
   d. Click the first corner of the rectangle and then click the diagonally opposite corner.

6. Which one of the following is NOT a method for drawing circles with the **Circle** command?
   a. Tan, Tan, Radius
   b. Center, Radius
   c. Tan, Tan, Point
   d. 2-Point

Command Summary

Button	Command	Location
	**Circle**	• **Ribbon:** *Home* tab>*Draw* panel • **Command Prompt:** circle or C
	**Dynamic Input**	• **Status Bar**
	**Erase**	• **Ribbon:** *Home* tab>*Modify* panel • **Command Prompt:** erase, E, or press <Delete>
	**Line**	• **Ribbon:** *Home* tab>*Draw* panel • **Command Prompt:** line or L
	**Ortho Mode**	• **Status Bar** • **Command Prompt:** ortho or <F8>
	**Polar Tracking**	• **Status Bar** • **Command Prompt:** <F10>
	**Rectangle**	• **Ribbon:** *Home* tab>*Draw* panel • **Command Prompt:** rectangle, rectang, or rec
	**Redo**	• **Quick Access Toolbar** • **Shortcut Menu:** redo • **Command Prompt:** redo
	**Undo**	• **Quick Access Toolbar** • **Shortcut Menu:** undo • **Command Prompt:** undo or U

Chapter 3

Projects: Creating a Simple Drawing

This chapter contains practice projects that can be used to gain additional hands-on experience in the topics and commands covered so far in this guide. These projects are intended to be self-guided and do not include step-by-step information.

Learning Objective

- Create simple drawings using basic shapes such as lines, circles, and rectangles.

3.1 Create a Simple Drawing

In this project, you will create a simple drawing using the commands **Open**, **Line**, **Circle**, **Rectangle**, **Save**, **Erase**, and **Undo**, as shown in Figure 3–1. You are not required to draw the dimensions. They are provided for reference only.

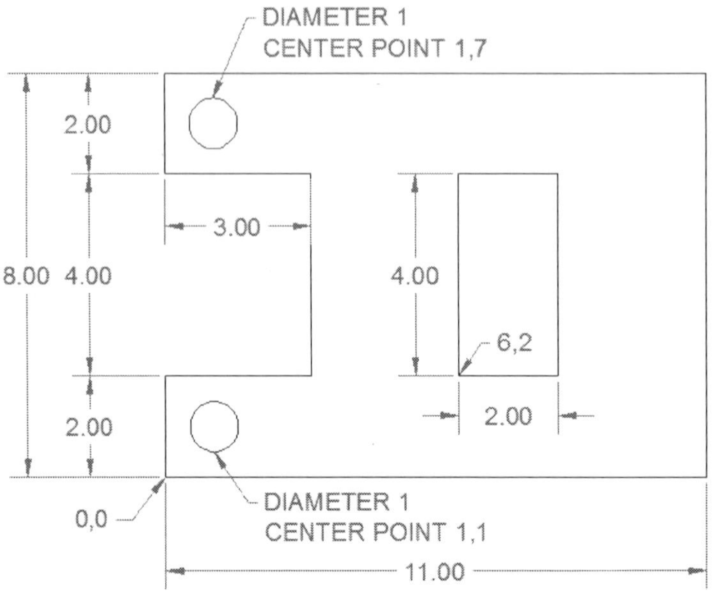

Figure 3–1

1. Open **Simple1.dwg** from your practice files folder. It is a blank drawing file.
2. Draw the object shown in Figure 3–1. Start with the lower left corner of the figure at point 0,0. Use exact coordinates to locate the centers of the circles and the first corner of the rectangle. Draw only the object, not the dimensions as they are for reference only.
3. Save and close the drawing.

3.2 Create Simple Shapes

In this project, you will create several simple shapes using the **Line** command, as shown in Figure 3–2. You are not required to draw the dimensions. They are provided for reference only.

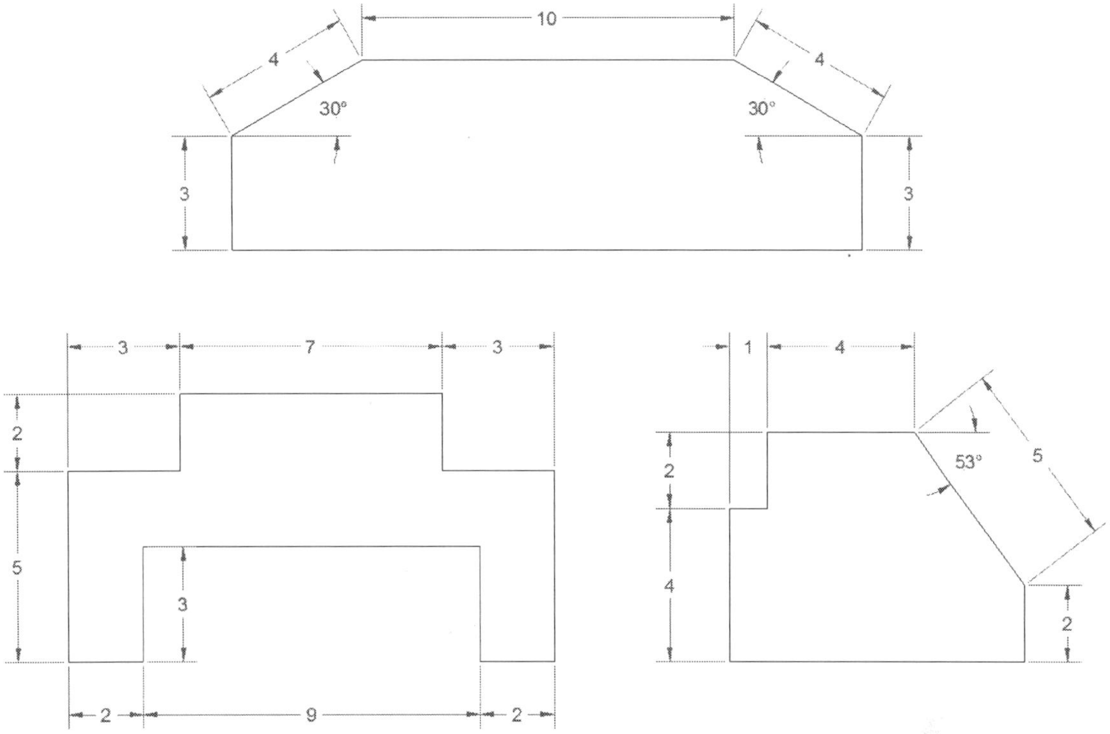

Figure 3–2

1. Open **Simple2.dwg** from your practice files folder. It is a blank drawing file.
2. Use the **Line** command to draw the shapes shown in Figure 3–2.
   - Use the lower left corner of each shape as the starting point and draw the shape clockwise.
   - Use the **Close** option for the last line segment.
   - You can select any point on the screen as the starting point, the exact coordinate location does not matter.
   - If you make a mistake on one segment, use the **Undo** option.
3. Save and close the drawing.

Chapter 4

Drawing Precision in AutoCAD

In this chapter, you learn to select exact points on objects using Object Snaps, use Object Snap overrides, draw lines at specific angles using Polar Tracking, specify distances using Polar Snap, find exact locations using Object Snap Tracking, and use Snap and Grid (optional).

Learning Objectives

- Snap to specific points on an object and set object snaps to remain toggled on.
- Override running object snaps with a specific object snap to select the correct part of an object.
- Draw lines at specific angle increments.
- Locate new points relative to existing ones.
- Restrict the crosshair movement to specific increments.
- Display a grid in the drawing window.

4.1 Using Running Object Snaps

When the AutoCAD® software saves information in a drawing file, it saves geometrical descriptions of the objects you have created. For example, a line is saved as two end points and a circle by its center point and radius. Object snaps enable you to take advantage of this geometrical precision by snapping to exact points on objects while you are in a command, as shown in Figure 4–1. You need some object snaps to be on most of the time, which can be set up as *running* object snaps.

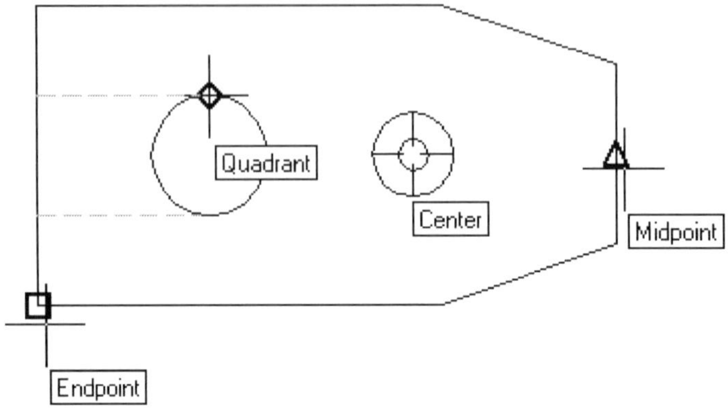

Figure 4–1

How To: Use Running Object Snaps

1. In the *Status Bar*, toggle on  (Object Snap).
   - You can also use <F3> to toggle object snaps on and off.
2. Start a command, such as **Line** or **Circle**.
3. Hover the cursor over an object. When the cursor is near a snap location, an icon displays that is specific to the object snap option that the cursor finds.
4. Click to select the object snap point.
5. Continue selecting other points, as required.

- When using an object snap on an object that might have more than one such point (e.g., **Endpoint** or **Midpoint**), select a point on the object that is close to the required point.

Object Snap Settings

You can set the various running object snap options that are available for use while picking a point. To use them, toggle on the Object Snap in the *Status Bar*. You can set the running object snaps at the following locations:

- In the *Status Bar*, in the 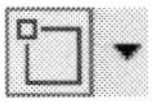 (Object Snap) drop-down list, as shown on the left in Figure 4–2. To display the *Object Snap* drop-down list, either click on the arrow symbol next to the icon or right-click on the icon. Clicking 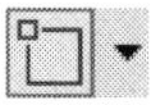 (Object Snap) toggles object snaps on or off.
- In the *Drafting Settings* dialog box, in the *Object Snap* tab, as shown on the right in Figure 4–2. To open the dialog box, expand 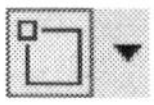 (Object Snap) in the *Status Bar* and select **Object Snap Settings....**

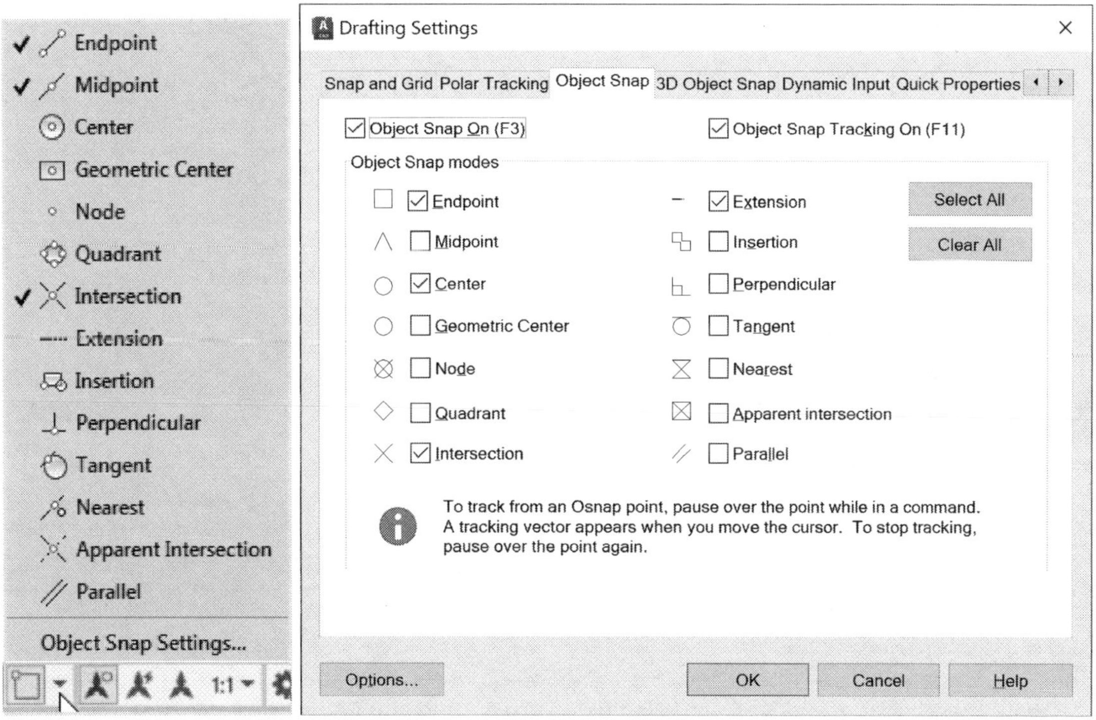

Figure 4–2

- Running object snaps are indicated by a checkmark.
- You can add or remove the object snap options when you are in the middle of a command.

- The symbol for each object snap mode displays in the drawing window when you hover the cursor over the snap location. After a short delay, a small tooltip also displays the name of the snap.
- Object snap settings are saved in the system (not in individual drawings) and remain set until changed.
- When you toggle  (Object Snap) on or off in the *Status Bar*, it does not change the settings.
- Clicking **Options** in the *Drafting Settings* dialog box opens the *Options* dialog box in the *Drafting* tab. Here, you can change the color of the Autosnap marker and modify other settings, as shown in Figure 4–3.
- You can also open the *Options* dialog box by right-clicking in the drawing window and selecting **Options**. Click on the *Drafting* tab to open it.

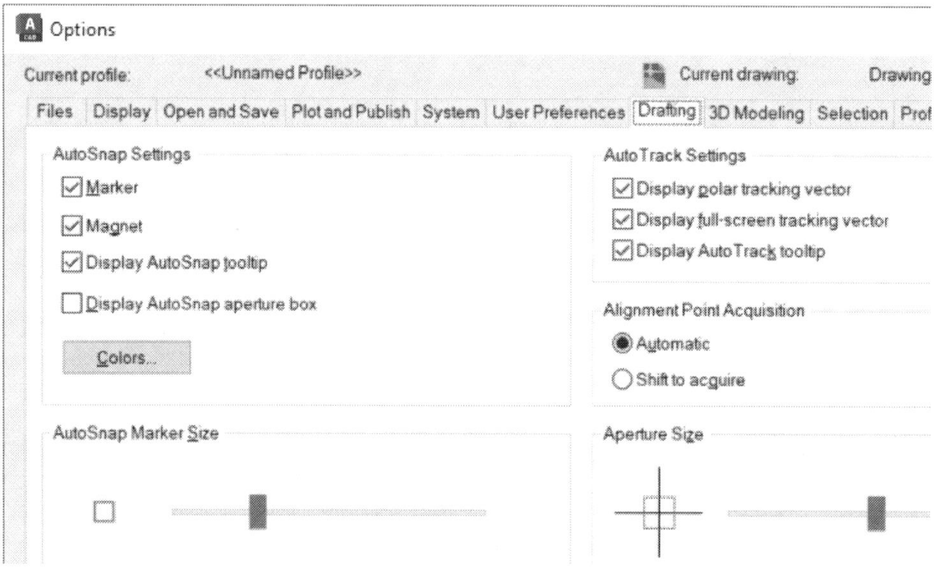

Figure 4–3

Primary Object Snaps

The most frequently used object snaps are **Endpoint**, **Center**, **Intersection**, and **Extension** where as **Quadrant**, **Midpoint**, and **Node** are also helpful in certain situations.

 Endpoint	Snaps to the end point of a line or arc.
 Midpoint	Snaps to the midpoint of a line or arc.

Center	Snaps to the center point of a circle or arc. You can hover the cursor over the edge of the circle or arc to get the center point, if **Quadrant** is not toggled on.
Node	Snaps to a permanent reference point.
Quadrant	Snaps to the quadrant point of a circle or arc (often described as clock positions, e.g., 12, 3, 6, and 9 o'clock).
Intersection	Snaps to the intersection of two objects. **Intersection** can be used in two ways: click directly on the intersection, or select the first object for the intersection and then the second. Intersections that do not actually exist, but would if the two lines were extended, can be selected in this manner.
Extension	Snaps to a point on the continuation of an object.

How To: Use the Extension Object Snap

The **Extension** object snap works differently than the rest of the primary object snaps. Instead of selecting a point, it enables you to specify a start point at a distance from another point. In the example shown in Figure 4–4, the **Extension** object snap is used to start a new wall at a distance from another wall.

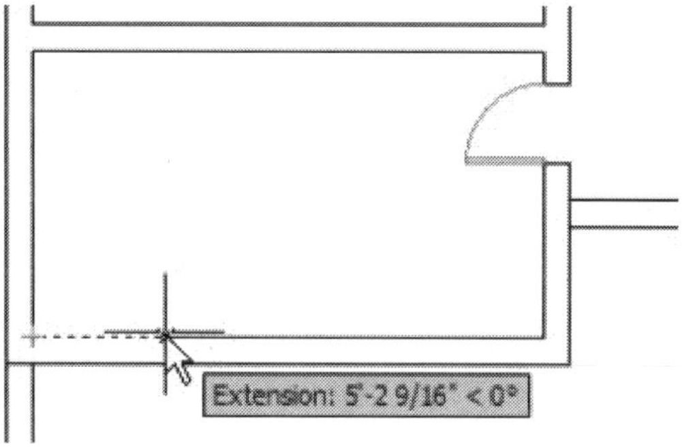

Figure 4–4

1. In the *Status Bar*, toggle on (Object Snap) and verify that the **Extension** object snap is selected.
2. Start a command, such as **Line** or **Circle**.
3. Hover the cursor over an object in the drawing. One of the standard object snap icons displays. Instead of selecting a point, move the cursor away. A small plus symbol (glyph) displays at the snap location.
4. When the cursor reaches a point along the line of the object, a dashed line displays from the end of the object to the crosshairs. In addition, a snap tip displays indicating the distance from the object and its angle. Enter the distance that you want to be from the original point.

Geometric Center Object Snap

The **Geometric Center** object snap tool finds the geometric center (centroid) of a closed polyline, as shown in Figure 4–5. It finds the geometric center of any closed irregular shape.

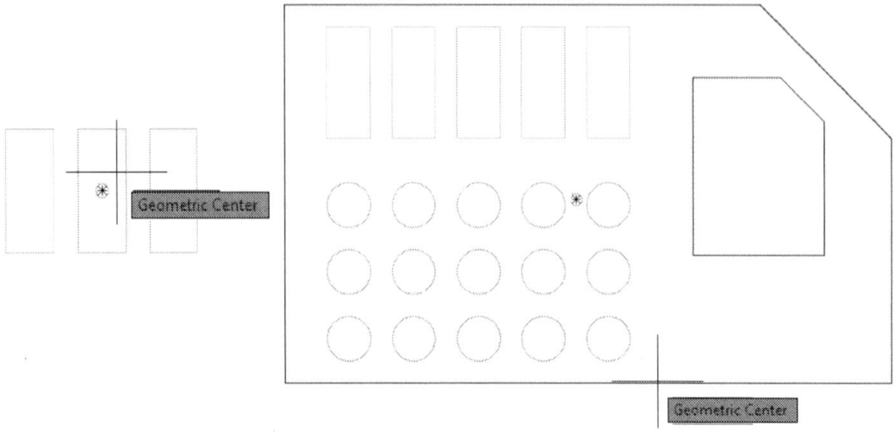

Figure 4–5

Practice 4a
Use Object Snaps

Practice Objective

- Draw a fence and rooflines using object snaps.

In this practice, you will set object snaps and use them to draw a fence line and rooflines, as shown in Figure 4–6.

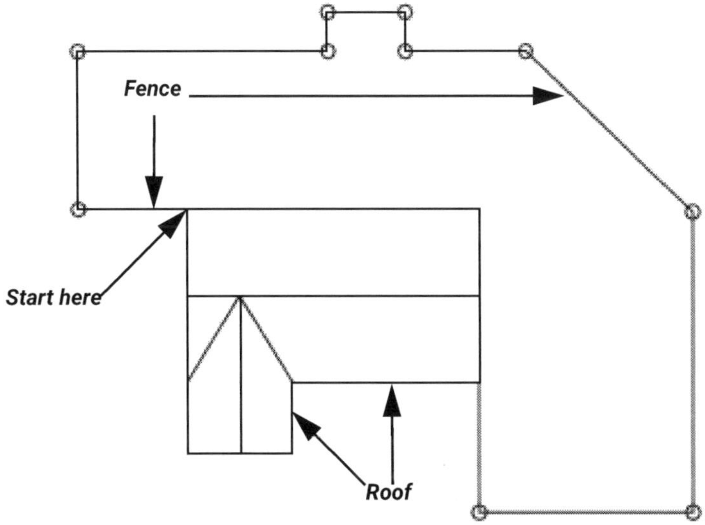

Figure 4–6

Task 1: Draw the fence.

1. Open **Fence-A.dwg** from your practice files folder.
2. In the *Status Bar*, click on the 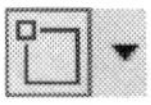 (Object Snap) arrow to display the object snaps list. Set the object snap modes to **Endpoint**, **Midpoint**, **Center**, and **Extension**. Toggle object snap on (highlighted).
3. Start the **Line** command to draw a fence as shown above in Figure 4–6. To locate the start point of the line, hover your cursor over the upper left corner of the house. The cursor snaps and displays an endpoint snap icon at that location. Click to start the line there. Moving clockwise, snap and click to the center of each of the fence posts (i.e., the small circles provided in the drawing). End the fence by snapping and clicking to the endpoint of the bottom right corner of the house. Press <Enter> to exit the **Line** command.

Task 2: Draw the roof lines.

1. In the *Status Bar*, click on the  (Object Snap) arrow and select **Intersection**.
2. In the *Status Bar*, toggle on  (Polar Tracking), if required.
3. Start the **Line** command again and hover your cursor near the middle of the right-side-line of the house till the midpoint object snap displays. Draw line (1) from the midpoint on the right side of the house straight left to the point where it intersects the left side, as shown in Figure 4–7. Press <Enter> to exit the **Line** command. This line indicates the main roof ridge.
4. Restart the **Line** command and hover your cursor near the midpoint on the right-side line of the house until the midpoint object snap displays. Draw line (1) from this midpoint to where it intersects on the left side of the house, as shown in Figure 4-7. Press <Enter> to exit the Line command. This line indicates the main roof ridge.

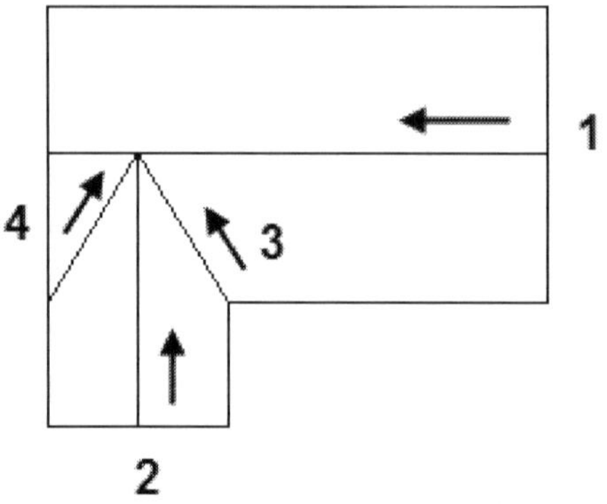

Figure 4–7

5. Draw line (2) from the midpoint of the front wing of the house straight up to the intersection of the ridge you just drew. This creates the ridge of the wing.
6. Draw line (3) from the top right corner endpoint of the wing to the intersection of the two ridge lines.
7. For line (4), after starting the **Line** command, hover the cursor over the bottom left corner (Endpoint object snap tooltip) of the house and then pull it up without selecting the point. A small plus symbol (glyph) displays at the corner location, along with a dotted line and the **Extension** object snap tooltip displays near the cursor indicating that it is enabled. Enter a distance of **10'-0"**. Press <Enter>. The line starts at this point. End it at the intersection of the two ridge lines. Press <Enter>.
8. Save and close the drawing.

End of practice

4.2 Using Object Snap Overrides

You can use 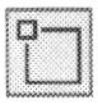 (Object Snap) for the points to which you normally snap. Other snaps, such as **Tangent** or **Perpendicular**, are required less often. Instead of selecting and then clearing those object snaps using the 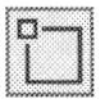 (Object Snap) list, you can apply them as one-time object snap overrides. Object snaps applied as overrides are only active for the next point you select. You can access overrides through the shortcut menu when you are in a command, as shown in Figure 4–8.

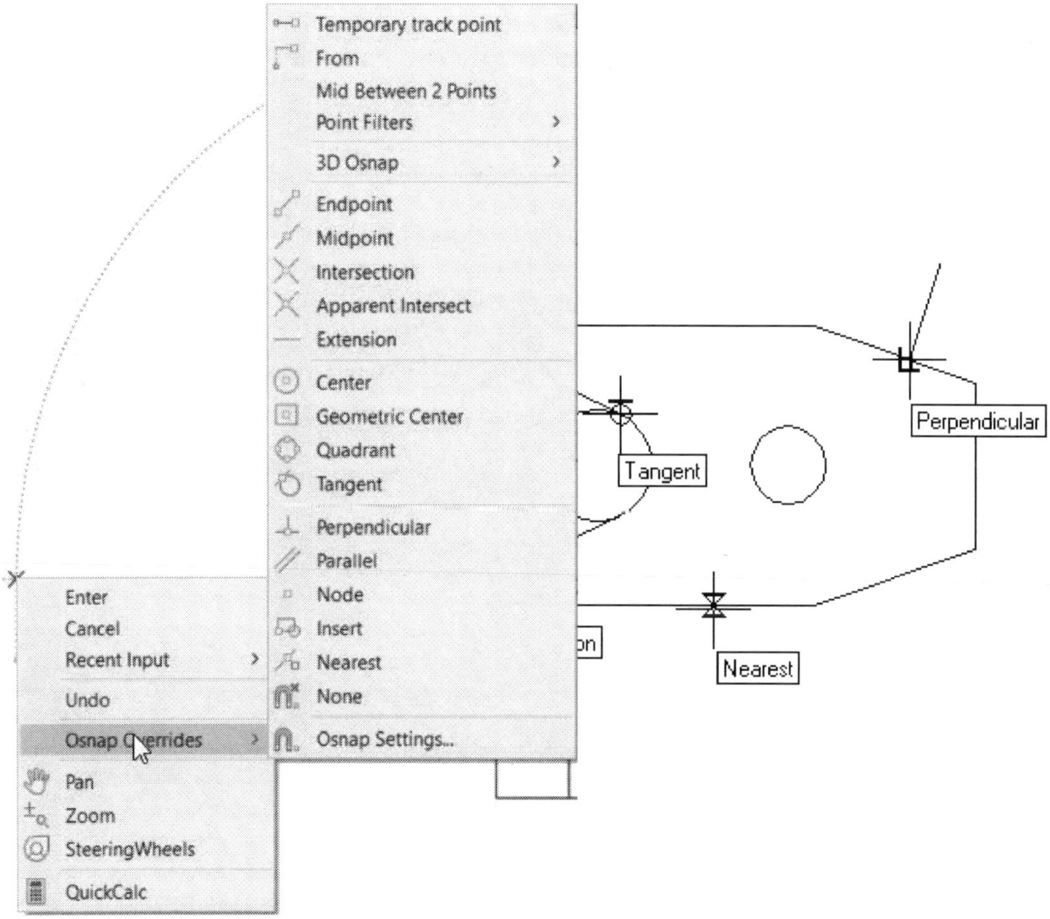

Figure 4–8

- You must start a command before using an object snap override. You can then set the object snap override in the shortcut menu by selecting **Osnap Overrides**, or by holding <Shift> while right-clicking.

How To: Use an Object Snap Override

1. Start a command where point input is required, such as **Line** or **Circle**.
2. Before selecting the point, hold down <Shift> and right-click. To display the object snap override menu, select the required object snap.
3. Move the crosshairs near the location of the object to which you want to snap. An icon for the running object snap displays at the snap location.
4. Click to select the point.

- If you select the wrong object snap, do not press <Esc> or use the **Undo** command (doing so would cancel the command). Instead, select the correct object snap override twice. The first time cancels the previous snap and the second sets the new snap.

Typical Object Snap Overrides

Tangent	Snaps to a point on a circle or arc that forms a line tangent to the object.
Perpendicular	Snaps to a point that creates a perpendicular line from one object to another.
Parallel	Snaps to a point that creates a line parallel to the selected object.
Insert	Snaps to the insertion point of text, a block, or an external reference.
Nearest	Snaps to the point on an object that is visually closest to the crosshairs.
None	Toggles off object snaps for the next point selected.

How To: Use the Parallel Object Snap

Parallel can only be used to draw linear objects. At least one point must be selected before **Parallel** can be used. The new line is drawn parallel to the selected object, as shown in Figure 4–9.

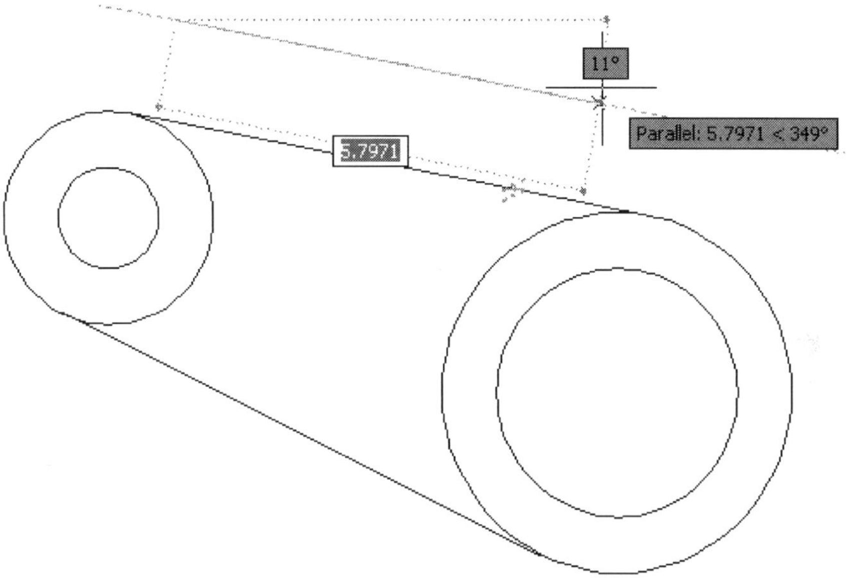

Figure 4–9

1. Start the **Line** command.
2. Select a starting point in the drawing.
3. Select the Parallel object snap override.
4. Hover the cursor over the object to which the new line should be parallel. First, the **Parallel** icon displays and when you move the cursor away a small plus symbol displays on the object.
5. Move the crosshairs away from the object. When you reach a point that makes the new line parallel to the selected object, a dashed line displays indicating the parallel direction. In addition, a parallel marker and snap tip display. Enter the distance or select the point that you want to use.

Practice 4b
Object Snap Overrides

Practice Objective

- Draw objects at precise locations with respect to already present objects in a drawing.

In this practice, you will use a variety of running object snaps and overrides in conjunction with the **Line** and **Circle** commands to complete the drawing (without the dimension), as shown in Figure 4–10.

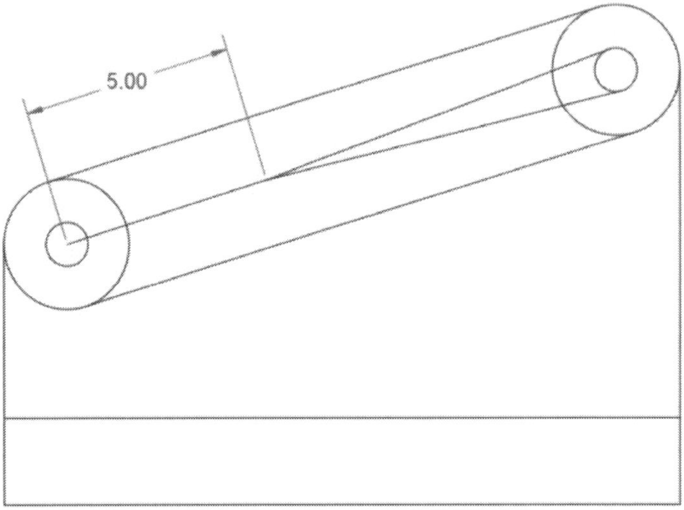

Figure 4–10

1. Open **Arm.dwg** from your practice files folder.
2. Set the object snaps to **Endpoint**, **Midpoint**, and **Center** and toggle  (Object Snap) on, if required.
3. With **Circle>**  (Center Radius), draw smaller circles with a radius of **0.5** at the center of the two existing circles. Hover your cursor over the circle for the center osnap to display.
4. Draw lines connecting the two outer large circles tangent to each circle. Start the **Line** command and at *Specify first point*, hold <Shift> and right-click to open the *object snap override* shortcut menu. Select **Tangent** override. Click anywhere along the upper edge of the bigger lower left large circle, as shown in Figure 4–11.

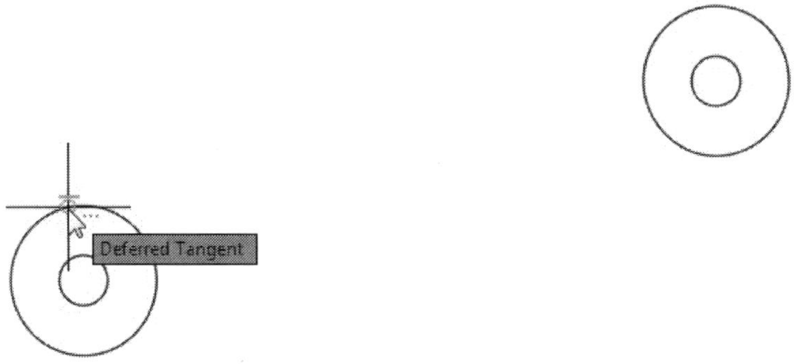

Figure 4–11

5. Use <Shift>+ right-click again and select the **Tangent** override again. Click anywhere along the upper edge of the bigger upper right large circle. Press <Enter> to exit the **Line** command. A line is drawn along the top tangent points of the two large circles.

   Note: *The object snap override must be selected each time you want to use it.*

6. Similarly, draw another line along the bottom tangent points of the two large circles.
7. Start the **Line** command and hold <Shift> and right-click to select the **Quadrant** override. Click along the 9 o' clock quadrant of the lower large circle, as shown in Figure 4–12. Click along the upper left end point of the rectangle to draw the line. (The **Endpoint** object snap is already selected.)

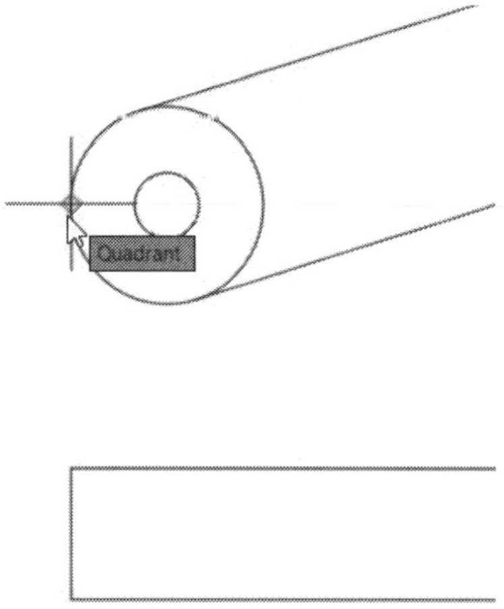

Figure 4–12

8. Draw a line from the 3 o' clock quadrant of the lower large circle perpendicular to the top line of the rectangle. Use the Osnap override menu to select both the **Quadrant** and **Perpendicular** overrides.

9. Draw a line that starts at the center of the small circle on the left, parallel (use the **Parallel** override) to one of the diagonal lines and **5 units** long (as shown in Figure 4–13).

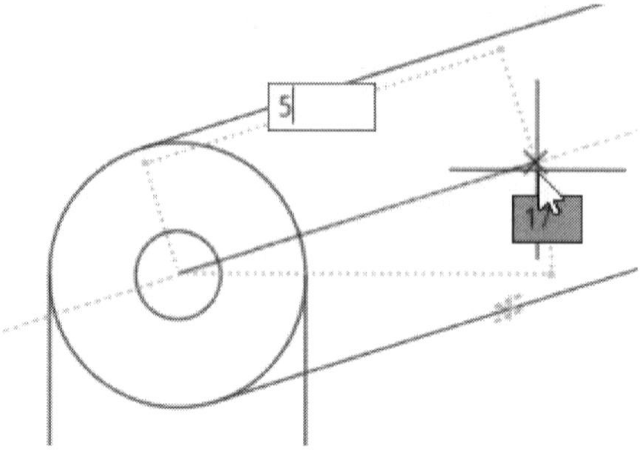

Figure 4–13

10. From the endpoint of the 5 units parallel line, draw a line tangent along the top of the small circle on the right.
11. Draw one more line from the endpoint of the parallel line that is tangent along the bottom of the small circle on the right.
12. Draw a line from the 3 o'clock quadrant of the upper right large circle to the upper right end point of the bottom rectangle.
13. Save and close the drawing.

End of practice

4.3 Polar Tracking at Angles

You can use Polar Tracking to draw horizontal lines, vertical lines, and lines at specific increment angles. (Polar Tracking) can be toggled on or off in the *Status Bar*. Right-click on (Polar Tracking) to select from the list of standard angles (as shown in Figure 4–14) to set the increment angles. You can also set the increment angle while working in a command.

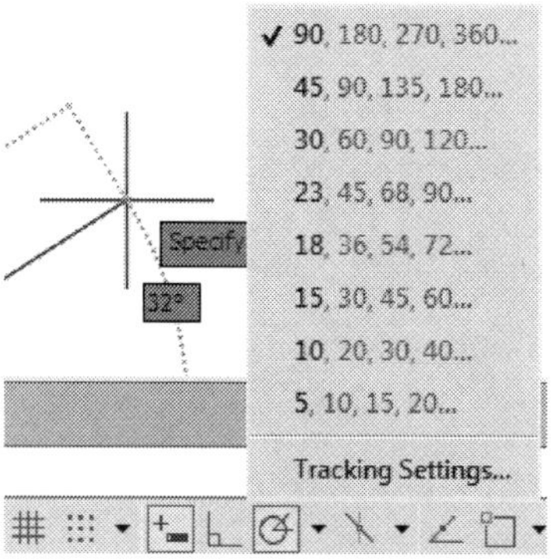

Figure 4–14

Polar Tracking Settings

For more Polar Tracking options, expand (Polar Tracking) (by right-clicking) and select **Tracking Settings...** to open the *Drafting Settings* dialog box, as shown in Figure 4–15. (You can also click on the arrow beside (Polar Tracking) and select **Tracking Settings....**) In this dialog box, you can specify additional angles and modify other settings.

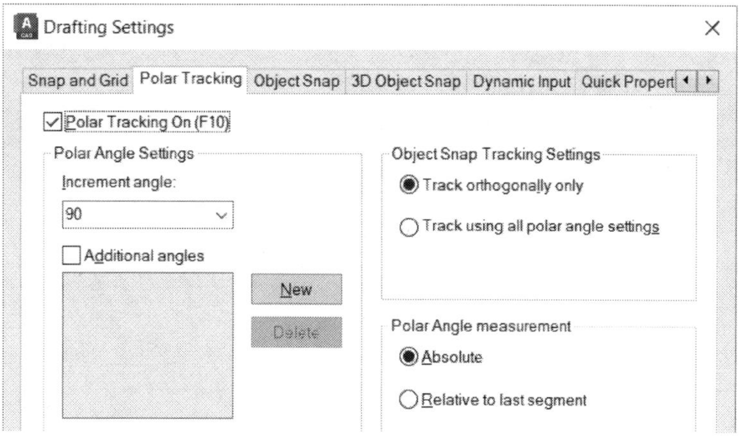

Figure 4–15

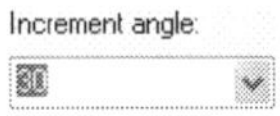	Select an angle in the Increment angle list. All these angles are listed in the Polar Tracking list, which is available in the *Status Bar*.
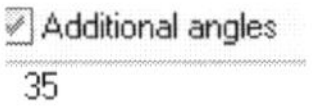	Select this option to use angles other than the one specified in the Increment angle list. You can only snap to this angle (not to its multiples) and to multiples from the Increment angle list. The angle gets added to the Polar Tracking list.
New	Click to add an additional angle. You can add up to ten additional polar tracking alignment angles.
Delete	Deletes selected additional angles.

- When the **Absolute** option is selected, Polar Tracking is relative to the current *X*- and *Y*- axes. For example, if the *Increment Angle* is set to **90** and you draw a diagonal line at 40° for the first segment, the subsequent line is still drawn in increments of 90° relative to the *X*- and *Y*-axes (to the right, left, up, or down), as shown on the left in Figure 4–16.
- When the **Relative to last segment** option is selected, Polar Tracking is relative to the last segment drawn or to a segment to which you snap using OSNAP. This means that you can draw the subsequent line in 90° increments from the diagonal line drawn, as shown on the right in Figure 4–16.

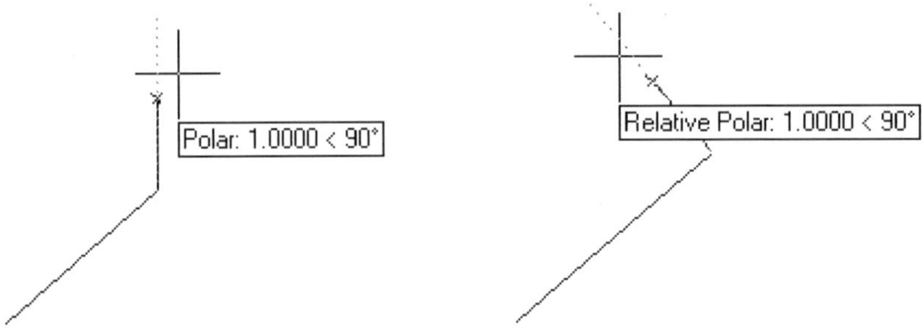

Figure 4–16

- In the Polar Tracking settings, you can select **Track orthogonally only** (i.e., horizontally and vertically) or **Track using all polar angle settings**.

Practice 4c
Polar Tracking

Practice Objective

- Draw an outline of a part using Polar Tracking and by setting the Polar Tracking options.

In this practice, you will adjust the *Polar Tracking* settings and then use **Polar Tracking** to draw the outline of the part, as shown in Figure 4–17. Do not draw the dimensions.

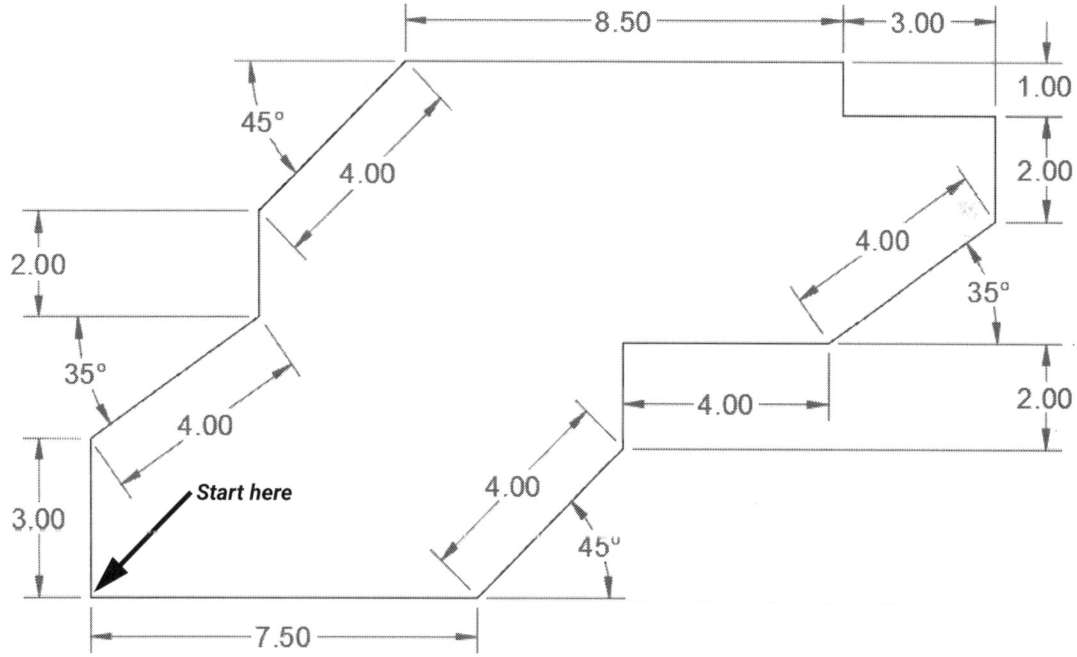

Figure 4–17

1. Open **Pattern.dwg** from your practice files folder. It is a blank drawing file.

2. In the *Status Bar*, expand (Polar Tracking) and note the various angles and increments. There is no angle increment for 35. Select **Tracking Settings...**.

3. In the *Drafting Settings* dialog box>*Polar Tracking* tab, select **Additional angles** and click **New.** In the edit box that is highlighted, enter **35** to add an additional angle, as shown in Figure 4–18. Click **OK**.

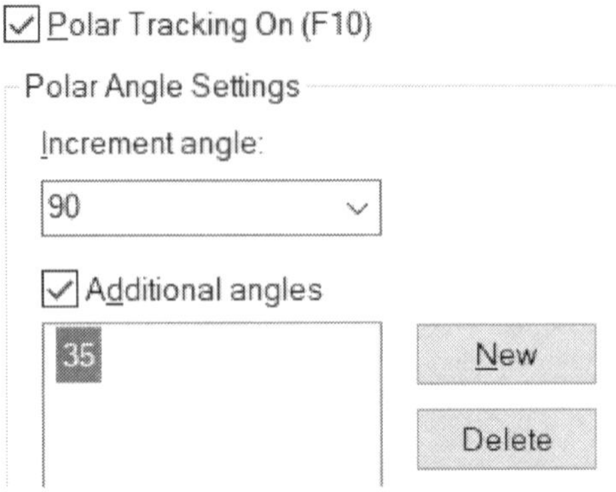

Figure 4–18

4. In the *Status Bar*, expand 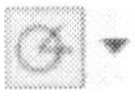 (Polar Tracking) and note that **35,70,105,140...** is added to the list. In the list, select **45,90,135,180....** Ensure that  (Polar Tracking) is toggled **On**.
5. Start the **Line** command and select any point on the screen as the lower left corner of the drawing (shown as "Start here" in Figure 4–17). Move the cursor straight to the right so that the tracking line at 0° displays. Enter **7.5** and press <Enter>.
6. Move the cursor up and to the right until the cursor snaps and a 45° tracking line displays. Enter **4** and press <Enter>.
7. Continue to draw the outline (as shown in Figure 4–17) snapping to the appropriate tracking angle and typing the distance for each segment. Note that you can snap to the 35° angle as well. The opposite (or complementary) angle for 45° is 135°.
8. For the last angled segment, the 35° tracking does not work (because the opposite or complementary angle for 35° is 145°, which was not set). Enter a distance of **4** (do not press <Enter>) and then press <Tab>. Note that the angle edit box is highlighted. Enter the angle as **145** and press <Enter>.
9. Draw the last vertical line of **3** units to complete the drawing.
10. Save and close the drawing.

End of practice

4.4 Object Snap Tracking

Object Snap Tracking enables you to locate new points in relation to one or two existing points, as shown in Figure 4–19. Using Object Snaps and Object Snap Tracking together can speed up your work.

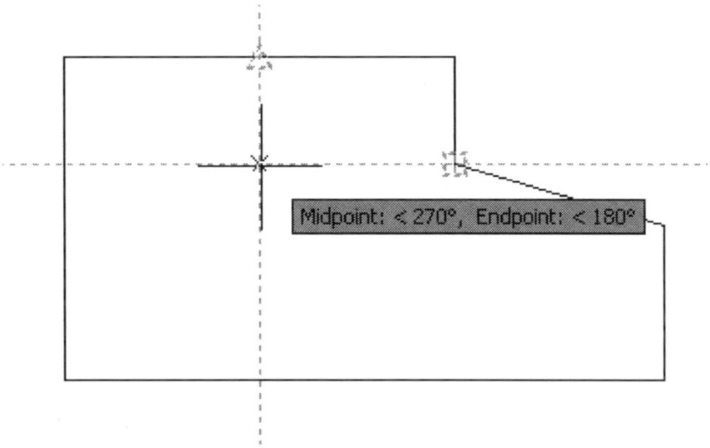

Figure 4–19

- Object Snaps must be toggled on to use Object Snap Tracking.
- Tracking builds a new point based on coordinates taken from two other points. The new X-coordinate is from one point and the new Y-coordinate is from another point.
- When a point is selected for Object Snap Tracking, a small plus (glyph) displays at the point. The point is said to be *acquired*. A dotted line displays from that point to indicate tracking.
- To clear an acquired point, move the cursor over the point again. Ensure that the small plus disappears.
- You can use Object Snap Tracking with Polar Tracking toggled on or off. However, in some cases Polar Tracking can interfere with the effects of Object Snap Tracking.

How To: Use Object Snap Tracking with One Point

1. In the *Status Bar*, toggle on both (Object Snap) and (Object Snap Tracking) and set the Object Snap options that you want to use.
   - You can also use <F11> to toggle object snap tracking on and off.
2. Start a command, such as **Line**.

3. Hover the cursor over the point from which you want to track (do not click on it). A small plus (glyph) marks the point, as shown in Figure 4–20.

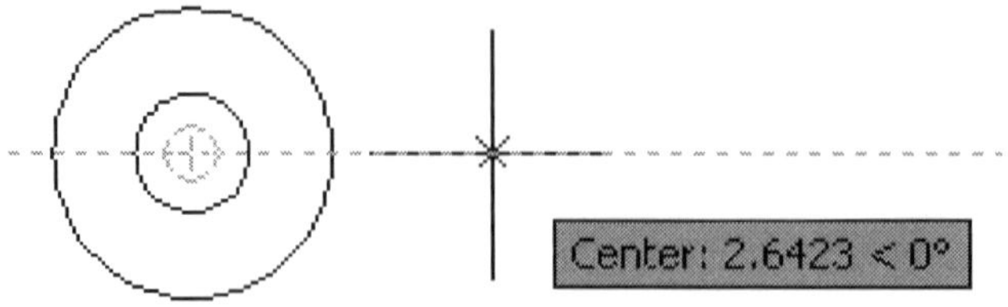

Figure 4–20

4. Move the cursor away from the point. A dotted line and tooltip display when the cursor locks into a tracking angle.
5. Enter the distance that you want to use and press <Enter>.

How To: Use Object Snap Tracking with Two Points

1. In the *Status Bar*, toggle on both  (Object Snap) and  (Object Snap Tracking) and set the Object Snap options that you want to use.
2. Start a command, such as **Line**.
3. Hover the cursor over the points from which you want to track (do not click on them). Small plus signs mark each point.
4. Two dotted lines display, each passing through an acquired point. Move the cursor to the point at which the lines intersect. A description of each dotted line displays in the tooltip, as shown in Figure 4–21.

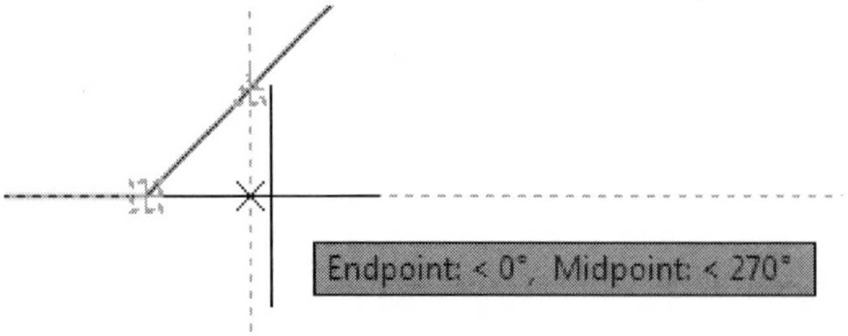

Figure 4–21

5. Select the point at the intersection of the tracking lines.

Practice 4d
Object Snap Tracking I

Practice Objective

- Create a top view of a part by using Object Snap Tracking.

In this practice, you will create a top view of a part by tracking the locations from the existing front and side views, as shown in Figure 4–22. Construction lines have been provided from the side view. The other construction lines, dimension, and the view labels do not need to be drawn.

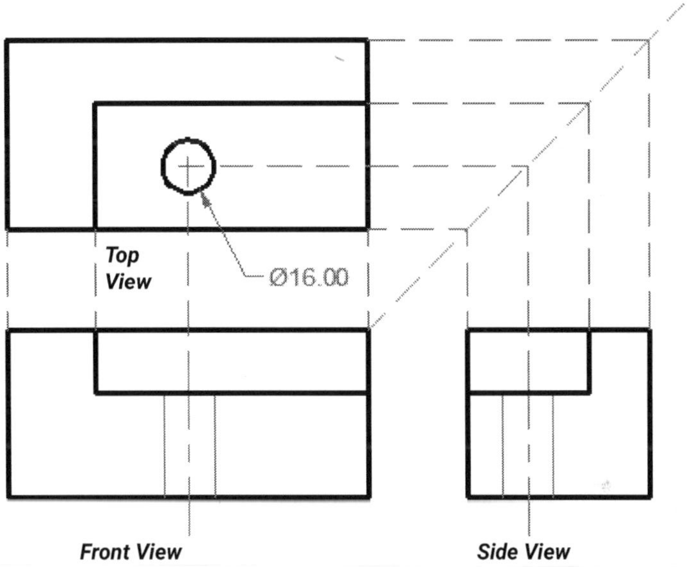

Figure 4–22

1. Open **Missing View.dwg** from your practice files folder.
2. Set the current object snaps as **Endpoint**, **Midpoint**, **Center**, **Quadrant**, and **Intersection**.
3. Toggle on 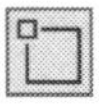 (Object Snap) and  (Object Snap Tracking), if required.
4. Start the **Line** command. At the *Specify first point:* prompt, hover the cursor over the top left corner of the front view, which displays the **Endpoint** object snap icon. Then, without clicking, move the cursor slightly up and then to the right. Note that a small green plus mark (glyph) displays at the top left corner of the front view. Move the cursor right and hover it over the top end point of the shortest construction line coming from the side view. Again without clicking, move the cursor left and note that a small green plus mark displays at this point as well.

5. Move the cursor left to where the two tracking lines intersect at a point, as shown in Figure 4–23. Click to select that point as the first point for the line.

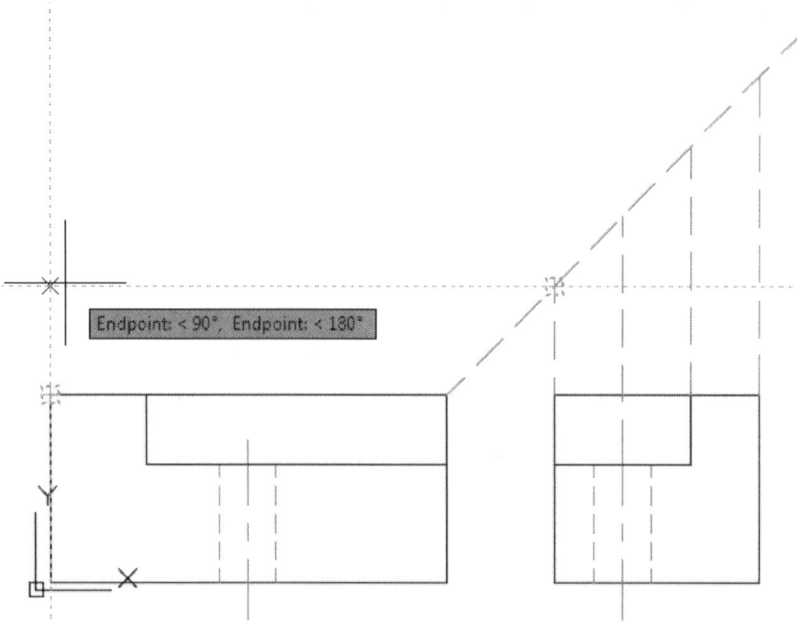

Figure 4–23

6. For the second point of the line, move the cursor right and hover it over the top right corner of the front view, which displays the **Endpoint** object snap icon. Then, without clicking, move the cursor up till it snaps with the right tracking line, as shown in Figure 4–24. Click to select that point and note the bottom line of the top view is created.

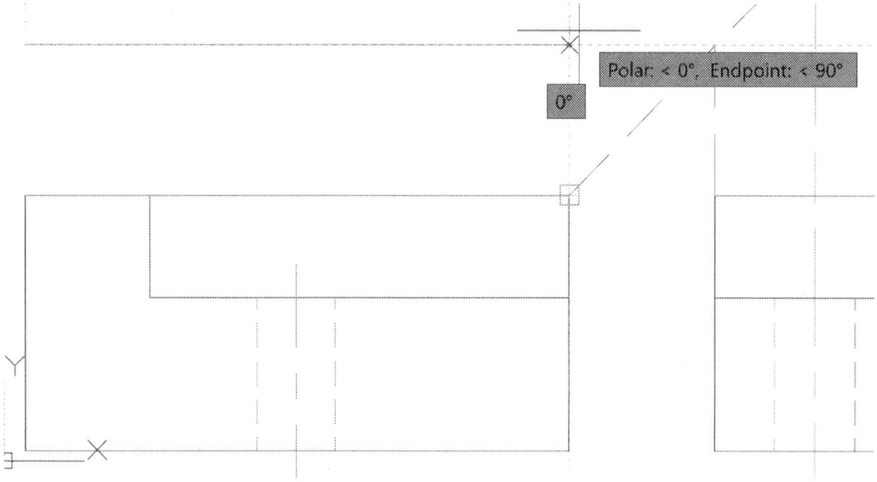

Figure 4–24

7. Continue to draw the rectangular outline of the top view, tracking from the appropriate points.
8. Draw the two interior lines on the top view (as shown in Figure 4–25) using tracking points.
9. Using the **Center, Diameter** option of the **Circle** command, draw a circle (diameter **16**) whose center point is established by tracking points, as shown in Figure 4–25.

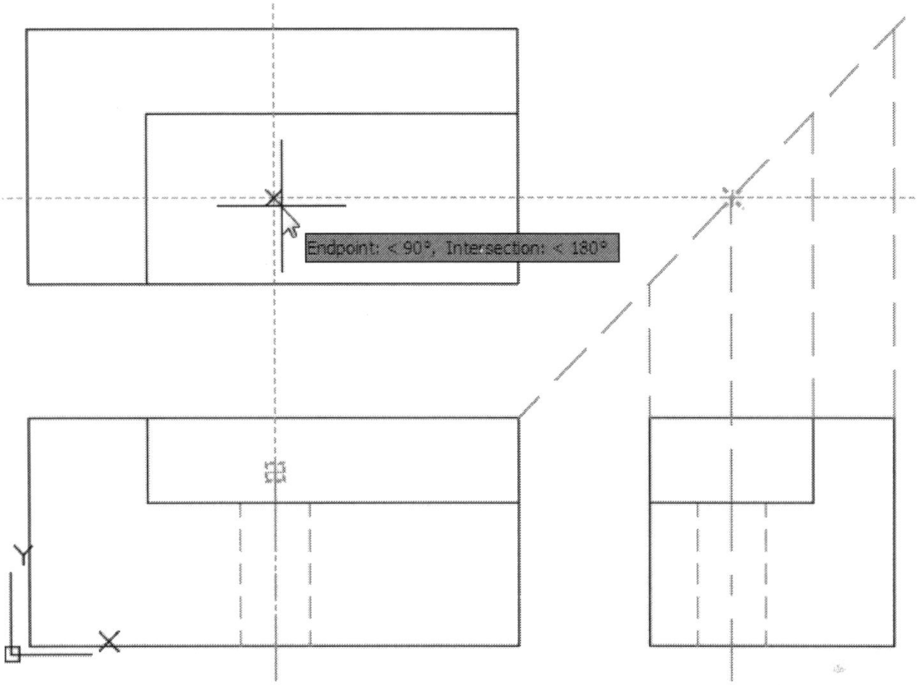

Figure 4–25

10. Save and close the drawing.

End of practice

Practice 4e
Object Snap Tracking II

Practice Objective

- Draw lines in a schematic diagram using Object Snap Tracking.

In this practice, you will use Object Snap Tracking to draw lines in a schematic diagram.

1. Open **Process.dwg** from your practice files folder.
2. Set the object snaps to **Midpoint** and **Quadrant**. Ensure that  (Object Snap) and  (Object Snap Tracking) are toggled on.
3. Use Object Snap Tracking to add lines between the Bleed Storage and Pump.
   - Zoom in on the two parts.
   - Start the **Line** command.
   - Select the midpoint on the bottom line of the Bleed Storage as the first point. Doing so also acquires the midpoint as a tracking point.
   - Hover the cursor over the left quadrant osnap of the Pump and then move the cursor away from that point (do not click). A small cross displays at the point.
   - Move the cursor to the left of the Pump. A snap tip and dotted tracking lines display from the Bleed Storage and Pump. When both tracking lines display (as shown on the left in Figure 4–26), click to place the second point of the line.
   - For the next point, select the left quadrant of the Pump, as shown on the right in Figure 4–26.

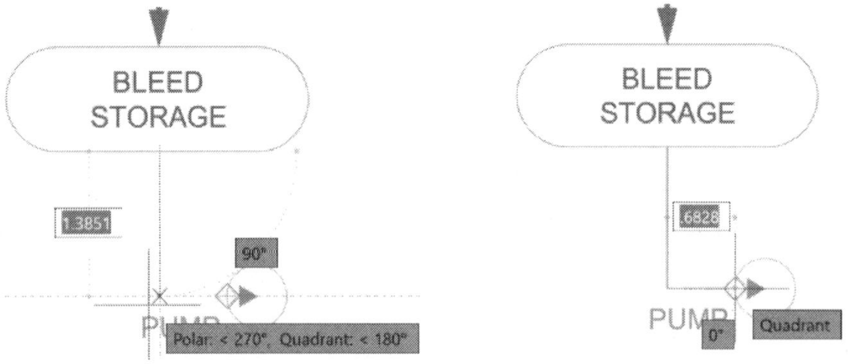

Figure 4–26

4. Similarly, using the object snaps and object snap tracking points, draw additional lines between the components, as shown in Figure 4–27.

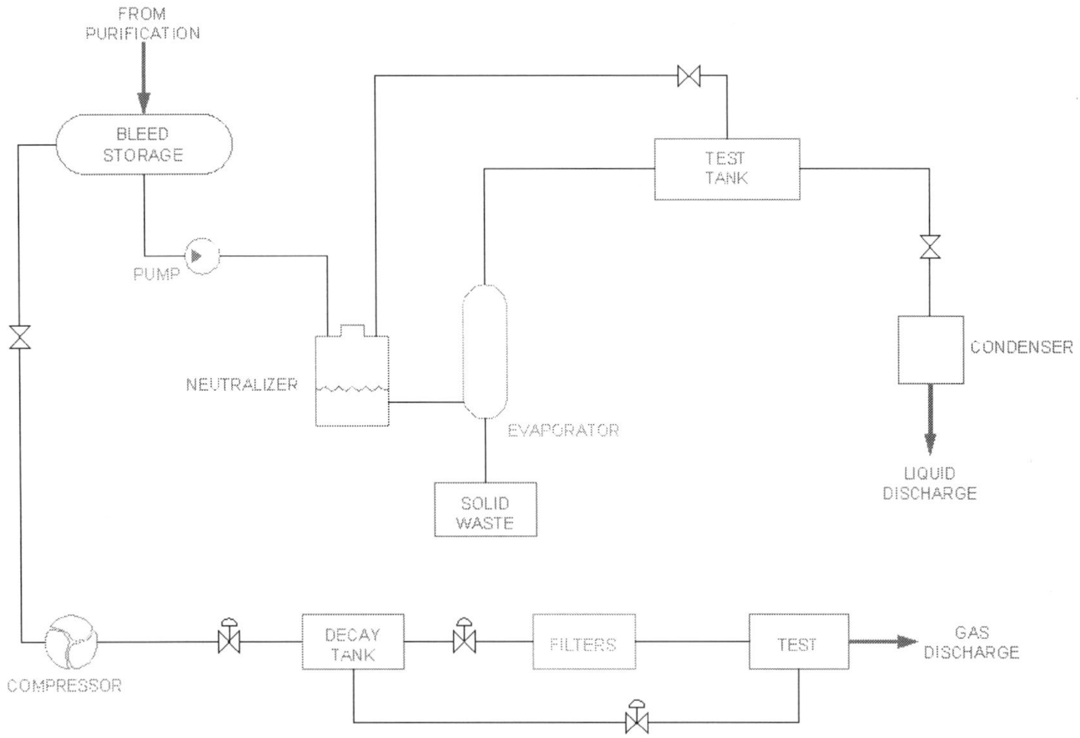

Figure 4–27

5. Save and close the drawing.

End of practice

4.5 Drawing with Snap and Grid

The AutoCAD Snap Mode and Grid Display are useful in schematic drawings, in which the objects are not drawn using real-world sizes or distances but are often lined up and evenly spaced, as shown in Figure 4–28.

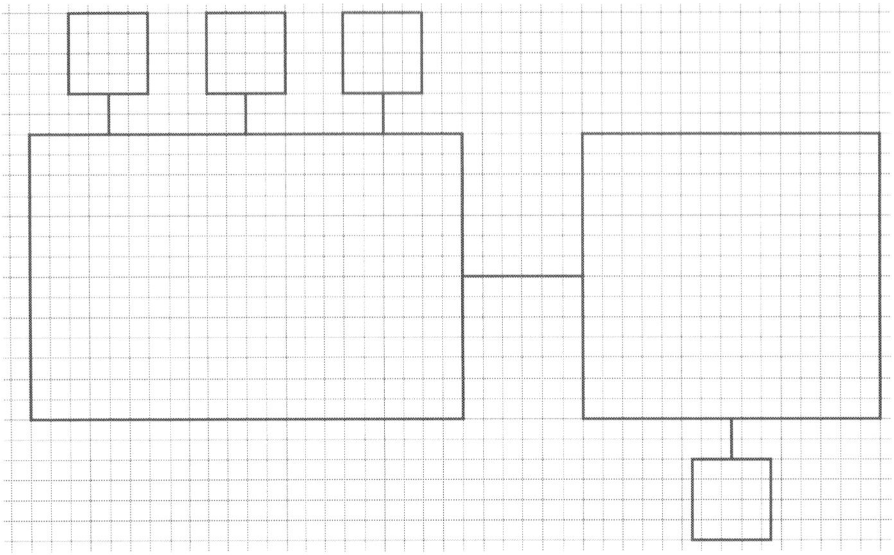

Figure 4–28

Snap Mode restricts the movement of the crosshairs to specific increments, such as 1 unit or 0.5 units. When **Snap Mode** is toggled on, objects you draw are forced to use an invisible snap grid based on the set *Snap spacing*. Click 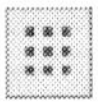 (Snap Mode) in the *Status Bar* or press <F9> to toggle it on or off, as shown in Figure 4–29.

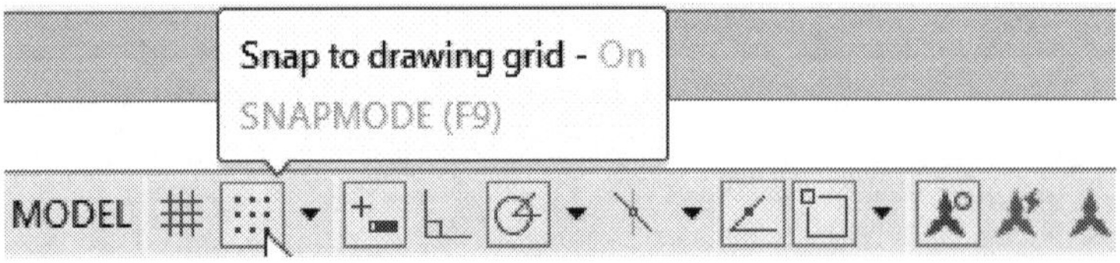

Figure 4–29

The **Grid Display** is a series of lines in the drawing window, which act as a visual reference. In appearance it is similar to engineering graph paper. The *Grid spacing* can be the same as or different to the Snap spacing. The command does not affect the movement of the crosshairs and does not print.

Click (Grid Display) in the *Status Bar* or press <F7> to toggle it on or off, as shown in Figure 4–30.

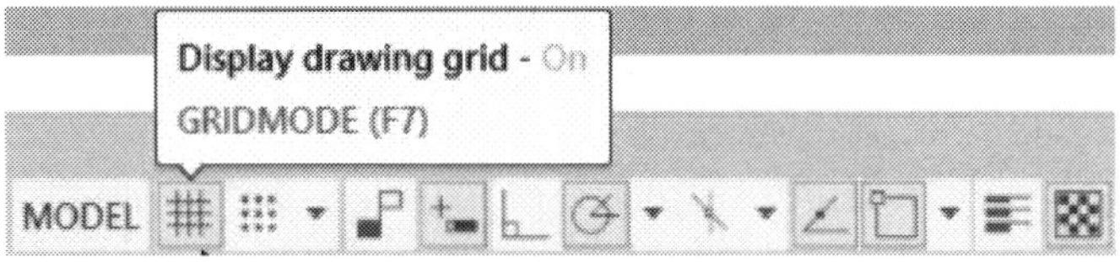

Figure 4–30

Snap and Grid Settings

You can set the various snap and grid options in the *Drafting Settings* dialog box, in the *Snap and Grid* tab, as shown in Figure 4–31. Expand (Snap Mode) and select **Snap Settings** to open the *Drafting Settings* dialog box in the *Snap and Grid* tab.

- To set the Snap or Grid spacing in a drawing, set the X- and Y-spacing for the Snap and/or Grid (these are usually the same).

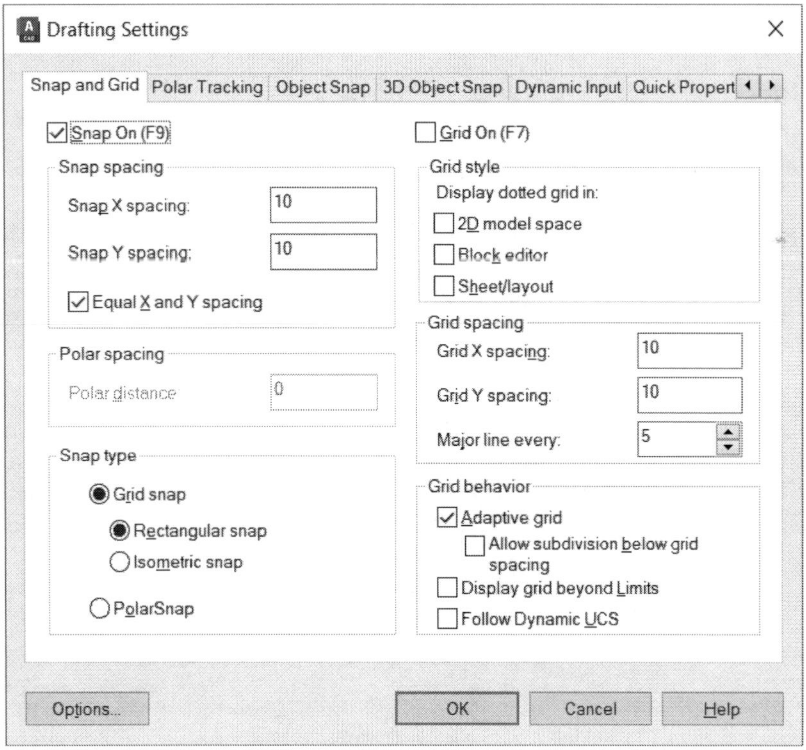

Figure 4–31

- The normal *Snap type* is **Grid snap>Rectangular snap**, which is a rectangular array similar to the grid. If the *Snap type* is set to **Polar Snap** instead, the snap increments are measured along the Polar tracking lines (this only works when Polar Tracking is on). In this case, you set the Polar spacing for the required increment.
- When the *Snap type* is set to **Isometric snap**, the grid and cursor become angled and can be used to draw 2D isometric parts.
- The *Snap type* options can also be set from the (Snap Mode) drop-down list, which can be displayed either by right-clicking on the **Snap Mode** icon or by clicking the arrow beside it.
- The *Grid style* options enable you to display the grid as a series of dots rather than lines and have it display differently for specific functions, such as the Block editor.
- You can use *Grid behavior* to further control how the grid is used. These tools are especially useful when you start working in 3D.
- You can use the **Legacy** option, which forces the cursor to always snap to the grid. If the **Legacy** option is toggled off, you cannot snap to the grid unless you are in an active command. Type **Snap** in the Command Line and select **Legacy**. Select **Yes** to toggle on the option. The **Legacy** option is only available as a Command Line option of the **Snap** command.

Isometric Drawing Environment

In the *Drafting Settings* dialog box (*Snap and Grid* tab), when the Snap type is set to **Isometric snap**, or in the *Status Bar*, when you toggle the (Isometric Drafting) on, the grid and cursor become angled. This enables you to draw 2D isometric parts quickly and efficiently, as shown in Figure 4–32. It is used to draw 3D representation of models in 2D space.

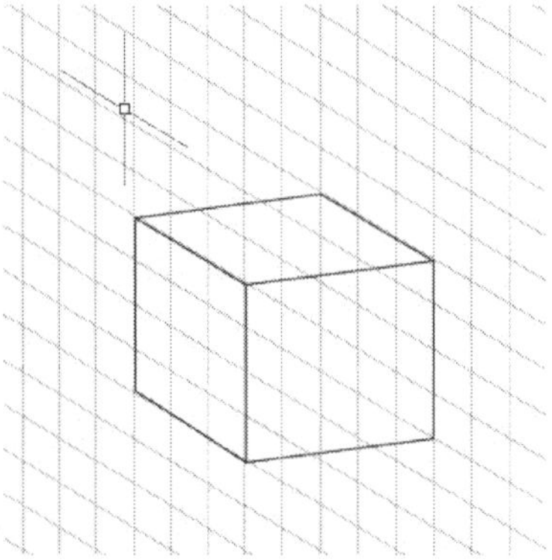

Figure 4–32

The rotation of the grid and the cursor is controlled using the **Isometric Drafting** tool in the *Status Bar*. When the **Isometric Drafting** is toggled on, the crosshairs display in red and green.

- Expand (Isometric Drafting) and click on one of the following options to set the required isometric drawing environment.
    - (Isoplane Left)
    - (Isoplane Top)
    - (Isoplane Right)
- The cursor (crosshairs) and grid display is oriented to suit the selected option, as shown for **Isoplane Top** in Figure 4–33.

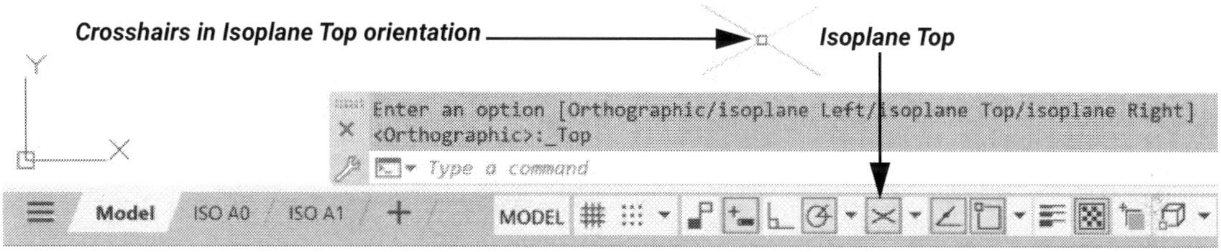

Figure 4–33

- You can use <Ctrl>+<E> or press <F5> to cycle through the different isoplanes.
- To represent holes in an isometric drawing in 2D, use the **Isocircle** option in the **Ellipse** command. In the *Home* tab>*Draw* panel, expand the *Ellipse* flyout and select (Axis,End). At the *Specify axis endpoint of ellipse* prompt, select the drop-down arrow and select **Isocircle**, as shown on the left in Figure 4–34. Select the required Isoplane and draw the circle as shown for Isoplane Top on the right in Figure 4–34.

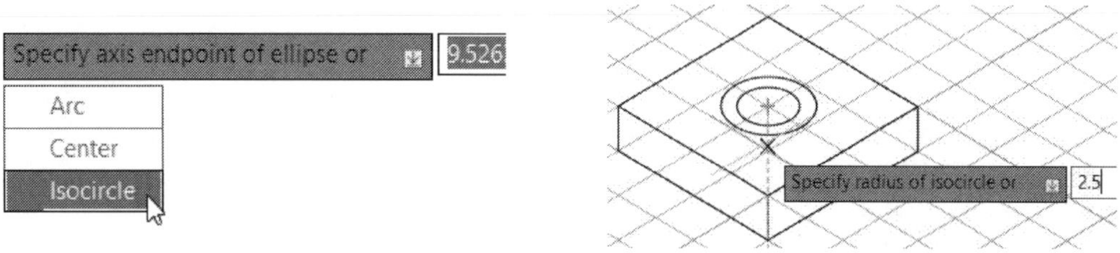

Figure 4–34

Practice 4f
Place Objects on a Drawing

Practice Objective

- Place objects in a drawing precisely.

In this practice, you will draw objects using Snap and Grid to help place them precisely, as shown in Figure 4–35.

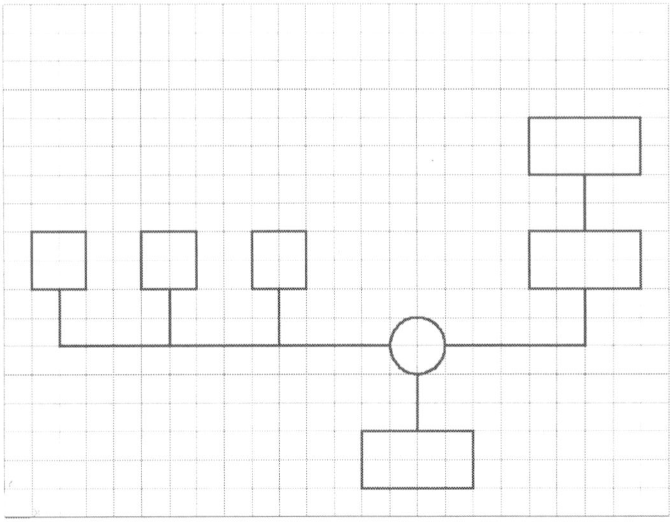

Figure 4–35

1. Open **Schematic.dwg** from your practice files folder. It is a blank drawing.
2. In the *Status Bar*, toggle on (Snap Mode) and (Grid Mode). Expand (Snap Mode) and select **Snap Settings**. Set the *Snap spacing* and *Grid spacing* (both X and Y Spacing) to **1.0** and click **OK**.
3. Toggle off (Object Snap).
4. Using the grid squares, draw the objects shown in Figure 4–35, starting with the circle (**radius=1**). The rectangles should be **2 x 2** and **4 x 2**. The exact distance between objects does not matter, only that they line up evenly.
5. Save and close the drawing.

End of practice

Chapter Review Questions

1. When you set Object Snap options in the *Drafting Settings* dialog box, the object snaps are:
   a. Tracking points for Object Snap Tracking
   b. Overrides to preset object snaps
   c. The same as the object snaps in the shortcut menu
   d. Available when you need to pick a point

2. What types of objects does the **Center** object snap work with?
   a. Circles and lines
   b. Circles, arcs, and rectangles
   c. Circles, arcs, and lines
   d. Circles and arcs

3. Which object snap enables you to position an object at the center of a rectangle that was created using the **Rectang** command?
   a. Center Object Snap
   b. Geometric Center Object Snap
   c. Midpoint Object Snap
   d. Intersection Object Snap

4. When can you use an object snap override from the shortcut menu?
   a. When Snap Mode is toggled on in the *Status Bar*
   b. When Object Snap Mode is toggled on in the *Status Bar*
   c. After you start a command and the software prompts you for a point
   d. Any time

5. If you set the Polar Tracking increment angles to 18, 36, 54,... you can track to the multiples of 18° in addition to horizontal and vertical lines.
   a. True
   b. False

6. Which settings in the *Status Bar* should be toggled on to use the Object Snap Tracking?
   a. Object Snap Tracking and Polar Tracking
   b. Object Snap Tracking and Object Snap
   c. Object Snap Tracking and Snap mode
   d. Only Object Snap Tracking

7. What happens when you type **Snap** in the Command Line, select **Legacy**, and then select **Yes** to toggle it on?
   a. It forces the cursor to always snap to the snap grid, even if you are not in an active command.
   b. It displays the grid as a series of dots rather than lines.
   c. The snap increments are measured along the Polar tacking lines and works when Polar Tracking is on.
   d. The grid and cursor become angled and makes it easier to draw a 2D isometric part.

8. When using **Isometric drafting**, which of the following isoplanes are available in the isometric drawing environment? (Select all that apply.)
   a. Isoplane Right
   b. Isoplane Left
   c. Isoplane Front
   d. Isoplane Top
   e. Isoplane Bottom

Command Summary

Button	Command	Location
	**Grid Mode**	• **Status Bar** • **Command Prompt:** (*toggle on/off*) <F7>
	**Isometric Drafting**	• **Status Bar** • **Command Prompt:** ISODRAFT
	**Object Snap**	• **Status Bar** • **Command Prompt:** (*toggle on/off*) <F3>
N/A	**Object Snap Overrides**	• **Shortcut Menu:** (*when in a command*) Snap Overrides or <Shift> + right-click • **Command Prompt:** (*when in a command*) *first three letters of the object snap name*
	**Object Snap Tracking**	• **Status Bar** • **Command Prompt:** (*toggle on/off*) <F11>
	**Polar Tracking**	• **Status Bar** • **Command Prompt:** (*toggle on/off*) <F10>
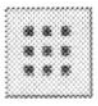	**Snap Mode**	• **Status Bar** • **Command Prompt:** (*toggle on/off*) <F9>

Chapter 5

Making Changes in Your Drawing

In this chapter, you learn how to select objects for editing, how to move, copy, rotate, scale, and mirror objects, and how to edit with grips.

Learning Objectives

- Select, move, scale, and rotate objects using various commands.
- Make copies of selected objects.
- Create reversed or symmetrical copies of objects around an axis line.
- Modify the location, number, and size of objects using grips options.

5.1 Selecting Objects for Editing

When you start most editing commands, the crosshairs display as a small selection box along with the Select objects prompt, as shown in Figure 5–1.

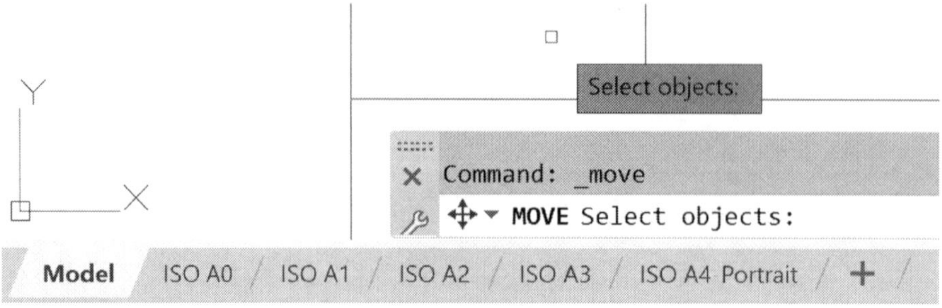

Figure 5–1

How To: Select Objects

1. After starting an editing command (such as **Move**, **Copy**, **Scale**, etc.), you are required to select the objects and the cursor crosshairs change to a selection box. Hover the small selection box over an object. The object is highlighted in a thicker line weight.
2. Click to select the object, which then highlights in blue, as shown in Figure 5–2.

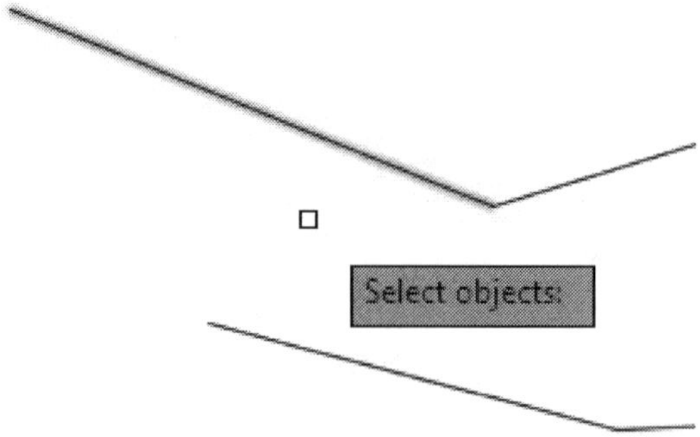

Figure 5–2

3. The cursor continues to display as the small selection box. You can click on another object to add to the selection.
4. Continue selecting objects if you want to add more objects to the selection.
5. When all of the objects have been selected, press <Enter> or right-click to exit the *Select objects:* prompt and continue with the command.

Implied Selection

You can select individual objects or draw a box, line, or lasso around multiple objects to select them together. When using any of the selection methods, the objects to be selected are highlighted in a thicker line weight before the selection is completed. Once the objects have been selected, they are highlighted in blue and a thicker line weight.

- **Window selection:** If you click to select the first point and then move the cursor to the right, a blue area with a solid border displays, as shown on the left in Figure 5–3. Any objects that are completely inside the boundary are selected.
- **Crossing selection:** If you click to select the first point and then move the cursor to the left, a green area with a dashed border displays, as shown on the right in Figure 5–3. Any objects inside or crossing the boundary are selected.
    - You can also start a Window or Crossing selection by typing **W** or **C** at the *Select objects:* prompt. With this method, it does not matter how you select the points to define the selection box.

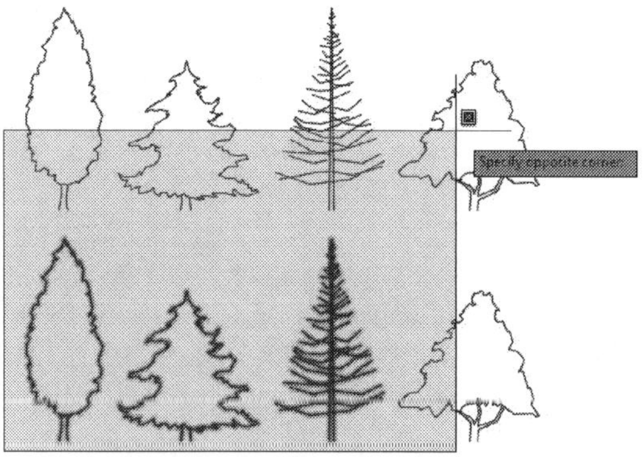

Window (blue)

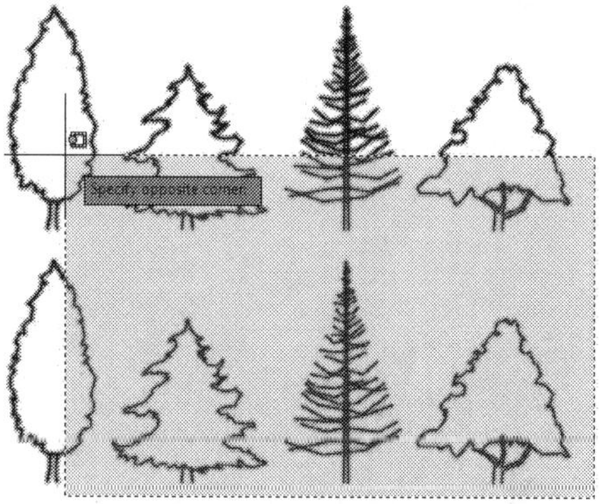

Crossing (green)

Figure 5–3

- **Lasso selection:** If you click and hold the mouse button to select the first point and then drag the cursor to the left or right, a lasso shape displays. If you drag to the right, the selection area displays in blue with a solid outline, as shown on the left in Figure 5–4. Objects are selected as they would be when using a Window selection. If you drag to the left, the selection area displays in green with a dashed border, as shown on the right in Figure 5–4. Objects are selected as they would be when using the Crossing selection. You can use the Lasso selection to create non-rectangular shapes. You can also press <Spacebar> to toggle between the Window, Crossing, and Fence selection modes when using the Lasso selection.

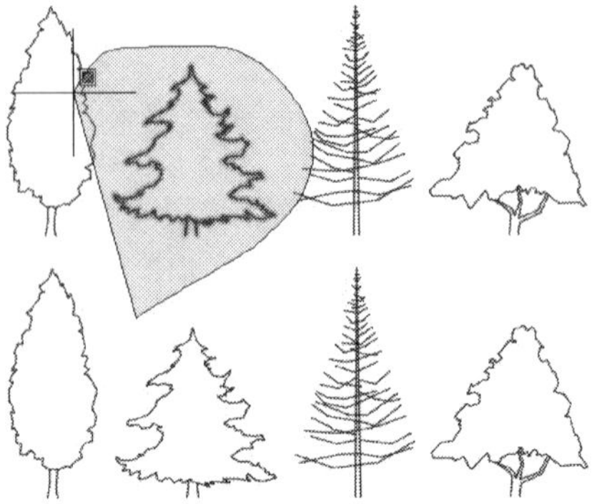

Lasso window (blue)

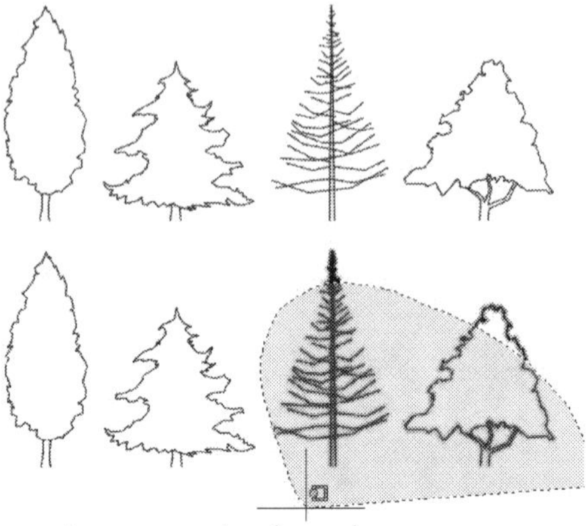

Lasso crossing (green)

Figure 5–4

- **Fence selection:** You can type **F** at the *Select objects:* prompt to start a Fence style object selection in which you pick a first point, and then continue to select additional points as if creating line segments. When you have finished creating the fence, press <Enter> to make the selection. Any object that the fence crosses is also selected.
- You can start a **Window** or **Crossing Polygon selection** by typing **WP** or **CP** at the *Select objects:* prompt. With this method, you pick a first point, and then various other points to define an irregularly shaped area.
- You can clear a selected object from a group of objects by pressing <Shift> and selecting the object. This enables you to select a group of objects quickly with a Window, Crossing, or Lasso, and then clear any object that you do not want to include in the selection set.
  - You can also type **R** at the *Select objects:* prompt and use any selection method to clear objects from the selection set. Type **A** at the *Select objects:* prompt to return to adding objects to the selection set.
- A variety of selection methods can be combined in a single command to build the selection set.

Selecting Objects Before the Command

The standard AutoCAD procedure is to start a command and then select the objects. However, you can select the objects before you start the command.

- When you select objects before starting the command, the objects highlight in blue, with a thicker line weight, and contain blue squares called *grips*, as shown in Figure 5–5.

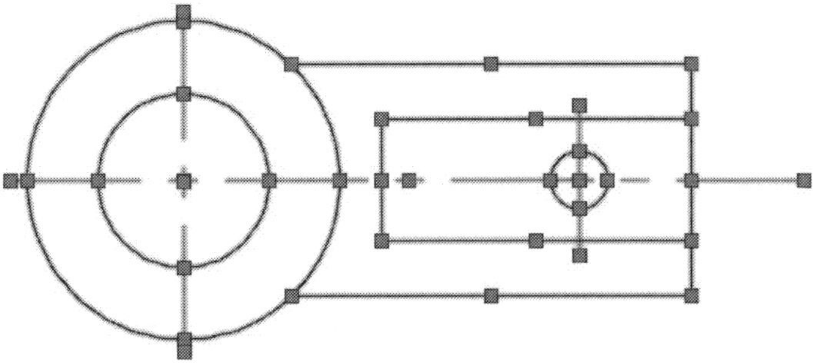

Figure 5–5

- If you have already selected objects and then you start a command, you are not prompted to *Select objects:* but the already selected objects are automatically used by the command.

5.2 Moving Objects

The **Move** command enables you to relocate a selected object or group of objects from one place in the drawing to another.

How To: Move an Object

1. In *Home* tab>*Modify* panel, click (Move).
2. Select the objects that you want to move.
3. Press <Enter> or right-click to end the object selection.
4. Specify the base point, which is the *handle* by which you hold the objects.
5. Move the cursor. displays at the cursor and the selected objects get attached to the cursor. A temporary rubber-band (dashed) line extends from the original location (basepoint) to the new location of the objects, as shown in Figure 5–6. A paler (light gray) version of the selected object(s) displays at its original location.

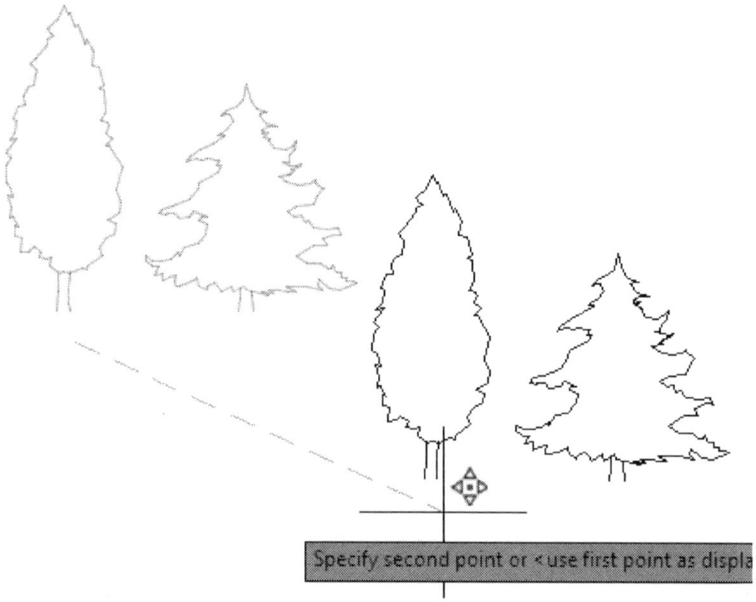

Figure 5–6

6. Specify a second point at which to place the objects. The original objects are moved to the new location.
   - You can select the objects first and then start the **Move** command.

- You can also move the objects without using the **Move** command. Select the objects first such that they are highlighted in blue with a thicker line weight and contains *grips*. Click anywhere on the object (ensure that you do not select any one of the grips) and drag them to a new location. This method does not permit you to move precisely.
- You can also select the objects first, press and hold <Ctrl>, and use the appropriate arrow key to **Nudge** the selected objects a few pixels in the specified direction.

Hint: Drawing Aids for Moving Objects

Several drawing aids can help you to move objects precisely including Object Snaps, Coordinate Entry, and Object Snap Tracking.

- **Object Snaps:** Start the **Move** command and select an object to move. Use Object Snaps to select a base point on the object, such as an end point. Then use Object Snaps to select the new location for the object, such as the center of a circle.
- **Coordinate Entry:** Start the **Move** command and select an object to move. Enter coordinates for the base point and press <Enter> when prompted for the second point. The coordinates determine the distances and directions in which the object is moved. For example, entering **2,5** for the base point moves the object 2 units in the X-direction and 5 units in the Y-direction.
- **Object Snap Tracking:** Start the **Move** command and select an object to move. With Osnap Tracking toggled on, hover the cursor over objects where the selected object is going to be placed and select two tracking points. Place the selected object at the intersection of the tracking points.

You can also combine these methods to move an object. For example, you can use Object Snaps to select the base point and then enter coordinates for the second point.

Hint: Rubber-band Line Color

By default, the rubber-band line that you get after selecting and moving the cursor in the **Move** and **Copy** commands, is a light orange color. You can control its color in the *Interface element* list in the *Drawing Window Colors* dialog box, which can be opened from *Options* dialog box>*Display* tab>**Colors**.

5.3 Copying Objects

The **Copy** command is used to make additional copies of selected objects. The prompts for this command are similar to those used for **Move**.

How To: Copy an Object

1. In the *Home* tab>*Modify* panel, click (Copy).
2. Select the objects that you want to copy.
3. Press <Enter> or right-click to end the object selection.
4. Select the base point.
5. Move the cursor to copy the objects to a new location. displays at the cursor and the selected object(s) get attached to it. A temporary rubber-band (dashed) line extends from the original location to the new location of the objects, as shown in Figure 5–7. A highlighted version of the selected object(s) displays at the original location.

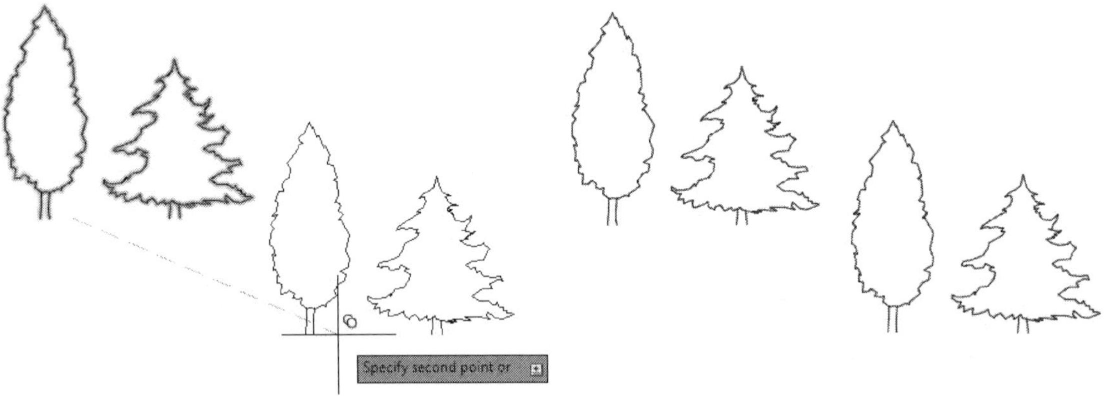

Select second point ***Original and copied objects***

Figure 5–7

6. Continue selecting points to create more copies, or press <Enter> or <Esc> to finish.
   - Copied objects have the same color, linetype, and layer properties as the original. This rule also applies to other commands that make duplicates of objects.
   - The **Undo** option enables you to undo the placing of a copy while remaining in the command.
   - You can select the objects first and then start the **Copy** command.
   - Similar to the **Move** command, you can use Object Snaps, Coordinate Entry, and Object Snap Tracking to select points for the **Copy** command.

You can also select the objects first, select a point on an object that does not touch a grip, drag the objects to a new location, and press <Ctrl> to make a copy. Do not press <Ctrl> until after you have started dragging, as it has a different purpose when you are selecting objects in 3D.

Hint: Editing Commands in the Shortcut Menu

If you select objects when a command is not active (selected objects are highlighted and grips are displayed) and then right-click, a shortcut menu displays with some basic editing commands, as shown in Figure 5–8. This is another way of starting these commands.

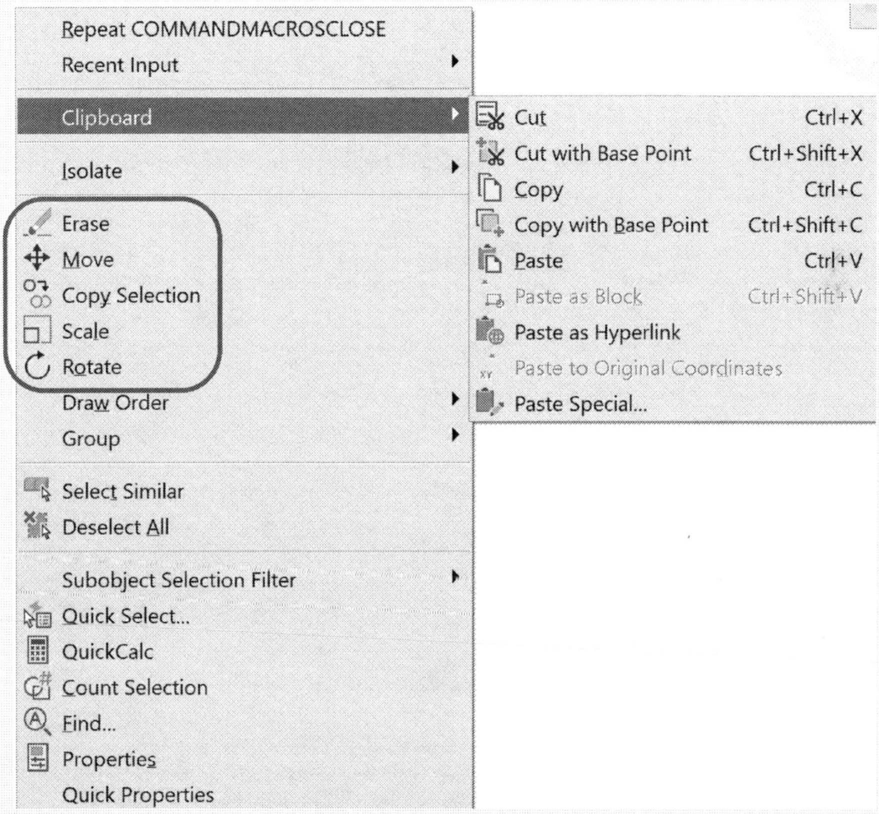

Figure 5–8

In the shortcut menu, expanding **Clipboard** opens the various **Cut**, **Copy**, and **Paste** options, as shown in Figure 5–8. These commands are different from the standard AutoCAD editing commands and are used to copy and paste selected objects into other AutoCAD drawings and programs, such as spreadsheets and documents. The **Copy** command in the expanded **Clipboard** menu is actually **Copy to Clipboard**. The **Copy Selection** command in the shortcut menu is the standard AutoCAD **Copy** command.

5.4 Rotating Objects

Design changes sometimes require modifying the placement angle of an object. The **Rotate** command rotates selected objects around a defined pivot point.

How To: Rotate an Object

1. In the *Home* tab>*Modify* panel, click (Rotate).
2. Select the objects to rotate.
3. Press <Enter> to end the object selection.
4. Select the base point around which the objects are going to rotate.
5. Move the cursor to rotate the objects. A dashed line indicates the location of the base point. displays at the cursor, indicating that the **Rotate** command is active, as shown in Figure 5–9. It also indicates the direction in which typed values are going to be rotated, in this case, counter-clockwise (default). The original objects fade to gray while the new objects maintain their original properties.

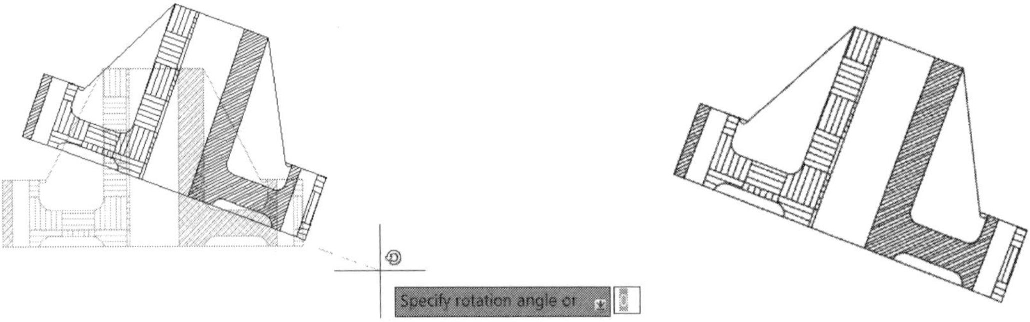

Enter an angle value ***Rotated object***

Figure 5–9

6. Enter a *Rotation Angle* or select a point to specify the rotation.
   - A negative rotation angle enables you to turn the object clockwise.
   - Polar Tracking can be used to constrain the rotation to a precise angle.
   - At *Specify rotation angle* prompt, you can access the **Copy** option, which leaves the original object in place and rotates a copy of it.
   - You can select the objects first and then start the **Rotate** command.

- You can change the default rotation direction used by the **Rotate** command by selecting or clearing the **Clockwise** option in the *Drawing Units* dialog box, as shown in Figure 5–10 (Application Menu>**Drawing Utilities**>**Units**).

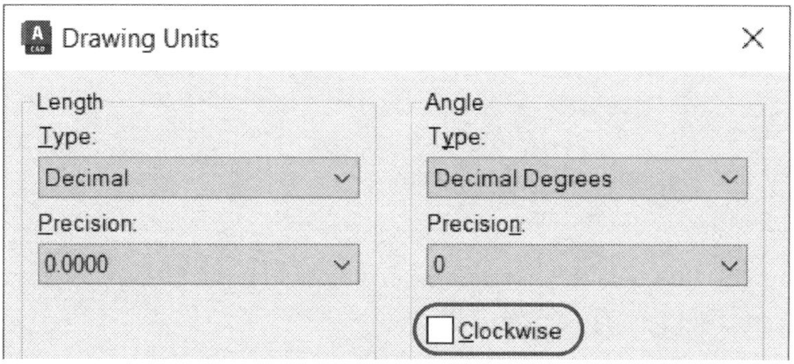

Figure 5–10

5.5 Scaling Objects

The **Scale** command enlarges or reduces the size of selected objects around a defined reference point.

How To: Scale an Object

1. In *Home* tab>*Modify* panel, click (Scale).
2. Select the objects to scale.
3. Press <Enter> or right-click to end the object selection.
4. Select the base point to be used for scaling.
5. Move the cursor to scale the objects. displays at the cursor, indicating that the **Scale** command is active, as shown in Figure 5–11. The original objects fade to gray while the new objects maintain their original properties.

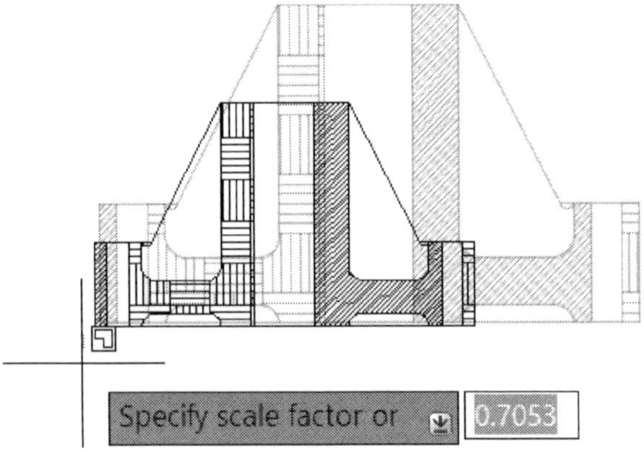

Figure 5–11

6. Enter a value for the scale factor.
    - The **scale factor** enables you to set the required level of enlargement or reduction in size. Scale factors smaller than 1 decrease the size and scale factors larger than 1 increase the size.
    - The **Copy** option in the **Scale** command leaves the original object unscaled and creates a scaled copy.

5.6 Mirroring Objects

The **Mirror** command creates reversed or symmetrical copies of objects across a user-specified mirror line.

How To: Mirror an Object

1. In the *Home* tab>*Modify* panel, click (Mirror).
2. Select the object(s) you want to mirror.
3. Press <Enter> to end the selection set.
4. Select the first point of the mirror line. The mirror line is the axis of symmetry or hinge about which the object(s) are mirrored.
5. Move the cursor to mirror the objects. A preview displays the mirror line and the potential location of the new mirrored object, as shown in Figure 5–12.

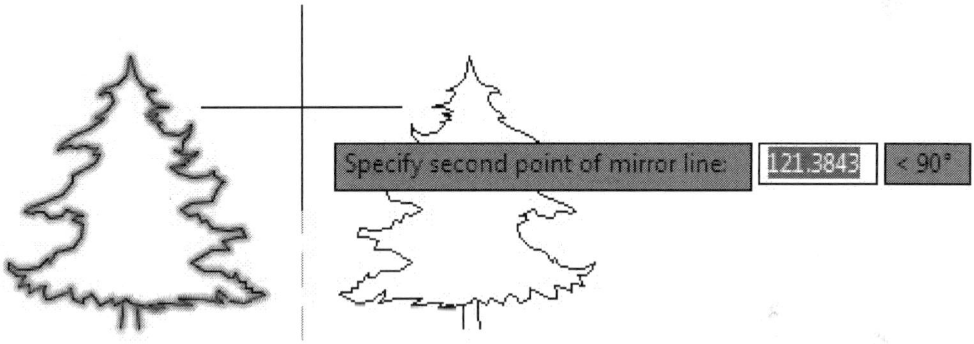

Figure 5–12

6. Select the second point of the mirror line.
7. At the *Erase source objects?* prompt, select **No** (default) to keep the original objects or **Yes** to delete them.
   - Polar Tracking is useful for controlling the angle of the mirror line.

Practice 5a
Select Objects

Practice Objective

- Select objects using the various selection methods.

In this practice, you will use the Crossing, Window, and Lasso methods to select the objects shown in Figure 5–13 for use with an editing command.

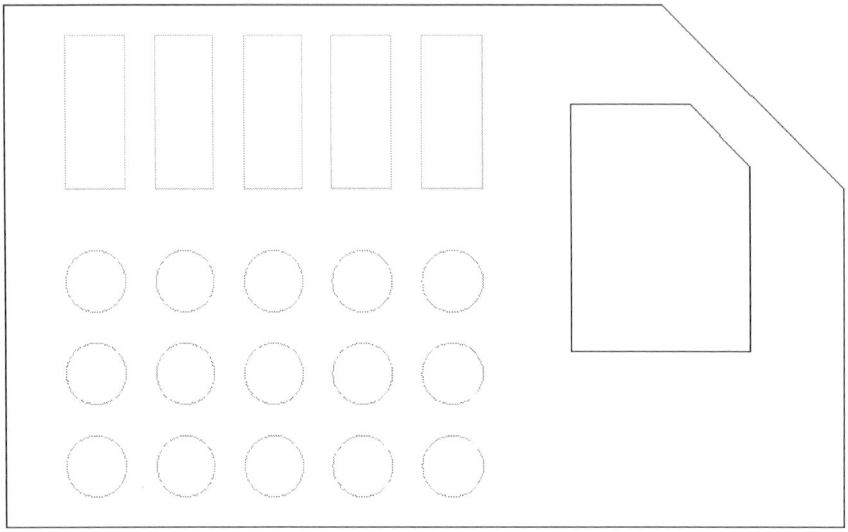

Figure 5–13

1. Open **Select.dwg** from your practice files folder.
2. Start an editing command, such as **Move,** by clicking (Move) in *Home* tab>*Modify* panel.
3. You will select the top two rows of circles using the crossing window. At the *Select objects:* prompt, click in an empty area near the right side of the top row of circles and then move the cursor diagonally (left and down) to create a crossing window (green), as shown on the left in Figure 5–14. Note that the objects (circles) that touch the crossing boundary are highlighted.
4. Click to complete the selection. Note that circles that were touched by the crossing window are selected and they display in blue with a thicker line weight, as shown on the right in Figure 5–14.

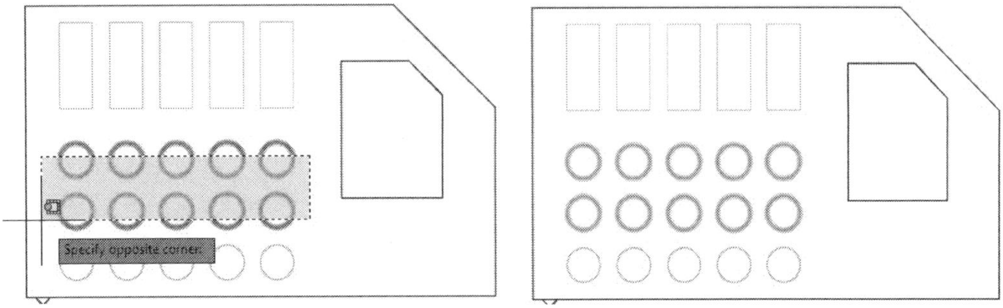

Crossing (green) *Selected objects*

Figure 5–14

5. Press <Esc> to abort the command and leave the circles intact.

6. Start the (Move) command again. At the *Select objects:* prompt, click in an empty area near the left side of the top edge of the shape and then move the cursor diagonally right to create a selection window (blue), as shown on the left in Figure 5–15. Click and note that only the objects that were entirely within the window boundary are selected, while the objects touching the window boundary remain unselected, as shown on the right in Figure 5–15.

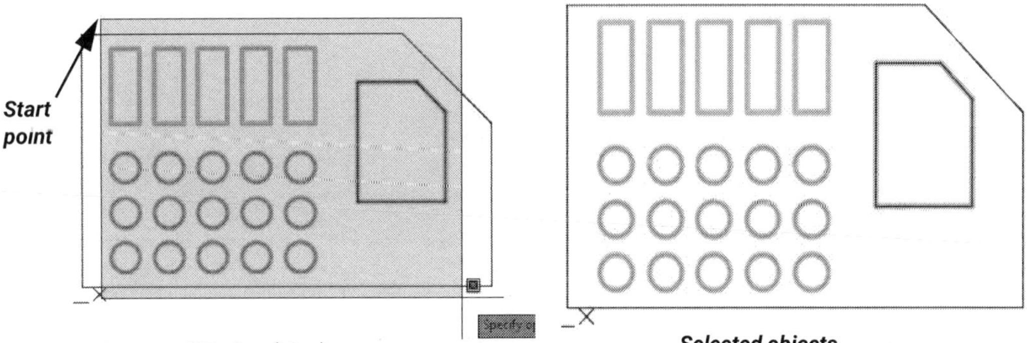

Window (blue) *Selected objects*

Figure 5–15

7. Hold <Shift> and create a window around the top row of rectangles to remove them from the selection.
8. Click on the middle rectangle to add it to the selection set.
9. Press <Esc> to abort the command and leave the geometry intact.
10. Close the drawing. Do not save changes.

End of practice

Practice 5b
Modify Objects

Practice Objective

- Modify the location, quantity, and size of objects.

In this practice, you will use the **Move**, **Copy**, **Rotate**, **Scale**, and **Mirror** commands to place furniture in a floorplan, as shown in Figure 5–16. Some of the objects in the drawing are locked in place so that you do not move them by mistake.

Figure 5–16

Task 1: Move an object.

In this task, you will use the **Move** command to place furniture in a floorplan, as shown in Figure 5–17.

Figure 5–17

1. Open **Arrange-A.dwg** from your practice files folder.
2. In the *Status Bar*, toggle off (Polar Tracking) and (Object Snap Tracking). Toggle on (Object Snap) and verify that **Endpoint** object snap is selected.
3. In the *Home* tab>*Modify* panel, click (Move).
4. Select the corner desk and press <Enter> to end the object selection.
5. For the base point, snap to the end point at the back corner (upper right) of the desk.
6. Hover the cursor and snap it (without clicking) to the inside corner of the top right cubicle, as shown in Figure 5–18. The original objects fade to gray while the new objects maintain their original properties.

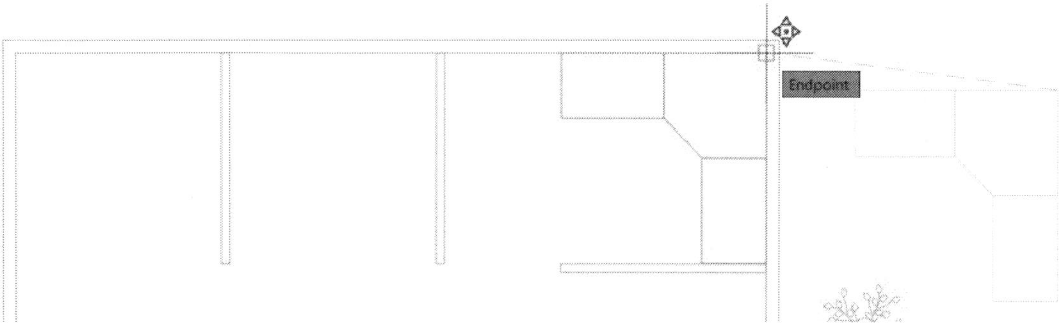

Figure 5–18

7. Click at that point to confirm the move.
8. Move the chair to place it in front of the desk (use approximate location) and move the laptop over the desk, as shown in Figure 5–17. Do not rotate the chair and laptop now.
   - You can toggle off (Object Snap) if it snaps to a point.
9. Move the plant to the open space next to the desk, as shown in Figure 5–17.

Task 2: Copy an object.

In this task, you will use the **Copy** command to copy several chairs and plants in the floorplan, as shown in Figure 5–19.

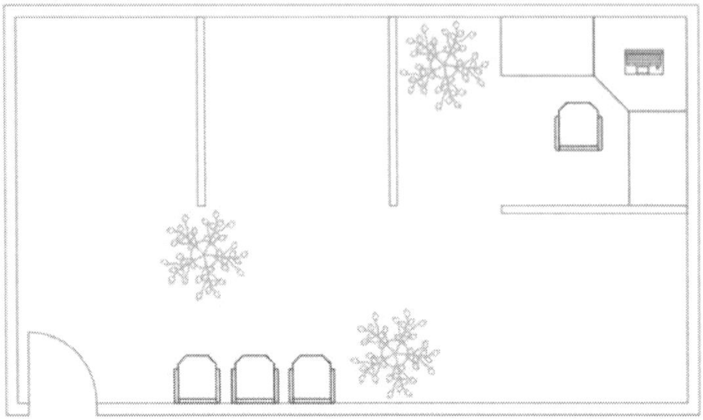

Figure 5–19

1. In the *Home* tab>*Modify* panel, click  (Copy).
2. Select the plant and press <Enter> to end the object selection.
3. For the base point, click near the center of the plant.
4. Move the cursor near the bottom of the left most inner wall, as shown in Figure 5–20. Note that a copy of the plant is attached with the cursor. A dashed line connects with the cursor indicating the new location with the original object highlighted, as shown in Figure 5–20. Once you locate the required location for the copy (bottom of the leftmost inner wall), click to place the plant.

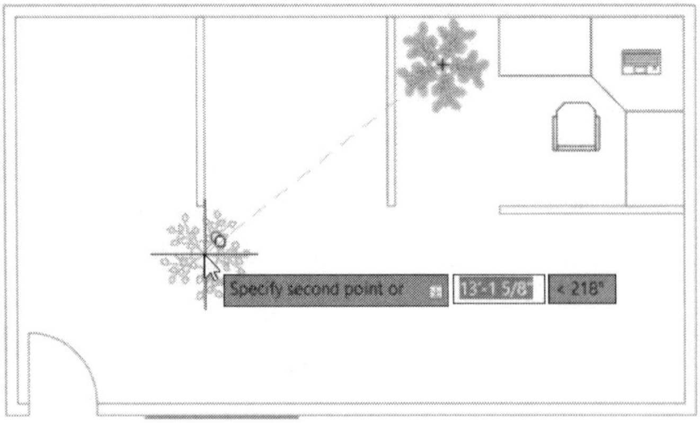

Figure 5–20

5. Move the cursor and note that the plant and the dashed line is still attached to the cursor. Move the cursor along the bottom wall and click to place another copy. Press <Enter> to exit the command.
6. Copy the chair to the locations shown in Figure 5–19. (Tip: To position the chairs flush along the wall, use the **Midpoint** or **Endpoint** object snap to select the base point at the back of the chair. Then, use the **Nearest** object snap override (<Shift>+ right-click) to select points along the wall.) After copying the three chairs, press <Enter> to exit the command.

Task 3: Rotate an object.

In this task, you will rotate the chair and laptop and then copy the entire set of furniture to other locations, as shown in Figure 5–21.

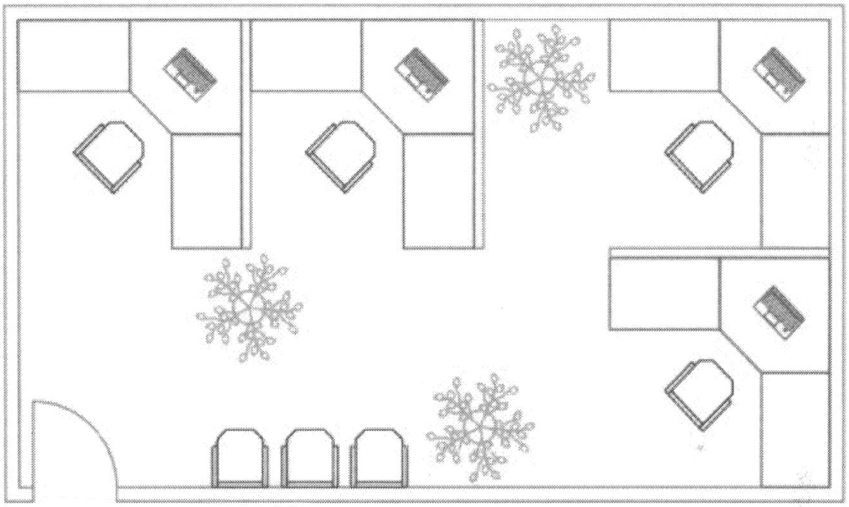

Figure 5–21

1. In the *Status Bar*, expand  (Polar Tracking) and select **45,90,135,180...**, if required.

   Toggle on  (Polar Tracking) and toggle off 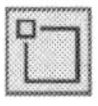 (Object Snap).

2. In the *Home* tab>*Modify* panel, click (Rotate) and select the chair near the desk. Press <Enter> and select the base point near the center of the chair's seat. Pull the cursor away from the chair until you see the 315° angle (multiple of 45) and the seat is facing the desk, as shown in Figure 5–22. Note that the original object fades to gray while the new object maintains the original properties. Click to accept the angle.

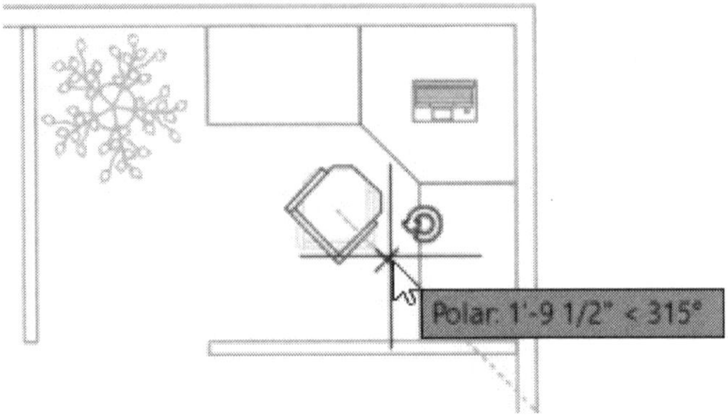

Figure 5–22

3. Repeat the process to rotate the laptop using the 315° angle so that the screen is facing the chair, as shown in Figure 5–21.
4. Move the chair as required, to place it correctly in front of the desk. Do the same for the laptop to center it on the desk.

   Note: *Select the object, hold <Ctrl>, and then use the required arrow key to nudge the objects in place.*

5. Toggle on (Object Snap) and verify that it is set to **Endpoint**.
6. Start the **Copy** command. Select the chair, desk, and laptop, and then press <Enter>. For the base point, select the back corner (top right) of the desk. Copy the objects to the other three cubicles, as shown in Figure 5–21.
7. Save the drawing.

Task 4: Scale an object.

In this task, you will copy and scale some of the plants, as shown in Figure 5–23.

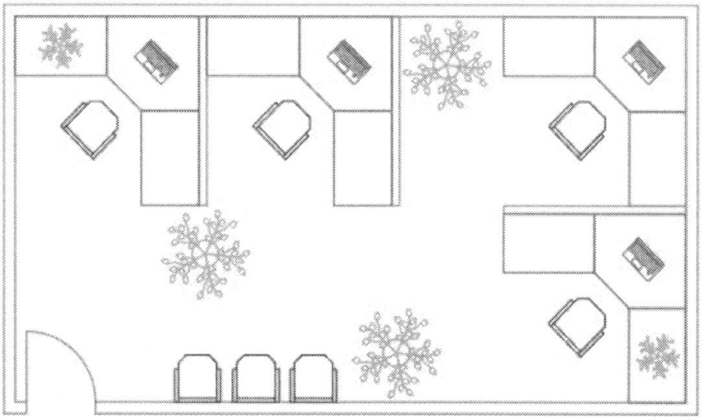

Figure 5–23

1. Copy one of the plants to the desk in the upper left cubicle.
2. In the *Home* tab>*Modify* panel, click (Scale). Select the plant, press <Enter>, and select the center of the plant as the base point. Enter **0.5** for the scale factor and press <Enter> to make it half of the original plant, as shown in Figure 5–23.
3. Copy the scaled plant to the desk in the lower right cubicle, as shown in Figure 5–23.

Task 5: Mirror objects.

In this task, you will use the **Mirror** command to mirror the contents of a cubicle, as shown in Figure 5–24.

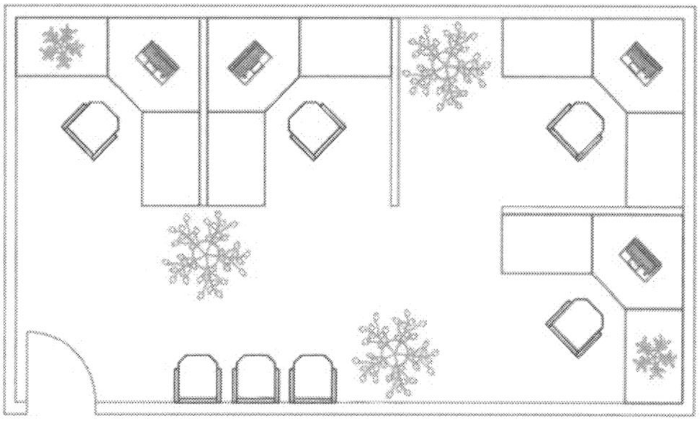

Figure 5–24

1. In the *Home* tab>*Modify* panel, click (Mirror).
2. At the *Select objects:* prompt, select the desk, laptop, and chair in the middle cubicle, and press <Enter>.
3. At the *Specify first point of mirror line:* prompt, select the end point of the line that separates the corner desk section from the straight desk section at the top of the cubicle, as shown on the left in Figure 5–25.
4. At the *Specify second point of mirror line:* prompt, select a bottom end point, as shown on the right in Figure 5–25. At the *Erase source objects?* select **Yes** from the drop-down list. The contents of the middle cubicle are mirrored and the original objects are deleted.

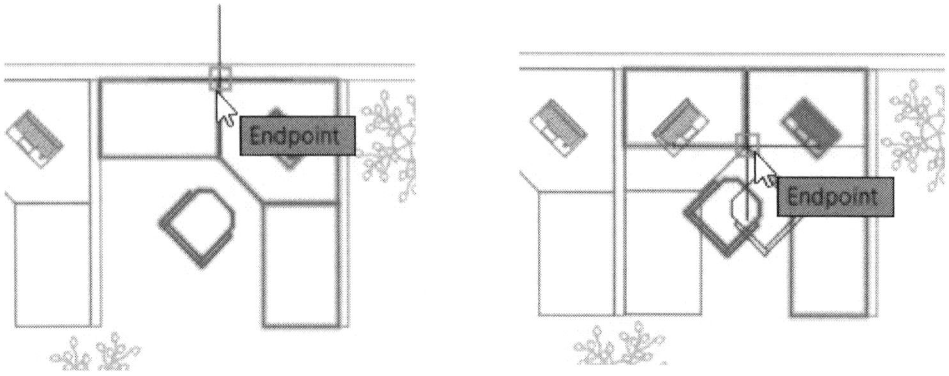

Figure 5–25

5. Save and close the drawing.

End of practice

5.7 Editing with Grips

You can modify objects by using their grips without using an editing command. The AutoCAD software stores information about objects as geometric formulas. Therefore, lines are defined by their end points, circles by their center and radius, etc. The software can easily compute additional points, such as the midpoint of a line or quadrants of a circle, and enable you to modify them, as shown in Figure 5–26.

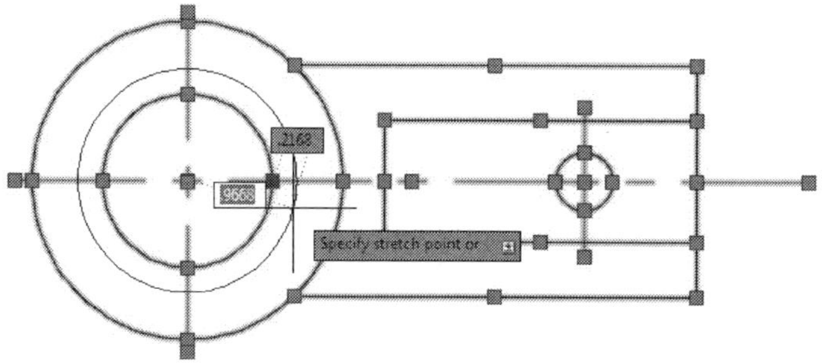

Figure 5–26

- By default, grips display as blue squares on an object when the object is selected without starting a command.
- If you hover the cursor over a grip but do not select it, the color changes to pink. Note that the color might look different depending on the monitor settings.

Working with Hot Grips

When you click directly on a grip, it changes to a selected or *hot grip* (red by default), as shown in Figure 5–27.

- Depending on the grip you make hot, the default mode is automatically enabled. For example, the quadrant grip of a circle stretches it, but the center grip moves the circle, as shown in Figure 5–27.

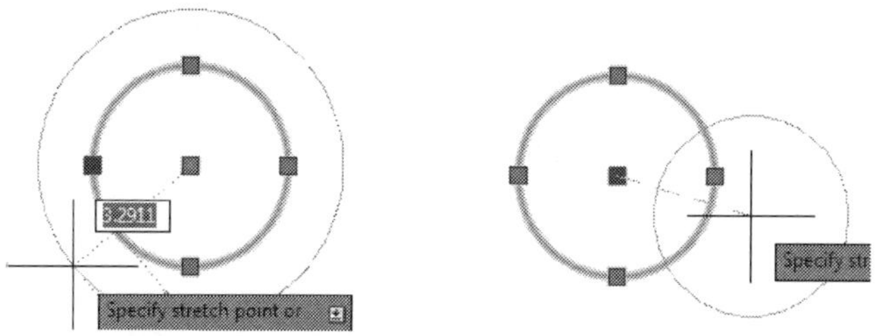

Hot grip selected on quadrant and used as Stretch

Hot grip selected in center and used as Move

Figure 5–27

- The grip options are dependent on the object that you have selected. Such grips are called multi-functional grips.
- Hover your cursor over the multi-functional grip to display its options, as shown in Figure 5–28. The options for the endpoint grips of line segments and arcs include **Stretch** and **Lengthen**, and for the middle grip of arcs include **Stretch** and **Radius**.

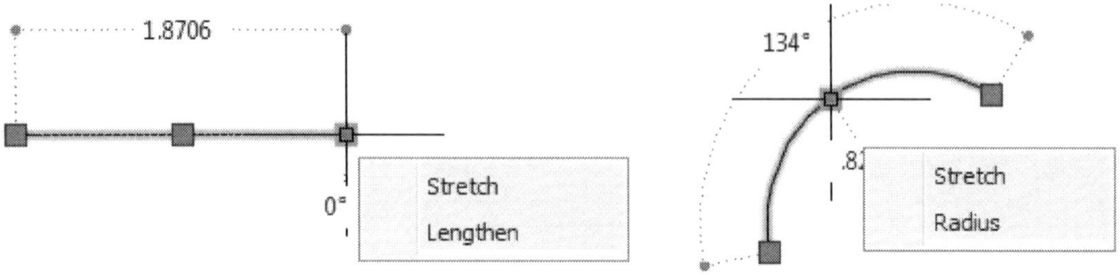

Figure 5–28

- Multi-functional grips are available for lines, polylines, arcs, splines and hatches.
- To select a different option after you make a grip hot, you can right-click to display the various editing commands in the shortcut menu, as shown in Figure 5–29. You can also press <Spacebar> to cycle through the available commands.

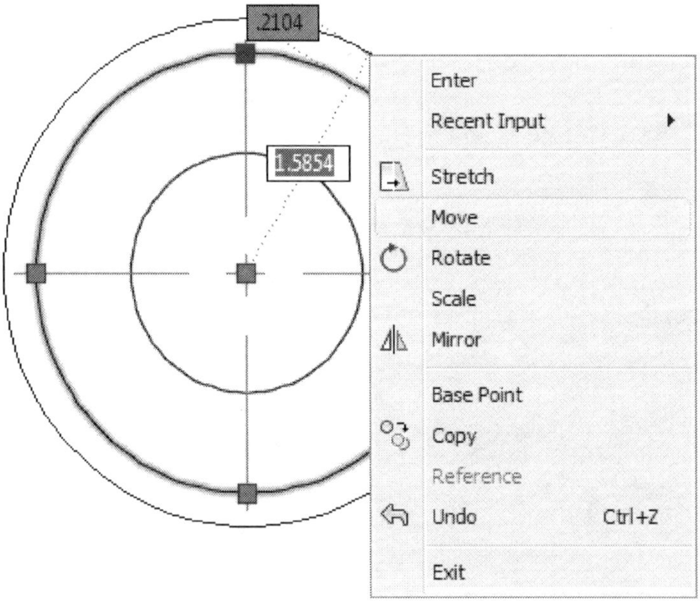

Figure 5–29

- Once a grip and an editing command have been selected, various advanced options (for the selected command) display by pressing <Down Arrow>, as shown in Figure 5–30.

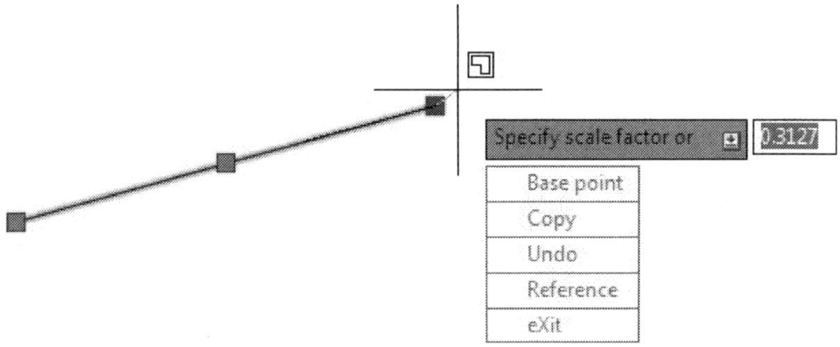

Figure 5–30

- To clear objects and their grips, press <Esc>.
- When using grips, their default mode and multi-functional mode only apply to the object with the hot grip. However, **Move**, **Mirror**, **Scale**, and **Rotate** affect all of the selected objects.
- You can hold <Shift> to activate multiple modes of grips.
- When using grips on a block, **Stretch** has the same effect as **Move**. This is because you cannot stretch a standard block object.
- You can change the display of grips (size and color) and other settings in the *Selection* tab in the *Options* dialog box (Application Menu>**Options**).

Grips with Dynamic Dimensions

Grips enable you to quickly check the dimensions of an object. For example, when you hover the cursor over the end point grip of a line, dynamic dimensions display the line's length and angle and the quadrant grip on a circle displays the circle's radius, as shown in Figure 5–31.

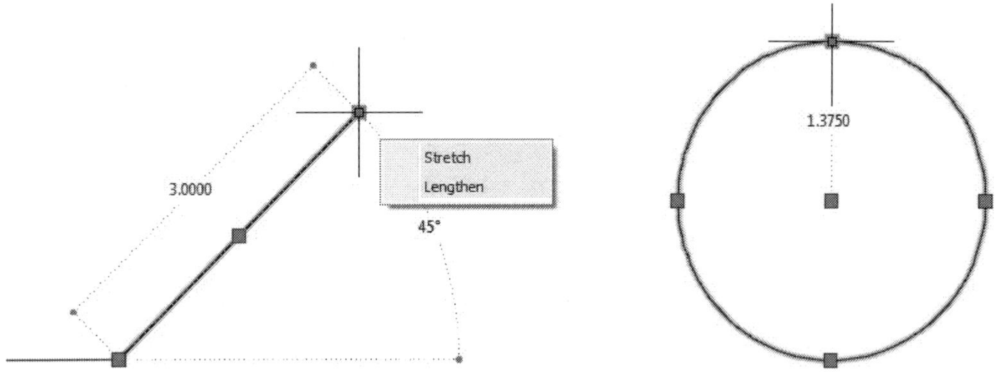

Figure 5–31

- (Dynamic Input) must be toggled on for the dimensions to be displayed.
- When you select the stretch grip of an object, you can edit the dimension instead of dragging the hot grip.

How To: Stretch a Line by 5 Units Using Grips

1. Select the line to display the grips.
2. Select the endpoint grip of the line, as shown in Figure 5–32.

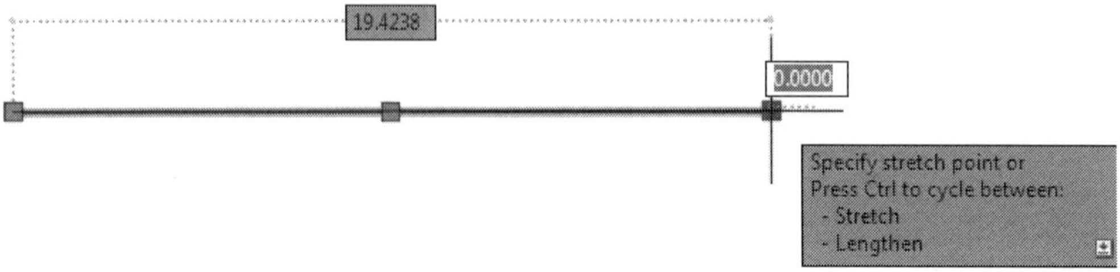

Figure 5–32

3. Two dimensions display for the length: one with the current overall length and the other with the change in length (which is 0 unless you move the cursor). The change in length can be edited.
4. Enter **5** (as shown in Figure 5–33), and press <Enter> to change the length. The line length increases by 5 units and the angle does not change.

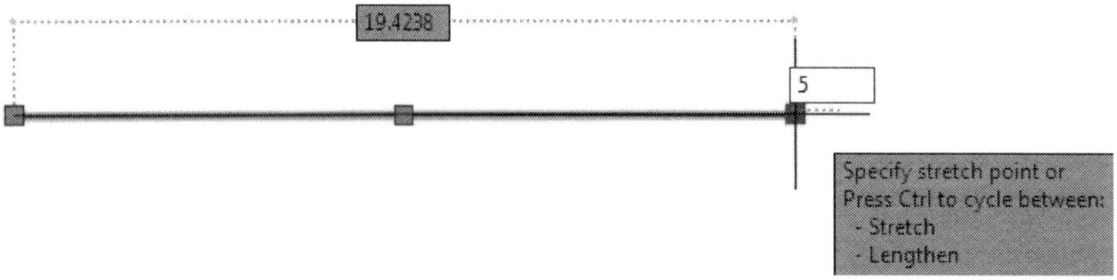

Figure 5–33

- Once you are in the change in length edit box, press <Tab> twice to change the angle (shown in Figure 5–34).

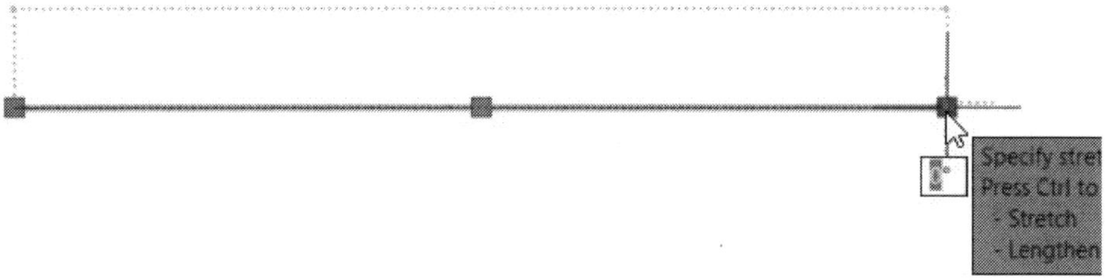

Figure 5–34

Practice 5c
Edit with Grips I

Practice Objective

- Modify objects using grips.

In this practice, you will use grips to move, copy, rotate, mirror, and scale objects on the façade of a building. You will also use <Shift> to copy and specify a new base point, as shown in Figure 5–35.

Figure 5–35

1. Open **Facade-A.dwg** from your practice files folder.
2. Set the object snaps to **Endpoint**, **Midpoint**, and **Intersection**, and toggle (Object Snap) on. Toggle (Polar Tracking) off. Toggle on (Dynamic Input), if it is not already on.
3. With no command active, select the double door. It has only one grip at the bottom endpoint of the middle section. Click on this grip to select it and make it hot (red by default). Move the door to the midpoint of the bottom line on the building. Press <Esc> to clear the object.
4. Repeat Step 3 with the arched window and place the grip at the midpoint of the top of the door.
5. Select the square window and select the grip. Right-click and select **Copy**. Select the intersections of the blue center lines (except the one inside the door) to place windows at each intersection (9 in total). Press <Esc> twice to finish.

6. Erase the blue center lines.
7. Select the four angled lines of the roof. Select the grip at the right end of any one of the lines. Right-click and select **Mirror**, then right-click again and select **Copy** to keep the original objects. Select the midpoint of the roofline (top horizontal line) as the second point for the mirror line. Press <Esc> twice to finish.
8. Select the center square window above the door and select the grip. Right-click and select **Base Point**. For the base point, select the intersection (or midpoint) of the mullions at the center of the window.
9. Right-click again and select **Rotate**. For the rotation angle, enter **45** and press <Enter>.
10. Select the window grip again. Right-click and select **Base Point** and select the intersection (or midpoint) of the mullions. Right-click and select **Scale**. For the scale factor, enter **0.7** to make it smaller and press <Enter>. Press <Esc> to finish.
11. Select the arched window above the door and select the grip. Right-click and select **Scale**. For the scale factor, enter **0.65** and press <Enter>. Press <Esc> to finish.
12. Select the bottom line along the base of the building. Hover the cursor over the grip at either end point to display the dimension. What is the length of the line?
13. Select the top roofline on the left side of the building, and hover the cursor over the end point at the top. What is the length and angle of the line?
14. Save and close the drawing.

End of practice

Practice 5d
Edit with Grips II

Practice Objective

- Modify objects using grips.

In this practice, you will use grips to move, copy, rotate, and scale objects, as shown in Figure 5–36.

Figure 5–36

1. Open **Arrange-Grips-A.dwg** from your practice files folder.
2. Use grips to move, copy, rotate, and scale objects (as shown in Figure 5–37) so that they are placed as shown above in Figure 5–36.

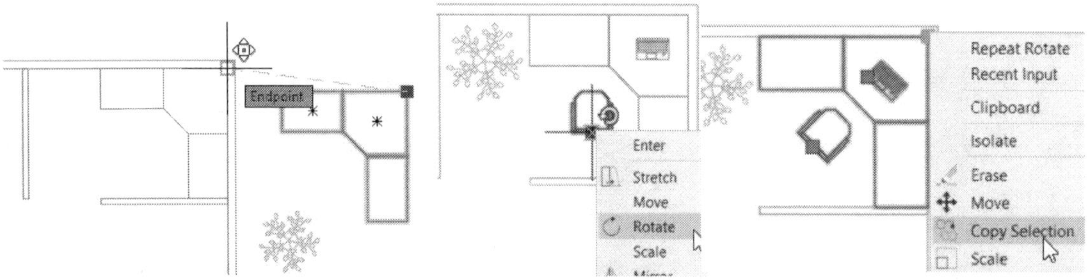

Hot grip used as Move ***Using Rotate in the hot grip Shortcut menu*** ***Using Copy Selection in the hover grip Shortcut menu***

Figure 5–37

End of practice

Chapter Review Questions

1. What is the difference between a Window and a Crossing selection box?
   a. Window selects everything inside the selection box and Crossing selects everything touching the selection box.
   b. Window selects everything inside or touching the selection box and Crossing selects everything inside the selection box.
   c. Window selects everything inside the selection box and Crossing selects everything inside or touching the selection box.
   d. Window selects everything touching the selection box and Crossing selects everything inside the selection box.

2. How can you clear a selected object from a group of selected objects?
   a. Pick the object again.
   b. Hold <Shift> and pick the object.
   c. Right-click on the object and select **Clear**.
   d. Hold <Ctrl> and pick the object.

3. What happens to objects when you select them before starting any command?
   a. They highlight in black with a thicker line weight.
   b. They highlight in blue with a thicker line weight and contain red squares.
   c. They highlight in blue with a thicker line weight and contain blue squares.
   d. They stay the same.

4. The **Move**, **Copy**, **Rotate**, and **Scale** commands use a base point, which is always the center or a midpoint of an object.
   a. True
   b. False

5. What happens to the selected objects in the active **Rotate** command?
   a. The original objects fade to gray and the new objects maintain their original properties.
   b. The original objects maintain their original properties and the new objects fade to gray.
   c. The original objects are highlighted with a thicker line weight and the new objects fade to gray.
   d. The original objects maintain their original properties and the new objects are highlighted with a thicker line weight.

6. Which Scale Factor should you use to make an object half of its current size?
   a. -2.0
   b. 0.5
   c. 0.2
   d. -0.5

7. When selecting objects for a command, such as **Move** or **Copy**, how do you end the object selection?
   a. Press <Alt>.
   b. Press <Esc>.
   c. Press <Ctrl>.
   d. Press <Enter>.

8. What is the default mode of the hot grips of a circle?
   a. A quadrant hot grip stretches the circle whereas the center hot grip moves the circle.
   b. A quadrant hot grip moves the circle whereas the center hot grip stretches the circle.
   c. Both the quadrant hot grip and the center hot grip stretch/scale the circle.
   d. Both the quadrant hot grip and the center hot grip move the circle.

Command Summary

Button	Command	Location
	**Copy**	• **Ribbon:** *Home* tab>*Modify* panel • **Command Prompt:** copy or CO
	**Mirror**	• **Ribbon:** *Home* tab>*Modify* panel • **Command Prompt:** mirror or MI
	**Move**	• **Ribbon:** *Home* tab>*Modify* panel • **Command Prompt:** move or M
	**Rotate**	• **Ribbon:** *Home* tab>*Modify* panel • **Command Prompt:** rotate or RO
	**Scale**	• **Ribbon:** *Home* tab>*Modify* panel • **Command Prompt:** scale or SC

Chapter 6

Projects: Making Your Drawings More Precise

This chapter contains practice projects that can be used to gain additional hands-on experience in the topics and commands covered so far in this guide. These projects are intended to be self-guided and do not include step-by-step information.

Learning Objectives

- *Schematic:* Create an electronic schematic using the editing commands with object snaps to help you to precisely place objects and symbols.
- *Architectural:* Develop a plot of land using the drawing tools, with Polar Tracking, object snaps, and editing commands, to help you to precisely draw and place buildings and landscape objects.
- *Mechanical:* Create mechanical parts and drawing components using the drawing tools, with Polar Tracking, object snaps, and editing commands, to help you to precisely draw and place features in the model.

6.1 Schematic Project: Electronics Diagram

In this project, you will copy and rotate electronic symbols to the appropriate places on a diagram, as shown in Figure 6–1. Use Object Snaps to position the objects precisely. Commands that you will use include **Copy**, **Rotate**, and **Move**. The color of the electronics diagram has been changed for printing clarity.

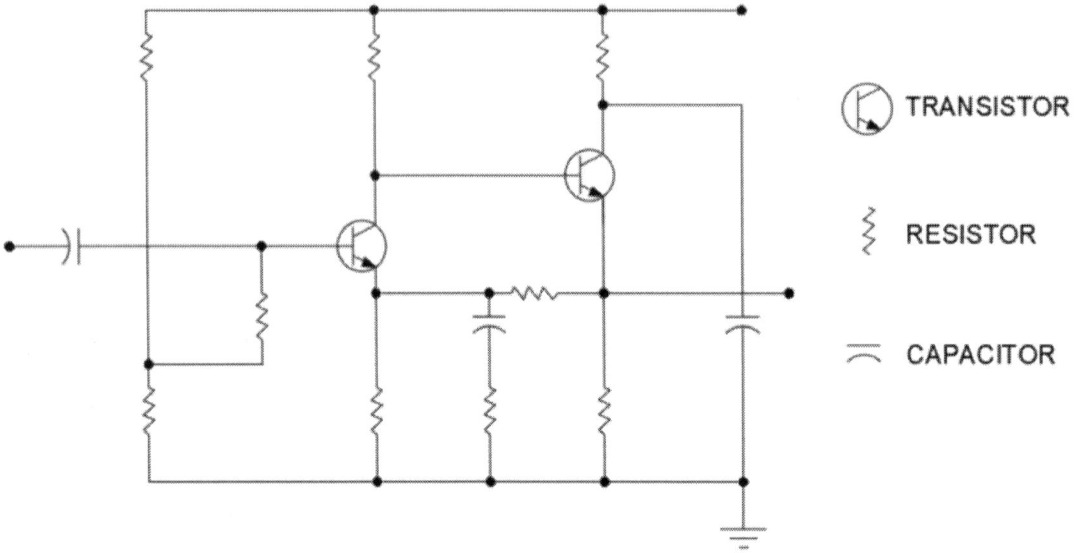

Figure 6–1

1. Open **Diagram.dwg** from your practice files folder.
2. Select the **Midpoint** and **Endpoint** object snaps and verify that 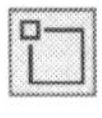 (Object Snap) is toggled on.
3. Copy the symbols from the key to the appropriate places on the diagram. Ensure that you snap to the exact base points to help position the objects precisely. For example, the base point for the transistor should be the midpoint of its vertical line. After copying, some objects need to be rotated and moved to the exact locations.
4. Save and close the drawing.

6.2 Architectural Project: Landscape

In this project, you will draw a house and garage, as shown in Figure 6–2, and landscape the yard by arranging trees and shrubs. Commands that you will use include **Line**, **Move**, **Copy**, **Scale**, and **Rotate**. Use Polar Tracking and Object Snap Tracking to help draw the buildings precisely. The dimensions provided are for reference only.

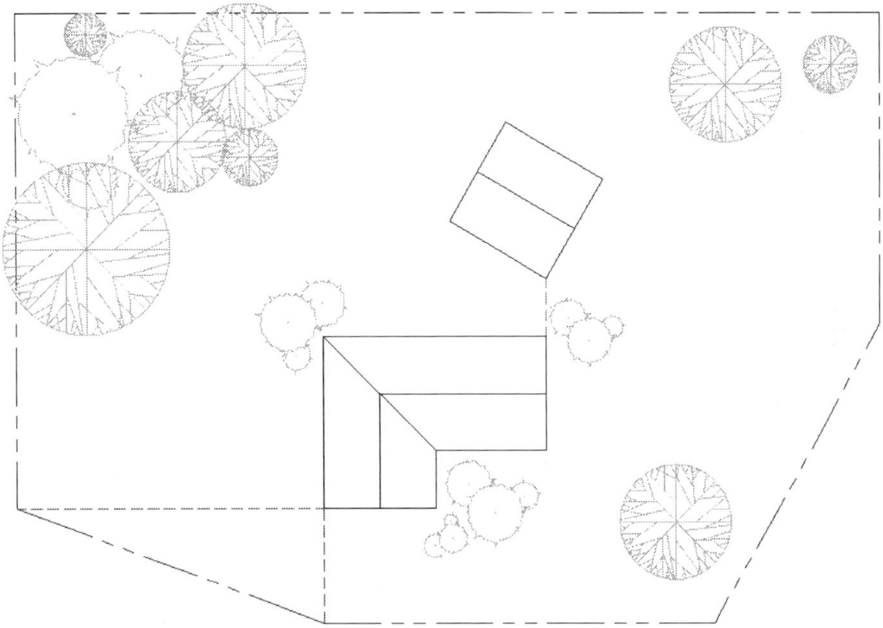

Figure 6–2

1. Open **Land-C.dwg** from your practice files folder. The dashed boundary is a plot of land. The green objects are shrubs and trees.

2. Set the Object Snap modes to **Endpoint** and **Midpoint**, and toggle on  (Object Snap),  (Object Snap Tracking), and  (Polar Tracking).

3. Use the **Line** command to draw the house for the given dimensions, as shown in Figure 6–3. Use Object Snap Tracking to establish point **A**, as shown in Figure 6–5.
   - Tip: When drawing the house and garage, type the ' **(feet)** symbol after the number to ensure that the value is entered in feet.

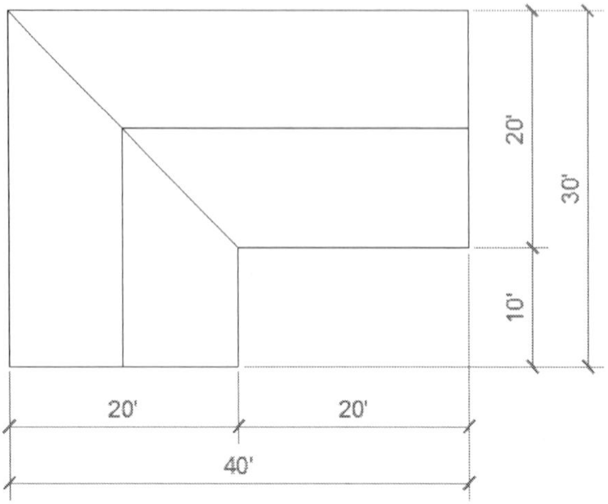

Figure 6–3

4. To draw the garage, expand  (Polar Tracking) and set a **30°** angle for the Polar Tracking angle. Use the **Line** command with Object Snap Tracking to position the first point **10'** above the top right corner of the house at point **B**, as shown in Figure 6–4 and Figure 6–5. Then use Polar Tracking to draw the **20' x 20'** garage at the angle shown in Figure 6–4.

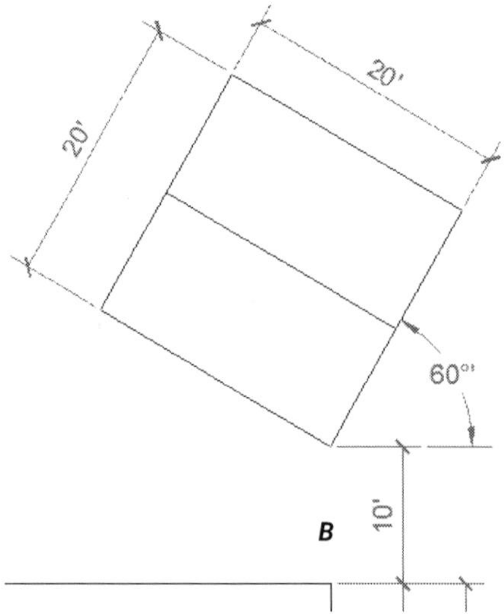

Figure 6–4

5. Place shrubs and trees in the yard, similar to that shown in Figure 6–5. Scale, rotate, copy, and move them as required.

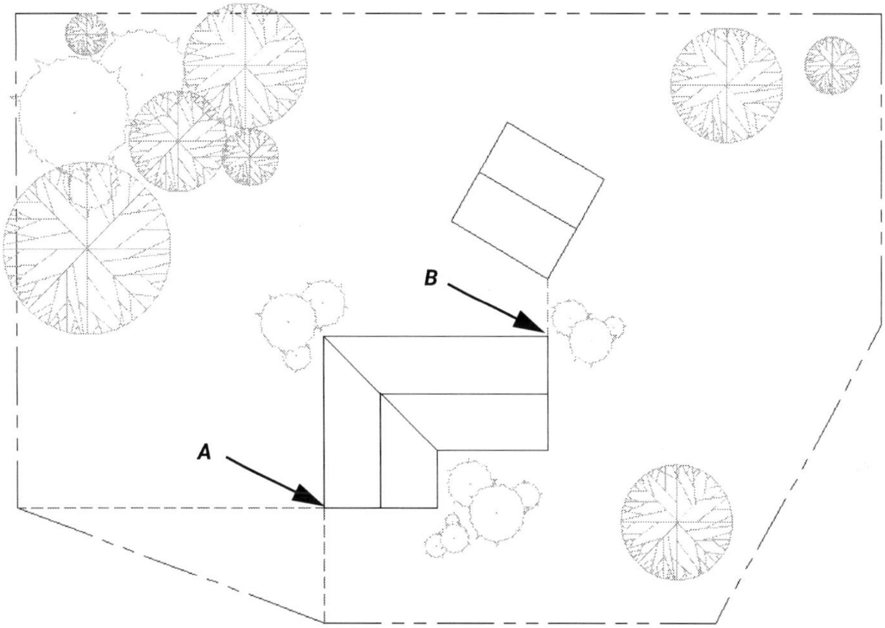

Figure 6–5

6.3 Mechanical Project: Using Polar and Object Snap Tracking

In this project, you will draw a mechanical part using **Line** and **Circle**, as shown in Figure 6–6. You will use Polar Tracking and Object Snap Tracking to draw them precisely. Draw only the object, not the dimensions. The dimensions provided are for reference only.

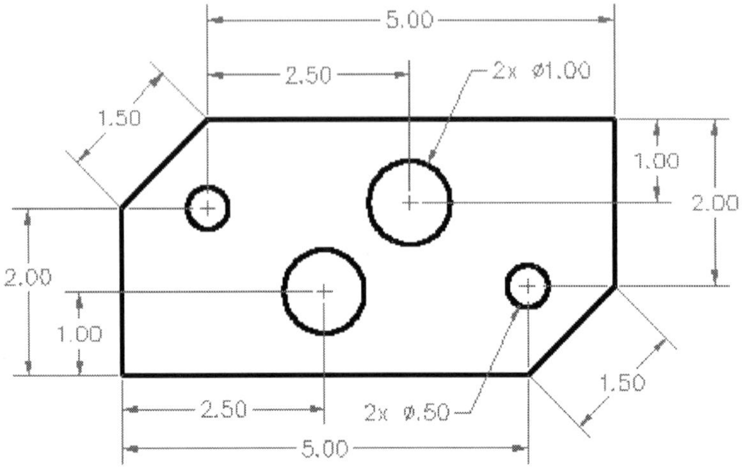

Figure 6–6

1. Open **Plate-I.dwg** from your practice files folder. It is a blank drawing.
2. Draw the object shown in Figure 6–6. Set the *Polar Tracking* angle to the increments of **45°** to draw the angled lines (the opposite angle for 45° is 135°). Use Object Snap Tracking to position the circles at the midpoints or endpoints of the nearby lines. The diameters of the circles are **0.5** and **1.0**.

6.4 Mechanical Project: Surge Protector

In this project, you will arrange objects in a drawing using the **Move**, **Copy**, **Rotate**, and **Scale** commands, as shown in Figure 6–7.

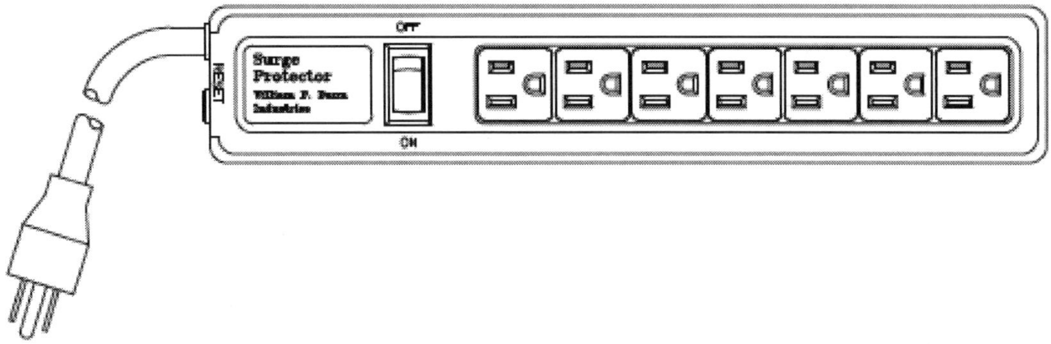

Figure 6–7

1. Open **Surge Protector-I.dwg** from your practice files folder.
2. Arrange the drawing as shown in Figure 6–7. Make copies of the objects as required. Position the outlets precisely using Object Snaps. Use the **Scale** command to make the text larger and then move it to the required location, similar to that shown in Figure 6–7.

- **Hint**: You can use the Geometric Center object snap as the basepoint for the switch and to place the outlets precisely.

6.5 Mechanical Project: Satellite

In this project, you will assemble drawing components using the **Copy**, **Move**, and **Rotate** commands, as shown in Figure 6–8.

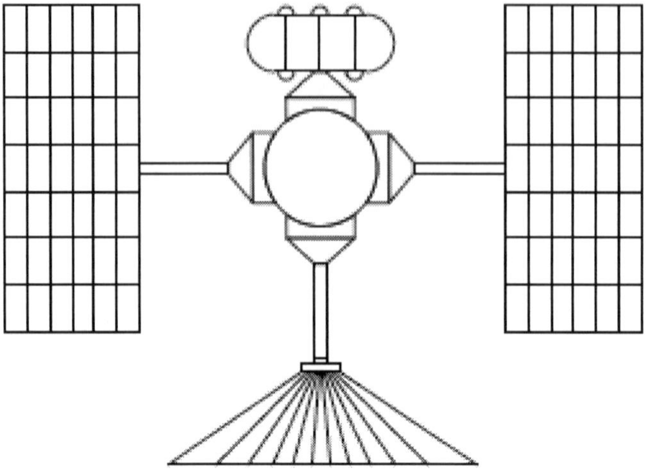

Figure 6–8

1. Open **Satellite-M.dwg** from your practice files folder.
2. Arrange the components as shown in Figure 6–8. Copy and rotate the objects as required. Use Object Snaps to place the components together precisely.
   - Tip: Set (Object Snap) to **Quadrant** and **Midpoint** to speed up the assembly process.

Chapter 7

Organizing Your Drawing with Layers

In this chapter, you learn how to create a new drawing with a template, make a layer current, draw on specific layers, control the state of a layer, and change the layer of an object.

Learning Objectives

- Create new drawings using templates.
- Organize a drawing into logical categories using layers.
- Control which parts of a drawing are displayed or plotted.
- Draw objects with specific saved properties.
- Modify object layers and layer states.

7.1 Creating New Drawings with Templates

What Is a Template?

When you start a new drawing, you are actually creating a copy of an existing *template* file. A template is a drawing that contains all of the objects and settings required in new drawings. Some of the settings stored in a template file include units, limits, layers, layouts with a border and titleblock, text styles, and dimension styles.

- In addition to the predefined templates that are supplied with the AutoCAD® software, you can also create your own custom templates.

Starting New Drawings from a Template

AutoCAD provides you with different ways for starting new drawings.

- Clicking + (New Drawing) in the *File Tabs* bar or clicking **New** in the *Start* screen starts a new drawing based on a most recently used template file or an AutoCAD default template file. Hovering your cursor over **New** in the Start window displays the name of the template that is being used to create the new drawing, as shown in Figure 7–1. The new drawing is automatically named as **Drawing** with the next available number appended to it, such as **Drawing1**, **Drawing2**, and so on.

  Note: *These methods start the* ***QNEW*** *command.*

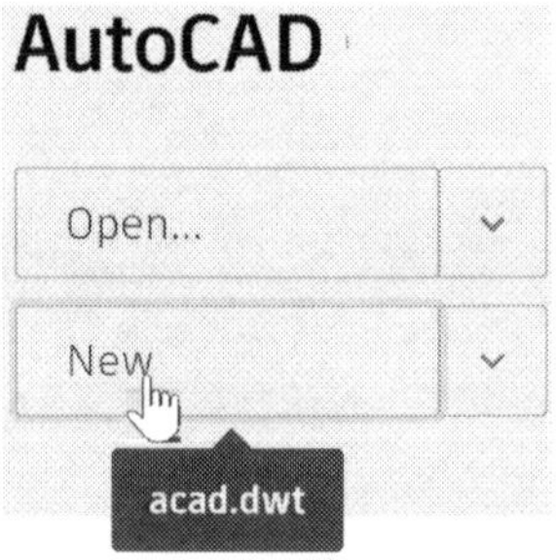

Figure 7–1

- If you want to create a new drawing from a different template, click (New) in the *Quick Access Toolbar* or click **New** in the Application Menu. Both of these methods open the *Select template* dialog box, where you can select the template file for creating the new drawing.
- You can also use the **Browse templates** option in the *New* drop-down list in the initial *Start* screen (as shown in Figure 7–2) to select a different template to create your new drawing.

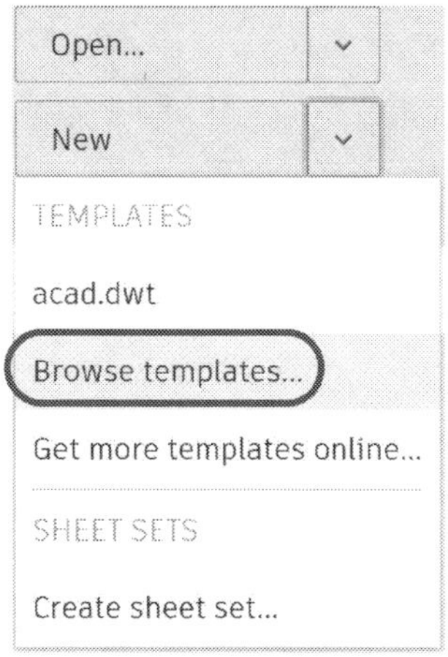

Figure 7–2

- By default, the *Select template* dialog box opens in the AutoCAD *Template* folder where all the templates provided with the software are displayed, as shown in Figure 7–3.
- Note that the *Files of type* displays **Drawing Template (*.dwt)** indicating that only the drawing templates are listed in the dialog box, as shown in Figure 7–3. AutoCAD template files have the extension .DWT. AutoCAD drawing files have the extension .DWG.

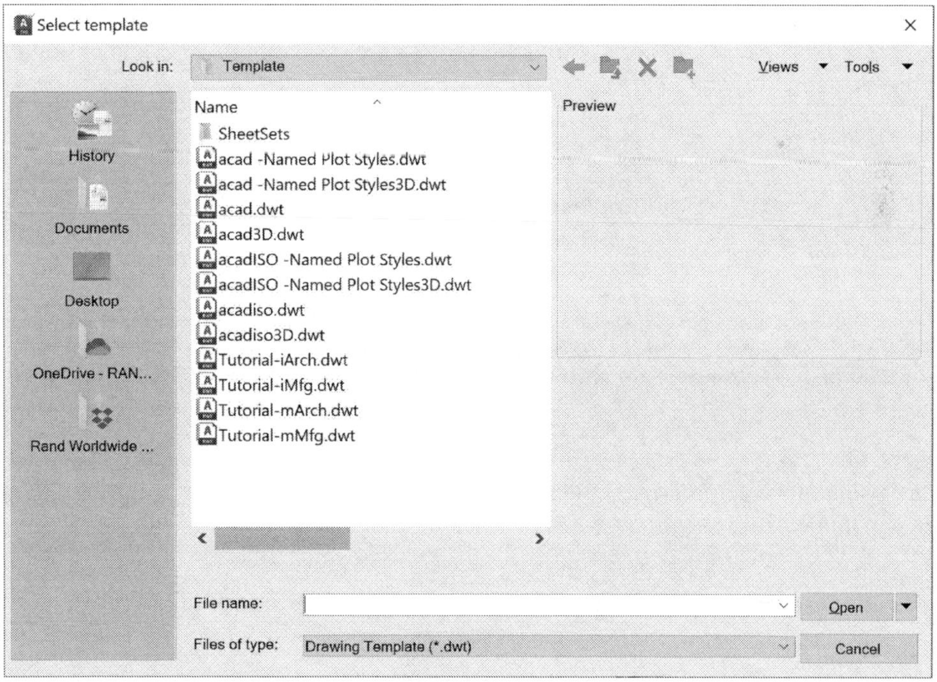

Figure 7–3

Hint: Setting the Default Template for QNEW

If you have a template that you use frequently, you can set it as the default for **QNEW** in the *Options* dialog box. In the *Application Menu*, click **Options**. In the *Files* tab, expand **Template Settings>Default Template File Name for QNEW**, and set the default filename (in place of **None**), as shown in Figure 7–4. As long as **None** is specified as the Default Template, typing **QNEW** in the Command prompt, or clicking (New) in the *Quick Access Toolbar* or in the *Application Menu*, opens the *Select File* dialog box.

Figure 7–4

Working with Different Types of Units

In the template file, you typically set the type of units to use in the drawing, as shown in Figure 7–5. For example, if you set the template file to feet and inches or decimal units, the same units are used in the drawing.

Architectural	3'-4 1/4"
Decimal	3.25
Engineering	3'-4.25"
Fractional	3 1/4"
Scientific	3.25E+01

Figure 7–5

- Decimal units can represent feet, inches, meters, kilometers, miles, or any other type of units you want to use.
- Measurements in feet and inches are called *architectural units* in the AutoCAD software. If you are using architectural units, the AutoCAD software assumes that any distance you enter is in inches, unless you type a foot symbol ('). The inch symbol (") is optional. Therefore, 37 or 37" is 37 inches, but 37' is 37 feet.
- The AutoCAD software does not accept distances with a foot symbol or an inch symbol if you are not using architectural or engineering units.

- The AutoCAD software usually accepts either a decimal or a fraction as input (it accepts 1/2 or 0.5). If you use fractions, separate the whole number from the fraction with a hyphen (1-1/2). If you do not use the hyphen, the software interprets the space as an <Enter>. Although you must enter 6'3-1/2" or 6'3 1/2", the distance displays as 6'-3 1/2".
- When typing decimals, leading zeros are not required (.5 is the same as 0.5), and trailing zeros do not affect the AutoCAD precision (0.5 is as precise as 0.50000).

Practice 7a
Use a Template to Start a Drawing

Practice Objective

- Start drawings using different templates.

In this practice, you will start drawings using different template files that were created for guide. The dimensions are for reference only.

Mechanical - Inches

1. In the Application Menu or in the *Quick Access Toolbar*, click (New). The *Select template* dialog box opens with the *Files of type* displaying **Drawing Template (*.dwt)**. In the *Select template* dialog box, navigate to your practice files folder. Note that only the drawing template files are listed here. Select **Mech-Inches.dwt**. and click **Open** to start a new drawing based on **Mech-Inches.dwt**.
2. Move the crosshairs in the drawing window and note the coordinate display in the *Status Bar*, similar to that shown in Figure 7–6. (If the coordinates are not displayed, expand (Customization) in the *Status Bar* and select **Coordinates**.) Note that the drawing is in Decimal units with a precision of four decimal places.

Figure 7–6

3. Create the sketch shown in Figure 7–7. **Tip:** You can toggle **ORTHOMODE** on to draw horizontal and vertical lines.

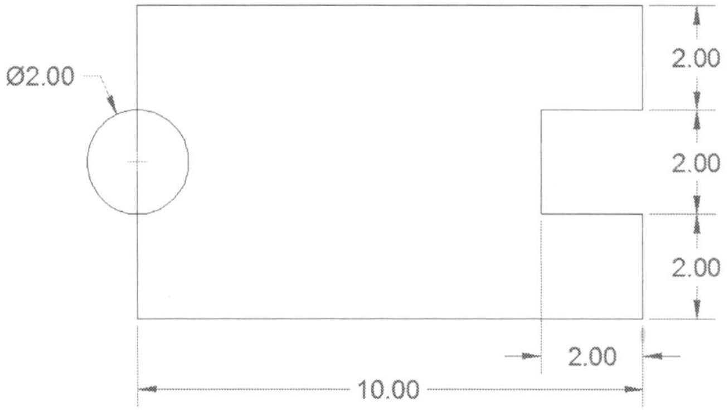

Figure 7–7

4. In the Application Menu or in the *Quick Access Toolbar*, click **Save As** and name the drawing **Mech1.dwg**.

Architectural - Feet and Inches

1. In the Application Menu or in the *Quick Access Toolbar*, click (New).
2. Start a new drawing based on **AEC-Imperial.dwt**, which is located in your practice files folder.
3. Move the crosshairs in the drawing window and note the coordinate display in the *Status Bar*. This drawing is in Architectural units, as shown in Figure 7–8.

Figure 7–8

4. Create the sketch shown in Figure 7–9. Note that you must type the foot symbol after each distance.

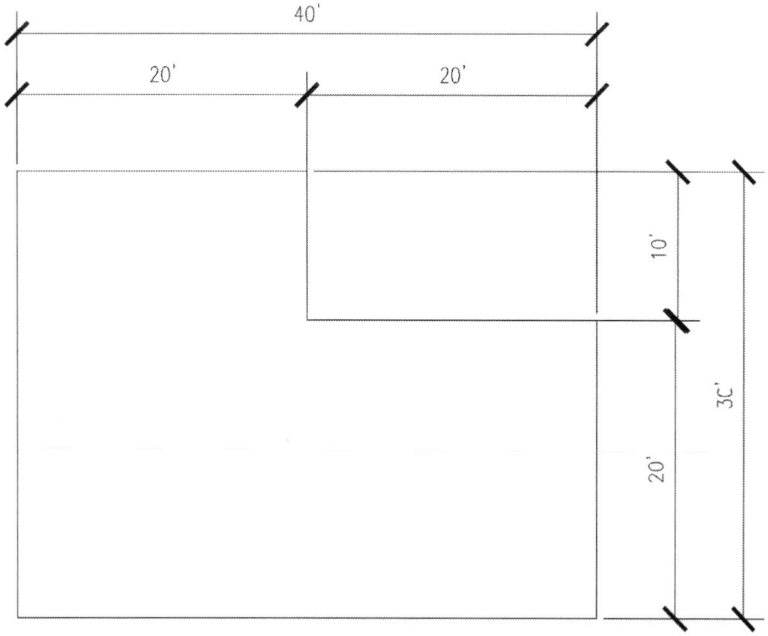

Figure 7–9

5. Save the drawing as **Plan1.dwg**.
6. Close both of the drawings.

End of practice

7.2 What Are Layers?

The AutoCAD software enables you to create an infinite number of layers in a drawing to organize the objects. Similar to overlays or transparencies, layers assist with editing, presentation, and system performance.

Layers organize a drawing into logical categories. For example, in mechanical drafting, views, hidden lines, sections, symbols, notes, and dimensions might be placed on separate layers. In an architectural drawing, there would be layers for walls, furniture, plumbing features, etc., as shown in Figure 7–10.

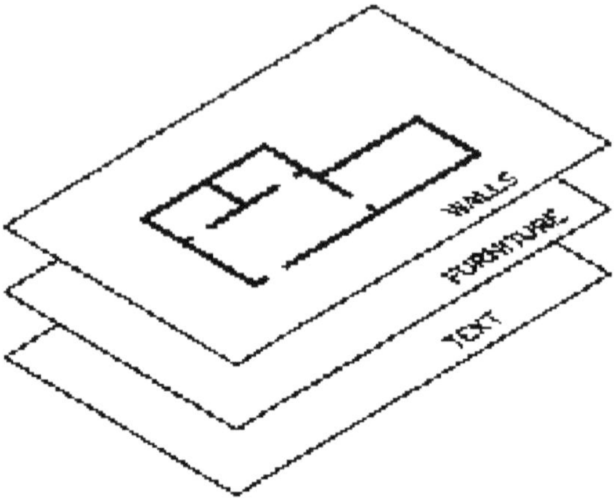

Figure 7–10

- The *current layer* is the layer on which newly drawn objects, such as lines, circles, and text, are placed.
- A color, linetype, and lineweight are assigned to each layer. When a layer is made current, you are automatically drawing in its assigned color, linetype, and lineweight.
- By toggling layers *on* or *off*, you can control which part of the drawing is displayed or is plotted.
- The layer **0** is present in every drawing and cannot be removed or renamed. It is normally not used like the other layers and has special properties for blocks.

Setting the Current Layer

The current layer displays in *Layer Control* in the *Home* tab>*Layers* panel, as shown on the left in Figure 7–11. Selecting the current layer name displays the drop-down list containing all of the existing layers in the current drawing, as shown on the right in Figure 7–11.

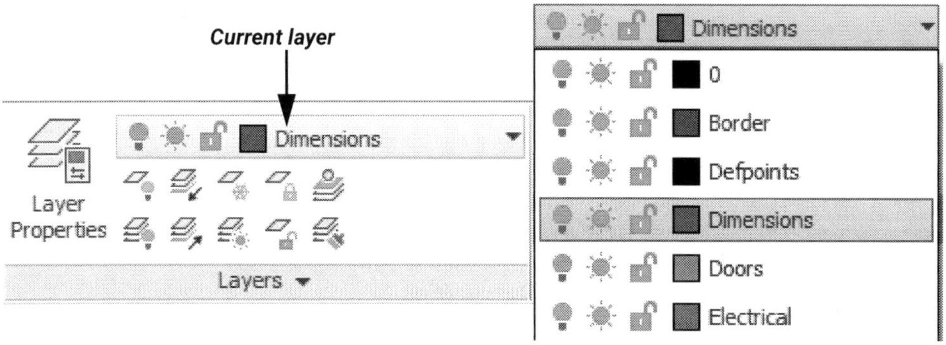

Figure 7–11

- To make a layer active, select its name in the *Layer Control* drop-down list.
- Another way to make a layer active is to select an object in the drawing and then in the *Home* tab>*Layers* panel, click (Make Current). This makes the selected objects' layer active. You can also click (Make Current) first and then select an object. Using (Make Current) indicates the active layer name in the Command Line as well.
- For easy access to various Layer tools, you can display the *Layer Control* bar in the *Quick Access Toolbar*, as shown in Figure 7–12. By default, *Layer Control* does not display in the *Quick Access Toolbar*, but you can display it by selecting **Layer** in the (Quick Access drop-down menu).

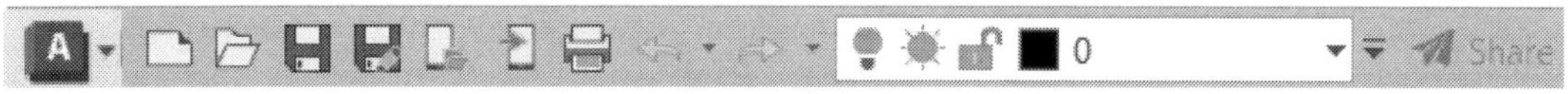

Figure 7–12

Hint: Properties Panel

You can change the layer and *color*, *linetype*, *lineweight*, *plot style*, and *transparency* of individual objects. In the *Home* tab, the *Properties* panel enables you to set these characteristics for objects (as shown in Figure 7–13), just as *Layer Control* enables you to set the layer.

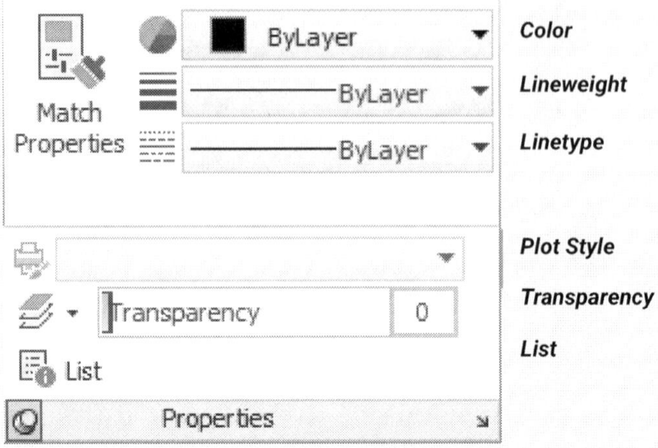

Figure 7–13

Normally, these properties are set to **ByLayer**, indicating that the objects do not have a specific color, linetype, lineweight, plot style, and transparency of their own. Instead, the layer that the objects are drawn on defines their properties.

Although you can assign colors, linetypes, lineweights, plot style, and transparency to individual objects, it is usually best to let the object take its properties from its layer. This method ensures consistency and control over properties. You can easily change the color, lineweight, linetype, plot style, and transparency of all of the objects on a specific layer by changing the properties of the layer.

7.3 Layer States

The state of the layer determines how the objects on it are displayed and selected.

- The following three aspects of a layer's state can be changed in *Layer Control* by selecting the appropriate symbol, as shown on the left in Figure 7–14.
- You can also use an object in the drawing to change its layer state by using the appropriate icon in the *Layers* panel, as shown on the right in Figure 7–14.

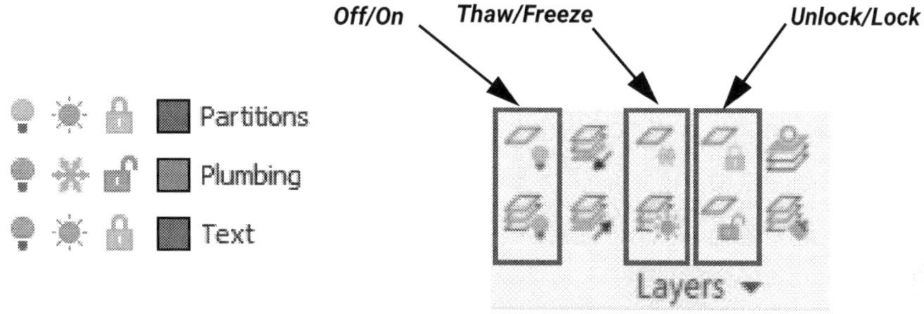

Figure 7–14

On/Off

A layer can be toggled on (displayed) or toggled off (hidden). Toggling a layer off is like temporarily removing it from the drawing. Layers that are toggled off are not displayed and are not plotted.

- The current layer can be toggled off, but the software warns you with an alert that provides you with options of either turning the current layer off or keeping it on. If the current layer is toggled off, you can draw but cannot see what you are drawing.

Thaw/Freeze

Layers that are not needed or displayed for a long time should be frozen. Freezing a layer is similar to toggling it off, except that the layer does not require calculation time when regeneration occurs.

- You cannot freeze the current layer and a frozen layer cannot be made current.
- The objects on the frozen layers are not displayed in the drawing and those objects are not regenerated as well.
- Once you thaw a layer, you might need to perform a regeneration operation to display the layer.

Lock/Unlock

Objects on layers that are locked can be viewed but not edited. When you hover the cursor over them, a small lock icon displays. By default, locked layers are also slightly grayed out.

- Locking a layer is useful when you do not want to accidentally edit the objects in the layer.

Returning a Layer to Its Previous State

You sometimes need to change the state of layers to edit a drawing and then change them back to their previous state. After you have changed the current layer or state of layers, in the *Home* tab>expanded *Layers* panel, use (Layer Previous) to return to the previous layer settings.

Practice 7b
Work with Layers and Layer States

Practice Objectives

- Draw objects on specific layers.
- Change the state of a layer using *Layer Control*.

In this practice, you will draw objects on specific layers and then change the state of the layers.

Task 1: Draw on and change layers.

In this task, you will draw an object on specific layers, as shown in Figure 7–15. The dimensions are for reference only.

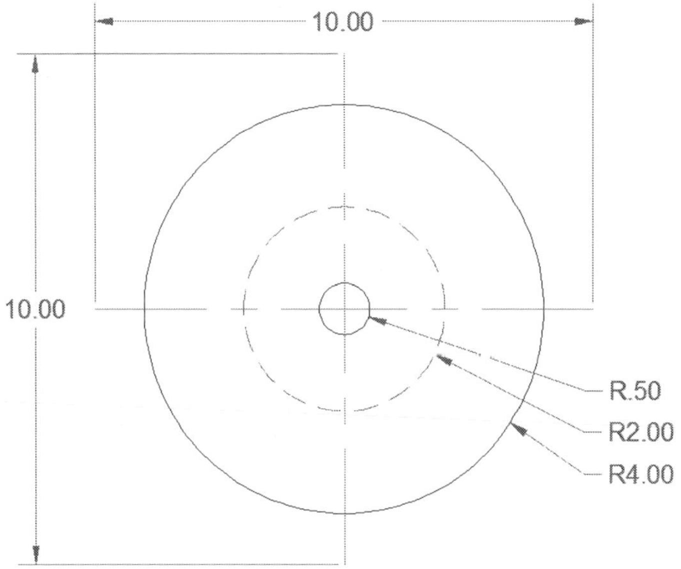

Figure 7–15

1. In the *Application Menu* or in the *Quick Access Toolbar*, click (New). Start a new drawing based on **Mech-Inches.dwt**, which is located in your practice files folder.
2. In the *Home* tab>*Layers* panel, expand *Layer Control* and select **Center** to set it as the current layer.

   ***Note:** For easy access to the Layer tools, display Layer Controls in the Quick Access Toolbar (select **Layer** in the drop-down menu).*

3. Draw a horizontal line, **10 units** long near the center of the screen and exit the command. Note that the line has a centerline style (dashed).
4. Draw a vertical line, **10 units** long separate from the line you just drew. Move it so that its midpoint is on the midpoint of the other line.
5. Change the current layer to **Object** by selecting it in *Layer Control*.
6. Draw a circle with a radius of **4** with its center point at the intersection of the two centerlines that you drew. The circle has a solid continuous linetype (white on a black background or black if the background is white).
7. Change the current layer to **Hidden**.
8. Draw another circle with a radius of **2** at the same center point as the first circle. It has a hidden line style.
9. In the *Home* tab>*Layers* panel, click (Make Current) and select the largest circle. Note in the *Layer Control* that the current layer changes to **Object**. (The layer of the largest circle)
10. Draw another circle with a **0.5** radius at the same center point. It should be white (or black) and continuous linetype of the **Object** layer.
11. Save the drawing as **Wheel.dwg**.

Task 2: Change the layer state.

In this task, you will change the state of layers.

1. Make layer **0** the current layer.
2. Use *Layer Control* to toggle off the layer **Center**, as shown in Figure 7–16. The two center lines disappear in the drawing.

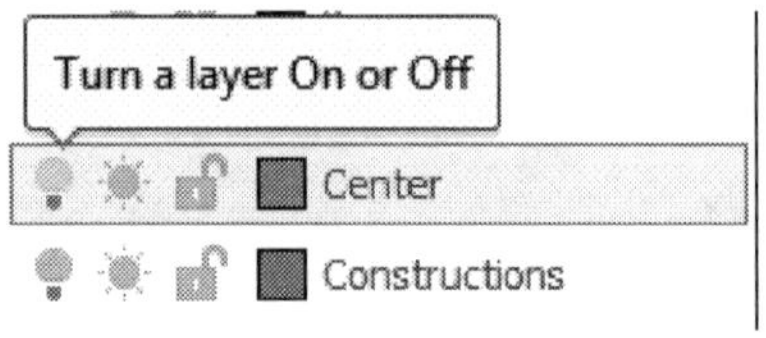

Figure 7–16

3. Use *Layer Control* to freeze the layer **Hidden**, as shown in Figure 7–17. The hidden linetype circle disappears.

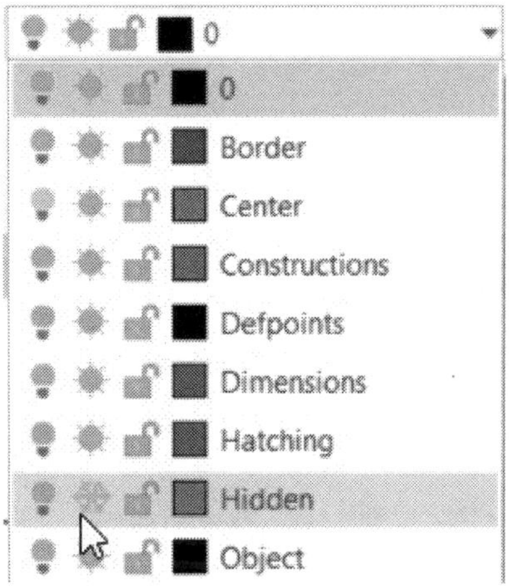

Figure 7–17

4. Use *Layer Control* to lock the layer **Object**. The circles on that layer stay displayed, but are slightly grayed out.
5. Try to erase the largest circle and then try to move it. You cannot modify the circle because it is on the locked layer **Object**.
6. Use *Layer Control* to unlock the layer **Object**.
7. Erase the largest circle. Use **Undo** to bring it back.
8. Save and close the drawing.

End of practice

7.4 Changing an Object's Layer

You can move objects from one layer to another so that they show differently in the drawing, as shown in Figure 7–18.

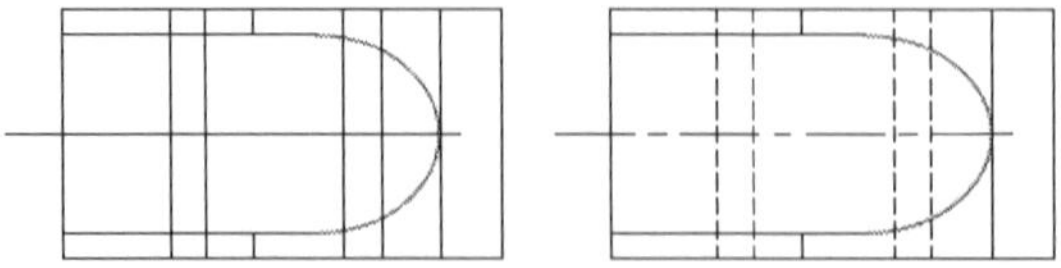

Figure 7–18

Change with Layer Control

You can change the layer of a selected object(s) using *Layer Control*.

How To: Change Object Layers with Layer Control

1. Select an object before you start a command. Layer Control displays the layer of the object.
2. Expand *Layer Control*, and hover the cursor on another layer. Note that the selected object previews with the new layer, as shown in Figure 7–19.

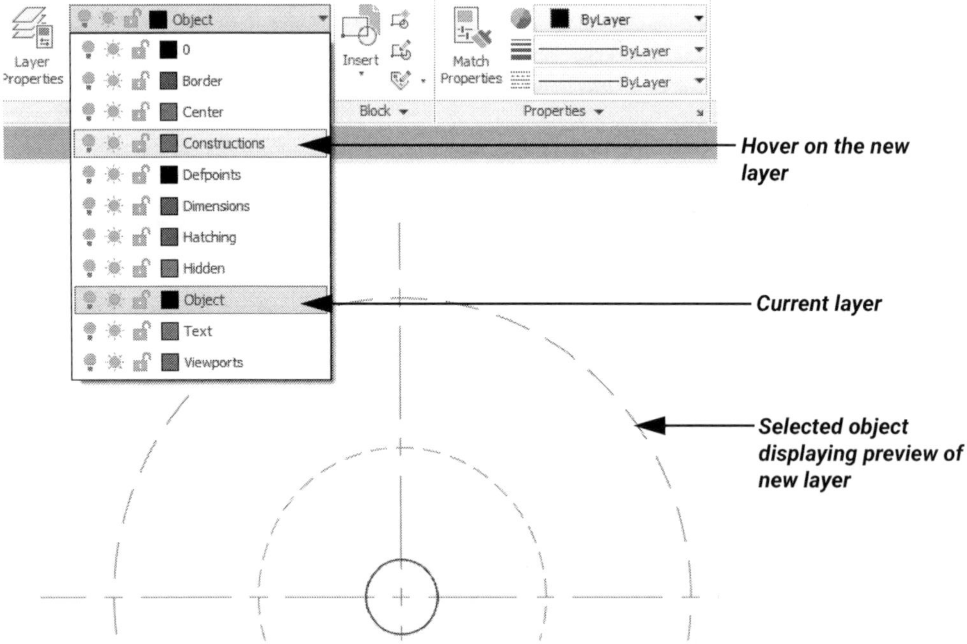

Figure 7–19

3. Select the layer to change it.

4. Press <Esc> to clear the selected object.

- You can select multiple objects to change their layers. If the selected objects are on different layers, a layer name does not display in *Layer Control*. You can still hover to preview and then select a layer to move all of the objects to that layer.

Match Layer

Another way to change the layer of an object is to use the **Match Layer** command. This command can be used when you have other objects on that layer in your drawing.

How To: Match Layers

1. In the *Home* tab>*Layers* panel, click (Match Layer).
2. Select the objects that you want to change.
3. Press <Enter> to finish the selection set.
4. Select an object on the destination layer.

   or

- Instead of selecting an object on the destination layer, you can press the <Down Arrow> which lists the **Name** option. Selecting **Name** opens the *Change to Layer* dialog box, in which you can select a layer name from a list, as shown in Figure 7–20. Use this option if you do not know which object layer to select. Otherwise, it is faster to select the objects and then select the layer in *Layer Control*.

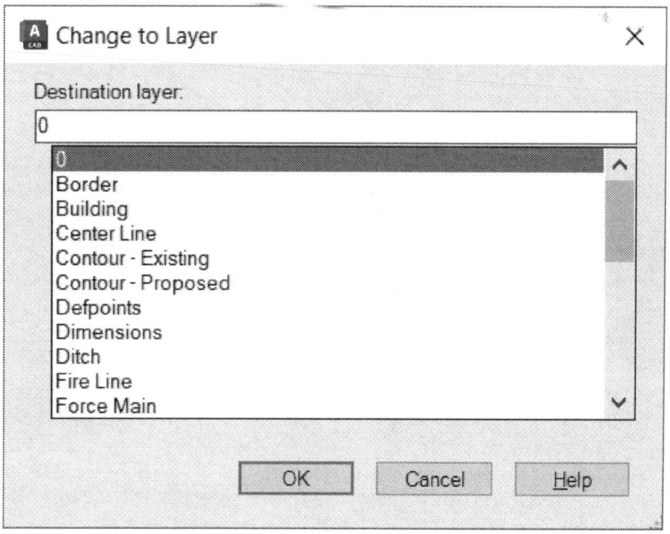

Figure 7–20

Practice 7c
Change an Object's Layer

Practice Objective

- Move objects to different layers.

In this practice, you will use *Layer Control* and the **Match Layer** command to move objects to different layers, as shown in Figure 7–21.

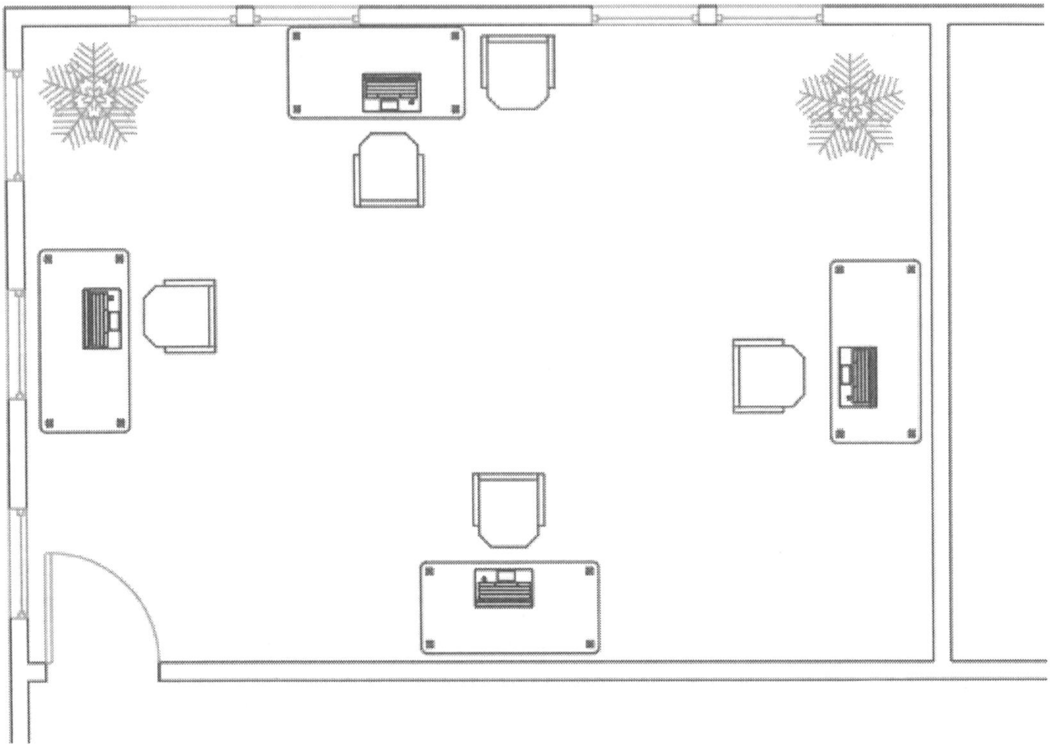

Figure 7–21

1. Open **Suite-A.dwg** from your practice files folder. Currently, all of the objects are on layer **0**.
2. With no command active, select any one line of the wall (blue grips display on the line and it highlights in blue with a thicker lineweight). The layer of that line (layer **0**) displays in *Layer Control*.
3. Expand *Layer Control* and hover the cursor over the layer **Walls**. The selected wall changes to blue color, which is the color of the layer **Walls**. Click to change the layer to **Walls**. Press <Esc> to clear the selection of the line.

4. Select one of the desks and repeat Step 3 to change its layer to the layer **Furniture** (it turns red). Press <Esc> to clear the selection.

5. In the *Home* tab>*Layers* panel, click (Match Layer). Select the other desks in the room as the objects to be changed, and then press <Enter> or right-click. Select the desk that you changed in Step 4 as the object on the destination layer. All of the desks change layers to match the destination desk.

6. Use (Match Layer) to change the remaining walls to the layer **Walls** using the changed wall as the destination layer. (Select the walls using a crossing window.)

7. With no command active, select the two plants. Use *Layer Control* to change their layer to **Misc**.

8. Change the remaining objects (chairs, laptops, door, and windows) to the appropriate layers. Use layer **Furniture** for chairs, layer **Electrical** for laptops, and layer **Windows** for windows.

9. Save and close the drawing.

End of practice

Chapter Review Questions

1. Objects on layers that are frozen stay displayed in the drawing but cannot be edited.
    a. True
    b. False

2. How do you move an existing object to a different layer?
    a. Recreate the object on the correct layer.
    b. Use the **Move** command.
    c. Change the current layer, select the object, and press <Enter>.
    d. Select the object and pick the required layer in *Layer Control*.

3. If you have finished drawing the walls in a floor plan drawing and want to display the objects, but do not want them to be erased or moved, what should you do?
    a. Lock the layer.
    b. Make a different layer current.
    c. Toggle the layer off.
    d. Freeze the layer.

4. After creating an object, how do you place it on another object's layer in the drawing?
    a. Use **Match Layer**.
    b. Change the current layer.
    c. Use **Make Current (Layer)**.
    d. Redraw it on the correct layer.

5. When objects do not display on a specific layer, and the layer does not regenerate with the drawing, the layer is ________.
    a. Thawed
    b. Current
    c. Frozen
    d. Locked

6. A drawing file designed to be the basis of new drawing is called a ________.
   a. Setup File
   b. Prototype
   c. Template File
   d. Seed File

Command Summary

Button	Command	Location
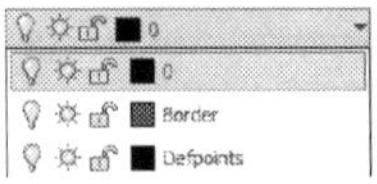	**Layer Control**	• **Ribbon:** *Home* tab>*Layers* panel • **Quick Access Toolbar**
	**Layer Previous**	• **Ribbon:** *Home* tab>*Layers* panel • **Command Prompt:** layerp
	**Make Current (Layer)**	• **Ribbon:** *Home* tab>*Layers* panel • **Command Prompt:** laymcur
	**Match Layer**	• **Ribbon:** *Home* tab>*Layers* panel • **Command Prompt:** laymch
	**New/Qnew**	• **Quick Access Toolbar:** New • **Application Menu:** New • **Command Prompt:** qnew or new

Chapter 8

Advanced Object Types

In this chapter, you learn how to draw and edit arcs, polylines, polygons, and ellipses.

Learning Objectives

- Draw arcs, polylines, and ellipses using various commands.
- Create complex single objects consisting of lines and arcs.
- Modify polylines to add or remove vertices, change widths, or convert lines to arcs and vice versa.
- Draw flowing shapes by blending together smooth curve segment.
- Create closed polygons containing three or more equal sides.
- Draw an ellipse by specifying the end points of the major and minor axes.

8.1 Drawing Arcs

The **Arc** command is used to add curved segments to a drawing, as shown in Figure 8–1. The information or geometry you have originally determines the option you use.

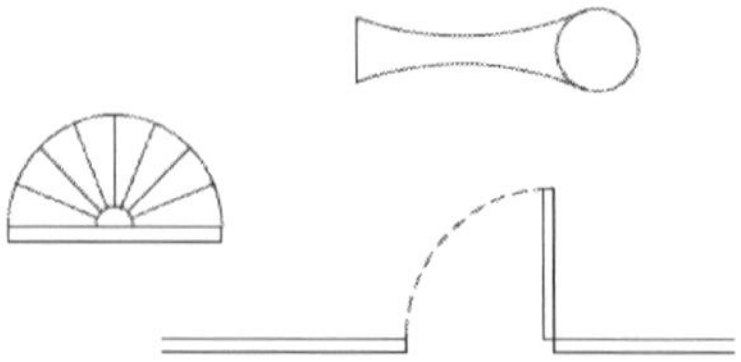

Figure 8–1

Arc Command Options

The **Arc** command has many options that enable you to create arcs. In the *Home* tab>*Draw* panel, expand  (Arc flyout) to access the different arc construction options available in the software, as shown on the left in Figure 8–2. The geometric definitions used for drawing arcs is shown on the right in Figure 8–2.

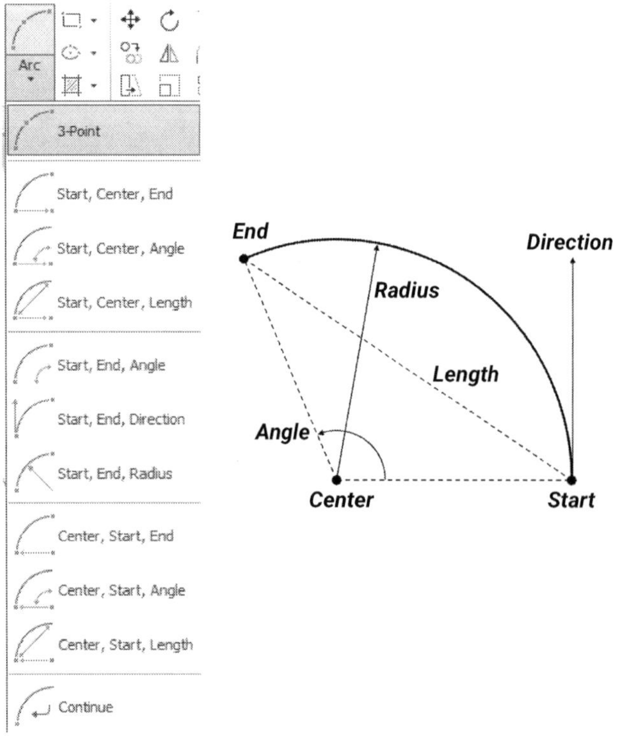

Figure 8–2

Start	Starting point of an arc.
Center	Center (or focal) point of an arc.
End	Ending point of an arc.
Radius	Radius of an arc.
Angle	Included angle turned by an arc.
Direction	Starting direction of an arc.
Chord (Length)	Chord length of an arc. (Distance between arc start and end points.)

Notes on Arcs

- By default, arcs in the AutoCAD software are drawn in a counter-clockwise direction from the starting point. You can hold <Ctrl> to reverse the direction when constructing an Arc.
- Pressing <Enter> at the *Specify start point:* prompt starts drawing the arc from the end point of the last line or arc segment drawn. (This feature is only available when the *Specify start point:* prompt is the first prompt for the type of arc being created.)
- You can also type, use the shortcut menu, or use the <Down Arrow> menu to access the arc options.

Practice 8a
Draw Arcs

Practice Objective

- Draw arcs using various options.

In this practice, you will draw door swings in a floorplan using the various options of the **Arc** command, as shown in Figure 8–3.

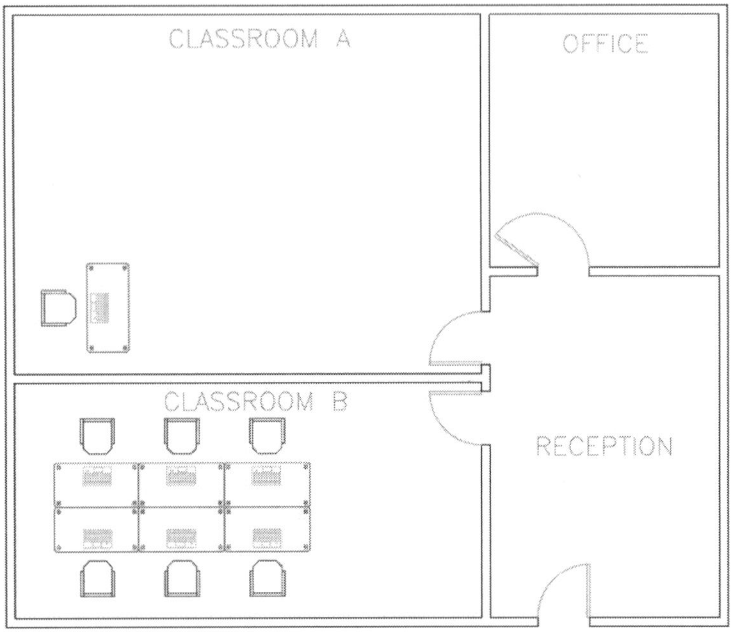

Figure 8–3

1. Open **Class-A.dwg** from your practice files folder. Note that the room doors do not have the door swings.
2. In *Layer Control*, set the current layer to **Doors**.
3. Set the **Endpoint** object snap, and toggle 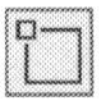 (Object Snap) on.
4. Zoom in on the office door.
5. In the *Home* tab>*Draw* panel, expand  (Arc flyout) and click  (Start, Center, End).
6. At the *Specify start point of arc:* prompt, select the upper right corner of the doorway wall, as shown in Figure 8–4.

7. At the *Specify center point of arc:* prompt, select the point where the door and wall meet, as shown in Figure 8–4.
8. At the *Specify end point of arc:* prompt, select the upper right corner of the door, as shown in Figure 8–4. The arc that represents the door swing is created, as shown in Figure 8–4.

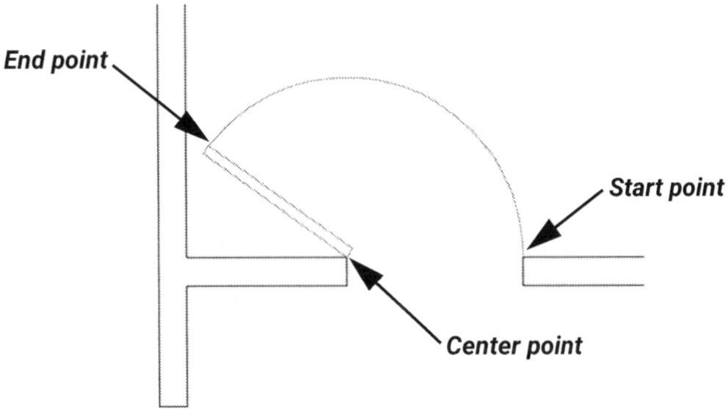

Figure 8–4

9. Pan over and zoom in to Classroom A's door.
10. In the *Home* tab>*Draw* panel, expand the *Arc* flyout and click (Start, Center, Angle).
11. At the *Specify start point of arc:* prompt, select the upper left corner of Classroom A's doorway wall.
12. At the *Specify center point of arc:* prompt, select the point where the door and wall meet.
13. For the angle, enter **90** and press <Enter>.
14. Pan over and zoom in to Classroom B's door.
15. In the *Home* tab>*Draw* panel, expand the *Arc* flyout and click (Start, Center, Angle).
16. For the start point, select the lower left corner of Classroom B's doorway wall. For the center point, select the point where the door and wall meet, and for the angle, enter **-90**. Press <Enter> to create the door swing and complete the command.
17. Pan over to the last door of the Reception room. Add the arc for the door swing using a **Start, Center, End**. **Tip:** To create the door arc in clockwise direction, press and hold <Ctrl> before selecting the end point of the arc.
18. Save and close the drawing.

End of practice

8.2 Drawing Polylines

Polylines are complex objects consisting of lines and arcs. Each segment in a polyline sequence is considered to be part of a single object. In addition, polylines can be assigned a width that can vary for each segment.

Polylines are ideal for drawing complex single objects, such as walls, transmission lines, ductwork, and schematic traces or area outlines, as shown in Figure 8–5.

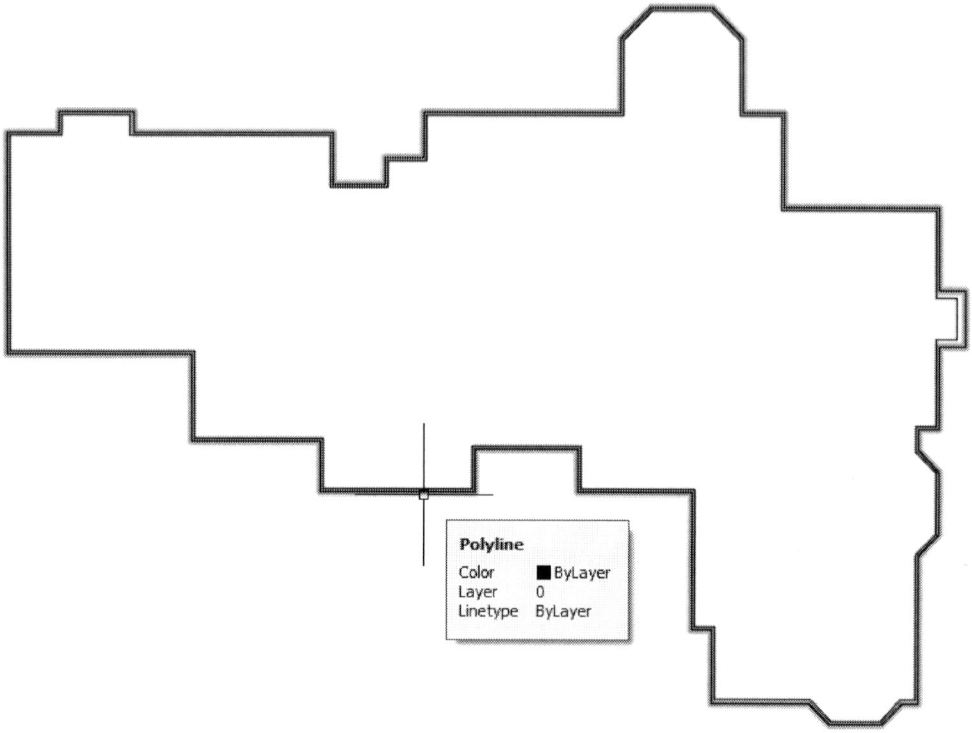

Figure 8–5

- Polylines can be used anywhere a regular line or arc can be used.
- When creating one continuous object, you cannot exit and then continue to complete the rest of the polyline object. It creates two separate objects.
- A polyline can be either open or closed. An open polyline has one start point and one end point.

How To: Draw a Polyline with Width and Arcs

1. In the *Home* tab>*Draw* panel, click (Polyline).
2. Select a start point. A darker point displays, indicating that it is the start point. This is useful when creating complex polylines. The point disappears when the polyline creation is completed.
3. (Optional) You can have different widths for each polyline segment. Select the **Width** option in the <Down Arrow> menu (as shown on the left in Figure 8–6), or type **W** and press <Enter>.
4. Enter a starting width or select two points to define the width.
5. Enter an ending width. If you want it to be the same as the starting width, you can press <Enter> to accept the default.
6. Select the next point(s).
7. (Optional) When you want to create an arc segment, do not end the **Polyline** command. Instead, select the **Arc** option in the <Down Arrow> menu or type **A** and press <Enter>.
   - In the Polyline arc, use <Down Arrow> to display the Arc options.
8. Follow the prompts to create the required type of arc. The prompts are similar to those in the **Arc** command. When drawing an arc, you can press <Ctrl> to draw in the opposite direction.
9. To switch back to line segments, type **L** and press <Enter> or select the **Line** option from the <Down Arrow> menu, or the shortcut menu, as shown on the right in Figure 8–6.

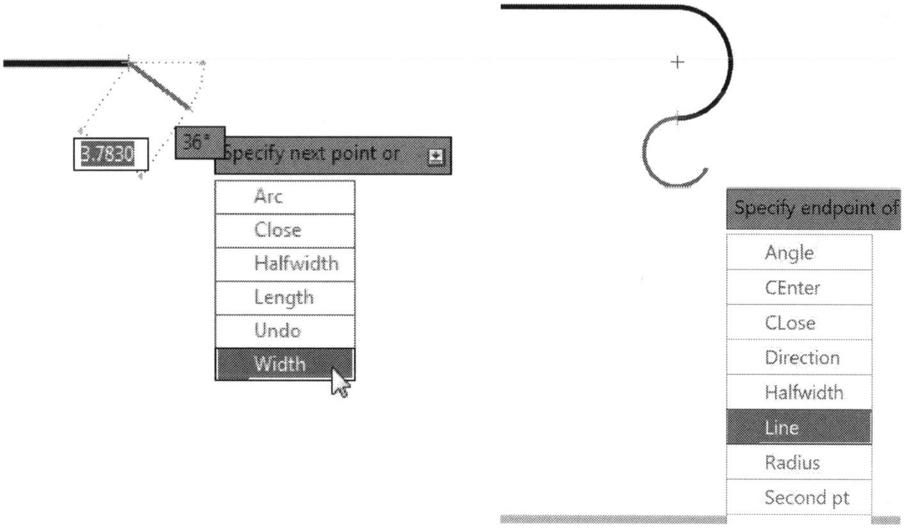

Figure 8–6

10. If you want to create a closed polyline, use the **Close** option (CL). It attaches the last segment back to the start point.

- You can use the **Undo** option to remove the last segment drawn without ending the command.
- Other options include **Halfwidth**, which specifies the distance from the center of a wide polyline to one of its edges, and **Length**, which draws a segment of the specified length at the same angle as the previous segment.

8.3 Editing Polylines

You can edit polylines by moving a vertex, changing its width, joining polylines or lines and arcs together, and converting polylines into individual segments. You can also add and remove vertices from existing polylines and convert arcs to lines and vice-versa.

How To: Change the Width of an Existing Polyline

1. In the *Home* tab>expanded *Modify* panel, click (Edit Polyline).
2. At the *Select polyline:* prompt, select the polyline. An options menu displays, as shown in Figure 8–7.
   - Without starting the **Edit Polyline** command, you can double-click on a polyline to display the options menu.

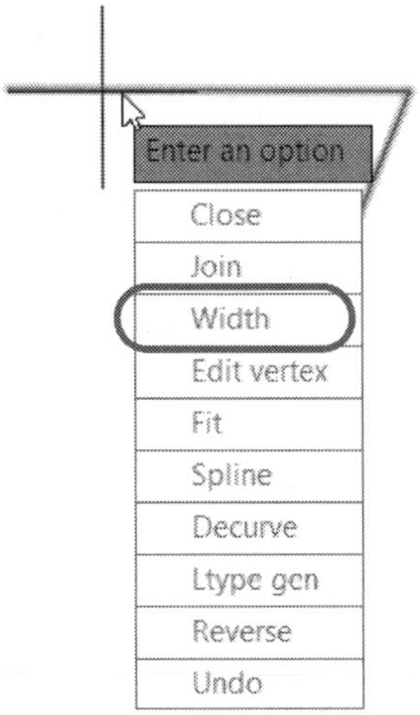

Figure 8–7

3. Select the **Width** option.
4. At the *Specify new width for all segments:* prompt, enter the new width and press <Enter>.
5. Press <Enter> to end the command.

How To: Modify Vertices in Polylines Using Edit Polyline

1. In the *Home* tab>expanded *Modify* panel, click (Edit Polyline).
2. Select the polyline that you want to edit. You can also double-click on a polyline to display the options menu.
3. Select the **Edit vertex** option.

4. An icon displays on the polyline, indicating the vertex that is currently being edited. To select a different vertex, select the **Next** option until the one you want to edit displays.
5. Select one of the following options to modify the current vertex:

Break	Breaks the polyline at the selected vertex, separating it from the rest of the polyline. If you break a polyline in more than one place, the separated objects remain polylines.
Insert	Inserts a new vertex at the selected point on the polyline. You can place the new vertex anywhere on the polyline.
Move	Moves a vertex to a new position on the polyline. You can move the current vertex to a new location, anywhere on the polyline.
Straighten	Deletes segments and vertices between two selected vertices, and replaces them with a single straight line segment.
Tangent	Attaches a tangent direction to the selected vertex to be used for curve fitting later.
Width	Modifies the width of the selected line or arc between two adjacent vertices.

6. Use the **Next** and **Previous** options to continue modifying vertices. Select **eXit** to return to the **Edit Polyline** command options, or press <Esc> to end the command.

Modifying Polyline Vertices Using Grips

If you select a polyline when you are not in a command, the vertex grips and midpoint vertex grips display. You can modify them by adding or deleting vertices, stretching them, extending them, and converting them from a line to an arc and vice-versa. You can access these options by hovering the cursor over a multifunctional grip and selecting an option in the list, as shown in Figure 8–8.

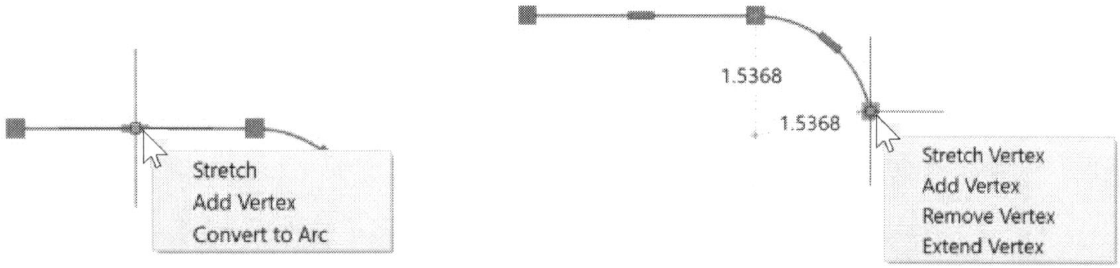

Figure 8–8

How To: Use Grips to Convert a Line to an Arc

1. When not in a command, select a polyline to display its vertices.
2. On the object, hover on the grip that you want to change. For example, if you want to change a line into an arc, hover on the midpoint vertex grip of the line.
3. Select **Convert to Arc**.

4. Drag the arc to the required size or enter the required dimension.
5. Continue selecting vertices and modifying them or press <Esc> to end the command.

Converting Lines and Arcs to Polylines

In some cases, creating lines and arcs and then turning them into a polyline is easier than using the **Polyline** command from the start. While separate lines and arcs work in most cases, having them work together as a polyline can be useful. For instance, selecting one object to move is easier than selecting all of the pieces from which it has been created, as shown in Figure 8–9.

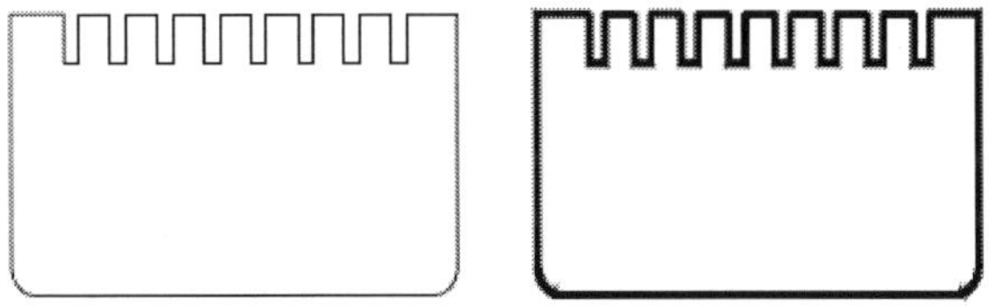

Figure 8–9

How To: Convert Lines and Arcs into a Single Polyline

1. In the *Home* tab>expanded *Modify* panel, click (Edit Polyline).
2. At the *Select polyline or:* prompt, select a line or arc.
3. At the *Do you want to turn it into one?:* prompt, press <Enter> to select the **Y** option.
4. Select **Join** in the options menu that displays.
5. Select the other objects that you want to join to the polyline, which get highlighted.
6. Press <Enter> once to end the *Select objects:* prompt.
7. Press <Enter> again to end the command.

- The **Multiple** option (at the *Select Polyline:* prompt) enables you to edit several polylines at once, or to convert multiple line segments into polylines at the same time.
- To be joined, each line segment or arc must be attached to the end point of the next.
- For open polylines, **Edit Polyline** displays the **Close** option; for closed polylines, it displays the **Open** option.

Turning Polylines into Lines and Arcs

When a polyline has been created, you might want to break it into all of its separate component parts, so that you can remove individual segments or make other changes.

- In the *Home* tab>*Modify* panel, click (Explode) to convert a polyline into individual arcs and lines.
- Exploding a wide polyline causes it to lose its width information.
- The **Explode** command works on other object types that are made from polylines, such as rectangles or polygons. It also works on blocks.

Practice 8b
Draw and Edit Polylines

Practice Objectives

- Draw polylines and convert a polyline into separate lines and arcs.
- Convert lines and arcs into a polyline.
- Change the width of a polyline.

In this practice, you will draw polylines. You will edit several polylines and change their width so that they will be used as symbols in a flowchart.

Task 1: Draw polylines for a flowchart.

In this task, you will create several polylines as symbols to be used in a flowchart, as shown in Figure 8–10. The dimensions are for your reference only.

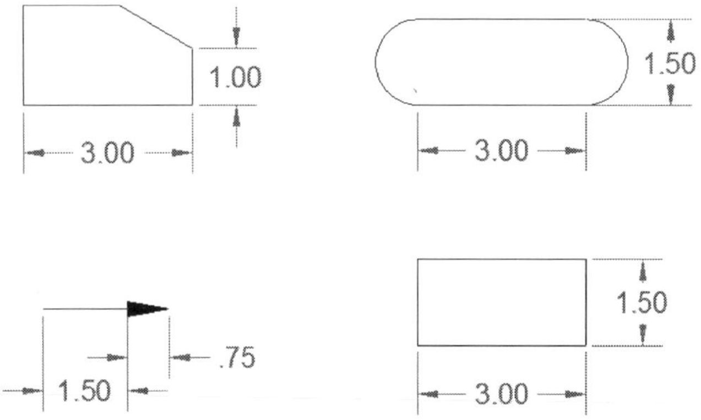

Figure 8–10

1. Start a new drawing based on **Mech-Inches.dwt**, which is located in your practice files folder, and save it as **Flowchart.dwg**.

2. Ensure that (Object Snap) and (Object Snap Tracking) are both toggled on. Set the **Endpoint, Midpoint**, and **Extension** object snaps.

3. Expand (Polar Tracking) and select **30,60,90,120...**. Ensure that it is toggled on.

4. In the *Home* tab> *Draw* panel, click (Polyline) and draw the top left symbol, as shown in Figure 8–11.
   - Specify the start point anywhere.
   - Move the cursor right, enter **3**, and press <Enter>.
   - Move the cursor straight up, enter **1**, and press <Enter>.
   - Move the cursor at an angle of **150°**, enter **1.5**, and press <Enter>.
   - Make the next point straight to the left, but track it to make it directly above (even with) the start point.
   - Type **C** and press <Enter> to close the figure and finish the command.
5. Start the **Polyline** command again and draw the top right symbol, as shown in Figure 8–11.
   - To specify the start point, track it from the lower right corner of the object drawn in Step 4.
   - Move the cursor right, enter **3**, and press <Enter>.
   - Type **A** and press <Enter> to switch to the **Arc** option.
   - Move the cursor straight up, enter **1.5**, and press <Enter>.
   - Type **L** and press <Enter> to switch to the **Line** option.
   - Move the cursor left, enter **3**, and press <Enter>.
   - Switch to the **Arc** option and type **CL** to close the figure and finish the command.
6. Start the **Polyline** command and draw the arrow below the symbol drawn in Step 4, as shown in Figure 8–11.
   - Specify the start point anywhere below the angled symbol.
   - Move the cursor right, enter **1.5**, and press <Enter>.
   - Type **W** and press <Enter> to switch to the **Width** option.
   - For the starting width, enter **0.25** and press <Enter>.
   - For the ending width, enter **0** and press <Enter>.
   - Move the cursor straight to the right, enter **0.75**, and press <Enter>.
   - Press <Enter> to finish the command.

7. The bottom right symbol shown in Figure 8–11 can be drawn using the **Rectangle** command or **Polyline** command.

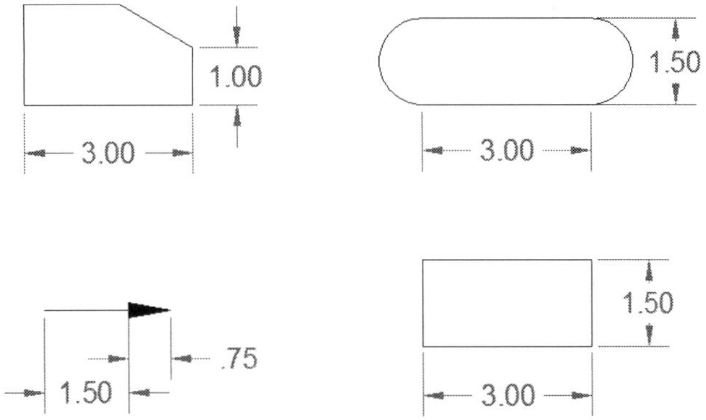

Figure 8–11

Note: A rectangle is also a polyline.

8. Arrange the objects to create the simple flowchart shown in Figure 8–12. Move, copy, and rotate the objects as required.

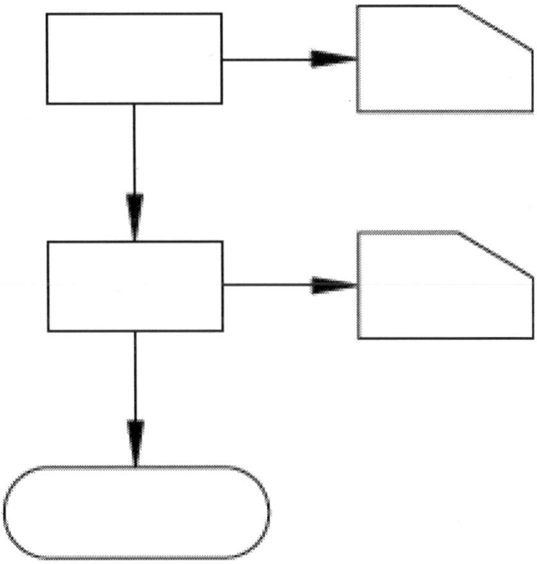

Figure 8–12

9. Save the drawing.

Task 2: Edit polylines.

In this task, you will explode a polyline, and then use the **Edit Polyline** command to join arcs and lines into a polyline and change the width, as shown in Figure 8–13. You will further convert the arcs back to straight lines.

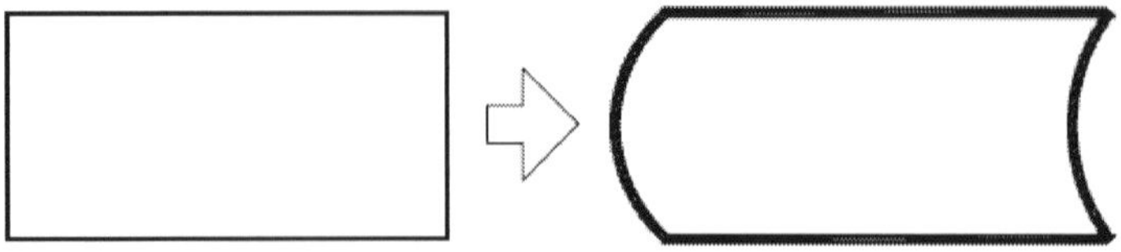

Figure 8–13

1. Make a copy of the rectangle.
2. Select the copied rectangle and explode it (in the *Home* tab>*Modify* panel, click (Explode)). Erase the two vertical lines. You can select the lines individually because the object is no longer a polyline.
3. Draw a 3-point arc along the left end of the two remaining horizontal lines. Use the **Endpoint** object snap to connect the arcs to the lines. (Tip: Using the **3 Point** arc option, select the left endpoint of the top horizontal line as the first point of the arc. For the second point of the arc, select an arbitrary point towards the left of the endpoints, as shown in Figure 8–14. For the third point of the arc, select the left endpoint of the bottom horizontal line.)

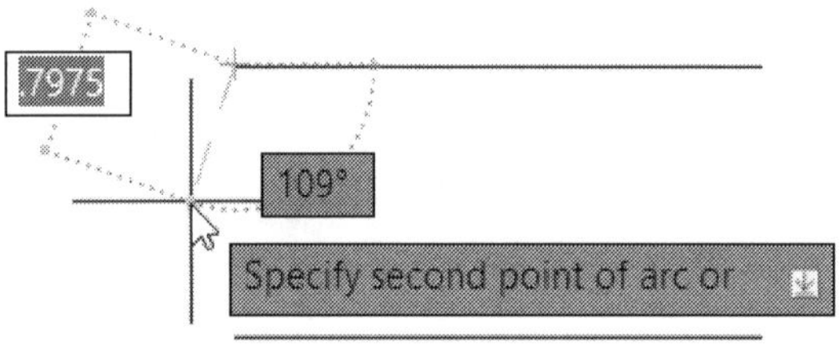

Figure 8–14

4. Copy the first arc to the other end.
5. In the *Home* tab>expanded *Modify* panel, click (Edit Polyline) and select any one of the lines. At the *Do you want to turn it into one?:* prompt, press <Enter> to select the **Y** (yes) option.
6. In the options menu, select **Join**.
7. At the *Select objects:* prompt, select the other line and the arcs and press <Enter>.
8. Select the **Width** option. Set the width to **0.05** and press <Enter>. Press <Enter> again to exit the command.

9. Use the **Move** command to move the shape. It is now all one object.
10. Verify that you are not in a command and select the polyline to display its grips.
11. Hover the cursor over one of the midpoint grip vertices on one of the arcs and select **Convert to Line**, as shown in Figure 8–15.

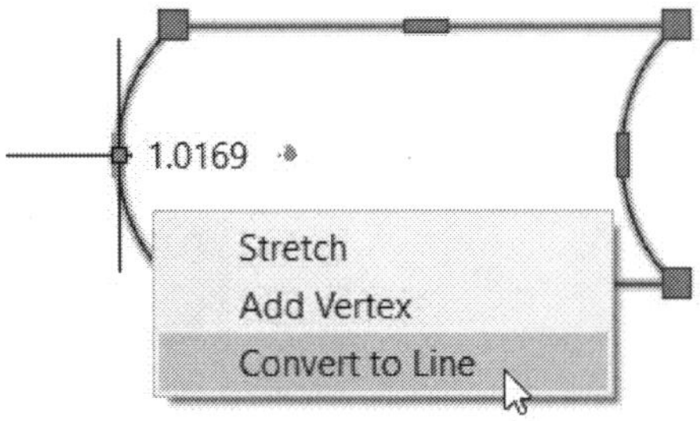

Figure 8–15

12. Repeat the previous step for the other arc. The shape is now a rectangle.
13. Save and close the drawing.

End of practice

8.4 Drawing Splines

A spline consists of smooth curve segments that are blended together to form a flowing shape. Splines are important in special drawing applications that use curves extensively (such as contour maps) or that require exact control of complex curves (such as the shape of a hull in shipbuilding or the aerodynamic surfaces of airplanes and cars). You can use (Spline Fit) or (Spline CV) in the *Home* tab>expanded *Draw* panel (as shown in Figure 8–16) for creating true spline curves.

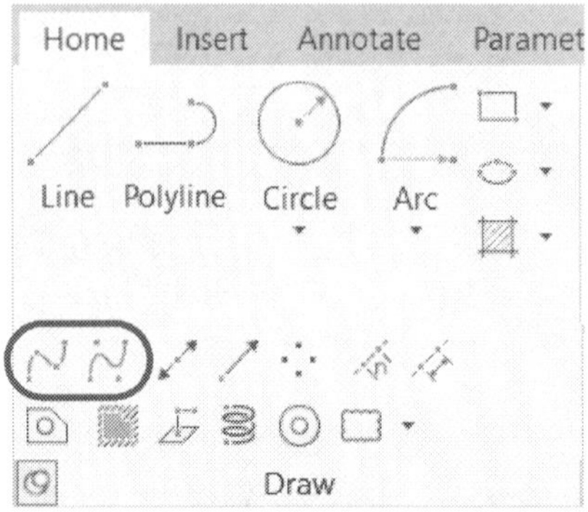

Figure 8–16

How To: Draw a Spline

1. In the *Home* tab>expanded *Draw* panel, click (Spline Fit).
2. Click to specify the start point of the spline.
3. Click to specify the next point of the spline. Move your cursor to display the shape of the curve, as shown in Figure 8–17.

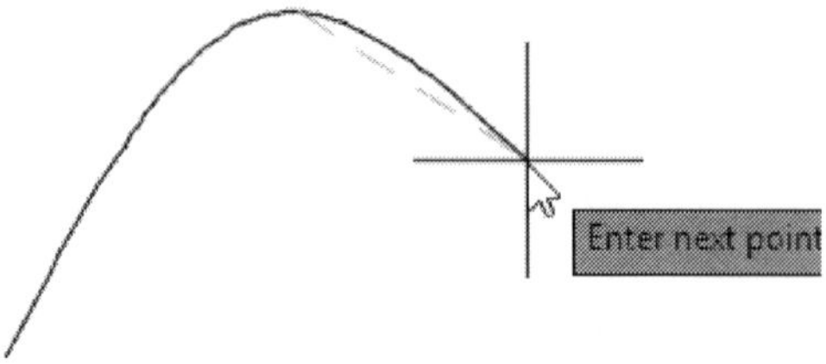

Figure 8–17

4. Continue clicking and specifying the points for the curves.

5. Press <Enter> to complete the creation of the spline, as shown in Figure 8–18.

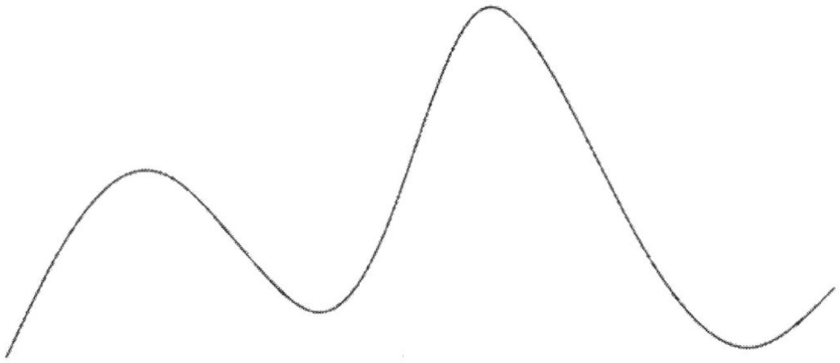

Figure 8–18

- The (Edit Polyline) command has a **Spline** option that converts a polyline into an approximation of a smooth curve, called a *spline curve*, as shown in Figure 8–19. (The **Fit** option is similar but the curve is not as smooth.)

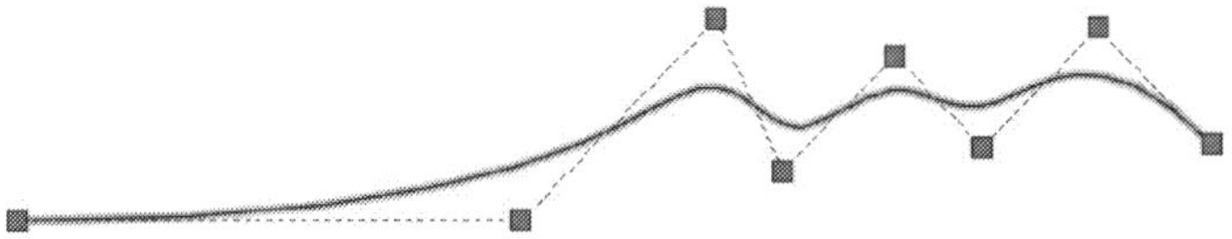

Figure 8–19

- (Spline Fit) and (Spline CV) create true spline curves. These are mathematically more exact and easier to control than splined polylines.
- After a spline has been created, its shape can further be refined using (Edit Spline) in the *Home* tab>expanded *Modify* panel.

Blend Command

The **Blend** command combines two selected lines or curves by creating a spline in the gap between them. The (Blend Curves) command is available in the *Home* tab>*Modify* panel, in the *Fillet* flyout. Start the command and select the first line or curve as shown in Figure 8–20.

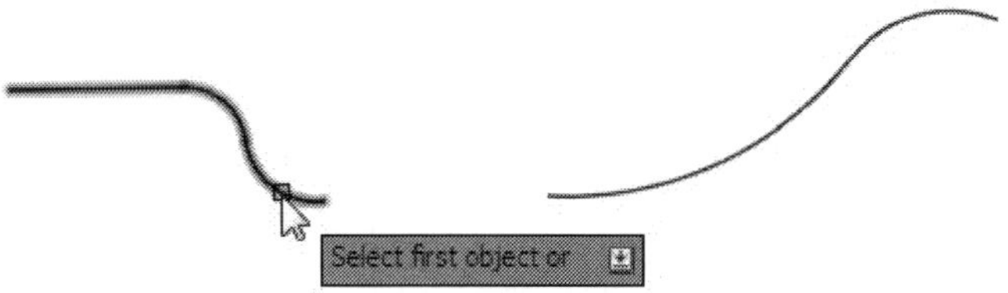

Figure 8–20

Select the second line or curve to create a new spline in the gap between the two curves, as shown in Figure 8–21.

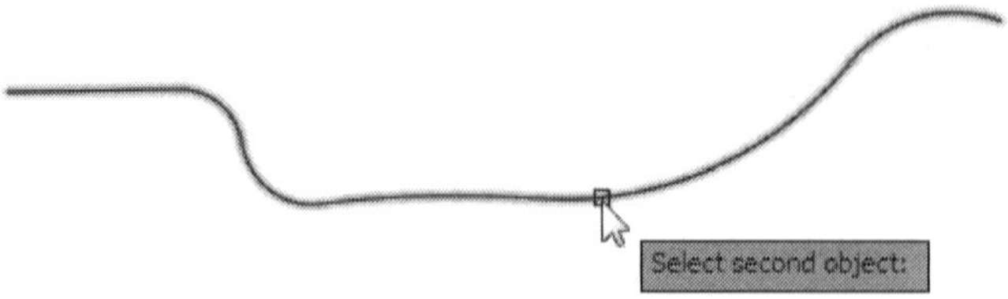

Figure 8–21

- Although a spline is added in the gap, the objects are three separate objects. Use (Join) to convert them into a single spline.
- You can use (Edit Spline)>*Convert to Polyline* to convert the spline into a polyline.

Joining Objects

In the *Home* tab>expanded *Modify* panel, (Join) joins broken polylines, lines, arcs, elliptical arcs, and splines, as shown in Figure 8–22. If you select two lines, they need to be touching each other end to end.

Figure 8–22

- You can join objects of different types (e.g., lines, polylines, and splines). The final joined object becomes the most complex of the selected objects. Therefore, if you select a line and a polyline, the final joined object is a polyline.
- With arcs, the **Close** option can be used to close arcs (e.g., to form circles).
- The source object determines the properties (e.g., layer, color, etc.) of the new object.

8.5 Drawing Polygons

The **Polygon** command generates closed geometric figures with three or more equal sides, such as triangles, hexagons, and diamonds, as shown in Figure 8–23.

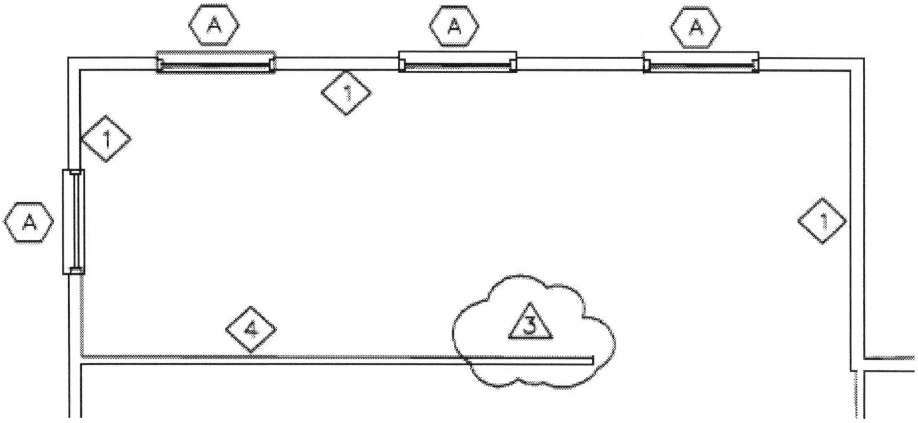

Figure 8–23

- The AutoCAD software builds these objects from polylines. Therefore, all of the sides form one unified object.
- Since polygons are made from polylines, you can use the **Edit Polyline** command to assign a width, explode them to create separate segments, or edit the vertices.

How To: Draw an Inscribed or Circumscribed Polygon

1. In the *Home* tab>*Draw* panel, expand the *Rectangle* flyout and click  (Polygon).
2. Enter the number of sides for the polygon, and press <Enter>.
3. Locate the center point anywhere in the drawing window.

4. Select **Inscribed in circle** or **Circumscribed about circle**, as shown in Figure 8–24.
    - An *inscribed* polygon is defined by the distance from the specified center to one of its vertices (inscribed in the imaginary circle).
    - A *circumscribed* polygon is defined by the distance from the specified center to one of the edges (circumscribed about the imaginary circle).

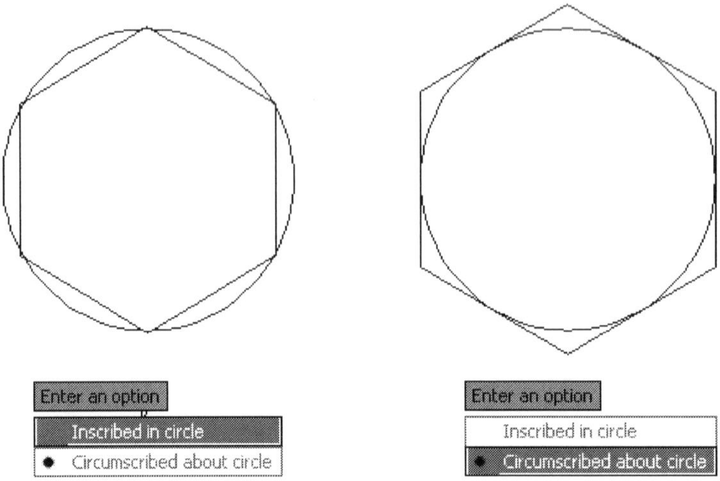

Figure 8–24

5. Enter the radius of the circle.

How To: Draw a Polygon by Edge

1. In the *Home* tab>*Draw* panel, expand the *Rectangle* flyout and click  (Polygon).
2. Enter the number of sides for the polygon, and press <Enter>.
3. At the *Specify center of polygon:*, type **E** for the **Edge** option.
4. At the *Specify first endpoint of edge:*, select a point to locate an endpoint of one of the sides of the polygon.

5. At the *Specify second endpoint of edge:* prompt, select a point to locate the other endpoint of the side of the polygon. This input defines the length of all of the sides (edges) and the angle at which the polygon is rotated, as shown in Figure 8–25. After entering the length of the side, press <Tab> to enter the angle.

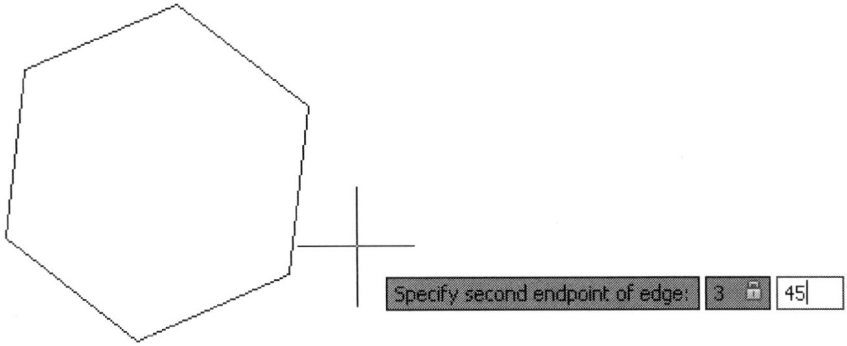

Figure 8–25

Practice 8c
Draw Polygons

Practice Objective

- Create polygons.

In this practice, you will create symbols using the **Polygon** and **Rectangle** commands, as shown in Figure 8–26. Draw only the objects. The text labels and dimensions are for reference only.

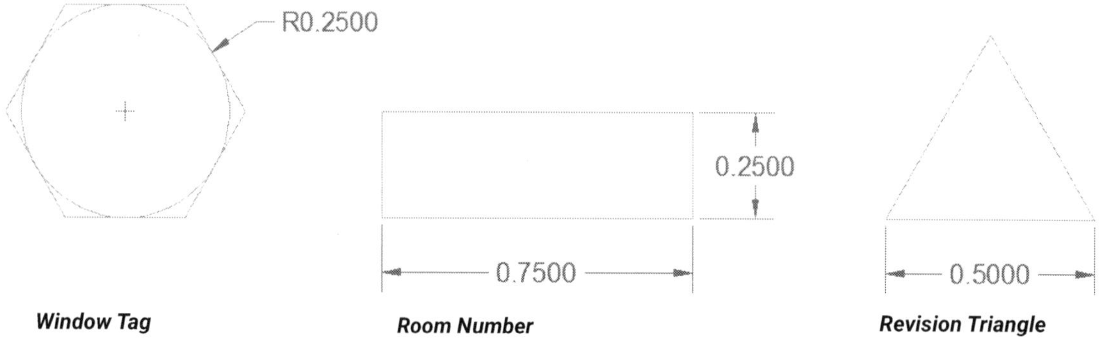

Figure 8–26

1. Start a new drawing based on **AEC-Imperial.dwt** which is located in your practice files folder. Save it as **Symbols.dwg**.
2. Draw the symbols shown in Figure 8–26. For the *Window Tag* object, start the **Polygon** command (in the *Home* tab>Draw panel, expand the Rectangle flyout and click  (Polygon)). For the number of sides, enter **6** and press <Enter>. Select anywhere in the drawing window as its center. Select **Circumscribed about circle** and enter **0.25** as the radius. Press <Enter> to complete the command. The polygon is not displayed. To see the polygon, zoom in using **Zoom Extents**.
    - In Figure 8–26, for the *Window Tag* object, the circle inside the polygon is for reference only. You do not have to draw it.
3. Draw the *Room Number* using the **Rectangle** command.
    - Zoom out and Pan to make space for other objects.
    - Start the **Rectangle** command and click near the right side of the hexagon to set the first corner.
    - At the *Specify other corner point.* prompt, enter **0.75,0.25**.
    - Press <Enter> to complete the command.

4. Draw the *Revision Triangle* using the **3-sided Polygon** command.

- Start the  (Polygon) command. For the number of sides, enter **3** and press <Enter>.
- Press <Down Arrow> and select the **Edge** option. Click anywhere to set the first endpoint of the edge.
- For the second endpoint, enter **0.50**, press <Tab>, and enter **0** as the angle.
- Press <Enter> to complete the command.

5. Save and close the drawing.

End of practice

8.6 Drawing Ellipses

The **Ellipse** command creates full ellipses or elliptical arcs. An ellipse is defined by two axes. You specify one axis first by selecting its two end points, or by selecting the center of the ellipse and an end point. The first axis can be either the major (longer) or minor (shorter) axis, as shown in Figure 8–27. You then specify the second axis.

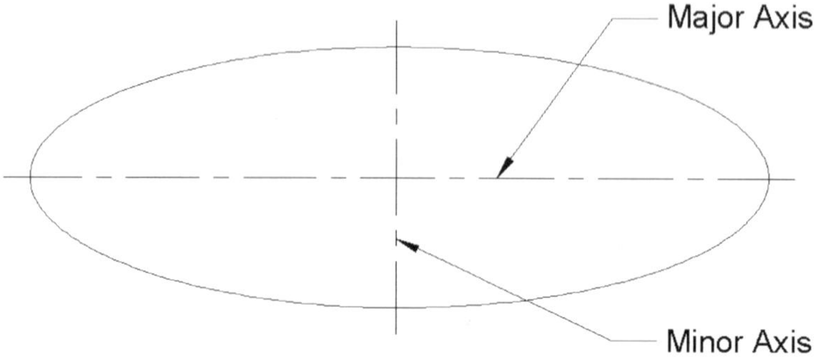

Figure 8–27

How To: Draw a Basic Ellipse

1. In the *Home* tab>*Draw* panel, expand the *Ellipse* flyout and click (Ellipse-Axis, End).
2. Specify the first axis end point of the ellipse and then the second axis end point. This describes the length of the ellipse.
3. Specify the distance to the other axis. This describes the width of the ellipse.
   - To create an elliptical arc, you define a full ellipse first, and then specify which portion of it is going to be included in the arc. In the *Home* tab>*Draw* panel, expand the *Ellipse* flyout and click (Elliptical Arc) to start the **Ellipse** command with the **Arc** option.
   - (Ellipse - Center) starts the **Ellipse** command with the **Center** option.

Additional Command Options

Rotation	Enables you to define the major to minor axis ratio by rotating a circle around the first axis. 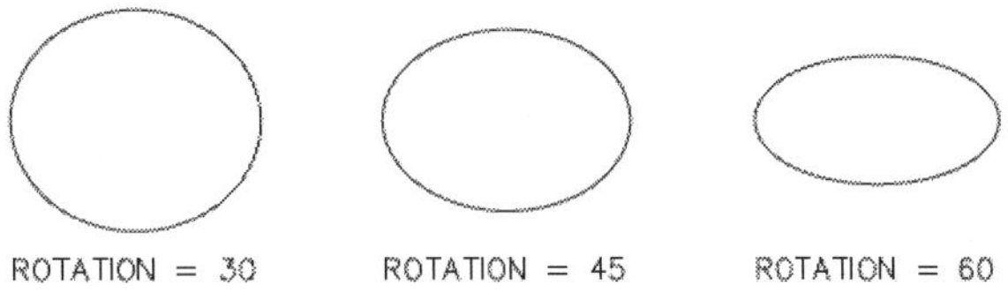
Center	Enables you to define the first axis by selecting the center of the ellipse and one end point of the axis.
Arc	Prompts you to create a full ellipse using any of the methods above, and then specify which portion to include in the arc.

Arc Options

Start Angle/ End Angle	Enables you to select or enter the starting and ending angles for the arc.
Included	Enables you to select or enter a value to define the included angle beginning at the start angle.
Parameter	Prompts for the same input as **Start Angle**. However, the software uses a parametric vector equation to calculate the elliptical arc. 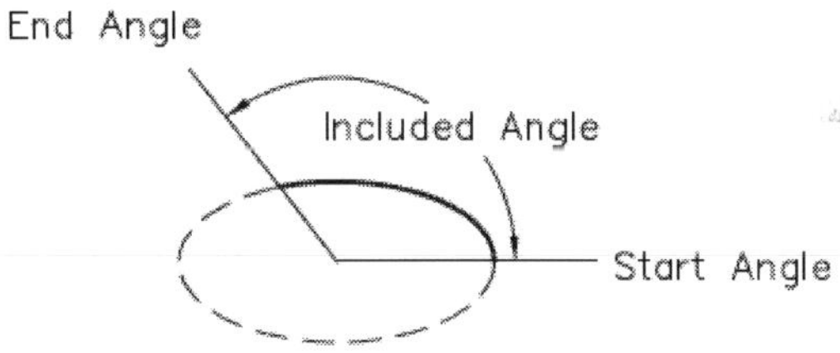

Hint: Isocircle Option

You can use the **Isocircle** option of the **Ellipse** command to represent holes in an isometric drawing in 2D, as shown in Figure 8–28. Using the  (Axis,End) option of the **Ellipse** command, at the *Specify axis endpoint of ellipse* prompt, click the drop-down arrow and select **Isocircle**. With the required Isoplane selected, drawing the ellipse creates a 3D representation of a hole in 2D.

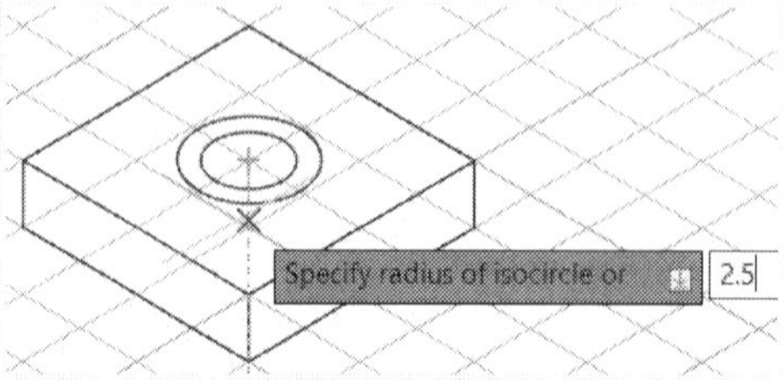

Figure 8–28

Practice 8d
Draw Ellipses

Practice Objective

- Create an ellipse and an elliptical angle.

In this practice, you will use the **Ellipse** command to create a 2D drawing of a cylinder, as shown in Figure 8–29.

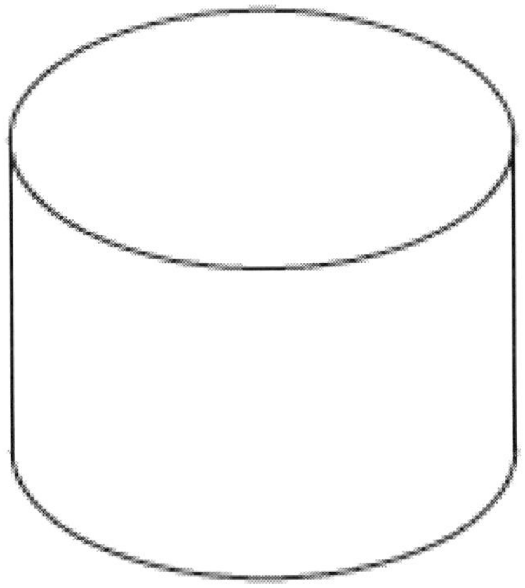

Figure 8–29

1. Start a new drawing based on **Mech-Inches.dwt**, which is located in your practice files folder, and save it as **Drum.dwg**.
2. Draw a vertical line **3** units long.
3. Copy that line **5** units to the right to create a parallel line.
4. In the *Home* tab>*Draw* panel>*Ellipse* flyout, click (Axis,End).
5. For the first axis end point, select the upper end point of the left line.
6. For the other axis end point, select the upper end point of the right line.
7. At the *Specify distance to other axis:* prompt, type **R** for Rotation and press <Enter>. Enter **60** and press <Enter>.
8. In the *Home* tab>*Draw* panel>*Ellipse* flyout, click (Elliptical Arc).
9. Select the lower end points of the lines as the axis end points.
10. At the *Specify distance to other axis:* prompt, type **R** for Rotation and press <Enter>. Enter **60** and press <Enter>.
11. At the *Specify start angle:* prompt, select the lower end point of the left line.

12. At the *Specify end angle:* prompt, select the lower end point of the right line.
13. Save and close the drawing.

End of practice

Chapter Review Questions

1. Which of the following is a valid method for constructing an arc in the AutoCAD software?
    a. 3 Points
    b. 2 Points
    c. 4 Points
    d. Center, Diameter

2. Which of the following is NOT true for a polyline?
    a. The segments are all considered to be one object.
    b. It cannot include arcs.
    c. Each segment can have different starting and ending widths.
    d. They can be open or closed.

3. Which command breaks a polyline into individual line and arc segments?
    a. Break
    b. Explode
    c. Edit Polyline
    d. Snap

4. Which command enables you to convert a single regular line into a polyline?
    a. Union
    b. Edit Polyline
    c. Blend
    d. Make Polyline

5. Polygons are built from polylines and can be modified using the **Edit Polyline** command.
    a. True
    b. False

6. How many axes are required to define and create an ellipse?
    a. 1
    b. 2
    c. 3
    d. 4

7. A series of continuous line and/or arc segments that act as one unified object is a:
    a. Ellipse
    b. Construction Line
    c. Polyline
    d. Block

Command Summary

Button	Command	Location
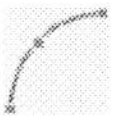	**Arc**	• **Ribbon:** *Home* tab>*Draw* panel • **Command Prompt:** arc or A
	**Blend Curves**	• **Ribbon:** *Home* tab>*Modify* panel • **Command Prompt:** blend
	**Edit Polyline**	• **Ribbon:** *Home* tab>expanded *Modify* panel • **Command Prompt:** pedit or PE
	**Edit Spline**	• **Ribbon:** *Home* tab>expanded *Modify* panel • **Command Prompt:** splinedit
	**Ellipse (Center)**	• **Ribbon:** *Home* tab>*Draw* panel • **Command Prompt:** ellipse or EL
	**Ellipse (Axis, End)**	• **Ribbon:** *Home* tab>*Draw* panel • **Command Prompt:** ellipse or EL
	**Ellipse (Elliptical Arc)**	• **Ribbon:** *Home* tab>*Draw* panel • **Command Prompt:** ellipse or EL
	**Explode**	• **Ribbon:** *Home* tab>*Modify* panel • **Command Prompt:** explode or X
	**Polygon**	• **Ribbon:** *Home* tab>*Draw* panel (*Rectangle flyout*) • **Command Prompt:** polygon or POL
	**Polyline**	• **Ribbon:** *Home* tab>*Draw* panel • **Command Prompt:** pline or PL
	**Join**	• **Ribbon:** *Home* tab>expanded *Modify* panel • **Command Prompt:** join
	**Spline Fit**	• **Ribbon:** *Home* tab>expanded *Draw* panel • **Command Prompt:** spline
	**Spline CV**	• **Ribbon:** *Home* tab>expanded *Draw* panel • **Command Prompt:** spline

Chapter 9

Analyzing Model and Object Properties

In this chapter, you learn how to locate information about objects and to measure exact distances and areas.

Learning Objectives

- Display and modify the basic properties of single or multiple objects.
- Match the properties of various objects and select objects based on their properties.
- Measure distances, radii, diameters, angles, and areas in a drawing.

9.1 Working with Object Properties

Every object in the AutoCAD® software has properties, such as layer, color, and linetype, and geometric information such as vertex points, length, etc. Many properties can be changed using *Quick Properties,* the *Properties* palette, or **Match Properties**. You can also use properties to help you select objects when using **Quick Select**.

- Hover the cursor over an object to display a tooltip containing basic information about the object, as shown in Figure 9–1.

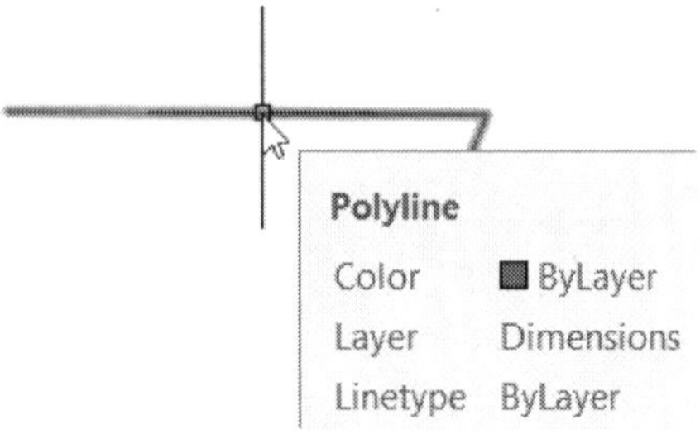

Figure 9–1

Quick Properties

If you select an object, when not in a command, and display its grips, the basic information about that object displays in the *Quick Properties* panel, as shown in Figure 9–2. These vary depending on the type of object selected.

- Press <Esc> to clear a selected object.

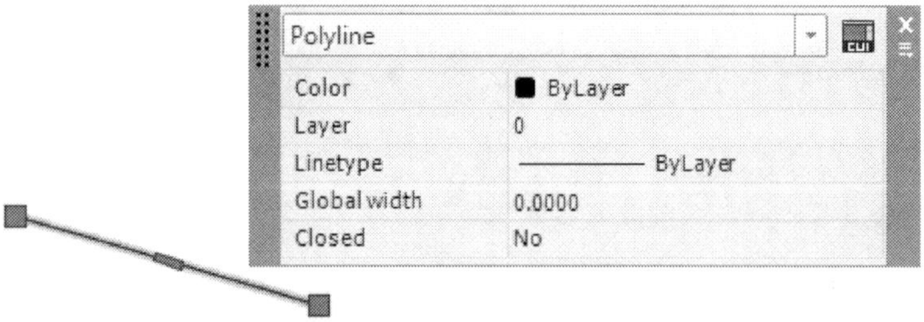

Figure 9–2

- The *Quick Properties* panel displays along with the selected object (in grip mode) when (Quick Properties) is toggled **On** in the *Status Bar*.

*Note: If (Quick Properties) is not displayed in the Status Bar, expand (Customization) and select **Quick Properties**.*

- When (Quick Properties) is toggled **Off**, you can display the Quick Properties for individual objects by selecting them (in grip mode), right-clicking, and selecting **Quick Properties** in the shortcut menu.
- In addition to viewing the information about the selected object, you can also change some properties in the *Quick Properties* panel. Click on a property and select a different option from the drop-down list, as shown on left in Figure 9–3. Clicking on some properties displays an edit box where you can enter a different value, as shown on the right in Figure 9–3.

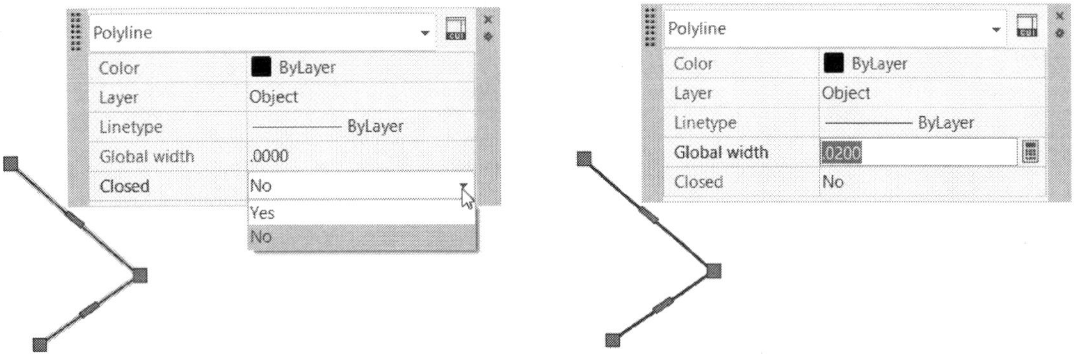

Figure 9–3

- You can also display a list of the basic properties for an object using (List) in the *Home* tab>expanded *Properties* panel. The AutoCAD Text window opens, displaying some of the properties of the selected object. You cannot change any properties using the **List** command. The **List** command can quickly provide the length of lines, and the area and perimeter of polylines.

Properties Palette

The primary way to get detailed information about the objects in your drawing is to use the *Properties* palette, as shown in Figure 9–4. It reports all of the properties of the object and enables you to change many of them.

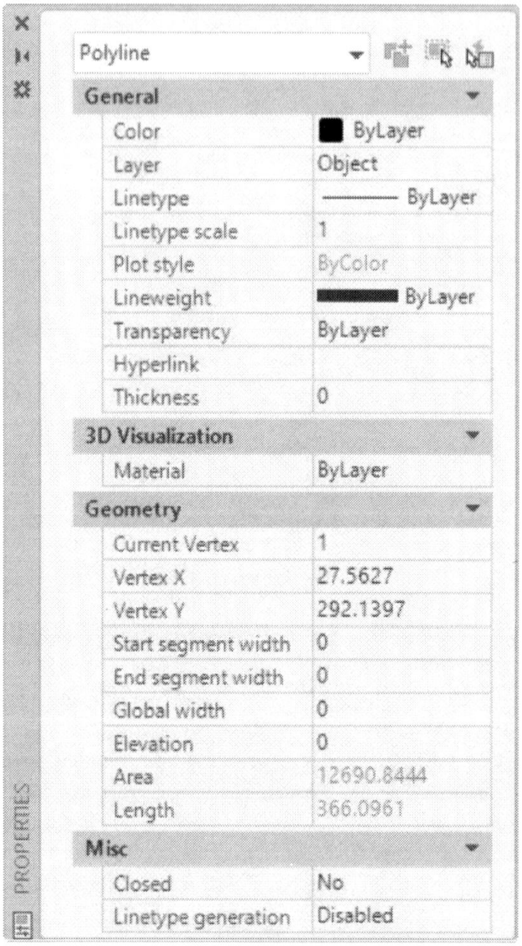

Figure 9–4

- You can toggle the *Properties* palette on or off using any of the following methods:
  - In the *View* tab>*Palettes* panel, click (Properties).
  - Press <Ctrl>+<1>.
  - In the *Home* tab>*Properties* panel, click .
  - In grip mode, right-click on an object and select **Properties** in the shortcut menu.
- You can have the *Properties* palette open even when an object is not selected. Once you select any object, its properties display in the open *Properties* palette.
- As with other palettes, you can dock the *Properties* palette to any side of the screen. Click, hold, and drag using its title bar and move it to either side of the screen. Once it shows the docking outline, leave the cursor as it automatically docks it in place. You can also hide the palette by clicking the (Auto-hide) icon located in the *Properties* title bar, as shown in Figure 9–5. Once hidden, it displays as a bar along the docked side and you can temporarily unhide it by hovering the cursor over the bar. You can also unhide it permanently by clicking in the title bar. Use **X** to close the palette.

Figure 9–5

How To: Modify Objects Using Properties

1. Open the *Properties* palette if it is not already open and select an object. The properties of the object display in the palette, as shown in Figure 9–6.

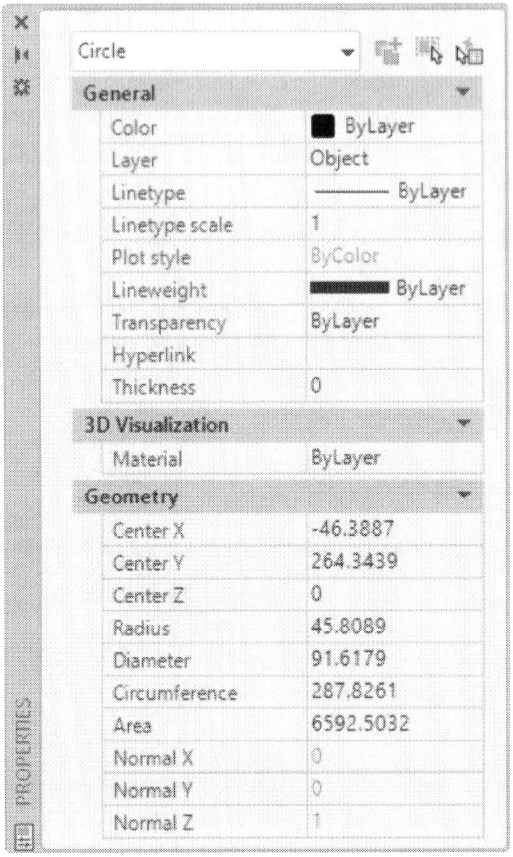

Figure 9–6

2. Change the properties as required by clicking in the value field of the property you want to change and then typing or selecting a new value.
   - As you move the cursor over the options in the drop-down lists, the object in the drawing window changes to provide a preview of the highlighted option.
3. To clear the object, move the cursor into the drawing window and press <Esc>.
   - Some properties display a list of options, such as the *Layer* property shown on the left in Figure 9–7.

- Some properties are numerical, as shown on the right in Figure 9–7. Once you click in the value field, you can enter a number, click (calculator) to open the *QuickCalc (calculator)* dialog box, or click (pick point) to modify the location of a point on the screen.

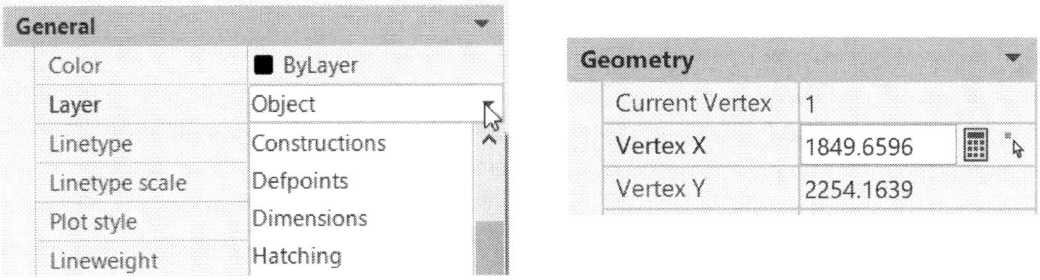

Figure 9–7

- Information in grayed-out cells cannot be changed.

Properties of Multiple Objects

- If you select more than one object of the same type (e.g., two circles), the AutoCAD software lists the types of properties that they have in common. If their values are different, they are listed as ***VARIES***, as shown in Figure 9–8. You can change these properties for all of the selected objects at the same time (e.g., select several circles and change their radius to 2.25).

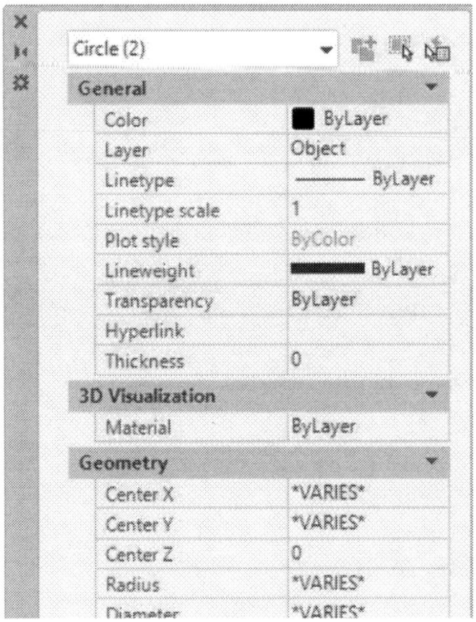

Figure 9–8

- If you select different types of objects (e.g., a circle and a line), the AutoCAD software displays the only types of properties that they have in common. If their values are different, they are listed as ***VARIES***. You can change the common properties of all of the selected objects at the same time. You can also switch between different types of objects using the drop-down list, as shown in Figure 9–9. (To select all of the objects in your drawing, in the *Home* tab>*Utilities* panel, click (Select All).)

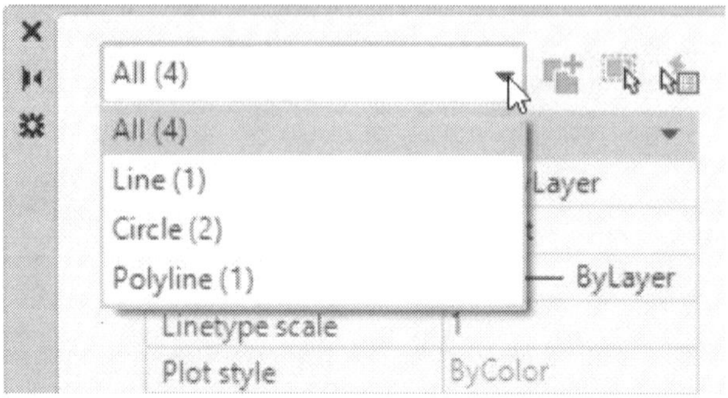

Figure 9–9

Matching Properties

To make objects in your drawing have the same properties as another object, use the **Match Properties** command. It enables you to select one object as a *model* and then copy its properties to any other object you select.

How To: Copy an Object's Properties

1. In the *Home* tab>*Properties* panel, click (Match Properties).
2. At the *Select source object:* prompt, select the object you want to use as a model. The cursor changes into a small square box with a paint brush.
3. As you move the cursor over the object that you are going to select, the object changes and displays a preview with the new properties. Select the objects to which you want the properties to be copied.
4. Press <Enter> to end the command.

- **Match Properties** works across drawings. Specify the source object in one drawing, and in the drawing tab bar click on another drawing to switch to it and select the destination objects. If the layer does not exist in the destination drawing, it is created. When you hover over the object in the second drawing, the object highlights but does not display a preview with the new properties.
- **Match Properties** enables you to match all or some of an object's properties. To control which properties are matched, use the **Settings** option (available in the shortcut menu or Command Line) when you have started the command and selected the source object. By default, all of the properties are selected, as shown in Figure 9–10.

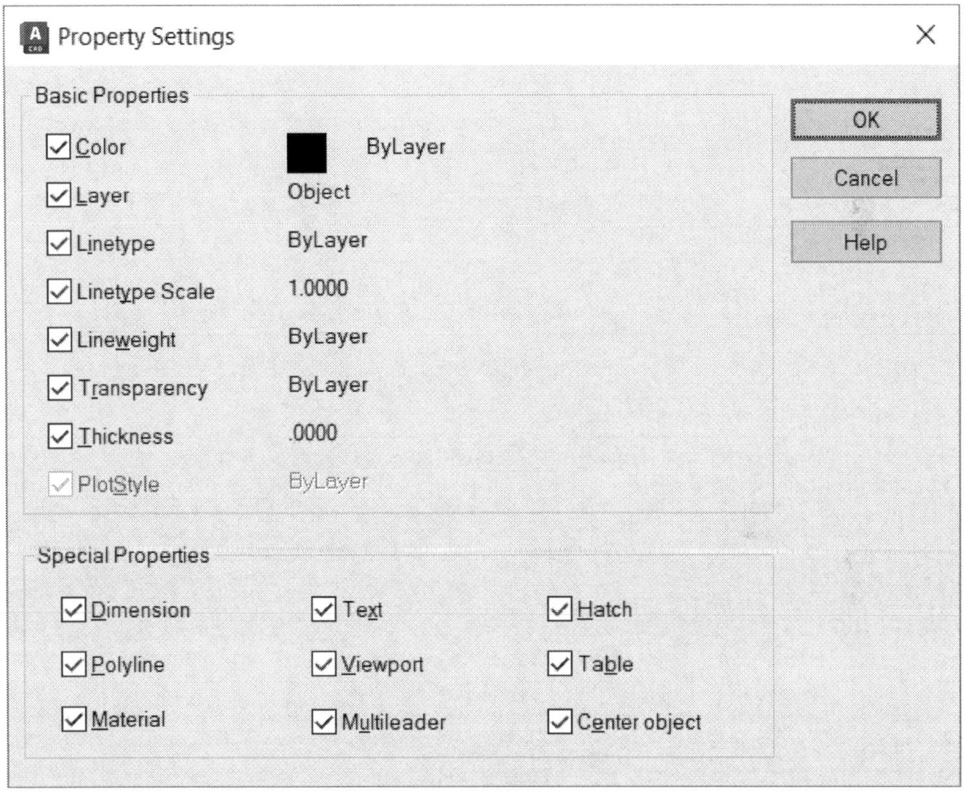

Figure 9–10

Quick Select

Quick Select can be used to select objects using their properties. It opens a dialog box in which you can specify a selection set by object type and/or properties (such as all of the circles with a radius of 0.25), as shown in Figure 9–11.

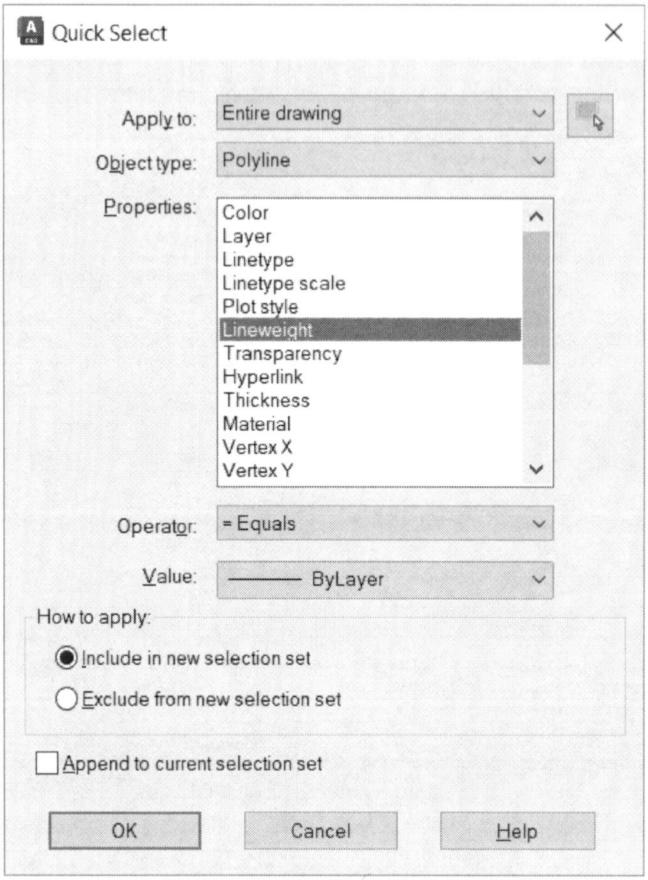

Figure 9–11

How To: Select Objects Using Quick Select

1. In the *Home* tab>*Utilities* panel or in the *Properties* palette, click  (Quick Select).
2. In the *Quick Select* dialog box, in *Apply to*, use **Entire drawing** or click  (Select objects) to create a selection set.
3. Select the required *Object type*. **Multiple** selects all of the object types. Only object types that are currently in the selection set display in the drop-down list.

4. In *Properties:*, select the property that you want to filter. This varies according to the selected object type.
5. Select an *Operator*, as shown in Figure 9–12. The available operators vary depending on the selected property type.
    - To select all of the objects of a specific type, regardless of their properties, use **Select All** for the *Operator*. For example, you can use this method to find all of the circle objects.

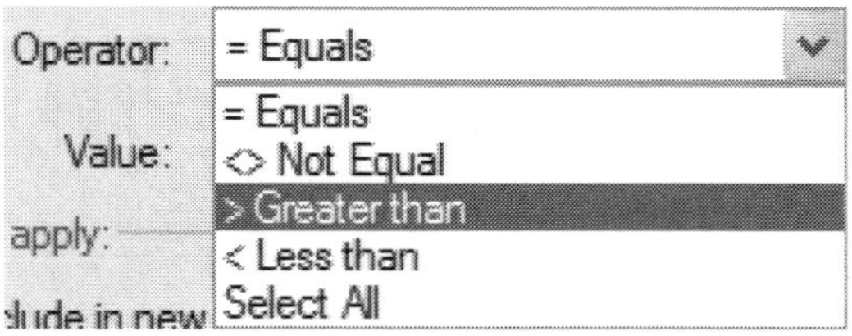

Figure 9–12

6. Specify the value that you want to find for the selected property. The available values vary depending on the selected property type. For example, values for the property **Layer** include all of the layers defined in the drawing. For the Radius value (of a circle), you need to enter a number.
7. Select an option for how the filter is going to be applied:
    - **Include in new selection set:** Places all of the objects that meet the criteria in a new selection set.
    - **Exclude from new selection set:** Places all of the objects that DO NOT meet the criteria in a new selection set.
8. If you want to build a selection set from several filters, select the **Append to current selection set** option, which adds the results to the current selection, rather than creating a new selection set.
9. Click **OK** to close the *Quick Select* dialog box. Objects that match the criteria are selected.
10. Use an editing command on the selected objects (such as **Erase** or **Properties**) to modify them.

Practice 9a
Work with Object Properties (Mechanical)

Practice Objective

- Obtain information about objects.

In this practice, you will get information about some objects (as shown in Figure 9–13) and then make changes to them, using the *Quick Properties* panel and the *Properties* palette.

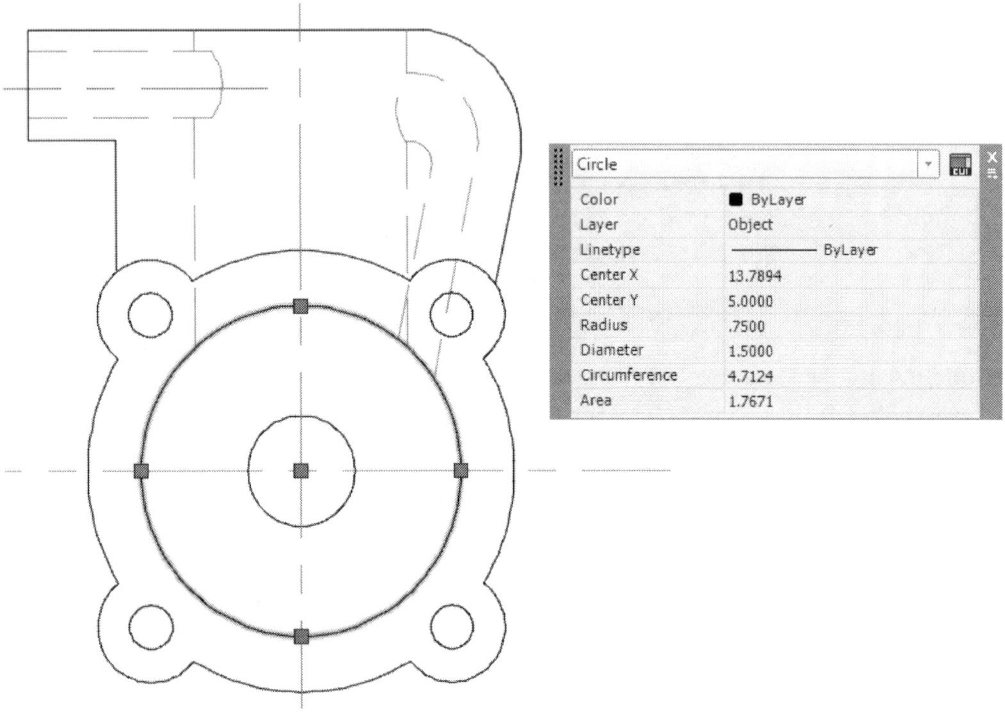

Figure 9–13

1. Open **Crank-I.dwg** from your practice files folder.
2. In the *Status Bar*, toggle on (Quick Properties).
3. Select the large full circle to display the *Quick Properties* panel, as shown in Figure 9–13. Press <Esc> to clear the selection.
4. Select the gray horizontal center line near the top left of the object. In its Quick Properties, note that it is drawn on the *Layer* **CONSTRUCTION**. Click anywhere in the *CONSTRUCTION* row to display it as an edit box and expand the *Layer* drop-down list. Hover the cursor over the **Center** layer and note how the gray line previews as orange, as shown in Figure 9–14. Select **Center** to change the layer of the line.

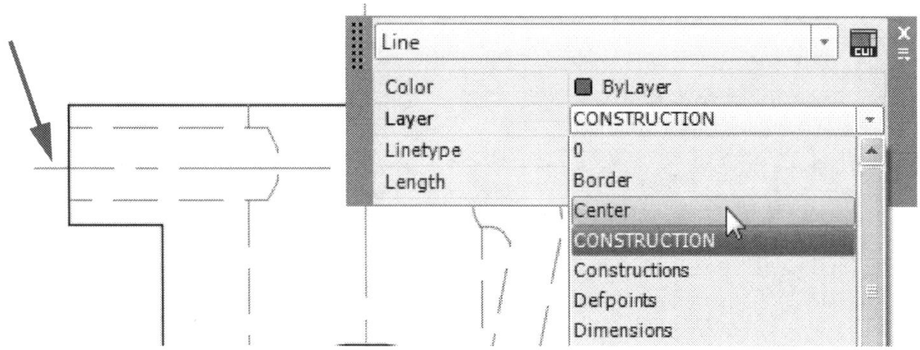

Figure 9–14

5. Clear your selection by pressing <Esc> and toggle (Quick Properties) off in the Status Bar.

6. In the *Home* tab>*Utilities* panel, click (Quick Select).

7. In the *Quick Select* dialog box, verify that *Apply to* is set to **Entire drawing**. Set the *Object type* to **Circle**, *Properties* to **Diameter**, and *Operator* to **= Equals**. In the *Value* edit box, enter **0.2** and click **OK**. The objects with the above properties (four small circles with the diameter 0.2) are selected and highlighted in the drawing.

8. Click in the *Home* tab>*Properties* panel to open the *Properties* palette. You can also click (Properties) in the *View* tab>*Palettes* panel to open the *Properties* palette. To dock the palette to one side of the screen, click, hold, and drag using its title bar and move it to either side of the screen. Once it disappears, leave the cursor as it automatically docks it in place.

9. In the *Geometry* area, click in the *Diameter* value field and enter **0.2750**, as shown in Figure 9–15. As soon as you press <Enter>, note that the selected circles become bigger.

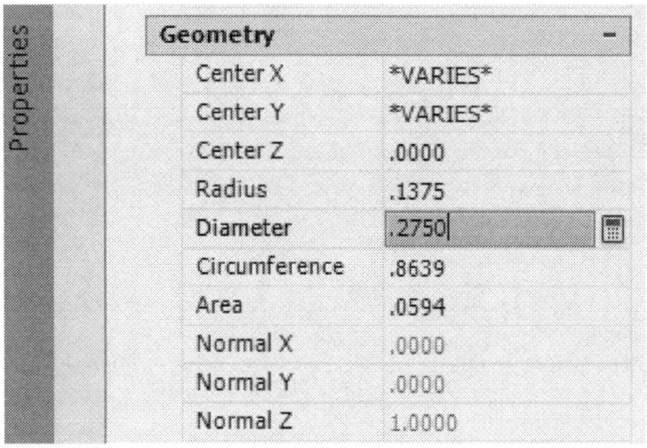

Figure 9–15

10. Clear the selection by pressing <Esc>.
11. Hover the cursor on the *Properties* title bar and click **X** to close the *Properties* palette.
12. Save and close the drawing.

End of practice

Practice 9b
Work with Object Properties (Architectural)

Practice Objective

- Locate objects based on their properties and change their values.

In this practice, you will use the *Properties* palette and *Quick Select* to find objects based on their layer, and then move them to the correct layer. You will also find text based on its height and change it to the correct height, as shown in Figure 9–16.

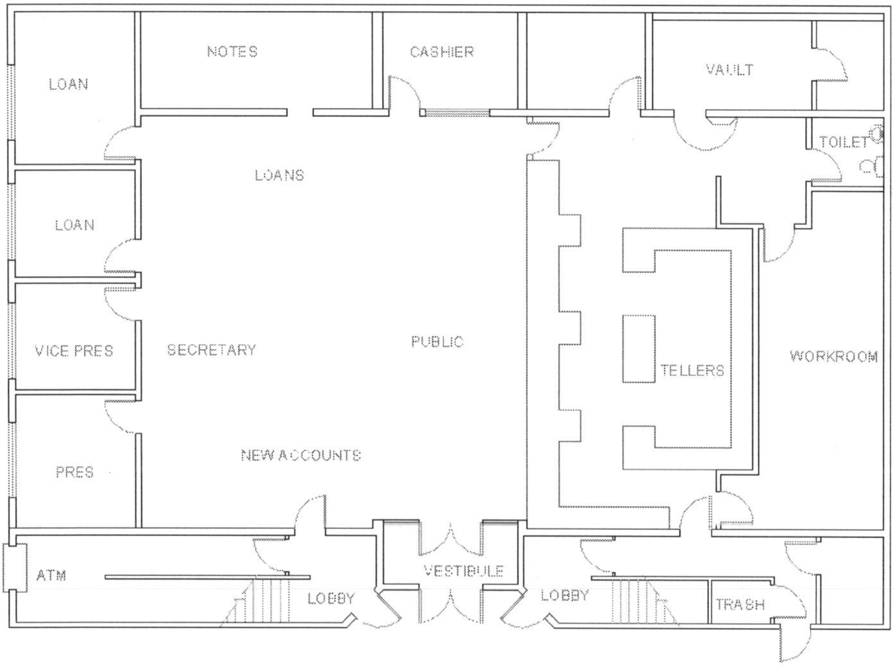

Figure 9–16

1. Open **Bank-Building-A.dwg** from your practice files folder.
2. In the *Home* tab>*Layers* panel, expand *Layer Control* and scroll through the names. Layer Control contains the layers **WALL** and **Walls**. You need to place all of the walls on the layer **Walls**.
3. Open the *Properties* palette, if it is not already open. (Click in the *Home* tab>*Properties* panel or use <Ctrl>+<1> to open the *Properties* palette.) Dock it to one side and hide it by clicking the icon located in the *Properties* title bar. Only the *Properties* tile bar remains visible.

4. In the *Home* tab>*Utilities* panel, click (Quick Select). To select everything on the layer **WALL**, in the *Quick Select* dialog box, set the *Object type* to **Multiple**. Select **Layer** in the *Properties* list, set *Operator* to **= Equals**, and set *Value* to **WALL**, as shown on the left in Figure 9–17. Click **OK**. All the objects on layer **WALL** are highlighted in the drawing, as shown on the right in Figure 9–17.

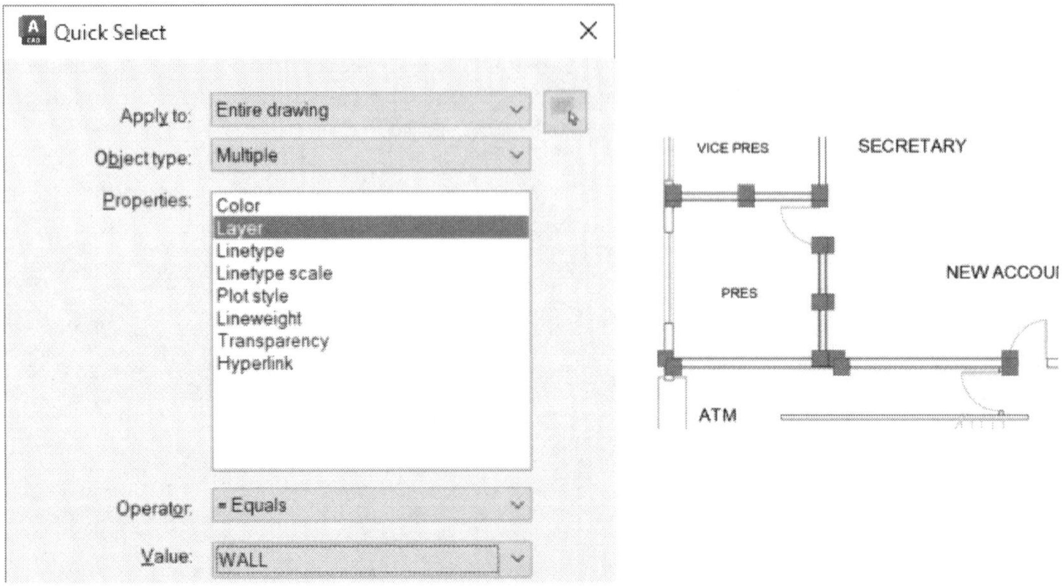

Figure 9–17

5. Hover the cursor over the title bar of the *Properties* palette to unhide it. In the *General* area, in the *Layer* edit box, open the *Layer* drop-down list and select **Walls** to change *WALL* to **Walls**, and press <Esc> to clear the object selection.

6. In the *Home* tab>*Utilities* panel, click (Quick Select), and in the dialog box, set the *Object type* to **Text** and the *Operator* to **Select All**. Click **OK**. All of the text in the drawing is highlighted. What layer is the text on? In the *Properties* palette, change the layer of the text objects to layer **Text** and press <Esc> to clear the object selection. All the text objects turn blue.

7. Use (Quick Select) and the *Properties* palette to select all of the text that is less than **11"** in height and change its *Height* to **1'-0"**.
8. Close the *Properties* palette.
9. Save and close the drawing.

End of practice

9.2 Measuring Objects

In drawings, you need to obtain the exact measurements of the objects that you create. For example, you need to check the diameter of a machine cylinder, the distance from the property line to the corner of a parking lot, or the area of a room in a house as shown in Figure 9–18.

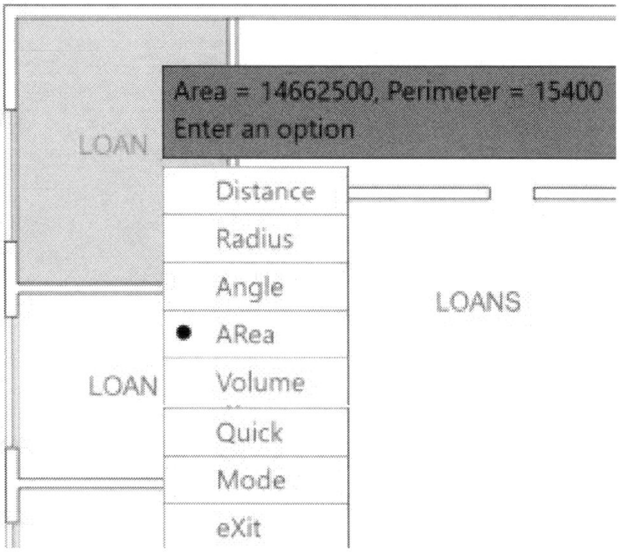

Figure 9–18

- Object snaps enable you to select points when measuring distances and areas to get exact and accurate measurements.

Using the Measure Tools

The various **Measure** tools enable you to measure distances, radii, diameters, angles, areas, or volumes. In the *Home* tab>*Utilities* panel, expand the *Measure* flyout and select an option, as shown in Figure 9–19.

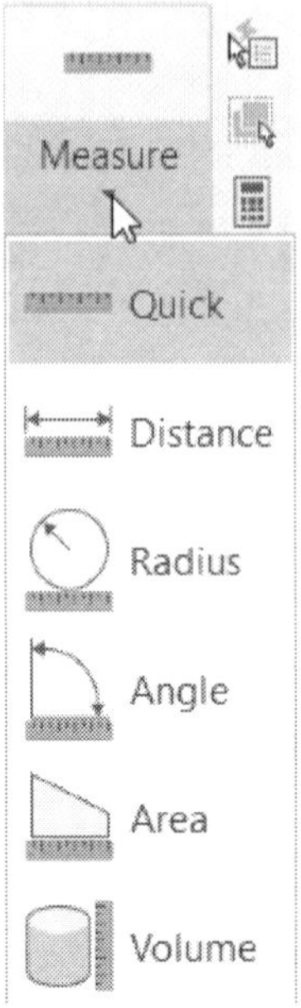

Figure 9–19

*Note: The **Measure** tool that you select automatically replaces the default measure tool until another one is selected or you end your current AutoCAD session.*

Quick Measure

The **Quick Measure** tool (**Measuregeom** command) provides you with multiple measurements in real-time. It is a quick and easy way of displaying the dimensions, distances, angles, areas/ perimeters, and volume within a single command.

How To: Quick Measure

1. In the *Home* tab>*Utilities* panel, expand the *Measure* flyout and click (Quick). The cursor displays an infinite plus mark.

2. As you hover the cursor over some objects, all the objects that are touching the cursor are highlighted and the appropriate measurements for those objects are displayed. As shown in Figure 9–20, the dimensions of the lines, the distances between lines, and the right angles along the corners are displayed.

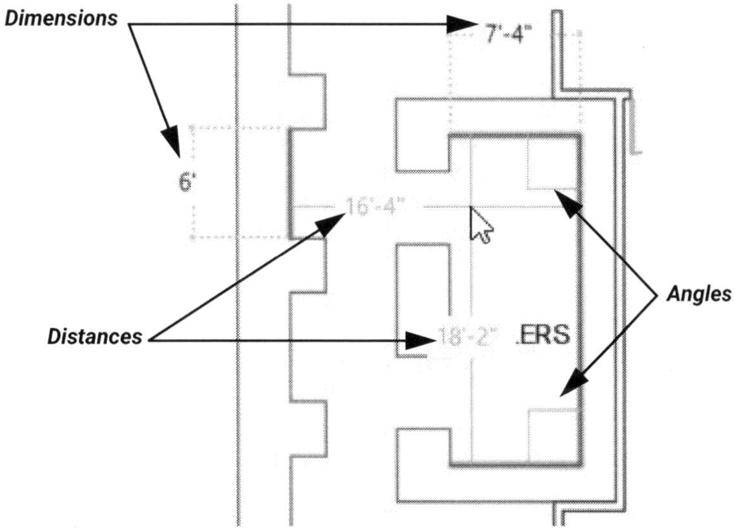

Figure 9–20

3. When you click inside a closed area, it is highlighted in green with the area and perimeter displayed near the cursor (as shown in Figure 9–21) and in the Command Line.

   - Hold down <Shift> and then click in various closed areas to display the cumulative area and perimeter.

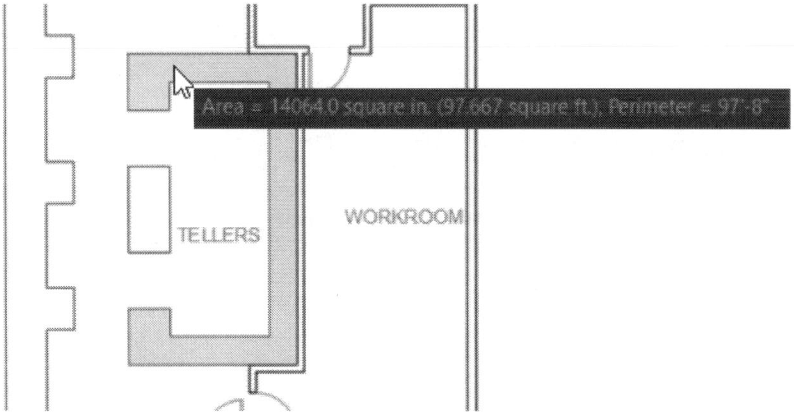

Figure 9–21

4. Press <Esc> to exit the command once you have finished reviewing the measurements.

Measuring Distances

One of the most basic measurements you need to make is the distance between points.

How To: Measure a Distance

1. In the *Home* tab>*Utilities* panel, expand the *Measure* flyout and click (Distance) or type **DIST** in the Command Line to start the distance measurement command. The cursor displays .
2. Select the first point and then the second point between which you want to measure the distance. The distance displays as shown in Figure 9–22.
   - For accurate measurements, use Object snaps to select the precise points to measure.

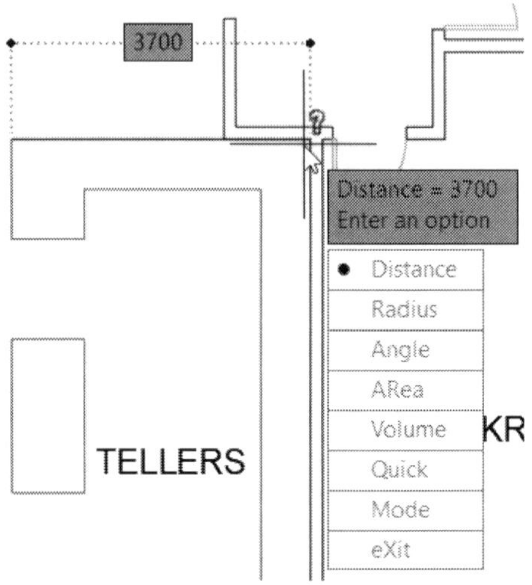

Figure 9–22

3. Press <Enter> to measure another distance or select a different option as shown in Figure 9–22.
4. Select the **eXit** option or press <Esc> to end the command.

How To: Get a Running Total of Distances

1. In the *Home* tab>*Utilities* panel, expand the *Measure* flyout and click (Distance). The cursor displays .
2. Select the first point to measure.
3. Select the **Multiple points** option (<Down Arrow> and select Multiple points or type **M**).
4. Select the other points that you want to measure.

5. Press <Enter> to end the command and display the total.

Hint: ID Point

(ID Point), located in the *Home* tab>expanded *Utilities* panel, provides the X-, Y-, and Z-axis coordinates of any selected point. Use object snaps to select a precise point.

Measuring Radius and Diameter

To find the radius and diameter data for circles or arcs you can expand the *Measure* flyout and click (Radius). Select the circle or arc to measure. A tooltip displays the information in the drawing area, as shown in Figure 9–23.

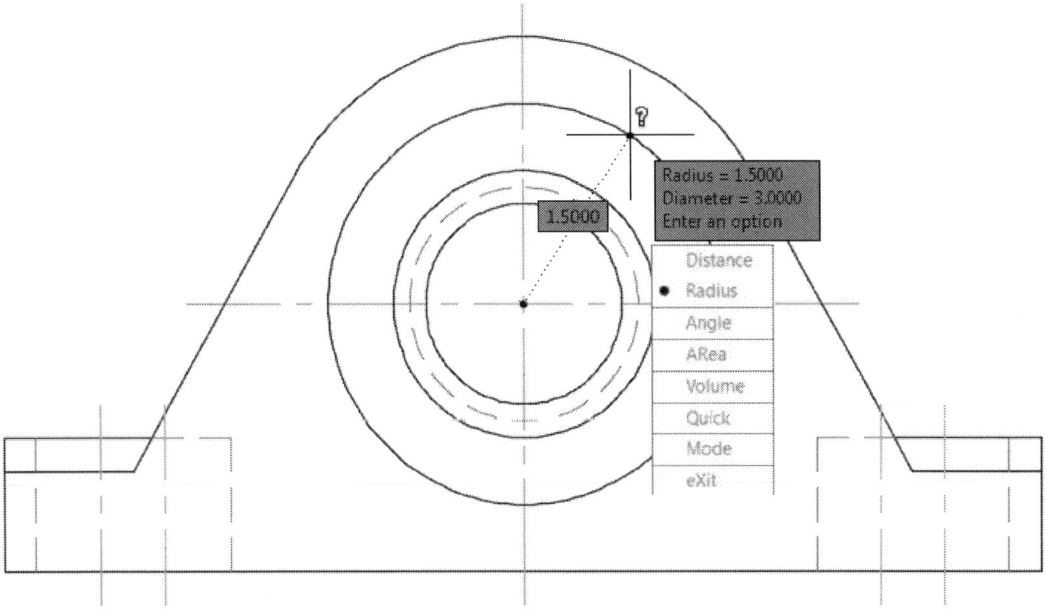

Figure 9–23

Measuring Angles

(Angle) in the **Measure** command can be used to display the angle between two lines, the opening angle of an arc, or any angle defined by a vertex and to other locations.

How To: Measure the Angle Between Two Lines

1. In the *Home* tab>*Utilities* panel, expand the *Measure* flyout and click (Angle). The cursor displays .
2. Select one line.
3. Select a second line. The angle displays, as shown in Figure 9–24.

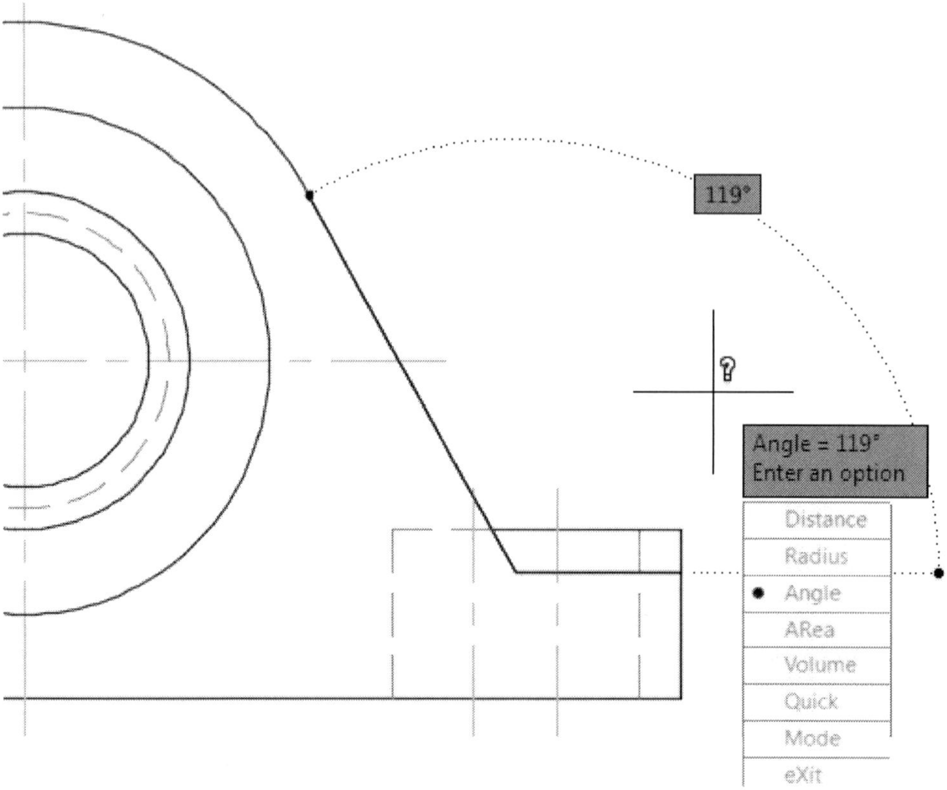

Figure 9–24

- To display the opening angle of an arc, click on the arc.

How To: Measure a Angle Using a Vertex

1. In the *Home* tab>*Utilities* panel, expand the *Measure* flyout and click (Angle).
2. At the *Select arc, circle, line or <Specify vertex>:* prompt, press <Enter> to specify a vertex.
   - If you click on a circle, it also enters the **Vertex** option. The first click on a circle also determines the first point of the angle. Selecting a second point on the circle or outside the circle completes the angle measurement.
3. Select a point (1) for the vertex, as shown in Figure 9–25.
4. Select a point (2) for the first angle end point.
5. Select a point (3) for the second angle end point.

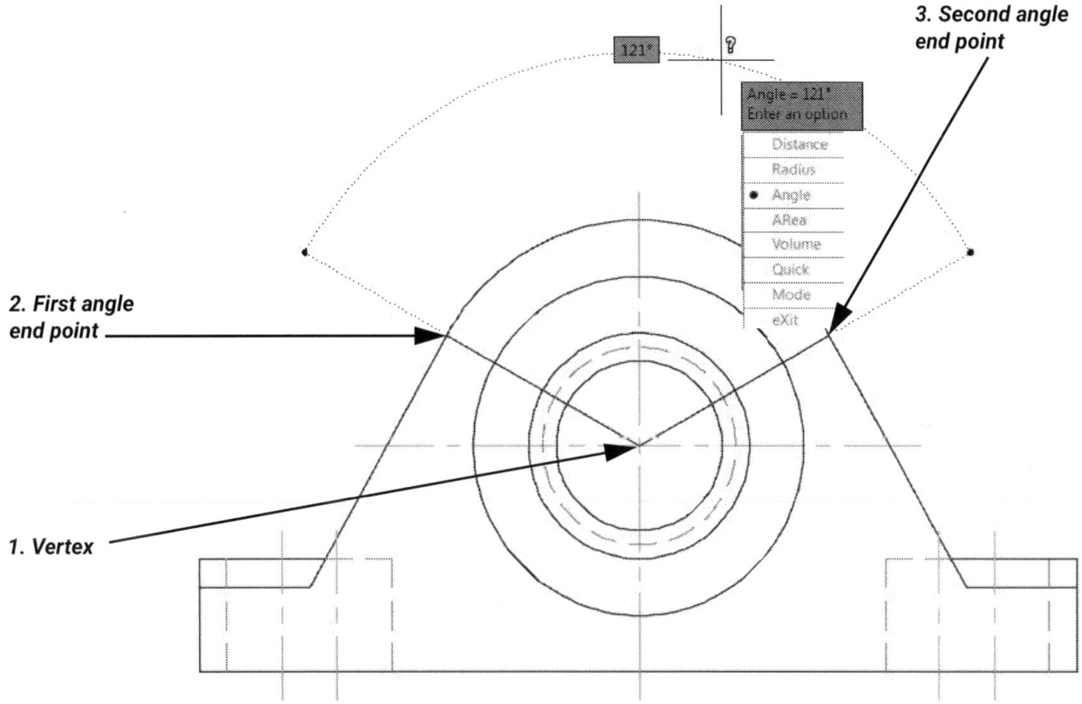

Figure 9–25

Measuring Areas

To measure the area of an object, you can either pick points or select objects (such as polylines or circles) to define the areas you want measured. You can also include or exclude areas by adding or subtracting them.

How To: Measure an Area by Picking Points

1. In the *Home* tab>*Utilities* panel, expand the *Measure* flyout and click (Area). The cursor displays . The temporary green fill automatically disappears when the **Measure** command is finished.
2. Select points around the area that you want to measure, as shown in Figure 9–26. A green fill indicates the selection for which the area is calculated.
   - For accurate measurements, use Object snaps to select the precise points to measure.

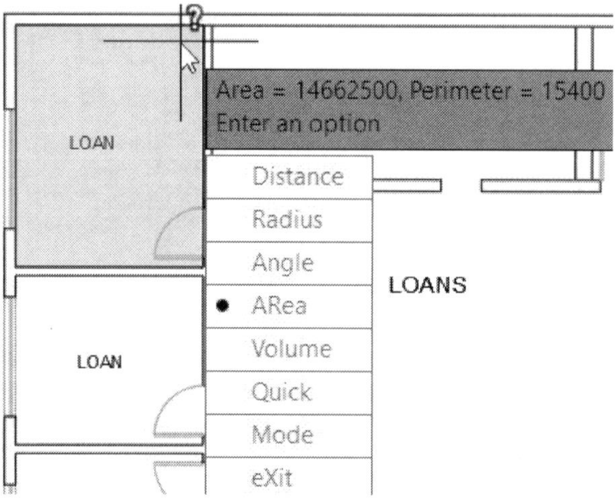

Figure 9–26

3. When you are finished, press <Enter> to display the total. The area and perimeter display.

How To: Measure the Area by Selecting an Object

1. In the *Home* tab>*Utilities* panel, expand the *Measure* flyout and click (Area). The cursor displays .
2. At the *Specify first corner:* prompt, type **O** and press <Enter> to select the **Object** option.
3. Select an object, such as a polyline, circle, or rectangle. The area displays, as shown on the left in Figure 9–27.
    - The polyline object can be both open or closed. If the object is open, the area is calculated by adding an imaginary line along the open section, as shown on the right in Figure 9–27.

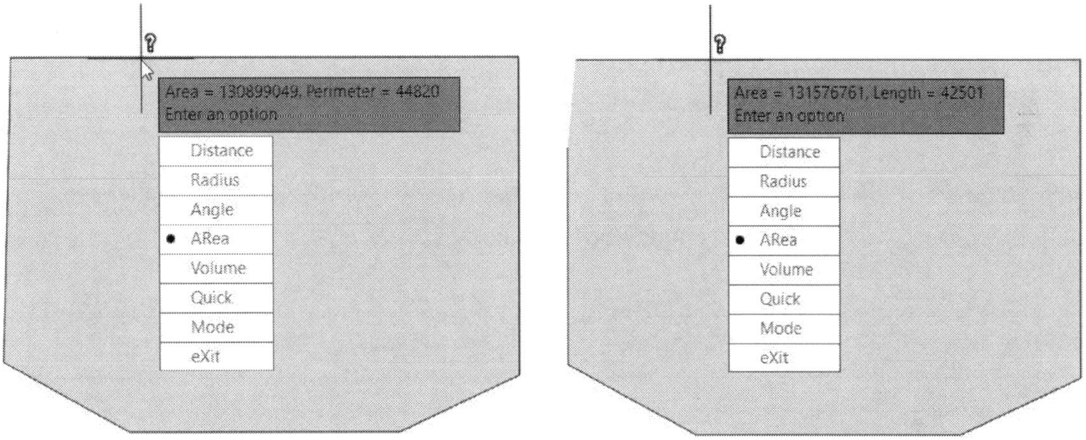

Closed Object ***Open Object***

Figure 9–27

How To: Add and Subtract Areas

1. In the *Home* tab>*Utilities* panel, expand the *Measure* flyout and click (Area). The cursor displays .
2. Select the **Add area** option first (<Down Arrow> and select **Add area**). You are placed in ADD mode and can select items to add by selecting points or using the **Object** option.
3. Press <Enter> to end ADD mode.
4. Select the **Subtract area** option (<Down Arrow> and select **Subtract area**).

5. Select the areas to subtract by selecting points or using the **Object** option. When you are in SUBTRACT mode, the selected areas display with a brown fill, as shown in Figure 9–28.

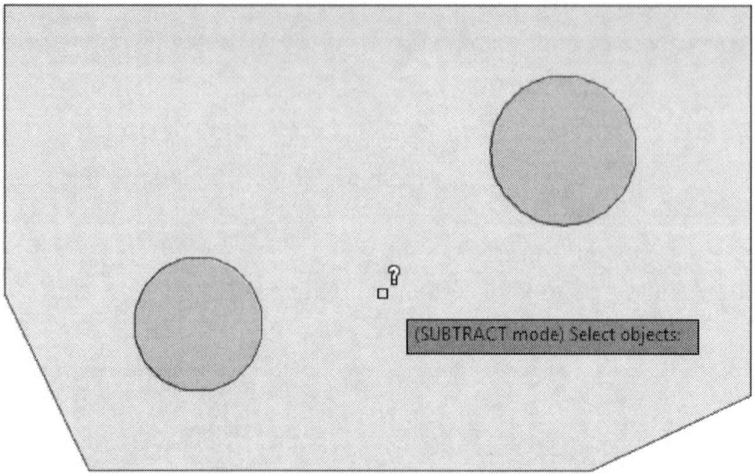

Figure 9–28

6. Press <Enter> to end SUBTRACT mode. The area and other information are displayed.
7. Select **eXit** or press <Esc> to end the command.

Note: *(Volume) calculates the volume of 3D objects using a method that is similar to the **Area** option. If you are working with 2D objects, set the boundaries as you do with area. You are then prompted to provide a height to complete the calculation.*

Practice 9c
Measure Objects (Architectural)

Practice Objective

- Check areas and distances in a floorplan.

In this practice, you will check areas and distances in a floorplan (shown in Figure 9–29) using the various Measure tools.

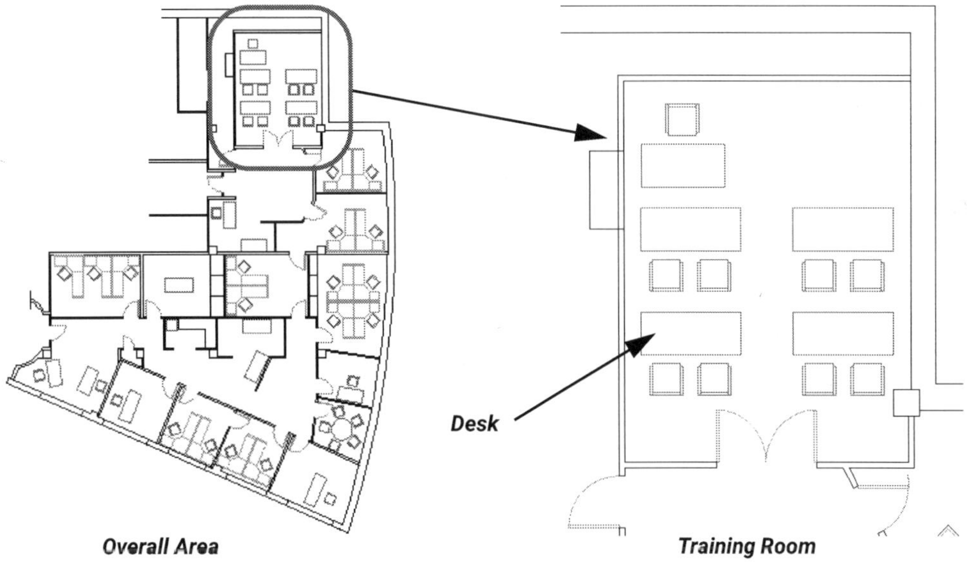

Figure 9–29

1. Open **Office Plan-A.dwg** from your practice files folder.
2. Zoom in on the training room at the back of the building (top of the floor plan), as shown in Figure 9–29. In the *Home* tab>*Utilities* panel, expand the *Measure* flyout and click (Quick). Hover your cursor inside one of the bigger desks (as shown in Figure 9–29) and review its size. The length and width respectively are:

    a. 6' and 2'-4"

    b. 6' and 2'-6"

    c. 6'-4" and 2'-4"

    d. 6'-4" and 2'-6"

3. While remaining in the **Quick** command, click inside the same desk. Being a closed area, it is highlighted in green with the area and perimeter displayed near the cursor. The perimeter of the desk is:

   a. 16'-0"

   b. 16'-8"

   c. 17'-0"

   d. 17'-4"

4. In the *Home* tab>*Utilities* panel, expand the *Measure* flyout and click (Area) to determine the area of the room in square feet (use the **Endpoint** osnap to pick the inner four corners of the training room and ignore the column and door opening). The area is:

   a. 374.23

   b. 369.57

   c. 375.833

   d. 376.125

5. In the training room, the size of the square column is (use the **Measure>Distance** command):

   a. 1'-4" x 1'4"

   b. 1'-6" x 1'-6"

   c. 1'-0" x 1'-0"

   d. 1'-8" x 1'-8"

6. Thaw the layer **Area**. It contains a magenta polyline that outlines a section of the building. Using the **Measure>Area** command with the **Object** option (pick the magenta polyline), what is the area rounded to the nearest square foot?

   a. 4068

   b. 4078

   c. 4073

   d. 4062

7. Close the drawing. Do not save changes.

End of practice

Practice 9d
Measure Objects (Mechanical)

Practice Objective

- Find the area of objects.

In this practice, you will find the areas of objects in a drawing (shown in Figure 9–30) using the Measure tools.

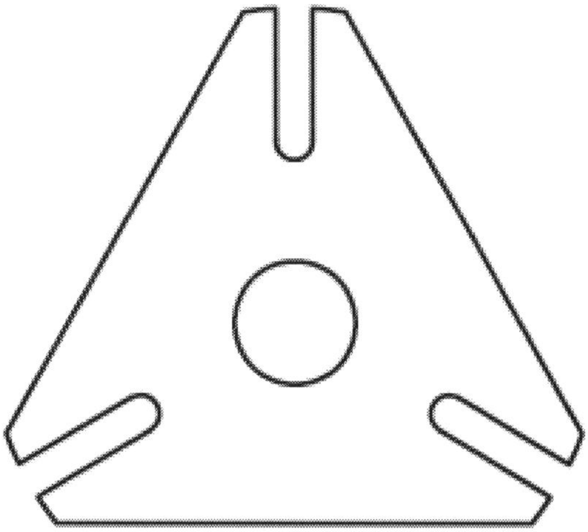

Figure 9–30

1. Open **Triangular-Plate-I.dwg** from your practice files folder.
2. Hover the cursor over various parts of the outline. Note that it consists of separate lines and arcs.
3. Use the **Edit Polyline** command with the **Join** option to turn the outside of the object into a single polyline.

4. Select the new polyline and review the information in *Properties* palette. To display the exact location of each vertex, click on the arrow buttons (as shown in Figure 9–31), to scroll through the vertices. This enables you to determine the X- and Y-coordinate points of each vertex. Cycle through the various vertices and note their respective coordinate locations. The vertex, whose information is displayed, is marked by an X. (The vertex number might be different for you as it depends on the selection of lines while joining them.)

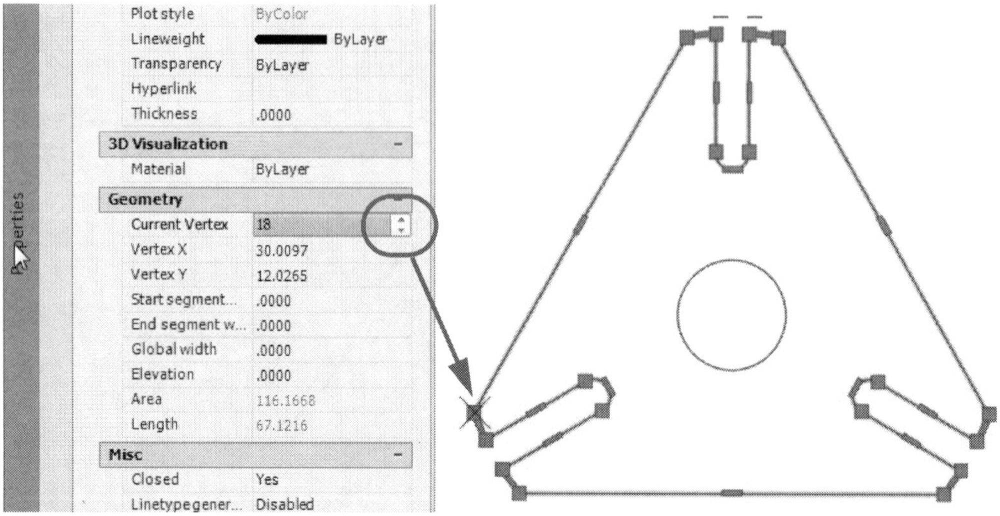

Figure 9–31

5. Use the **Measure>Area** command with the **Object** option to find the area of the outside shape.

   a. 115.9875

   b. 116.1668

   c. 116.2007

   d. 115.9725

6. Use the **Measure>Area** command to find the area of the shape with the hole removed. First use the **Add area** and **Object** options, and then select the outline to find the total area, including the circle. Press <Enter> to exit the ADD mode. Then use the **Subtract area** and **Object** options and select the circle, as shown in Figure 9–32. Press <Enter>. The total area of the shape minus the hole is:
   a. 108.4118
   b. 108.2791
   c. 107.4608
   d. 107.6538

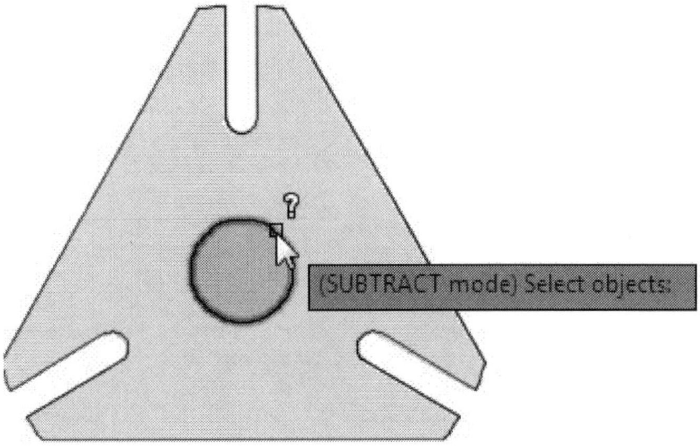

Figure 9–32

7. Close the drawing. Do not save changes.

End of practice

Chapter Review Questions

1. Which tool reports the length of a line?
   a. ID Point
   b. Measure>Length
   c. Quick Select
   d. Properties

2. Which tool should you use when measuring distances and areas to get exact measurements?
   a. Object Snap
   b. Object Snap Tracking
   c. Grid
   d. Polar Tracking

3. How do you find the area of an object? (Select all that apply.)
   a. Using the **Measure>Area** command and picking points to define the boundary of the area.
   b. Using the **Object** option of the **Measure>Area** command and picking a single point on the boundary of the area.
   c. Using the **Object** option of the **Measure>Area** command and double-clicking inside a closed area.
   d. Using the **Measure>Area** command and picking any point inside a closed area.

4. One of the differences between *List* and the *Properties* palette is that with *List* you can only view the information, while with the *Properties* palette you can edit some of the information to modify the object.
   a. True
   b. False

5. Which of the following cannot be measured using the **Measure>Angle** command?
    a. The angle between two lines.
    b. The opening angle of an arc.
    c. The distance between the centers of two circles.
    d. Any angle defined by a vertex or other locations.

6. When you select multiple objects, the *Properties* palette only displays which of the following?
    a. Their colors and layers.
    b. Their lineweights and linetypes.
    c. The properties that they have in common.
    d. Their X and Y coordinate points.

Command Summary

Button	Command	Location
	ID Point	• **Ribbon:** *Home* tab>expanded *Utilities* panel • **Command Prompt:** ID
	List	• **Ribbon:** *Home* tab>expanded *Properties* panel • **Command Prompt:** list
	Match Properties	• **Ribbon:** *Home* tab>*Properties* panel • **Command Prompt:** matchprop or MA
	Measure>Angle	• **Ribbon:** *Home* tab>*Utilities* panel, expand *Measure* • **Command Prompt:** measuregeom (*select Angle option*)
	Measure>Area	• **Ribbon:** *Home* tab>*Utilities* panel, expand *Measure* • **Command Prompt:** measuregeom (*select Area option*)
	Measure>Distance	• **Ribbon:** *Home* tab>*Utilities* panel, expand *Measure* • **Command Prompt:** measuregeom (*select Distance option*)
	Measure>Quick	• **Ribbon:** *Home* tab>*Utilities* panel, expand *Measure* • **Command Prompt:** measuregeom
	Measure>Radius	• **Ribbon:** *Home* tab>*Utilities* panel, expand *Measure* • **Command Prompt:** measuregeom (*select Radius option*)
	Properties	• **Ribbon:** *Home* tab>expanded *Properties* panel • **Ribbon:** *View* tab>*Palettes* panel • **Shortcut Menu:** (*on a selected object*)>Properties • **Command Prompt:** properties, PR, or <Ctrl>+<1>
	Quick Properties	• **Double-click:** (*on certain types of objects*) • *Status Bar*: expanded Customization
	Quick Select	• **Ribbon**: *Home* tab>*Utilities* panel • **Shortcut Menu:** Quick Select • **Command Prompt:** qselect • **Properties Panel:** top
	Select All	• **Ribbon:** *Home* tab>*Utilities* panel

Chapter 10

Projects: Drawing Organization and Information

This chapter contains practice projects that can be used to gain additional hands-on experience in the topics and commands covered so far in this guide. These projects are intended to be self-guided and do not include step-by-step information.

Learning Objectives

- *Architectural:* Create a building outline with interior walls and measure the various distances and areas.
- *Mechanical:* Create a mechanical part with layers and investigate the properties of the objects.
- *Civil:* Create a property outline using polylines and verify the various properties.

10.1 Architectural Project

In this project, you will draw an outline of a building using a polyline and add lines for interior walls, as shown in Figure 10–1. (Note that the dimensions are for reference only. Do not draw the dimensions.) When you have finished the drawing, use the **Properties** and **Measure** commands to answer the questions in Task 2.

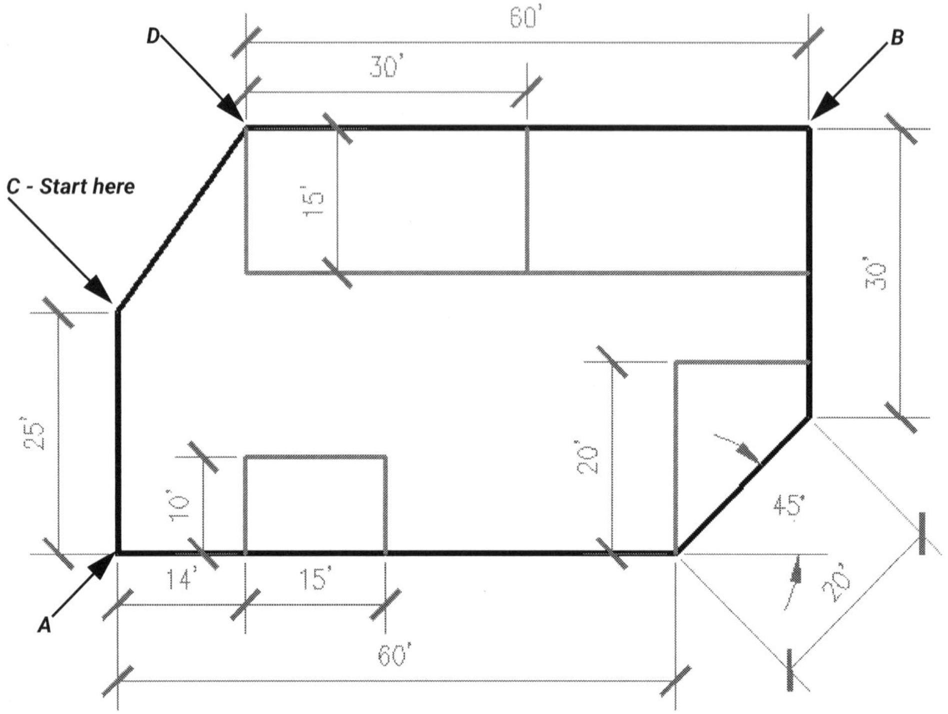

Figure 10–1

Task 1: Draw the building outline.

1. Start a new drawing based on **AEC-Imperial.dwt**, which is located in your practice files folder. Save it as **Office1.dwg**.
2. Set the layer to **Walls**.
3. Use the **Polyline** command to draw the outside wall starting at point **C** at **10',10'**, drawing counter-clockwise, as shown in Figure 10–1.
4. Set the layer to **Partitions**.
5. Draw the inside walls using the **Line** command and use Object Snaps and Polar Tracking to place the walls correctly.

Task 2: Measure objects in the drawing.

1. What is the direct distance between points **A** and **B**?
   a. 86'-3 1/2"
   b. 87'-2 1/8"
   c. 86'-4 1/4"
   d. 87'-3 1/2"

2. Set the current layer to **0** and toggle off the layer **Partitions**. What is the area (to the nearest square foot) inside the outer wall polyline?
   a. 3032
   b. 3034
   c. 3035
   d. 3037

3. Select the outer wall polyline and open the *Properties* palette. Scroll through the Vertex numbers to point **B**. The current vertex displays an **X** at the point. What are the exact X,Y coordinates of point **B**?
   a. 85'-2 1/2", 28'-1 1/2"
   b. 84'-1 3/4", 29'-1 3/4"
   c. 84'-2 3/8", 28'-1 1/4"
   d. 85'-2 1/2", 29'-1 1/2"

4. Explode the polyline. Select the line **CD** and open the *Properties* palette. What is the angle of the line?
   a. 125
   b. 234
   c. 60
   d. 167

10.2 Mechanical Project

In this project, you will draw the outline of a mechanical part using a polyline, and then add other objects on a different layer, as shown in Figure 10–2. (Note that the dimensions are for reference only. Do not draw the dimensions.) Once you have finished the drawing, answer the questions in Task 2 using the *Properties* palette and **Measure** command.

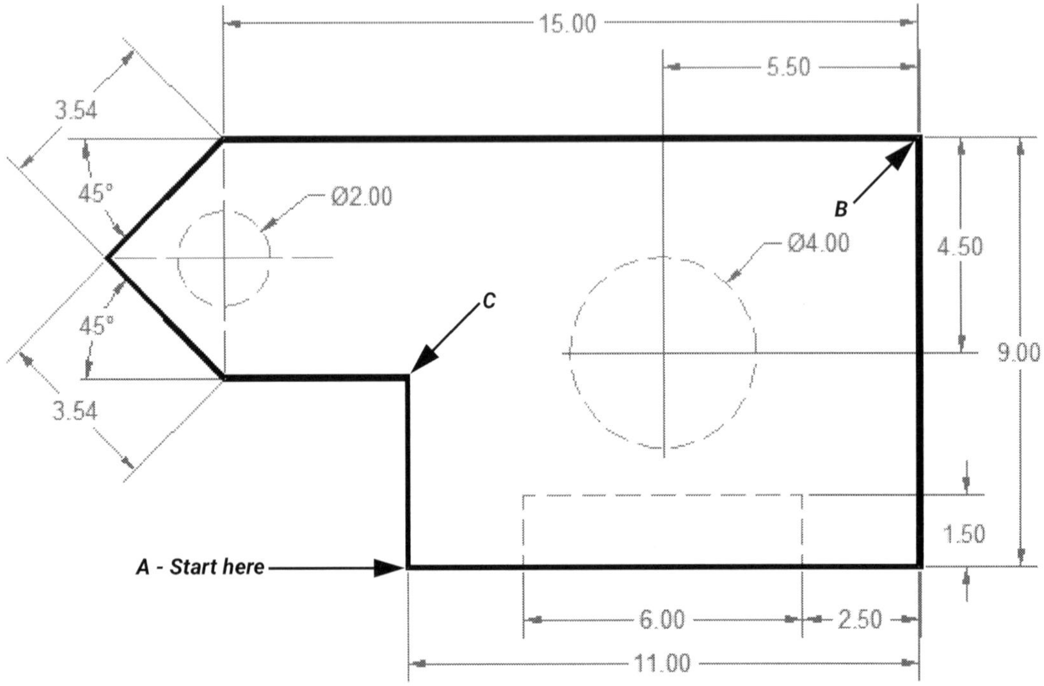

Figure 10–2

Task 1: Draw the mechanical part.

1. Start a new drawing based on **Mech-Inches.dwt**, which is located in your practice files folder. Save it with the name **Part1.dwg**.
2. Set the current layer to **Object**, if required.
3. Use the **Polyline** command to draw the outside of the object, starting with **point A** at **10,2** and drawing counter-clockwise, as shown in Figure 10–2.
4. Set the current layer to **Hidden**.
5. Draw the objects shown with hidden lines in Figure 10–2.

Task 2: Measure objects in the drawing.

1. What is the direct distance between points A and B?
   a. 15.0025
   b. 14.2534
   c. 14.2127
   d. 15.2379

2. Select the **Ø4.00** circle. Open the *Properties* palette. What are the precise X,Y coordinates of its center point?
   a. 15.5, 5.5
   b. 15.5, 6.5
   c. 14.6, 12.90
   d. 14.6, 6.5

3. Toggle off the layer **Hidden**. What is the area of the outline object?
   a. 125.3015
   b. 126.2821
   c. 126.2313
   d. 125.2911

4. Select the outside polyline and open the *Properties* palette. Scroll through the Vertex numbers to point **C**. The current vertex displays with an **X** at the point. What are the exact X,Y coordinates of point **C**?
   a. 10, 6
   b. 10, 5.9937
   c. 9.995, 5.9937
   d. 9.995, 6

10.3 Civil Project

In this project, you will draw the outline of a building and a property line using polylines and different layers, as shown in Figure 10–3. (Note that the dimensions are for reference only. Do not draw the dimensions.) Once you have finished the drawing, answer the questions in Task 2 using the *Properties* palette and **Measure** command.

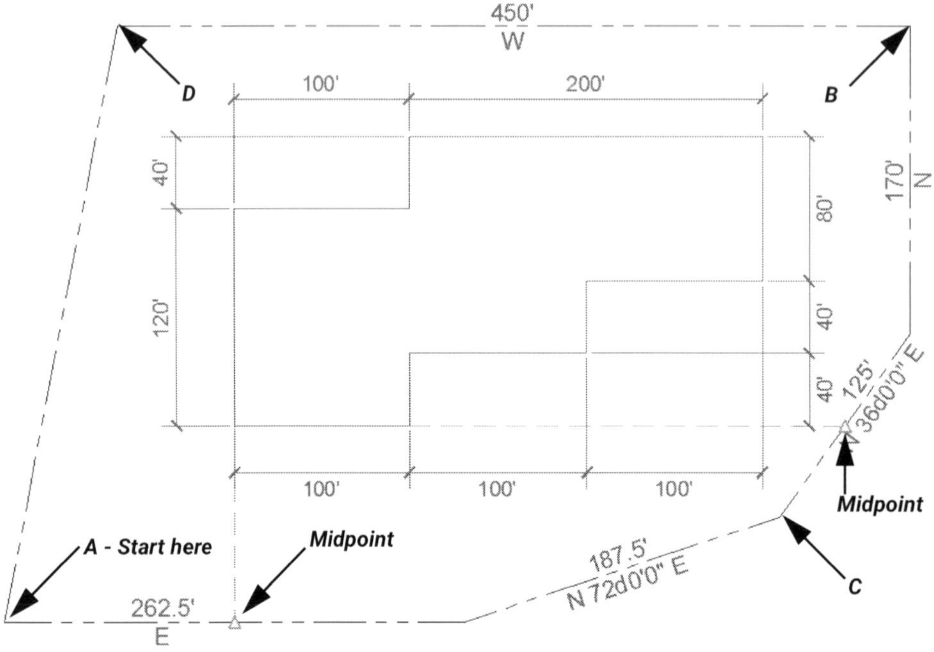

Figure 10–3

Task 1: Draw the property line and building outline.

1. Start a new drawing based on **Civil-Feet.dwt**, which is located in your practice files folder. Save it with the name **Plat1.dwg**.
2. Set the current layer to **Property Line**.
3. Draw the outer boundary shown in Figure 10–3, starting with **point A** at **0,0**, and going counter-clockwise.
    - The drawing is in decimal feet. Therefore, you do not need to type the foot sign after the distances.
4. The angles in this civil drawing are expressed in Surveyor's Units. Set the *Polar increment angle* to **18°** (18° matches the Cartesian coordinate angle for **N 72d0'0" E**) and **54°** (54° matches the Cartesian coordinate angle for **N 36d0'0" E**).
5. Set the current layer to **Building**.

6. Draw the building outline, as shown in Figure 10–3. Use Polar Tracking with the **Midpoint** object snap for the start point.

Task 2: Measure objects in the drawing.

1. What is the direct distance between points **A** and **B**?
   a. 611.45
   b. 609.23
   c. 610.56
   d. 610.75

2. Turn the property lines into a polyline if they were created using the **Line** command. Select the polyline and open the *Properties* palette. Scroll through the Vertex numbers to point **C**. The current vertex displays with an **X** at the point. What are the exact X,Y coordinates of point **C**?
   a. 442.26, 60.20
   b. 449.26, 58.96
   c. 440.08, 56.87
   d. 440.82, 57.94

3. Toggle off the layer **Building**. What is the perimeter of the outline (layer **Property Line**)?
   a. 1529.39
   b. 1530.29
   c. 1529.40
   d. 1530.40

4. Explode the property line and select the line **DA**. What is the angle of the line?
   a. S 11d3'21.26"W
   b. S 11d3'20.48"W
   c. S 11d3'20.46"W
   d. S 11d3'21.28"W

Chapter 11

Advanced Editing Commands

In this chapter, you learn how to trim, extend, stretch, fillet, and chamfer objects.

Learning Objectives

- Remove part of an object that extends past a cutting edge.
- Break objects and extend parts of objects.
- Stretch portions of objects while leaving other portions fixed at their original positions.
- Create rounded corners and beveled edges on an object.
- Create objects parallel or concentric to other objects.
- Create a rectangular pattern of duplicate objects in rows and columns.
- Create a radial pattern of duplicate objects.
- Create a pattern of duplicate objects along a path.

11.1 Trimming and Extending Objects

Trim and **Extend** commands can be used to modify already existing objects to ensure that they have the correct size and length, as shown in Figure 11–1.

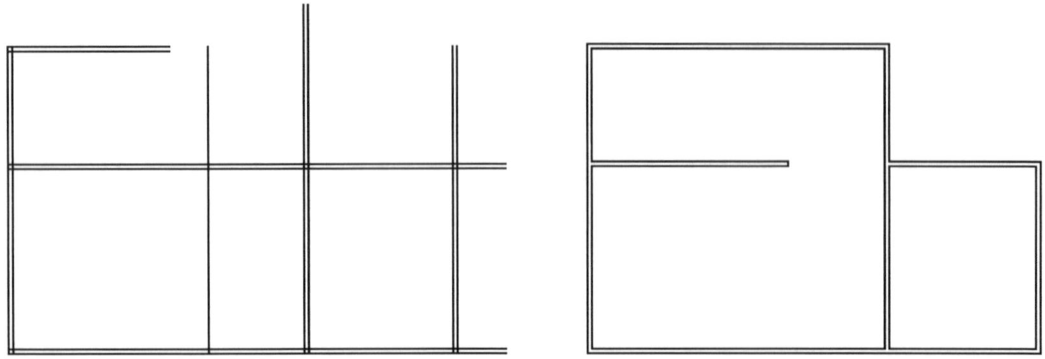

Figure 11–1

The commands are located in the *Home* tab>*Modify* panel, in the *Trim/Extend* flyout, as shown in Figure 11–2.

Figure 11–2

Trimming Objects

The **Trim** command erases any part of an object that extends past a cutting edge. It simplifies many drawing tasks. For example, an easy way to create an arc is to draw a circle and then trim it.

How To: Trim Objects

1. In the *Home* tab>*Modify* panel, click (Trim).
2. Hover the cursor over the part of the object that you want to trim. The software determines all the potential cutting edges by default and displays the trimming portion as faded in a light gray line weight. This provides a preview of the part that is going to be removed, as shown in Figure 11–3.
   - You can also use the **Trim** command to extend an object. At the *Select object to trim or Shift-select to extend* prompt, hold <Shift> to switch to the **Extend** command.

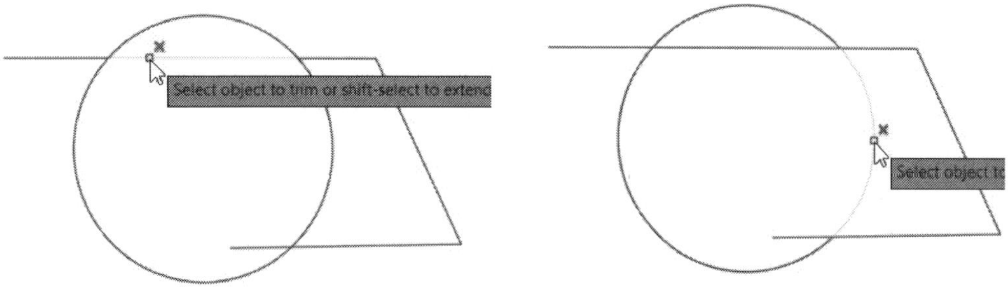

Figure 11–3

3. Select the part to be removed.
4. Press <Enter> to complete the command.

Extending Objects

Using the **Extend** command, any object that does not reach a boundary edge is lengthened until it meets the boundary, as shown in Figure 11–4.

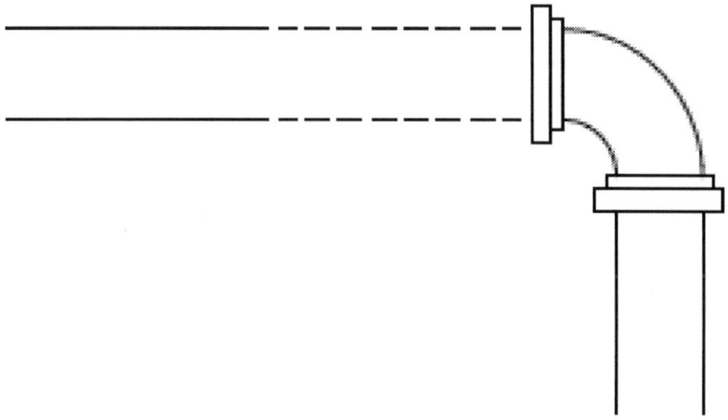

Figure 11–4

How To: Extend Objects

1. In the *Home* tab>*Modify* panel, click (Extend).
2. Hover the cursor over the object that you want to extend (closer to the boundary edge), and a preview of the part that is going to be added displays. The extended part is highlighted in blue with a thicker line weight.
   - You can also use the **Extend** command to trim an object. At the *Select object to extend or Shift-select to trim* prompt, hold <Shift> to switch to the **Trim** command.
3. Select to extend the object.
4. Press <Enter> to complete the command.

Selecting Objects to Trim and Extend

By default, objects to be trimmed or extended can be selected using the following methods:

- **Individual selection**: Select the objects by picking them individually.
- **Freehand Selection**: Press and hold the left mouse button, then drag the cursor over the objects you intend to trim or extend, as shown in Figure 11–5.

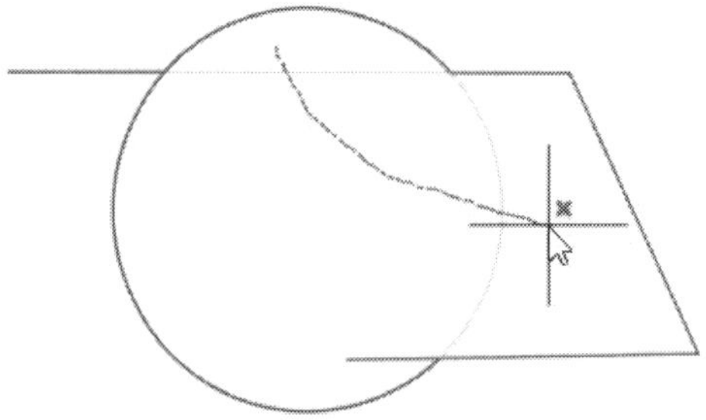

Figure 11–5

- **Two-Point Fence selection:** Click two points to create a segment that passes through the objects to be trimmed or extended, as shown in Figure 11–6.

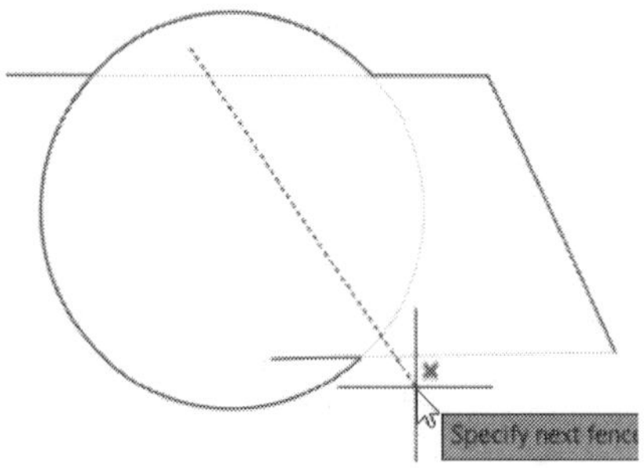

Figure 11–6

If you select something by mistake, you can use the **Undo** option in the command (<Down Arrow> menu) to restore the last object trimmed/extended. You can also click (Undo) in the *Quick Access Toolbar* for the **Trim** and **Extend** commands, however this loses all of the trimming/extending you have done to that point.

Hint: Trim or Extend Additional Options

When you start the **Trim** or **Extend** command, you are provided with various options (<Down Arrow> menu or Command Line selection) before you select objects for trimming/extending. These options for selecting objects are not the default options and need to be explicitly selected from the menu.

When you select the **Crossing** option, you are prompted to select two opposite corners, as shown in Figure 11–7. Everything touching or in the box is previewed (faded light gray) and is then trimmed or extended when you select the second corner. You remain in the command so that you can select more objects as required.

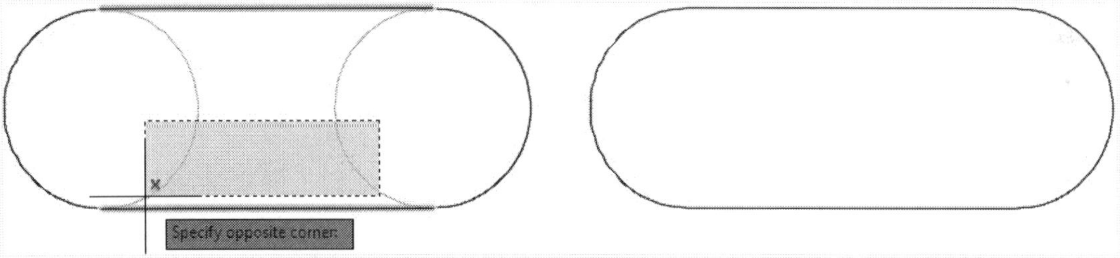

Figure 11–7

When you select the **cuTting edges** (for trimming)/**Boundary edges** (for extending) option, you are prompted to select the required edges first. The selected cutting or boundary edges are highlighted in blue with a thicker line weight, as shown in Figure 11–8. Select the objects that need to be trimmed or extended.

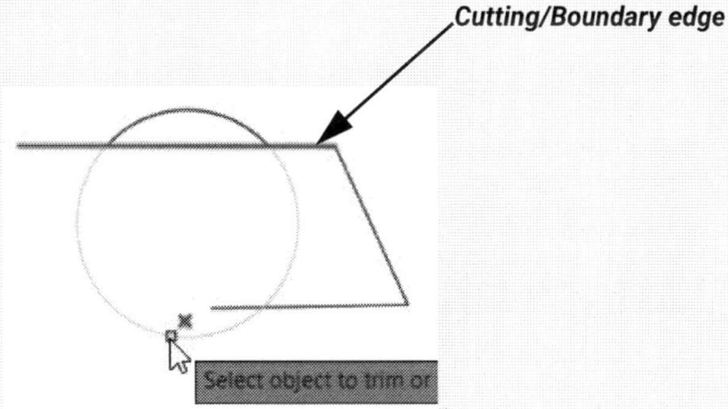

Figure 11–8

Hint: Breaking Objects

The **Break** command can be used to cut an object without any overlapping edges. Two different options of the command are available in the *Home* tab>expanded *Modify* panel, as shown in Figure 11–9:

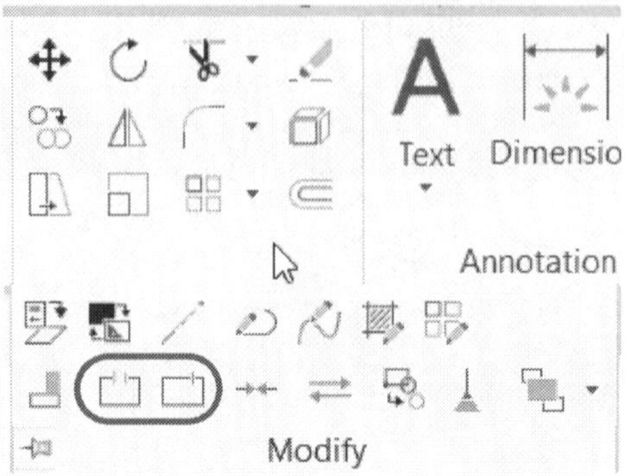

Figure 11–9

- **(Break):** Removes a portion of an object between two user-defined points, leaving a gap. This has the same effect as trimming between two cutting edges.
- **(Break at Point):** Breaks an object at one point so that it becomes two pieces, but does not have a gap. This option is useful if you need to change a portion of a line into a different linetype. This command can be repeated by pressing <Enter>.

Practice 11a
Extend and Trim Objects

Practice Objective

- Remove and extend objects.

In this practice, you will extend and trim lines to complete a drawing, as shown in Figure 11–10.

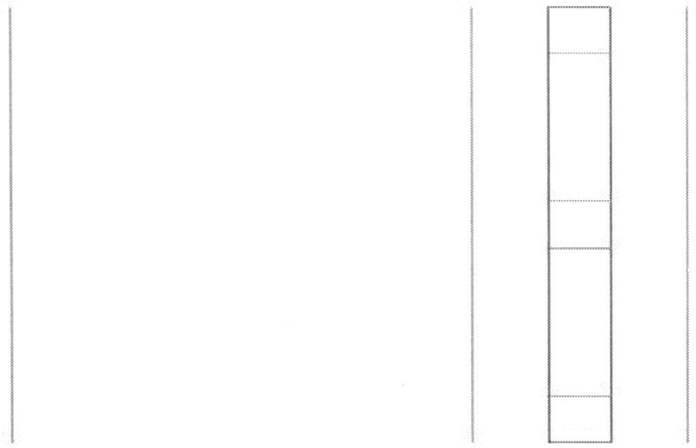

Before

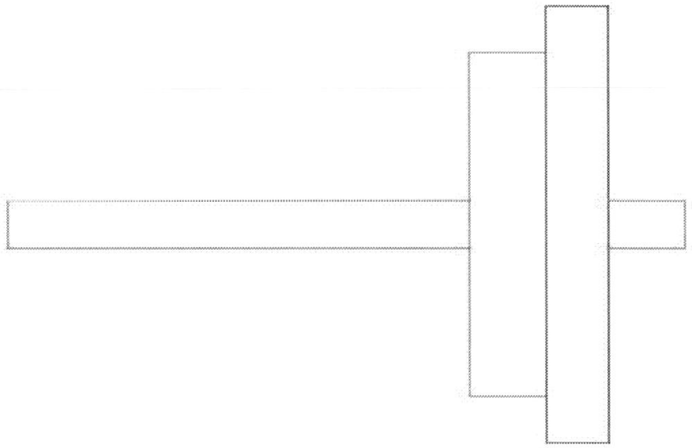

After

Figure 11–10

1. Open **Shaft-M.dwg** from your practice files folder.
2. In the *Home* tab>*Modify* panel, click (Extend).
3. Click above and then below the two short horizontal red lines (to create a fence line), closer to their right endpoints, such that they extend until the red vertical line (last line) located on the right hand side, as shown in Figure 11–11.

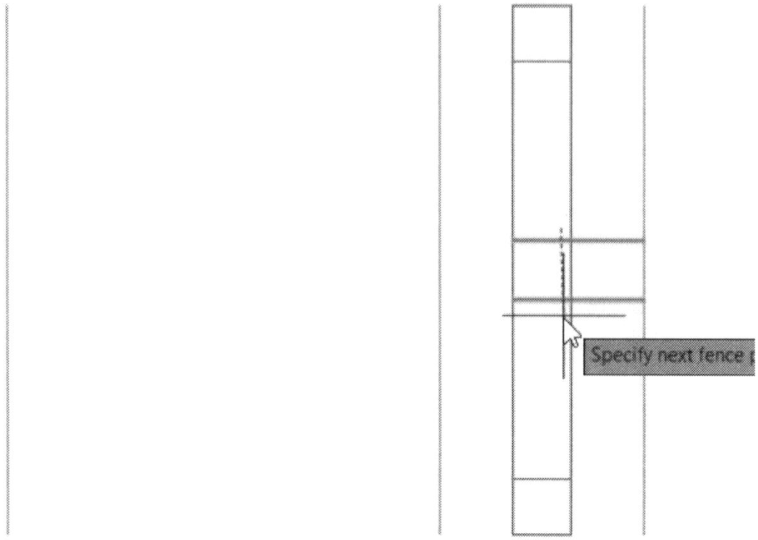

Figure 11–11

4. While remaining in the **Extend** command, open the <Down Arrow> menu or at the Command prompt, select **Boundary edges**.
   - If you exited the command, select it again in the ribbon or press <Enter> to repeat it.
5. Select the vertical red line on the far left hand side as the boundary edge, and press <Enter>. Note that it is highlighted in blue and has a thicker line weight.
6. Using a fence line, select the pair of short horizontal red lines closer to their left endpoints, to extend them all the way to the selected red line. Press <Enter> to complete the command.
7. Start the **Extend** command again and individually select the pair of short horizontal blue lines along their left endpoints, to extend them to the vertical blue line. Press <Enter> to complete the command.
8. In the *Home* tab>*Modify* panel, click (Trim). Select the top and bottom portions of both vertical red lines to trim their top and bottom portions.
9. While remaining in the **Trim** command, select the top and bottom portions of the vertical blue line to trim its top and bottom portion.

10. You are still in the **Trim** command. Inside the black rectangular area, select two fence selection points, above and below the blue horizontal lines, (as shown in Figure 11–12) to trim the inner four lines.

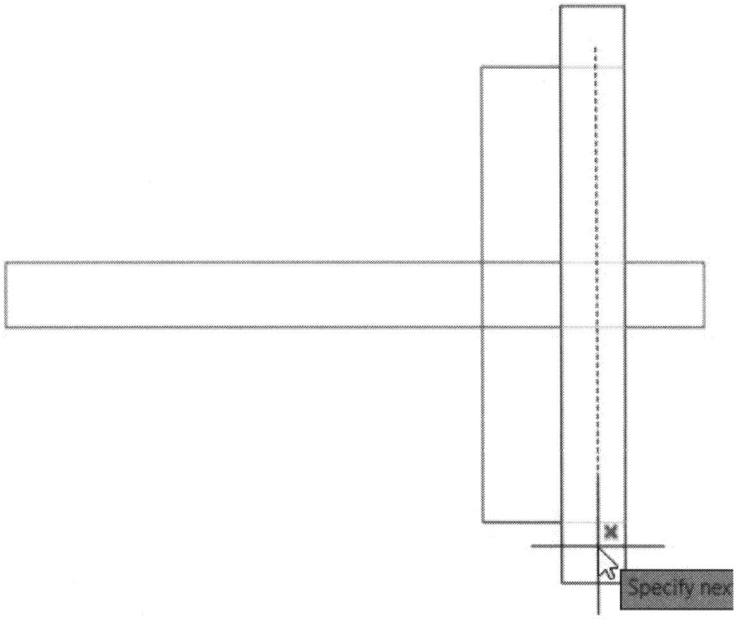

Figure 11–12

11. Similarly, trim the two red horizontal lines within the blue rectangular area. Press <Enter> to complete the command.
12. Save and close the drawing.

End of practice

Practice 11b
Trim Objects on a Drawing

Practice Objective

- Remove parts of objects.

In this practice, you will use the different options of the **Trim** command to remove parts of lines and to trim circles to create empty slots, as shown in Figure 11–13.

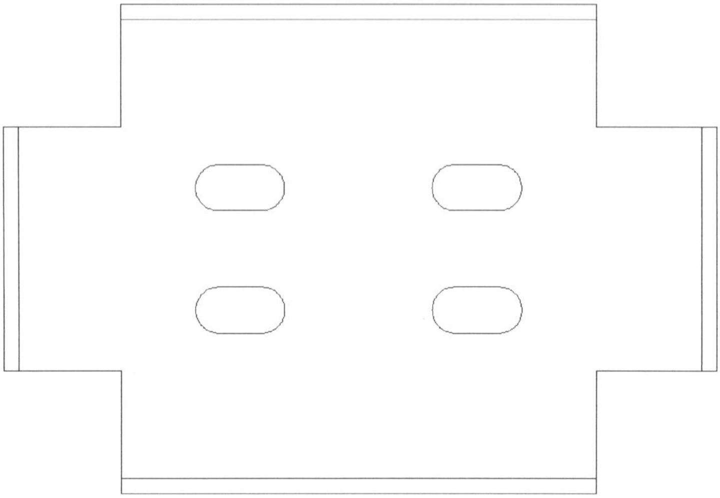

Figure 11–13

1. Open **Bracket-I.dwg** from your practice files folder.
2. Start the **Trim** command.
3. Starting from the outside of the top horizontal line of the inner rectangle, click and hold the left mouse button and drag it to create a freehand line over the four lines that create the inner rectangle, as shown in Figure 11–14. Let go of the left mouse button to trim all the four lines in one go.

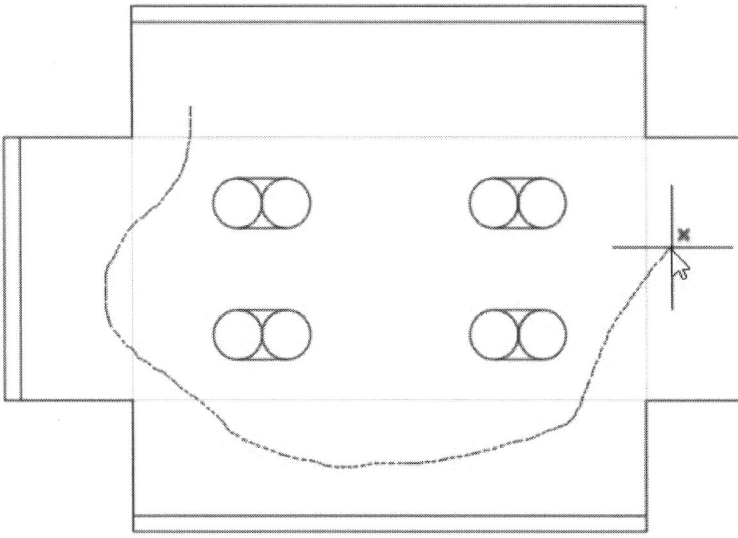

Figure 11–14

4. While remaining in the **Trim** command, open the <Down Arrow> menu or at the Command prompt, select **Crossing**.
5. Create a crossing window inside each slot to trim the inner portions of the circles, as shown in Figure 11–15. Individually select the small portion left behind to clean the slot.

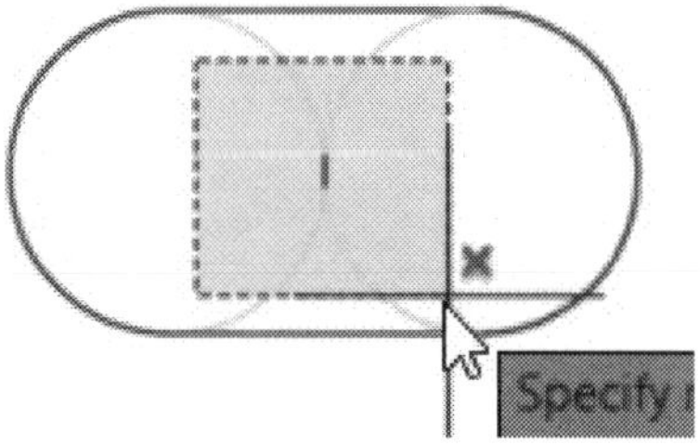

Figure 11–15

6. Similarly, trim the other three slots. You have to select the **Crossing** option each time you want to use it. Clean up the three slots as well.
7. Press <Enter> to exit the command.
8. Save and close the drawing.

End of practice

Practice 11c
Break at Point

Practice Objective

- Break lines into segments and change the linetype of the new segments.

In this practice, you will use the **Break at Point** command to break lines into separate segments and then change the linetype of the new segments using Quick Properties, as shown in Figure 11–16.

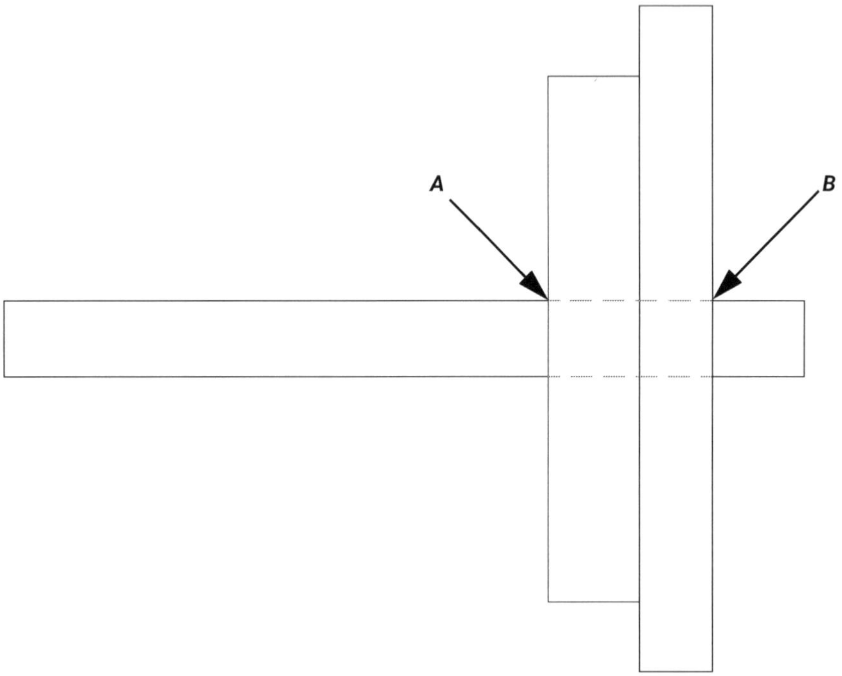

Figure 11–16

1. Open **Shaft2-M.dwg** from your practice files folder.
2. Select the two long horizontal lines. Note that they are single line segments. Press <Esc> to clear the selection.
3. In the Object snap menu, select **Intersection** and toggle (Object Snap) on.
4. In the *Home* tab>extended *Modify* panel, click (Break at Point).
5. At the *Select object:* prompt, select the top long horizontal line.
6. For the break point, select the Intersection labeled **A** in Figure 11–16.

7. Press <Enter> to continue in the **Break at Point** command. At the *Select object:* prompt, select the broken off portion of the same horizontal line, along the right side of point **A**.
8. For the break point, select the Intersection labeled **B** in Figure 11–16.
9. Select the horizontal line between points A and B. It is now a separate segment. In the *Quick Properties* panel, click in the *Layer* row and expand the drop-down list. Select **Construction** to change the layer, as shown in Figure 11–17. Clear the selection.
   - Ensure that  (Quick Properties) is toggled on in the *Status Bar*.

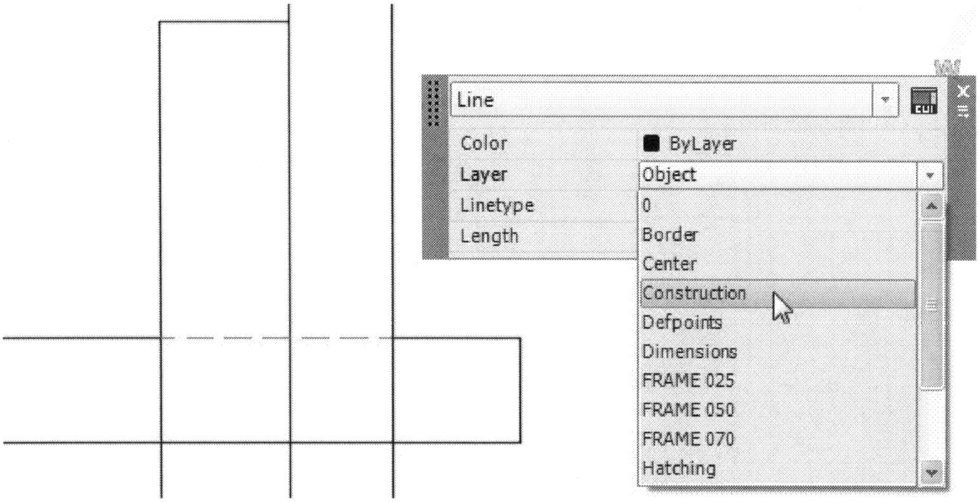

Figure 11–17

10. Repeat the procedure on the lower horizontal line.
11. Save and close the drawing.

End of practice

11.2 Stretching Objects

The **Stretch** command enables objects and/or parts of objects to be moved and/or extended, leaving other objects and parts of objects stationary.

How To: Stretch Objects

1. In the *Home* tab>*Modify* panel, click (Stretch).
2. Use a *Crossing* selection to select the objects to stretch. The objects are highlighted in blue.
3. Press <Enter> to finish the selection set.
4. Select the base point (the *handle* by which you hold the objects).
5. Move the cursor in the direction in which you want to stretch the object. A preview displays of the original objects now faded to gray, while the new objects have maintained their original properties, as shown in Figure 11–18.

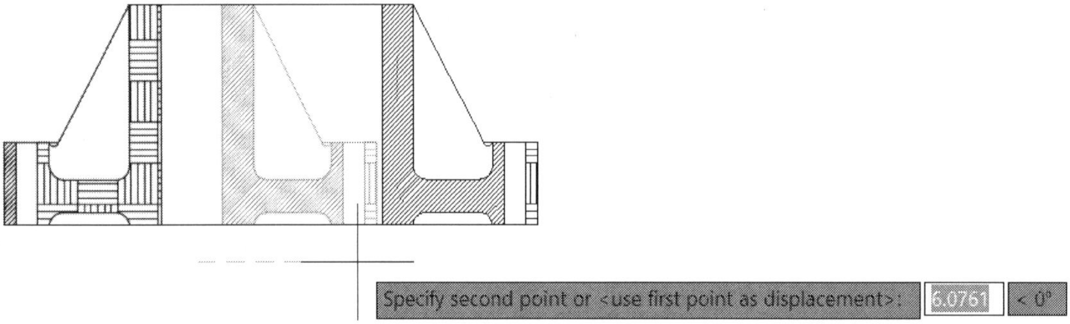

Figure 11–18

6. Select the second point (which in conjunction with the base point defines the distance and direction to which you are stretching) or enter a distance and press <Enter>.

Notes on Stretching Objects

- Objects to be stretched must be selected using the **Crossing** or **Crossing Polygon** selection methods. A Crossing Polygon enables you to draw an irregularly shaped polygon by selecting each of the polygon's vertices (it displays in green), as shown in Figure 11–19. Anything inside or touching the polygon is selected.

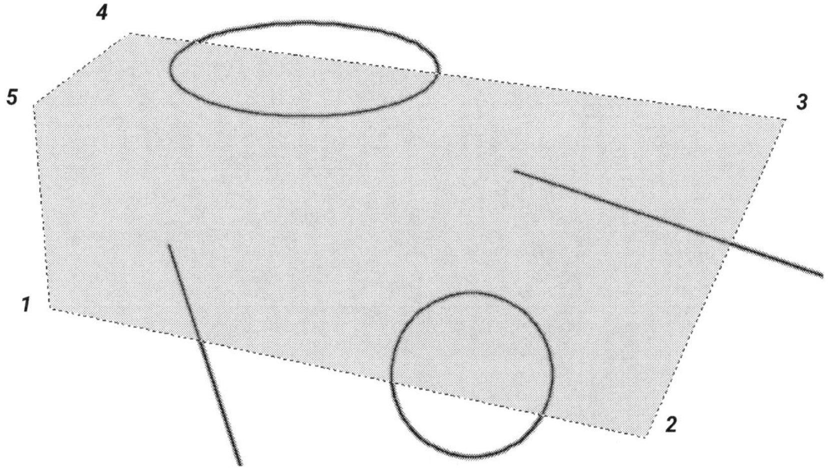

Figure 11–19

*Note: Circles, ellipses, and blocks do not stretch because they do not have end points. The **Stretch** command moves them instead.*

- The stretching of objects is based on their end points or their insertion point.
  - Objects *outside* the crossing window are unchanged.
  - Objects *crossing* the crossing window are stretched or contracted accordingly.
  - Objects *inside* the crossing window are moved.
- While **Scale** reduces or enlarges an entire object proportionately in all directions, **Stretch** only changes it in one direction.

Practice 11d
Stretch Objects

Practice Objective

- Increase the width of objects by stretching them.

In this practice, you will use the **Stretch** command to increase the width of the entire building and then increase the width of the office and reception area, as shown in Figure 11–20.

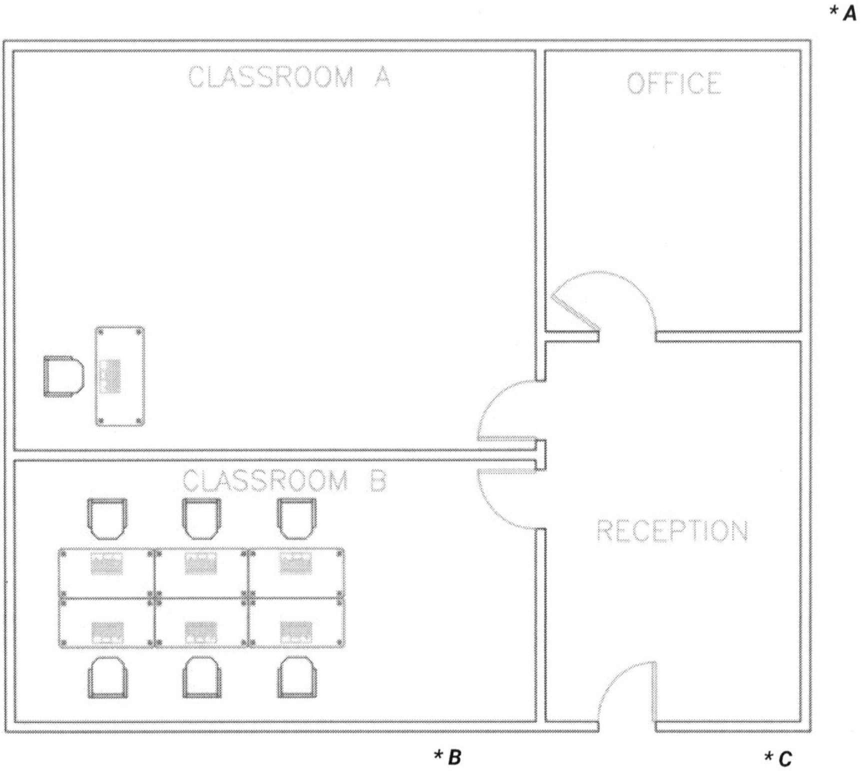

Figure 11–20

1. Open **Class2-A.dwg** from your practice files folder. Distances in the drawing are in feet and inches.

2. In the status bar, toggle on (Orthomode) to restrict the movement of objects orthogonally.

3. In the *Home* tab>*Modify* panel, click (Stretch). At the *Select objects:* prompt, use a Crossing selection to create a crossing window with its first corner at point **A** and the diagonally opposite corner at point **B**, as shown in Figure 11–20 (ensure that the doors to both the classrooms are fully enclosed within the crossing window). Press <Enter>.

4. At the *Specify base point:* prompt, select a point near the upper right corner of the office. At the *Specify second point:* prompt, pull the cursor to the right, enter **8'** (make sure to enter the ' feet sign after 8), as shown in Figure 11–21. Press <Enter> and note that only the horizontal Classroom walls are stretched, making the two classrooms larger (elongated).

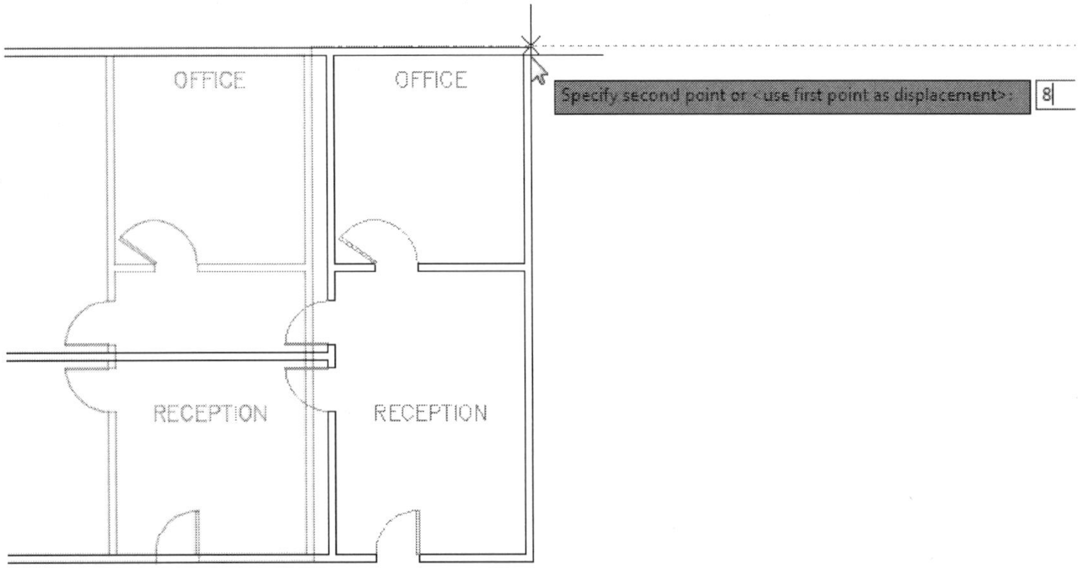

Figure 11–21

5. Start the **Stretch** command again. At the *Select objects:* prompt, use a *Crossing* selection with corners at points **A** and **C**, as shown in Figure 11–20. (Make sure that the crossing window does not touch the text.) Press <Enter>.

6. At the *Specify base point:* prompt, select a point near the upper right corner of the office. At the *Specify second point:* prompt, pull the cursor to the right, enter **4'**, and press <Enter>. This makes the office and the reception rooms larger.

7. Save and close the drawing.

End of practice

11.3 Creating Fillets and Chamfers

Fillets and chamfers are used to create rounded corners and beveled edges respectively, as shown in Figure 11–22.

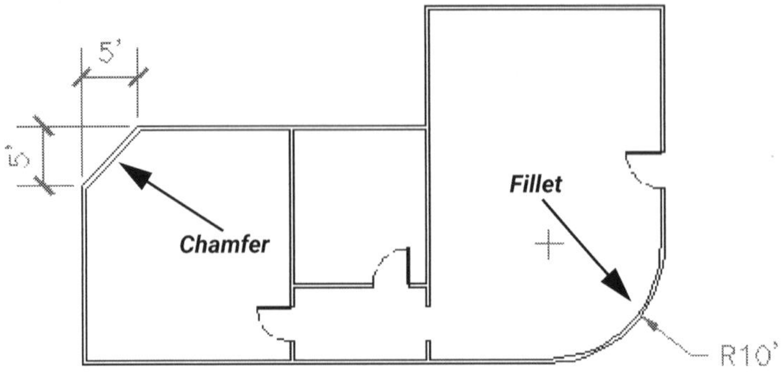

Figure 11–22

Filleting Objects

The **Fillet** command modifies the intersection of two objects and can be used to create inside and outside rounded corners, as shown in Figure 11–23. It can also be helpful in cleaning up a drawing by forcing lines to meet at an exact intersection.

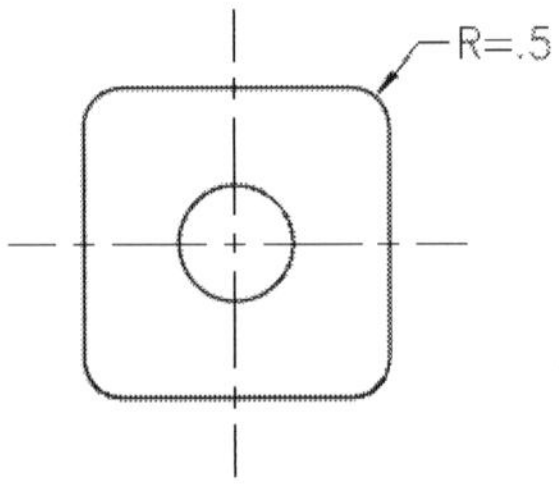

Figure 11–23

How To: Fillet Objects

1. In the *Home* tab>*Modify* panel, click (**Fillet**).
2. Select the **Radius** option (<Down Arrow> menu), enter the new radius, and press <Enter>.
   - The **Radius** option enables you to specify the fillet radius. This value should be selected and set before you pick the objects to fillet.
3. If you are filleting several sets of objects, select the **Multiple** option (<Down Arrow> menu).
4. Select the first line that you want to fillet.

5. Hover the cursor over the second line that you want to fillet. A preview displays the fillet being highlighted in blue and the original object faded in light gray, as shown in Figure 11–24.

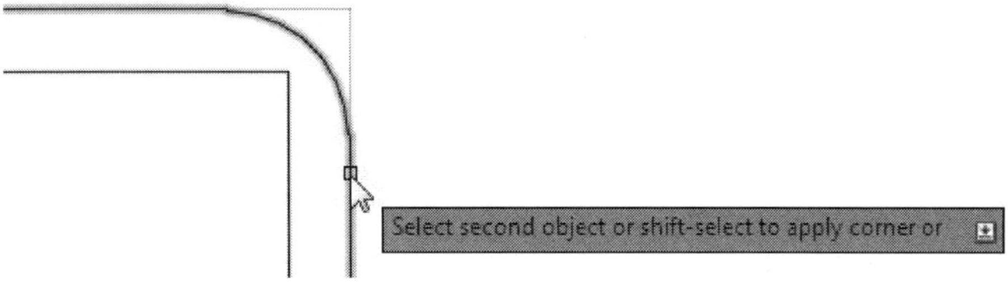

Figure 11–24

6. Select the second line to confirm the fillet.
7. If you have selected the **Multiple** option, you can continue selecting two lines to fillet until you press <Enter> to complete the command.
   - A fillet with the **Radius** option set to **0** can be used to make lines meet at a square corner. You can also hold <Shift> as you select the two lines without having to change the radius.
   - You can fillet two parallel lines. In this case, the radius is automatically calculated so that the arc is tangent to both lines.
   - The **Undo** option undoes the last fillet without exiting the command.
   - The **Polyline** option fillets all of the vertices of a selected polyline. You can still fillet one vertex by selecting segments to fillet.
   - The **Trim/NoTrim** option determines whether selected lines are trimmed after the arc is added.
   - You can fillet both lines and arcs in a polyline.

Chamfering Objects

The **Chamfer** command angles or bevels the intersection of two lines to create an angled corner, as shown in Figure 11–25.

Figure 11–25

How To: Chamfer Objects

1. In the *Home* tab>*Modify* panel, click  (Chamfer).
2. Select the **Distance** option and enter two distances.
   - The first chamfer distance is used on the first line that you select and the second chamfer distance is used on the second line that you select. Distances are measured from the intersection of the two lines.
3. If you are chamfering several sets of objects, select the **Multiple** option.
4. Select the first line that you want to chamfer, which is highlighted in blue.

5. Hover the cursor over the second line that you want to chamfer. A preview displays the chamfer being highlighted in blue and the chamfered portion being faded in light gray, as shown in Figure 11–26.

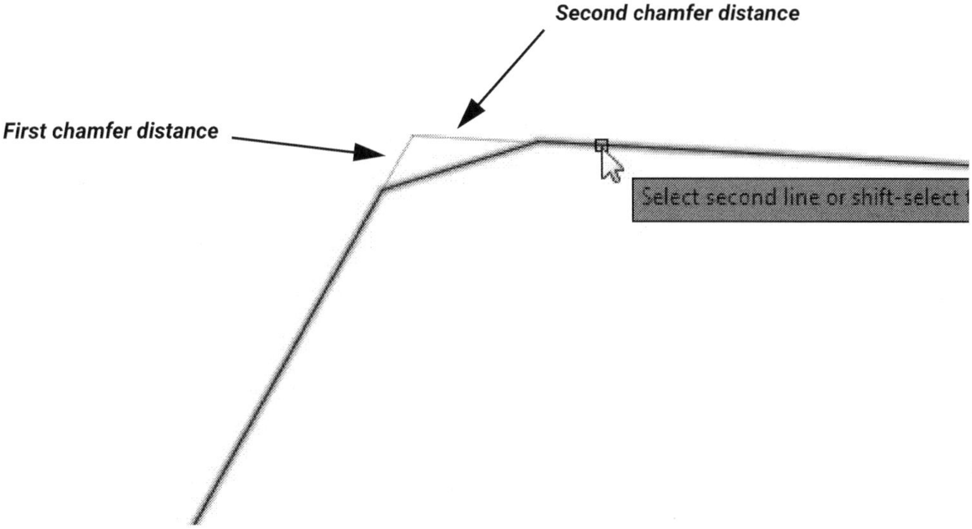

Figure 11–26

6. Select the second line.
7. If you selected the **Multiple** option, you can continue selecting two lines to chamfer until you press <Enter> to complete the command.

- Another way to specify the chamfer is to set the **Angle** option, which sets the chamfer length of the first line you select and then the angle between the original line and the chamfered edge.
- The distance and angle information are stored separately. Therefore, you can use the **Method** option to change between the two options in the same command. The last method you selected is used when a new command is started.
- The **Undo**, **Trim/NoTrim**, and **Polyline** options work the same way as when using the **Fillet** command.

Practice 11e
Fillet Objects

Practice Objective

- Create rounded corners and fillet parallel lines.

In this practice, you will use the **Fillet** command to round the outer corners of a part with two different radius sizes, as shown in Figure 11–27. You will also fillet parallel lines to create slots.

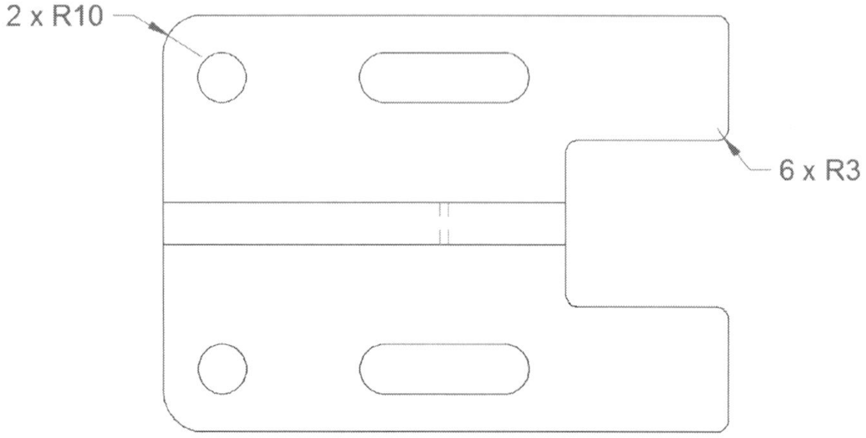

Figure 11–27

1. Open **Visebase-M.dwg** from your practice files folder.
2. In the *Home* tab>*Modify* panel, click (Fillet). Set the **Radius** option (select **Radius** in the <Down Arrow> menu or type **R**). Set *Radius* to **10**.
3. Near the upper left corner, select the horizontal line and then hover your cursor on the left vertical line, as shown in Figure 11–28. Note the fillet preview.

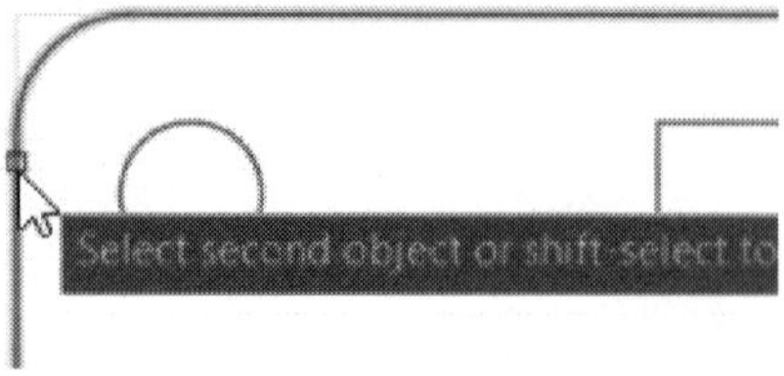

Figure 11–28

4. Select the left vertical line to fillet the upper left corner.
5. Repeat the command to fillet the lower left corner with the same radius. Select the lines without entering the **Radius** option as the radius has already been set in Step 2.

6. Start the **Fillet** command again. In the <Down Arrow> menu, select the **Radius** option and enter the radius as **3**. Display the <Down Arrow> menu again and select the **Multiple** option to repeat the prompts. Fillet the six corners on the right side of the object. Press <Enter> to exit the **Multiple** option.
7. Continue in the **Fillet** command and select the top horizontal line of the rectangle that is located in the upper area of the part. Select the bottom horizontal line of the rectangle closer to the left corner to create a fillet, as shown in Figure 11–29. Repeat for the right end of the lines.
   - The fillet radius is automatically calculated between the two parallel lines of the rectangle.

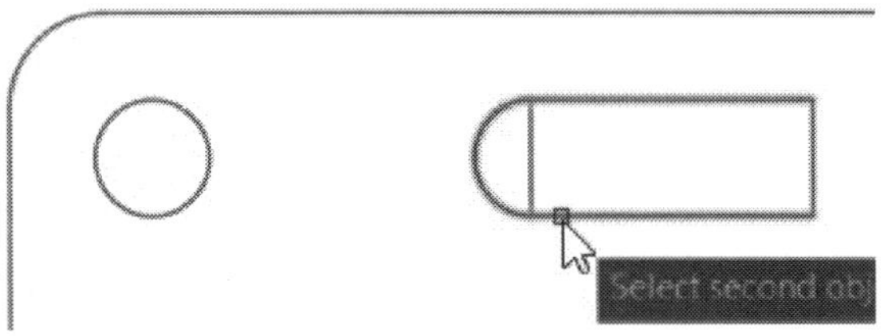

Figure 11–29

8. Repeat Step 7 for the bottom rectangle.
9. Erase the short vertical lines to clear out both the slots.
10. Save and close the drawing.

End of practice

Practice 11f
Chamfer Objects

Practice Objective

- Create different sizes of angled edges.

In this practice, you will use the **Chamfer** command with several different distances to create the angled edges on a part, as shown in Figure 11–30.

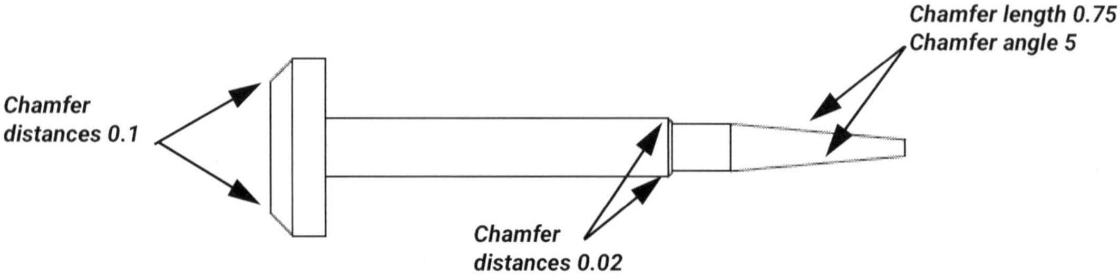

Figure 11–30

1. Open **Punch-I.dwg** from your practice files folder.
2. In the *Home* tab>*Modify* panel, click (Chamfer). In the <Down Arrow> menu, select **Distance** or type **D** to use the **Distance** option. Set both *Chamfer distances* to **0.1**.
3. Select the horizontal and vertical lines in the top left corner of the part to apply the chamfer.
4. Repeat the command to chamfer the bottom left corner using the same distances.
5. Start the **Chamfer** command and select the **Distance** option. Set both *Chamfer distances* to **0.02**. Select the **Multiple** option to repeat the prompts. Chamfer both corners where the shaft changes size.
6. While remaining in the **Chamfer** command, select **Angle** in the <Down Arrow> menu or type **A** to set the **Angle** option. Set the *Chamfer length* on the first line to **0.75**. Set the *chamfer angle* to **5**. Apply the chamfer to the right end of the part, selecting the top horizontal line first, and then the short vertical line. Repeat for the bottom corner of the right end.
7. Add vertical lines to indicate the edges of the three chamfers, as shown in Figure 11–30. (Use the Endpoint object snap.)
8. Save and close the drawing.

End of practice

11.4 Offsetting Objects

The AutoCAD software enables you to create parallel shapes with a single editing command called **Offset,** as shown in Figure 11–31.

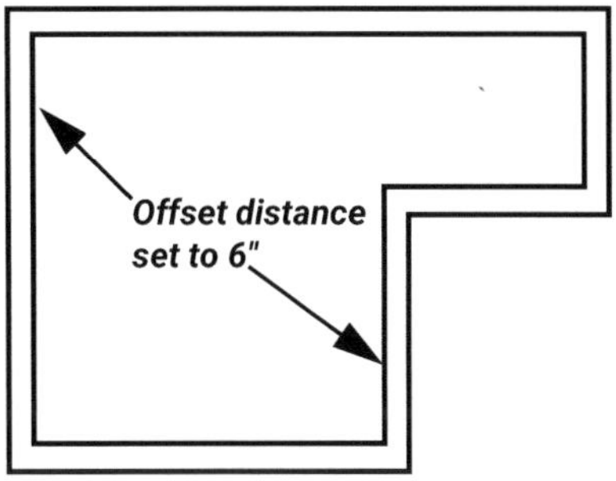

Figure 11–31

- The **Offset** command works with lines, circles, arcs, and polylines.
- You can specify a distance between the original object and the offset copy, or select a point through which the copy is going to pass.

How To: Offset Objects Using a Distance

1. In the *Home* tab>*Modify* panel, click (Offset).
2. Enter the offset distance and press <Enter>.
3. Select the object to offset.
4. Hover the cursor on either side of the object to display a preview of the offset copy.
    - You can change the offset distance before selecting the side to place the offset copy.
5. Select a point on either side of the object to place the offset copy on that side.
6. Select another object to offset by the same distance, or press <Enter> to complete the command.
    - If you want to offset one object multiple times, select the **Multiple** option before you select the side you want to offset. The new objects are placed at the same distance from the last object that was offset.
    - The **Through** option enables you to select a point through which the offset object must pass. You can drag the cursor on either side of the object to display a preview of the offset copy before placing the offset.

- The **Erase** and **Layer** options are settings that remain active until you change them. By default, objects from which you offset are not erased, and the layer of the new object matches the layer of the source object rather than the current layer.
- If you offset a polyline, all of the sides are offset equally, as shown in Figure 11–32. To only offset one side of a polyline, you need to explode it first.

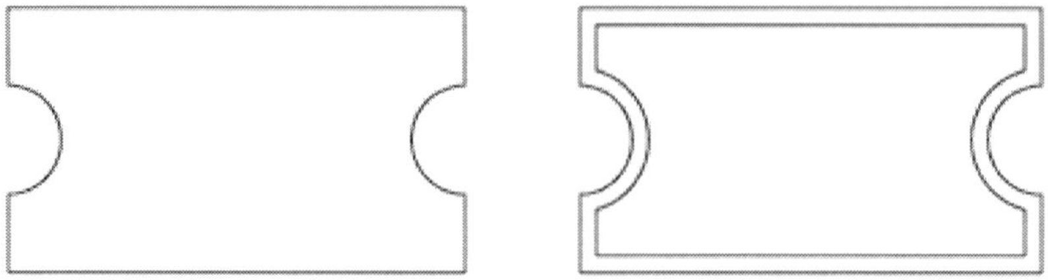

Figure 11–32

Practice 11g
Offset Objects

Practice Objective

- Offset polylines, lines, and arcs.

In this practice, you will use the **Offset** command on polylines, lines, and arcs to create walls and steps, as shown in Figure 11–33. The color of the arc steps has been changed for printing clarity.

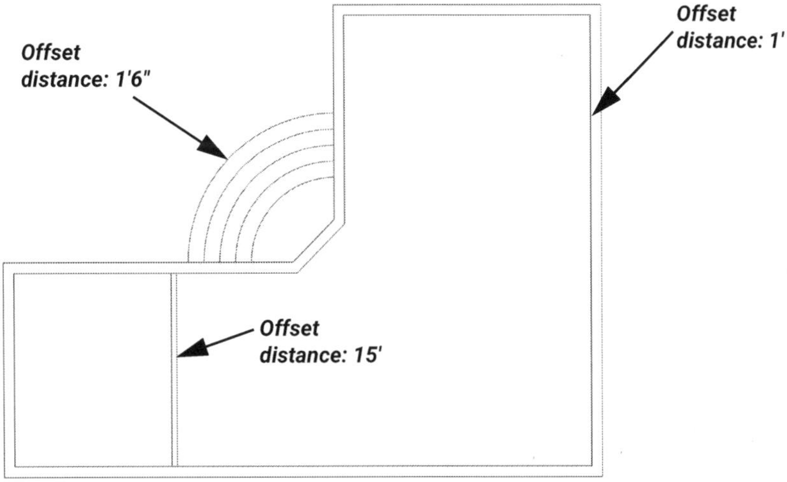

Figure 11–33

1. Open **Offset-A.dwg** from your practice files folder. Distances in the drawing are in feet and inches.
2. In the *Home* tab>*Modify* panel, click (Offset). Enter the *offset distance* as **1'** and press <Enter>. Select the large polyline as the object to offset. Move the cursor inside the polyline to display the preview of the offset copy towards inside.
3. Select a point inside the polyline to create the offset copy on the inside. Press <Enter> to complete the command.
4. Start the **Offset** command again. Enter the *offset distance* as **1'6"** and press <Enter>. Select the yellow arc as the object to offset. Drag the cursor outside (above) the arc to display the preview and select a point outside (above) the arc to create the offset copy.
5. Note that you are still in the **Offset** command and at the *Select object to offset:* prompt, select the arc you just created. At the *Specify point on side to offset:* prompt, press <Down Arrow> and select the **Multiple** option to make the command repeating. Select three points above the arcs to have a total of five arcs. Press <Enter> twice to exit the command.

6. In the *Home* tab>*Modify* panel, click (Explode) and select the inner black polyline, that you created in Step 3. Press <Enter>. The polyline is turned into multiple single line objects.
7. Start the **Offset** command again, and set the *offset distance* to **15'**. Select the inside vertical line on the left bottom as the object to offset. Move the cursor to right of the line to preview the offset line (as shown on the left in Figure 11–34). Select a point to place the offset line.
8. Note that you are still in the **Offset** command. At the *Select object to offset:* prompt, select the line you just created. Note that an offset line is previewed at **15'**. In the offset distance edit box, enter **6"**, (as shown on the right in Figure 11–34) to change the offset distance. Press <Enter> to place the offset line to make an interior wall. Press <Enter> again to exit the command.

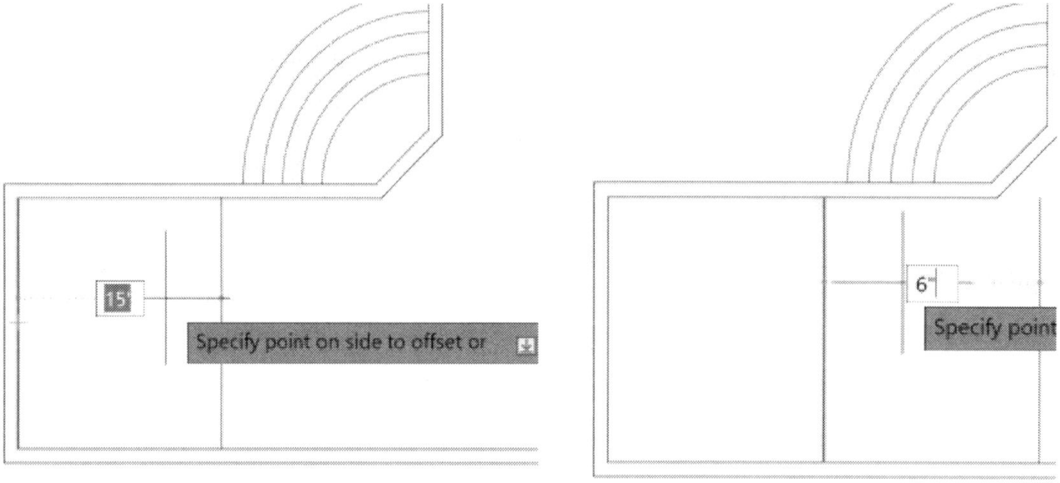

Figure 11–34

9. Save and close the drawing.

End of practice

11.5 Creating Arrays of Objects

The **Array** commands generate copies of selected objects at fixed intervals of rows and columns, around a center point, or along a path, as shown in Figure 11–35. For example, a rectangular array can be used to create light fixtures in a ceiling grid. Holes around a circular gasket or radial wings of a building are examples of a polar array. A path array can be used for lights along a walkway or the edge of an irregular shaped pool.

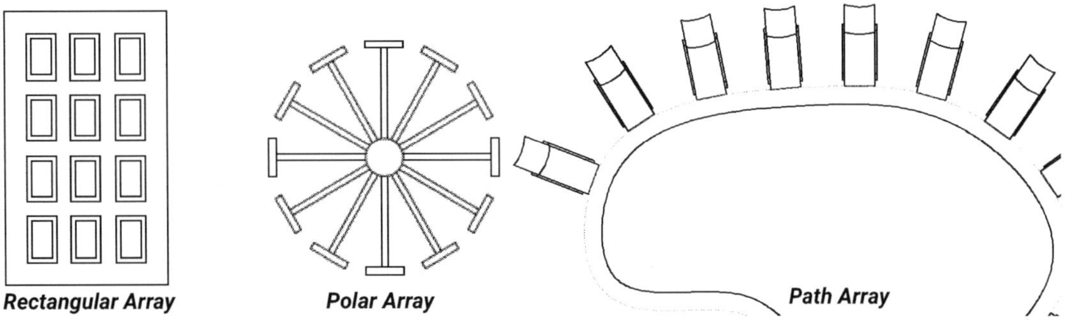

Figure 11–35

- The different methods of Array can be accessed in the *Home* tab>*Modify* panel>*Array* flyout, as shown in Figure 11–36.

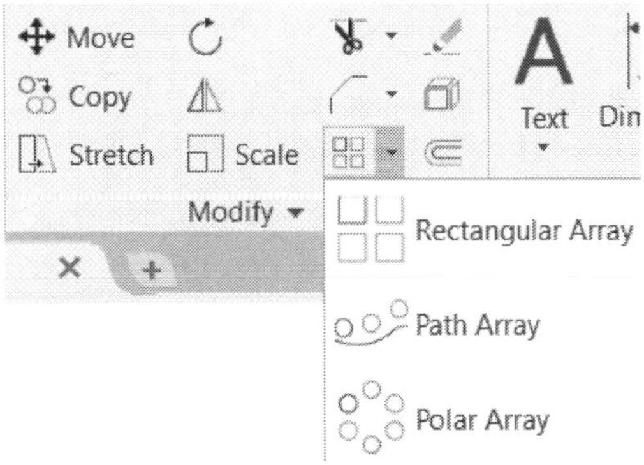

Figure 11–36

- You can create arrays using two methods: using grips, or using the *Array Creation* contextual tab. Once the required objects have been selected to be arrayed in any array style, the grips display on the array and the *Array Creation* contextual tab displays in the ribbon. You can use either method to set the number of items, rows, columns, levels, or other options. The *Array Creation* contextual tab for creating a Rectangular array is shown in Figure 11–37.

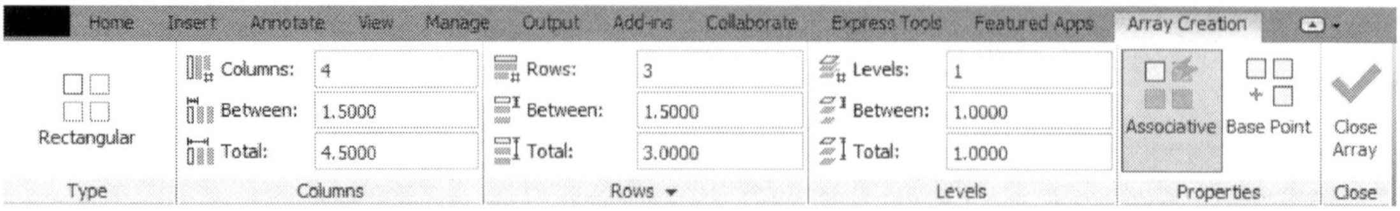

Figure 11–37

Associative Arrays

You can control whether an array is associative or non-associative by selecting/clearing **Associative** in the *Properties* panel of the *Array Creation* contextual tab. By default, arrays are created as associative arrays where all the objects of the array maintain a relationship with each other. This is useful if you want to adjust the array patterns, spacing, and the location. This way you can easily modify all the objects in the array together and with respect to each other.

Rectangular Array

A rectangular array consists of a pattern of objects that are divided into rows and columns.

How To: Create a Rectangular Array Using Grips

1. In the *Home* tab>*Modify* panel, expand the *Array* flyout and click (Rectangular Array).
2. At the *Select objects:* prompt, select the object(s) that you want to array and press <Enter>.
    - You can use windows or crossing selection to select objects.
3. A preview of the array displays a default number of objects in rows and columns, as shown in Figure 11–38. It also displays grips that enable you to modify the array.

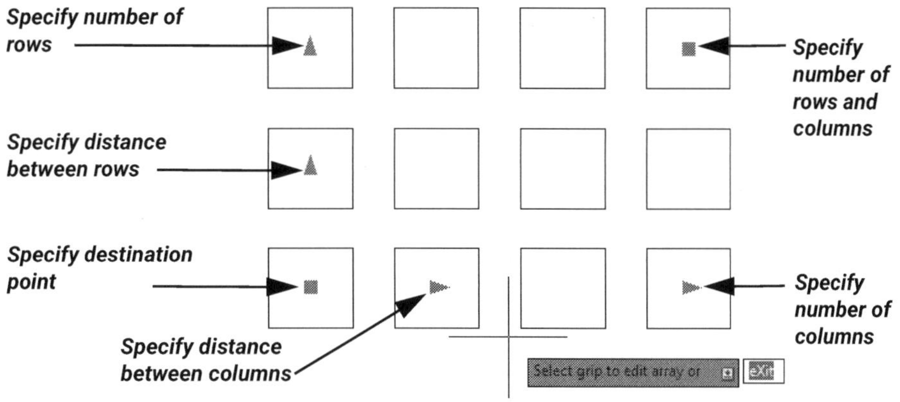

Figure 11–38

4. To specify the number of items to be in the array, use one of the following methods:
   - Use the *Specify number of rows*, *Specify number of columns*, and *Specify number of rows and columns* grips to change the number of columns and rows.
   - At the *Select grip to edit array or:* prompt, type **COU** and press <Enter> to use the **Count** option. Enter a value for the number of columns, and then for the number of rows. Press <Enter> after each value.
5. Specify the spacing between the arrayed items, using one of the following methods:
   - Use the *row* spacing and *column spacing* grips to change the number of columns and rows.
   - At the *Select grip to edit array or:* prompt, type **S** and press <Enter> to use the **Spacing** option. Enter a value for the distance between the columns and then for between the rows. Press <Enter> after each value.
6. If required, you can modify the location of the array by selecting the *Specify destination point* grip and then picking a destination point in the drawing window.
7. Press <Enter> to complete the command.

Polar Array

A polar array consists of a pattern of objects that are copied about a central radius.

How To: Create a Polar Array Using the Array Creation Contextual Tab

1. In the *Home* tab>*Modify* panel, expand the *Array* flyout and click (Polar Array).
2. At the *Select objects:* prompt, select the object(s) that you want to array. Press <Enter> to end the selection of objects.

3. At the *Specify center point of array:* prompt, select a point on the screen to be the center of the polar array.
4. A preview of the array displays a default number of objects in a radial pattern, as shown in Figure 11–39. Additionally, it displays grips and an *Array Creation* contextual tab in the ribbon that enable you to modify the array.

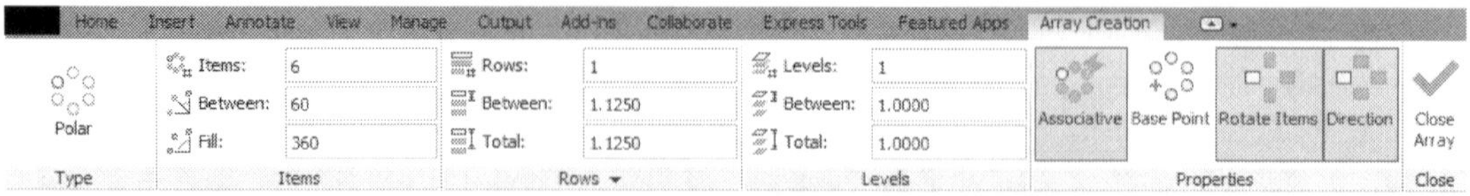

Figure 11–39

5. Specify the number of items in the *Items* panel.
6. Depending on the number of items and the *Fill* angle, the *Between* angle value changes to fit the specified number.
    * Using the **Fill** option, enter the angle that you want the arrayed items to fill.
7. If required, you can modify the rotation of the items and the direction of the array using the **Rotate Items** and **Direction** buttons in the contextual tab.
8. Press <Enter> to complete the command.

* When creating polar arrays, you can use the **ROWs** option to add additional offset rows around the center point and the **Rotate Items** option to change the orientation of the arrayed items, as they are being placed around the center point.

Path Array

A path array consists of a pattern of objects that are copied along a straight, curved, or irregular linear path.

How To: Create a Path Array

1. In the *Home* tab>*Modify* panel, expand the *Array* flyout and click  (Path Array).
2. At the *Select objects:* prompt, select the object(s) that you want to array. Press <Enter> to end the selection of objects.
3. At the *Select path curve:* prompt, select the object that you want to use as the path.
4. A preview of the array displays a default number of objects copied along a path, as shown in Figure 11–40. It also displays grips that enable you to modify the array.

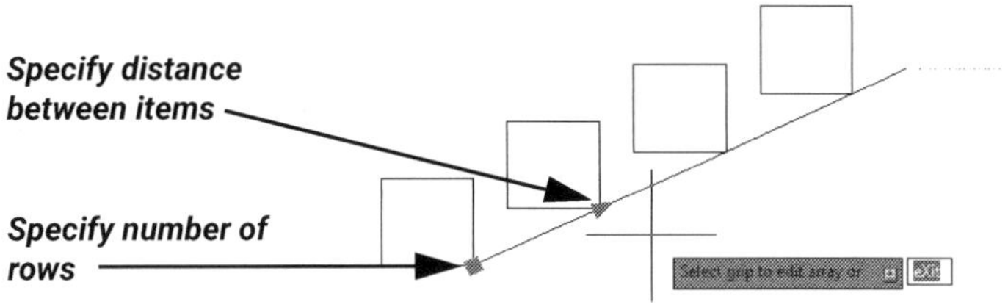

Figure 11–40

5. Specify the number of items in the array by selecting the square grip (as shown in Figure 11–40), typing a value, and pressing <Enter>.
6. Specify the distance between the items along the path by selecting the arrow grip (as shown in Figure 11–40), typing a value, and pressing <Enter>. You can also select the grip and drag the cursor to change the value.
7. Press <Enter> to complete the command.
   - When using the path array, you might want to place the arrayed object in its final orientation and position. You need to place it near the start point of the path. Otherwise, you need to use the **Orientation** option to indicate how the object is to be oriented and positioned along the path.
   - You can use the **Method** option, with its **Divide** option to evenly space the objects along the path.

Modifying Arrays

After an associative array has been created, you can modify their items individually.

- To remove an individual item from the array, click on the array to display its grip and the *Array* contextual tab. Press and hold <Ctrl> and select the required item in the array group, as shown on left in Figure 11–41. Press <Delete> to remove the item. Click on the array and note that it is still associative, as shown on the right in Figure 11–41.

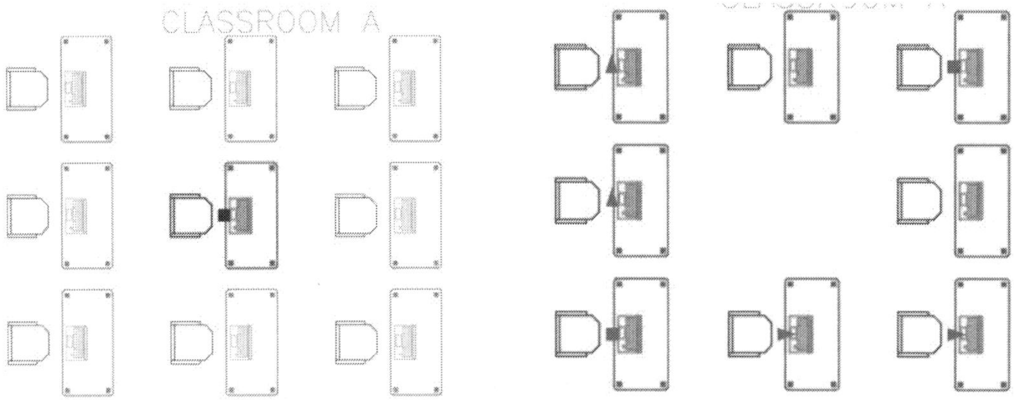

Figure 11–41

- To replace an item in the array with another separate item, click on an array to display its grip and the *Array* contextual tab, as shown in Figure 11–42. Note that the *Array* contextual tab contains additional options than the *Array Creation* contextual tab that is displayed while creating an array. Select  (Replace Item) in the *Array* contextual tab, as shown in Figure 11–42.

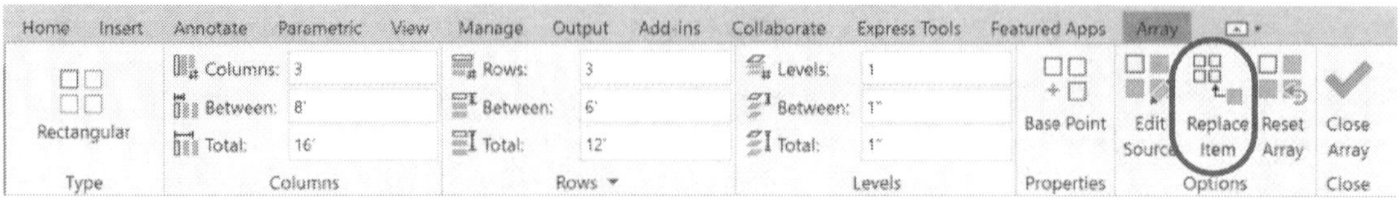

Figure 11–42

  - Select the replacement object and its base point, as shown on the top in Figure 11–43. Select the item in the array to be replaced, as shown on the bottom in Figure 11–43. Press <Enter> and select **eXit** in the drop-down list to complete the command.

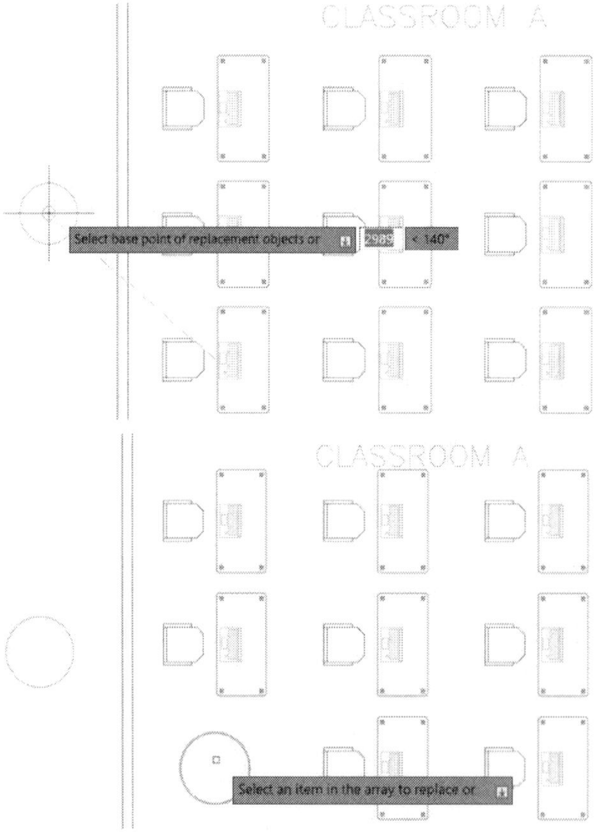

Figure 11–43

Practice 11h
Rectangular Array

Practice Objective

- Make copies of objects at fixed intervals of rows and columns.

In this practice, you will use a **Rectangular Array** to make copies of a workstation in a classroom, as shown in Figure 11–44. (You will create the array using grips.)

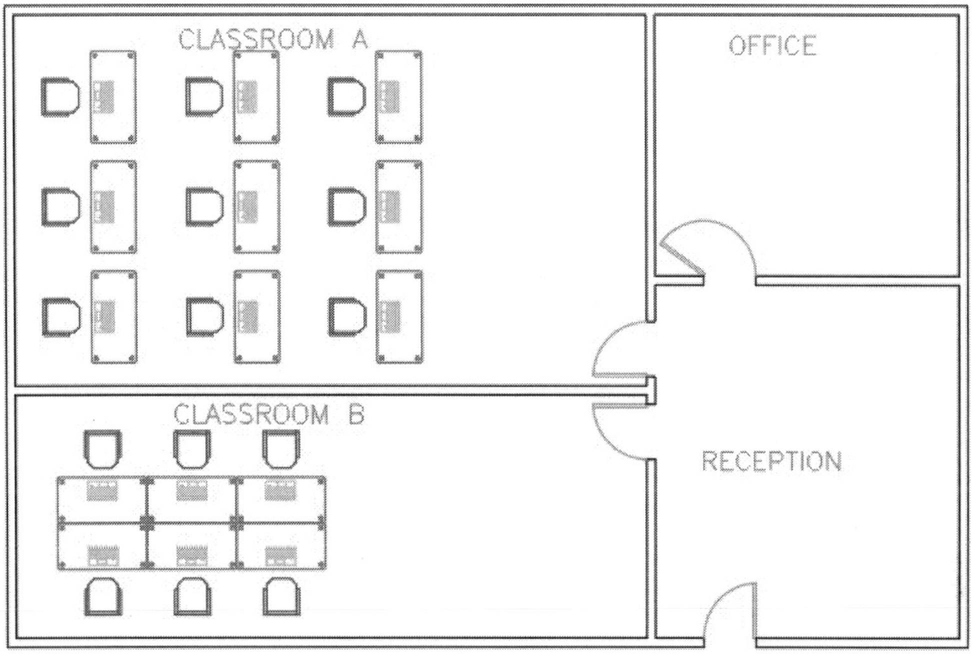

Figure 11–44

1. Open **Class3-A.dwg** from your practice files folder.
2. In the *Home* tab>*Modify* panel, expand the *Array* flyout and select (Rectangular Array).
3. At the *Select objects:* prompt, select the desk, chair, and laptop in Classroom A and press <Enter>.
   - You can use the window or crossing selection to select the three objects.

   Note: *You can use the Array Creation contextual tab instead of grips to enter the values used in Steps 4, 5, and 6.*

4. At the *Select grip to edit array*, select the top-right corner grip (square grip) and enter **3**, as shown in Figure 11–45. Press <Enter>.
   - The top right square grip specifies the number of rows and columns.

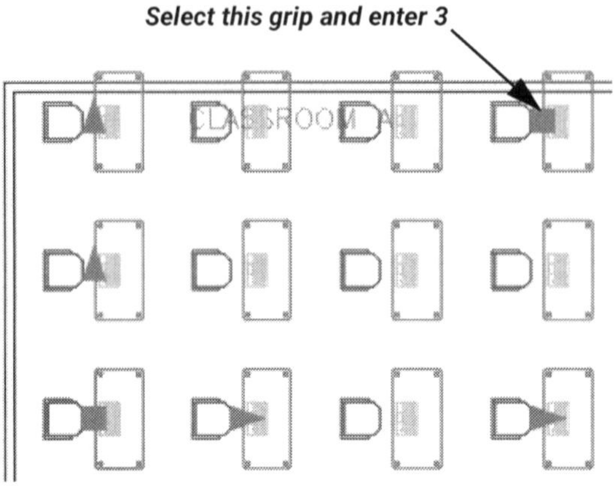

Figure 11–45

5. Select the middle grip along the left side (upward-pointing arrow grip) and verify that **ROW SPACING** displays at the cursor prompt. Enter **6'**, as shown on the left in Figure 11–46. Press <Enter>. (In the ribbon, in the *Array Creation* contextual tab>*Rows* panel>**Between** edit box.)
   - The middle left arrow grip specifies the row spacing.
6. Select the middle grip along the bottom (right-pointing arrow grip) and verify that **COLUMN SPACING** displays at the cursor prompt. Enter **8'**, as shown on the right in Figure 11–46. Press <Enter>. (In the ribbon, in the *Array Creation* contextual tab>*Columns* panel>**Between** edit box.)
   - The middle bottom arrow grip specifies the column spacing.

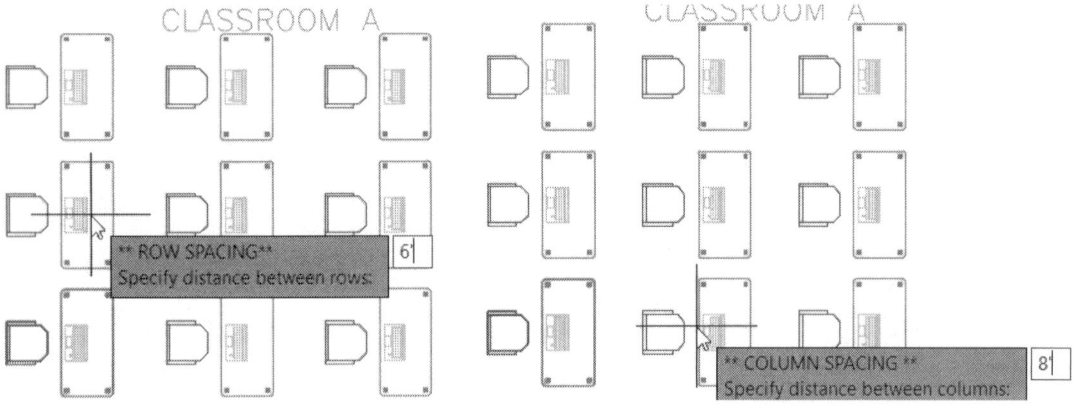

Figure 11–46

7. Press <Enter> to exit the command.
8. Save and close the file.

End of practice

Practice 11i
Polar Array

Practice Objective

- Make copies of an object around a center point.

In this practice, you will use **Polar Array** to make copies of the nut around the flange, as shown in Figure 11–47.

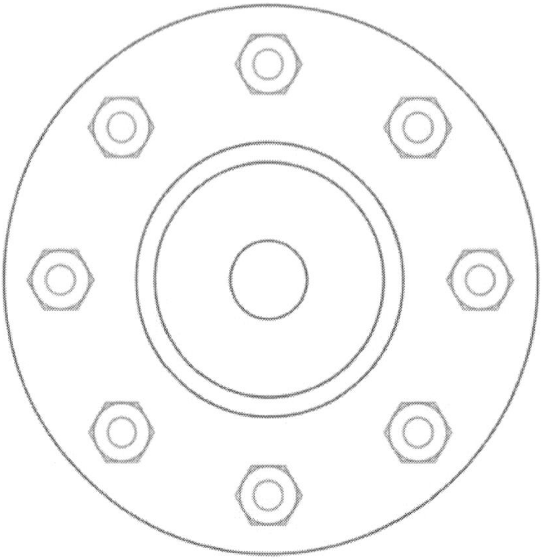

Figure 11–47

1. Open **Flange-I.dwg** from your practice files folder.
2. Select the **Center** object snap option and verify that **Object Snap** is toggled on in the Status Bar.
3. In the *Home* tab>*Modify* panel>*Array* flyout, click  (Polar Array).
4. At the *Select objects:* prompt, select the nut. Press <Enter> to finish selecting objects.
5. At the *Specify center point of array:* prompt, select the center of any circle.

6. Note that the *Array Creation* contextual tab displays in the ribbon. In the *Items* panel, for *Items*, enter **8** and press <Enter>. Note that the *Between* angle value changes to 45 so that it accommodates the specified number of items, as shown in Figure 11–48. Note how the nuts are rotated around the center of the circles.

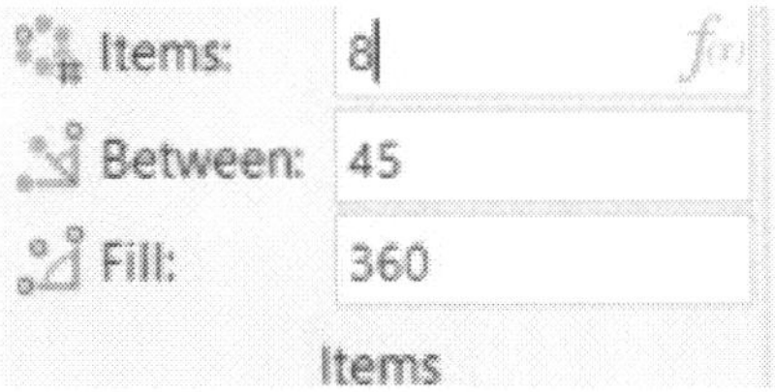

Figure 11–48

7. In the preview of the array, note that the nuts are rotated in different directions and are not oriented correctly. In the *Array Creation* contextual tab>*Properties* panel, click (Rotate Items) to clear it. Note that the nuts are correctly oriented around the flange.
8. Press <Enter> or click (Close Array) to complete the command.
9. Save and close the file.

End of practice

Practice 11j
Path Array

Practice Objective

- Make copies of an object along a selected path.

In this practice, you will use a **Path Array** to make copies of a deck chair around the edge of a pool, as shown in Figure 11–49.

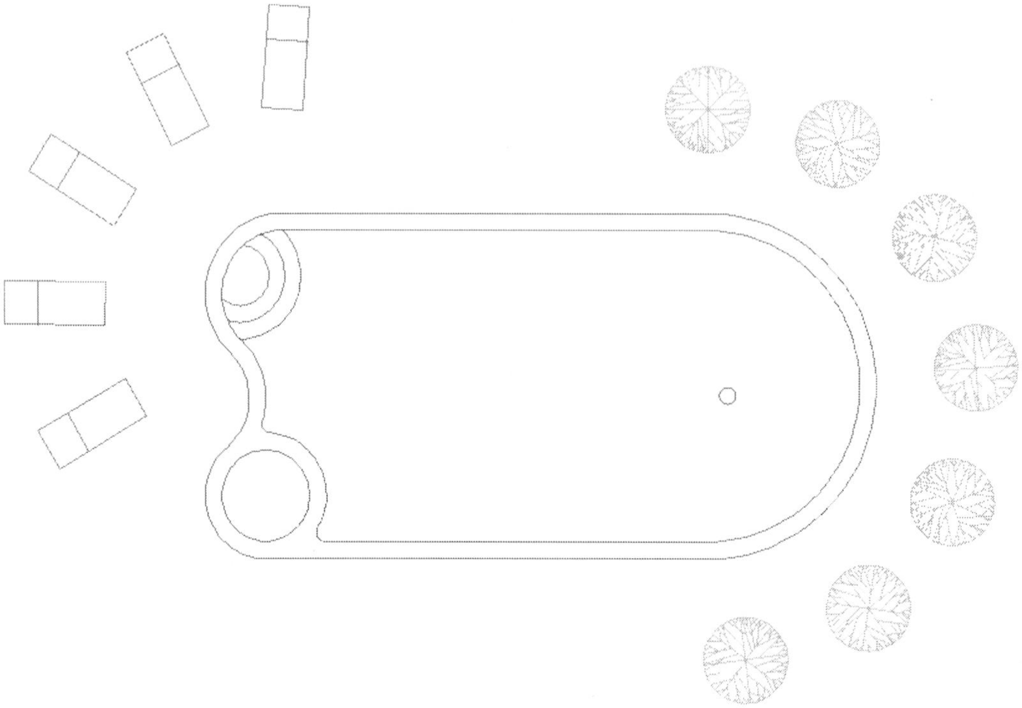

Figure 11–49

1. Open **Deckchair-I.dwg** from your practice files folder.
2. In the *Home* tab>*Modify* panel>*Array* flyout, click (Path Array).
3. At the *Select objects:* prompt, select the tree near the top right of the pool. Press <Enter> to finish selecting objects.
4. At the *Select path curve:* prompt, select the magenta arc that starts at the tree.

5. Note in the *Array Creation* contextual, in the *Items* panel, the **Items** are displayed as **7** which is the correct number, but the trees do not cover the arc fully. In the Items panel, for *Between* enter **8'** (as shown in Figure 11–50) and press <Enter>. Note how the 7 trees space out to cover the arc completely.

Figure 11–50

6. Press <Enter> again to exit the command.
7. Start the **Path Array** command again.
8. At the *Select objects:* prompt, select the chair to the left of the pool. (Select both the rectangle and the line that makes up the chair.) Press <Enter> to finish selecting objects.
9. At the *Select path curve:* prompt, select the magenta arc that starts at the chair. Note that 3 chairs (Items: 3) are placed along the arc.
10. In the *Array Creation* contextual tab, in the *Properties* panel, expand the *Measure* flyout and click  (Divide). The chairs are now evenly spaced along the path.
11. In the *Array Creation* contextual tab>*Items* panel, in the *Items* field, enter **5** (as shown in Figure 11–51), and then press <Enter>. Note that there are now 5 chairs that are placed along the path at an equal distance from each other.

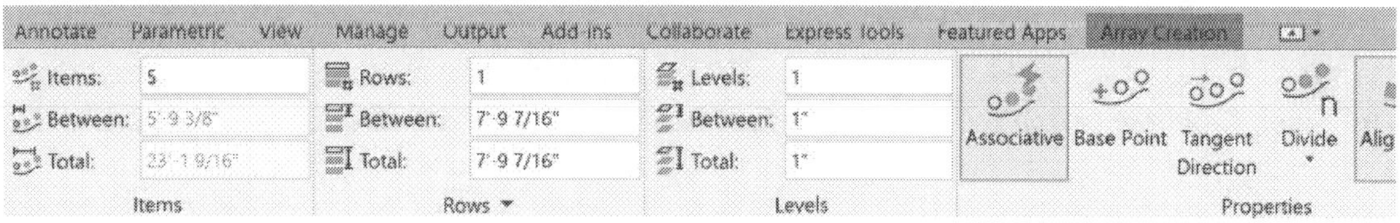

Figure 11–51

12. Press <Enter> to end the command.
13. Toggle off the layer **Path** to hide the paths that were used to create the arrays.
14. Save and close the file.

End of practice

Chapter Review Questions

1. By default, which of the following methods can be used for selecting objects to be trimmed or extended? (Select all that apply.)
   a. Two point fence selection
   b. Window selection
   c. Lasso selection
   d. Freehand selection

2. What method do you use for selecting objects to **Stretch**?
   a. Any selection method
   b. Window selection
   c. Crossing selection
   d. Pick individual objects

3. Which of the following objects cannot be stretched? (Select all that apply.)
   a. Circles
   b. Rectangles
   c. Blocks
   d. Polygons

4. Which **Chamfer** option creates beveled edges at all of the vertices of a selected polyline?
   a. Angle
   b. Multiple
   c. Method
   d. Polyline

5. What do you need to set before you apply a fillet in your drawing?
   a. Distance
   b. Radius
   c. Angle
   d. Thickness

6. You can fillet two parallel lines to add an arc tangent to both lines.
   a. True
   b. False

7. Which command would you use to array a number of trees around an irregularly-shaped pond?
   a. Polar Array
   b. Path Array
   c. Spline Array
   d. Rectangular Array

8. Which of the following commands creates parallel objects of the selected objects?
   a. Fillet
   b. Mirror
   c. Offset
   d. Extend

Command Summary

Button	Command	Location
	**Break**	• **Ribbon:** *Home* tab>expanded *Modify* panel • **Command Prompt:** break
	**Break at Point**	• **Ribbon:** *Home* tab>expanded *Modify* panel • **Command Prompt:** break
	**Chamfer**	• **Ribbon:** *Home* tab>*Modify* panel>expand *Trim* and select **Chamfer** • **Command Prompt:** chamfer or CHA
	**Extend**	• **Ribbon:** *Home* tab>*Modify* panel • **Command Prompt:** extend or EX
	**Fillet**	• **Ribbon:** *Home* tab>*Modify* panel • **Command Prompt:** fillet or F
	**Offset**	• **Ribbon:** *Home* tab>*Modify* panel • **Command Prompt:** offset or O
	**Path Array**	• **Ribbon:** *Home* tab>*Modify* panel (*expanded Array drop-down list*) • **Command Prompt:** arraypath
	**Polar Array**	• **Ribbon:** *Home* tab>*Modify* panel (*expanded Array drop-down list*) • **Command Prompt:** arraypolar
	**Rectangular Array**	• **Ribbon:** *Home* tab>*Modify* panel (*expanded Array drop-down list*) • **Command Prompt:** arrayrect
	**Stretch**	• **Ribbon:** *Home* tab>*Modify* panel • **Command Prompt:** stretch or S
	**Trim**	• **Ribbon:** *Home* tab>*Modify* panel • **Command Prompt:** trim or TR

Chapter 12

Introduction to Blocks

In this chapter, you are introduced to blocks and dynamic blocks, and how to insert them using the *Insert* gallery, the *Blocks* palette, *Tool Palettes*, and *DesignCenter*.

Learning Objectives

- Convert a group of objects into a single block.
- Add blocks to a drawing and modify dynamic blocks.
- Insert blocks using various tools.

12.1 What Are Blocks?

A group of objects can be converted into a single symbol or block. Blocks can be anything from furniture (as shown in Figure 12–1) to schematic symbols, to entire drawings, such as a roof detail. Different types of drawings use different blocks. For example, architects need blocks, such as doors, windows, and roof sections. Mechanical designers would have a stock of nuts, bolts, and reusable parts.

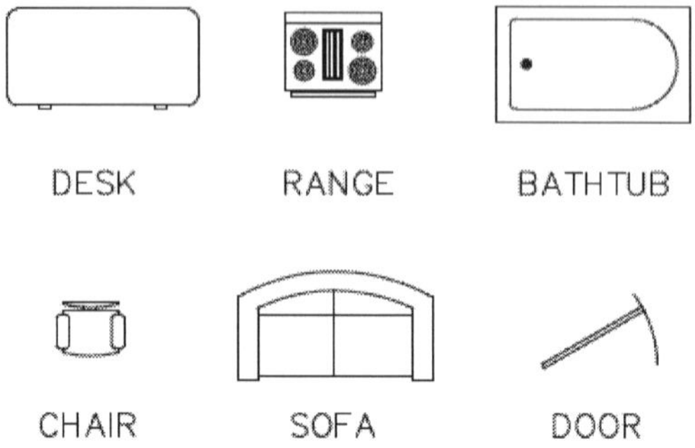

Figure 12–1

The benefits of using blocks in the AutoCAD software:

- Ease of manipulating the blocks in a drawing, since they are unified objects. Some blocks, called *dynamic blocks*, are designed so that you can adjust their size or other features after inserting them.
- Consistency of standard details or parts.
- Reduced file size, since each instance of the block in a drawing refers to a single block definition.

The block creation commands are located in the *Insert* tab>*Block Definition* panel.

- (Create Block) creates a local block which is saved in the current drawing and can be reused multiple times in the same drawing.
- (Create Block) is also available in the *Home* tab>Block panel.
- (Write Block) creates a global block that is saved as a drawing file to be used in other drawings as well.
- There are several ways to insert a block, such as the *Insert* gallery, the *Blocks* palette, *Tool Palettes*, and *DesignCenter*.

Creating Simple Blocks

The **Create Block** command converts a group of selected objects into a single named object that belongs to the current drawing.

How To: Create a Block

1. Draw the objects that you want to include in a block.
2. In the *Insert* tab>*Block Definition* panel or in the *Home* tab>*Block* panel, click  (Create Block).
3. In the *Block Definition* dialog box (shown in Figure 12–2), specify the *Name*, *Base point*, *Objects*, *Behavior*, *Settings*, and *Description*.

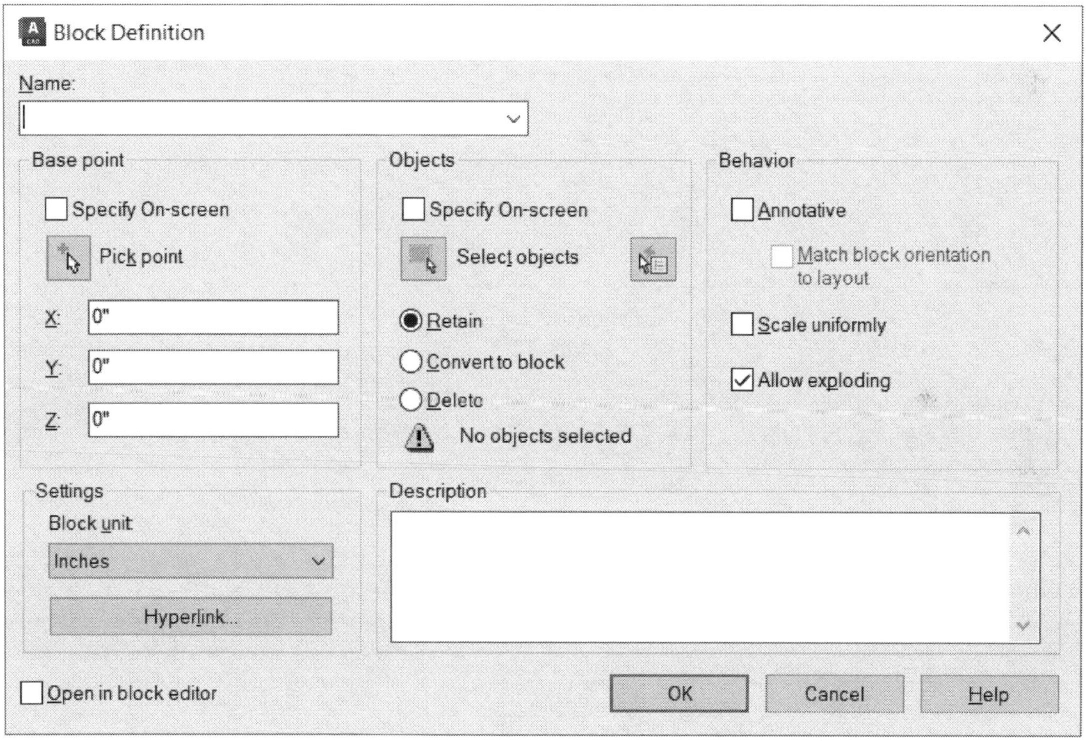

Figure 12–2

4. Click **OK**.

- The block is saved in the drawing and is listed in the *Insert* gallery and the *Blocks* palette.

Hint: Blocks and Layers

When you insert a block, the insertion point is always placed on the current layer. The way the block was created determines whether the block objects use the properties of the current layer, or have a layer or layers that are already associated with objects in the block. Block objects created on layer **0** use the properties of the current layer. Block objects created on other layers use the properties of those layers, no matter which layer is current when the block is inserted.

While there is no absolute standard for how blocks are created, you are most likely to use multilayer compound blocks. For example, you might create a detail that includes hatching, text and the objects, as shown in Figure 12–3. These blocks should be inserted on layer **0**.

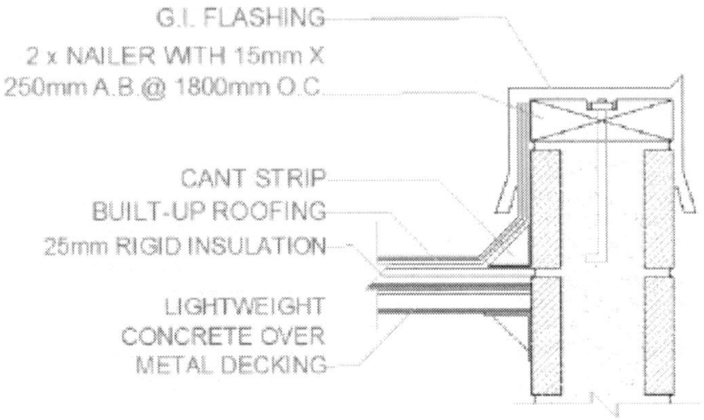

Figure 12–3

Simple blocks, such as a symbol or screw (as shown in Figure 12–4), are more likely to be created on layer **0** and inserted on the required layer.

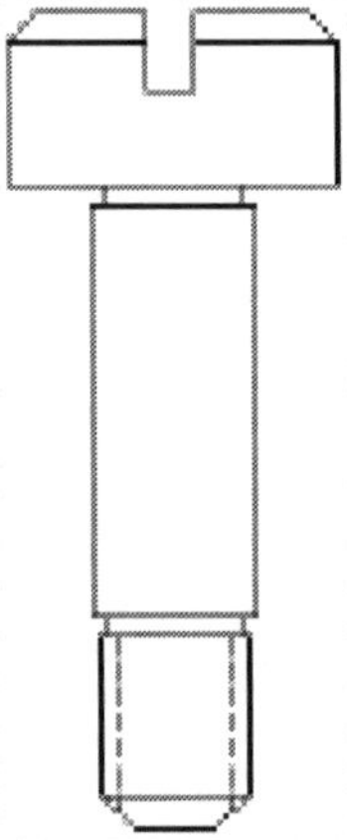

Figure 12–4

Practice 12a
Create Simple Blocks

Practice Objective

- Create a local block.

In this practice, you will define a block for a desk using the **Create Block** command.

Task 1: Create a local block.

In this task, you will create a simple block for a table, first drawing the objects shown in Figure 12–5, and then using the **Create Block** command.

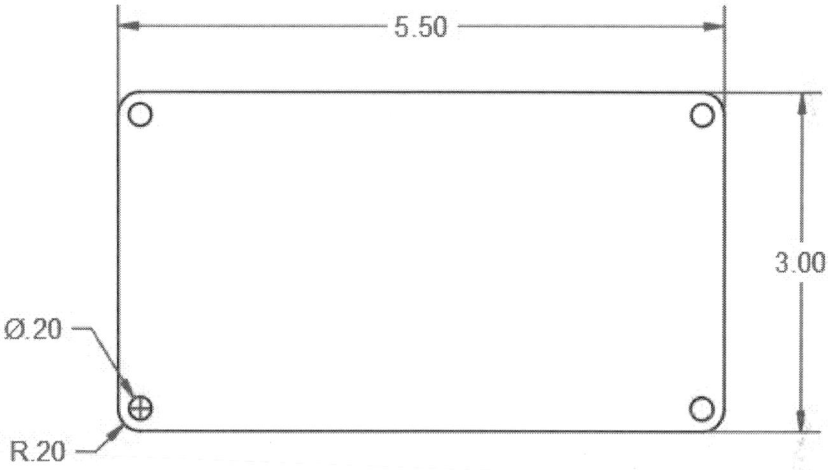

Figure 12–5

1. Open **Block.dwg** from your practice files folder. It is a blank drawing.
2. Draw the block for the table as shown in Figure 12–5. Using the **PLine** command, draw a rectangular shape of **5.50 x 3.00** unitsunits.
3. Start the **Fillet** command. Enter **R** to start the *Radius* option and enter **0.20**. Use the <Down Arrow> menu to select the **Polyline** option and select the polyline of the table. All four corners of the table are filleted.
4. Draw one of the circles with a diameter of **0.20 (radius 0.10)** such that its center is at the center of the fillet. Copy the circle to the other three corners (centered to the fillet).
5. In the *Insert* tab>*Block Definition* panel or in the *Home* tab>*Block* panel, click (Create Block). In the *Block Definition* dialog box, name the block **Table**.

6. In the *Base point* area, click  (Pick point). Select the geometric center of the table as the base point. (Select **Geometric Center** in the Osnap menu and toggle the **OSNAP** on in the *Status Bar*.)

7. In the *Objects* area, click  (Select objects), select all of the objects, and press <Enter>. Select the **Delete** option, as shown in Figure 12–6.
8. Ensure that *Block unit* is set to **Inches**, as shown in Figure 12–6.
9. Ensure that **Open in block editor** is NOT selected, as shown in Figure 12–6.

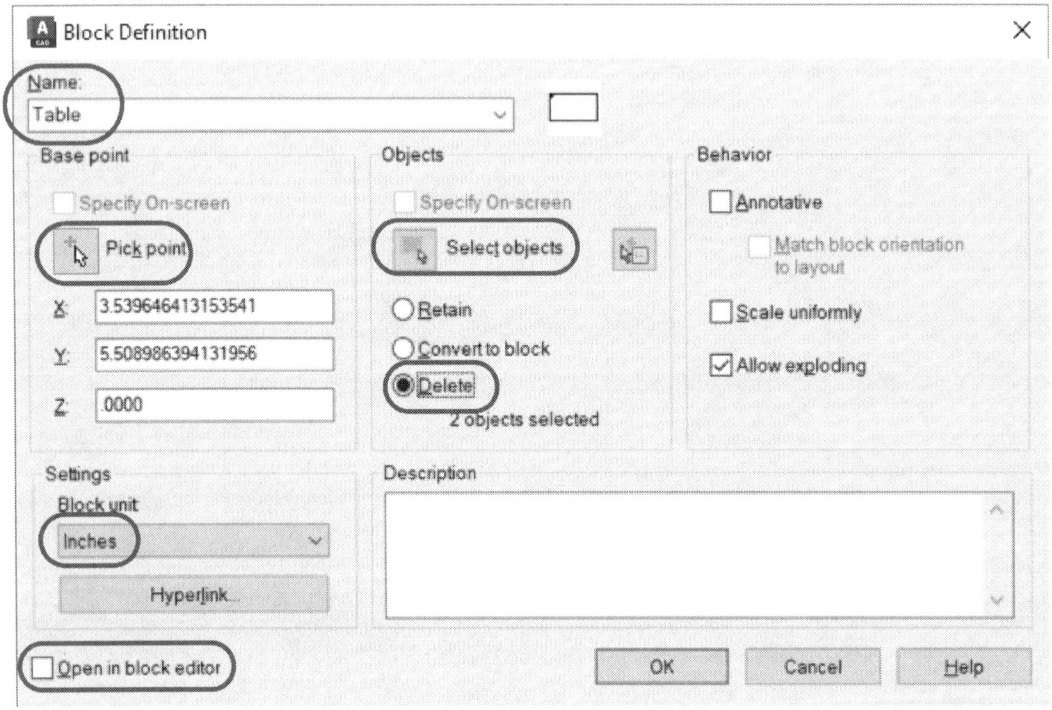

Figure 12–6

10. Click **OK**. The block is created and objects are deleted from the active drawing.

11. In the *Insert* tab>*Block* panel, expand  (Insert Block) and note that the block **Table** is saved in the *Insert* gallery. The block is also saved in the *Blocks* palette, which is an extended version of the gallery.
12. Save and close the drawing.

End of practice

12.2 Inserting Blocks Using the Blocks Palette

Once the block has been created, it can be reused in the drawing. A defined block is saved in the *Insert* gallery and the *Blocks* palette. All the other blocks in the current drawing are also listed in the *Insert* gallery and in the *Blocks* palette and can be quickly inserted into the current drawing. While inserting a block, you are required to specify the insertion point, scale, and rotation.

Insert Gallery

In the *Insert* tab>*Block* panel, when you expand the *Insert* gallery, the list of blocks present in the current drawing are displayed, as shown in Figure 12–7.

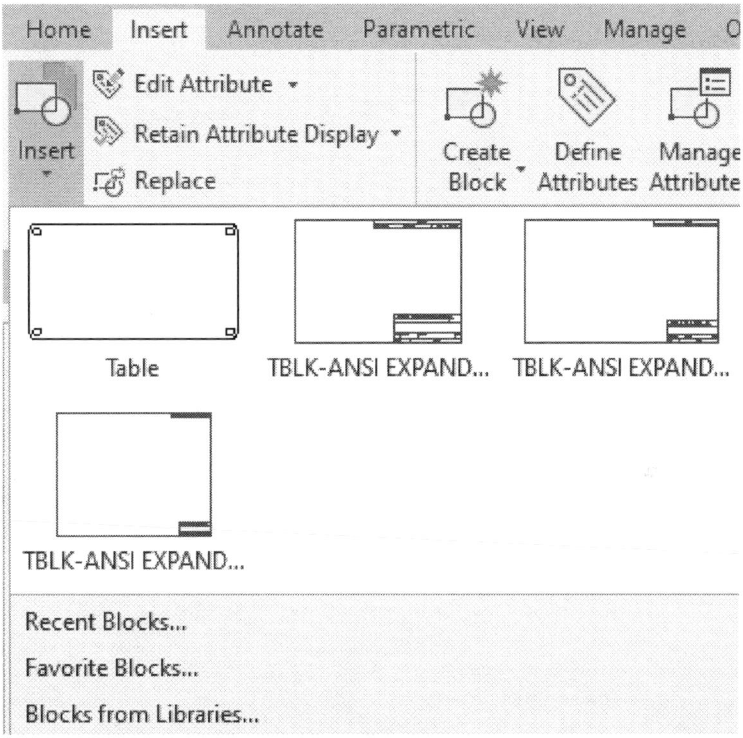

Figure 12–7

How To: Insert a Block from the Gallery

1. In the *Home* tab>*Block* panel or *Insert* tab>*Block* panel, expand  (Insert Block) and select a block from the list.

2. In the drawing, either click to place the block at the required location or select one of the insertion options.

- When you click on the block in the gallery, the block image gets attached to the cursor along with the *Specify insertion point:* prompt. You can either click to place the block at the required location or select one of the insertion options (<Down Arrow>), as shown in Figure 12–8.

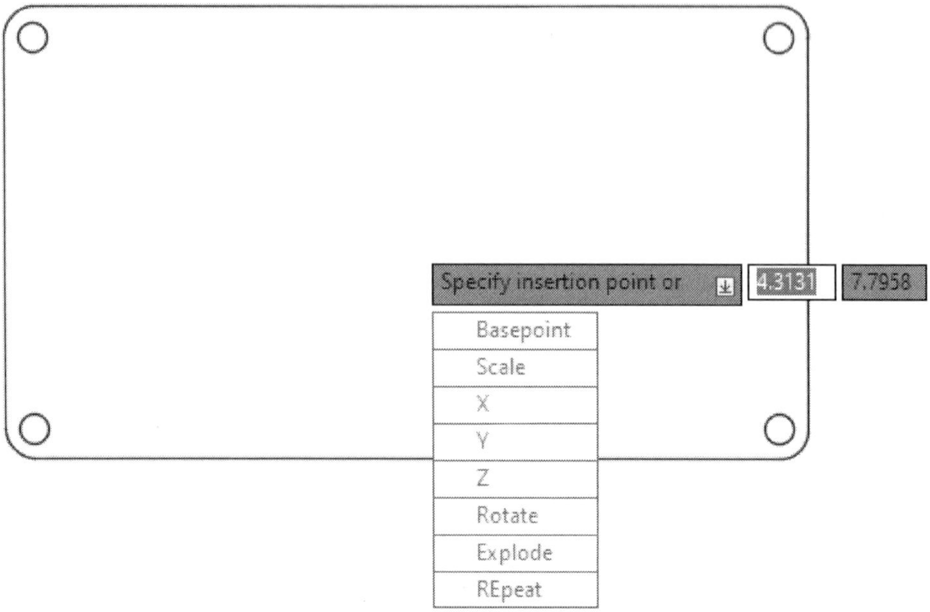

Figure 12–8

- In the *Insert* gallery, **Recent Blocks, Favorite Blocks,** and **Blocks from Libraries** open the *Blocks* palette in their respective tabs.
- The *Insert* gallery and the *Blocks* palette>*Current Drawing* tab displays the same list of blocks.

Blocks Palette

The *Blocks* palette (shown in Figure 12–9) provides you with a convenient and efficient way of inserting blocks and drawings into the current drawing.

- In the *Insert* tab>*Block* panel, expand (Insert) and select the **Recent Blocks, Favorite Blocks**, or **Blocks from Libraries** to open the *Blocks* palette.
- In the *View* tab>*Palettes* panel, click (Blocks) to open the *Blocks* palette.

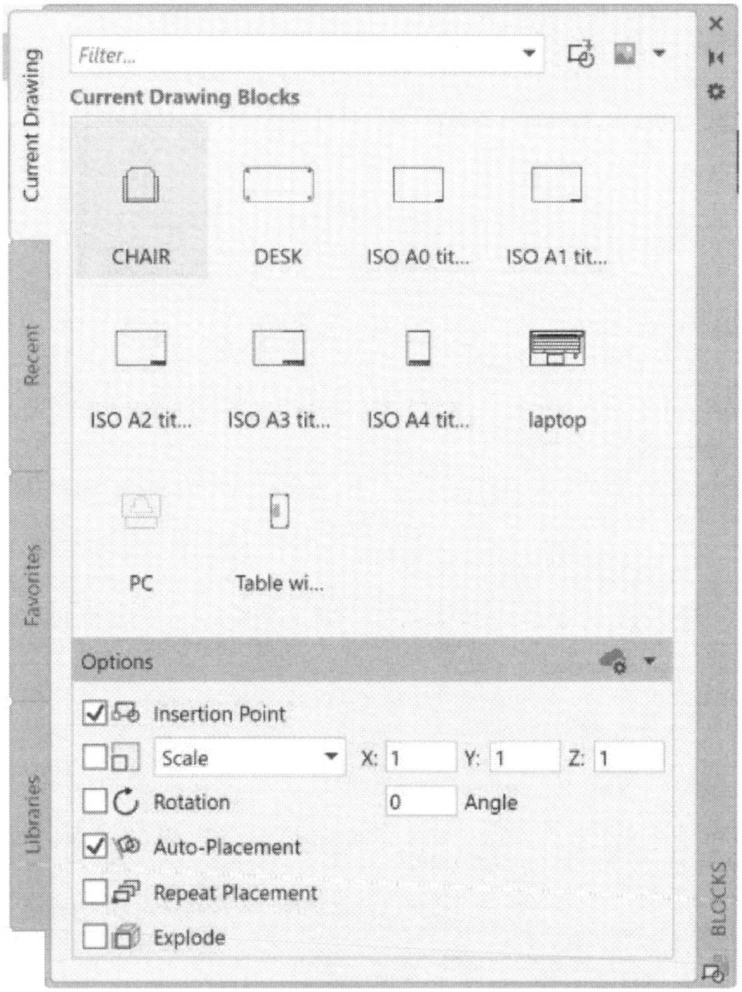

Figure 12–9

The *Blocks* palette contains four tabs:

- ***Current Drawing* tab:** All the blocks in the current drawing are displayed in this tab. It is a replica of the Insert gallery.
- ***Recent* tab:** All the blocks that were inserted recently in the current drawing are displayed in this tab. It includes all the inserted blocks whether they are from the current drawing or inserted from other drawings. The blocks displayed in this tab also include the blocks that were inserted while working in other drawing sessions. To remove a block from this tab, right-click on the block and select **Remove from Recent List**.

- ***Favorites* tab:** You can group your most commonly used blocks in the *Favorites* tab. In any other tab, right-click on the required block, and select **Copy to Favorites**, as shown in Figure 12–10.

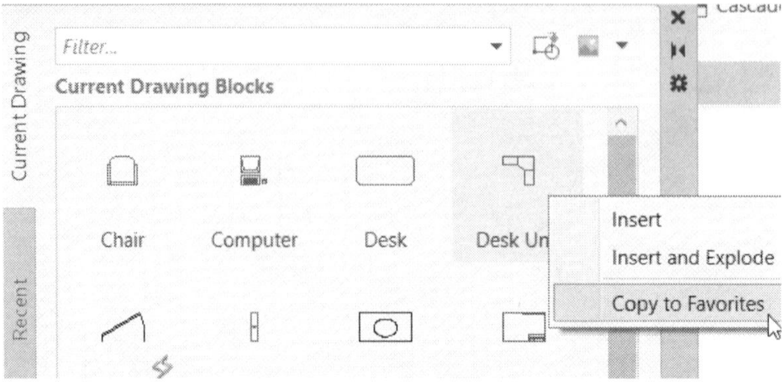

Figure 12–10

- ***Libraries* tab:** You can insert any AutoCAD drawing as a block or insert blocks from other drawings. The file becomes a block in the current drawing and is then listed in the *Libraries* tab. The tab also displays the drawings that were inserted while working in other drawing sessions. You can use the  (navigation tool) near the top right corner of the palette to navigate to the drawing that you want to insert. In addition to a drawing file, you can also insert a folder or any other block definition stored in the drawing. These blocks are listed in the *Libraries* tab.

  When you open the folder from the *Blocks* palette, it brings all the drawings in that folder into the *Libraries* tab to be used as blocks in the current drawing. To save time and to increase work efficiency, you can store all the drawings (which in turn can contain multiple block definitions) together in a folder and then access them at the same time by opening the folder in the *Blocks* palette.

Insertion Options

Along the lower portion of the palette are the Insertion options, and these options remain persistent in all the tabs. These options can be used while inserting the blocks.

- The drag-and-drop method inserts the block without any options. The block is placed where you drop it. Since you do not usually know the precise X,Y coordinates of the *Insertion Point*, you can specify them in the drawing rather than by entering them in the *Blocks* palette.
- If you want to rotate the object before you insert it, enter the rotation angle in the *Rotate* edit box. Click and drop the rotated block.
- Most blocks are correctly scaled for the drawing in which you are inserting them. However, the **Scale**, **X**, **Y**, and **Z** options enable you to change the scale.
- Blocks are normally created at the appropriate size for the drawing and the insertion scale should generally be set to **1**.

- The **Repeat Placement** option enables you to insert multiple blocks in a single step.
- The **Auto-Placement** option provides you with automatic placement points based on similar placements of the blocks that have been previously placed in the drawing. If a block has already been placed in the drawing, while inserting another instance of the same block you are automatically provided with similar placement points in other areas of the drawing. If that is not the required position, you can press <Tab> to switch to other placement options or move the cursor away and select a new position.
- The **Explode** option converts the block into its component parts when it is inserted into the drawing. If you use this option, the block is hidden while you specify its insertion point, scale, and rotation on-screen (you can also explode a block after it has been inserted using the **Explode** command).
- If a block is inserted into a drawing that uses different units, the block is scaled automatically.

How To: Insert a Block from the Blocks palette

1. In the *View* tab>*Palettes* panel, click (Blocks), or in the *Insert* tab>*Block* panel, expand (Insert) to open the gallery. Select **Recent Blocks**, **Favorite Blocks**, or **Blocks from Libraries** to open the *Blocks* palette.
2. In the *Blocks* palette, open the required tab and select the block or the drawing for insertion.
3. Specify the *Insertion Point*, *Scale*, *Rotation*, *Explode*, *Repeat Placement*, and other options as required. You can set these in the *Blocks* palette or on-screen (using the <Down Arrow>).
4. Click **OK**.

Hint: Cloud Accessibility

The *Blocks* palette enables you to store all the blocks that are located in the *Recent* and *Favorites* tabs in a cloud location with a supported cloud storage provider such as Box, Dropbox, One Drive, and Google Drive. By storing the blocks on the cloud, you can now access and use them with Internet-enabled devices anytime and from anywhere. You are required to be signed in to your Autodesk account to allow the application to access your blocks.

Use the Settings icon ( ) in the *Options* area of the *Blocks* palette to open the *Block Sync Settings* dialog box. Here you can select the location on the cloud and manage your sync settings.

Once you save the blocks on the cloud, the Settings icon is replaced by the Cloud icon ( ), indicating that the blocks in the *Recent* and *Favorites* tabs are available on the cloud and can be accessed on devices anytime and from anywhere.

Hint: Blocks and Object Snaps

You can snap to Object snap points (**Endpoint**, **Midpoint**, etc.) on the objects in a block. Additionally, the **Insert** object snap snaps to the insertion base point of a block, as shown in Figure 12–11.

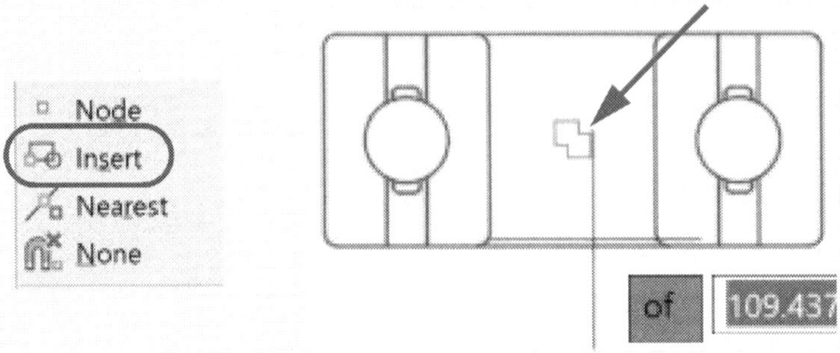

Figure 12–11

12.3 Inserting Blocks Using Tool Palettes

The AutoCAD software comes with many blocks, which are stored in the *Tool Palettes* window (*View* tab>*Palettes* panel> (Tool Palettes) or press <Ctrl>+<3>). After you locate the required block in one of the *Tool Palettes* tabs, you can drag and drop it from the palette into the drawing.

- The AutoCAD software comes with example blocks that are located on several tabs of the palette, as shown in Figure 12–12. You can also create custom palettes.
- In *Tool Palettes,* dynamic blocks are indicated by a lightning bolt symbol, as shown in Figure 12–12.

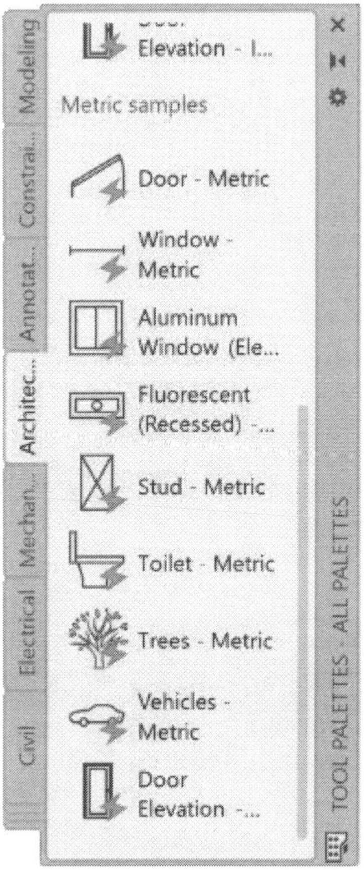

Figure 12–12

- If there are more objects than can fit in the window, a scroll bar displays next to the title bar, enabling you to scroll through the list.

Controlling the Tool Palettes Window

It is useful to display *Tool Palettes* as you are working. For efficient use of screen space, you can dock and hide the palette to one side of the drawing window with either the icon or text displayed. When you need to display the full palette, hover the cursor over the icon (or text depending on your setting), as shown in Figure 12–13. (This process also applies to other palettes, such as the *Properties* and the *Blocks* palettes.)

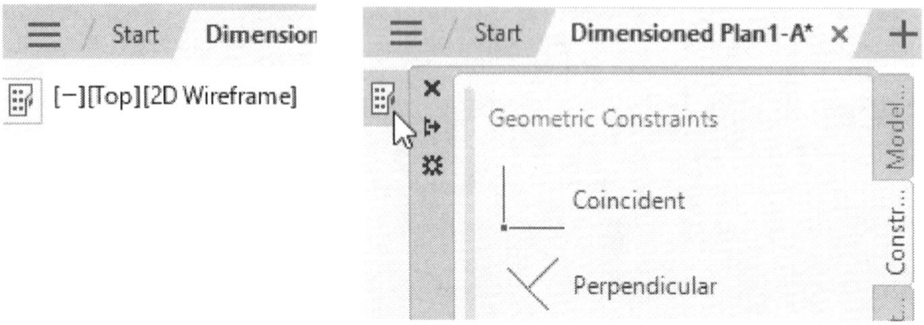

Figure 12–13

How To: Dock and Hide a Palette

1. Open *Tool Palettes*.
2. Place the cursor over the title bar of the palette and drag it to one side of the screen. It should dock. If it does not, right-click on the title bar, select **Allow Docking**, and try again.
   - Right-click on the title bar of an undocked palette, and select **Anchor Left** or **Anchor Right** to dock and auto-hide the palette. (**Allow Docking** must be selected first for anchoring to work.)
3. Minimize the palette by clicking (Auto-hide). The palettes stack if more than one is docked.
4. Move the cursor over the title bar or icon to display the full-size palette.

- When a palette is hidden, right-click on the palette title bar and set the docked view to **Icons only** or **Text only**, as shown in Figure 12–14.

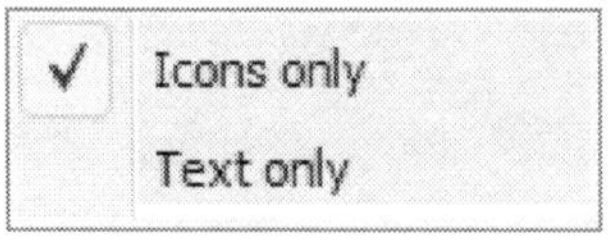

Figure 12–14

12.4 Inserting Dynamic Blocks

Dynamic blocks are special kinds of blocks that can be changed dynamically. Once they are in your drawing, they can be manipulated in a variety of ways, including lengthening a side, flipping the direction, aligning to other objects, rotating, or selecting from a list of options, as shown in Figure 12–15. Dynamic blocks are powerful tools and in many cases, several standard blocks can be replaced by one dynamic block.

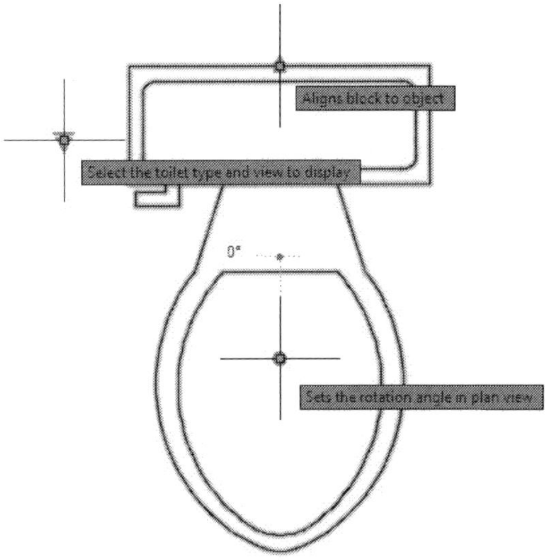

Figure 12–15

Manipulating Dynamic Blocks

When you select a dynamic block, special grips display indicating the types of modifications that are available. Hover the cursor over one of the grips to display its tooltip. Click on the required grip to change the block, as shown in Figure 12–16.

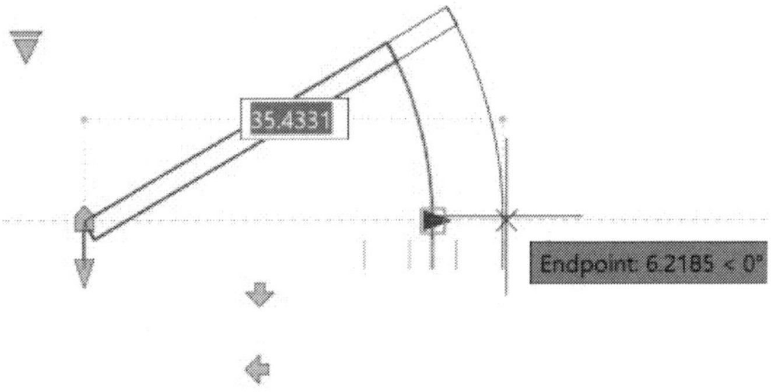

Figure 12–16

- The modification features in dynamic blocks can differ from one block to another. For example, one block might only have the *Lengthen/Shorten* grip, while another might have the *Flip*, *List*, and *Rotate* grips.

Dynamic Block Grips

The available block grips are described as follows.

	**Lengthen/Shorten**	Enables you to scale, stretch, or array a block. The action depends on how the block was defined.
	**List**	Opens a list of options from which to select, such as size, number of items, view displayed, etc.
	**Insert/Move**	Indicates the insertion point of the block and other points that might have been assigned in the block. It can move the entire block or just one entity in the block.
	**Flip**	Flips the entire block in the direction of the arrow.
	**Align**	Aligns the entire block at the angle of an object when you move the block near that object. Use <Tab> to cycle through placement of dynamic blocks to orient it in the required direction.
	**Rotate**	Enables you to rotate the block or specific objects in the block. The objects that rotate are preset in the block definition.

- Blocks that are not dynamic only have an *Insert/Move* grip, which you can use to drag the block to a new location.
- After you have finished modifying the dynamic block, press <Esc> to clear it and its grips from modification.
- Dynamic blocks are indicated by a lightning bolt symbol.

12.5 Inserting Blocks Using DesignCenter

DesignCenter is available to manage your standards. It enables you to access named objects in any drawing to copy them into the current drawing and is also used for inserting blocks. You can have a library of drawings that include typical blocks grouped in a useful order, as shown in Figure 12–17. From *DesignCenter*, you can open the drawing and then drag and drop the blocks into your current drawing.

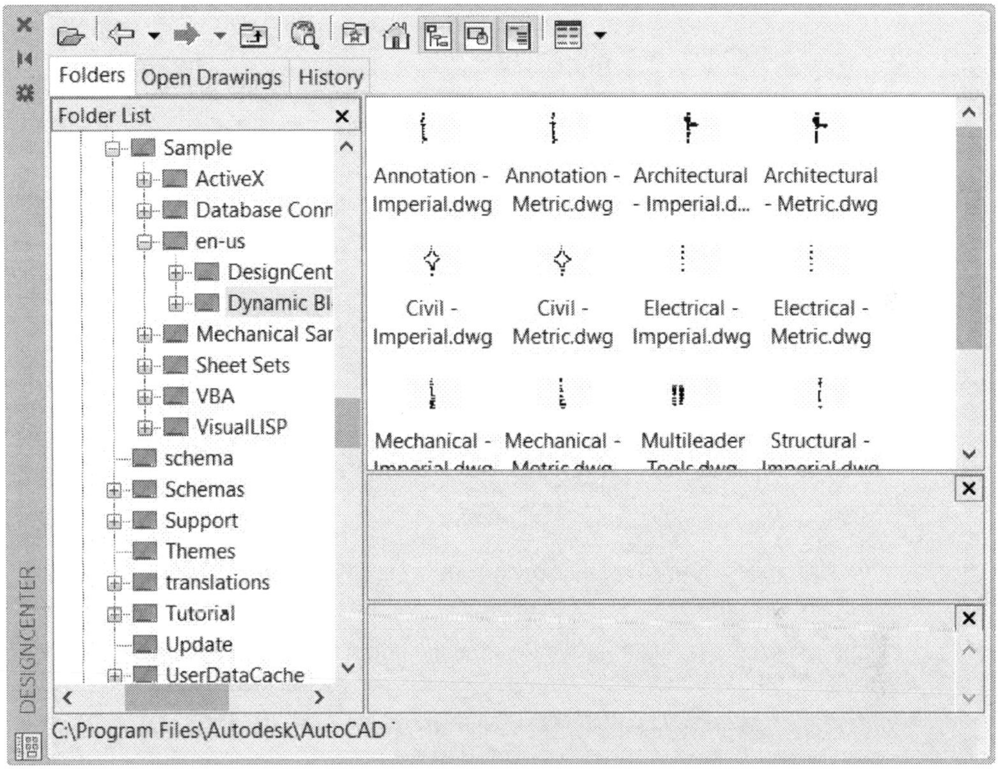

Figure 12–17

- In addition to blocks, you can copy other named objects using *DesignCenter*, including layers, linetypes, layouts, reference files (Xrefs), and text, table, or dimension styles. Open *DesignCenter*, locate the drawing containing the objects you want to use, and drag them into your current drawing.
- You can open *DesignCenter* by clicking (DesignCenter) in the *View* tab>*Palettes* panel.
- Press <Ctrl>+<2> to toggle open or close *DesignCenter*. *DesignCenter* is a palette and can be docked and hidden in the same way as *Tool Palettes* and the *Properties* palette.

DesignCenter Content

Three tabs across the top of *DesignCenter* provide access to different parts of its content. These tabs are:

Folders	Enables you to use the *Folder List* to navigate to drawings on your computer or network drives.
Open Drawings	Provides access to drawing(s) that are open in the AutoCAD software. You can copy components from any of the open drawings into your current drawing window.
History	Lists several of the last drawings used in *DesignCenter*. Double-click on the filename to load the drawing in the *Folders* tab.

Navigation and Display Options

The *DesignCenter* palette contains tools for navigating to drawings and changing the display, as shown in Figure 12–18.

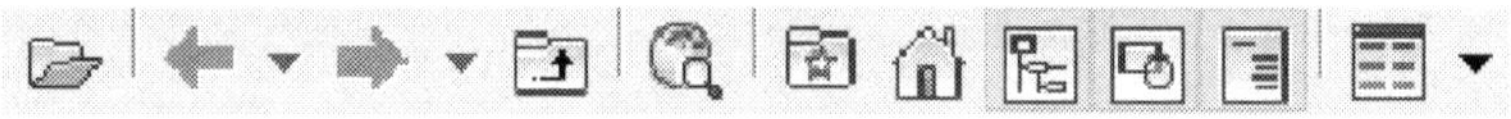

Figure 12–18

	**Load:** Opens the *Load* dialog box. When you select a drawing, it opens in *DesignCenter* without opening in the AutoCAD software.
	**Back/Forward:** Returns to the previous drawing selected. Click to expand the list of the available drawings.
	**Up:** Backs up one folder level each time the button is clicked. Use this if you have toggled off the tree view.
	**Search:** Opens the *Search* dialog box in which you can search for drawings, blocks, layers, etc., by name.
	**Favorites:** Similar to other Windows programs, you can specify favorite places from which to get drawings or web sites. Right-click in *DesignCenter* to add items to your favorites list.
	**Home:** Switches to the *DesignCenter* folder.
	**Tree View Toggle:** Toggles on and off the tree view of the folder structure (on the left side of *DesignCenter*). When the tree view is off, only the components in the folder that you have selected are displayed.
	**Preview:** Displays a preview of the selected block.

	Description: Displays a description of the selected block if one is available.
	Views: Toggles through the various types of views. Use the **Large Icons** option to display a thumbnail image of the blocks.

- Set the drawings or folders that you need to access most often as **Favorites**. Right-click on the file or folder in *DesignCenter* and select **Add to Favorites**. Click (Favorites) in the toolbar for quick access.

Practice 12b
Work with Blocks

Practice Objective

- Add blocks and dynamic blocks using the *Blocks* palette, *Tool Palettes*, and *DesignCenter*.

In this practice, you will add blocks and dynamic blocks using the *Blocks* palette and *Tool Palettes*. You will also add landscaping blocks using *DesignCenter*, as shown in Figure 12–19.

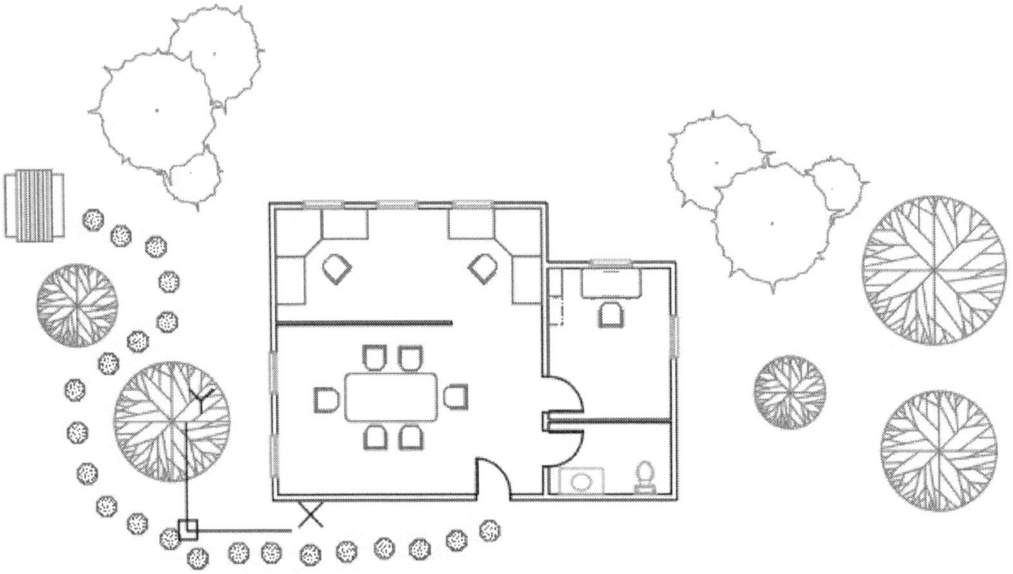

Figure 12–19

Task 1: Insert blocks.

In this task, you will insert blocks in a floor plan, as shown in Figure 12–20. You will use the various tabs and options in the *Blocks* palette. The blocks in this drawing were created on their own layers. You will insert them all on layer **0**.

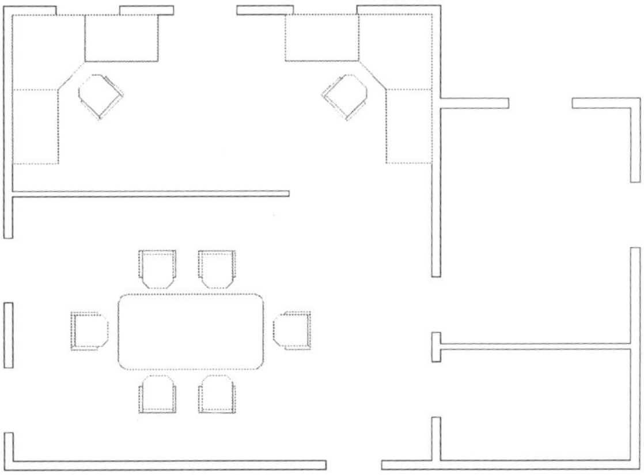

Figure 12–20

1. Open **Plan-A.dwg** from your practice files folder.
2. Select layer **0** in the *Layer* drop-down list.
3. Ensure that (Object Snap) is toggled on and **Endpoint** is selected.
4. In the *Insert* tab>*Block* panel, expand (Insert). In the gallery, select the block named **Desk Unit,** as shown in Figure 12–21.

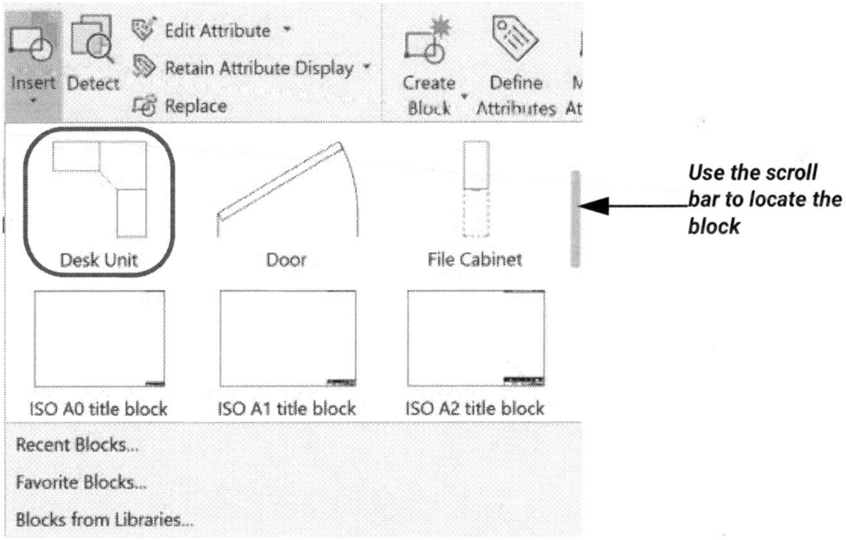

Figure 12–21

5. The desk is attached to the cursor. Type **R** and press <Enter> or use the <Down Arrow> menu to select the **Rotate** option. Ensure that **0** is set for rotation angle, and press <Enter>.
6. Type **X** and press <Enter>. Ensure that **1** is set as the *X* scale factor, and press <Enter>.

7. Similarly, ensure that both for the *Y* and *Z* scale factors are set as **1**.
8. Place the desk in the top right corner of the office, as shown in Figure 12–20.
9. Expand  (Insert) and select **Recent Blocks** in the gallery. Note that the *Blocks* palette opens in the *Recent* tab with the Desk Unit listed there.If the *Block Sync Settings* information box opens, close it.

   Note: *Using the Blocks palette is an efficient way of inserting blocks.*

10. In the *Options* area, select the **Insertion Point**, if required. Set the *Rotation Angle* to **90**, as shown in Figure 12–22. Click on the Desk Unit. In the *Redefine Block* dialog box that opens, select **Don't redefine "Desk Unit"**. Move your cursor and note that the desk is attached to the cursor and is already rotated at 90°. Move it to the top left corner (as shown in Figure 12–22) and click to place it.
    - There might be other blocks in your *Recent Blocks* gallery of your *Blocks* palette.

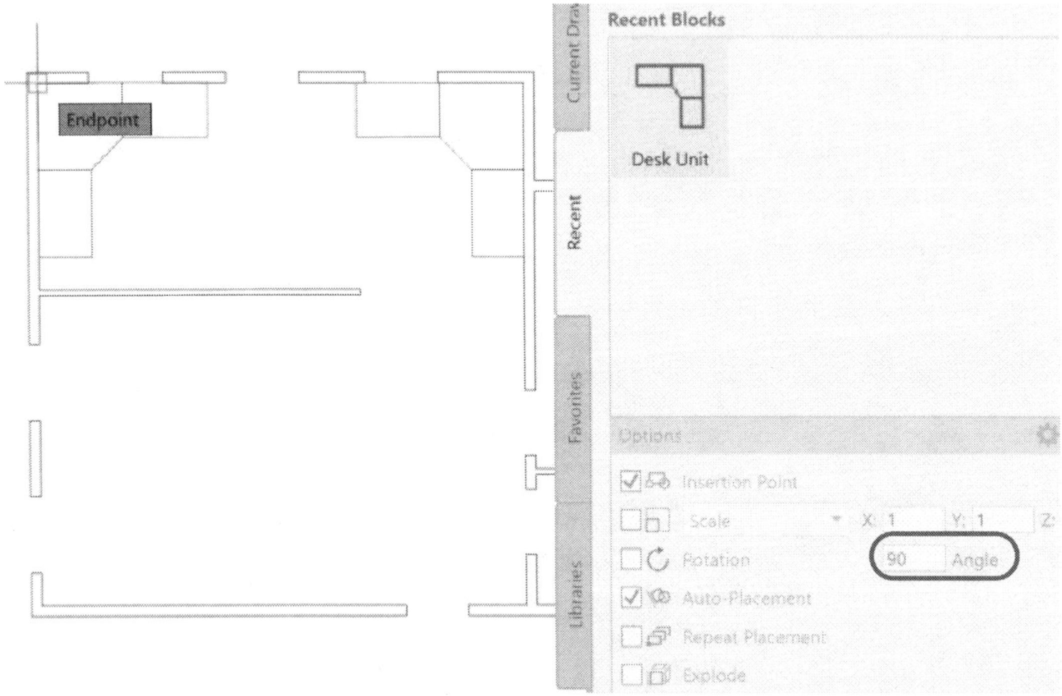

Figure 12–22

11. Click on the *Current Drawing* tab of the *Blocks* palette.
12. Locate the **Chair** block, right-click and select **Copy to Favorites**.

13. Click on the *Favorites* tab and note that the Chair block is listed there. In the *Options* area, set the *Rotation Angle* to **45**. Click on the Chair block. In the *Redefine Block* dialog box that opens, select **Don't redefine "Chair"**. Move your cursor and note that the chair is attached to the cursor and is already rotated at 45°. Place it facing the top left corner Desk Unit.
14. Change the *Rotation Angle* to **-45**. Click and place the Chair facing the top right corner Desk Unit.

    Note: *Use the* ***Don't redefine*** *option whenever the Redefine Block dialog box is displayed.*

15. Click on the *Libraries* tab of the *Blocks* palette.
16. Click the  (navigation tool) which opens the *Select a folder or a file for Block Library* dialog box. Select **Table-A.dwg** (in your practice files folder) and click **Open**. It is listed in the *Libraries* tab.
17. Set the *Rotation Angle* to **0** and select **Table-A** block and place it near the middle of the largest room.
18. Switch to the *Favorites* tab.
19. Click to set the **Repeat Placement** option.
20. Select the block **Chair** and place the chair facing the lower horizontal edge of the table. Note that the block is still attached with the cursor because of the **Repeat Placement** option. Click to place another chair adjacent to the first chair (facing the lower horizontal edge of the table).
21. The block remains attached with the cursor. Click <Down Arrow> and select **Rotate** in the menu. Enter **90** at the *Specify rotation angle* prompt and press <Enter>. Place a chair facing the right vertical edge of the table.
22. Similarly, using the **Rotate** option in the <Down Arrow> menu, insert chairs around the table. Use the rotation angles of **-90** and **180**. Press <Esc> to exit the Block Insertion command.
23. Leave the *Blocks* palette open.

Task 2: Work with dynamic blocks.

In this task, you will add dynamic blocks from *Tool Palettes* to the floor plan and then manipulate them, as shown in Figure 12–23.

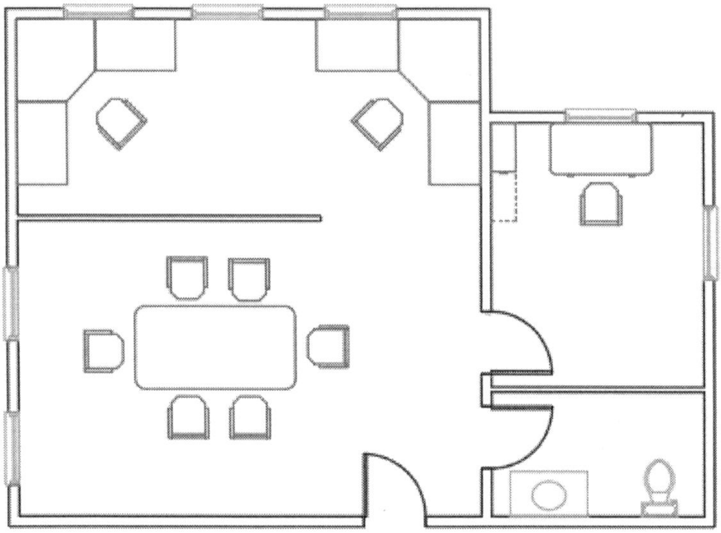

Figure 12–23

1. Zoom in on the opening along the bottom wall of the plan.

2. In the *View* tab>*Palettes* panel, click  (Tool Palettes) to open *Tool Palettes*. Note the types of blocks that are available in the different tabs.

3. In *Tool Palettes*, select the *Architectural* tab and select **Door-Imperial**. Note that it is attached to the cursor. Hover the cursor so that the door snaps to the upper endpoint of the left wall of the opening. If the door snaps vertically, press <Tab> until it aligns horizontally along the wall (as shown in Figure 12–24), and then click to place it. Note that the door does not fit in the opening.

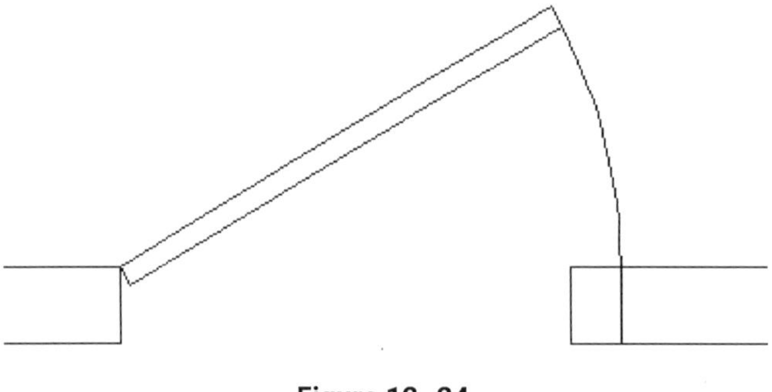

Figure 12–24

4. Select the inserted door to display the grips. Click the (Lengthen) grip at the right end of the door and note the current length (**3'-4"**). Drag the cursor to the left to make the length **3'** (as shown in Figure 12–25), and click to place it at that location.

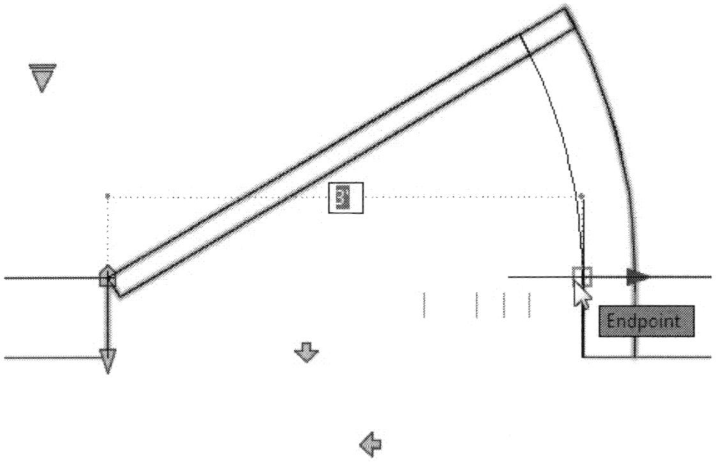

Figure 12–25

5. Click the (List) grip and select **Open 90°**. The door swing changes to this angle. Press <Esc> to clear the door selection.
6. Add doors (**Door-Imperial** in *Tool Palettes*) to the bathroom (smallest room) and the small office, as shown in Figure 12–23. Place one door, rotate it, and resize it using the (Lengthen) grip, as required. Then, copy it to create the other door and flip it using the (Flip) grip.
7. Pan to the smallest room, and then from *Tool Palettes*, click and drop a **Toilet-Imperial** into it. The toilet displays as a front view.
8. Select the toilet to display the grips. Click the (List) grip and select **Elongated (Plan)**. A plan (top) view of the toilet displays.
9. Click the (Align) grip and move the cursor to place the toilet along the bottom wall. It aligns with the wall. Press <Esc> once it is at the correct location.
10. From the *Blocks* palette>*Current Drawing* tab, add a **Sink** along the bottom wall on the left side of the toilet.
11. Move the sink and toilet to the layer **Plumbing**.
12. Set the layer to **Windows**.
13. Add windows using the **Window** block in the *Current Drawing* tab of the *Blocks* palette. Use the **Repeat Placement** option and then use the **Rotate** option in the <Down Arrow> menu with rotation angles of **90** and **-90** to place the windows along the sides of the plan.

14. You can also add a desk, chair, and a file cabinet to the office from the *Blocks* palette.
15. Close *Tool Palettes* and the *Blocks* palette.

Task 3: Insert blocks using DesignCenter.

In this task, you will insert landscaping blocks using *DesignCenter*, as shown in Figure 12–26.

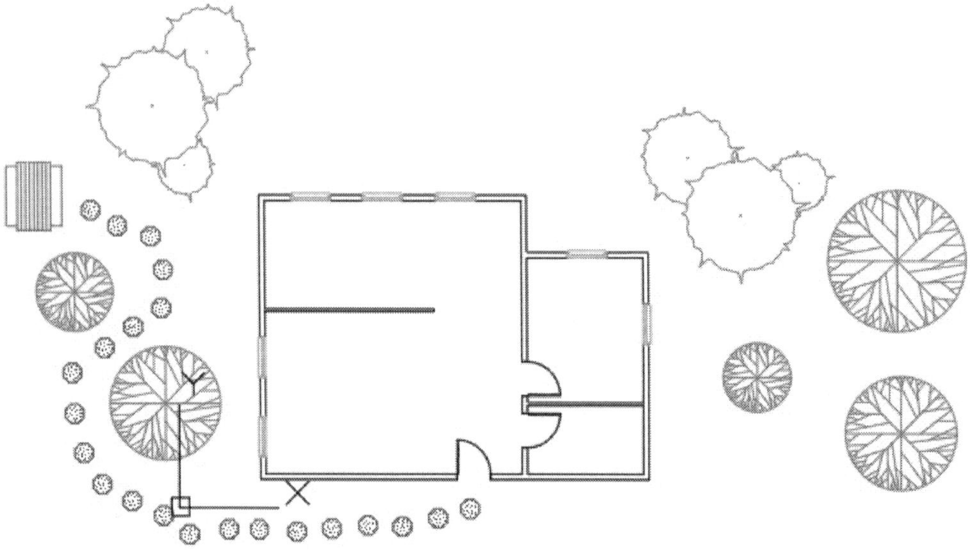

Figure 12–26

1. Toggle off the layers **Furniture** and **Plumbing**.
2. In *Layer Control*, make the layer **Planting** as the current layer.

   Note: *The blocks in DesignCenter are created on layer* ***0***. *Therefore, you need to select the layer on which you want to place them.*

3. Zoom out so that there is room around the outside of the building.
4. In the *View* tab>*Palettes* panel, click (DesignCenter) to open the *DesignCenter* palette.
5. In the *DesignCenter* folder supplied with the AutoCAD software (usually in the *Sample>en-us>DesignCenter* folder), find the file **Landscaping.dwg**. Expand it and select **Blocks** to open it.
6. Drag and drop several **Tree - deciduous** and **Clump of Trees or Bushes** (in plan view) into the drawing. **Move**, **Rotate**, and **Scale** them similar to that shown in Figure 12–26.
7. Set the current layer to **Furniture-Outdoor**. Place a **Picnic Table** similar to that shown in Figure 12–26.
8. Set the current layer to **Hardscape**.

9. Create a path of **Stepping Stone-hexagonal** blocks around the trees, similar to that shown in Figure 12–26.
10. Save and close the drawing.

End of practice

Chapter Review Questions

1. What are some advantages of using blocks? (Select all that apply.)
   a. Consistency of standard details and parts.
   b. Easier to select and manipulate unified objects.
   c. Contains built-in snaps to snap to objects in the drawing.
   d. Reduced file size.

2. Which of the following are tabs in the *Blocks* palette? (Select all that apply.)
   a. Directories
   b. Libraries
   c. Favorites
   d. Folders

3. Using the *Blocks* palette, how can you insert multiple blocks in a single step?
   a. Click on the block and the hold the <Ctrl> key while placing.
   b. Right-click on the block and select **Multiple**.
   c. Use the **Repeat Placement** option.
   d. You cannot insert multiple blocks in a single step.

4. You can use *Tool Palettes* to insert blocks into the drawing by dragging and dropping.
   a. True
   b. False

5. What can you do using *DesignCenter*?
   a. Return a layer to its previous state.
   b. Search for and drag and drop a block into your drawing.
   c. Create template files.
   d. Explode blocks into separate line segments.

6. Some dynamic blocks display the following modification grips:
    a. The grips are the same in every dynamic block.
    b. Explode, Move, and Align.
    c. Explode, List, and Scale.
    d. Flip, Rotate, and List.

Command Summary

Button	Command	Location
	**Blocks Palette**	• **Ribbon:** *View* tab>*Palettes* panel • **Command Prompt:** insert or I
	**Create Block**	• **Ribbon:** *Home* tab>*Block* panel or *Insert* tab>*Block Definition* panel • **Command Prompt:** block
	**DesignCenter**	• **Ribbon:** *View* tab>*Palettes* panel • **Command Prompt:** adcenter (*on*), adcclose (*off*) or <Ctrl>+<2> (*toggle on/off*)
	**Insert (Insert Blocks gallery)**	• **Ribbon:** *Insert* tab>*Block* panel • **Ribbon:** *Home* tab>*Block* panel
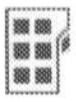	**Tool Palettes**	• **Ribbon:** *View* tab>*Palettes* panel • **Command Prompt:** toolpalettes (*open*), toolpalettesclose or <Ctrl>+<3> (*toggle on/off*)

Chapter 13

Projects: Creating More Complex Objects

This chapter contains practice projects that can be used to gain additional hands-on experience in the topics and commands covered so far in this guide. These projects are intended to be self-guided and do not include step-by-step information.

Learning Objectives

- *Mechanical:* Create several machine parts using draw commands along with advanced editing tools such as, chamfers, fillets, offsets, and arrays.
- *Architectural:* Create floor plans using draw commands along with advanced editing tools and insert blocks.
- *Civil:* Create a parking lot using draw commands along with advanced editing tools and insert blocks.

13.1 Mechanical Project 1: Plate

In this project, you will construct a mechanical plate, as shown in Figure 13–1. Commands you can use include **Line**, **Offset**, **Circle**, **Trim**, **Fillet**, and **Chamfer**. Dimensions are for reference only.

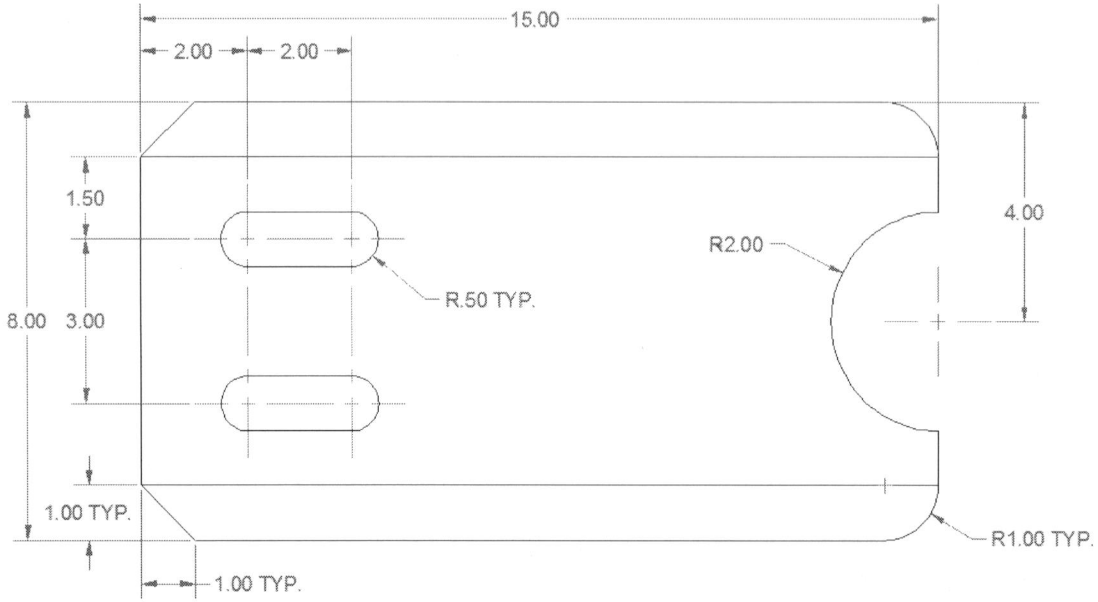

Figure 13–1

1. Start a new drawing called **Plate1.dwg** based on **Mech-Inches.dwt**, which is located in your practice files folder.
2. Draw the object shown in Figure 13–1. Commands you can use to construct the object include **Line**, **Offset**, **Circle**, **Trim**, **Fillet**, **Chamfer**, and **Copy**.
   - Tip: To locate the slots, you can offset the lines from the side and top of the object to locate the center points of the **R0.50** arcs. Draw one slot and copy it to the required location. Delete the offset lines.

13.2 Mechanical Project 2: Gasket

In this project, you will draw a gasket, as shown in Figure 13–2, using commands such as **Circle**, **Array**, **Trim**, and **Fillet**. Dimensions are for reference only.

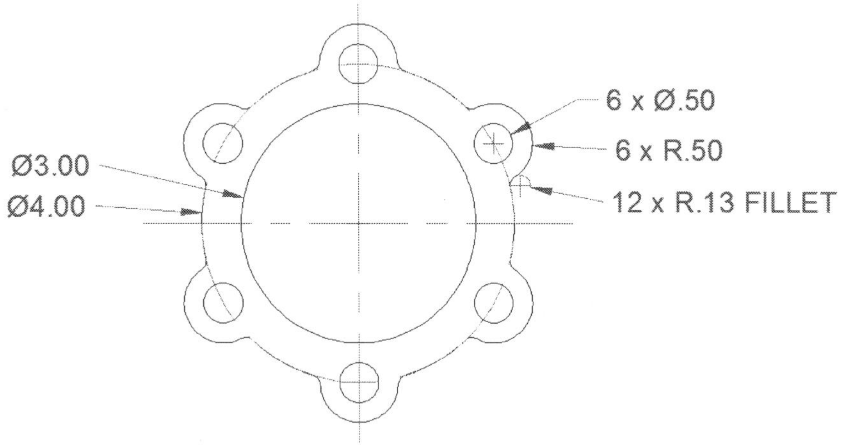

Figure 13–2

1. Start a new drawing called **Gasket.dwg** based on **Mech-Inches.dwt**, which is located in your practice files folder.
2. Draw the object shown in Figure 13–2. Commands you should use to construct the object include **Circle**, **Polar Array**, **Trim**, and **Fillet**.

13.3 Mechanical Project 3: Plate

In this project, you will draw a plate with slots and holes, as shown in Figure 13–3. Commands you can use to construct the object include **Line**, **Offset**, **Circle**, **Mirror**, **Trim**, and **Array**. Dimensions are for reference only.

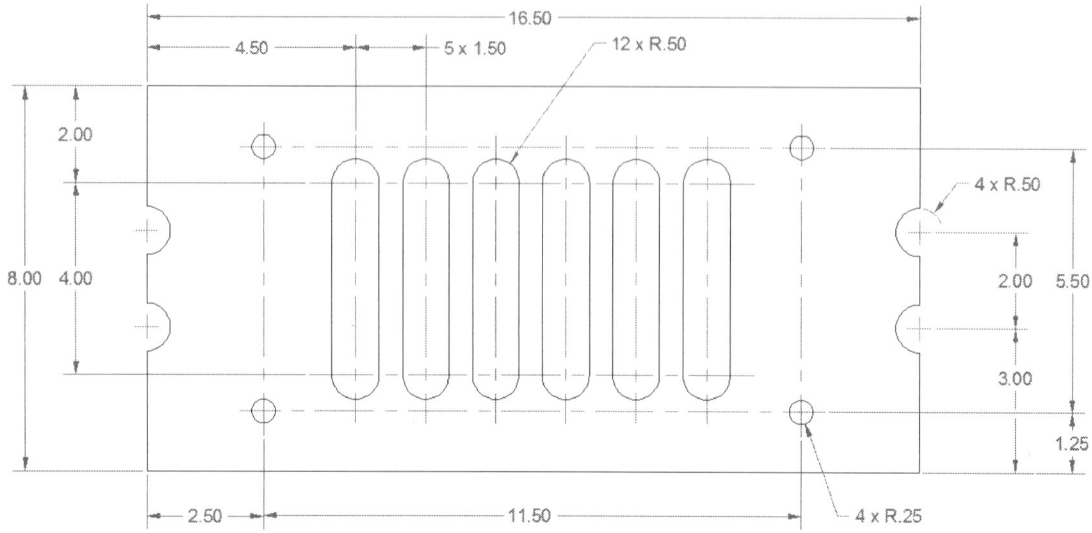

Figure 13–3

1. Start a new drawing called **Plate2.dwg** based on **Mech-Inches.dwt**, which is located in your practice files folder.
2. Draw the object shown in Figure 13–3. Commands you should use to construct the object include **Line**, **Offset**, **Circle**, **Mirror**, **Trim**, and **Rectangular Array**.
   - Tip: To locate the circles or arcs for the holes and slots, you can offset the lines from the side and top of the object to locate the center points.
   - An alternative way of creating the arcs of the slots is to draw two vertical parallel lines of the slots and then use the **Fillet** command.

13.4 Mechanical Project 4: Rocker Arm

In this project, you will draw a rocker arm, as shown in Figure 13–4. Commands you can use include **Circle**, **Line**, **Offset**, **Trim**, and **Polyline Edit**. Dimensions are for reference only.

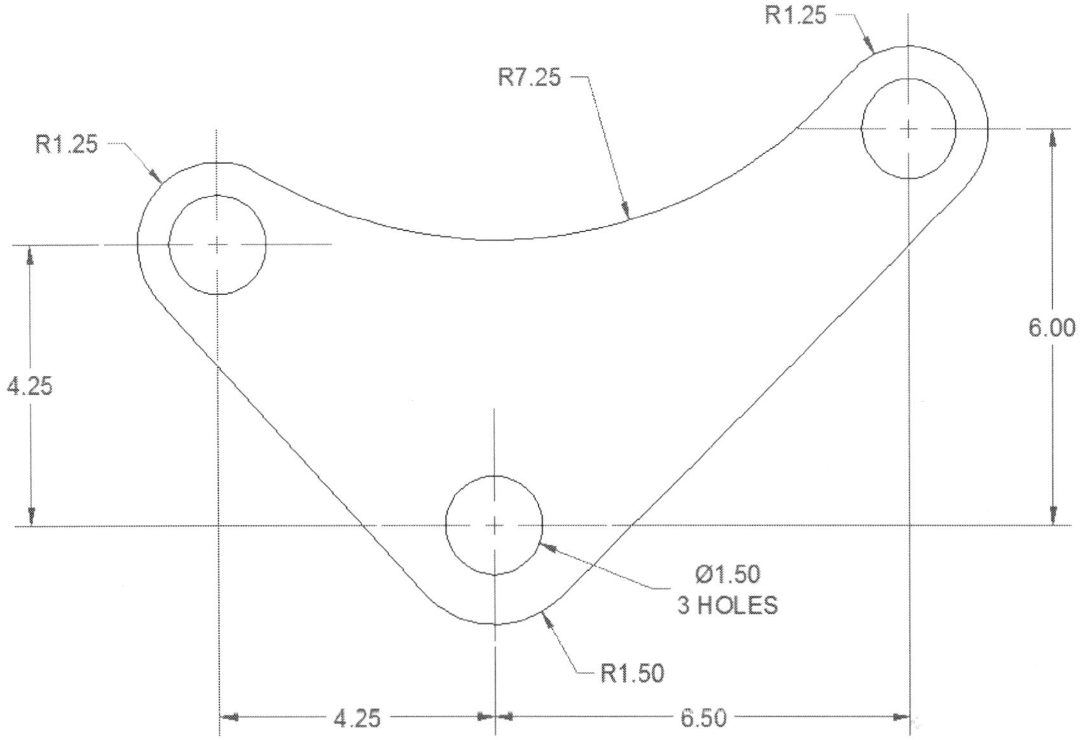

Figure 13–4

1. Start a new drawing called **Rocker.dwg** based on **Mech-Inches.dwt**, which is located in your practice files folder.
2. Draw the object shown in Figure 13–4. Commands you should use to construct the object include **Circle**, **Line**, **Offset**, **Trim**, and **Polyline Edit**.

- Tip: Start by drawing a circle of **R1.50**. Draw horizontal and vertical lines from the center of the circle. Offset the lines by the required distances to locate the centers of the **R1.25** circles, as shown in Figure 13–5.

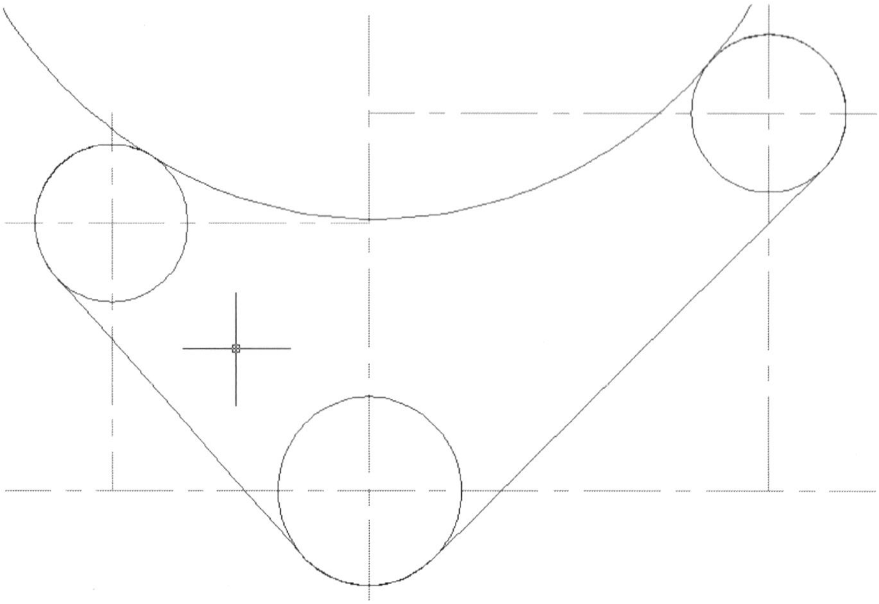

Figure 13–5

- Tip: For the **R7.25** arc, use a **Tan, Tan, Radius** circle. After trimming, join the outline of the object into a polyline.

13.5 Architectural Project 1: Floor Plan

In this project, you will draw the office floor plan shown in Figure 13–6. Commands you can use include **Polyline**, **Fillet**, **Offset**, and **Trim**. You will then insert dynamic blocks for the doors and windows from *Tool Palettes*. Dimensions are for reference only.

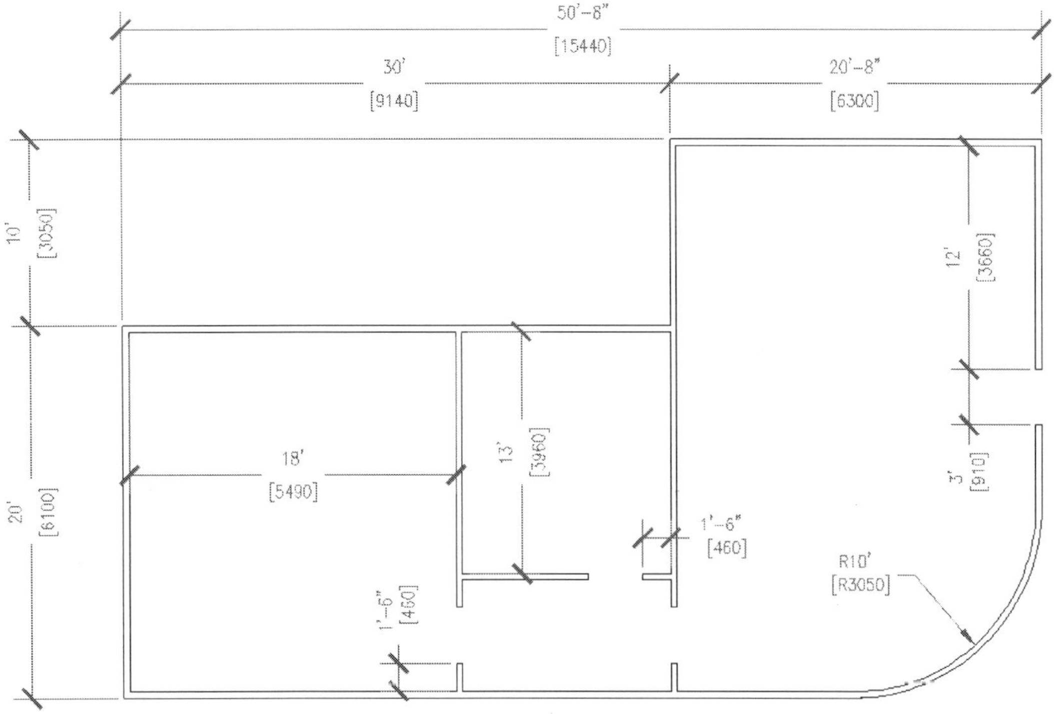

Figure 13–6

- This drawing can be created in either Imperial units (feet and inches) or Metric units (millimeters). In the drawing shown in Figure 13–6, Metric units are included in brackets after the Imperial units.
- All walls are **4" [100mm]** wide. All door gaps are **3' [900mm]** wide.

Task 1: Draw the walls and door openings.

1. Start a new drawing based on **AEC-Imperial.dwt** (or **AEC-Millimeters.dwt** for Metric), which are located in your practice files folder.
2. Save the drawing as **Office3.dwg**.

3. Verify that the layer **Walls** is current and draw the walls.
   - Tip: To create the door gaps, offset the wall lines to create cutting edges at the required distances and then trim the doors.
4. Save the drawing.

Task 2: Insert door and window blocks.

1. Open *Tool Palettes* and select the *Architectural* tab.
2. Add doors and windows from the Tool Palette to the drawing, as shown in Figure 13–7. Use the dynamic blocks in the appropriate units, either Imperial or Metric Tool Palettes. Use grips to modify the locations and sizes of the doors and windows, and the swing of the doors.
   - Change the current layer to **Doors** as you place the doors and to **Windows** as you place the windows. The color of doors and windows has been changed for printing clarity.

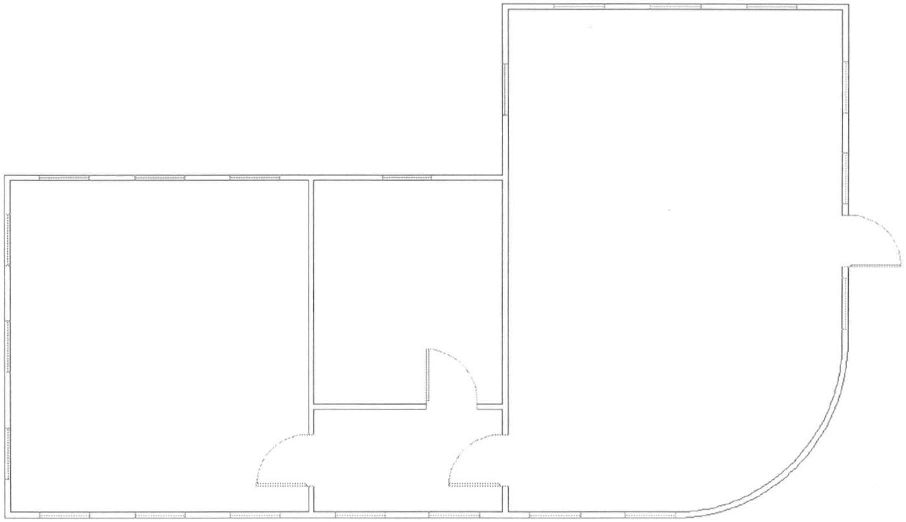

Figure 13–7

   - Tip: To locate the windows along the walls, use (Object Snap Tracking) and track from the outside corner of the wall. For example, along the bottom wall, the first window on the left side is placed **2'** (**600mm**) from the outside corner of the building.
   - Tip: When you have positioned the first window along a wall, use **Rectangular Array** to evenly space the others. For example, to place windows along the bottom wall (as shown in Figure 13–7), use a **Rectangular Array** of **1** row and **7** columns (there are 7 windows) and a *Column offset* distance of **6'** (**1800mm**).

13.6 Architectural Project 2: Floor Plan

In this project, you will draw the office floor plan shown in Figure 13–8. Commands you can use include **Line**, **Polyline**, **Polygon**, **Offset**, **Explode**, **Trim**, and **Array**. You will then insert blocks for the doors and windows. Dimensions are for reference only.

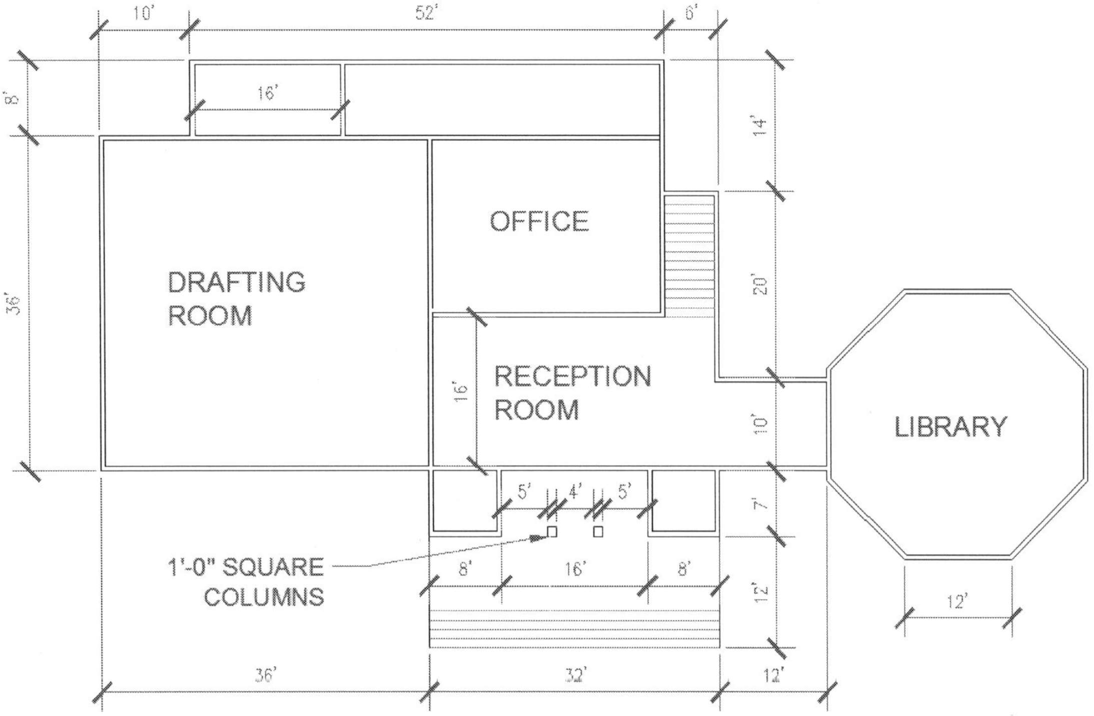

Figure 13–8

Task 1: Draw walls and stairs.

1. Start a new drawing based on **AEC-Imperial.dwt**, which is located in your practice files folder. Save it with the name **Wright Office.dwg**.
2. Draw the walls as shown in Figure 13–8 on the layer **Walls**. All walls are **6"** thick. Clean up intersections by trimming.
3. To draw the Library, use the **Polygon** command with the **Edge** option.
4. Put the stairs on the layer **Misc**. The stairs are spaced **1'** apart.

Task 2: Insert door and window blocks.

1. Create openings for the doors, as shown in Figure 13–9, by trimming. The opening should be **3' wide** for *single doors* and **6' wide** for *double doors*.
2. Open *Tool Palettes* and select the *Architectural* tab.
3. Add doors and windows from the palette to the drawing, as shown in Figure 13–9. Use grips to modify the locations, lengths and widths of the doors and windows, and the swing of the doors.
    - Change the current layer to **Doors** as you place the doors and to **Windows** as you place the windows.

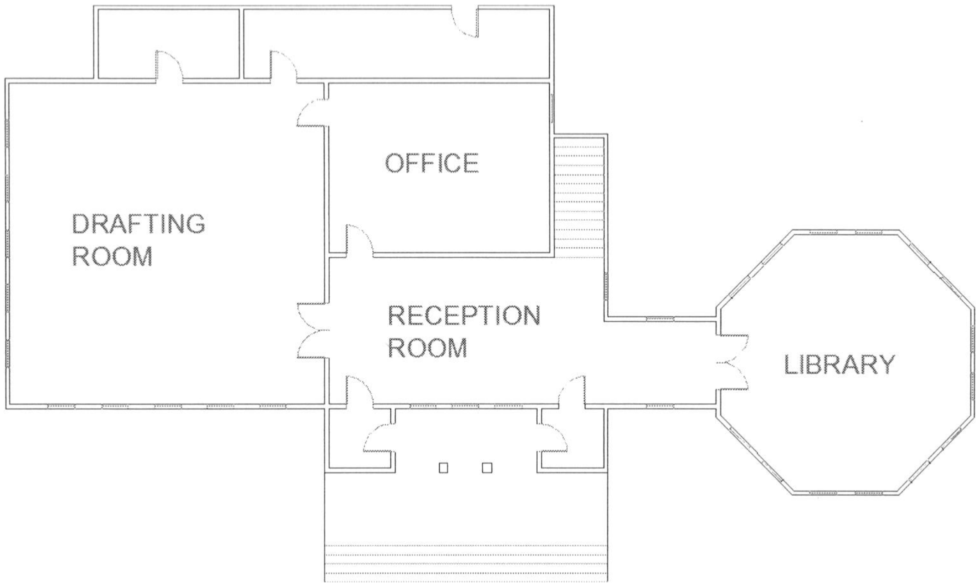

Figure 13–9

- Tip: Use **Mirror** to create the double doors.
- Tip: To quickly add windows in the library, place two along one wall and then use **Polar Array**. Erase the windows where the door is required.

13.7 Civil Project: Parking Lot

In this project, you will draw a building, sidewalk, driveway, and parking spaces, as shown in Figure 13–10. Use commands such as **Trim**, **Extend**, **Fillet**, and **Offset** and use blocks to add trees and shrubs as required. Dimensions are for reference only.

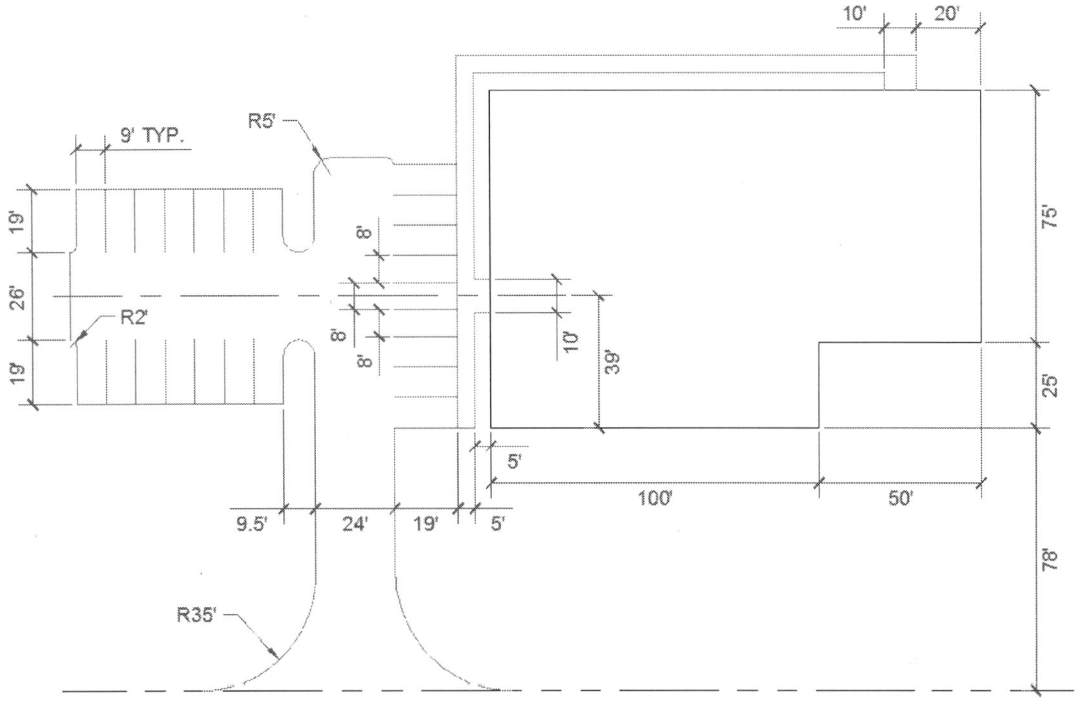

Figure 13–10

Task 1: Draw the building, sidewalk, and parking spaces.

1. Start a new drawing using **Civil-Feet.dwt**, which is located in your practice files folder. Save it as **Parking1.dwg**.

2. Draw the objects shown in Figure 13–10. Dimensions in the drawing are in decimal feet, so you do not have to type the foot symbol. Place objects on the appropriate layers: the building on **Building**, the sidewalk on **Pavement Edge New**, the parking lot on **Parking**, and the property line on **PropertyLine**. Some of the colors in the image has been changed for printing clarity.
   - Use the example shown in Figure 13–11 to help construct some of the fillets.

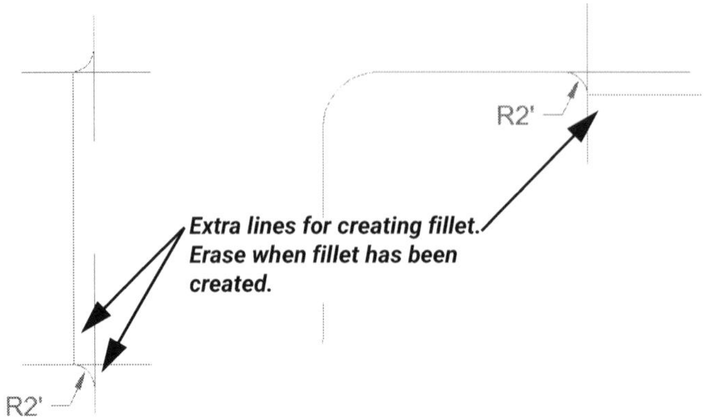

Figure 13–11

Task 2: Insert landscape blocks.

1. Set the current layer to **Tree Line**.
2. Open *DesignCenter* and use the various tree blocks included with **Landscaping.dwg** in the AutoCAD® *DesignCenter* folder, as shown in Figure 13–12.

Figure 13–12

3. Save and close the drawing.

Chapter 14

Setting Up a Layout

In this chapter, you learn about using layouts, how to switch between Paper Space and Model Space, how to create viewports in a layout, how to scale and manipulate viewports, and how to copy a layout.

Learning Objectives

- Modify objects in Model Space and Paper Space.
- Create new layouts by copying existing layouts or by using templates.
- Create rectangular and irregular shaped viewports in a layout.
- Create viewports from existing objects in a layout.
- Create single or multiple viewports in a layout.
- Modify viewports using grips and various commands.
- Learn the guidelines for setting up layouts.

14.1 Working in Layouts

When you first enter a layout, you are in a mode called Paper Space by default. You can identify this mode by the **Paper Space** icon displayed in the lower left corner of the screen and **Paper** displayed in the *Status Bar*, as shown in Figure 14–1.

- In Paper Space, you can add or edit the border and title block, add notes, and create or manipulate the viewports that display the model.

Paper Space icon

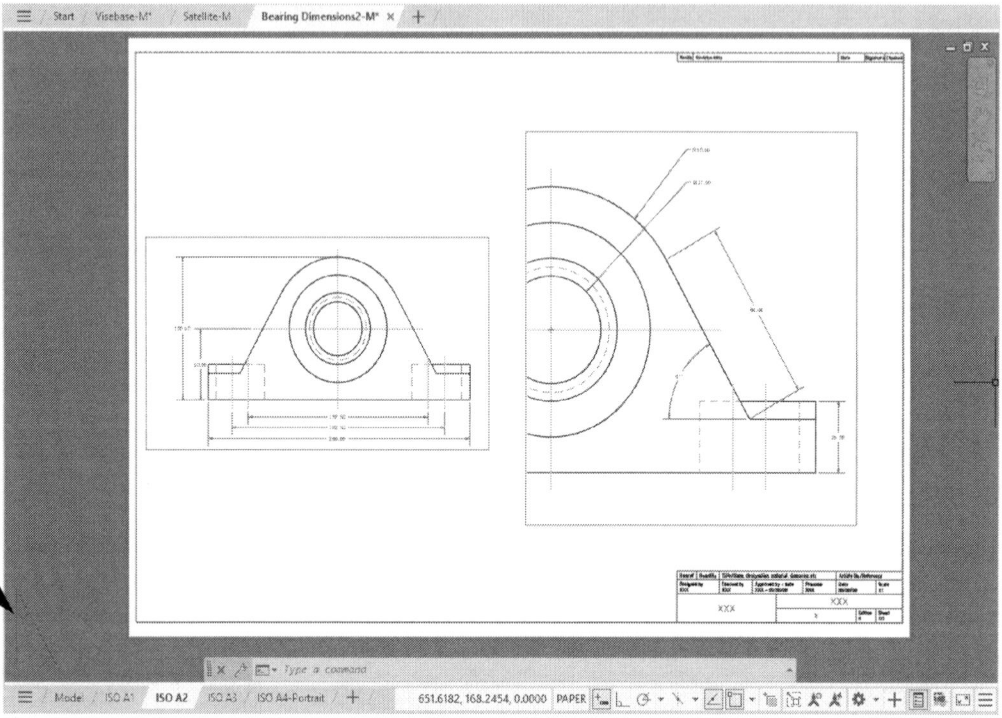

Figure 14–1

- Paper Space displays a graphic representation of the drawing sheet. A dashed boundary on the sheet represents the printable area (if a border is already inserted, it might hide the dashed boundary). The size of the layout reflects the actual sheet size specified in the layout settings. The model displays in one or more viewports in the layout.
- When working in layouts, you can use any of the AutoCAD commands.

- If several layout tabs are available, you can hover the cursor over a tab to display a thumbnail view of the layout, as shown in Figure 14–2. Select a tab to make it active.

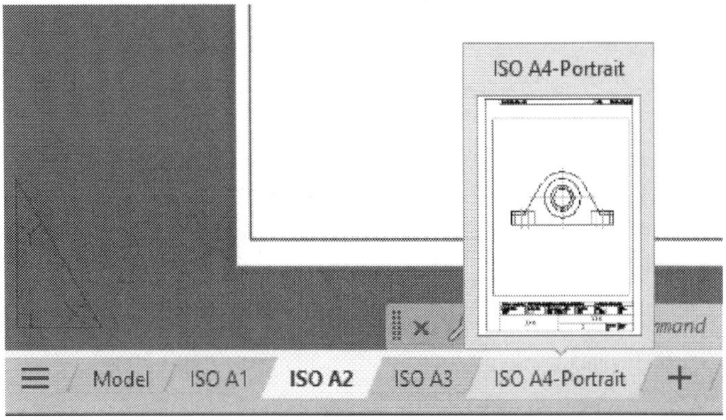

Figure 14–2

- If there are more layouts that cannot be accommodated in the *Status Bar*, you can click  (Layout tab menu) to display a list of all the layouts, as shown in Figure 14–3. Select a different layout to make it active.

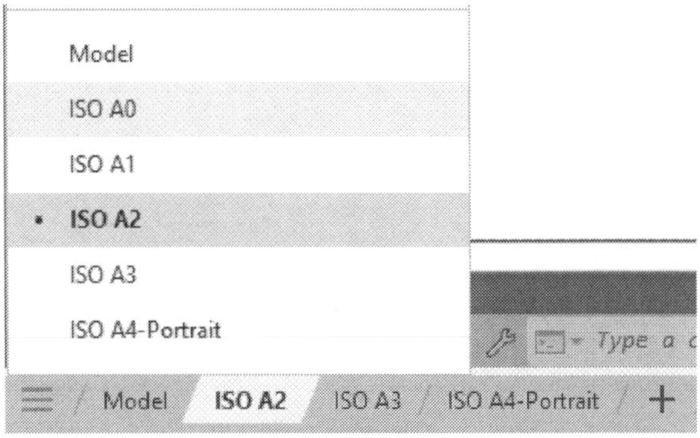

Figure 14–3

- When repositioning layout tabs, you can drag layouts into positions that are currently hidden. As you click on a layout to drag, an ellipsis along the edges might display, indicating that there are hidden layouts. As a layout is dragged to the edge of the displayed layout tab, either on the left or right ellipsis (as shown in Figure 14–4), tabs automatically scroll to show hidden layouts. This enables you to drop a layout to any location, even if it is hidden.

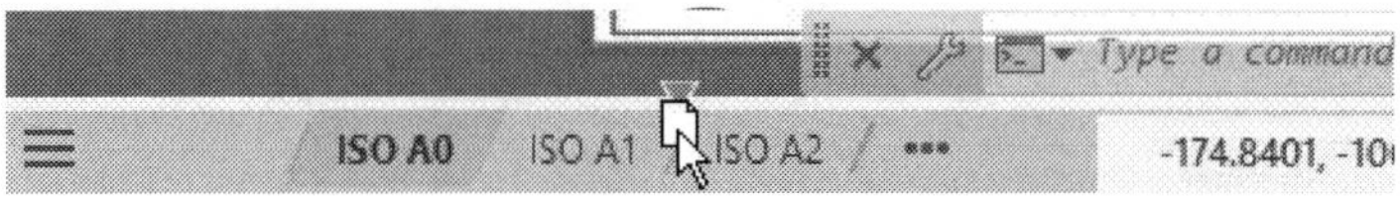

Figure 14–4

Switch Between Paper Space and Model Space

While making changes in a layout, you often switch between working on the sheet of paper and working on the model through the viewport to adjust the view.

Working Inside a Viewport (Model Space)

- When in a layout tab, you can switch to Model Space by double-clicking inside a viewport. It makes that viewport the active work area. The active viewport displays with a thicker border (as shown in Figure 14–5), and the *Status Bar* displays **Model**.

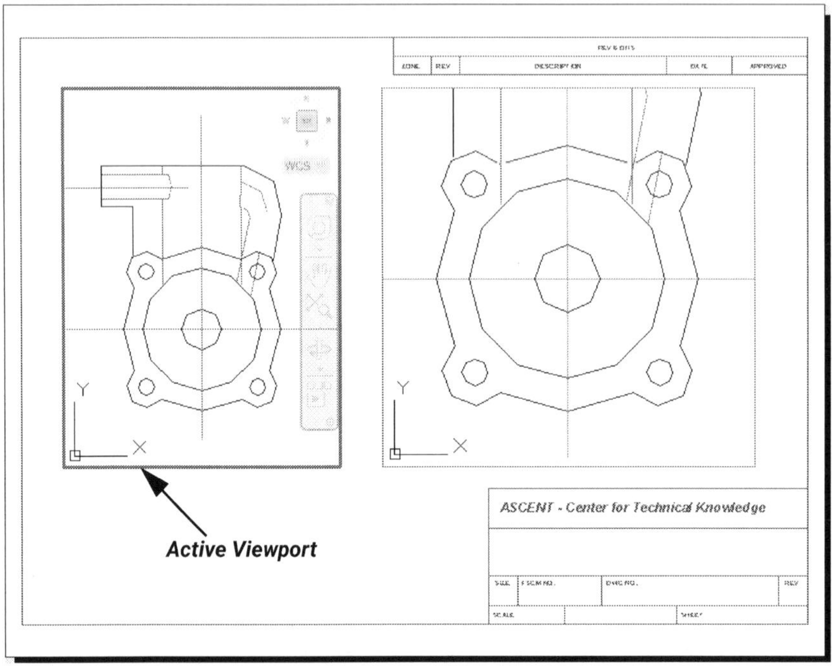

Figure 14–5

- Only one viewport can be active at a time. The active viewport has a thicker boundary and displays the crosshair cursor. In other viewports and in the paper area, the cursor is an arrow. To make a different viewport active, click inside its border.
- In the active viewport, you can **Zoom** or **Pan** to display any part of the model.
- Any change you make to the model's objects through a viewport, such as moving or deleting them, is reflected in the model, the drawing, and all other viewports.

Returning to Paper Space

Double-click on the paper area of the layout to change from Model Space back to Paper Space, as shown in Figure 14–6. This makes the paper the active work area again. The **Paper Space** icon displays in the drawing window and the *Status Bar* displays **Paper**. The viewport border returns to its default thickness.

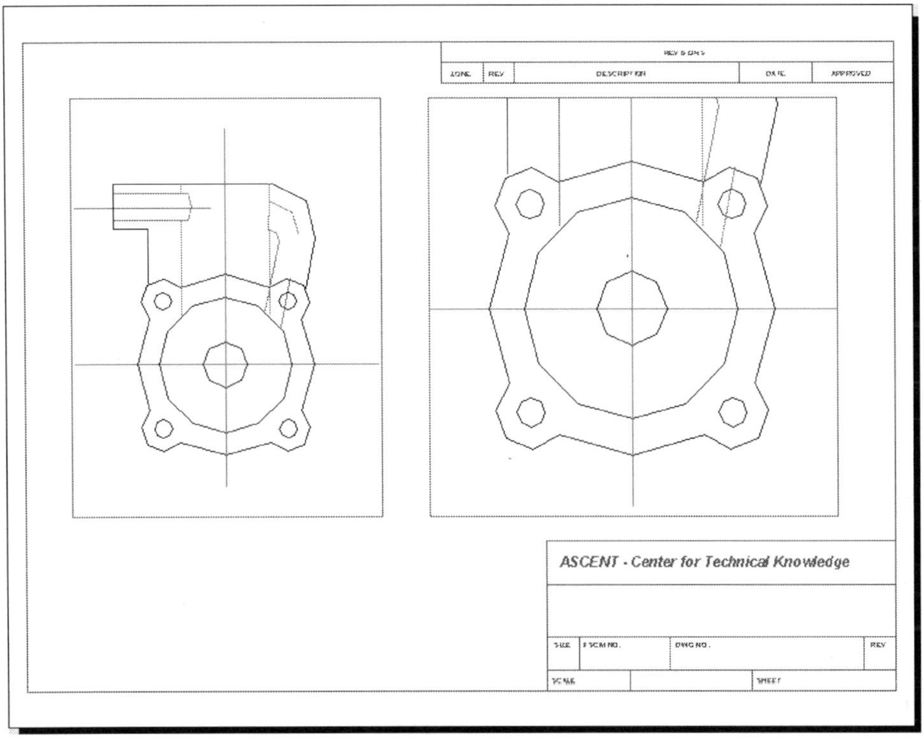

Figure 14–6

- If you double-click on the edge of the viewport, it opens the view in Model Space and fills the screen. This is called *maximizing* the viewport and makes it easier for you to modify the drawing. You can also click (Maximize Viewport) in the *Status Bar* to maximize the viewport and then click (Minimize Viewport) to return to Paper Space.

14.2 Creating Layouts

When you are working with small projects, you need to have as many layouts in your drawing as the number of printed sheets required to describe the model. You can create new layouts from scratch (empty layouts), by copying existing layouts in your drawing, or create them from template files. You can then add viewports and other objects to the new layout.

> **Note:** *If you are working with large projects that contain many layouts, use the Sheet Sets Manager to coordinate the project.*

How To: Copy and Rename a Layout

1. In the *Status Bar*, right-click on the layout tab that you want to copy and select **Move or Copy....**
2. In the *Move or Copy* dialog box, select the layout before which the copied layout is to be added, as shown on the left in Figure 14–7. Alternatively, you can select the **(move to end)** option to add the copied layout as the last layout tab. Select the **Create a copy** option and click **OK**. The new layout is added before the selected layout (as shown on the right in Figure 14–7) or as the last layout, depending on the selected option.

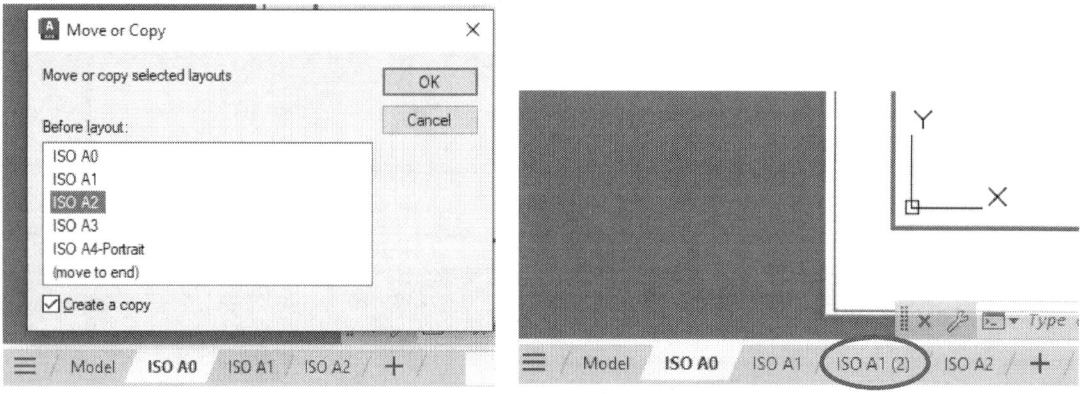

Figure 14–7

3. To rename the layout, double-click on the tab. It is highlighted in blue and you can type the new name, as shown in Figure 14–8. You can also right-click on the tab and select **Rename**.

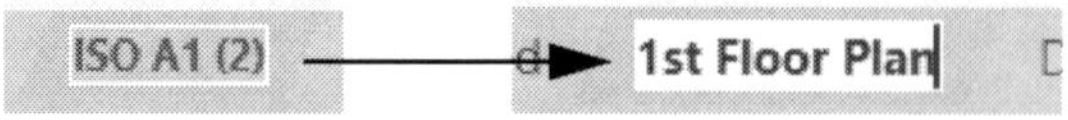

Figure 14–8

When you copy a layout, all of the related plotting information and any objects on the layout (such as titleblock, viewports, and notes) are copied as well.

Hint: Best Practice for Layouts

The best way to create a new layout is to copy an existing one that includes all of the settings that you want to use. It is recommended that you have standard layouts containing company title blocks and page setups available in template files, so the parameters do not have to be recreated every time you are ready to set up a sheet.

How To: Create a Layout from a Template

1. In the *Layout* tab>*Layout* panel, expand (New) and click **From Template**. You can also right-click on a layout tab and select **From Template...**.

   Note: *You can also copy layouts from template files or other drawings.*

2. In the *Select Template From File* dialog box, locate the template file you want to use and click **Open**.
3. In the *Insert Layout(s)* dialog box, select the layout you want to use, as shown in Figure 14–9.

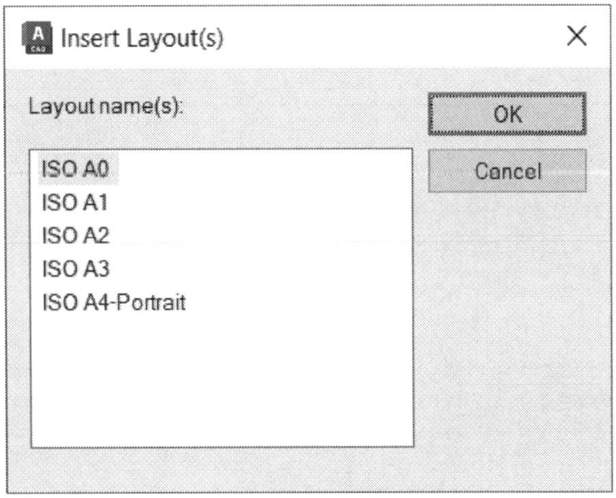

Figure 14–9

4. The new layout is added to the end of the row of tabs.

How To: Create a New Layout

1. Click  at the end of the layout tabs or right-click on a layout tab and select **New Layout** to create a new layout. It creates a new layout with the name **Layout 1** or the next available layout number.
   - Alternatively, use  (New Layout) in the *Layout* tab>*Layout* panel. This prompts you to enter a new name or accept the Layout 1 name.
2. Rename the layout (double-click or right-click and select **Rename**).

14.3 Creating Layout Viewports

You can create the required viewports in a layout using one of several viewport commands, or the *Viewports* dialog box. You can insert a single viewport, a standard configuration of multiple viewports, a polygonal viewport, or convert an object to a viewport. Each viewport in a layout can contain a different view of the model, displayed at any scale.

- Viewports should be placed on a layer that is used specifically for storing viewports. Toggling the layer off (or making it a non-plotting layer) hides the viewport border, but not the model objects inside the viewport.
- You can create multiple viewports in various shapes and sizes in a layout.
- You can create multiple viewports that overlap, but you should not place one completely inside another's boundaries.
- The various viewport commands can be accessed through the *Layout* tab in the ribbon (as shown in Figure 14–10), which is displayed when you are in a layout and in Paper Space.

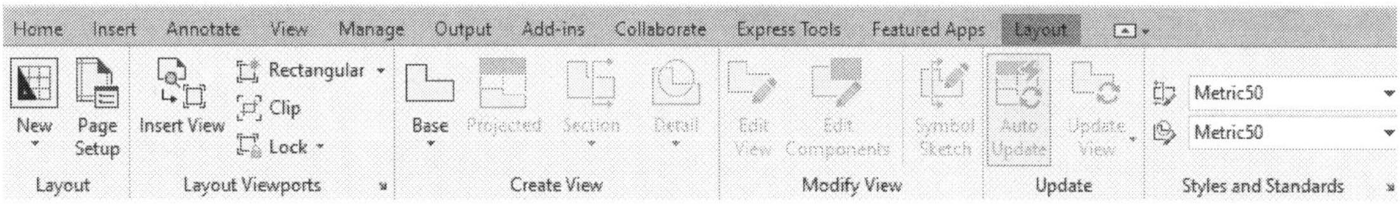

Figure 14–10

Rectangular Viewports

How To: Create a New Rectangular Viewport

1. Verify that you are in a layout and in Paper Space.
2. Set the layer to which you want to add the viewports to be current.
3. In the *Layout* tab>*Layout Viewports* panel, expand the *Viewports* drop-down list and click  (Rectangular).
4. Select the first corner of the viewport.
5. Select the opposite diagonal corner of the viewport.

- After starting the **Viewports, Rectangular** command, you can use the options at the Command Prompt to switch to the **Polygonal** or **Object** viewport creation by typing **P** for **Polygonal** or **O** for **Object**.

- Other options available at the start of the **Viewports, Rectangular** command are as follows:

ON/OFF	Toggle an existing viewport on or off.
Fit	Fits an entire rectangular viewport in the printable area of the layout sheet.
Shadeplot	Sets how viewports are plotted. Select from the **As Displayed**, **Wireframe**, **Hidden**, **Visual Styles**, and **Render Presets** options.
Lock	Locks or unlocks a viewport's view and scale.
Restore	Restores the settings of a saved viewport.
Layer	Removes any layer overrides in the selected viewport and resets them to the global layer properties.
2/3/4	Creates multiple preconfigured viewports.

Polygonal Viewports

How To: Create a New Polygonal Viewport

1. Verify that you are in a layout and in Paper Space.
2. Set the layer to which you want to add the viewports to be current.
3. In the *Layout* tab>*Layout Viewports* panel, expand the *Viewports* drop-down list and click  (Polygonal).
4. Select a start point for the viewport.
5. Select the next point(s).
6. If you want to create an arc segment, select the **Arc** option in the <Down Arrow> menu or press <A>, and follow the prompts to create the arc. To switch back to straight line segments, select the **Line** option or press <L>.
7. Complete the command, using the **Close** option or by pressing <Enter>.

Object Viewports

How To: Convert an Object to a Viewport

1. Verify that you are in a layout and in Paper Space.
2. Set the layer to which you want to add the viewports to be current.
3. In the *Layout* tab>*Layout Viewports* panel, expand the *Viewports* drop-down list and click  (Object).
4. Select a closed object to convert to a viewport.

Viewports Dialog Box

How To: Create a Viewport Using the Viewports Dialog Box

1. Verify that you are in a layout and in Paper Space.
2. Set the layer to which you want to add the viewports to be current.
3. In the *Layout* tab>*Layout Viewports* panel, click  on the right corner of the panel title. The *Viewports* dialog box opens.
4. Verify that you are in the *New Viewports* tab, as shown in Figure 14–11.
5. In the *Standard viewports* area, select the configuration you want to use. A preview of the arrangement displays in the *Preview* pane on the right, as shown in Figure 14–11.

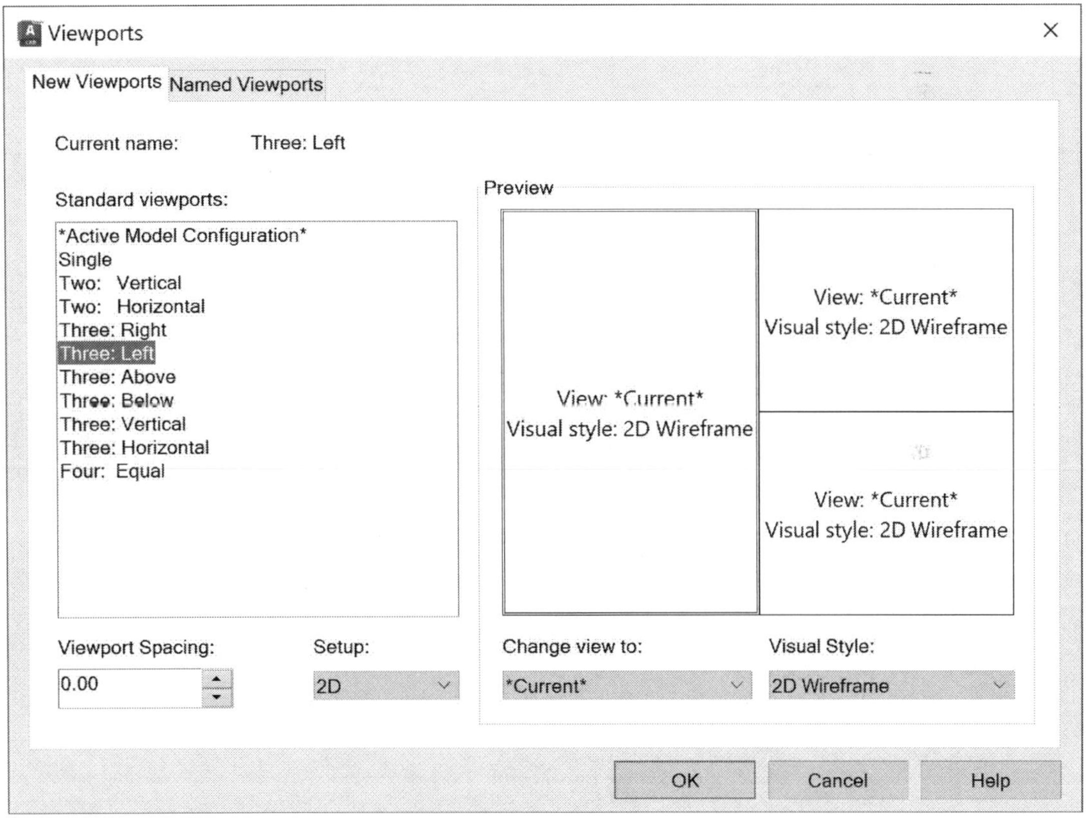

Figure 14–11

6. If you are creating multiple viewports, set the *Viewport Spacing*, which is the space or gap between viewports. The other options are primarily used in 3D drawings.

7. Click **OK**.
8. Select two corners to define the size and location of the viewport(s) in the layout.

Modifying Viewports with Grips

Once you have created and placed viewports in the layout, you can move, resize, and scale them using grips. To modify a viewport, you must be in Paper Space. When you select the edge of a layout viewport, three types of grips display. If the **Quick Properties** option is toggled on, the layout viewport property palette also displays, as shown in Figure 14–12.

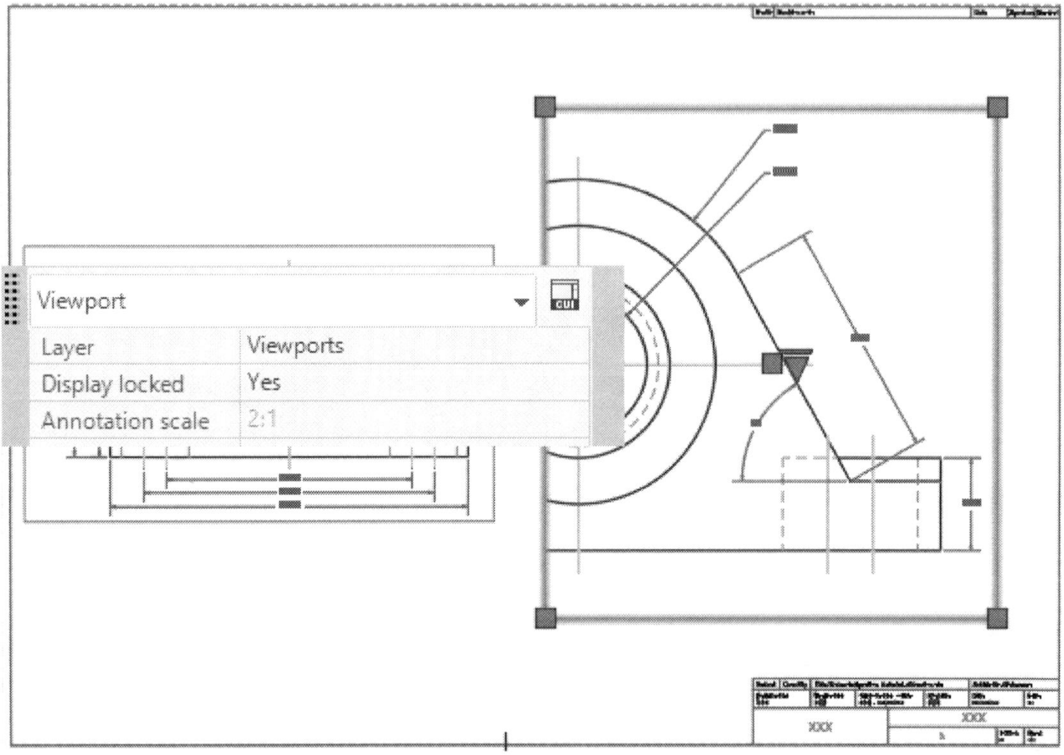

Figure 14–12

The available viewport grips are:

- **Corner square grip** ■: The corner grips are used to resize the viewport, as shown in Figure 14–13.

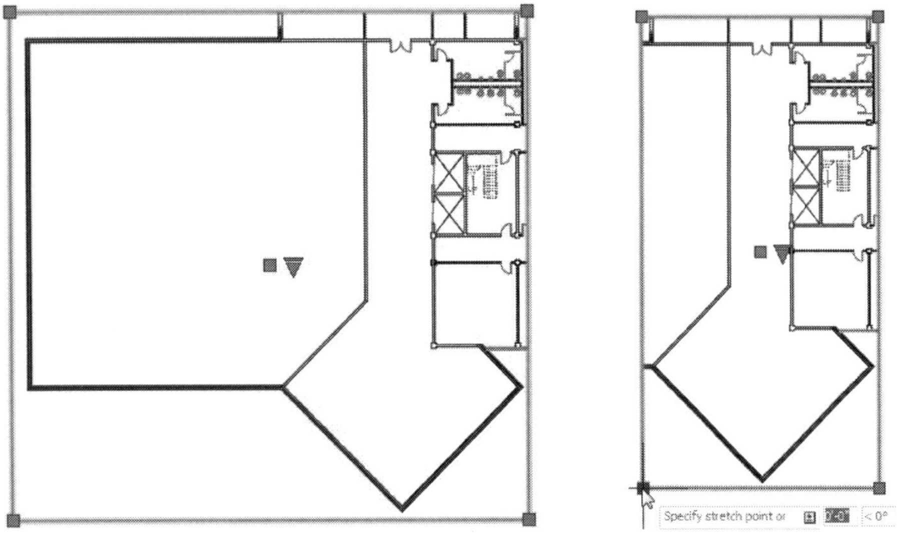

Original viewport ***Resized viewport***

Figure 14–13

- **Middle square grip** : The middle square grip is used to move and place the viewport at a new location in the layout, as shown in Figure 14–14.

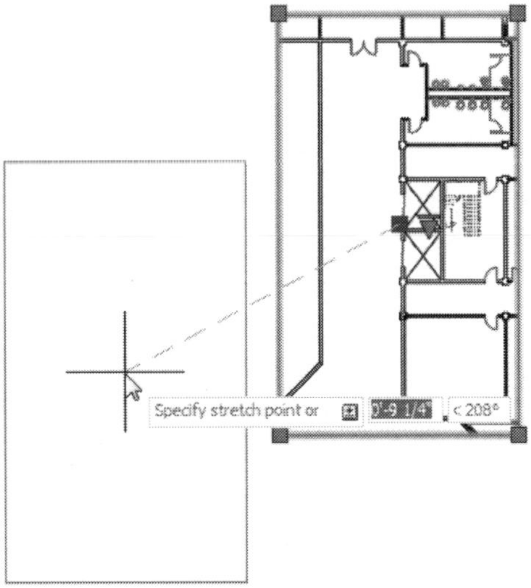

Figure 14–14

- **Middle arrow grip**: The middle arrow grip is a list grip which lists the various scales that you can use to set the viewport scale, as shown in Figure 14–15.
    - You can scale the objects in a viewport to print at a specific scale factor relative to the paper. The scale sets the size of the drawing relative to the Paper Space and sets the Annotation scale to match. This becomes critical when you need to dimension and annotate the drawing.

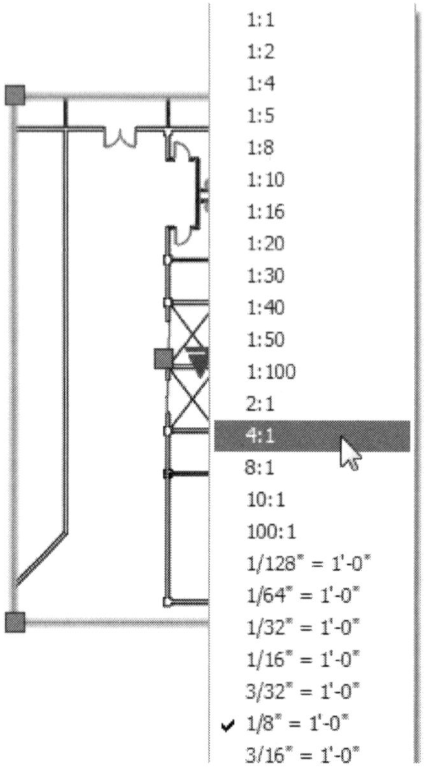

Figure 14–15

- *Status Bar*: You can also set the scale factor of the layout view using the *Status Bar*. Select the edge of the viewport or make the viewport active to display the viewport tools in the *Status Bar*, as shown on the left in Figure 14–16. Expand 1/8" = 1'-0" (Scale of the selected viewport) and select a scale, as shown on the right in Figure 14–16.

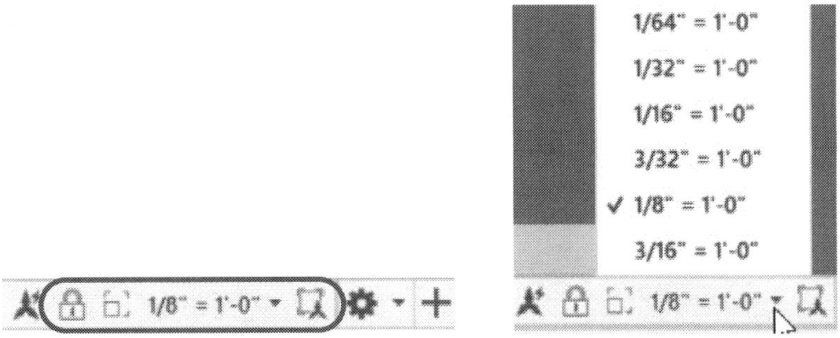

Figure 14–16

- It is useful to activate the viewport and zoom in on the part of the drawing you want to display before setting the scale.

  Note: *You can use* ***Regen*** *or* ***Regenall*** *to regenerate the views.*

- Once you have set the scale, you can pan in the viewport without changing the scale. However, using the **Zoom** command modifies the scale.
- If the scale you want to use is not in the list, you can add a custom scale factor (e.g., **1:200** or **1"=6"**) by selecting **Custom...** in the Scale of the selected viewport list. In the *Edit Drawing Scales* dialog box, click **Add**, type a name for the scale, and enter the values for the *Paper units* and *Drawing units*. Click **OK** to add the custom scale to the list.

Locking the Viewport

When the viewport is displaying the correct view and scale, you should lock the display so that it is not changed by accident. When you try to **Zoom** or **Pan** in a locked viewport, the entire layout zooms or pans instead.

- To lock a viewport, select it and click (Lock/Unlock Viewport) in the *Status Bar*. To unlock a viewport, click (Lock/Unlock Viewport).
- You can also use the shortcut menu to lock and unlock viewports. In Paper Space, select the viewport border, right-click, and select **Display Locked>Yes or No**, as shown in Figure 14–17.

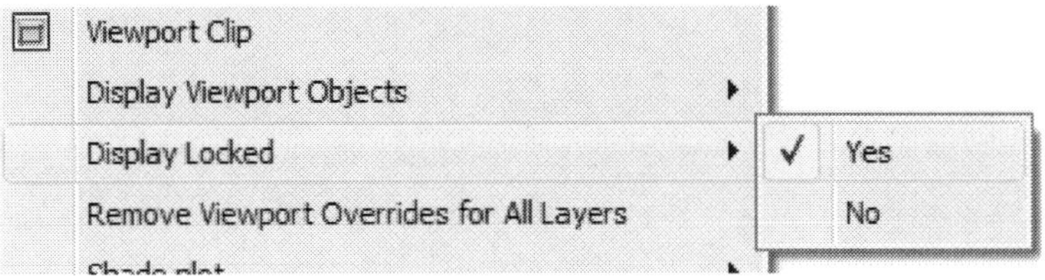

Figure 14–17

14.4 Named Views

If you are working on a complex drawing, you might want to break it into views so that you can access the Model Space and Paper Space viewports. Named views are areas of the drawing that are saved under specific names. For example, you can use named views to define a view of each quadrant in a map, or an area in a large mechanical assembly or architectural plan. Once saved, you can switch to these views for quick reference. Although these named views are created in the Model Space, you can also insert the views as viewports into a layout. The (New View) command can be used to create named views of the drawing currently displayed on the screen. You can either save the entire drawing or a specific area of the drawing, by creating a window around that area. This command is available in the *View* tab>*Named Views* panel, as shown in Figure 14–18.

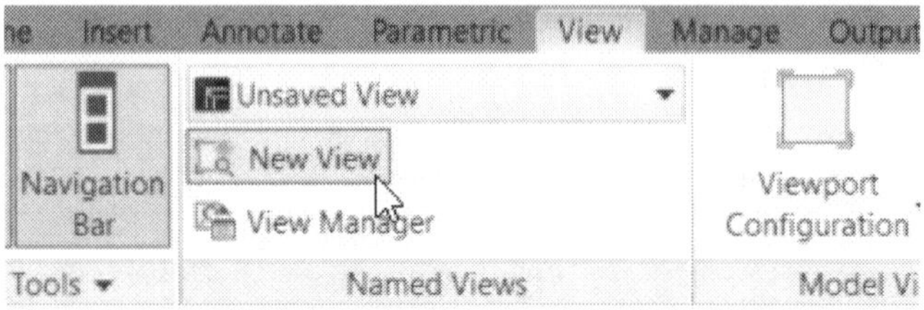

Figure 14–18

How To: Create a Named View

1. In the *View* tab>*Named Views* panel, click (New View).
2. In the *New View/Shot Properties* dialog box that opens, in the *View name* field, enter the name for the view.
3. In the *Boundary* area, select **Define window**, as shown in Figure 14–19. This option enables you to create a window around the area of the model that you want to work on or make a viewport of in the layout.
   - The **Current display** option enables you to save the current screen view.

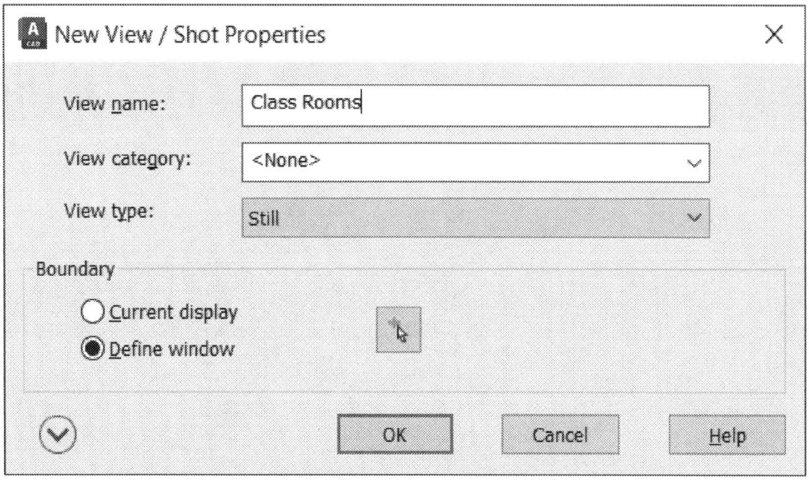

Figure 14–19

4. Using **Zoom** and **Pan**, create a window around the portion of the drawing that you want to save as a named view, as shown in Figure 14–20.

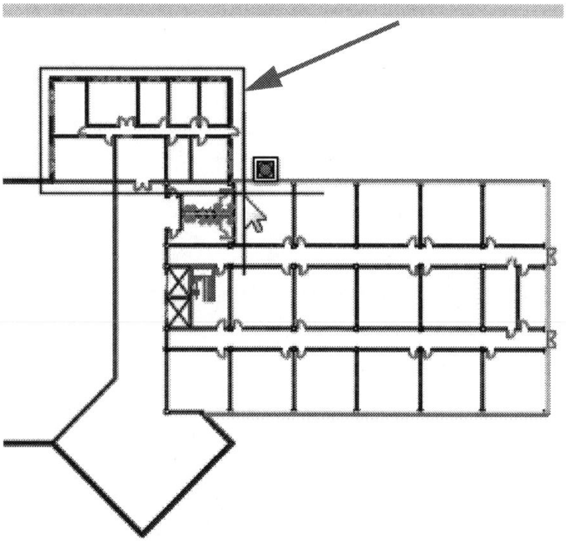

Figure 14–20

5. Press <Enter>.
6. In the *New View/Shot Properties* dialog box, click **OK.**

7. In the *View* tab>*Named Views* panel, expand the *Views* drop-down list to display the named views that you created, as shown in Figure 14–21.

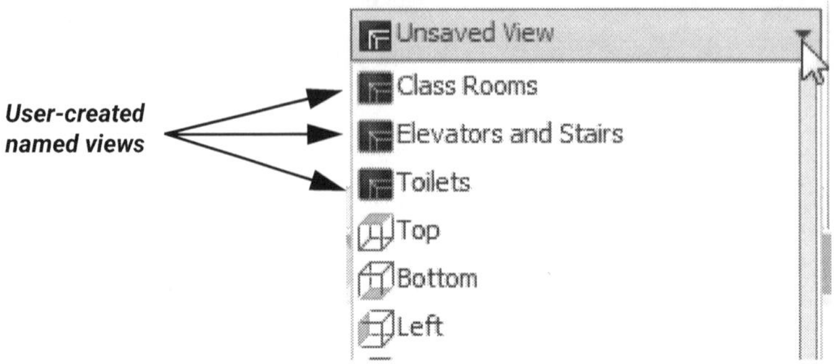

Figure 14–21

8. Click on any named view to restore it and zoom in to the area that you have saved as that view. This is useful when you are working in big drawings, as it becomes easier to locate and work on specific areas.

Insert Views

When inserting a view of the model on paper, you can set the scale at which the model should be printed. The (Insert View) command enables you to create viewports of the named views. This command also enables you to create a new view directly from a layout, if a named view of the desired area has not been created.

The advantage of using the (Insert View) command is that it enables you to set the scale before placing the view. This can help you understand how the view fits on the sheet. When using the Viewport commands to create views, you set the scale after you place the view on the sheet.

The (Insert View) command is located in the *Layout* tab>*Layout Viewports* panel, as shown in Figure 14–22. To access the *Layout* tab, you must be in a layout and in Paper Space.

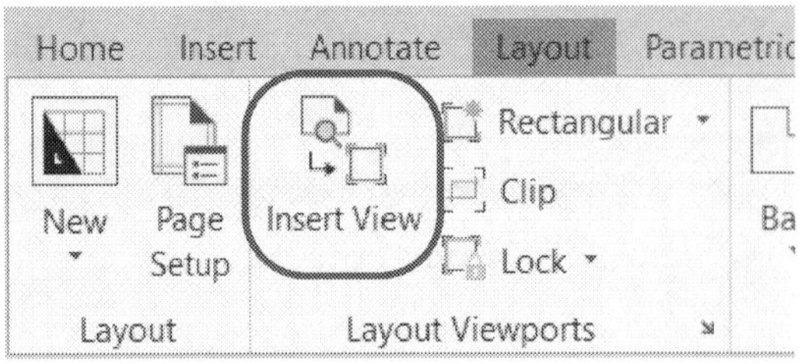

Figure 14–22

How To: Insert a Named View into a Layout

1. Ensure that you are in a layout and in Paper Space.

2. In the *Layout* tab>*Layout Viewports* panel, expand the 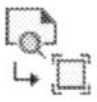 (Insert View) drop-down list. The user-created named views are displayed in the gallery, as shown in Figure 14–23.

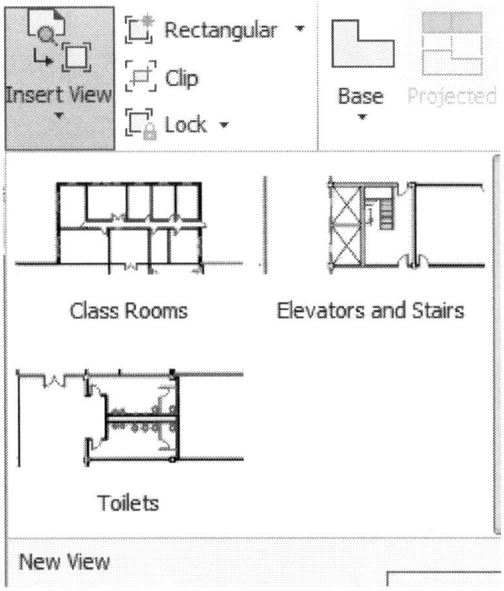

Figure 14–23

3. In the gallery, select the view that you want to insert. The view window attaches to the cursor, as shown in Figure 14–24. Click to place the view inside the Paper Space.

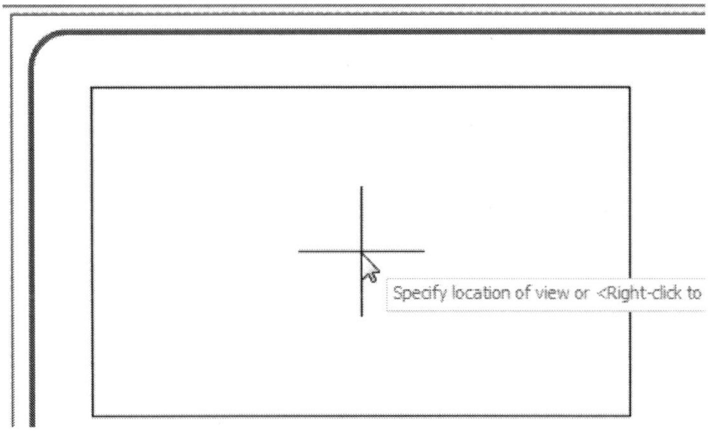

Figure 14–24

4. Depending on the preview window, you can change the size of the view so that it fits on the layout as required. To set the scale of the view, right-click on the view and select the scale, as shown in Figure 14–25.

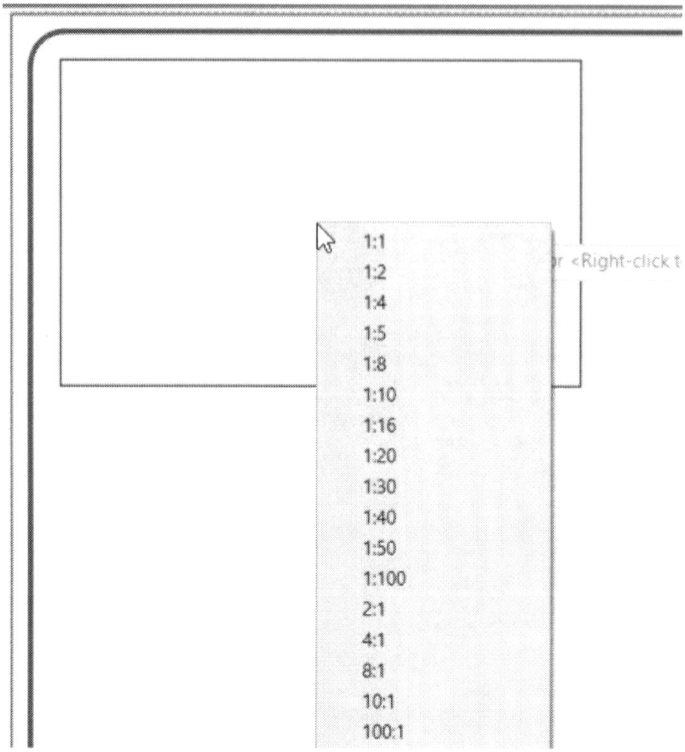

Figure 14–25

5. Click to place the viewport of the defined view in the layout.
6. Press <Enter>.

How To: Insert a View When the Desired Named View Does Not Exist

1. Ensure that you are in a layout and in Paper Space.
2. Determine the layer on which you want to add the viewports. Set that layer to be the current layer.
3. In the *Layout* tab>*Layout Viewports* panel, expand the (Insert View) drop-down list.
4. If the required view was not created as a named view, then it is not located in the gallery. Create a new view by selecting **New View**, as shown in Figure 14–26.

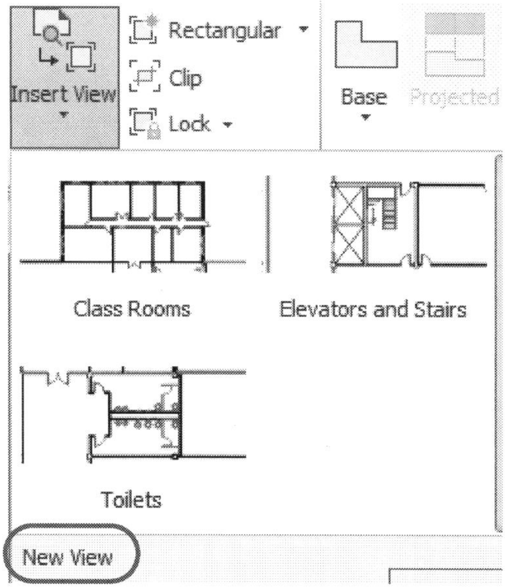

Figure 14–26

5. Note that you are now in the Model Space. You are prompted to specify how much of the model you want to display in Paper Space. Create a window around the portion of the drawing that you want to define as a view, as shown in Figure 14–27.
   - If you plan to create dimensions in the Model Space, ensure that you leave enough space to fit them.

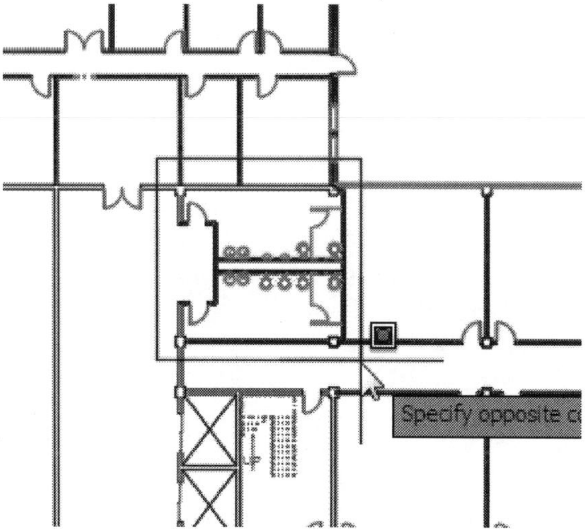

Figure 14–27

6. Press <Enter>. You are switched back to Paper Space, and the view window is attached to the cursor.

7. Depending on the preview window, you can change its size so that it fits on the layout as required. Right-click to select the view scale.
8. Click to place the viewport of the defined view in the layout.
   - Note that this view is not saved in the gallery as a named view. To ensure that the view can be reused, you must save it as a named view.

14.5 Guidelines for Layouts

Model Space geometry should be drawn at full scale in real-world units. Paper Space layout objects (e.g., border, titleblock, title text, etc.) should be drawn at the actual size required for them to fit on the paper at a one-to-one scale.

Use the following guidelines to help when using layouts:

1. Create the drawing in Model Space at full scale in its real-world units.
2. Switch to a layout by selecting the *Layout* tab.
3. Insert a titleblock into the layout if it is not already there. The titleblock should be a block, rather than individual objects.
4. Create as many viewports in the layout as required to display the model.
5. Switch between Model Space and Paper Space to complete the rest of the steps.
6. Pan inside the viewport to center the required displayed area of the drawing. You must be in Model Space to be able to pan.
7. Set the scale factor for each viewport.
8. When the view is correct, lock the viewport so that the scale cannot be changed.
9. Annotate the drawing. General notes that are not linked to objects in the viewports, titleblocks, and titles are typically added in Paper Space. Add dimensions and some other annotations in Model Space.
10. When the drawing is finished, plot the layout in Paper Space mode at a 1:1 scale.

Practice 14a
Work with Layouts

Practice Objectives

- View Model Space and Paper Space in layouts.
- Create, update, modify, and delete viewports in a layout.

In this practice, you will note the differences between Model Space and Paper Space and switch between Model Space and Paper Space in a viewport in a layout. You will create, scale, and lock viewports in a layout. You will then create copies of the layout, rename the new layouts, and update them with different viewport information, such as the **Auditorium Wing** layout shown in Figure 14–28. You will also delete unused layouts.

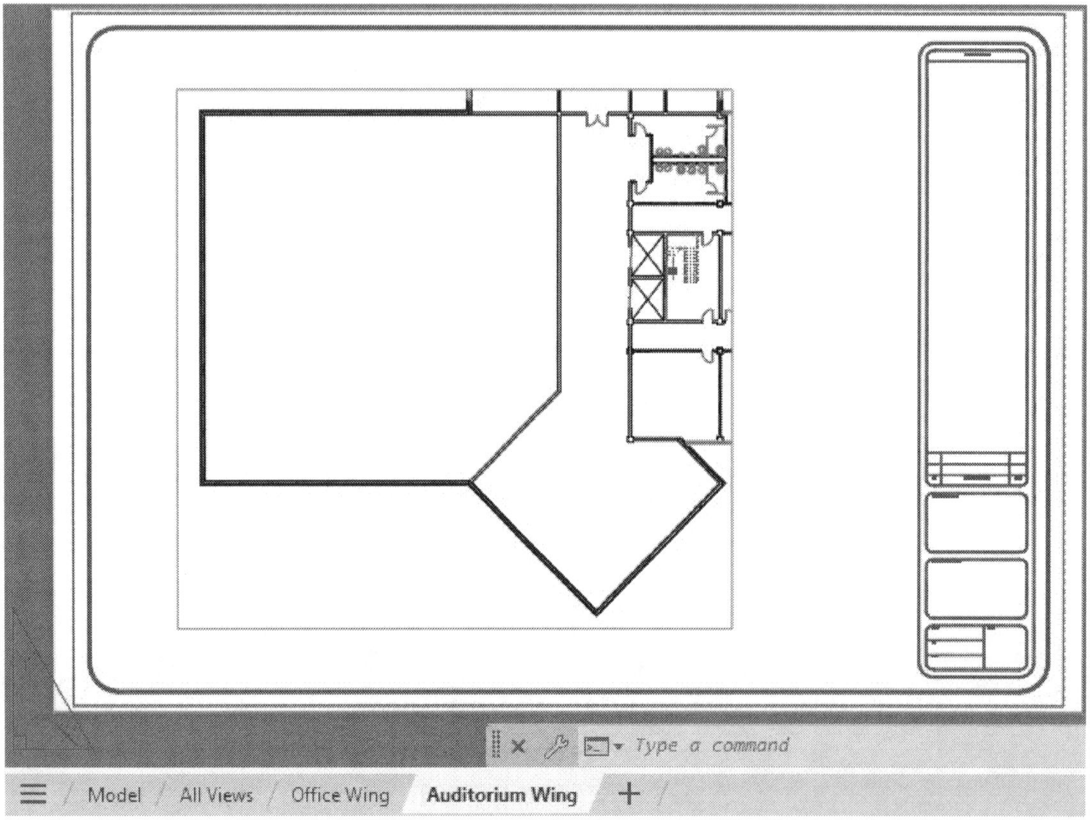

Figure 14–28

Task 1: View Model Space and Paper Space in layouts.

In this task, you will note the differences between Model Space and Paper Space, and switch between Model Space and Paper Space in a viewport on a layout tab.

1. Open **College Building-A.dwg** from your practice files folder. Note that the *Model* tab is active, as shown in Figure 14–29, and that you are in Model Space.

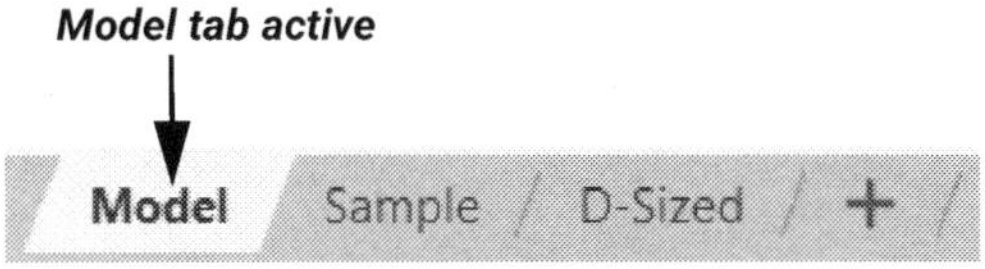

Figure 14–29

2. Zoom in on one of the single doors. Use the **Measure>** (Quick) command (*Home* tab> *Utilities* panel) to measure its opening. Note that it displays as **3'**, which is the *real-world* distance in Model Space.
3. Select the **Sample** layout tab. The layout view has a title block and one viewport (gray rectangle) inside it. Note that the model is displayed inside the viewport. Also note that you are in Paper Space. This is indicated by the viewport boundary being faded. Additionally, the Paper Space icon displays along the bottom left corner of the screen and PAPER label displays in the *Status Bar*.
4. Ensure that (Object Snap) is toggled on and is set to **Endpoint** osnap.
5. Zoom in on one of the open single doors and using the **Measure>Distance** command, check the distance of the door. It displays the actual size of the door (**3'**).
6. Toggle off (Object Snap) and check the distance again. It displays the approximate length of its printed size on the paper.
7. Toggle (Object Snap) back on.
8. Zoom out and measure the length of the border. It is drawn at the actual size required to fit on an A-sized sheet of paper.
9. Double-click inside the viewport boundary (faded rectangle) to make it active. Note that the viewport boundary around the model turns thick, indicating that you are in viewport Model Space and will be working on the model through the viewport. This is also indicated by the MODEL displayed in the *Status Bar*.
10. In the *Status Bar*, note that the (Lock/Unlock Viewport) is toggled off. Note the viewport scale.

11. **Zoom** and **Pan** so that only the Office Wing, near the top of the building displays, as shown in Figure 14–30. (You can use one of the Zoom options in the Navigation Bar that is displayed inside the viewport window.) In the *Status Bar*, note the viewport scale. The scale factor of the viewport is changed.

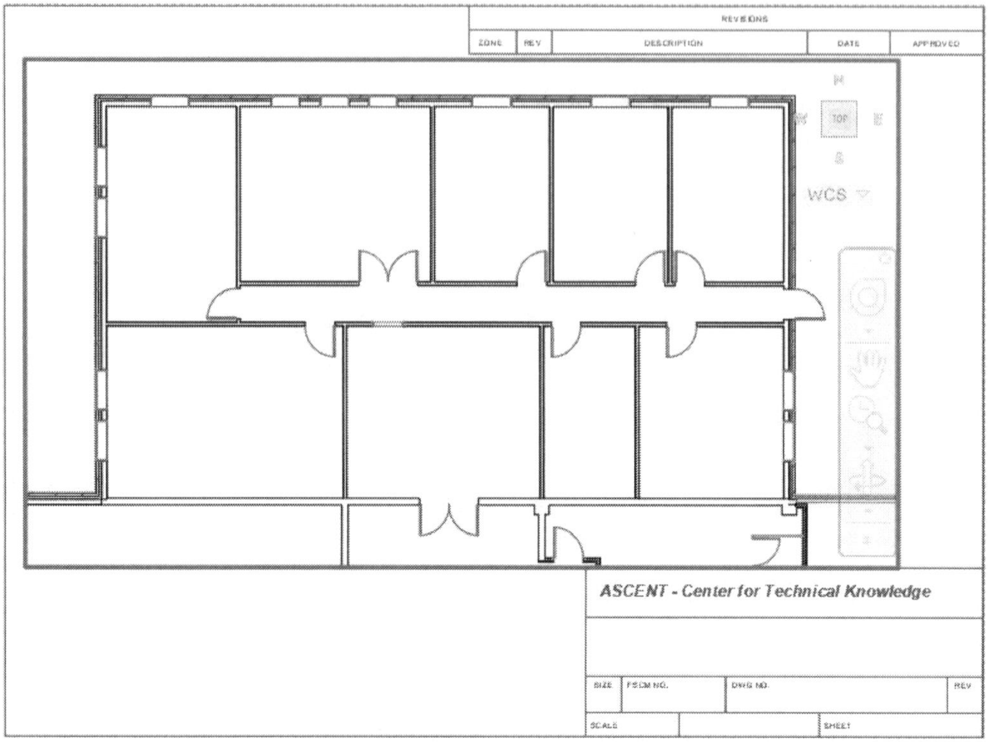

Figure 14–30

12. Save the drawing.

Task 2: Create named views.

In this task, you will create named viewports in the Model Space.

1. Enter Model Space by clicking on the *Model* tab in the layouts tab bar. Zoom to the extents of the drawing.

2. In the *View* tab>*Named Views* panel, expand the *Unsaved View* drop-down list, as shown in Figure 14–31. Note that there are no user-created named views.

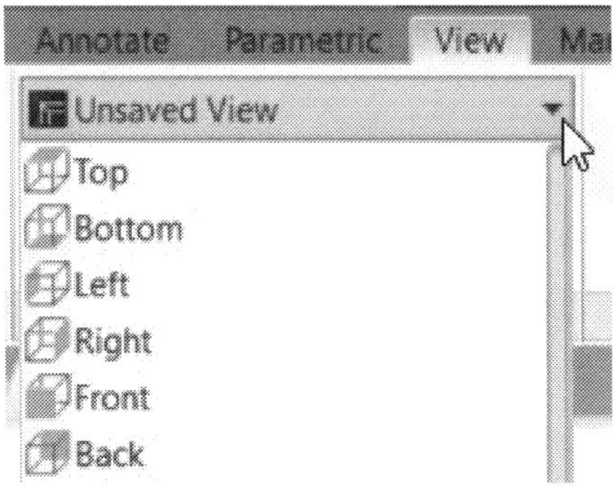

Figure 14–31

3. In the *View* tab>*Named Views* panel, click (New View).
4. In the *New View/Shot Properties* dialog box, in the *View name* field, type **Offices**. In the *Boundary* area, select **Define window**, as shown in Figure 14–32.

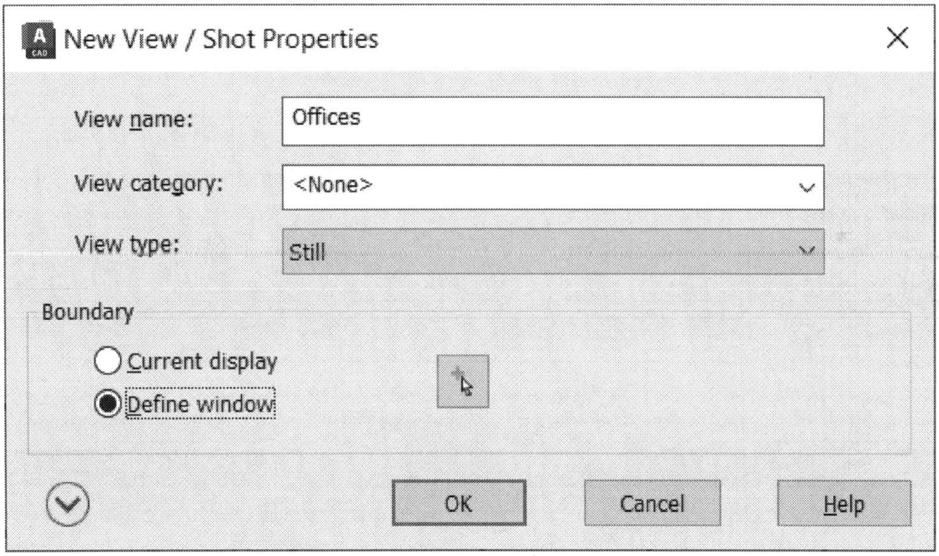

Figure 14–32

5. Create a window around the offices near the top of the drawing, as shown in Figure 14–33. Press <Enter>.

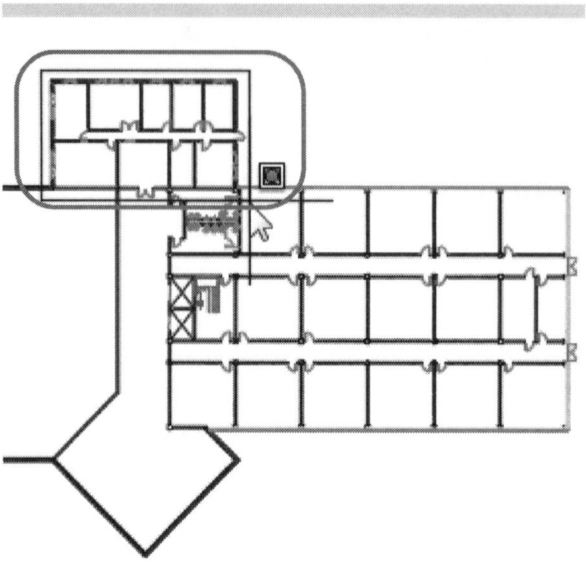

Figure 14–33

6. In the *New View/Shot Properties* dialog box, click **OK**.
7. Repeat Steps 3 to 6 to create the two additional views shown in Figure 14–34:
   - For the first view, name it **Toilets**, and then, using **Define window** create a window around the toilets area.
   - For the second view, name it **Elevators and Stairs** and using **Define window** create a window around the area containing elevators.

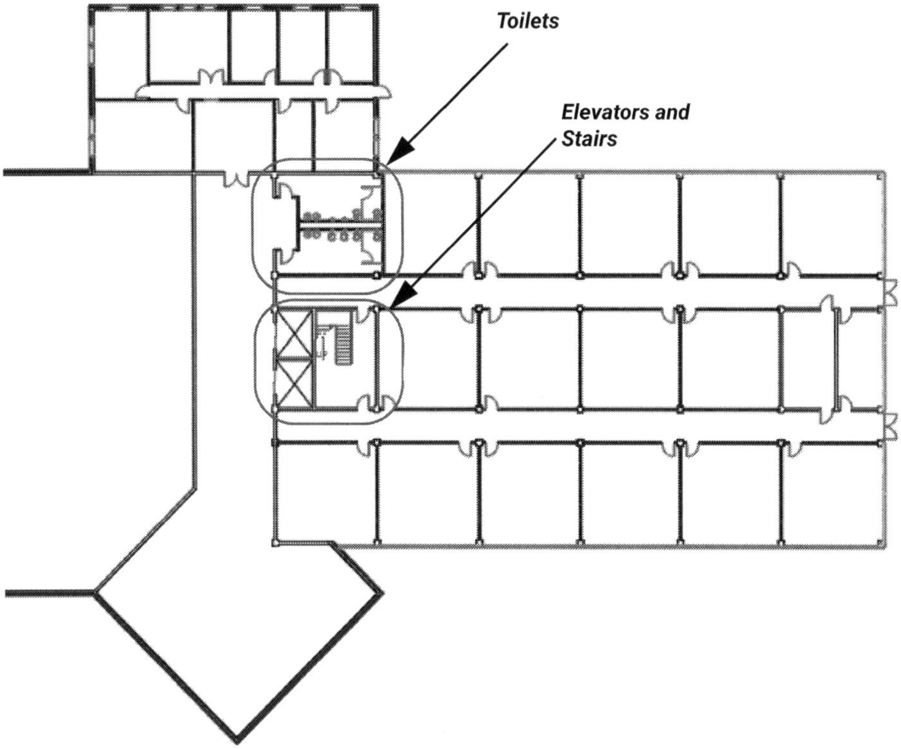

Figure 14–34

8. Expand the *Unsaved View* drop-down list. Note that the three named views have been added as shown in Figure 14–35.

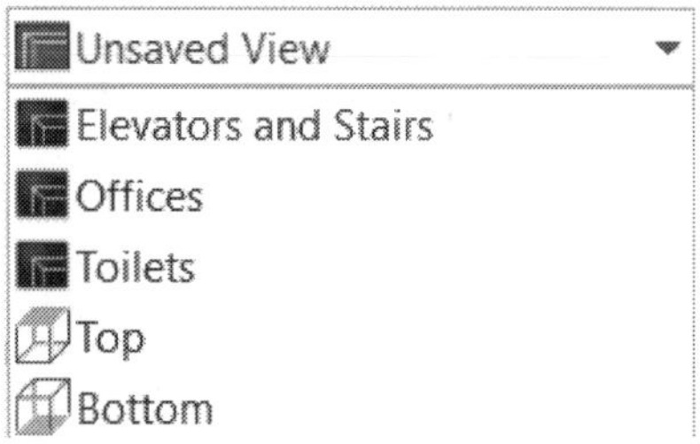

Figure 14–35

9. In the *Unsaved View* drop-down list, select **Elevators and Stairs** and note how the drawing zooms into the *Elevators and Stairs* area that you have selected for the named view.
10. Similarly, select **Toilets** and note the area you are zoomed in to.
11. Zoom to the extents of the drawing.
12. Save the drawing.

Task 3: Insert views in a layout.

In this task, you will insert named views in a layout.

1. Switch to the **D-Sized** layout tab.
2. Delete the existing viewport in this layout by selecting the gray rectangle and pressing <Delete>. Only the titleblock is left in the Paper Space.
3. In the *Layout* tab>*Layout Viewports* panel, expand the (Insert View) drop-down menu. The three named views are displayed in the gallery, as shown in Figure 14–36.

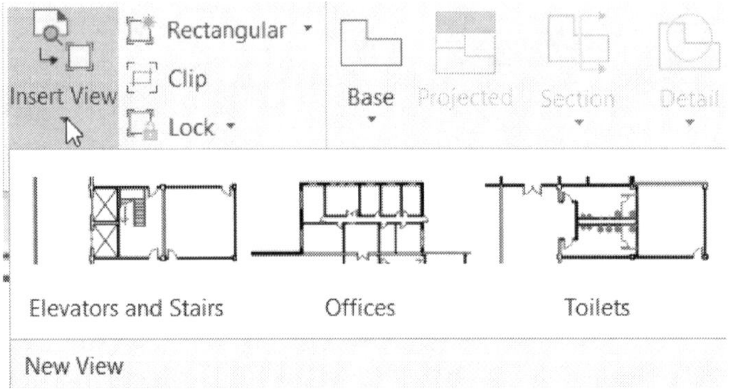

Figure 14–36

4. Select the **Offices** view and note how it attaches to the cursor, as shown in Figure 14–37.

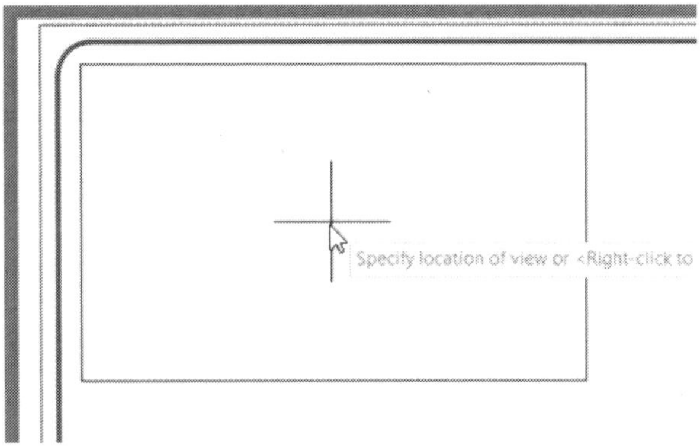

Figure 14–37

5. Without clicking, right-click and select **1/4"=1'-0"**. Place the new viewport near the upper left corner inside the title block border.

6. Click on the **Offices** border (gray border) to display its grips. Click on the *Middle arrow* grip ( ): to display the scale list, and then select **1/8"=1'-0"**, as shown in Figure 14–38.

   - In the *Status Bar*, note that (Lock/Unlock Viewport) is highlighted, indicating that the selected viewport is locked.

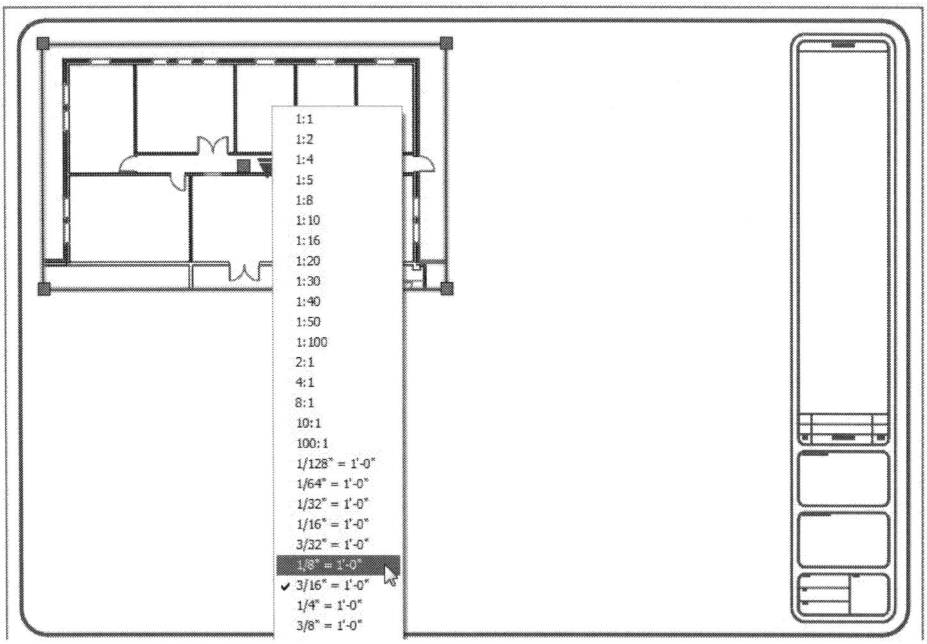

Figure 14–38

7. Using the square grip in the middle, move the viewport closer to the upper left corner of the title block border, as shown in Figure 14–39.

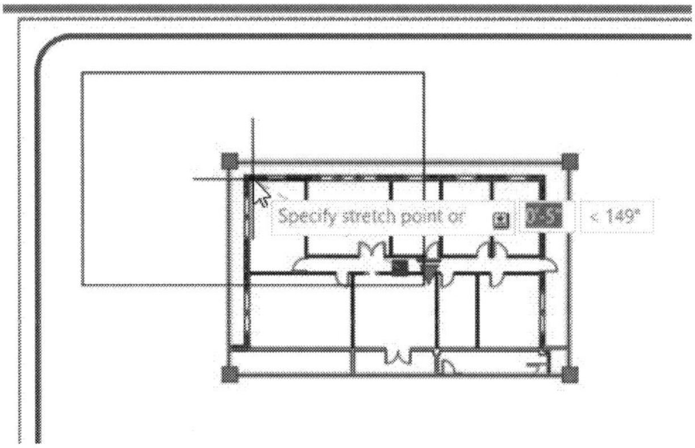

Figure 14–39

8. Press <Esc> to clear the viewport selection.
9. From the (Insert View) gallery, insert the other two views (**Toilets** and **Elevators and Stairs**).
10. Right-click and set the viewport scales to **1/4"=1'-0"** for each of the views and arrange the viewports inside the border similar to that shown in Figure 14–40.

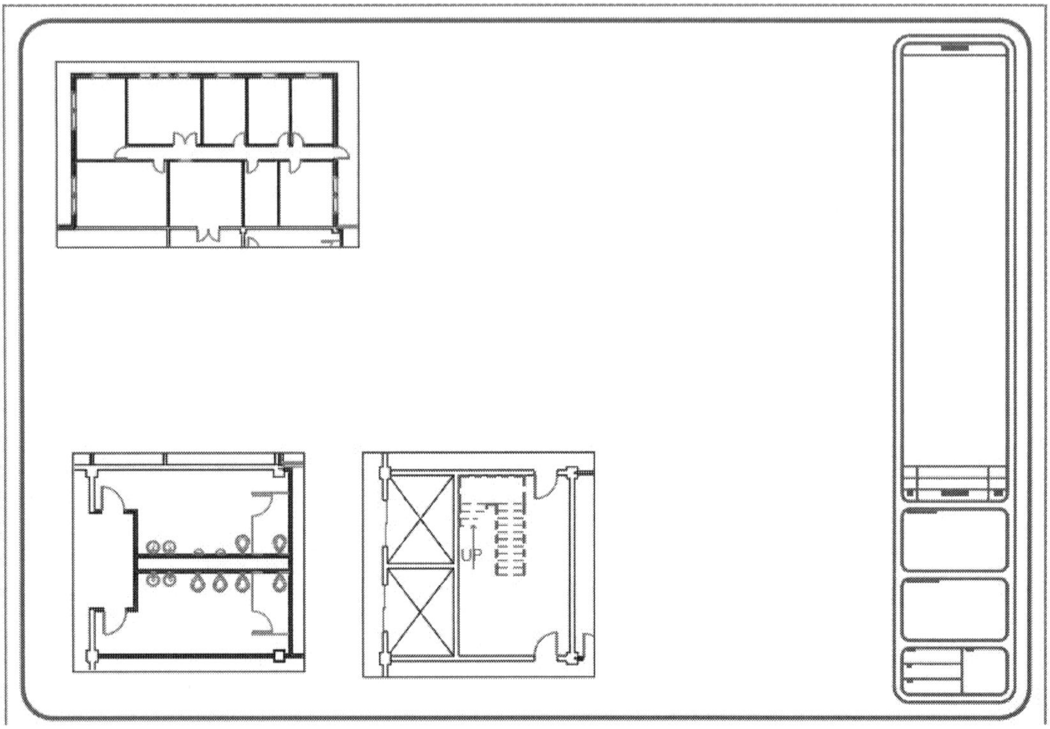

Figure 14–40

Task 4: Create a view from the layout.

In this task, you will create and insert a view from the layout.

1. Make the **Viewports** layer current.
2. In the *Layout* tab>*Layout Viewports* panel, expand the (Insert View) gallery and select **New View**.
3. Note that you are now switched to the Model Space. You are prompted to specify how much of the model you want to display in Paper Space. Create a window around the foyer portion of the drawing as shown in Figure 14–41.

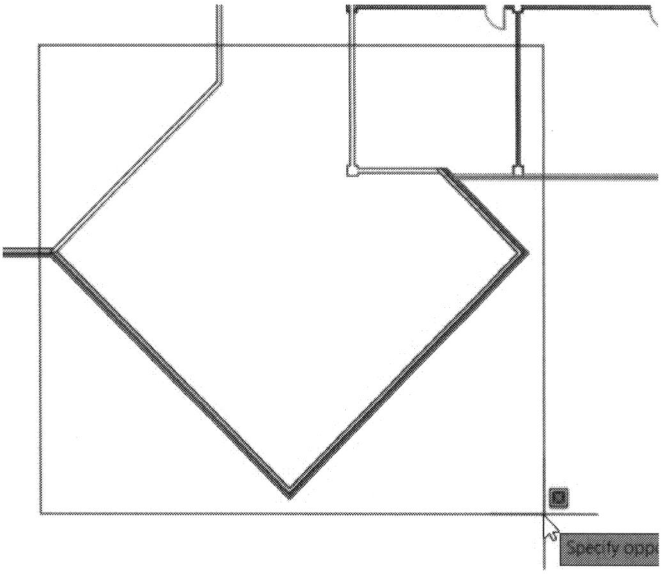

Figure 14–41

4. Press <Enter>. You return to Paper Space, and the preview window is attached to the cursor.
5. Click to place the viewport in the top right corner of the layout, as shown in Figure 14–42.
   - The foyer viewport might overlap the **Elevators and Stairs** viewport. You will fix it in the next task.

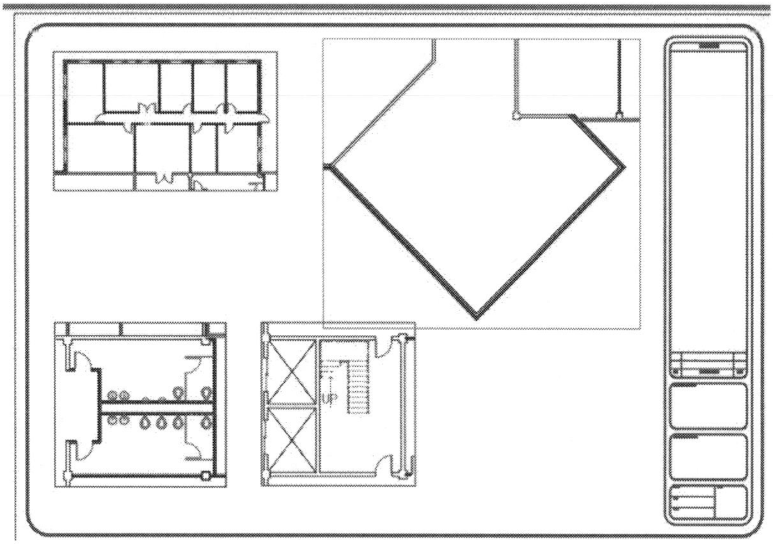

Figure 14–42

6. Expand the 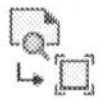 (Insert View) gallery and note that the view you just created is not available in the gallery. The view is not a saved view.

   *Note: The **New View** command creates a view on the fly and does not save it.*

7. Save the drawing.

Task 5: Work in a layout.

In this task, you will create, scale, and lock viewports in a layout.

1. Double-click inside the *Foyer* viewport that you inserted in Task 4. It becomes active.
   - The active viewport has a thicker boundary edge.
2. Try to **Pan** and **Zoom** inside the window. The whole Paper Space is panned as the viewport scale is locked at **3/16" = 1'-0"**, as shown in the Figure 14–43.

Figure 14–43

3. In the *Status Bar*, toggle off the Viewport Lock.
4. Now **Zoom** and **Pan** the view inside the foyer viewport. Note how the viewport scale changes.
5. With the viewport activated, **Zoom** and **Pan** until the auditorium (i.e., the large, empty room) and the foyer display. Note that some other areas might also display.
6. In the *Status Bar*, use the Viewport Scale Control list and select several different scales. Finish with a scale of **1/16"=1'-0"**, as shown in Figure 14–44.

   Note: If you pan and zoom before locking the viewport, the scale changes.

Figure 14–44

7. Switch to Paper Space by double-clicking in an empty area outside any viewport. Select the viewport boundary and use the corner grips to adjust the viewport size, so that only the auditorium and the foyer are inside the viewport, as shown in Figure 14–45. Make sure not to pan or zoom.

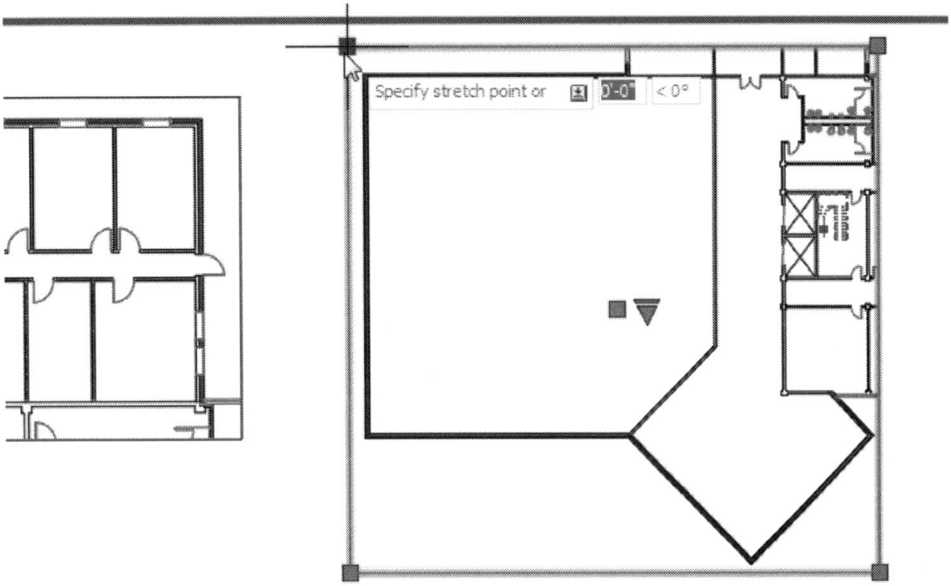

Figure 14–45

8. Use the middle square grip to move this viewport in line with the Offices viewport.
9. When you are satisfied with the way the viewport looks, verify that its boundary is still selected and, in the *Status Bar*, the Scale displays as **1/16"=1'-0"**, click (Lock/Unlock Viewport) to lock the viewport.
10. Press <Esc> to clear the viewport selection.
11. Save the drawing.

Task 6: Copy and modify layouts.

In this task, you will create copies of the layout, rename the new layouts, update them with different viewport information, and delete unused layouts.

1. Make a copy of the **D-Sized** layout by right-clicking on its tab name in the *Status Bar* and selecting **Move or Copy...**. In the dialog box, select **(move to end)** and **Create a copy**, as shown in Figure 14–46. Click **OK** to add a copy of the tab, named **D-Sized (2)** to the end of the row. Repeat the process to create one more (**D-Sized (3)**) layout.

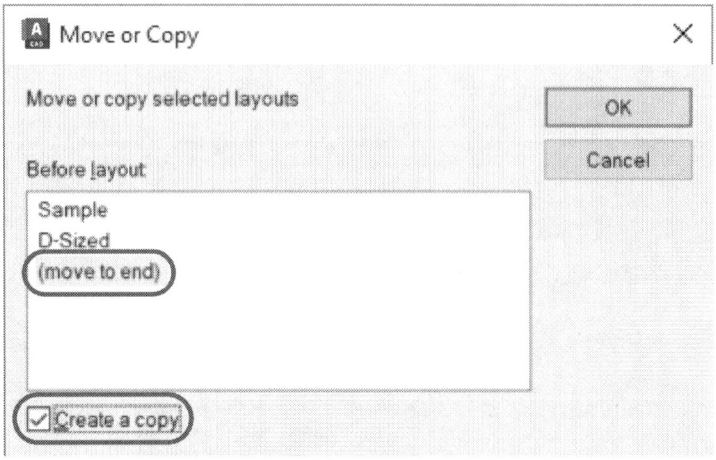

Figure 14–46

2. Double-click on the **D-Sized** tab name so that it highlights in blue. Type the name **All Views** to change it. Rename the other two layouts based on the **D-Sized** layout as **Office Wing** and **Auditorium Wing**, as shown in Figure 14–47.

Figure 14–47

3. Select each of the new layouts and note that they contain the same information.
4. Open the **Office Wing** layout and delete the upper right viewport and bottom two viewports by selecting the boundary of each viewport and then pressing <Delete>.

5. Click the boundary of the Offices viewport to display its grips. In the *Status Bar*, note that the (Lock/Unlock Viewport) is locked and the scale factor is grayed out. Using the middle arrow grip, set the scale to **1/4"=1'-0".**

   Note: *Even though the (Lock/Unlock Viewport) is locked in the* Status Bar, *you can easily use the middle arrow grip to change the scale.*

6. Use the middle square grip to place the viewport in the center of the layout. Press <Esc> to clear the selection.
7. Open the **Auditorium Wing** layout and delete the upper left and the bottom two viewports.
8. Select the auditorium viewport boundary to display the grips and using the middle arrow grip, set the scale to **1/8"=1'-0"**. Using the middle square grip, place the viewport in the center of the layout. Press <Esc> to clear the selection.
9. Delete the **Sample** layout by right-clicking on the layout tab in the *Status Bar*, selecting **Delete**, and then clicking **OK** in the confirmation dialog box.
10. Save the drawing.

End of practice

Chapter Review Questions

1. Once you have scaled a viewport, how do you prevent the scale from being changed?
   a. Explode the viewport.
   b. Lock the viewport.
   c. Freeze all layers in the drawing.
   d. Lock the layer that the viewport is on.

2. When you copy a layout, which of the following is true of the new layout?
   a. Everything in the new layout matches the original layout.
   b. The new layout is always added at the end of all of the other layouts.
   c. The new layout is always empty and you need to set up the new layout.
   d. Only the title block is copied over from the original layout into the copied layout.

3. How can you modify viewports?
   a. Using grips.
   b. Using the *Insert Layout* dialog box.
   c. Using the **Edit Viewport** tool.
   d. You cannot modify the viewports once they are created.

4. Which of the following is true with respect to viewports in a layout?
   a. You cannot create multiple overlapping viewports.
   b. You can create multiple viewports only if they are of the same shape and size.
   c. You can create multiple viewports in various shapes and sizes.
   d. You can create only one viewport per layout.

5. Which of the following is true for the (Insert View) command? (Select all that apply.)
   a. The command enables you to create named views in Model Space.
   b. The command enables you to create named views in Paper Space layouts.
   c. The command enables you to create viewports of the named views in the layout.
   d. The command enables you to set the scale of the viewports before placing the view in a layout.

6. When you select the edge of a viewport in Paper Space layout, different grips display. What does the middle square grip do?
   a. Resizes the viewport.
   b. Moves the viewport.
   c. Scales the viewport.
   d. Rotates the viewport.

Command Summary

Button	Command	Location
	Insert View	• **Ribbon:** *Layout* tab>*Layout Viewports* panel
/	**Lock/Unlock Viewport**	• **Status Bar**
	Maximize Viewport	• **Status Bar**
	Minimize Viewport	• **Status Bar**
MODEL	**Model Space**	• **Status Bar**
	New View	• **Ribbon:** *View* tab>*Named View* panel
PAPER	**Paper Space**	• **Status Bar**
1:2	**Viewport Scale**	• **Status Bar**
	Viewports, Object	• **Ribbon:** *Layout* tab>*Layout Viewports* panel • **Command Prompt:** -vports or mview
	Viewports, Polygonal	• **Ribbon:** *Layout* tab>*Layout Viewports* panel • **Command Prompt:** -vports or mview
	Viewports, Rectangular	• **Ribbon:** *Layout* tab>*Layout Viewports* panel

Chapter 15

Printing Your Drawing

In this chapter, you learn about printing in the AutoCAD® software, how to select what to print or plot, how to select a plotter, and how to preview a printed drawing.

Learning Objectives

- Print a drawing from Model Space as a check plot or finished drawing plot.
- Print a layout drawing in Paper Space based on a paper size.
- Preview and plot layouts.
- Set options for printing and plotting.

15.1 Printing Concepts

As you work on a drawing, it sometimes needs to be printed. For example, you can print a check plot while the drawing is in progress, and when the drawing is finished, you can print a full set of working drawings with dimensioning, text, and titleblocks, as shown in Figure 15–1. Depending on the size of your project, you can do all of these things from one or several drawing files.

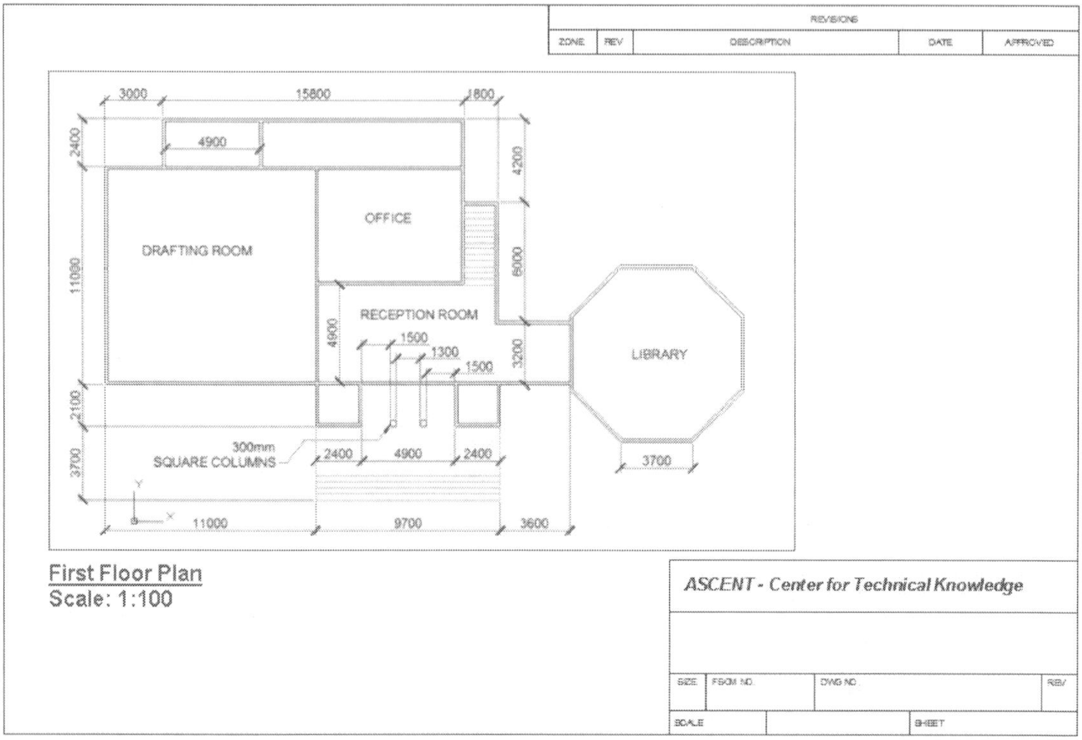

Figure 15–1

There are two methods of printing in the AutoCAD software:

- From Model Space
- From Paper Space Layouts

Hint: Printing vs. Plotting

Both of these terms are used to describe the process of getting an AutoCAD drawing onto a piece of paper. Most of what you do now is technically printing, but many people refer to large format printing as plotting because of the old plotters that were used before laser technology. Printing and plotting mean essentially the same thing today.

Model Space Printing

Everything you have done so far has been in AutoCAD Model Space. In Model Space, you draw the model full-size in its real-world units. You can print directly from Model Space for a quick *check plot* of all or part of the drawing, as shown in Figure 15–2.

- When you print from Model Space, you set a scale in the **Plot** command. DO NOT scale the objects in the drawing.

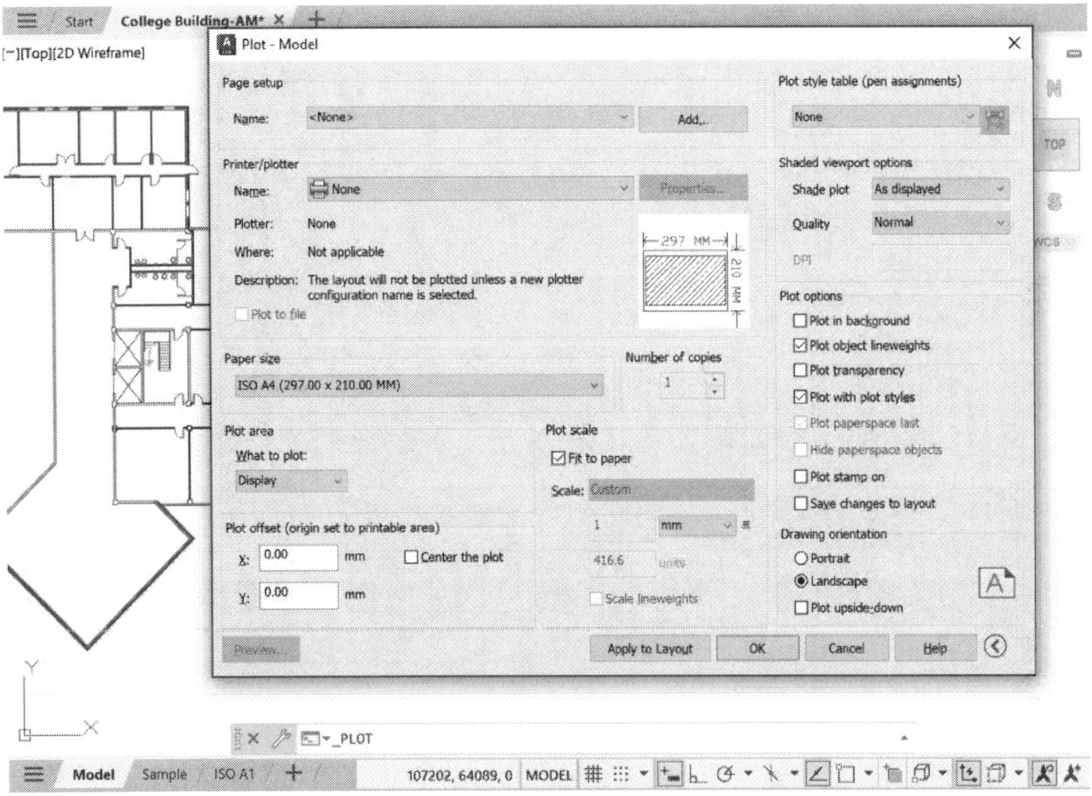

Figure 15–2

- You can set the scale in the **Plot** command to print the model at a precise scale factor, such as **1/4"=1'-0"**.
- If you need a border, titleblock, dimensions or other annotations to be printed at a specific size, these non-representational objects need to be scaled up to the scale of the drawing. This ensures that when the drawing is shrunk down to fit on the sheet of paper during the **Plot** command, their sizes are printed correctly.
- With Model Space printing, you cannot easily print multiple views of the same drawing at different scales.

Paper Space Layout Printing

The primary way to print in the AutoCAD software is to use Paper Space Layouts. Think of the layout as a sheet of paper on which you can place snapshots of your model in *viewports*. These snapshots can be any size and at any scale, as shown in Figure 15–3. You can arrange, enlarge or crop them, as required.

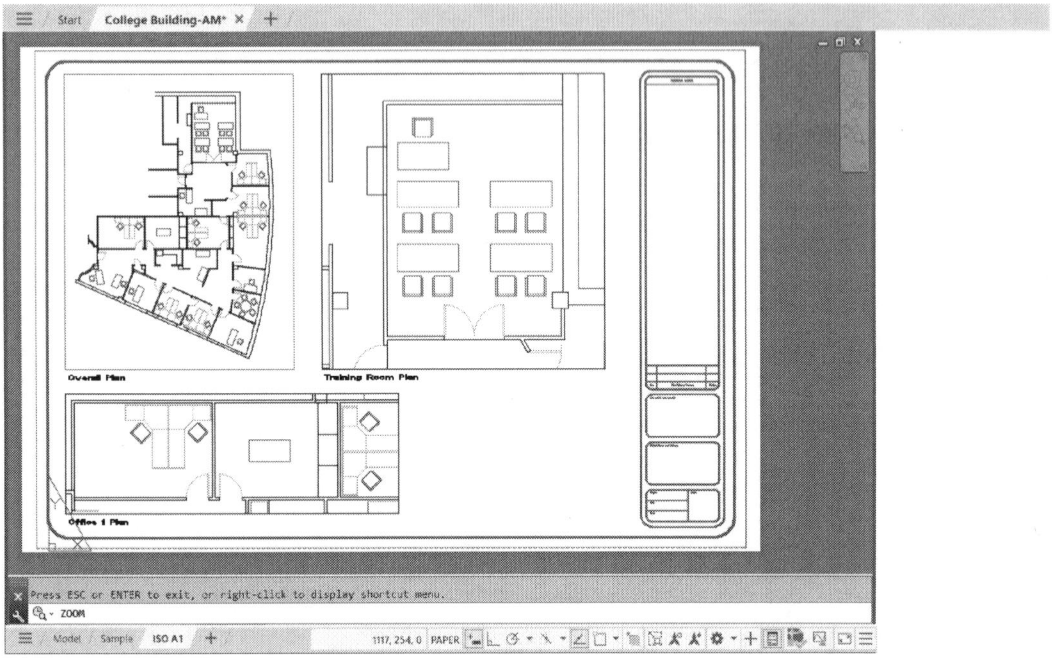

Figure 15–3

Using this method of printing separates the tasks of drawing into two stages:

1. In Model Space, all of the elements are drawn full scale (i.e., at their actual real-world size).
2. In Paper Space Layouts, all of the elements are drawn at the appropriate size for the sheet of paper and you add viewports to display the model.

- The border, titleblock, general notes, schedules, and titles are placed on the layout. They should be drawn at the actual size at which you want them to print on the sheet of paper. Most dimensions and text can be added through the viewport on the model. Their size is controlled by the scale of the viewport and the associated annotation scale.

Only one model can be displayed per drawing, but you can have multiple layouts. Each layout can have a different sheet size, scales, and plotter and these settings are stored in the layout.

15.2 Printing Layouts

When creating layouts in a drawing, each layout represents one sheet, as shown in Figure 15–4. By creating the layout, you define what should be printed. The layout is based on a paper size that is determined by the printer. If the layout is set up correctly, you can plot it without reviewing any additional information in the *Plot* dialog box.

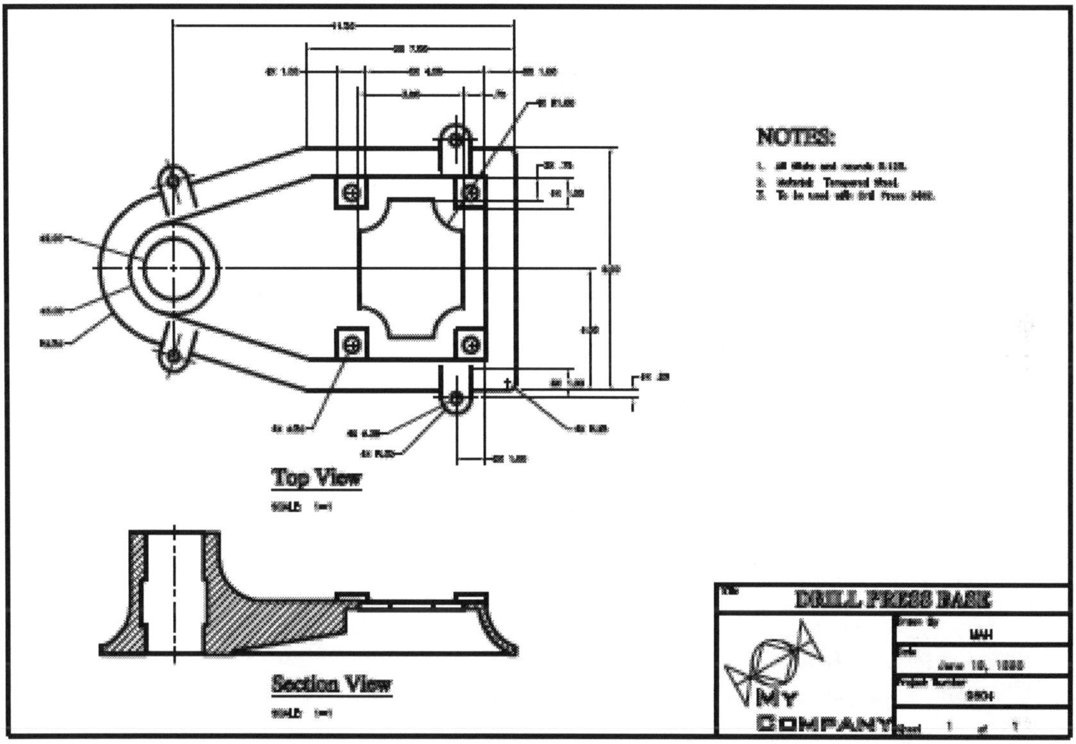

Figure 15–4

How To: Plot a Layout

1. Select the layout that you want to plot.
2. In the *Output* tab>*Plot* panel, click (Plot).
   - You can also start the **Plot** command in the *Application Menu* by selecting **Print**.

3. If everything is set up as required, in the *Plot* dialog box, click **OK**.

- If the drawing has multiple layouts, a *Batch Plot* notification dialog box opens where you can either use the **Try Batch Plot (Publish)** or select **Continue to plot a single sheet**, as shown in Figure 15–5.

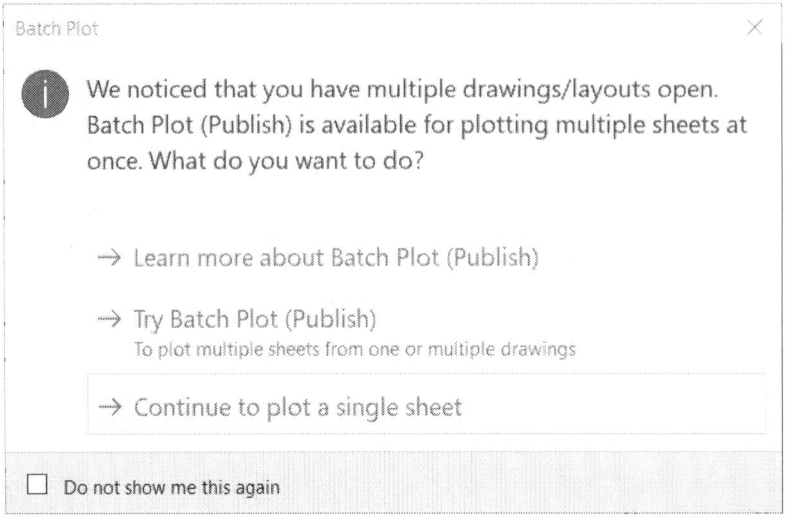

Figure 15–5

- If you are plotting to a DWF plotter or creating a PDF file (which creates a file rather than a paper plot), you are prompted for a name and location for the file in the *Browse for Plot File* or a *Save PDF File As* dialog boxes respectively.
- When the plot is finished, a balloon notification displays in the *Status Bar*, as shown in Figure 15–6. You can click on the link in the balloon to display details about the plot job.

Figure 15–6

Previewing the Plot

Previewing your plot can be helpful to ensure that you are plotting the correct objects before wasting paper and ink.

- You can access the preview in the *Output* tab>*Plot* panel by clicking (Preview), or in the *Application Menu* by selecting **Print>Plot Preview**.
- You can also click **Preview** in the *Plot* dialog box. This is useful when you are making changes in the dialog box and want to display the results before printing.
- In Preview mode, viewing tools, such as Pan and various Zoom options display instead of the ribbon. You can also right-click and select an option, as shown in Figure 15–7.

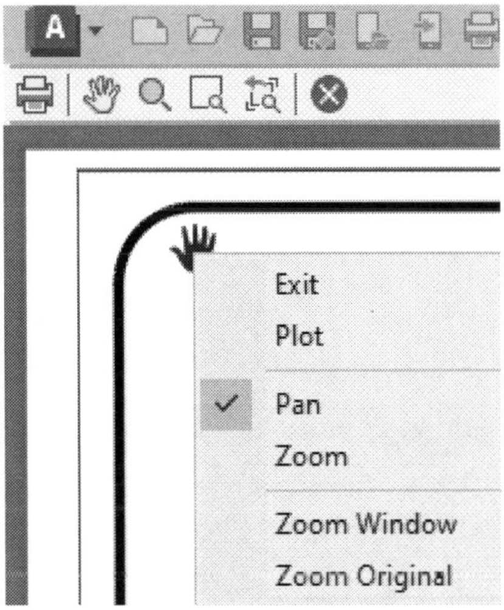

Figure 15–7

Batch Plot

If a drawing has multiple layouts, you can use **Batch Plot** to publish a group of drawings that are compressed together in a selected electronic format. This makes them easy to work with, maintain, and distribute.

- You can create a batch plot by clicking (Batch Plot) located in the *Output* tab>*Plot* panel or in the *Application Menu* by selecting **Print>Batch plot**.
- You can also batch plot by selecting **Try Batch Plot (Publish)** in the *Batch Plot* dialog box, which opens while using the **Plot** command with a multi-layout drawing.

- In the *Publish* dialog box, you can set the electronic drawing set as **DWF**, **DWFx**, or **PDF** file, as shown in Figure 15–8.

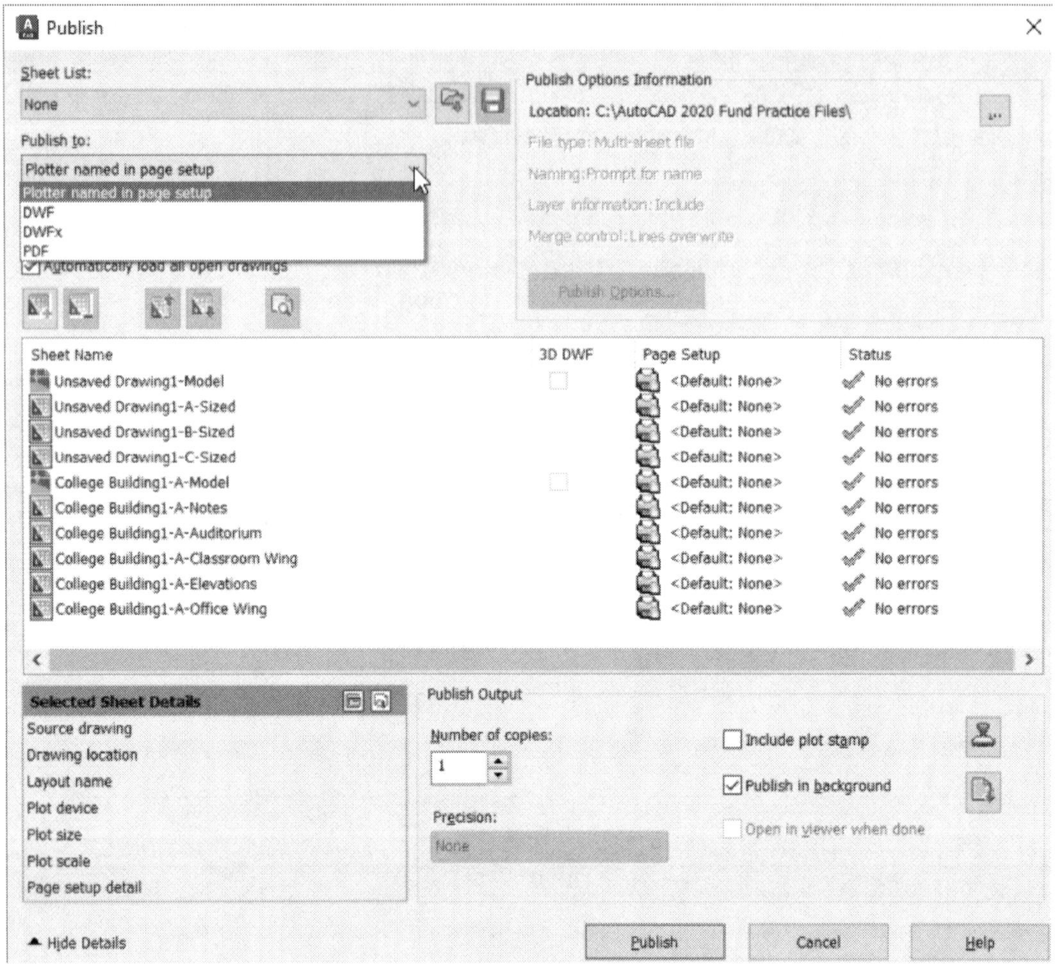

Figure 15–8

15.3 Print and Plot Settings

While most of the options are typically set in a layout, you can adjust some additional options when plotting. For example, you might want to make a half-sized plot or just plot part of a layout or model so that you can check the design, as shown in Figure 15–9. You can make changes in the *Plot* dialog box without impacting the layout.

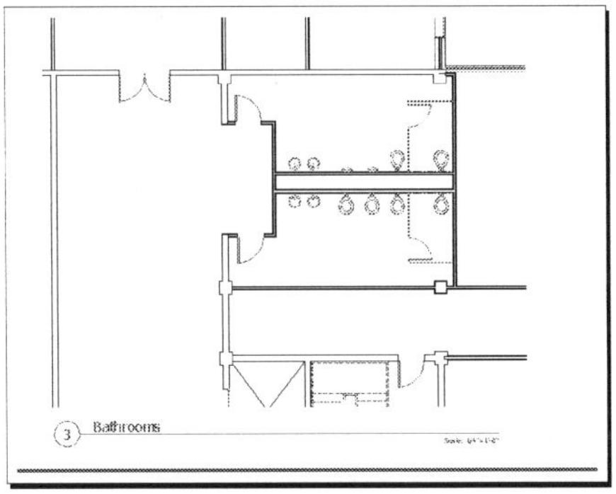

Figure 15–9

You can modify the plot settings in the *Plot* dialog box, as shown in Figure 15–10.

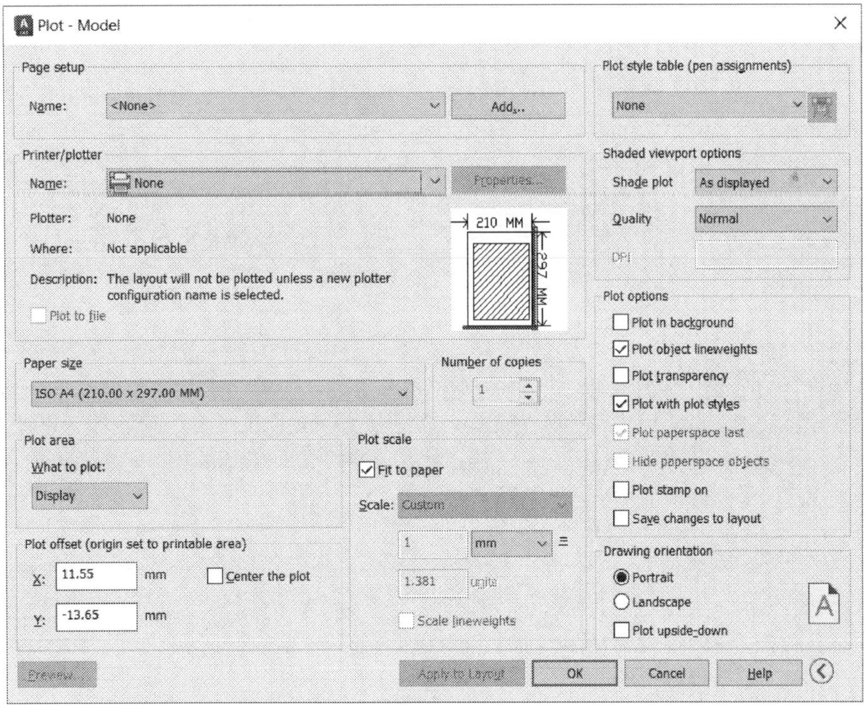

Figure 15–10

Printer/Plotter

- You need to select the plotter first because it determines the paper size.
- Depending on the type of plotter specified, the *Number of copies* area might be available, to set the number of copies to print, as shown in Figure 15–11. It is grayed out when you are using a DWF plotter and some options of PDF version because it plots to a file, rather than directly to paper.

Figure 15–11

What to Plot

The *Plot area* controls the part of the drawing that is plotted.

- The **Display** or **Window** options, as shown in Figure 15–12, can be used to plot part of a layout or model. While the **Display** option plots the objects that display on the screen, the **Window** option enables you to create a window around the area that you want to plot.

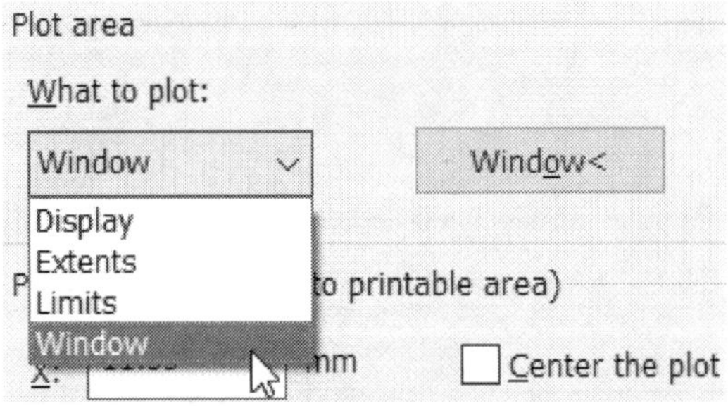

Figure 15–12

- The **Extents** option plots a view that includes every object in the drawing. It includes any objects that might be outside your main drawing. Note that with this option, the objects in the plot might be very small depending on how far apart they are in the drawing.
- The **Limits** option is only available in Model Space and plots an area that is defined by the limits that have been set in the drawing.

Setting the Plot Scale

- While you typically print layouts at a 1:1 scale, you can print half-sized plots by selecting a *Scale* of **0.5=1.0**.
- The **Fit to paper** option, as shown in Figure 15–13, can be used when printing a check plot to a letter-sized plotter. Note that the drawing is not to scale when this option is selected.

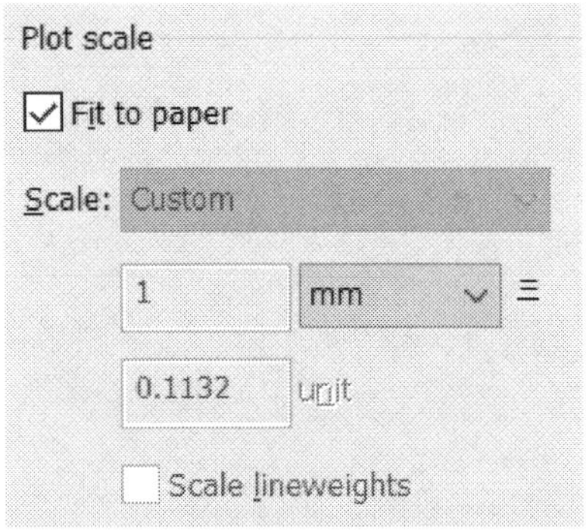

Figure 15–13

- You can also specify a *Scale* of **1/4"=1'-0"**. This is typically done if you are plotting from Model Space and want to have it to scale.
- The **Scale lineweights** option scales the lineweights in proportion to the plot scale. If not selected (the default), the lineweights plot at the line width size.

Plot Offset

- By default, the lower left corner of the plot area starts printing at the lower left corner of the page margin. You can move the plot area to the left or up from the lower left margin by specifying an X- or Y-offset, as shown in Figure 15–14.

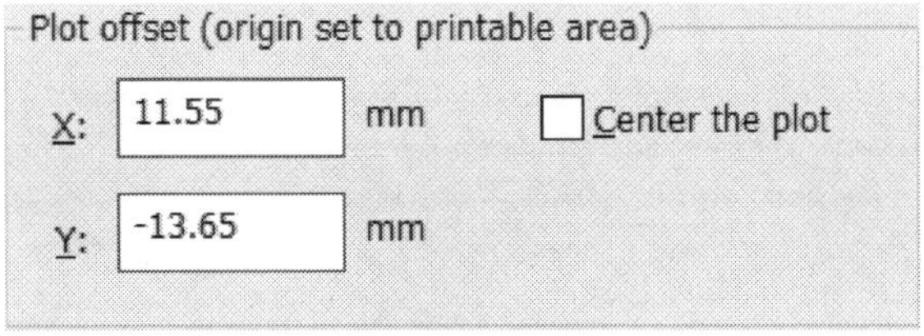

Figure 15–14

- The **Center the plot** option is not available (grayed out) when the *Plot area* is set to **Layout** because the layout fills the printable area completely.
- The **Center the plot** option automatically calculates X- and Y-offsets so that the plot is centered on the paper.

More Options

If the dialog box displays in the compressed form, click (More Options) in the lower right corner to display more options. Some of the options are shown in Figure 15–15.

> ***Note:*** *Most of the options relate to advanced features.*

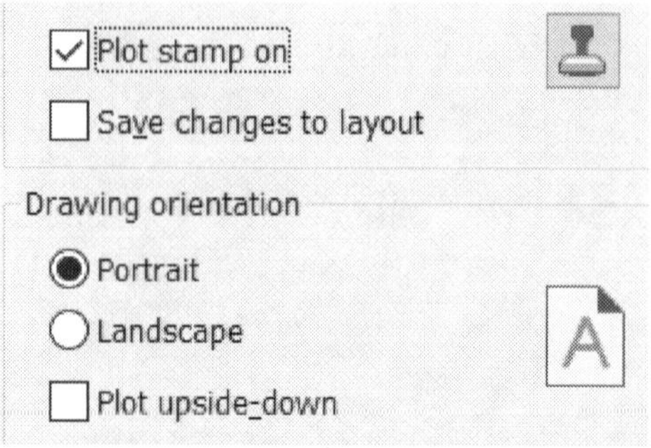

Figure 15–15

Plot stamp on	Adds a plot stamp with standard information, such as drawing name, date and time, etc. The (Plot Stamp Settings) icon becomes available when the **Plot Stamp On** is selected.
Save changes to layout	Automatically saves any changes you make to the plot settings with the layout, which become the new defaults when you plot the layout.

- **Apply to Layout** is similar to the **Save changes to layout** option, except that it only saves changes to the layout when you click the button, rather than automatically, all the time.
- You can also select the *Drawing orientation* options such as printing with **Portrait** or **Landscape** orientation, as shown above in Figure 15–15.

Practice 15a
Print Layouts and Check Plots

Practice Objectives

- Plot a layout to a file.
- Print a check plot from Model Space.

In this practice, you will plot a layout to a file and create a check plot, as shown in Figure 15–16.

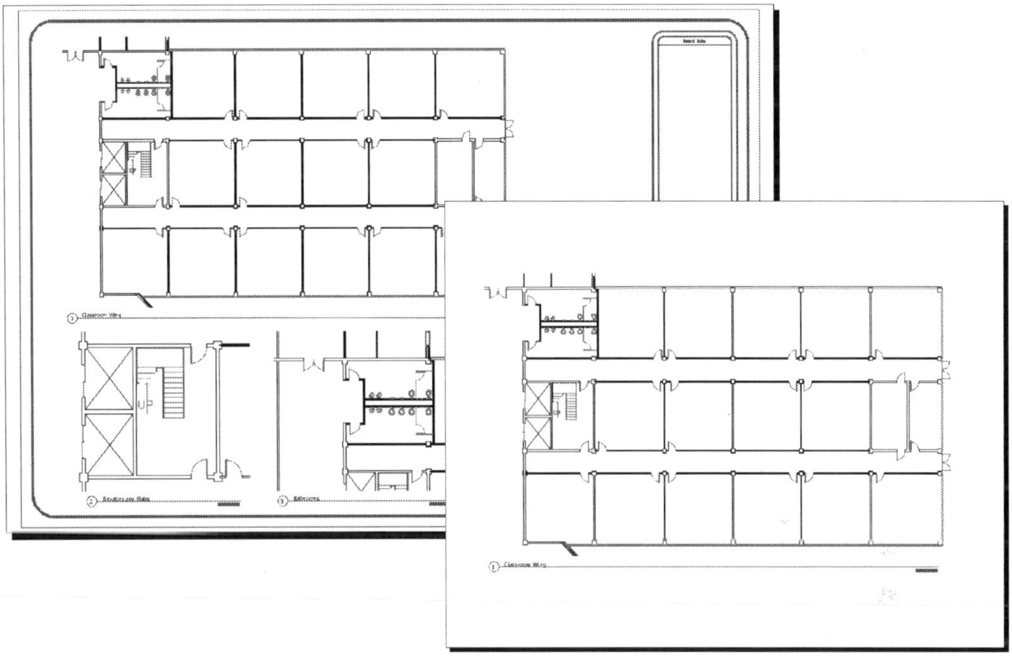

Figure 15–16

Task 1: Print layouts.

In this task, you will plot a layout (shown in Figure 15–17) to a file.

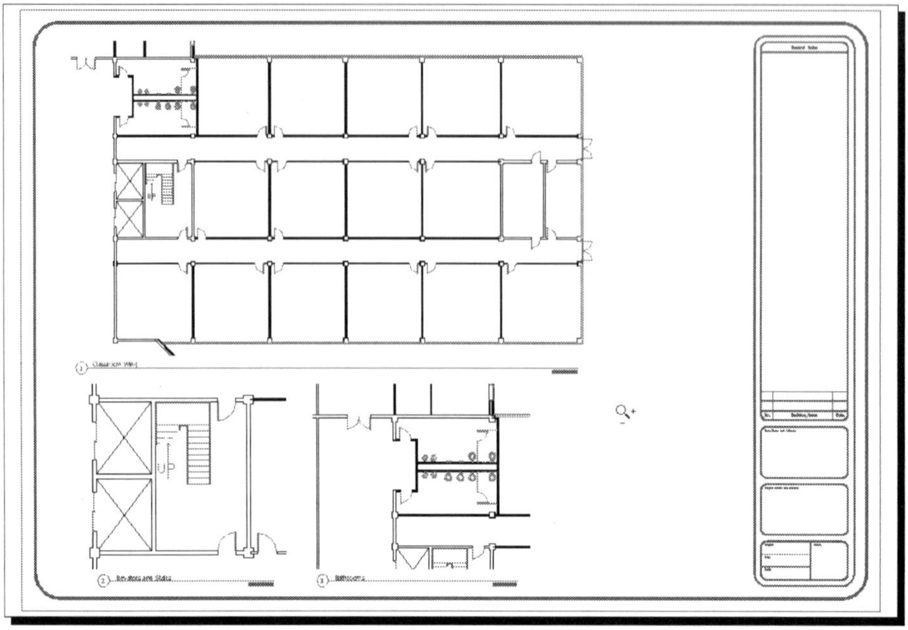

Figure 15–17

1. Open **College Building1-A.dwg** from your practice files folder.
2. Switch to the **Classroom Wing** layout tab and verify that you are in Paper Space.
   - If **Classroom Wing** is not displayed in the layout tabs bar, click and select it from the list, as shown in Figure 15–18.

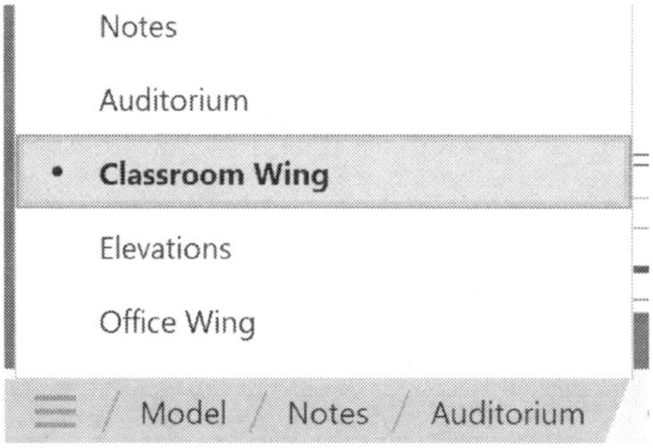

Figure 15–18

3. In the *Output* tab>*Plot* panel, click (Plot). As there are multiple layouts in the drawing, the *Batch Plot confirmation* dialog box opens. Click **Continue to plot a single sheet**.
4. In the *Plot* dialog box, note that *Printer/plotter*, *Paper size*, and other options are all set according to the page setup for this layout. The layout is set to use the **DWF6 ePlot.pc3** plotter, which automatically plots to a file.
5. Click **Preview**. Note that your cursor changes to a magnifying glass, indicating that you are in **Zoom Realtime** mode. Zoom in a little, right-click, and select **Pan**.
6. After experimenting with panning and zooming, right-click and select **Zoom Original**. Right-click again and select **Exit** to return to the *Plot* dialog box.
7. Click **OK** to create the plot file. Note that the *Files of type* is set to **DWF (*.dwf)**. Accept the default file name for the .DWF file and save it in your practice files folder.
8. When the plot is complete, in the *Status Bar*, a balloon message displays along with the Plot icon, as shown in Figure 15–19. Select **Click to view plot and publish details...** to display the plot details. Click **Close**.

Figure 15–19

Task 2: Print check plots.

In this task, you will create a check plot, as shown in Figure 15–20.

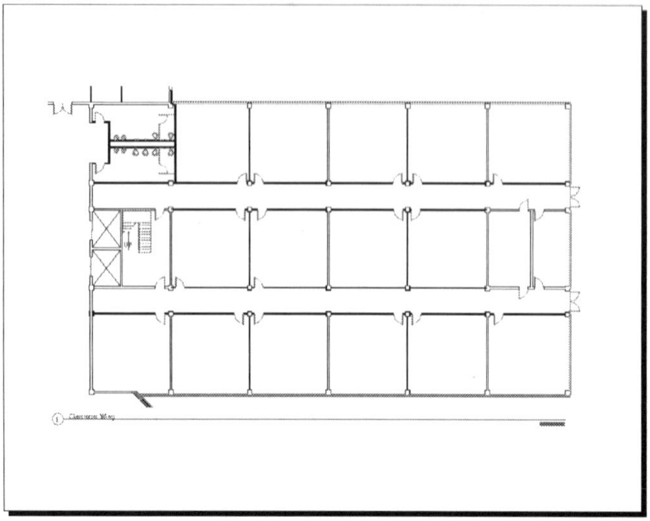

Figure 15–20

1. Start the **Plot** command again. In the *Batch Plot confirmation* dialog box, click **Continue to plot a single sheet**.
2. Set the *Paper size* to **ANSI A (8.50 x 11.00 Inches)** and click **Preview**. Only a small portion of the entire plot displays, as shown in Figure 15–21. Right-click and select **Exit**.

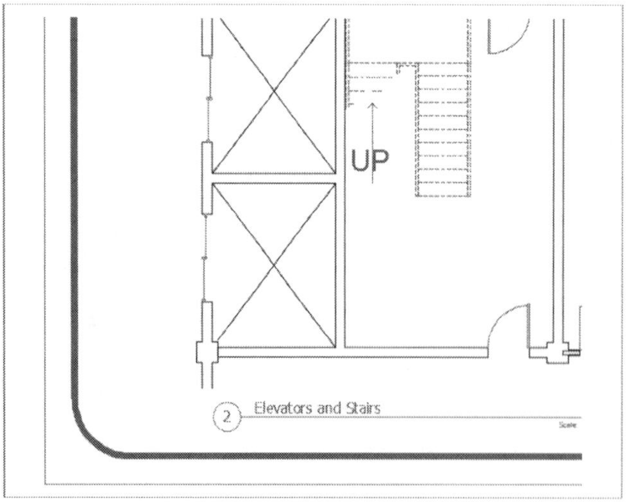

Figure 15–21

3. In the *Plot area*, expand the *What to plot* drop-down list and select **Window**. Draw a window around the Elevators and Stairs viewport, and preview again. The selected viewport displays as it fits on an 8.5 x 11 sheet of paper at a 1/4"=1'0" scalewhich . Exit the preview.
4. Click **Window<**, draw a window around the *Classroom Wing* viewport at the top of the layout, and preview the plot. Only a portion of the selected viewport is displayed. Exit the preview.
5. Set the *Plot scale* to **Fit to paper** and the *Plot offset* to **Center the plot**. Preview again. The whole viewport displays. Exit the preview.
6. Click **OK** to plot the drawing. Name the file **Check Plot.dwf** and click **Save** to save it in the practice files folder.
7. Ensure that you are in the **Classroom Wing** layout tab. In the *Output* tab>*Plot* panel, click **Preview**. The preview indicates that the entire layout is going to be plotted as was intended. The changes you just made to the **Plot** command did not change the layout information.
8. Exit the preview. Save and close the drawing.

End of practice

Chapter Review Questions

1. With Model Space printing, it is very easy to print multiple views of the same drawing at different scales.
   a. True
   b. False

2. Which of the following is true for Model Space and Paper Space printing?
   a. In both Model Space and Paper Space, all of the elements are drawn full-scale at their real-world size.
   b. In both Model Space and Paper Space, all of the elements are drawn at an appropriate size for the sheet of paper.
   c. In Model Space, all of the elements are drawn at an appropriate size for the sheet of paper.
   d. In Paper Space, all of the elements are drawn at an appropriate size for the sheet of paper.

3. To plot a layout, what scale should you typically use in the *Plot Scale* area in the *Plot* dialog box?
   a. 1:1
   b. Custom
   c. Any standard scale
   d. Scale to fit

4. What is determined when you select the plotter first in the *Plot-Model* dialog box?
   a. Plot area
   b. Paper size
   c. Plot Scale
   d. Plot offset

5. When you plot from the *Model* tab, which *What to plot* option in the *Plot* area automatically plots all of the drawn objects?
   a. Display
   b. Window
   c. Extents
   d. View

6. Which of the following can you do using the preview of a plot?
   a. Modify objects in the drawing.
   b. Zoom or pan around the drawing.
   c. Only preview a portion of the entire drawing.
   d. Delete viewports from a layout.

7. In the *Plot* dialog box, which *What to plot* option do you set in the *Plot* area to plot the objects that are currently displayed in the drawing window?
   a. Extents
   b. Window
   c. Layout
   d. Display

Command Summary

Button	Command	Location
	**Batch Plot**	• **Ribbon:** *Output* tab>*Plot* panel • **Application Menu:** Print>Batch Plot
	**Plot**	• *Quick Access Toolbar* • **Ribbon:** *Output* tab>*Plot* panel • **Application Menu:** Print • **Command Prompt:** print, plot, or <Ctrl>+<P>
	**Plot Preview**	• **Ribbon:** *Output* tab>*Plot* panel • **Application Menu:** Print>Plot Preview • **Command Prompt:** preview

Chapter 16

Projects: Preparing to Print

This chapter contains practice projects that can be used to gain additional hands-on experience in the topics and commands covered so far in this guide. These projects are intended to be self-guided and do not include step-by-step information.

Learning Objective

- *All:* Create named views, insert viewports, adjust viewport views using grips, and then plot the layout to a file.

16.1 Mechanical Project

In this project, you will set up a drawing in a layout. You will create named views and insert them in the layout. Then, you will scale, resize, and move the viewports to place them, as shown in Figure 16–1.

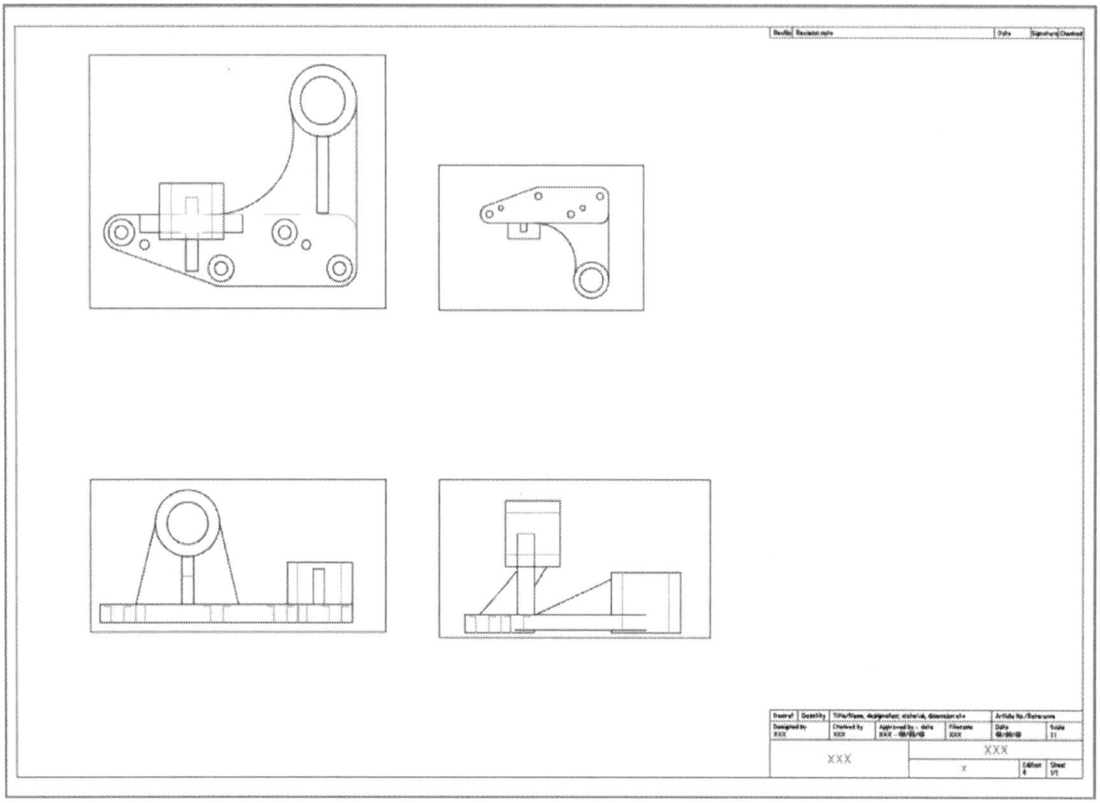

Figure 16–1

1. Open **Leverbracket-M.dwg** from the practice files folder.
2. In the Model Space, in the *View* tab>*Named Views* panel, use the (New View) command and the **Define window** option to create four named viewports: **Top**, **Front**, **Side**, and **Bottom**.
3. Switch to the **ISO A2** layout.
4. Erase the existing viewport.

5. In the *Layout* tab>*Layout Viewports* panel, use the **Insert View** gallery (shown in Figure 16–2) to insert the four named viewports as shown in Figure 16–1.

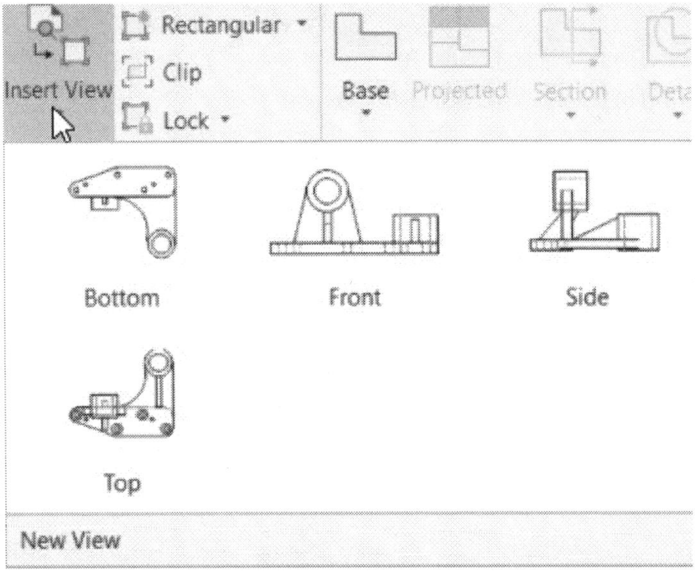

Figure 16–2

6. Using the Scale grip, set the scale for the **Front**, **Top**, and **Side** views to **1:2**.
7. Scale the **Bottom** view to **1:4**.
8. Using the **Resize** and **Move** grips, align the views, similar to that shown in Figure 16–1.
    - **Hint:** Use (Object Snap Tracking) to track from a second point in another view.
9. Save the drawing.
10. Preview and then plot to a file.

16.2 Architectural Project

In this project, you will set up a drawing in a layout by creating the named views and inserting them in the layout. You will scale, resize, and move the viewports, and use **Plot** to plot the drawing to a file, as shown in Figure 16–3.

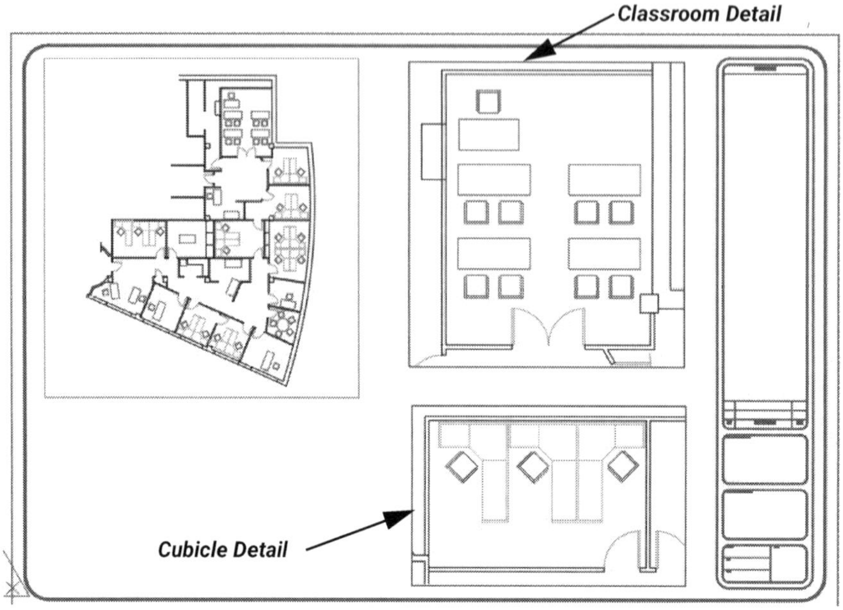

Figure 16–3

1. Open **New Office-A.dwg** from your practice files folder.
2. In the Model Space, create two named viewports (**Classroom Detail** and **Cubicle Detail**), as shown in Figure 16–3.
3. Switch to the **D-Sized** layout.
4. Resize the existing floor plan viewport and move it to the top left corner of the layout, as shown in Figure 16–3. Ensure that it has a scale of **1/8" = 1'**.
5. Insert the **Classroom Detail** near the top right side of the layout. Scale it to **1/2" = 1'** and then use the **Resize** and **Move** grips to place it as shown in Figure 16–3.
6. Insert the **Cubicle Detail** near the bottom right side of the layout. Scale it to **1/2" = 1'** and then use the **Resize** and **Move** grips to place it as shown in Figure 16–3.
7. Preview and then plot to a file.

Chapter 17

Text

In this chapter, you learn how to set up and use annotation scales and how to create, edit, and format multiline text.

Learning Objectives

- Work with annotative objects and scales.
- Create, edit, import and format paragraphs of text.
- Check and correct the spelling of the text in a drawing.
- Modify text styles, existing multiline text, and multilinear objects.
- Format the paragraph style, change the line spacing in a paragraph, and create columns.
- Add and remove leader lines to a multileader object.
- Combine, align, and evenly space leader lines.
- Create a unified table object that includes title, column headers, and multiple rows and columns.
- Populate table cells with text, blocks, and fields, and add calculations in a table.
- Add and remove columns, merge and unmerge cells, and modify cell properties in a table.

17.1 Annotation Basics

When you set up layouts with viewports at various scales, the parts of the model display at different sizes. However, the final printed sheet should have text and dimensions that are all of the same size when they are plotted, as shown in Figure 17–1. The *Annotation Scale* feature enables you to add text and dimensions to a drawing with views at many different scales. These annotation objects are scaled to suit and do not display in viewports with other annotation scales.

- Annotation objects include text, dimensions, hatches, and multileaders.

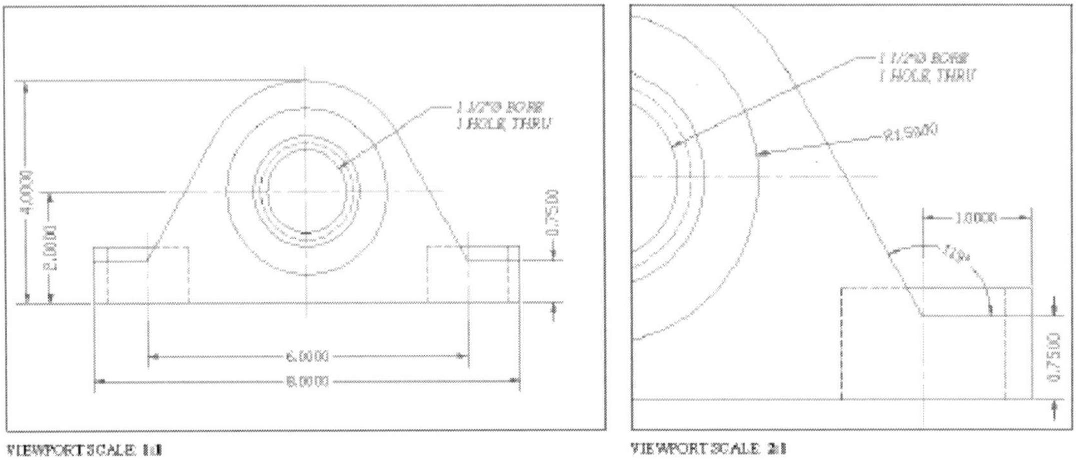

Figure 17–1

- When you create each viewport, set the viewport scale by using the (Middle arrow grip) of the selected viewport boundary or 1:2 (Viewport Scale) in the *Status Bar*, as shown in Figure 17–2. The Annotation Scale is automatically matched to the viewport scale.

Figure 17–2

***Note:** Click (Lock/Viewport) to lock the viewport so that the scale and location are not changed by mistake.*

- To add annotation objects, double-click inside the viewport to make it active and select the annotation tool. It is automatically scaled to match the viewport/annotation scale.

- To understand the differences between annotations placed in Model Space and Paper Space, open the *Properties* palette and note the two parameters: **Paper text height** and **Model text height**. For example, in the room shown in Figure 17–3, the text **Service Area** is placed in a viewport at a scale of **1/4"=1'-0"**, while the text for the title and scale is placed in Paper Space at a scale of 1:1. Note that the two text objects look the same size.

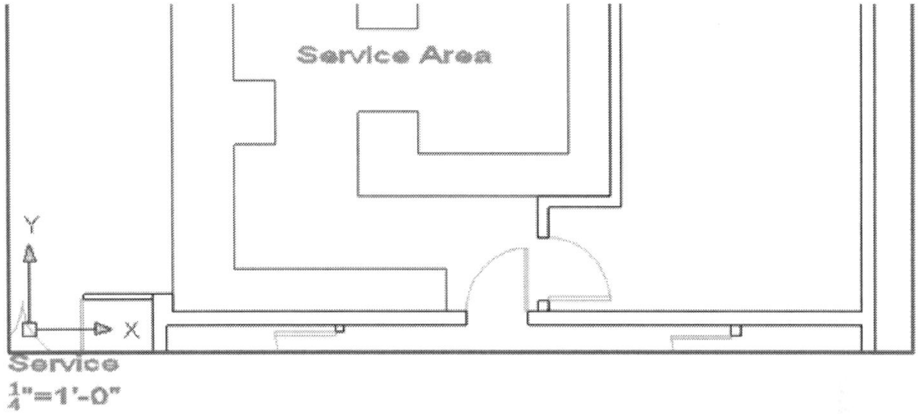

Figure 17–3

- Many annotation objects are created using styles. The annotation styles (Text Styles, Dimension Styles, and Multileader Styles) can be made annotative. You should select a style that is designed to work with the Annotation Scale so that objects are correctly placed in each viewport.

- (Annotation) displays next to annotative style names in the Text Style, Dimension Style, and Multileader Style Controls, as shown in Figure 17–4.

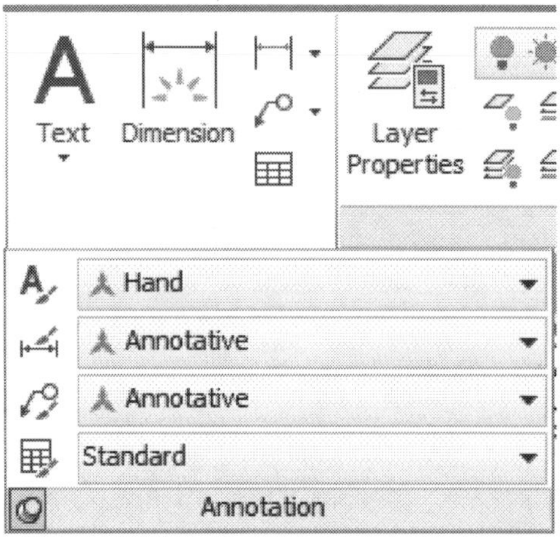

Figure 17–4

- When you have objects in your drawing that are annotative, (Annotation) symbol displays when you hover the cursor over them, as shown in Figure 17–5.

Figure 17–5

- You must change the Viewport Scale in the *Status Bar* for the annotative objects to change scale.

- You can annotate objects in Model Space by setting the 1:1 (Annotation Scale) in the *Status Bar*, as shown in Figure 17–6. It is linked to the Viewport Scale and the annotation displays in viewports that have the same annotation scale.

Figure 17–6

- When you use annotation styles, the *Model text height* in the *Properties* palette is read-only.

17.2 Adding Text in a Drawing

Many drawings include notes about the objects and about the project, as shown in Figure 17–7. This might be a set of general notes in the titleblock or notes specific to a particular view.

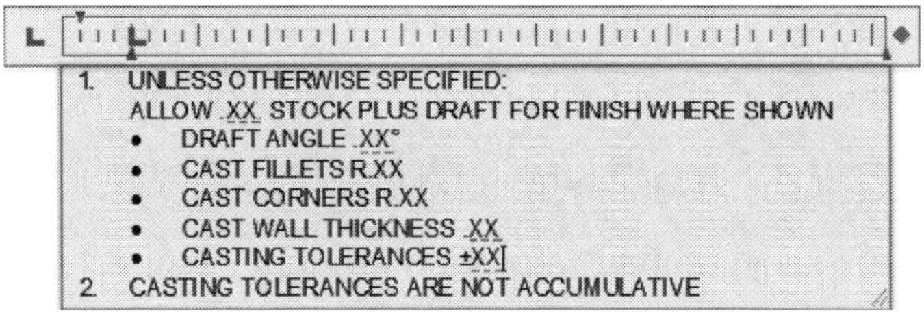

Figure 17–7

Multiline Text

You can use the **Multiline Text** (Mtext) command to create, edit, and format paragraphs of text.

- Any text created in the *Text Editor* becomes one object, no matter how many lines it contains. Because you are typing it in a Text Editor, the text automatically wraps at the end of the line.
- Text should be placed on its own layer.
- Set the layer and the text style before you start the **Multiline Text** command. The text style sets the default font of the text.

How To: Add Multiline Text

1. In the *Annotate* tab>*Text* panel or in the *Home* tab>*Annotation* panel, click A (Multiline Text).

   Note: *If you are creating an annotative object, you might be prompted to set the annotation scale.*

   - An example text string (abc) displays near the cursor as shown in Figure 17–8. This preview indicates the current text height and font.

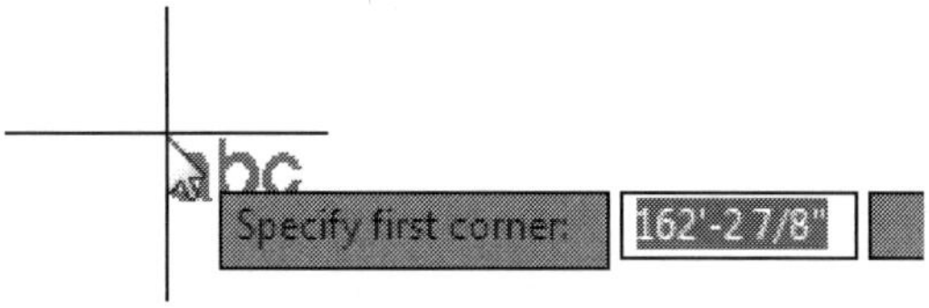

Figure 17–8

2. Select two points in the drawing to define a boundary box for the text. The *Text Editor* opens, as shown in Figure 17–9.

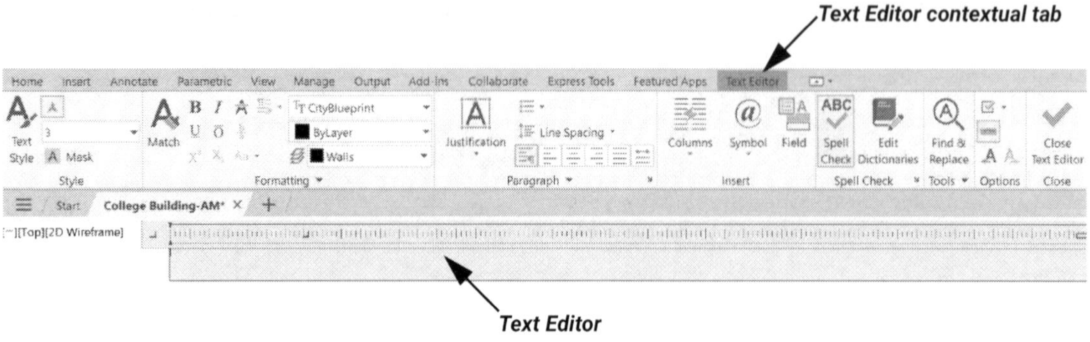

Figure 17–9

- When creating the boundary box for the text, an arrow displays indicating the direction in which the text is going to flow, based on the current vertical justification. The boundary determines the location of the text and its width (i.e., the length of a line before words wrap to the next line), but does not limit the number of lines you can type.

3. Type the text in the *Text Editor* and apply formatting options from the contextual tab.
4. Click (Close Text Editor) or click in the drawing window to finish creating the text. The text is inserted in the drawing as one object.

- The background of the *Text Editor* is transparent. This enables any drawing objects that are covered by the text box to be displayed.

How To: Set the Text Height

1. In the *Annotate* tab>*Text* panel or in the *Home* tab>*Annotation* panel, click A (Multiline Text).
2. Select the first point of the boundary box.
3. Select **Height** from the Command Line or shortcut menu (<Down Arrow>), as shown in Figure 17–10.
    - The text height specified with the **Height** option becomes the default text height for that text style. If you change the text height in the *Text Editor*, it is not saved.

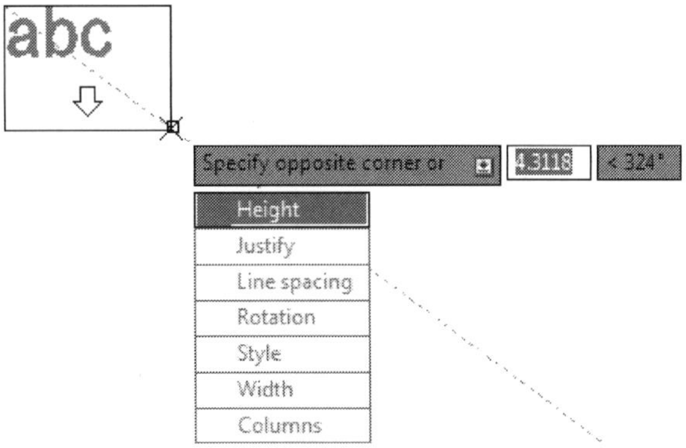

Figure 17–10

4. Enter the text height and press <Enter>.
5. Select the other point of the boundary box.

- Text can be placed in Paper Space or Model Space. In most cases, and especially if you are using an annotative text style, you should specify the height of the text to be the final plotted size.

Copying and Importing Text

You can copy text from a word processing software or other text editor and paste it directly into the *Text Editor*, as shown in Figure 17–11. You can also import text files that are saved in the ASCII or RTF format.

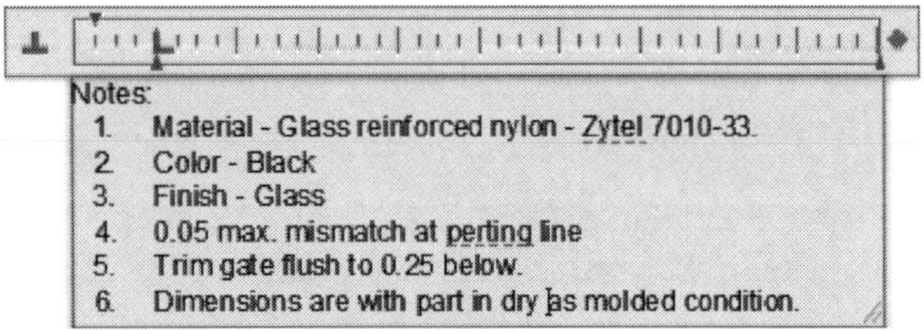

Figure 17–11

How To: Copy and Paste Text into the Text Editor

1. In a document file, copy the text to the Windows Clipboard.

   Note: *If you are creating an annotative object, you might be prompted to set the annotation scale.*

2. In the AutoCAD software, in the *Annotate* tab>*Text* panel or in the *Home* tab>*Annotation* panel, click A (Multiline Text).

3. Select points for the boundary box.
4. In the *Text Editor*, right-click and select **Paste**. The text you copied is pasted into the Text Editor.

- If you use **Paste Special**, you can set the copied text to be pasted without character or paragraph formatting, as shown in Figure 17–12.

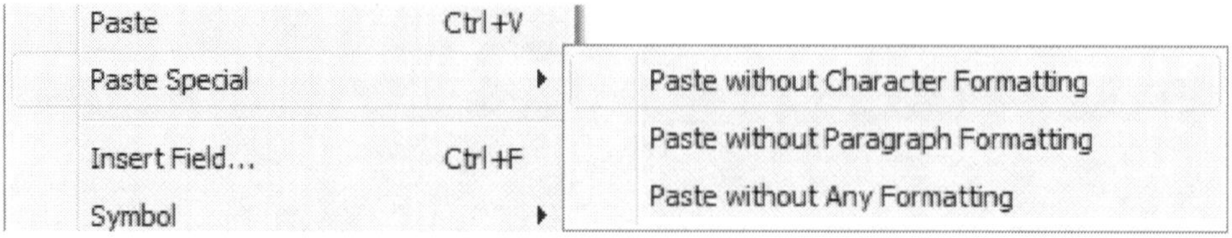

Figure 17–12

- When you copy and paste text created with Microsoft Word, it keeps the formatting from the document, including numbering or bullets and specific headings.

How To: Import Text

1. In the *Annotate* tab>*Text* panel or in the *Home* tab>*Annotation* panel, click A (Multiline Text).
2. Select points for the boundary box.
3. In the *Text Editor* contextual tab>expanded *Tools* panel, click **Import Text**. You can also right-click in the *Text Editor* and select **Import Text**.
4. In the *Select File* dialog box, select the file that you want to use and click **Open** to import the text.
   - Imported text does not include formatting.

Hint: Text Symbols

You can add symbols to your text. In the *Text Editor* contextual tab>*Insert* panel, expand @ (Symbol) and select a symbol in the list. You can select **Other...** at the end of the list to open the *Character Map* dialog box to access specialty symbols in different fonts.

In the *Text Editor* contextual tab>*Insert* panel, click (Field) to add text objects that gather their information from objects or system variables, such as the date or drawing name in the AutoCAD software.

Spell Checking

The spellings are checked by default when you are in the *Text Editor*. It can be toggled on and off in the *Text Editor* contextual tab>*Spell Check* panel, as shown in Figure 17–13.

Figure 17–13

- Any misspellings are underlined with a dashed red line, but only in the *Text Editor*. Right-click on the word to display a list of suggestions, as shown in Figure 17–14. You can also add words to the dictionary or ignore the misspelled words.

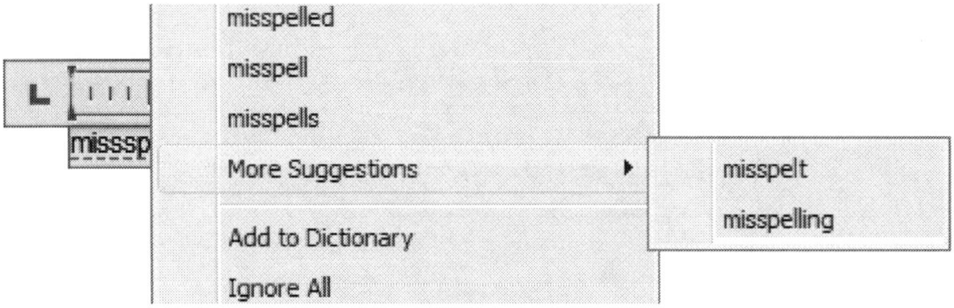

Figure 17–14

- Click  in the *Spell Check* panel title to open the *Check Spelling Settings* dialog box.

Practice 17a
Add Text in a Drawing

Practice Objectives

- Add text to a cover sheet with different text styles and sizes.
- Import text into the *Text Editor*.

In this practice, you will use the **Multiline Text** command to place text on a cover sheet using two different text styles and sizes, as shown in Figure 17–15. You will also import text into the *Text Editor*.

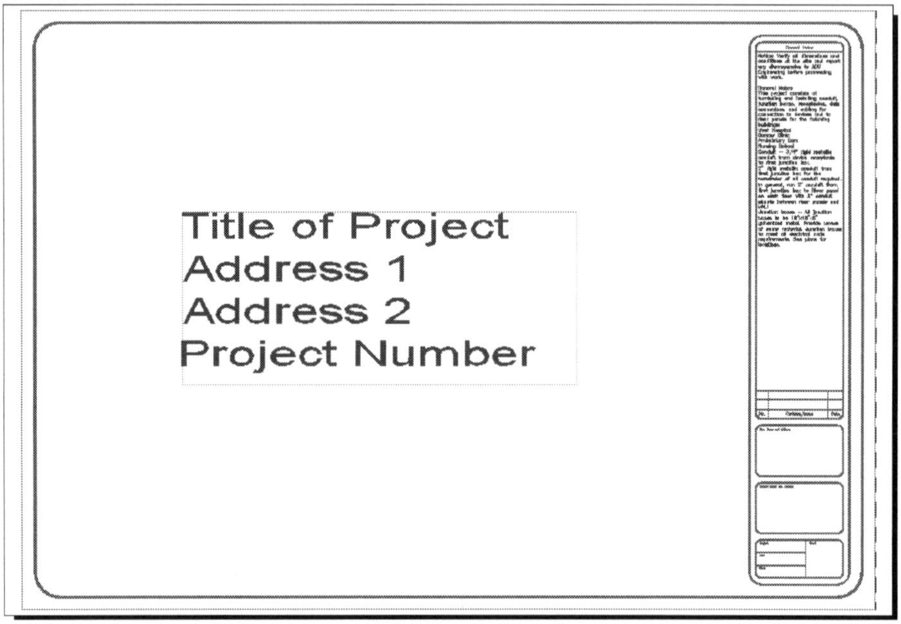

Figure 17–15

Task 1: Add General Notes to the cover sheet.

1. Open **Cover Sheet-A.dwg** from your practice files folder.
2. Ensure that you are in the **Cover Sheet** layout tab.
3. Set the current layer to **Notes**.
4. In the *Home* tab>expanded *Annotation* panel, set the current text style to **Standard**, as shown in Figure 17–16. The text style can also be set in the *Annotate* tab>*Text* panel.

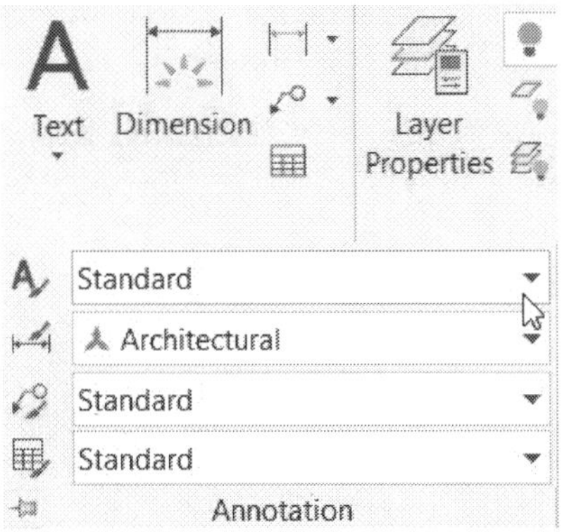

Figure 17–16

5. Zoom in on the top right corner of the layout, where it says **General Notes**.
6. In the *Home* tab>*Annotation* panel, click **A** (Text), which is the **Multiline Text** command. (The **MText** command can also be accessed in the *Annotate* tab>Text panel.) The alphabet is attached to the cursor indicating the height of the text.
7. To avoid snapping to the lines in the titleblock, toggle off **Object Snap** if required.
8. In the *General Notes* area of the titleblock, select near the upper left corner under the General Notes line as the first point of the boundary box. Right-click, select **Height**, enter **1/8"**, and press <Enter>. For the second point, click approximately in a diagonally opposite corner in the *General Notes* area, as shown in Figure 17–17. The *Text Editor* displays for the width of the boundary box that you selected, and the *Text Editor* contextual tab also opens.

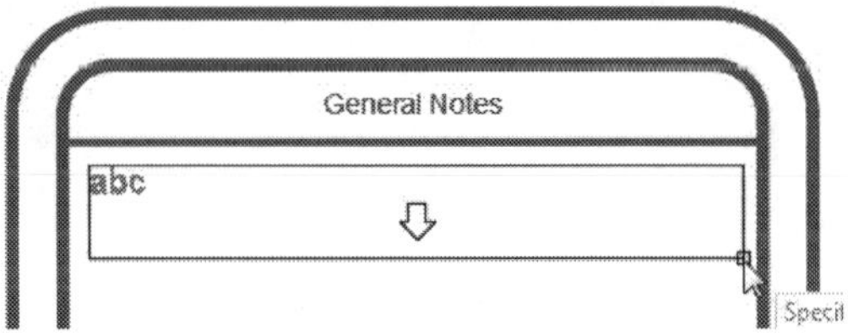

Figure 17–17

9. Type the text shown in Figure 17–18 and remain in the *Text Editor*.

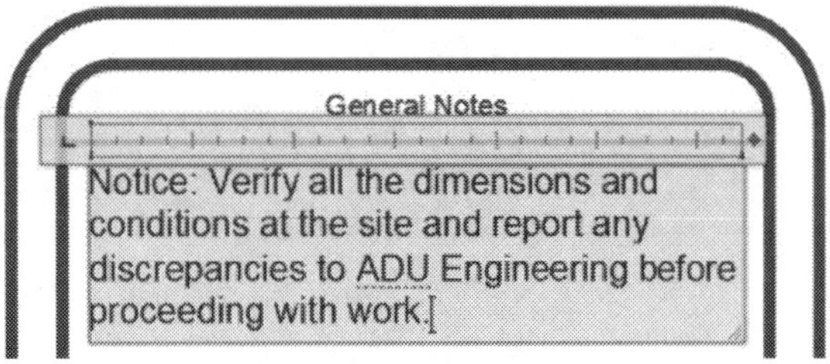

Figure 17–18

10. Note that **ADU** is underlined in red because the word is not recognized by the spell checker. Select it, right-click, and select **Add to Dictionary**.

    Note: *For the words to be underlined, in the Text Editor tab>Spell Check panel,* ***Spell Check*** *must be toggled on (highlighted).*

11. Move the cursor to the end of the text, and press <Enter> twice to go to the next line and add a new empty line.
12. Right-click in the *Text Editor* and select **Import Text**.
13. In the *Select File* dialog box, select the **General Notes.txt** file from your practice files folder and click **Open**. The text from the file is added.
14. Select a point anywhere on the screen, outside of the *Text Editor*, to close it. The text displays as shown in Figure 17–19.
    * Your word wrap might be different because the size of your text boundary box might be different.

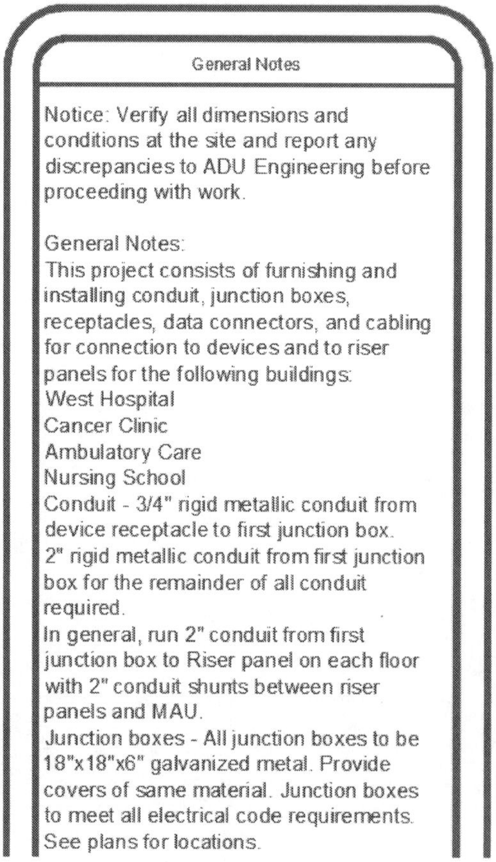

Figure 17–19

Task 2: Add project information to the cover sheet.

1. Zoom out to display the entire cover sheet layout.
2. In the *Annotate* tab>*Text* panel, set the text style to the **Title** text style.
   - The text style can also be set in the *Home* tab>expanded *Annotation* panel.
3. Click A (Multiline Text).
4. For the first corner, select the top left corner of the green rectangle at the center of the layout. (Use **Object Snap.**) Right-click, select **Height**, enter **1"**, and press <Enter>. Then, select the bottom right corner of the green rectangle.
5. In the *Text Editor,* type the text shown in Figure 17–20, pressing <Enter> at the end of each line to go to the next one.

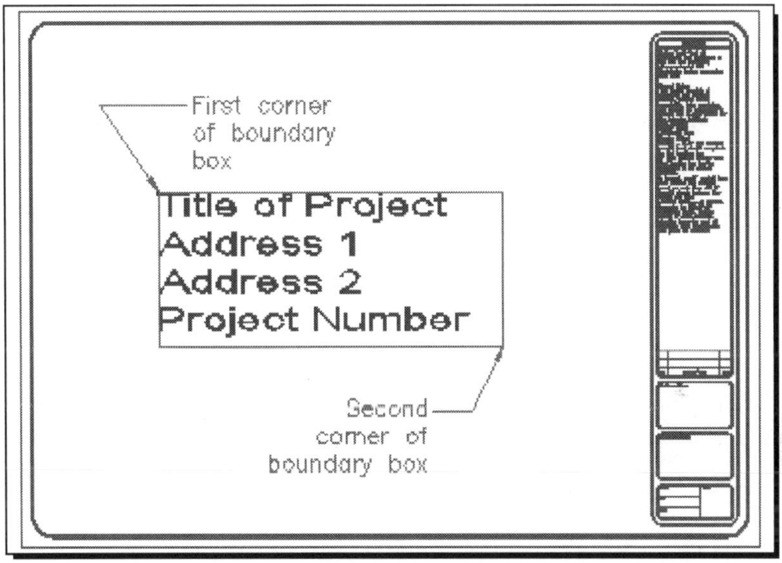

Figure 17–20

6. After entering the last line of text, in the *Text Editor* contextual tab, click ✔ (Close Text Editor) to end the command and close the *Text Editor*.
7. Save and close the drawing.

End of practice

17.3 Modifying Multiline Text

You can manipulate multiline text with grips and adjust its various settings in the *Properties* palette. However, changing the text's layer, and copying, moving, and rotating the text can be achieved by using standard AutoCAD commands and processes.

Editing Multiline Text

You can edit the already existing multiline text in the *Text Editor*.

How To: Edit Multiline Text

1. Double-click on a text object to open the *Text Editor*. The *Text Editor* contextual tab also opens.
   - You can also right-click on the selected text and select **Mtext Edit**.
2. Edit the text, as shown in Figure 17–21.

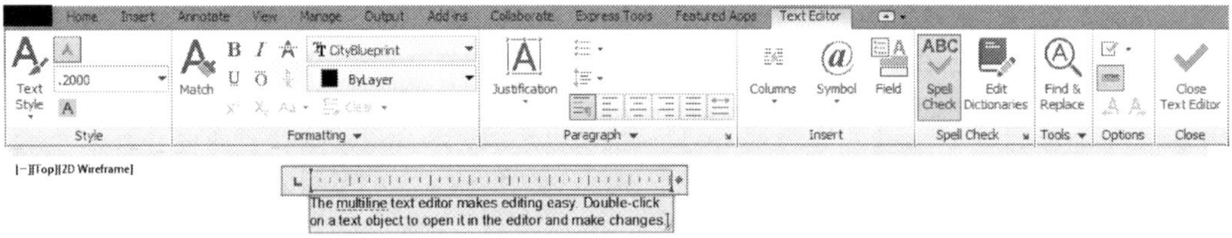

Figure 17–21

3. In the *Text Editor* contextual tab, click (Close Text Editor) or click in the drawing window to finish editing the text.

- If you press <Esc> to close the *Text Editor*, you are prompted to save your text changes.

Changing Text Width and Length

After you have placed multiline text in your drawing, you can control the text boundary box width and length using grips or the *Text Editor*.

- Select some multiline text without any commands running. Grips display at the location point and at the column width and height, as shown in Figure 17–22. Click on a grip to select it (it turns red), and then move the cursor and select another point to stretch the column width or height to a different size. To clear the grips, press <Esc>.

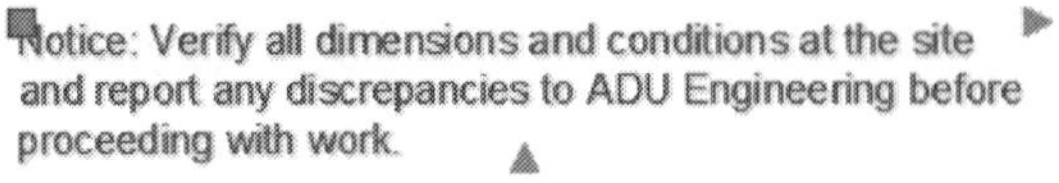

Figure 17–22

- The location grip (square grip box) moves the entire multiline text. It also designates the justification of the object.
- You can modify the text width and length in the *Text Editor* by hovering the cursor over the edges or the corner of the *Text Editor* and then dragging the double-arrows. You can also use the horizontal diamond on the right end of the ruler to modify the text box *Width*, as shown in Figure 17–23.

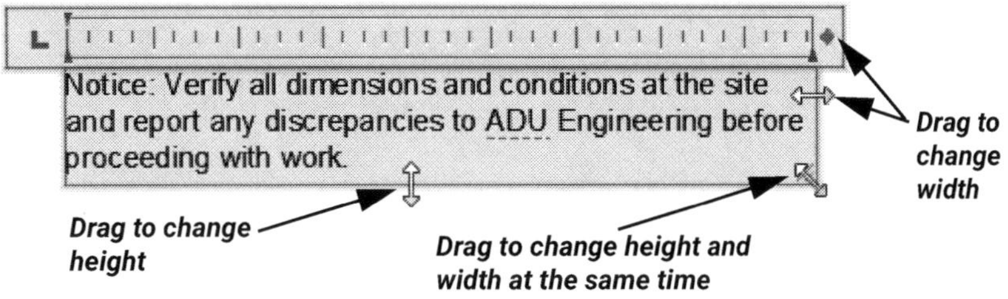

Figure 17–23

Changing Text Properties

The *Properties* palette is useful for changing multiple instances of text. You can change general properties (such as the layer) or specific properties (such as style, height, or justification).

- You can also add a text frame around multiline text, as shown in Figure 17–24.

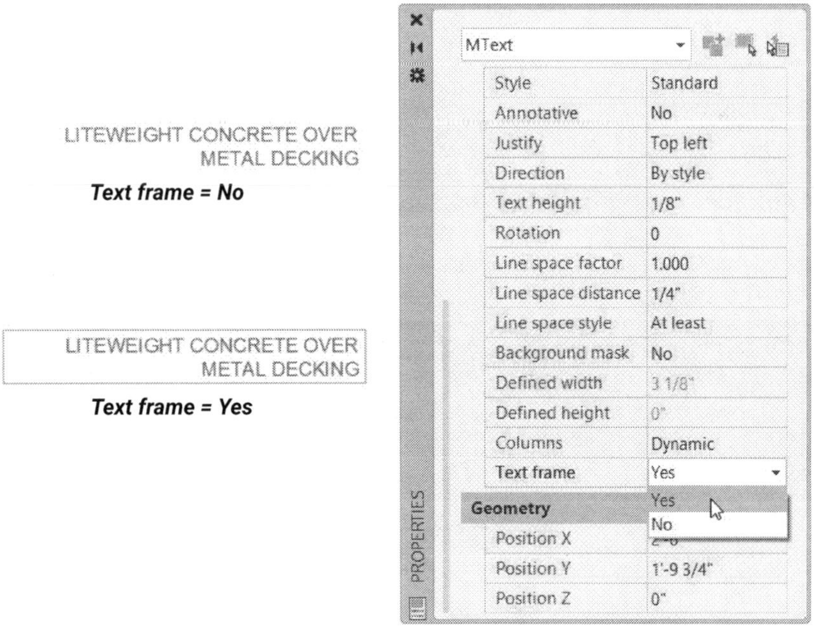

Figure 17–24

How To: Add a Text Frame

1. Select the multiline text.
2. Right-click and select **Properties**.
3. In the *Properties* palette, change the *Text frame* field to **Yes**.

Hint: Frame Offset Value

The text frame is offset from the text by the value of the **Border offset factor** in the *Background Mask* dialog box, as shown in Figure 17–25.

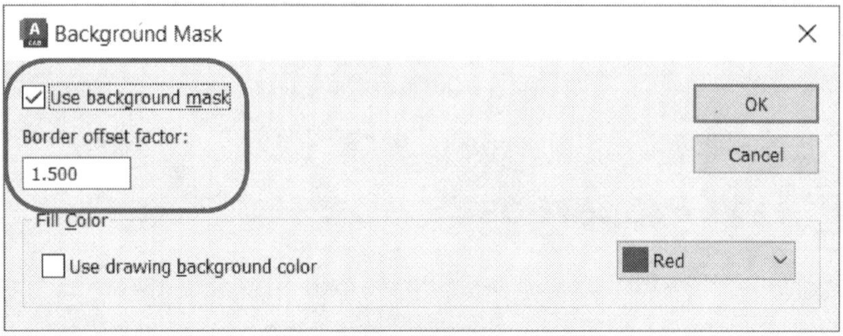

Figure 17–25

Spell Checking

While you are in the *Text Editor*, you can have spell checking on and fix spelling errors on the fly. You can also check the spelling in an entire drawing or part of a drawing.

How To: Check the Spelling in a Drawing

1. In the *Annotate* tab>*Text* panel, click ABC (Check Spelling).
2. In the *Check Spelling* dialog box (shown in Figure 17–26), expand the *Where to check* drop-down list and select **Entire drawing, Current space/layout**, or **Selected objects**.

   - You can also click (Select Objects) to specify which objects to check.

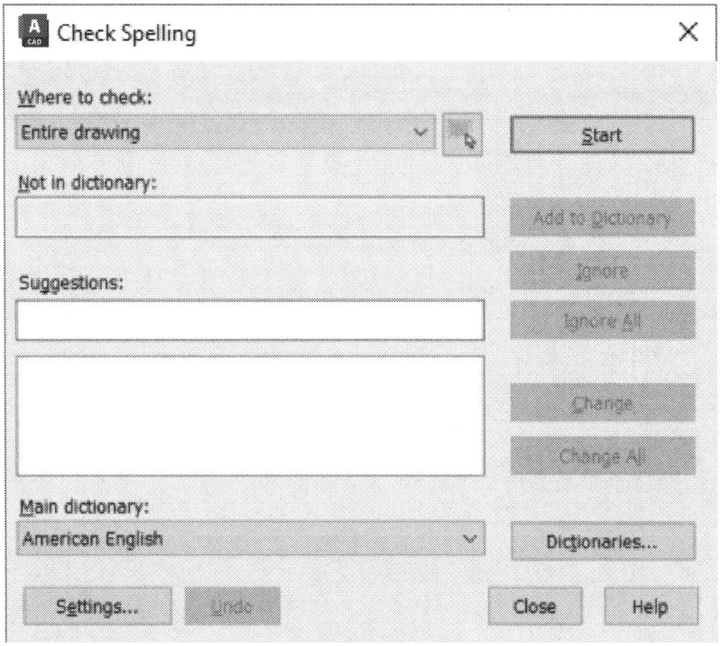

Figure 17–26

3. Click **Start**.
4. The AutoCAD software zooms to the text being checked and highlights any misspelled words. As with other spell checkers, you can:
    - Click **Change** or **Change All** to change the word to the selected suggestion.
    - Click **Ignore** or **Ignore All** to maintain the spellings.
    - Click **Add to Dictionary** to add a word to your custom dictionary.
    - Click **Undo** if you modify a spelling error by mistake.
5. When the spelling check is complete, a message box opens. Click **OK** and then **Close** in the *Check Spelling* dialog box.
    - Click **Dictionaries...** to specify the Main and Custom dictionaries, and add words to your custom dictionary.
    - Click **Settings...** to specify the types of items you want to check and how you want the checker to deal with specific variations of words.

Practice 17b
Modify Multiline Text

Practice Objectives

- Modify multiline text objects.
- Check the spelling in the drawing.

In this practice, you will modify text using grips, the *Text Editor*, and the *Properties* palette to clean up a redlined detail, as shown in Figure 17–27. You will also check the spelling in the drawing file.

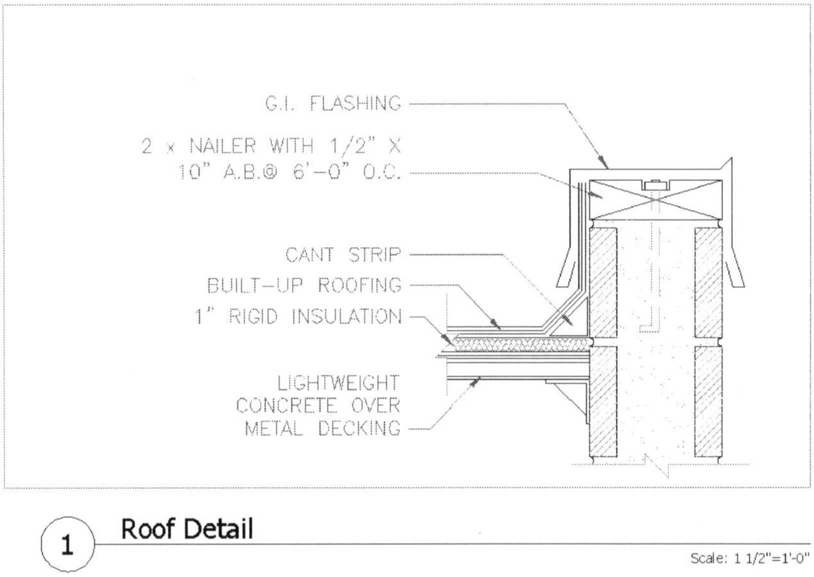

Figure 17–27

Task 1: Edit multiline text in a drawing.

1. Open **Detail Sheet-A.dwg** from your practice files folder.
2. Ensure that you are in the **Detail Sheet** layout.
3. Zoom in on the *Roof Detail* viewport located near the upper left corner of the layout. It contains a section view with labels. The red text and markings are for reference only.
4. Double-click inside the viewport to make it active.
5. Click once on the text that ends with **O.C.** Select the top left grip and select a point farther to the left to make the text fit in two lines, as shown in Figure 17–28. Press <Esc> to clear the grips.

Figure 17–28

6. Double-click on the same piece of text. In the *Text Editor*, change **8**" to **10**", as shown in Figure 17–29. Verify that the complete text is still in two lines, and use the left double-arrows to adjust the width as required. Press <Esc>.

   Note: *Pressing <Esc> in the Text Editor requires you to save the changes whereas clicking outside the Text Editor automatically saves the changes.*

Figure 17–29

7. Click **Yes** to save the text changes.
8. Press <Shift> and select the two pieces of text for the lower two leaders (starting with **1"** and **Liteweight**), right-click and select **Properties**.
9. In the *Properties* palette, in the *Text* area, note that the *Paper text height* is **1/16"**. Click on it, change it to **1/8"** (as shown in Figure 17–30), and press <Enter>.

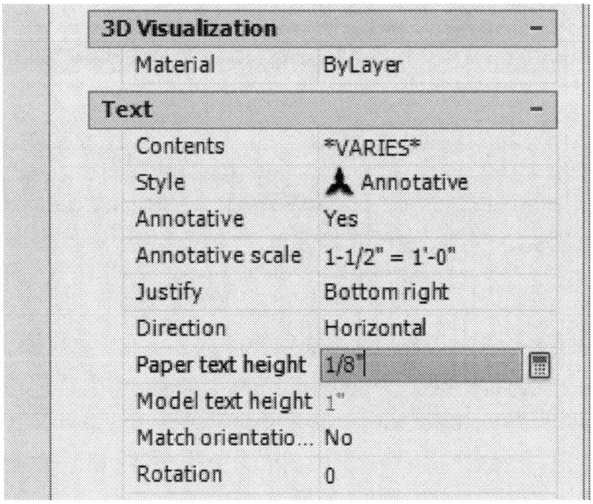

Figure 17–30

10. Close the *Properties* palette. Note that the selected text has become larger. Press <Esc> to clear the text.
11. Select the text **1" RIGID INSSULATION**. Use grips to stretch the text to the left so that it fits on one line. Press <Esc> to clear the text.

Task 2: Check the spelling.

1. Remain in the *Roof Detail* viewport.
2. In the *Annotate* tab>*Text* panel, click  (Check Spelling).
3. In the *Check Spelling* dialog box, in the *Where to check* drop-down list, select **Current space/layout**. Click **Start**.
4. Work through each of the spelling errors, correcting them as required and ignoring proper names. Note that the word **NAILER** is highlighted although it is spelled correctly. It is a technical term that is not found in the standard dictionary. Click **Ignore**.
5. Next, **INSSULATION** is highlighted. Correct it by clicking **Change** to use the spelling in the *Suggestions* area, as shown in Figure 17–31.

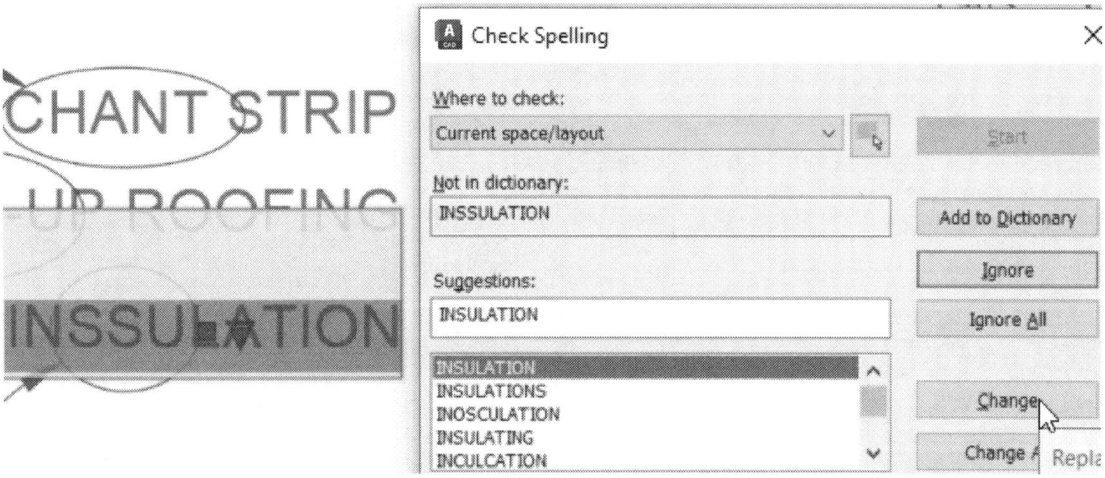

Figure 17–31

6. Similarly, the word **LITEWEIGHT** should be corrected.
7. In the message box, click **OK** to finish checking the spelling.
8. Click **Close** to close the *Check Spelling* dialog box.
9. Two of the misspelled words are not picked up by the Spell Checker because they are actual words. You need to modify these directly.
10. Double-click on the text *CHANT* and in the *Text Editor*, correct the spelling to **CANT** and then save the change.
11. Similarly, change the text *BUILD-UP* to **BUILT-UP**.

12. Toggle the layer **redline** off.
13. Double-click outside the viewport to return to Paper Space.
14. Save the drawing.

End of practice

17.4 Formatting Multiline Text

Multiline text offers formatting features similar to those found in word processing software. For example, you can bold, underline, or strikeout specific text, use bullets or numbered lists, and create columns of information, as shown in Figure 17–32.

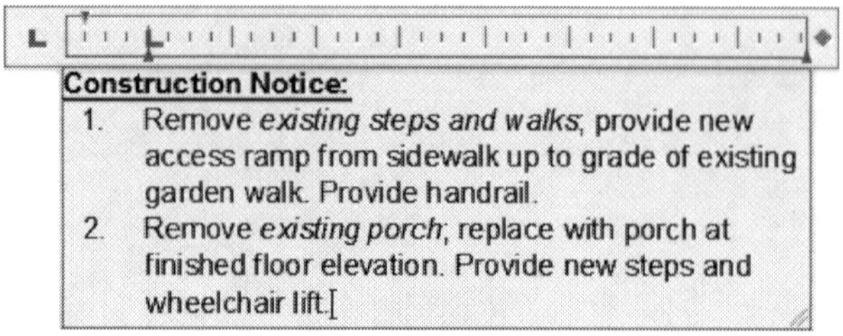

Figure 17–32

- Some options affect the entire multiline text object, some modify specific paragraphs in the text, and some only change selected text.

Formatting the Multiline Text Object

Changing the *Text Style* and *Justification* affects the entire multiline text object. If you need to change these features, do so before you make any other modifications to the formatting.

Changing the Text Style

You can change the *Text Style* of the overall text object once you are in the *Text Editor*.

- Changing the style overrides any other formatting you have done. A warning box opens if you select a different style, as shown in Figure 17–33.

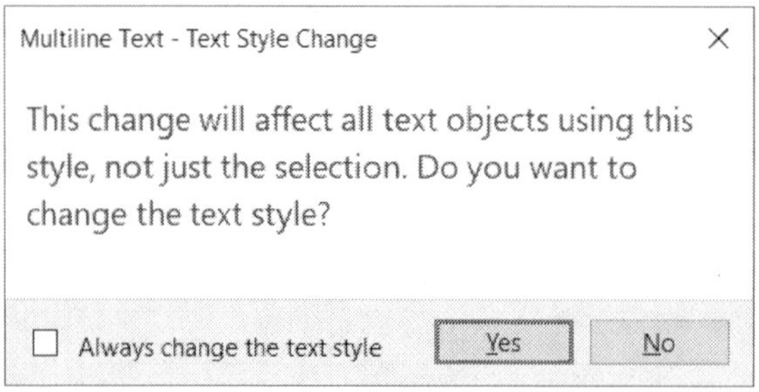

Figure 17–33

- If you are not using an annotative text style, you can click (Annotative) in the *Text Editor* contextual tab to make that instance of the text annotative without changing the text style.

Changing the Justification

The *Justification* sets the overall justification for the entire text object. In this case, the width and height of the boundary box are considered. For example, if you set the *Justification* to **Middle Center**, the text is centered in the middle of the boundary box, as shown in Figure 17–34. To change the multiline text object, use the **Justification** tools located in the *Text Editor* contextual tab>*Paragraph* panel in the ribbon.

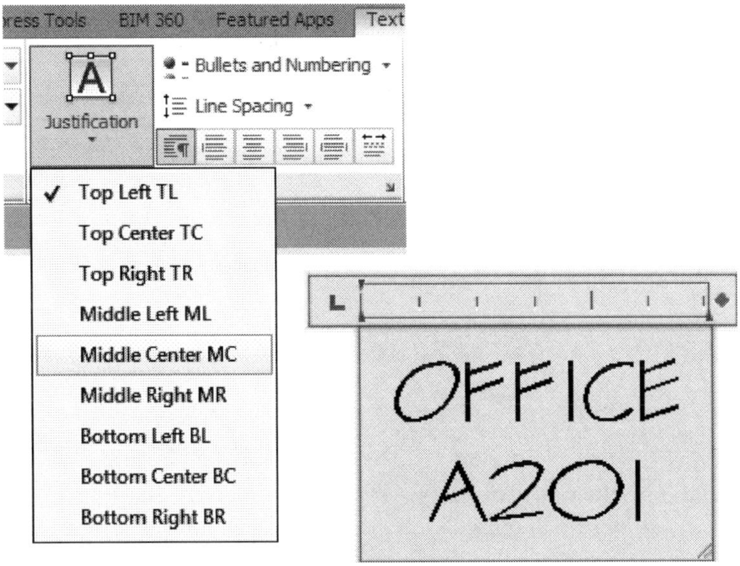

Figure 17–34

- (Background Mask) in the *Style* panel places a masking element behind the text so that other objects do not show through. You can use the drawing background color or a specific color, as shown in Figure 17–35.

  Note: *Setting a background mask applies it to the entire multiline text object.*

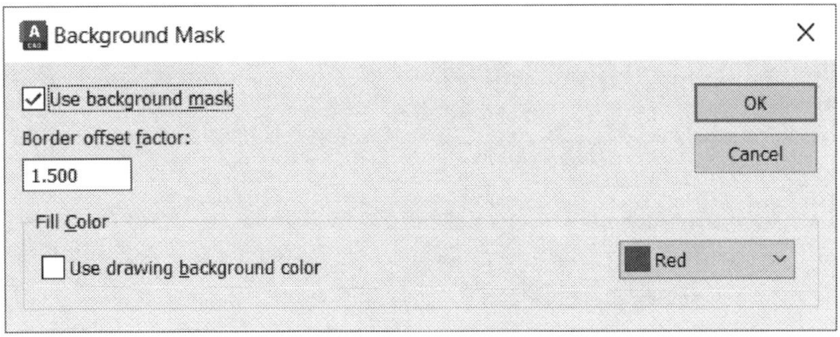

Figure 17–35

Formatting Selected Text

The *Formatting* panel in the *Text Editor* contextual tab enables you to change the font of individual text that you have selected, as well as bold, italicize, underline, overline, strikethrough, and change the case of the text, as shown in Figure 17–36.

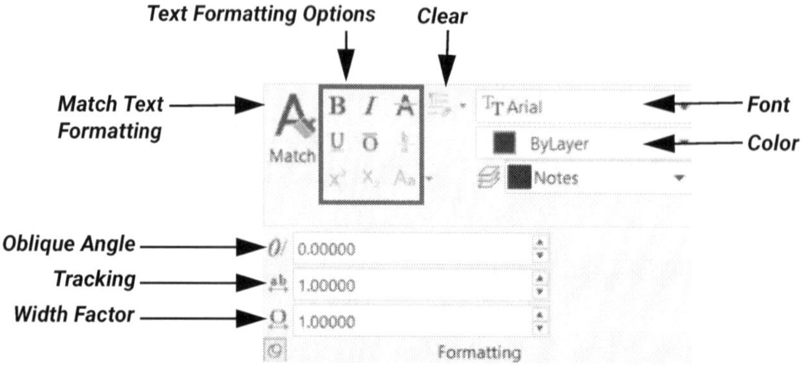

Figure 17–36

- Buttons are grayed out if the text is not selected or if the font does not support an option, such as **Bold** or *Italic*.
- In many cases, setting the color impacts the printed weight of the text, because colors are often used to control plotted line width.
- Three other text modification tools in the expanded area in the *Formatting* panel enable you to modify the text angle or spacing: **Oblique Angle**, **Tracking**, and **Width Factor**.
- You can use **Match Text Formatting** to copy the formatting from one set of text to another while using the *Text Editor*. You can also use this option to modify dimensions and tables.
- To remove the formatting from an mtext object, expand (Clear) and select the required option, You can remove the formatting from selected characters, from selected paragraphs, or from all of the text in a text object, as shown in Figure 17–37.

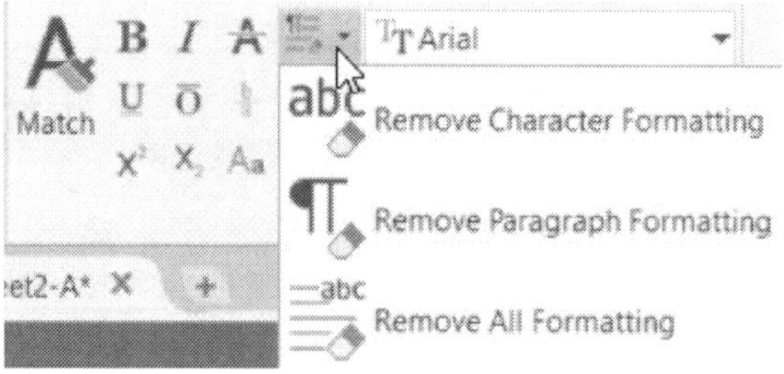

Figure 17–37

Hint: Fractions in Multiline Text

To display a fraction as stacked, use (Stack) when you enter a fraction in the *Text Editor*.

Click on the stacked number to display . Click to display the basic **Stack** options, as shown in Figure 17–38.

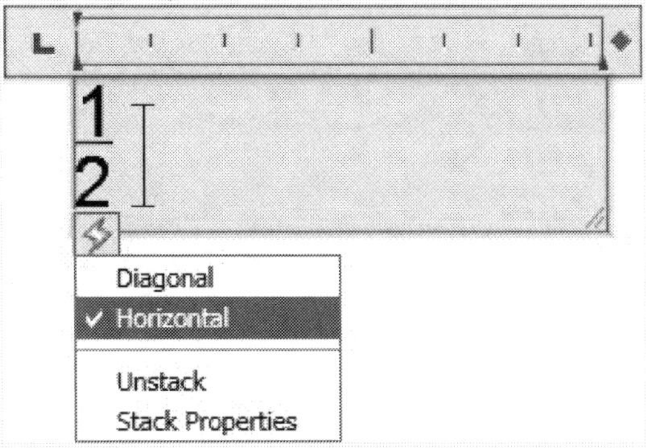

Figure 17–38

Double-click on the stacked number to open the *Stack Properties* dialog box, where you can modify the more advanced settings, as shown in Figure 17–39.

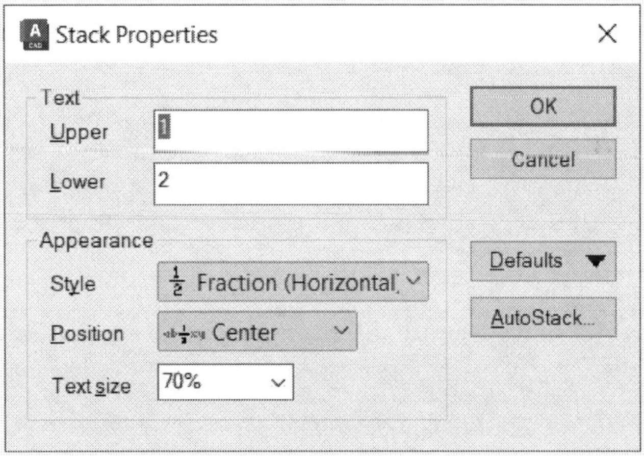

Figure 17–39

Formatting Paragraph Text

You can modify entire paragraphs of text, including changing paragraph level justifications, line spacing, indents, bullets, and numbering, as shown in Figure 17–40.

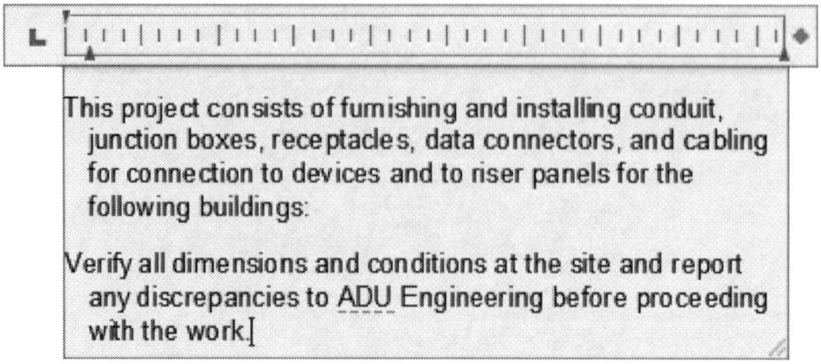

Figure 17–40

- The paragraph formatting tools are located in the *Text Editor* contextual tab>*Paragraph* panel, as shown in Figure 17–41.

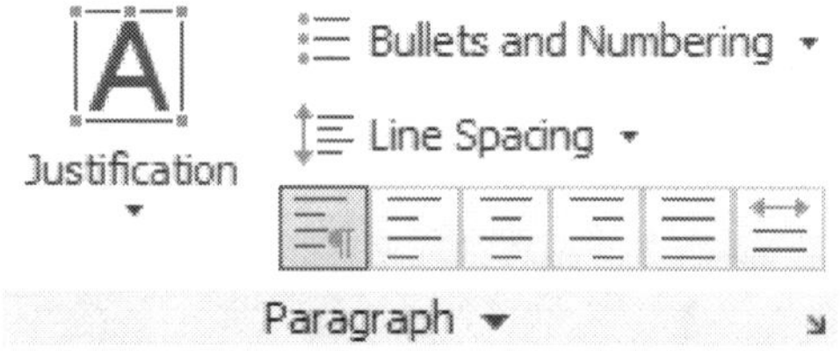

Figure 17–41

- A paragraph is any text that is typed before you press <Enter> to create a new line.
- To modify paragraphs, you can either select the entire paragraph or place the cursor somewhere in the paragraph.

Justifications

You can set justifications for individual paragraphs in a multiline text object. The options are as follows:

-  (Default)
-  (Left)
-  (Center)
-  (Right)

- (Justify (Fit))
- (Distribute)

An example of some of the justifications is shown in Figure 17–42.

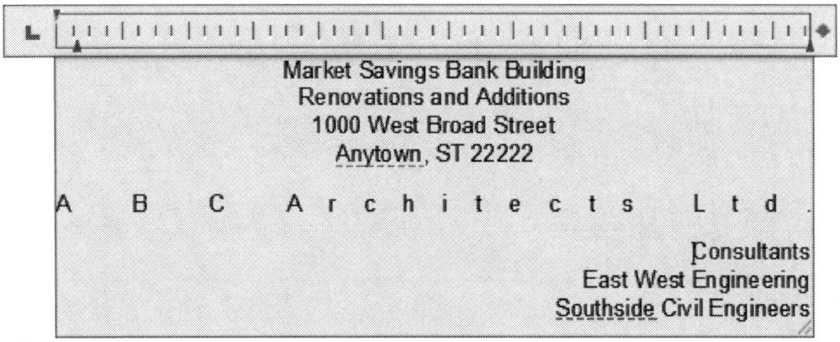

Figure 17–42

- **Justify (Fit)** spreads out the text so that the sentences are left- and right-justified. **Distribute** justifies to the left and right sides and spreads out whole words and individual letters across the space.

Line Spacing

You can set the line spacing using the supplied multiples of the text height, as shown in Figure 17–43, or select **More...** to create custom line spacing in the *Paragraph* dialog box. **Clear Line Spacing** returns the distance to the default setting.

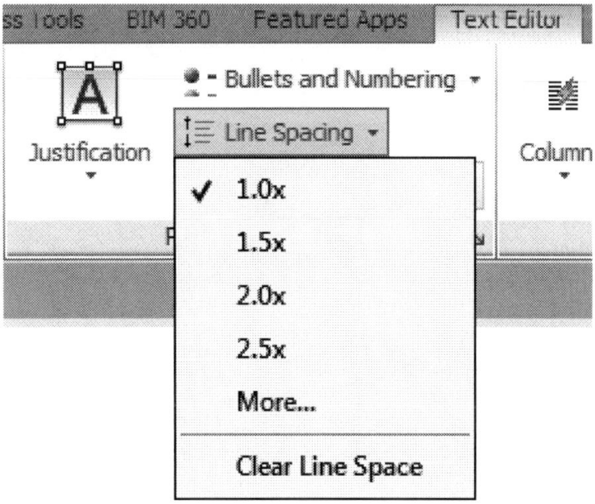

Figure 17–43

Bullets and Numbers

You can add bullets, numbers, or letters to text as you are typing, or add them to paragraphs that are already in the text object.

Select the type of list from the **Bullets and Numbering** list in the *Text Editor* contextual tab, as shown in Figure 17–44.

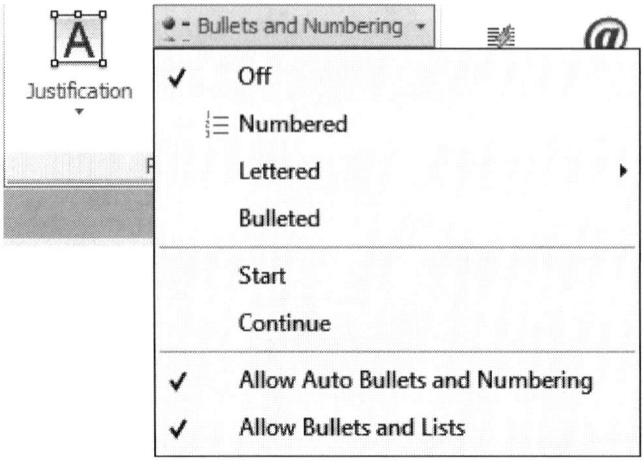

Figure 17–44

- The list can be in upper or lowercase letters, numbers, or bullets. Each time you press <Enter>, a new paragraph is created and numbered appropriately.
- To create a sub-list of a list, press <Tab> at the beginning of the line. Press <Shift>+<Tab> to back up.
- You can **Restart** or **Continue** a numbered list and modify the default methods of using lists in the menu.
- Modify the indent and tab settings to set the locations of the numbers and text.
- Bullets and numbering are automatically applied to the text as you type if the line begins with a symbol or number followed by a space or <Tab>.

Setting Indents and Tabs

You can set the indents and tabs by using the ruler at the top of the *Text Editor*.

- Select the text that you want to indent and slide the markers to locate the indent. The top marker controls the first line of a paragraph and the bottom marker controls subsequent lines in the paragraph, as shown in Figure 17–45.

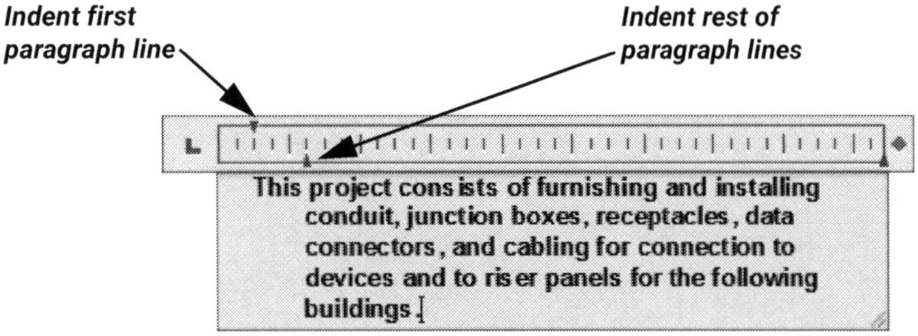

Figure 17–45

- The heavy **L** in the ruler marks preset tab stops, as shown in Figure 17–46. To add a manual tab, click on the ruler at the required location. You can drag the tab marker along the ruler to move it, or drag it off the ruler to delete it.

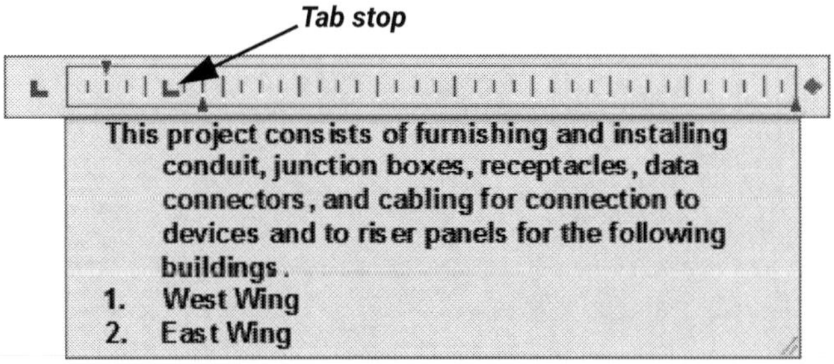

Figure 17–46

- There are tabs for ⌞ (Left), ⊥ (Center), ⌟ (Right), and ⊥ (Decimal). Click the tab box on the left side of the ruler to switch between the different types of tabs.
- You can also modify the tab settings in the *Paragraph* dialog box.

Creating Paragraph Formats

To modify the *Paragraph* settings, click ↘ in the *Paragraph* panel title. You can set the paragraph format options at any time using the *Paragraph* dialog box, as shown in Figure 17–47.

- You can only set the *Paragraph Spacing* in the *Paragraph* dialog box. It controls the distance before or after any paragraph.

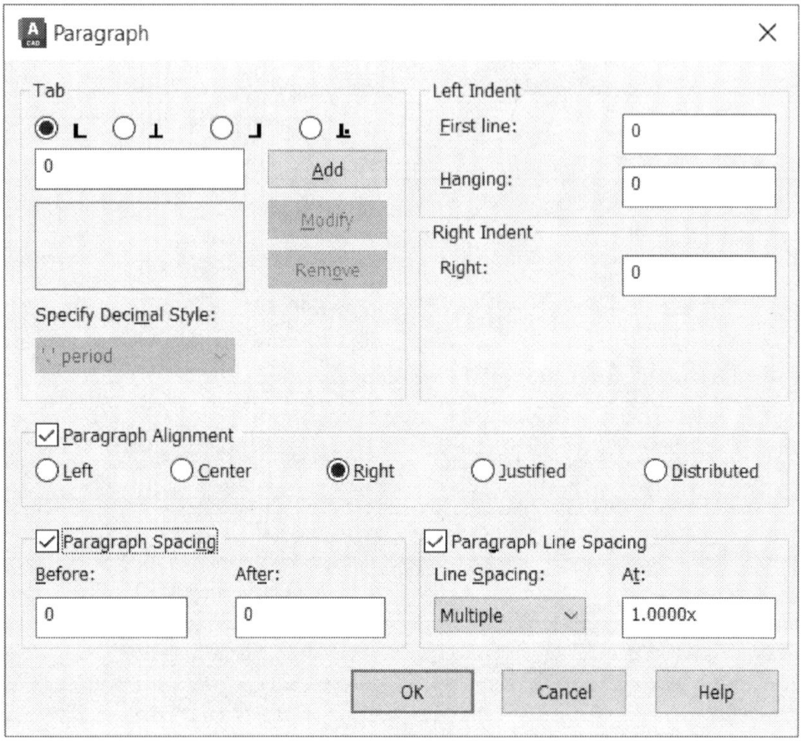

Figure 17–47

Creating Columns

You can place the text in a column format, as shown in Figure 17–48, using the column options in the *Text Editor*. There are two methods of column creation: **Dynamic** and **Static**.

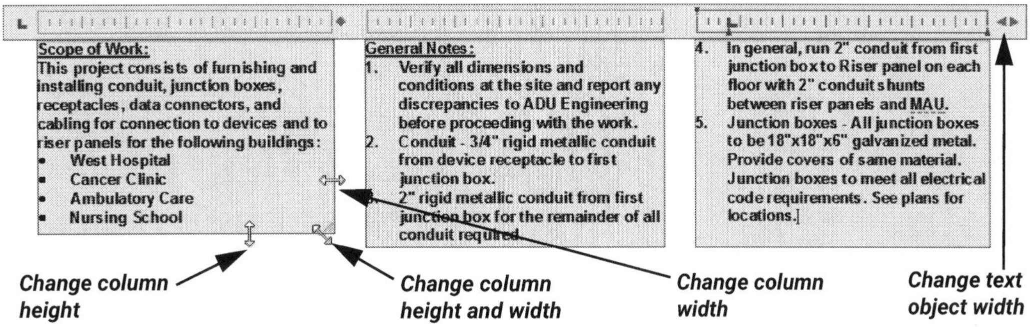

Figure 17–48

Note: *Column settings affect the entire multiline text object.*

- By default, all of the multiline text is set up to display dynamic columns with a manual height. This can be adjusted with grips or by dragging the edges of the first column to adjust the height and width separately, or both at the same time, as shown in Figure 17–48.

Static Columns

With **Static Columns**, you can specify the number of columns in the list, as shown in Figure 17–49. The columns are evenly divided in the text box.

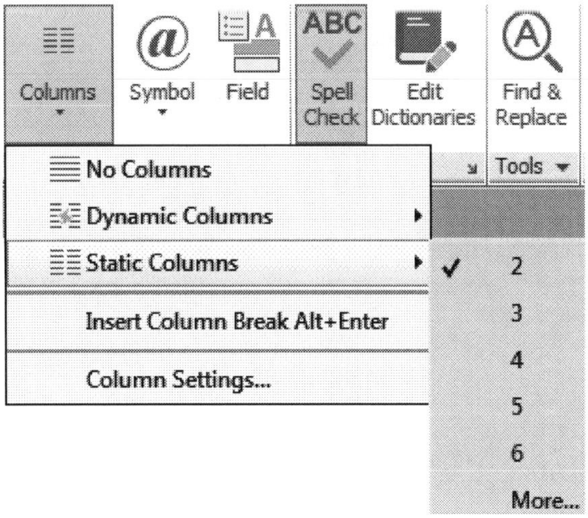

Figure 17–49

- If you need more than six columns, select **More...** or **Column Settings...**. In the *Column Settings* dialog box, you can set the number of Static Columns, their height and width, and the gutter width.

Dynamic Columns

With **Dynamic Columns**, you can specify an automatic or manual height, as shown in Figure 17–50. The number of columns varies depending on the amount of text.

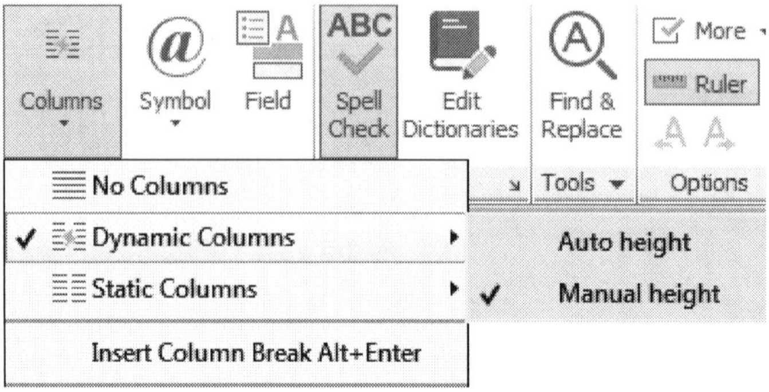

Figure 17–50

- You can also set the height and width of columns in the *Column Settings* dialog box and modify them with grips.
- After you start typing column information in the Mtext boundary, you can select **Insert Column Break** or type <Alt>+<Enter> to add a break before the end of the column. This enables you to control the flow of text in the Mtext object.
- When you have columns in your drawing, you can control the spacing with grips, depending on the type of columns and their settings.

Practice 17c
Format Multiline Text in a Drawing

Practice Objectives

- Change the formatting options of text objects.
- Add text and create columns.

In this practice, you will use formatting options in the *Text Editor* to set the style, modify individual objects, add numbering and indents, and set the justification of the text, as shown in Figure 17–51. If you have time, you can also add text and create columns.

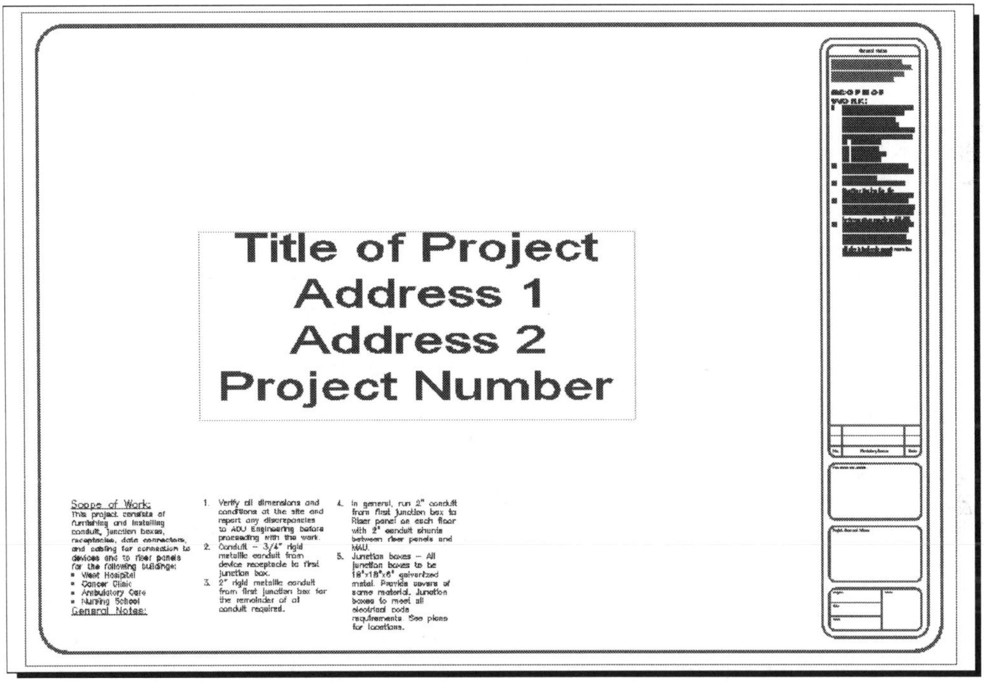

Figure 17–51

Task 1: Format multiline text in a drawing.

1. Open **Cover Sheet2-A.dwg** from your practice files folder.
2. Zoom in on the *General Notes* area near the upper right corner of the titleblock.
3. Double-click on the text below the General Notes to open it in the *Text Editor*. All the lines and paragraphs are selected.

4. In the *Text Editor* contextual tab>*Style* panel, click on the **Text Style** icon and select the style **Hand** in the gallery. In the *alert* dialog box, click **Yes**. The entire text object updates to the new style.

5. Highlight (select) the first sentence (four lines), which starts with **Notice**. In the *Text Editor* contextual tab>*Formatting* panel, click U (Underline) to make the sentence underlined, and in the Color list, select **Red,** as shown in Figure 17–52.

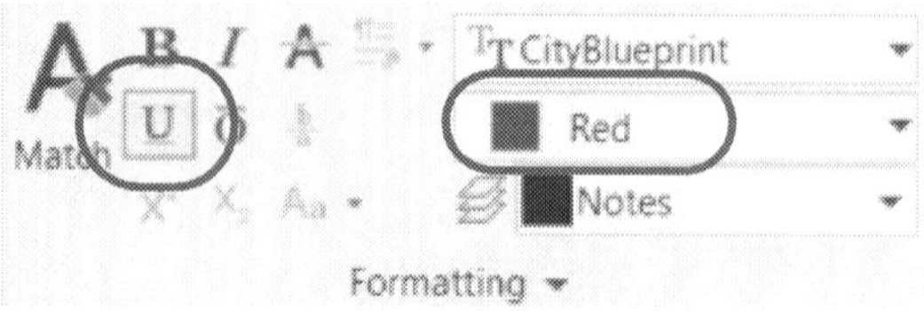

Figure 17–52

6. In the next paragraph of the text, highlight the text **General Notes** and change it to read **Scope of Work**. Highlight **Scope of Work** and change its *Font* to **Arial**, *Text Height* to **3/16"**, and make all of the words **Uppercase,** as shown in Figure 17–53.

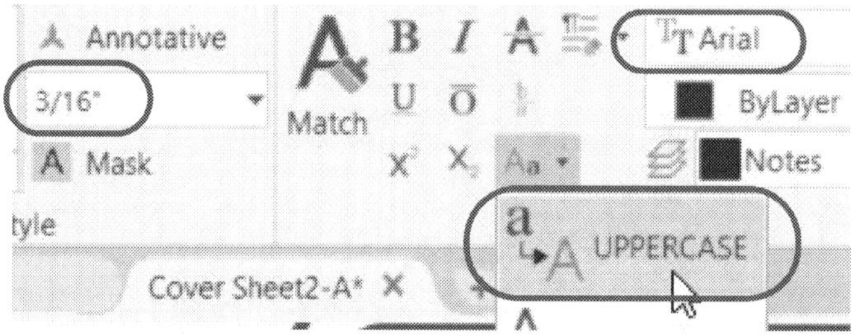

Figure 17–53

7. Highlight all of the lines of text below **SCOPE OF WORK**. In the *Text Editor* contextual tab>*Paragraph* panel, expand **Bullets and Numbering** and select **Numbered** to apply autonumbering. Each paragraph becomes numbered.

8. Items 2-5 in the list should be sub-items under the first bullet point. Select the insertion point in front of the text *West Hospital* and press <Tab>. The line becomes a sub-item as 1.1. Repeat for the next three lines until you get to 1.4.

9. To adjust the indent for the sub-items, highlight those four lines. In the ruler, drag the first line indent marker to the **3/8" mark**, as shown in Figure 17–54.

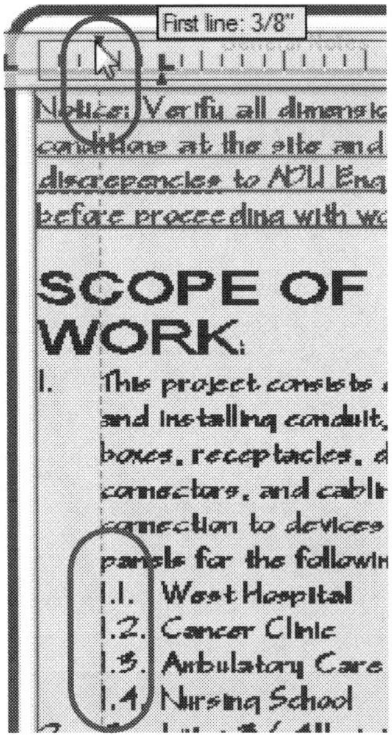

Figure 17–54

10. Click (Close Text Editor) to close the *Text Editor*.
11. Zoom out to display the entire layout.
12. Double-click anywhere on the four lines of *Title* text in the center of the cover sheet.
13. In the *Text Editor* contextual tab>*Paragraph* panel, change the *Justification* to **Middle Center MC**, as shown in Figure 17–55.

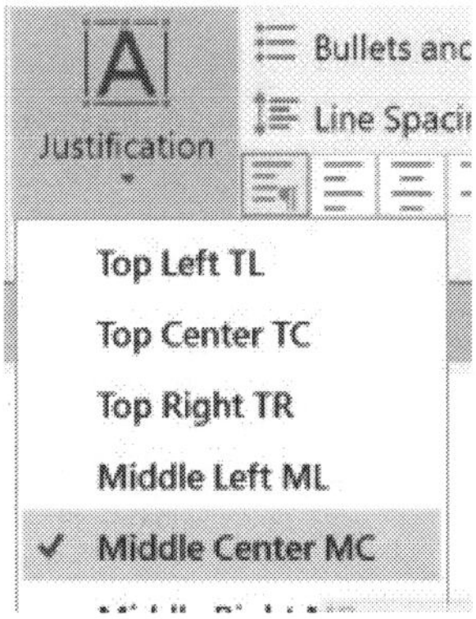

Figure 17–55

14. Close the *Text Editor*.
15. Save the drawing.

Task 2: (Optional) Create columns.

In this task, you will import a text file, apply formatting, and divide the text into columns, as shown in Figure 17–56.

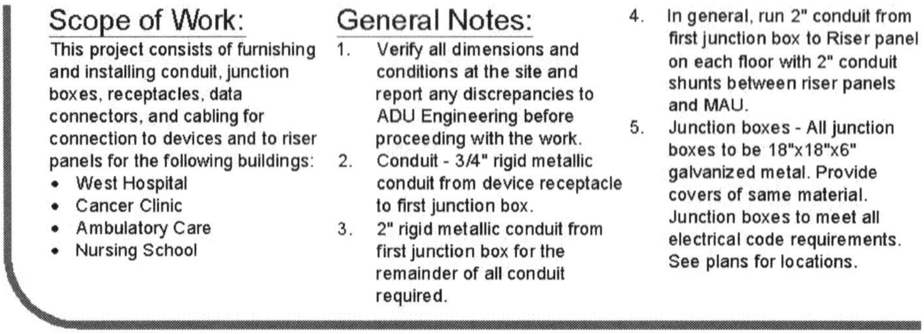

Figure 17–56

1. In the lower left corner of the cover sheet, use the **Multiline Text** command to create a new multiline text object. Set the current text style to **Standard** with a *Height* of **3/16"**.
2. In the *Text Editor*, right-click and select **Import Text.** From the practice files folder, import the text file **Scope of Work.txt**. (This is similar to the text you placed under General Notes.)
3. Modify the formatting so that the items are bulleted and numbered (as shown in Figure 17–57). Use **1/4"** for the height and underline the titles *Scope of Work* and *General Notes*. Use a numbered list for the text under *General Notes* and use bullets for the buildings under *Scope of Work*.

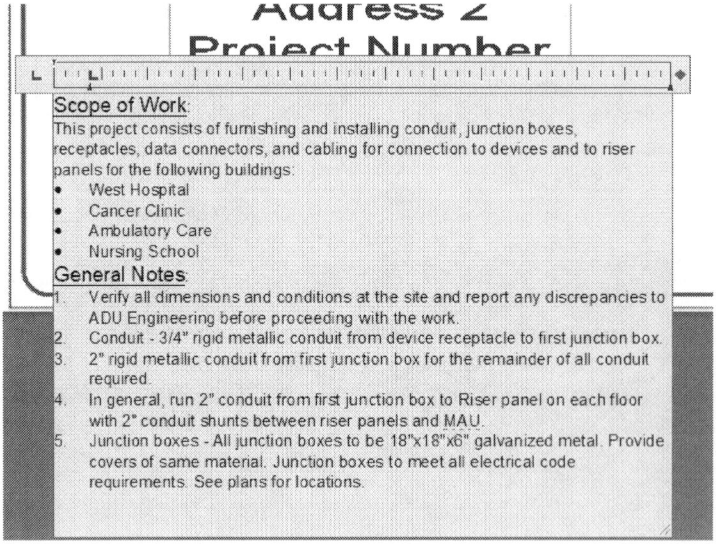

Figure 17–57

4. In the *Text Editor* contextual tab>*Insert* panel, expand the (Columns flyout) and select **Static Columns>2**. The text is divided into two columns.

5. Click (Columns flyout)) and select **Column Settings**. The *Column Settings* dialog box opens.

6. In the *Width* area, set the *Column* to **3"** and *Gutter* to **1/2"**, as shown in Figure 17–58.

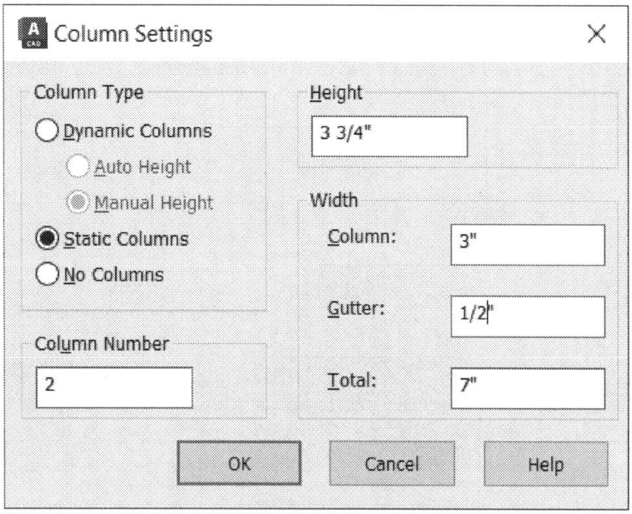

Figure 17–58

7. Click **OK** to close the *Column Settings* dialog box. The columns adjust to match the new values. The text is not completely on the sheet.

8. Expand (Columns flyout)), and select **Dynamic Columns>Manual height**. Close the *Text Editor*.

9. The text is a single column flowing below the sheet. Click on the text to display the grips. Use the top right pointing arrow grip to widen the column width slightly (the text **furnishing** to display at the end of first line), then drag and drop the upward facing arrow at the bottom of the column to just above the *General Notes* section. This creates two columns.

10. In the second column, drag and drop the upward facing arrow just below the point 3, creating the third column. Use the arrows to adjust the columns, as shown in Figure 17–59. Press <Esc> to exit the selection.

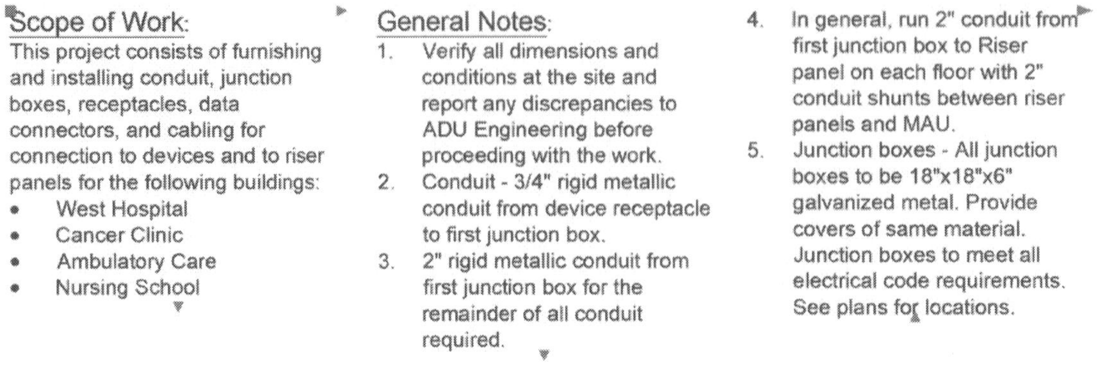

Figure 17–59

11. Save and close the drawing.

End of practice

17.5 Adding Notes with Leaders to Your Drawing

In a drawing, you often need to use an arrow to point to objects in the drawing and add either text or keynotes. This can be done using the **Multileader** command. Multileaders consist of straight lines or splines and can contain multiple leaders. You can use multiline text or blocks for content, as shown in Figure 17–60.

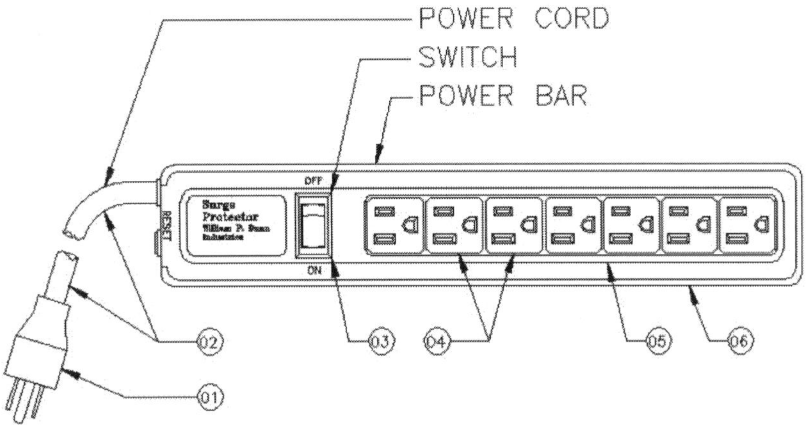

Figure 17–60

- As with other text and dimension objects, multileaders use a style and can be annotative.
- The style of a multileader determines whether it uses text for the note or a block, such as a circle.

How To: Add a Text Note

1. Select a Multileader style that uses text. Both the Standard and Annotative styles provided with the AutoCAD templates are designed this way.
2. In the *Annotate* tab>*Leaders* panel or in the *Home* tab>*Annotation* panel, click  (Multileader).
3. Select a point for the leader arrowhead location.
4. Select a point for the leader landing. By default, a horizontal tag is attached to the end.
5. Type the text. To specify the text width so that it word-wraps, you can use the Text Width arrows in the Text Formatting ruler.

6. Click (Close Text Editor) in the *Text Editor* contextual tab or click away from the text in the drawing. The multileader displays as shown in Figure 17–61.

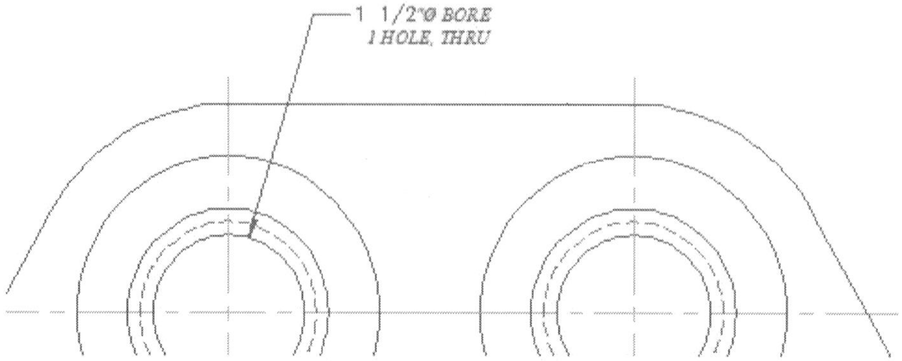

Figure 17–61

- The *Text Editor* contextual tab displays when you place multiline text using the **Multileader** command.
- You can change the order in which you place the leader using the **Leader Landing first** or **Content first** options, as shown in Figure 17–62. If you change the method of placing the leader, it becomes the default and is used the next time you start the command.

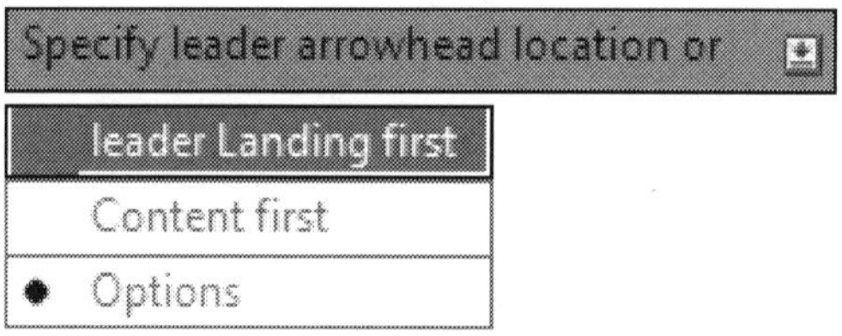

Figure 17–62

- You can use **Options** to modify the appearance of the leader, but creating Multileader Styles is recommended.

Drawing Keynotes

You can draw multileaders with numbers in a block that are related to a list of keynotes located elsewhere in the drawing, as shown in Figure 17–63. You need to use a multileader style that uses blocks.

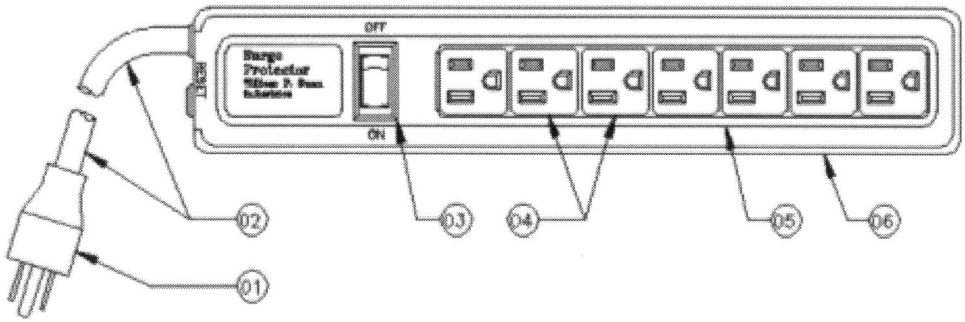

Figure 17–63

Modifying Multileaders

The leader and text (or block) of a multileader are one object. Multileaders can be modified using grips and text editing tools.

Grip Editing

You can use grips to modify the landing length (as shown in Figure 17–64), leader length and angle, and to move the multileader.

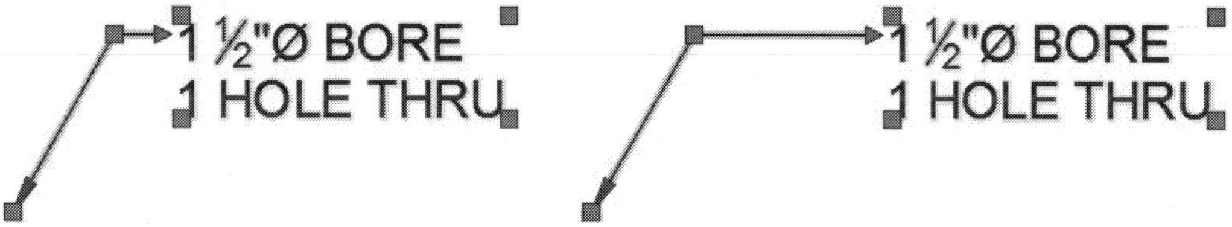

Figure 17–64

- The square grip at the end of the leader line changes the location at which the leader line is pointing.
- The square grip at the top left of the text moves the multileader.
- The arrow grip on the landing changes its length.

- If you hover over the square multi-functional grips on the leader line, as shown in Figure 17–65, additional options display, such as **Add Vertex** and **Add/Remove Leader**.

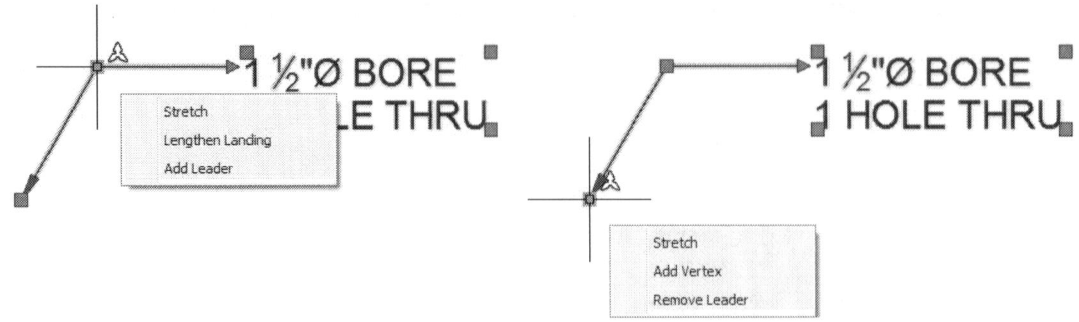

Figure 17–65

- If you are working with text leaders that have a specific text length, you can modify the text boundary using grips, as shown in Figure 17–66.

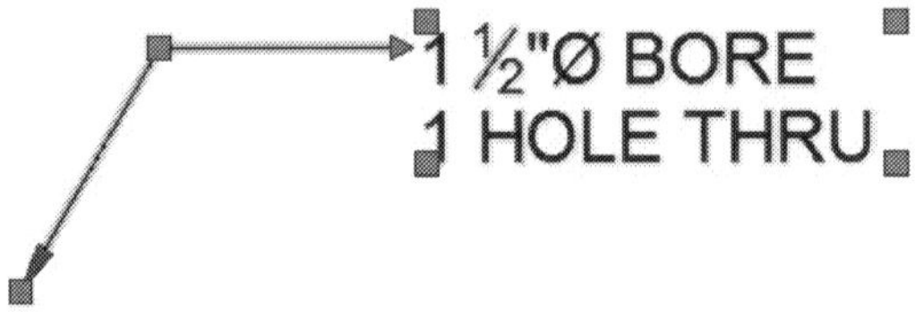

Figure 17–66

- If the text does not have a specified boundary, you can create one by clicking on the text again and modifying the boundary box using the *Text Width* ruler, as shown in Figure 17–67.

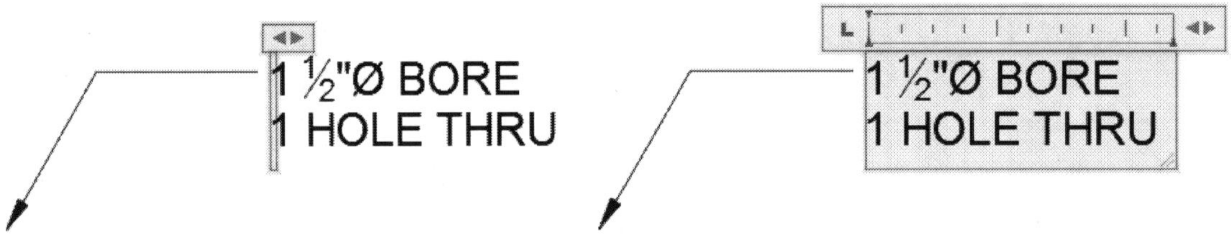

Figure 17–67

Adding and Removing Leaders

You can add or remove leader lines to create a single leader object, which points to multiple locations in the drawing, as shown in Figure 17–68.

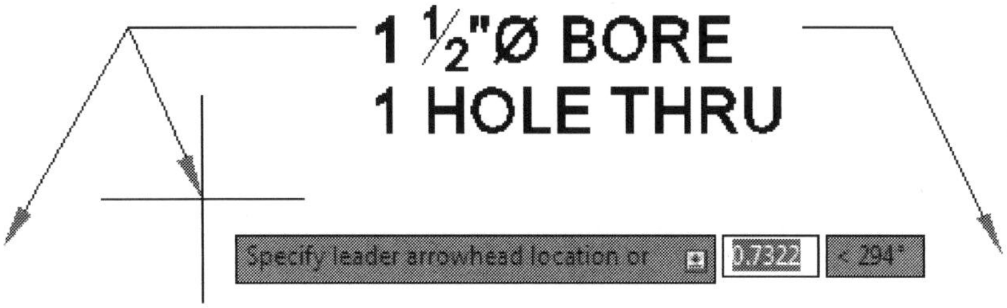

Figure 17–68

How To: Add Leaders

1. In the *Annotate* tab>*Leaders* panel, click (Add Leader).
2. Select an existing multileader.
3. Select the location at which you want to add the new leader.
4. Continue adding leaders as required.
5. Press <Enter> to complete the command.

How To: Remove Leaders

1. In the *Annotate* tab>*Leaders* panel, click (Remove Leader).
2. Select an existing multileader.
3. Select the leaders that you want to remove.
4. Press <Enter> to complete the command.

Select Individual Leaders to Edit

You can select individual leaders and modify them. For example, in Figure 17–69, several leaders were modified to distinguish new plants from existing plants of the same type.

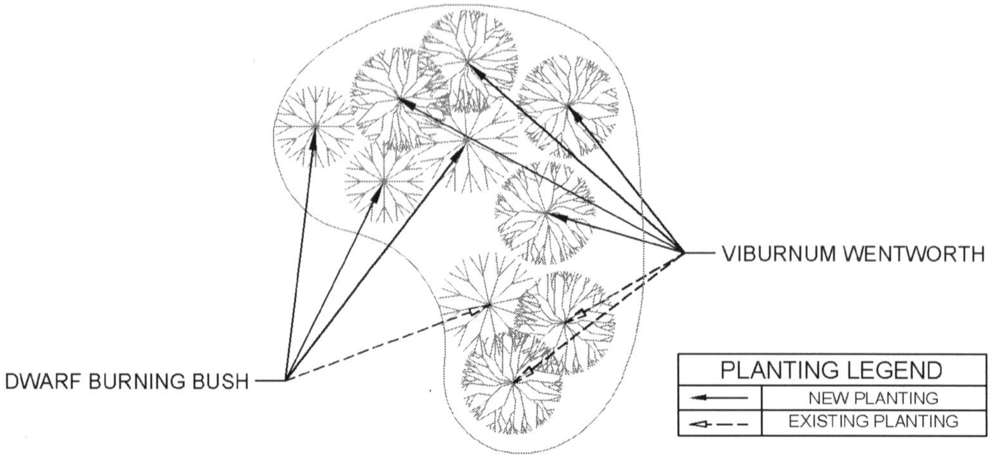

Figure 17–69

How To: Select and Edit Individual Leaders

1. Select an existing multileader.
2. Hold <Ctrl> and click to select one or more leaders in a multileader. The leaders display with red grips.
3. Once selected, right-click and select **Properties**. Use the *Properties* palette to change the properties of the selected leaders, such as their color, leader, or arrowhead size, as shown in Figure 17–70.

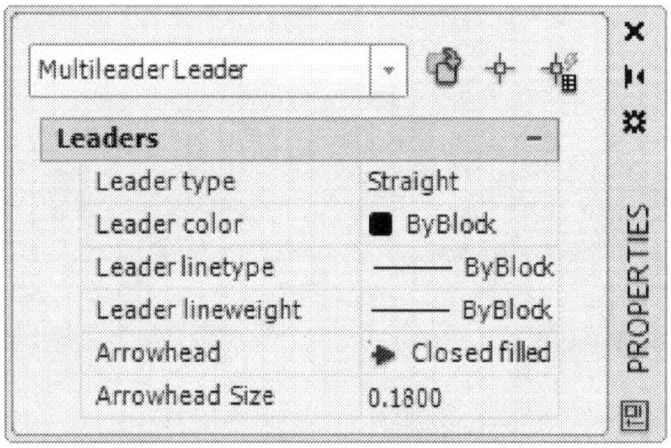

Figure 17–70

Aligning Multileaders

You can use the **Multileader Align** command to arrange multileaders so that they are evenly spaced and aligned, as shown in Figure 17–71.

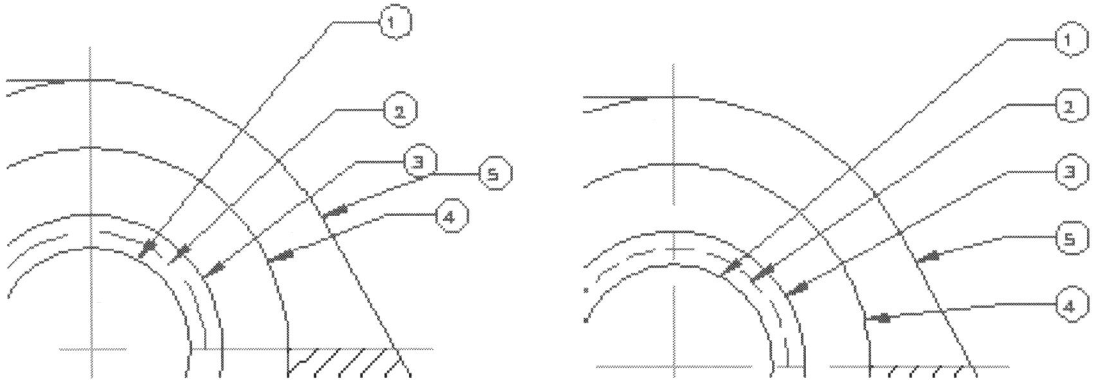

Figure 17–71

How To: Align Multileaders

1. In the *Annotate* tab>*Leaders* panel, click (Align, Multileader).
2. Select the multileaders that you want to align and press <Enter>.
3. You can change the current mode of aligning by pressing <Down Arrow>, selecting **Options**, and selecting an option.
   - The last option used becomes the default when you use the command again.
4. Select the multileader or points to which you want to align.

Distribute	Select two points. The multileaders are evenly spaced between them.
Make leader segments Parallel	Select a multileader to which to make the other leader segments parallel. The content remains in place and the leaders' angles are made parallel to the selected leader.
Specify Spacing	Select to type a distance for the spacing and then select a multileader to which to align and direction for alignment.
Use current spacing	Select to use the current spacing settings. The content is aligned and the spacing between the multileaders does not change.

Collecting Multileaders

You can collect several multileaders together using one leader, as shown in Figure 17–72. This only works with multileaders that have block content, not those with text content. This enables you to combine multiple blocks into a string. The blocks can be displayed vertically, horizontally, or wrapped to fit into a selected space.

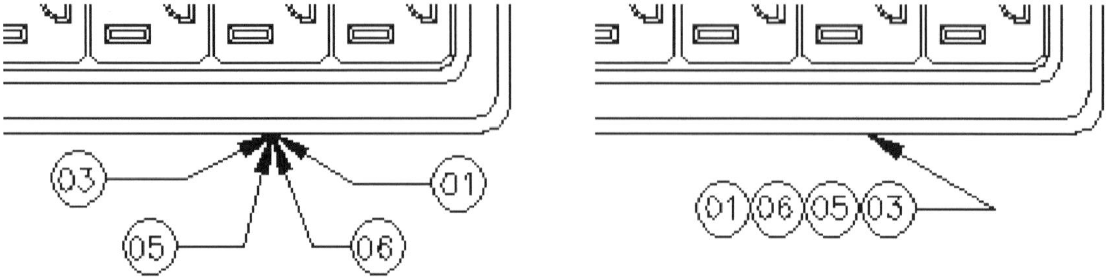

Figure 17–72

How To: Collect Multileader Blocks

1. In the *Annotate* tab>*Leaders* panel, click  (Collect).
2. Select the leaders that you want to group together and press <Enter>.
3. Select a location for the newly collected leaders.

- The default layout is **Horizontal**, but you can change it to **Vertical** using the shortcut menu. If there is a long line of bubbles, select the **Wrap** option and specify the wrap distance.

Practice 17d
Add Notes to Your Drawing

Practice Objectives

- Add text and block-based multileaders to a drawing.
- Add leaders to multileaders.
- Align and modify multileaders.

In this practice, you will add text and block-based multileaders. You will add leaders to multileaders and then align and modify leaders with grips as required, as shown in Figure 17–73.

- The multileader style **Keynotes** was created for this drawing.

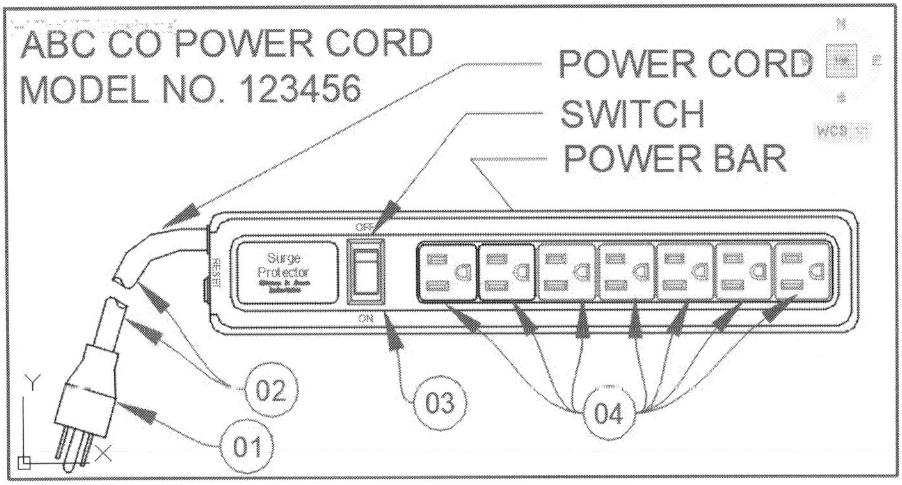

Figure 17–73

Task 1: Draw multileaders.

1. Open **Power Protector-I.dwg** from your practice files folder.
2. Switch to the **A-Sized** layout and activate the viewport. Use **Zoom Extents** to display the drawing in the viewport. Pan the model down so that more empty space is left at the top. You can also use the viewport grips to add space around the surge protector. Set the scale to 1:2 and lock the viewport.
3. Set the *current layer* to **Text**.
4. In the *Annotate* tab>*Leaders* panel, in the *Multileader style* list, click **Annotative**.

5. In the *Annotate* tab>*Leaders* panel, click (Multileader).
6. Add multileaders as shown in Figure 17–74, and label them as **POWER CORD**, **POWER BAR**, and **SWITCH**. Place the multileaders so they are not aligned.

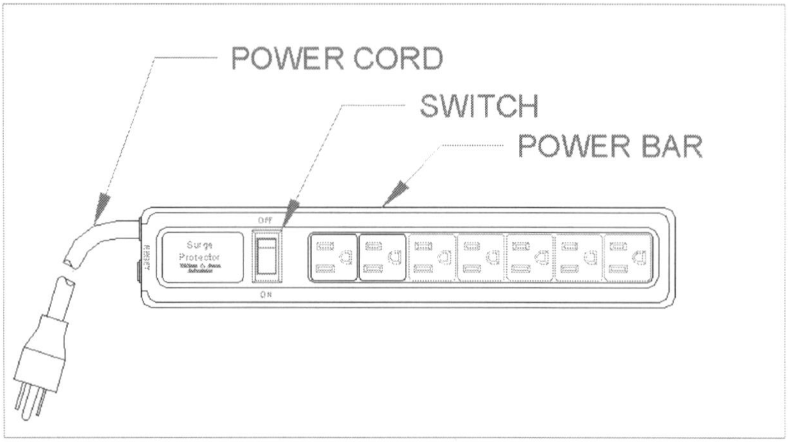

Figure 17–74

7. Set the current *Multileader style* to **Keynotes**.
8. Start the **Multileader** command. Add several multileaders and with each multileader, in the *Edit Attributes* dialog box, enter tag numbers to label the components as **01**, **02**, **03**, and **04**, as shown in Figure 17–75.

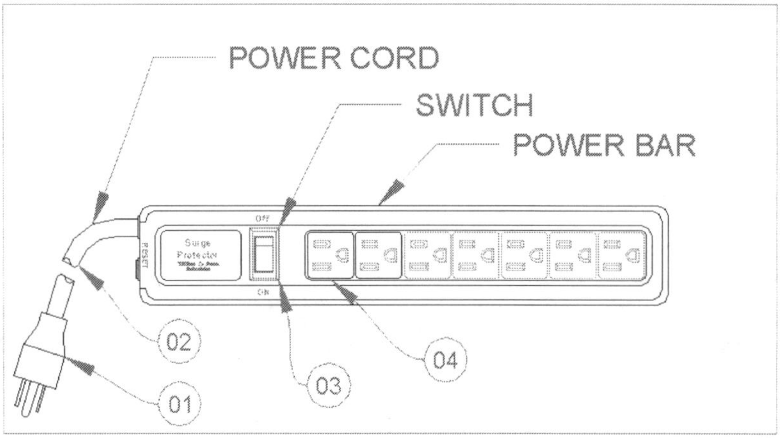

Figure 17–75

Task 2: Modify multileaders.

1. Select the multileader with the label **02** and then in the *Annotate* tab>*Leaders* panel, click (Add Leader). A leader is attached to the cursor and to the label. Click to place a leader to the other half of the power cord (as shown in Figure 17–76) and press <Enter>.
2. Similarly, add leaders to the multileader labeled **04** to point to each of the remaining sockets.
3. In the *Annotate* tab>*Leaders* panel, click (Align, Multileader).
4. Press <Shift> and select the multileaders **POWER CORD**, **SWITCH,** and **POWER CORD**, then press <Enter>. Align the multileaders to **SWITCH** by selecting it. To set the direction, move the cursor perpendicularly above the **SWITCH** multileader. Click to place the multileaders.
5. Use grips to modify the exact locations of the leaders and text, as required.

Task 3: Add text.

1. Set the current *Text style* to **Annotative** (*Annotate* tab>*Text* panel).
2. Start the **Multiline Text** command.
3. Use a height of **0.125** and then add a note above and to the left of the power bar, as shown in Figure 17–76. Use the grips to place the note in two lines.

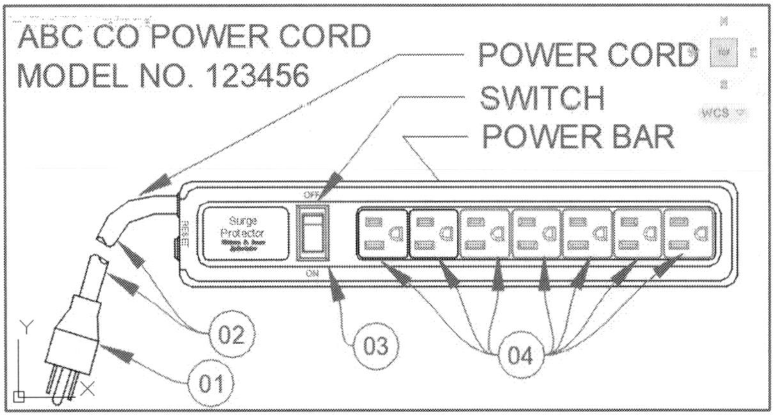

Figure 17–76

4. Save the drawing.

End of practice

17.6 Creating Tables

The **Table** command creates a unified table typically containing title and column headers with any number of rows/columns of data, as shown in Figure 17–77.

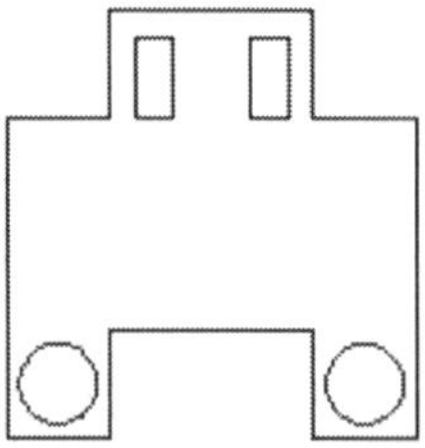

DESCRIPTION OF HOLES		
SIZE	DESCRIPTION	QTY
A	⌀.375 THRU	2
B	.187X.375 RECT	2

Figure 17–77

- You can create table styles that define custom standard properties. When you insert a table object, you add the values for each of the cells.
- You can also create tables to which you can add custom information by linking external Excel spreadsheet files, or by extracting AutoCAD object data and creating a table from the information.
- Tables can include calculations.

How To: Create an Empty Table

The **Table** command is used to create tables from scratch, and from links and data extractions.

1. In the *Annotate* tab>*Tables* panel or in the *Home* tab>*Annotation* panel, click 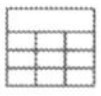 (Table).
2. The *Insert Table* dialog box opens, as shown in Figure 17–78. In the *Table style* drop-down list, select the table style.

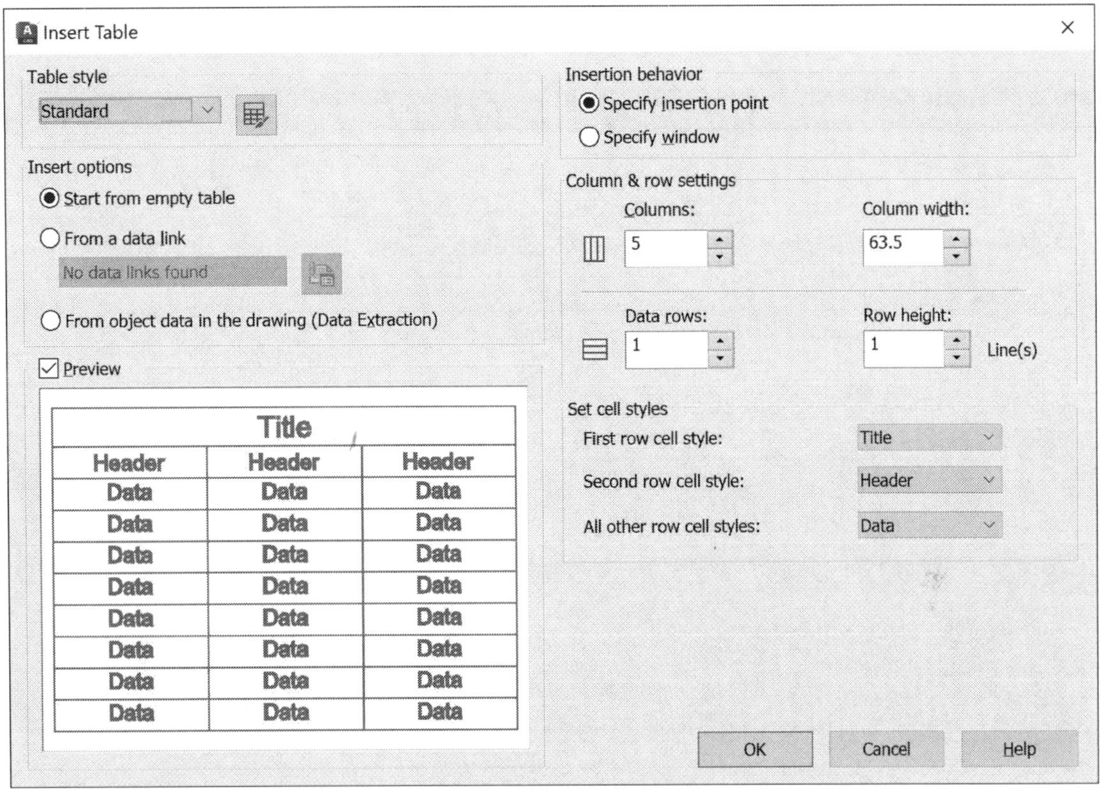

Figure 17–78

3. In the *Insert options* area, select **Start from empty table**.
4. In the *Insertion behavior* and *Column & row settings* areas, select the required options.
   - If you select the **Specify insertion point** option, you can set the number of columns and rows and their sizes.
   - If you select the **Specify window** option, you can set either the number of columns or the column width, and the number of rows or the row height (where the information not specified is automatically calculated by the size of the window).
5. In the *Set cell styles* area, select the required styles.
6. Click **OK** to place the table in the drawing.
7. Select a point in the drawing window to place the table or select two points to draw a window, depending on the option that you selected in the *Insertion behavior* area.

8. The *Text Editor* contextual tab opens and the title bar of the table is highlighted, as shown in Figure 17–79. Type the title.

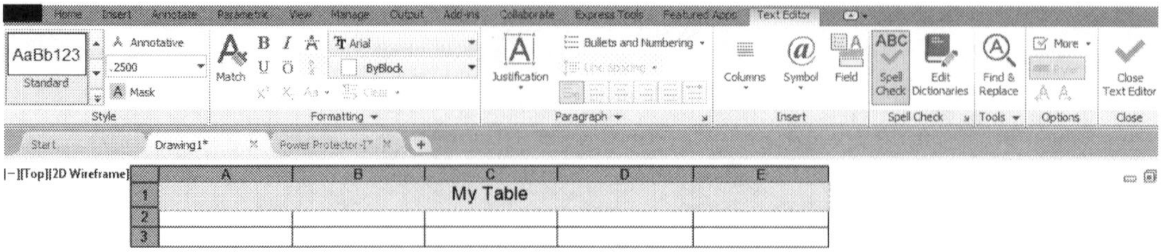

Figure 17–79

9. Press <Tab>. The first column and row highlight. Type the column heading or other information.

10. Continue to press <Tab> to move through the cells. You can also use the arrow keys on the keyboard to move from cell to cell. Press <Enter> to move down a row.

11. Click (Close Text Editor) to end the command.

- In the *Insert Table* dialog box, click (Launch the Table Style dialog) in the *Table style* area to create a table style.

Populating Table Cells

Table cells can contain plain text, blocks, and fields (which can contain mathematical equations). The example shown in Figure 17–80 has blocks in the *Room #* column, fields that are linked to the area of polyline objects in the *Area* column, and the total area of the building using a formula next to the *Total Area* cell.

Occupancy Table			
Room #	Department	Area	Use
101	Marketing	452.0 SQ. FT.	Office
102	Marketing	463.2 SQ. FT.	Office
103	Sales	452.0 SQ. FT.	Office
104	Engineering	2712.8 SQ. FT.	Drafting Room
105	Engineering	463.9 SQ. FT.	Office
106	Engineering	466.9 SQ. FT.	Office
107	Engineering	463.9 SQ. FT.	Office
	Total Area:	5474.6876 SQ. FT.	

Figure 17–80

- Click once in a cell to open the *Table Cell* contextual tab. It contains a variety of tools for adding and modifying cells. The current cell is highlighted with a gold edge, as shown in Figure 17–81.

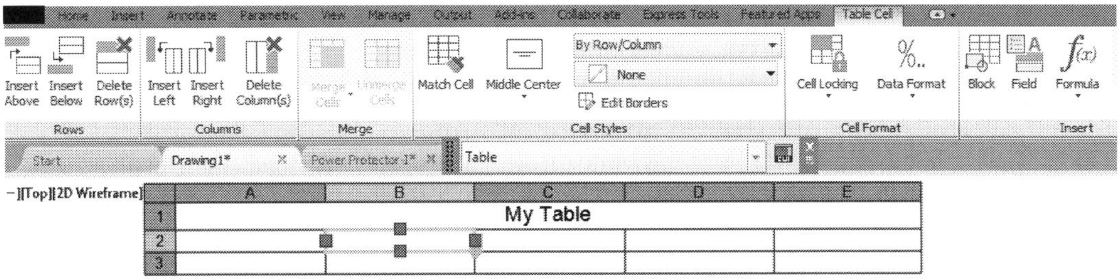

Figure 17–81

- Double-click in a cell to place the text and open the *Text Editor* contextual tab.

Inserting Blocks, Fields, and Formulas

Table cells can include text, blocks, fields, and formulas. Tools for inserting them are located in the *Table Cell* contextual tab>*Insert* panel and in the shortcut menus.

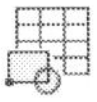

Insert Block: Opens the *Insert a Block in a Table Cell* dialog box. Select the name of the block or browse for a file. Then set the properties and cell alignment. The **AutoFit** option scales the size of the block to fit the cell size.

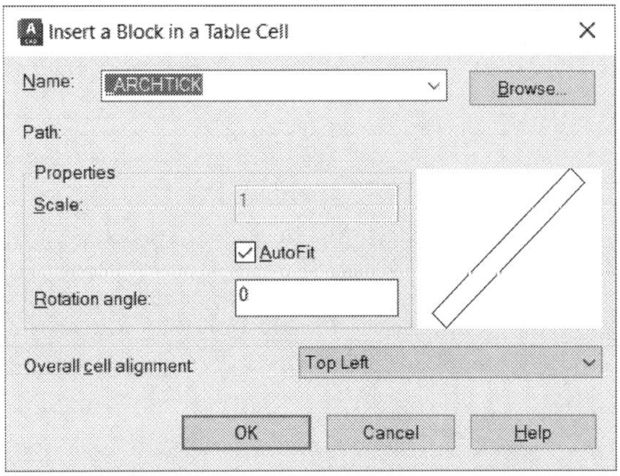

Insert Field: Adds a field selected in the *Field* dialog box into the cell. Hyperlinks are added using fields.

Insert Formula: Select **Sum**, **Average**, **Count**, **Cell**, or **Equation** to add a formula to the cell.

- To remove cell content, select the cell(s) and press <Delete>. You can also right-click and select **Delete All Contents**. This only deletes the selected cell(s).
- Tables are typically created in Paper Space. However, you sometimes need to access information in Model Space, such as the area of a hatch or polyline. When you are working with Object fields in a text object or table, you can select an object in a viewport even if the table is in Paper Space.

Calculations in Tables

You can make calculations directly in an AutoCAD table and the basic mathematical calculations are available, such as addition, subtraction, multiplication, division, and exponents, as well as **Sum** (as shown in Figure 17–82), **Average**, and **Count**. You can combine arithmetic functions, including parentheses, to create formulas.

	A	B	C	D
1	Replacement Costs			
2	Item #	Cost	Count	Total
3	AZ–408	255.45	12	3065.40
4	DG–411	18.29	22	402.38
5	DA–862	35.30	8	282.40
6			Grand Total:	=Sum(D3:D5)

Figure 17–82

- When the table is in edit mode, it displays letters for the columns and numbers for the rows. As in a standard spreadsheet, you specify a cell by its location, such as D3 (Column D, Row 3). When you finish editing, the table displays without this information.
- Cells used for calculations must only contain numeric information. The numeric information can be text or fields that have a numeric value (i.e., the area of a hatch or polyline).

Types of Calculations

Sum	Adds up numbers in the selected table cells.
Average	Computes the average of the numbers in the selected table cells. It adds up all of the numbers and divides the sum by the number of cells selected.
Count	Adds the number of selected cells, not the information in the cells. The cells must only contain numerical information.
Cell	Repeats the information from a selected cell in the current cell. The selected cell can be in another table. The selected cell must have numerical information; otherwise, #### displays in the field.
Equation	Computes the entered equation. You can add (+), subtract (-), multiply (*), divide (/), and set exponents (^). You can also group items together in parentheses, such as =(B3 / B7) * 2. The calculation in parentheses is computed first.

How To: Add Calculations to a Table

1. Create a table containing the numeric information that you want to calculate.
2. Click once in the cell in which you want the calculated value to be placed.
3. In the *Table Cell* contextual tab>*Insert* panel, expand $f(x)$ (Formula) and select the type of formula that you want to calculate, as shown on the left in Figure 17–83. Alternatively, right-click and select **Insert>Formula** and select the type of formula, as shown on the right in Figure 17–83.

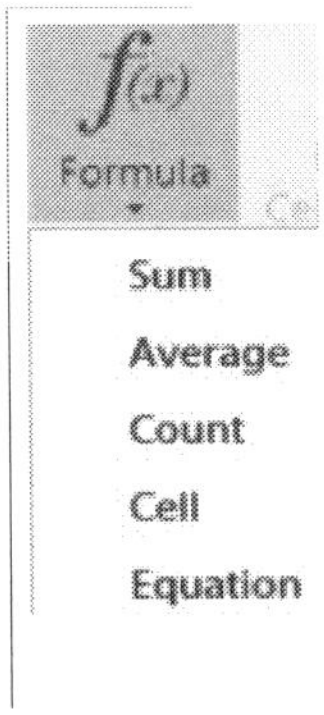

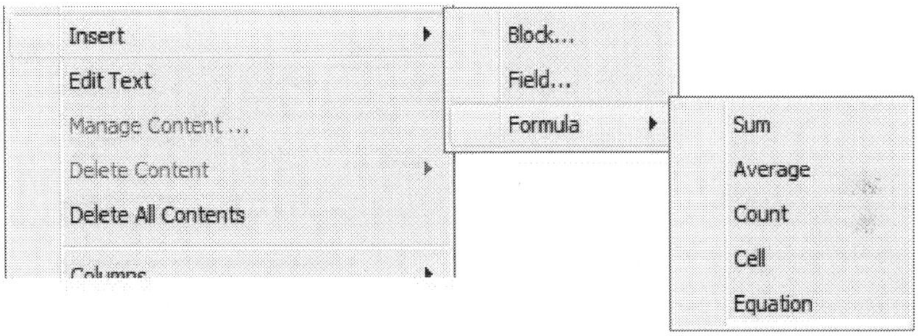

Figure 17–83

- **For Sum, Average, and Count:** Select two points for the corners of the table cell range. Click in the cells to be calculated when you select the points.
- **For Cell:** Click in another cell to place its value in the current cell. This can be a cell in another table.
- **For Equation:** Enter an equation using the cell coordinates, such as = B4 * C4.
- You can modify the equations created by any of the formulas. For example, you might select a cell range and want to add a cell or group of cells that are not in that range. In such a case, separate the new cell or range of cells by a comma, as follows:

=SUM (B3:E3)	Original formula
=SUM (B3:E3,C4)	Adding an additional cell
=SUM (B3:E3,C4:E4)	Adding a range of cells

- The calculated value in the cell is a formula field. It displays with a shaded background. You can edit the field to display the formula or change the formatting by double-clicking on the text.

Practice 17e
Create Tables

Practice Objective

- Create a table and add a formula.

In this practice, you will create a table that includes text, blocks, fields, and a hyperlink using the **Table** command. You will also add a formula summing up the values in one column using the **Formula** command.

1. Open **Occupancy-A.dwg** from your practice files folder.
2. Switch to the **Occupancy** layout.
3. Make the layer **0** current, and freeze all of the layers except **0**, **A-Area**, **A-Room-Symb**, and **Viewports**.
4. In the *Annotate* tab>*Tables* panel, start the **Table** command.
5. In the *Insert Table* dialog box, verify that the **Standard** table style and the **Specify insertion point** option are selected.
6. In the *Column & row settings* area, set the *Columns* to **4**, set the *Column width* to **2 1/2"**, and set the *Data rows* to **8**. Click **OK** and place the table in the drawing below the Floor Plan viewport.
7. Double-click inside the top row and type **Occupancy Table** for the title, as shown in Figure 17–84. Type the remaining titles for each of the column headings shown, using <Tab> to move to the next column.

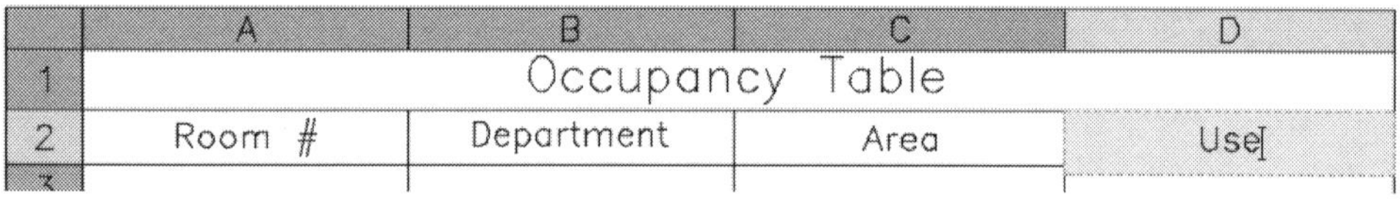

Figure 17–84

8. For the cells in each column, add the following information, as shown in Figure 17–85.
   - Click once on a cell until the individual cell is highlighted and grips display. The *Table Cell* contextual tab also displays. The tools (**Block** and **Field**) required are located in the *Insert* panel. (**Hint:** Use the **Auto-Fill** cells grip for similar content.)

Room #	Use (Block) to open the *Insert a Block in a Table Cell* dialog box. Select **Room Number** as the block name. Set the *Overall cell alignment* to **Middle Center**. Toggle on **Auto-Fit**. Click **OK**. Change the attribute to be the correct room number. Click **OK**.
Department	Type the text shown in Figure 17–85 for the departments.
Area	Use (Field) to insert a field in each cell in the column (for the 7 rooms). In the *Field* dialog box, set the *Field category* to **Objects** and the *Field names* to **Object**. In the *Object type* area, click (Select object) and then select the magenta polyline around the corresponding room in the floor plan. In the *Property* area, select the **Area** property. Set the *Format* to **Architectural** and the *Precision* to **0.0**.
Use	Type the text shown in Figure 17–85 into each cell in the column.

9. In the bottom cell of the *Area* column, add a formula using **Sum** (select the cell, right-click, and select **Insert>Formula> Sum**). Using a window, select the room areas in that column as the range and then press <Enter>. The calculated sum displays in the last *Area* column, as shown in Figure 17–85. (If the area does not fit in a single row, click on the table and use the move grip of the column to widen it.)

Occupancy Table			
Room #	Department	Area	Use
101	Marketing	452.0 SQ. FT.	Office
102	Marketing	463.2 SQ. FT.	Office
103	Sales	452.0 SQ. FT.	Office
104	Engineering	2712.8 SQ. FT.	Drafting Room
105	Engineering	463.9 SQ. FT.	Office
106	Engineering	466.9 SQ. FT.	Office
107	Engineering	463.9 SQ. FT.	Office
	Total Area:	5474.6876 SQ. FT.	

Figure 17–85

10. Select the cell with the sum, right-click, and select **Insert>Edit Field**. Set the *Precision* to **0.0**.
11. Thaw all of the layers that you had previously frozen.
12. Save the drawing.

End of practice

17.7 Modifying Tables

You can modify tables and table data in a variety of ways. Modifications can be made to individual cells, rows, columns, or to the entire table.

Modifying Cells, Rows, and Columns

When you select multiple cells, rows, or columns, you can add and remove rows and columns, merge and unmerge cells, and modify cell properties. You can also modify an individual cell using grips.

- To select more than one cell, hold <Shift> or click and drag across the cells that you want to select.
- To select an entire row or column, select the corresponding letter or number that displays (gold) when a cell is selected with grips.
- You can also **Cut**, **Copy**, and **Paste** cell contents using the shortcut menu.

Cell Grips

The square grips around a cell change its height and width. If you modify the grips of a selected cell, it impacts all of the rows or columns in which it is located. The diamond shaped grip is used to click and drag to automatically fill the selected cells with the contents of the current cell. First select, and then right-click on the diamond grip to change the options, as shown in Figure 17–86.

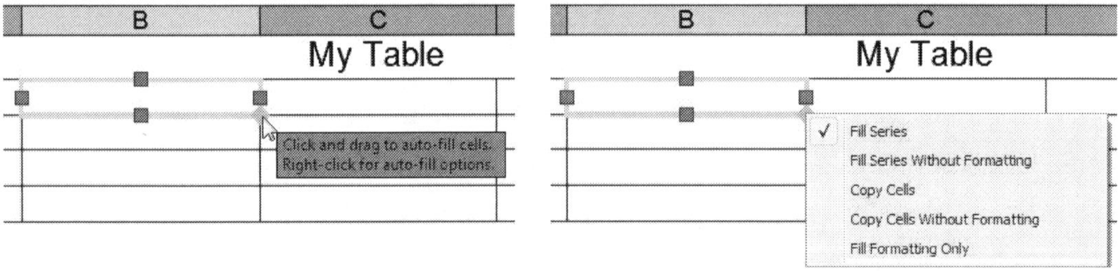

Figure 17–86

Modification Tools

With a cell selected, use the various tools available in the *Table Cell* contextual tab (as shown in Figure 17–87) to modify the tables.

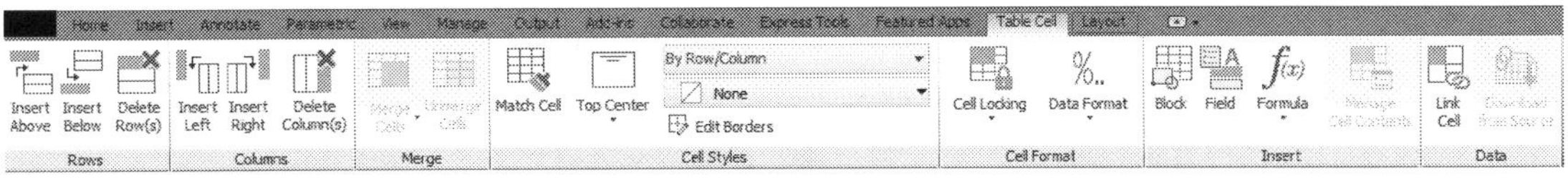

Figure 17–87

Adding and Removing Rows and Columns

	**Insert Above:** Inserts a row above the selected cell or row.
	**Insert Below:** Inserts a row below the selected cell or row.
	**Delete Row(s):** Deletes the selected row(s).
	**Insert Left:** Inserts a column to the left of the selected cell or column.
	**Insert Right:** Inserts a column to the right of the selected cell or column.
	**Delete Column(s):** Deletes the selected column(s).

Merging and Unmerging Cells

	**Merge Cells:** Merges selected cells depending on the selected option (**All**, **By Row**, or **By Column**). Multiple cells must be selected for this to be available.
	**Unmerge Cells:** Returns merged cells to an unmerged state. Merged cells must be selected for this option to be available.

Modifying Cell Properties

Match Cell: Applies the properties of a selected cell to other cells, similar to the **Match Properties** command.

Alignment: Applies the alignment selected from a list to the objects in the cell. You can align multiple cells at the same time. The current cell alignment icon might be displayed.

N/A

Cell Styles: Changes the style of the cell to the one selected from the list.

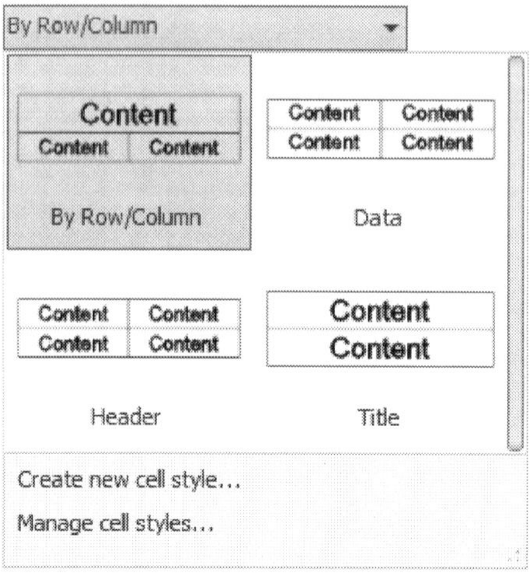

N/A

Background Fill: Changes the background color of the cell to the color selected from the list.

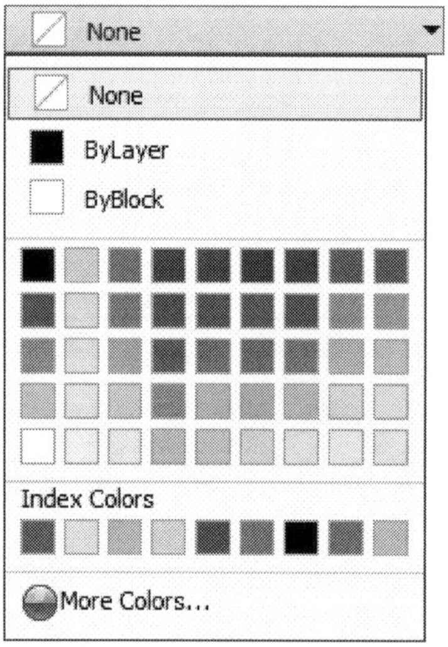

Cell Locking: Sets cells to be **Unlocked**, **Content Locked**, **Format Locked**, or **Content and Format Locked**.

%..	**Data Format:** Sets the data format of items in a cell. It is set to **General** by default. However, you can change the numerical data to **Angle**, **Currency**, **Data**, **Decimal Number**, **General**, **Percentage**, **Point**, **Text**, and **Whole Number**. If you need to customize the data format, right-click in the cell and select **Custom Table Cell Format** to open the *Table Cell Format* dialog box.
	Manage Cell Contents: Controls the location and flow of objects if there is more than one type of content in a cell, such as a block and text. This opens the *Manage Cell Content* dialog box.
	Edit Borders: Opens the *Cell Border Properties* dialog box, in which you can specify lineweights, linetypes, color, and border types for individual cells, rows, or columns. Toggle on **Lineweight** in the *Status Bar*, expanded Customization list to display the lineweights.

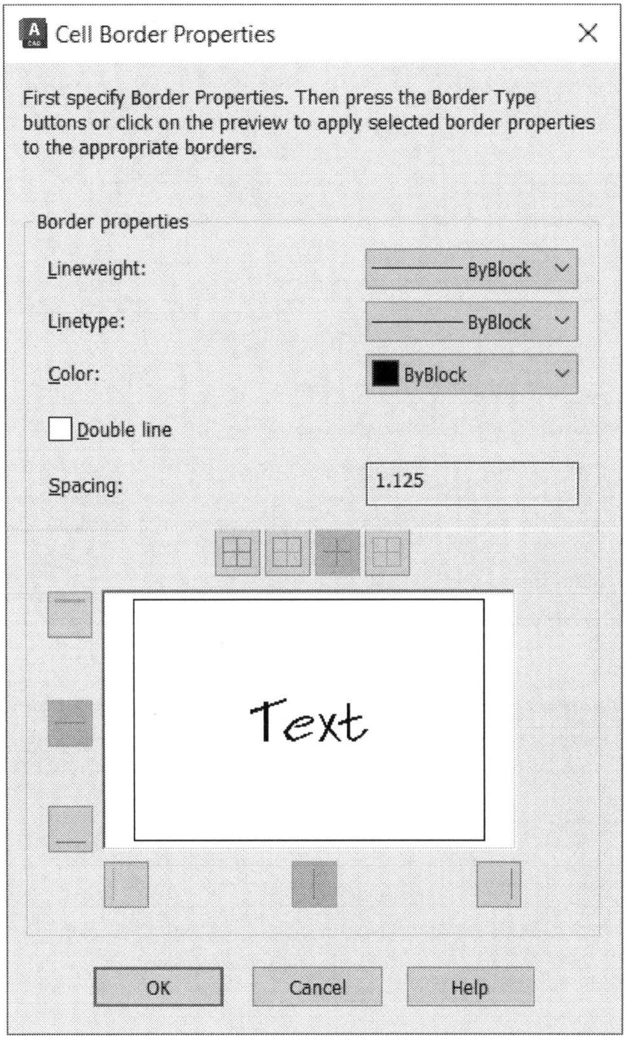

Modifying the Entire Table

When you select the entire table (click the edge of the table), as shown in Figure 17–88, you can use grips to modify its overall size, the width of columns, the height of rows, and to break the table into columns. You can also modify some of these options in the *Properties* palette or through the shortcut menu.

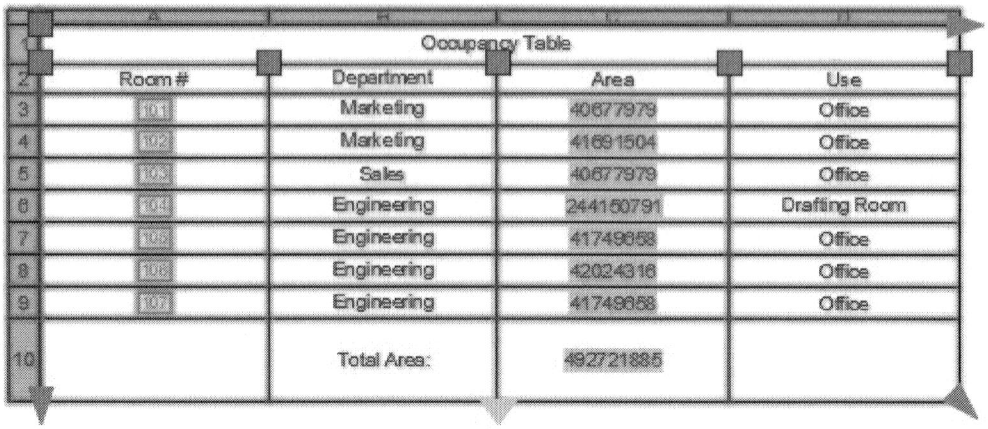

Figure 17–88

- Table-specific shortcut options include **Table Style**, **Size Columns Equally**, **Size Rows Equally**, **Remove All Property Overrides**, **Export**, and **Table Indicator Color**.
- **Table Indicator Color** is the color of the row numbers and column letters that display when the table is selected.

Table Grips

Tables can be extensively modified with grips, as shown in Figure 17–89. You can use them to adjust the width, height, and columns to fit the available space as required.

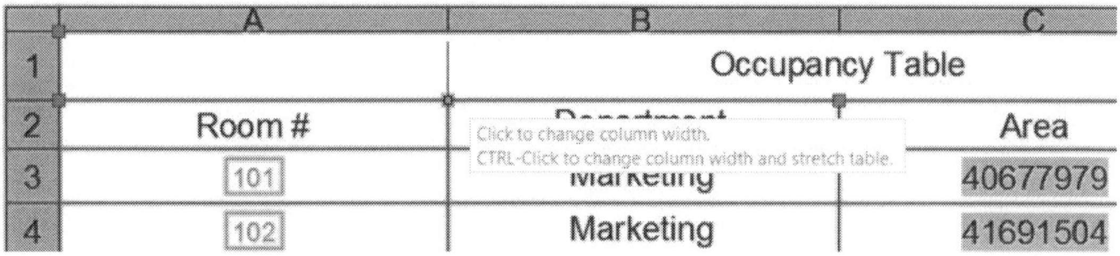

Figure 17–89

	Column Width: Controls the column width. Click the grip to change the width without changing the overall table width. The adjacent columns resize accordingly. Hold <Ctrl> to modify the overall width of the table. The upper left square grip moves the entire table.
	Table Height: Uniformly stretches the table height. The height of each row changes, including the title and headers. Rows are not added.
	Table Width: Uniformly stretches the table width. The width of each column changes. Columns are not added.
	Table Height and Width: Uniformly stretches both table height and width.
	Table Breaking: Activates table breaking, enabling you to control where the table is broken when it is in columns.

Breaking a Table

When a table is too long to fit on a sheet, you can break it and change its overall height. Click the grip (Table breaking) and drag it upwards until it reaches the required location in the table, as shown in Figure 17–90. The rest of the table is placed next to it in as many columns as required to contain all of the rows.

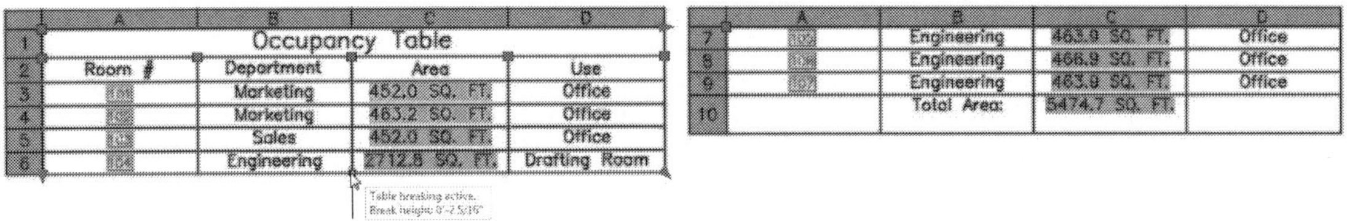

Figure 17–90

Practice 17f (Optional) Modify Tables

Practice Objective

- Modify the table using various modification tools.

In this practice, you will use grips to modify the width and height of rows and columns, add and merge rows to create a new header, insert rows, copy and paste information, use Auto-fill to add information to cells, and break the table into columns. The completed table is shown in Figure 17–91.

Occupancy Table			
First Floor			
Room #	Department	Area	Use
101	Marketing	452.0 SQ. FT.	Office
102	Marketing	463.2 SQ. FT.	Office
103	Sales	452.0 SQ. FT.	Office
104	Engineering	2712.8 SQ. FT.	Drafting Room
105	Engineering	463.9 SQ. FT.	Office
106	Engineering	466.9 SQ. FT.	Office
107	Engineering	463.9 SQ. FT.	Office
	Total Area:	5474.7 SQ. FT.	

Second Floor			
Room #	Department	Area	Use
201	Engineering		Office
202	Engineering		Office
203	Engineering		Office
204	Engineering		Office
205	Engineering		Office
206	Engineering		Office
207	Engineering		Office

Figure 17–91

1. Open **Occupancy1-A.dwg** from your practice files folder.
2. Zoom in to the **Occupancy Table** area of the drawing.
3. Select the table to display the grips. Hold <Ctrl>, click and drag the right side square grip of the *Area* column to the right to increase the *Area* column width while also stretching the table, as shown in Figure 17–92. Click again to accept the stretch.

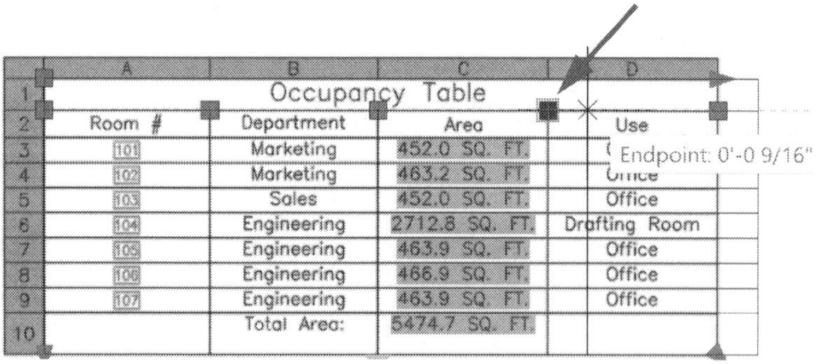

Figure 17–92

4. Click on number 10 to select the last row and use the bottom middle grip to decrease its height such that it is similar to the height of other rows.

5. Select the Row 2 of the table. In the *Table Cell* contextual tab>*Rows* panel, click (Insert Above) to place a new row above Row 2. Double-click inside the first cell of the new row and enter the text **First Floor**.
6. Select the newly created Row 2. Right-click and select **Merge>By Row**.
7. With the row still selected, in the *Table Cell* contextual tab>*Cell Styles* panel, expand the *Table Cell Styles* list, and set the *style* to **Title**, as shown in Figure 17–93.

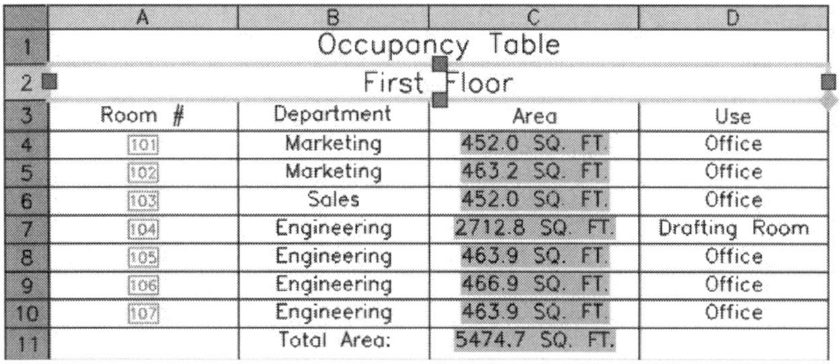

	A	B	C	D
1	Occupancy Table			
2	First Floor			
3	Room #	Department	Area	Use
4	101	Marketing	452.0 SQ. FT.	Office
5	102	Marketing	463.2 SQ. FT.	Office
6	103	Sales	452.0 SQ. FT.	Office
7	104	Engineering	2712.8 SQ. FT.	Drafting Room
8	105	Engineering	463.9 SQ. FT.	Office
9	106	Engineering	466.9 SQ. FT.	Office
10	107	Engineering	463.9 SQ. FT.	Office
11		Total Area:	5474.7 SQ. FT.	

Figure 17–93

8. Select the bottom row. In the *Table Cell* contextual tab>*Rows* panel, click (Insert Below) to add a row. Continue to click until the last row number displays as **21**.
9. Select one of the cells containing a room number block. Right-click and select **Copy** to copy the cell to the clipboard.
10. Leave two open rows after the *Total Area* row and paste the block into the cell in the *Room #* column (*Row 14*).
11. Select the copied cell and click on the Auto-fill grip (cyan diamond) of the cell. Drag it to the *Room #* cell of *Row 20*, as shown in Figure 17–94. Click to copy the block to the next six cells below.

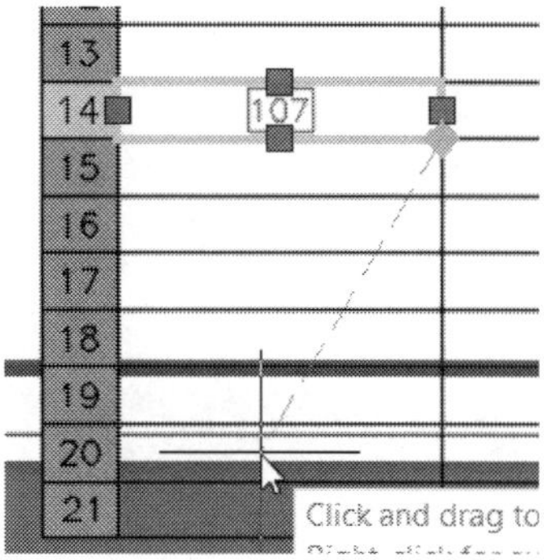

Figure 17–94

12. Double-click on the first new block to open the *Edit Block* in a *Table Cell* dialog box. Click **OK**. In the *Enter Attributes* dialog box, change the *Room Number* to **201** and click **OK**.
13. Modify the rest of the room numbers with subsequent numbers.
14. Enter **Engineering** in the *Department* column for **Room 201**. Use **Auto-fill** to fill the rest of the *Department* cells till **207** (leave the last row blank).
15. Repeat the **Copy** and **Auto-fill** process to fill the *Use* columns with **Office**. Do not fill in the *Area* column.
16. Select the entire table and break it under the *Total Area* row. Click (Table breaking) and drag it up till under **Total Area** row. Note that as you keep on moving it up the rows are added along the right side. Click under the *Total Area* row to break the table at this point, as shown in Figure 17–95.

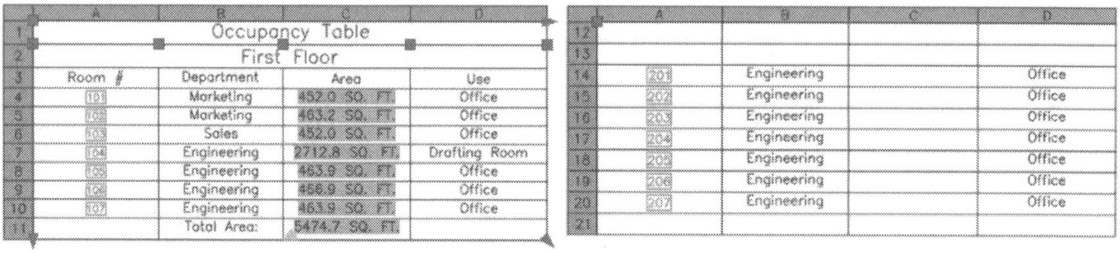

	A	B	C	D
1	Occupancy Table			
2	First Floor			
3	Room #	Department	Area	Use
4	101	Marketing	452.0 SQ. FT.	Office
5	102	Marketing	463.2 SQ. FT.	Office
6	103	Sales	452.0 SQ. FT.	Office
7	104	Engineering	2712.8 SQ. FT.	Drafting Room
8	105	Engineering	463.9 SQ. FT.	Office
9	106	Engineering	456.9 SQ. FT.	Office
10	107	Engineering	463.9 SQ. FT.	Office
11		Total Area:	5474.7 SQ. FT.	

	A	B	C	D
12				
13				
14	201	Engineering		Office
15	202	Engineering		Office
16	203	Engineering		Office
17	204	Engineering		Office
18	205	Engineering		Office
19	206	Engineering		Office
20	207	Engineering		Office
21				

Figure 17–95

17. You can add and merge rows to specify an additional title and headers for the Second Floor, as shown in Figure 17–96. Set the cell styles as required.

Second Floor			
Room #	Department	Area	Use
201	Engineering		Office
202	Engineering		Office
203	Engineering		Office
204	Engineering		Office
205	Engineering		Office
206	Engineering		Office
207	Engineering		Office

Figure 17–96

18. Save the drawing.

End of practice

Chapter Review Questions

1. When creating multiline text, you pick two points. What do those points determine?
    a. The text height.
    b. The text location.
    c. The rotation angle of the text.
    d. The thickness of the text.

2. Using the **Import Text** tool located in the *Text Editor* contextual tab>expanded *Tools* panel, the text that is imported does not include formatting.
    a. True
    b. False

3. What happens when you double-click on a text object?
    a. It opens the *Properties* palette.
    b. It opens the text for editing.
    c. It explodes the text.
    d. It updates the text to the current text style.

4. How do you add a text frame around a multiline text?
    a. By drawing a rectangle separately and adding it to the multiline text properties.
    b. Selecting **Outline** in the *Text Editor* contextual tab.
    c. Setting the *Text Frame* to **Yes** in the *Properties* palette.
    d. You cannot add a text frame to the multiline text.

5. When editing text, how do you change the justification of the multiline text object (left, right, centered, etc.)?
    a. Edit the Text Style.
    b. Click the ruler above the editing frame.
    c. You cannot change the justification after the text is created.
    d. Tools in the *Text Editor* contextual tab>*Paragraph* panel in the ribbon.

6. Which of the following statements is true regarding multileaders?
   a. The leader and text (or block) of a multileader are separate objects.
   b. The square grip at the end of the leader line moves the multileader.
   c. The square grip at the top left of the text moves the multileader.
   d. The arrow grip on the landing of the leader line changes the location to which the leader line is pointing.

7. To collect several multileaders together into one leader, the multileaders should have:
   a. Block content only.
   b. Text content only.
   c. String content only.
   d. Both block and text content.

8. What object types can be contained in a table? (Select all that apply.)
   a. Text
   b. Blocks
   c. Fields
   d. Lines

9. When a table is selected, what does the square grip do?
   a. Breaks the link between the table and the Excel spreadsheet.
   b. Resizes the column width in the table.
   c. Uniformly stretches the table width.
   d. Uniformly stretches the table height.

Command Summary

Button	Command	Location
	Annotation	• **Ribbon:** *Text Editor* contextual tab
1:1	**Annotation Scale**	• **Status Bar** (*in Model Space*)
	Columns	• **Ribbon:** *Text Editor* contextual tab
	Field	• **Ribbon:** *Text Editor* contextual tab
	Justify: Center	• **Ribbon:** *Text Editor* contextual tab
	Justify: Default	• **Ribbon:** *Text Editor* contextual tab
	Justify: Distribute	• **Ribbon:** *Text Editor* contextual tab
	Justify: Fit	• **Ribbon:** *Text Editor* contextual tab
	Justify: Left	• **Ribbon:** *Text Editor* contextual tab
	Justify: Right	• **Ribbon:** *Text Editor* contextual tab
	Mtext Edit	• **Shortcut Menu:** (*on selected text*) Mtext Edit • **Double-click** (*on text*) • **Command Prompt:** mtedit
	Multileader	• **Ribbon:** *Home* tab>*Annotation* panel or *Annotate* tab>*Leaders* panel • **Command Prompt:** mleader
	Multileader: Add Leader	• **Ribbon:** *Home* tab>*Annotation* panel or *Annotate* tab>*Leaders* panel
	Multileader: Align	• **Ribbon:** *Home* tab>*Annotation* panel or *Annotate* tab>*Leaders* panel • **Command Prompt:** mleaderalign
	Multileader: Collect	• **Ribbon:** *Home* tab>*Annotation* panel or *Annotate* tab>*Leaders* panel • **Command Prompt:** mleadercollect
	Multileader: Remove Leader	• **Ribbon:** *Home* tab>*Annotation* panel or *Annotate* tab>*Leaders* panel

Button	Command	Location
A	**Multiline Text**	• **Ribbon:** *Home* tab>*Annotation* panel or *Annotate* tab>*Text* panel • **Command Prompt:** mtext or T
ABC	**Spell Check**	• **Ribbon:** *Annotate* tab>*Text* panel • **Command Prompt:** spell
@	**Symbol**	• **Ribbon:** *Text Editor* contextual tab
	Table	• **Ribbon:** *Home* tab>*Annotation* panel or *Annotate* tab>*Tables* panel • **Command Prompt:** table
	Table Column: Delete Column(s)	• **Ribbon:** *Table Cell* contextual tab>*Columns* panel
	Table Column: Insert Left	• **Ribbon:** *Table Cell* contextual tab>*Columns* panel
	Table Column: Insert Right	• **Ribbon:** *Table Cell* contextual tab>*Columns* panel
	Table Row: Delete Row(s)	• **Ribbon:** *Table Cell* contextual tab>*Rows* panel
	Table Row: Insert Above	• **Ribbon:** *Table Cell* contextual tab>*Rows* panel
	Table Row: Insert Below	• **Ribbon:** *Table Cell* contextual tab>*Rows* panel
	Table: Alignment	• **Ribbon:** *Table Cell* contextual tab>*Cell Styles* panel
	Table: Cell Locking	• **Ribbon:** *Table Cell* contextual tab>*Cell Format* panel
%..	**Table: Data Format**	• **Ribbon:** *Table Cell* contextual tab>*Cell Format* panel
	Table: Edit Borders	• **Ribbon:** *Table Cell* contextual tab>*Cell Styles* panel
	Table: Insert Block	• **Ribbon:** *Table Cell* contextual tab>*Insert* panel
	Table: Insert Field	• **Ribbon:** *Table Cell* contextual tab>*Insert* panel
fx	**Table: Insert Formula**	• **Ribbon:** *Table Cell* contextual tab>*Insert* panel
	Table: Manage Cell Content	• **Ribbon:** *Table Cell* contextual tab>*Insert* panel

Button	Command	Location
	**Table: Match Cell**	• **Ribbon:** *Table Cell* contextual tab>*Cell Styles* panel
	**Table: Merge Cells**	• **Ribbon:** *Table Cell* contextual tab>*Merge* panel
	**Table: Unmerge Cells**	• **Ribbon:** *Table Cell* contextual tab>*Merge* panel

Chapter 18

Hatching

In this chapter, you learn how to hatch areas of your drawing and to edit applied hatching.

Learning Objectives

- Apply hatch patterns to fill specific areas of a drawing.
- Set hatch pattern properties and hatch options.
- Modify a hatch pattern, scale, angle, and boundaries.

18.1 Hatching

Hatching is a pattern of lines or shapes that is used to distinguish certain areas of a drawing from other areas. For example, hatching might be used to indicate which rooms on a floor plan are occupied by a specific department, as shown in Figure 18–1. In mechanical design, hatching is typically used to indicate section views. The AutoCAD® software contains many predefined hatch patterns.

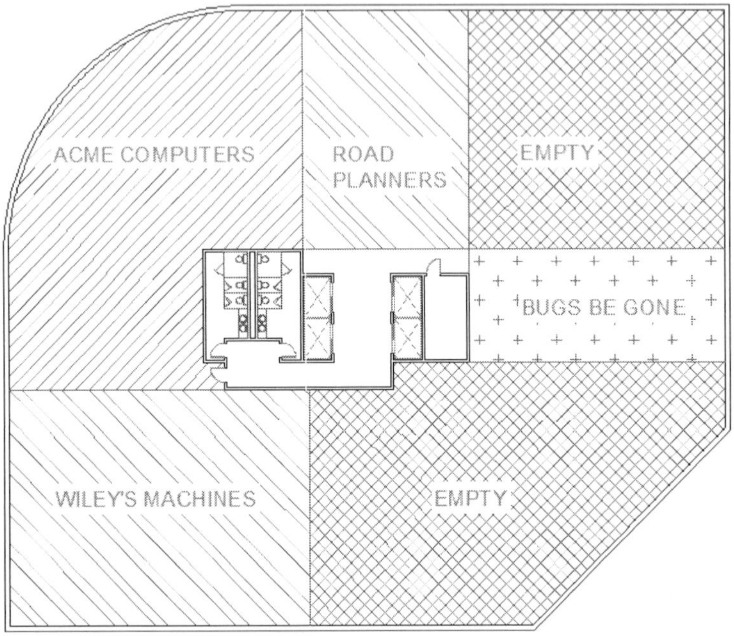

Figure 18–1

- There are two ways to apply hatching: *Tool Palettes* and the **Hatch** command.
- Hatching should be placed on a separate hatch layer so that it can be easily toggled off or frozen.
- Hatching can be annotative, so you should apply it after a viewport has been prepared and scaled.
- Many patterns for specific applications can be purchased from commercial third-party developers.

Applying a Hatch: Tool Palettes

Tool Palettes (*Hatches and Fills* tab) contain several hatch patterns that can be used for hatching a closed area in a drawing.

- Click on a pattern. It is attached to the cursor, as shown in Figure 18–2. Move the cursor inside the closed area that you want to hatch. A preview of the hatch in the area displays. Click to hatch the area.

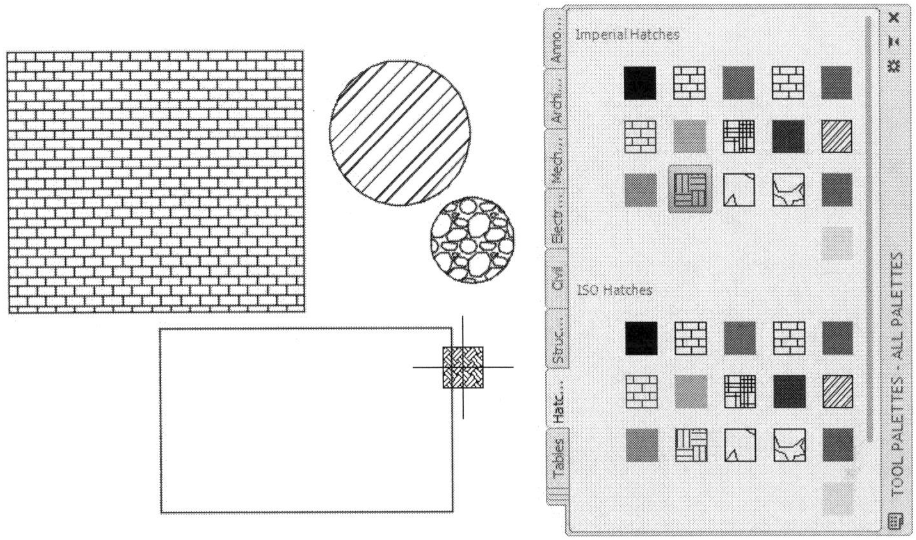

Figure 18–2

- The area for hatching should be completely bounded, with no gaps.
- Closed objects and text inside the bounded area (known as *islands*) are not normally hatched.
- The default *Hatches and Fills* tab in *Tool Palettes* comes with hatches that are scaled for Imperial and ISO (Metric) drawings, and several gradient hatches, as shown in Figure 18–2.

  Note: *In Tool Palettes, if the tab is hidden, click on the area just below the bottom tab( ) and select* ***Hatches and Fills****.*

- By default, the hatch patterns provided are not annotative. You can change that after the hatch has been applied to the object by opening its *Properties* palette, and changing *Annotative* to **Yes**, as shown in Figure 18–3.

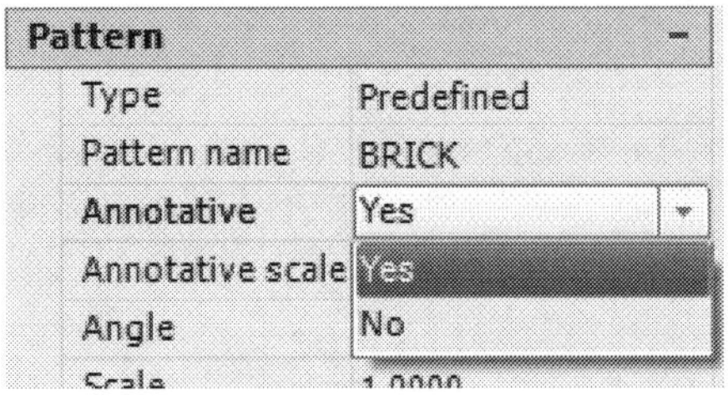

Figure 18–3

Applying a Hatch: Hatch Command

The **Hatch** command provides more control and options than hatching using *Tool Palettes*. Using this command, you can select from many different patterns and adjust the scale or angle of the hatch as you apply it, as shown in Figure 18–4.

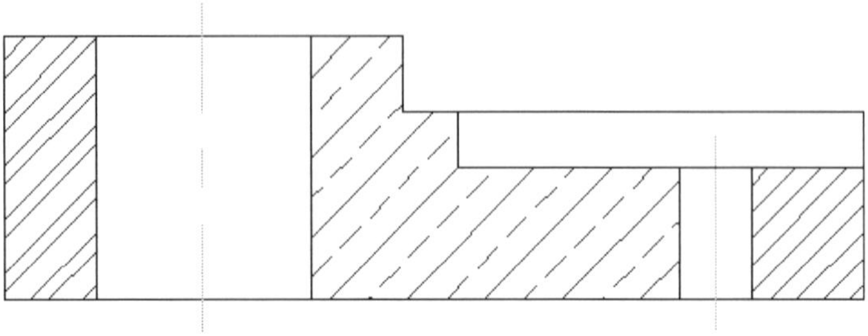

Figure 18–4

How To: Hatch Objects

1. In the *Home* tab>*Draw* panel, click  (Hatch), located in the *Hatch* flyout.
2. In the *Hatch Creation* contextual tab, set the *Pattern*, *Scale*, *Angle*, and *Transparency*, as shown in Figure 18–5.

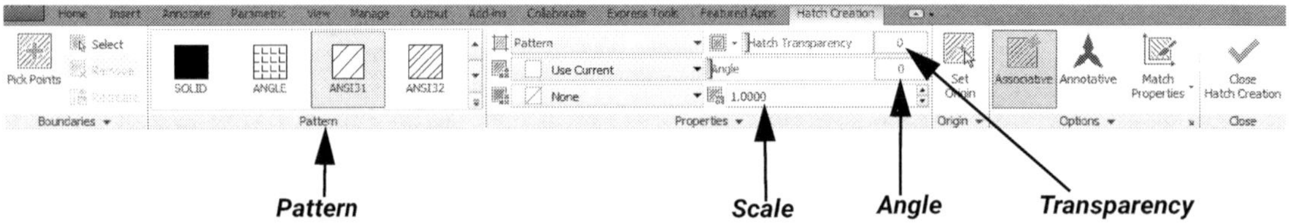

Figure 18–5

3. Click  (Pick Points) and hover the cursor inside the bounded area to preview the hatch. Click to add the hatch or modify the settings until the correct results display in the preview.
   - You can also click  (Select Boundary Objects) and select a closed object or group of objects that form a closed boundary.
   - If the hatch cannot be created due to invalid hatch boundaries, an alert box opens, as shown in Figure 18–6. Red circles are also displayed at the places that the software detects as gaps in the boundary. Use **REGEN** command to remove them.

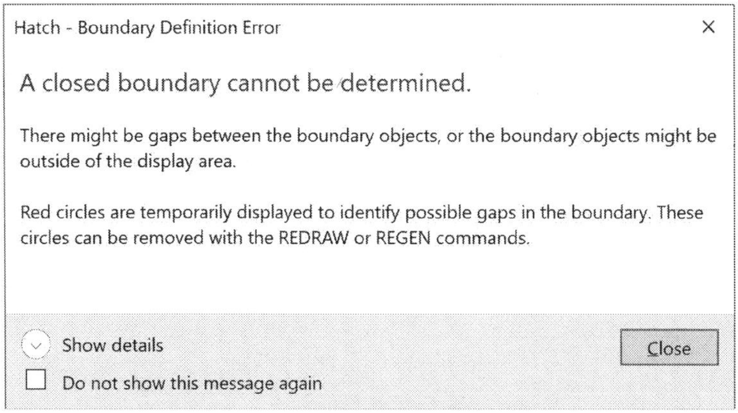

Figure 18–6

- Click (Remove Boundaries) to select objects in the drawing to remove them from the selection.

4. Press <Enter> or click (Close Hatch Editor) to end the command.

Hatch Pattern and Properties

In the *Hatch Creation* contextual tab, you can set the *Pattern*, *Scale*, *Angle*, and *Transparency* of the hatch.

Pattern Panel

In the *Pattern* panel, select a pattern from the list. You can expand the list by clicking , as shown in Figure 18–7.

> ***Note:*** *If your ribbon is reduced in size due to the size of the interface, you might need to expand (Hatch Pattern) in the Pattern panel first.*

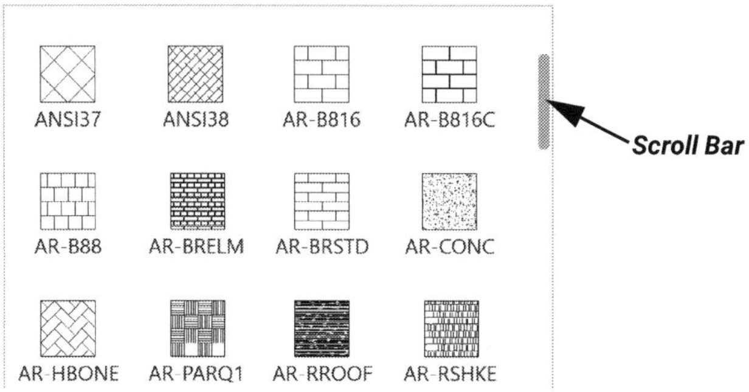

Figure 18–7

Properties Panel

In the *Properties* panel, you can set the *Hatch Type*, *Hatch Color*, *Background Color*, *Hatch Transparency*, *Hatch Angle*, *Hatch Pattern Scale*, and *Hatch Layer Override*. These enable you to customize how the hatch displays in the drawing.

Hatch Type

The type of hatch can be **Solid**, **Gradient**, **Pattern**, or **User defined,** as shown in Figure 18–8. Select the hatch type, and then select a pattern in the *Pattern* list.

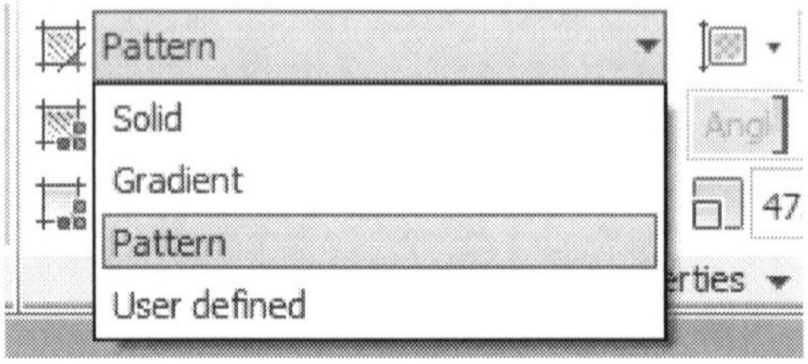

Figure 18–8

- User-defined patterns are parallel lines with a spacing and angle that you specify. You can create a cross-hatch by expanding the *Properties* panel and clicking  (Double).
- To create a solid fill, set the *Hatch Type* to **Solid** and the *Hatch Color* to **ByLayer** or a color.
- To create a gradient fill, set the *Hatch Type* to **Gradient** and set the colors for *Gradient Color 1* and *Gradient Color 2*.

Hatch Color

Use this option to set the color of the hatch. You can select a specific color, use the current color, or set the color to **ByLayer**, where the color of the hatch is controlled by the color of the layer.

Background Color

Use this option to add a background color to the hatch. For example, if you have two hatches of the same pattern, you can set a different background color for each one.

Hatch Transparency

Use this option to control the level of transparency for the hatch. This is useful for displaying objects below the hatch, such as furniture, walls, or annotations. You can use the slider or enter the value, as shown in Figure 18–9. You can also expand (Transparency Values) and set the transparency to **ByLayer Transparency** or **ByBlock Transparency**.

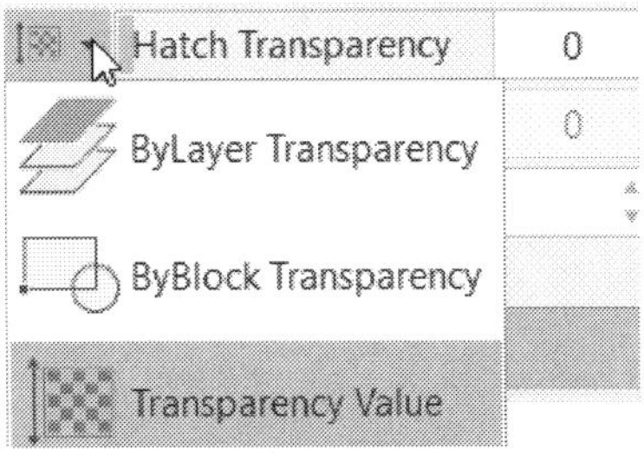

Figure 18–9

Hatch Angle

The *Hatch Angle* sets the rotation angle of the hatch pattern. An angle of **0** creates the pattern at its original angle. Increase the value to get an angled pattern, as shown in Figure 18–10.

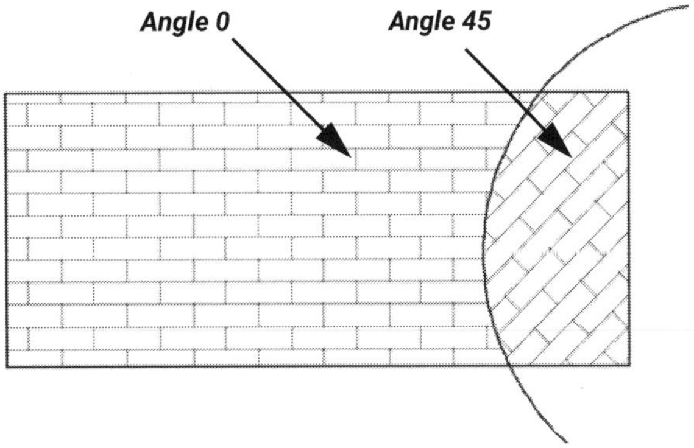

Figure 18–10

Hatch Pattern Scale

The *Hatch Pattern Scale* controls the space between the lines in the pattern (which are normally based on the drawing's plot scale factor). Enter the scale required to correctly display the hatch pattern so that its lines and spaces display clearly.

- If you are working in a viewport and using Annotative scaling, you should expand the *Properties* panel and click (Relative to Paper Space). It calculates the scale based on the viewport scale. **Annotative** maintains the hatch scale relative to Paper Space if the viewport scale is changed.

Hatch Layer Override

You can set the layer on which the hatch is placed, overriding the current layer.

- You can use the **HPLAYER** system variable to set the layer on which the hatch is placed, overriding the current layer.
- If the layer you want to use does not exist in the drawing, type the new layer name. The next time you start the **Hatch** command, the layer is created and the hatch is placed on it.

Hatch Origin

The hatch origin determines how the hatch fits into the selected area. If you are using a pattern (such as brick hatching), the hatch origin enables you to start and end the pattern appropriately inside the boundary.

- Click  (Set Origin), select the point at which the pattern is going to start, and then select an internal point to set the boundary. You can use the preset options to set the origin to the **Bottom Left**, **Bottom Right**, **Top Left**, **Top Right**, or **Center**, as shown in Figure 18–11.

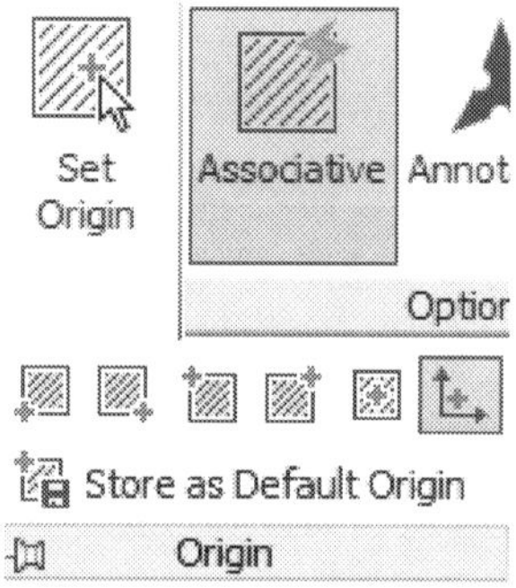

Figure 18–11

- You can select **Use Current Origin** to return to the default origin point.
- You can select **Store as Default Origin** to save the current location as the default origin.

Hatch Options

You can set the hatch to be **Annotative**, so that it uses the annotative scale of the viewport in which it displays, as shown in Figure 18–12.

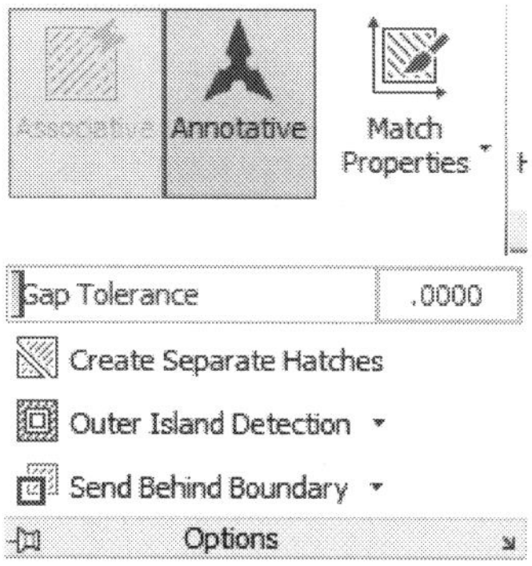

Figure 18–12

- Hatches are typically set to **Associative** (the default if **Annotative** is selected). This means that the hatch is associated with the boundary. If the boundary is changed (e.g., moved, stretched, etc.), the hatch pattern area changes to fill the new boundary.
- Click (Create Separate Hatches) if you want each boundary selected during one command to be created as individual hatches. Otherwise, they are all one hatch object no matter how many boundaries you select.
- (Send Behind Boundary) drop-down options (shown in Figure 18–13) control whether the hatch is behind or in front of overlapping objects or boundaries. You can specify the relationship for any overlapping objects or just the boundary.

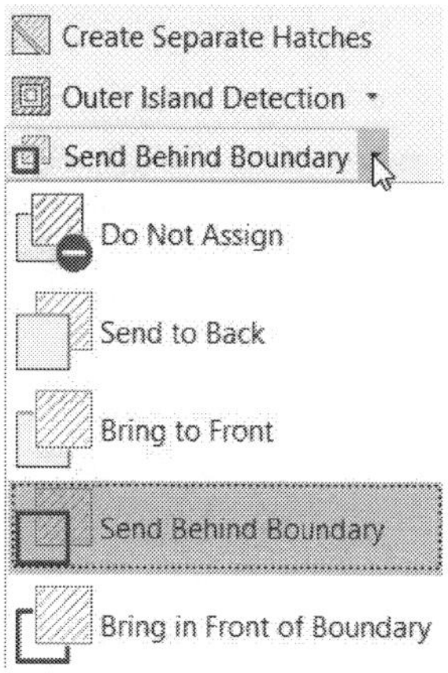

Figure 18–13

- Click (Match Properties) to select an existing hatch object in the drawing and use it to hatch other areas.
- **Island Detection** sets whether or not the areas in overlapping or complex objects are hatched. Expand the drop-down list and select the required type of detection, as shown in Figure 18–14.

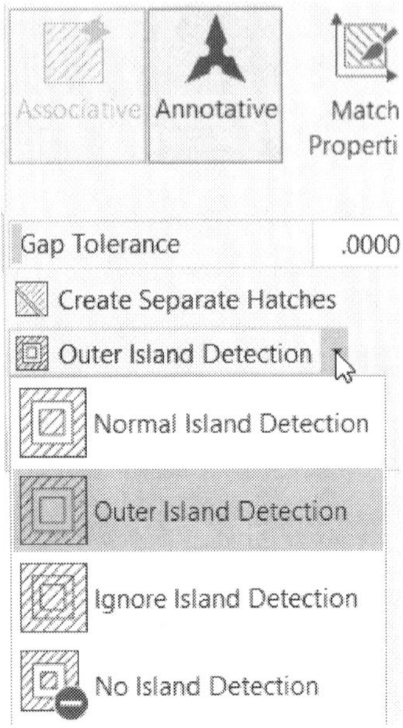

Figure 18–14

- **Gap Tolerance** sets the largest gap permitted in the boundary of an area to be hatched. If set to **0** (the default), no gaps are permitted.

Hint: Finding the Area of a Hatch

The *Area* of a hatch displays in the *Properties* palette, as shown in Figure 18–15. It can be used as a quick way to find the area of an object with holes.

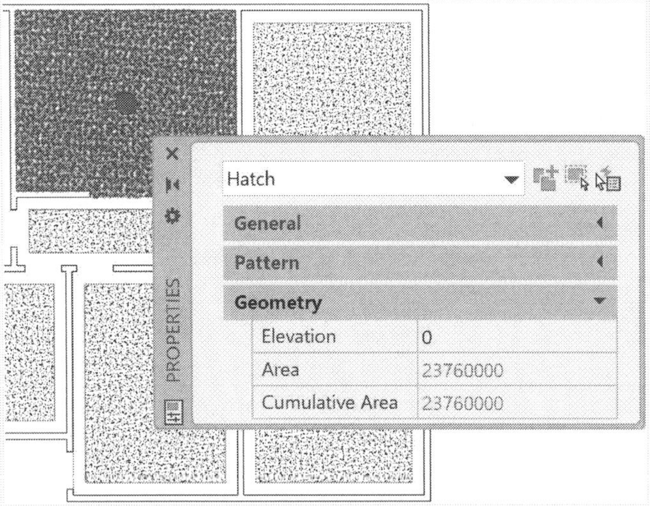

Figure 18–15

If more than one hatch is selected, it provides the cumulative area. For example, you might want to know the area of several rooms in a building. Hatch the rooms, select the hatches, and note the *Cumulative Area* in the *Properties* palette, as shown in Figure 18–16.

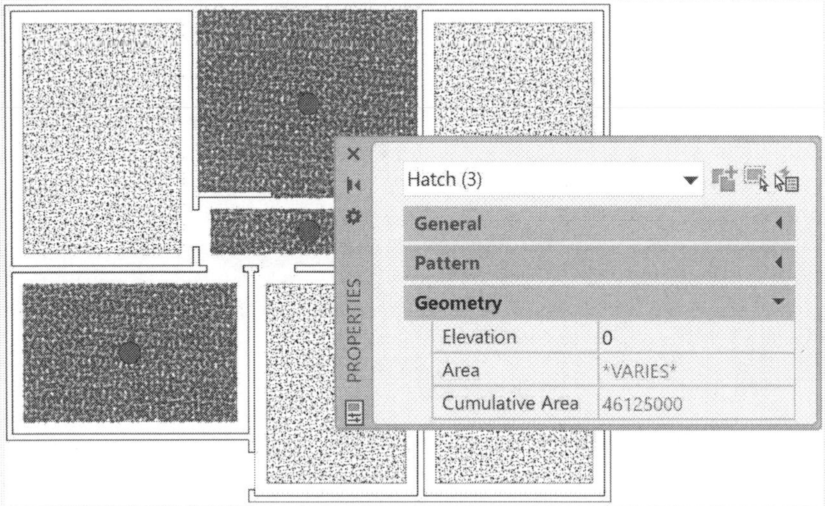

Figure 18–16

Hint: Path Hatching

You can now apply hatching along a specified path. This is a mode of hatching which is available through the Command Line. Once you start the **Hatch** command, instead of selecting an internal point, select the **Draw** option at the Command Line. Note that the *hatch mode* is **Area**. Select the **Mode** option and then select the **Path** mode, as shown in Figure 18–17. The *hatch mode* changes to **Path** and you can specify the Width and Alignment.

```
Command: _hatch
Pick internal point or [Select objects/Draw/Undo/seTtings]: D
Current hatch mode: Area
Specify start point or [picK internal point/Select objects/Rectangle/Circle/Mode/seTtings]: M
Specify draw hatch mode [Area/Path] <Area>: P
Current hatch mode: Path, Width = 600, Alignment = Outside
HATCH Specify start point or [picK internal point Select objects Rectangle Circle ALignment
Width Mode seTtings]:
```

Figure 18–17

After the hatch mode is set to path, you can pick two points to define the path, as shown in Figure 18–18.

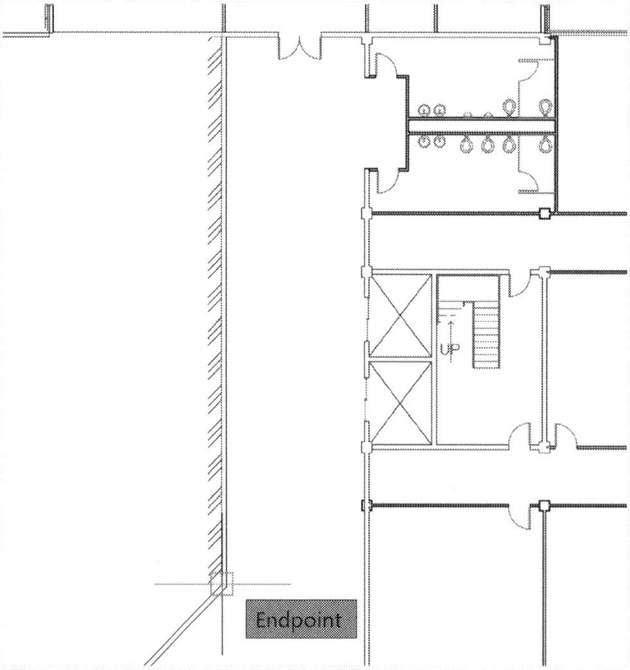

Figure 18–18

18.2 Editing Hatches

Instead of erasing and reapplying hatching to change the pattern or scale, you can adjust the hatch using:

- The *Hatch Editor* contextual tab in the ribbon
- The **Edit Hatch** command
- Grips

You can change the hatch pattern, scale, or angle, and add or remove areas from the existing hatch boundary.

When you modify the boundaries of associative hatches, the hatch automatically updates, as shown in Figure 18–19.

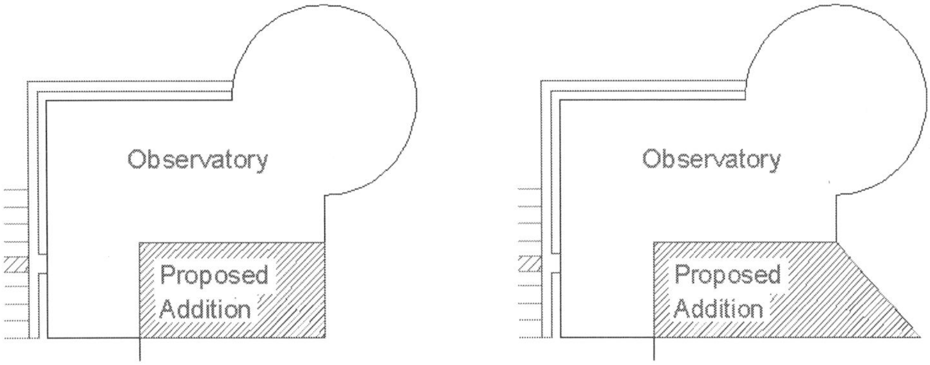

Figure 18–19

Hatch Editor Tab

To edit an existing hatch, select a hatch by clicking on it to display the *Hatch Editor* contextual tab.

How To: Edit a Hatch Using the *Hatch Editor* Tab

1. Select the hatch to be modified.
2. In the *Hatch Editor* contextual tab, change the properties as required.
   - The options in this contextual tab are the same as those available for placing the hatch.

3. If required, modify the boundaries using  (Recreate Boundary) or  (Display Boundary Objects).

	**Recreate Boundary:** Creates a new object around the hatch area, and associates the hatch with the new object separate from the original boundary.
	**Display Boundary Objects:** Displays the selected objects and their boundary with grips. Modifying the grips changes both the boundary and the hatch if the hatch is associative. If the hatch is not associative, different grips display and you can modify the hatch separately from the original boundary.

4. Press <Enter> to apply the changes.

Edit Hatch Command

To open the *Hatch Edit* dialog box (shown in Figure 18–20), in the *Home* tab>expanded *Modify* panel, click  (Edit Hatch) and then select the hatch object. The dialog box contains tools that are similar to the *Hatch Editor*.

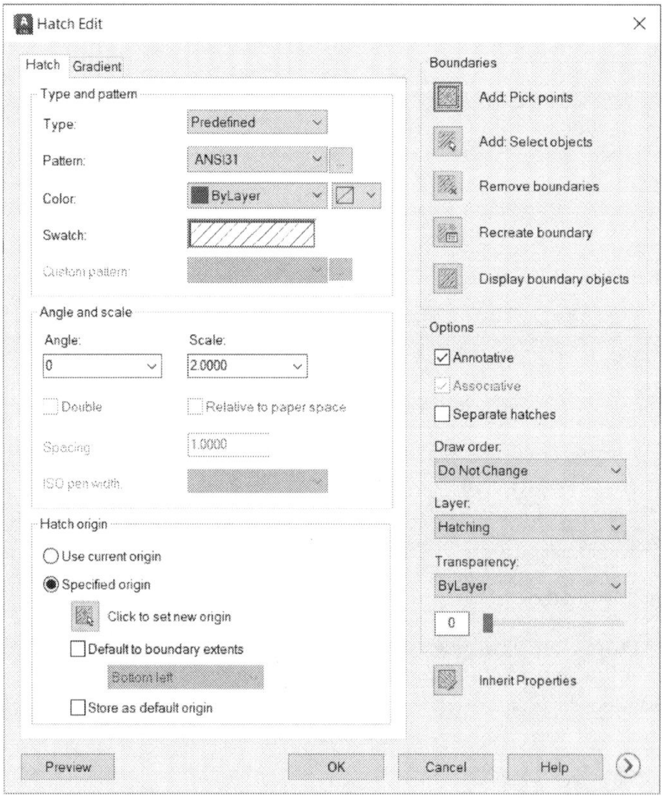

Figure 18–20

Grip Editing Hatch Boundaries

When associative hatches are selected, a single grip displays for the hatch, as shown on the left in Figure 18–21. However, non-associative hatch boundaries display grips at each of their corners and at the midpoint of the edges, as shown on the right in Figure 18–21.

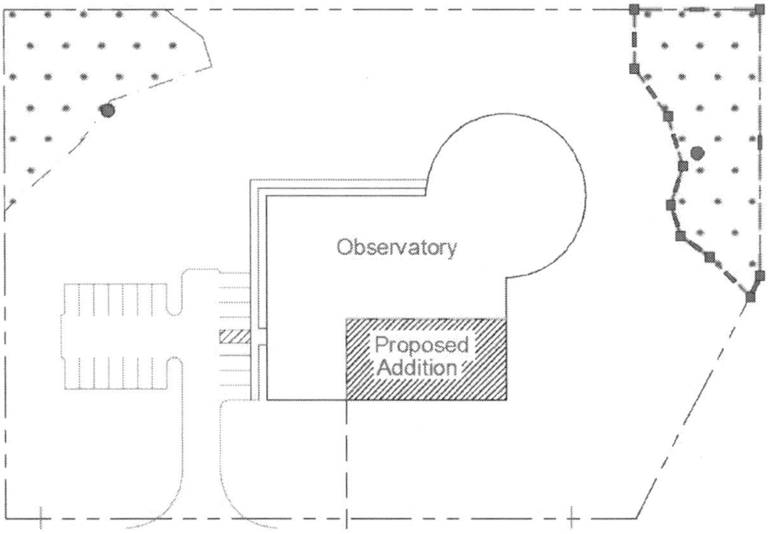

Figure 18–21

Non-Associative Hatch Boundaries

- **Add Vertex:** To add a vertex to the boundary, hover over a multifunctional edge grip at the required location and select **Add Vertex** in the dynamic list, as shown in Figure 18–22. Drag and place the new vertex point.

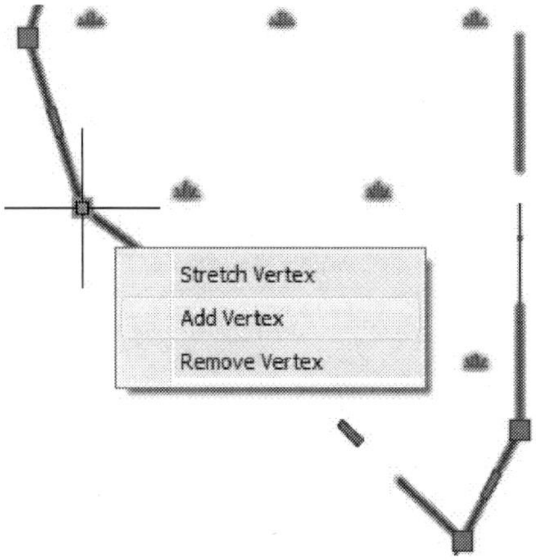

Figure 18–22

- **Convert to Arc:** To change an edge to an arc, hover over the multifunctional edge grip and select the **Convert to Arc** option, as shown in Figure 18–23. Drag and place the midpoint of the arc.

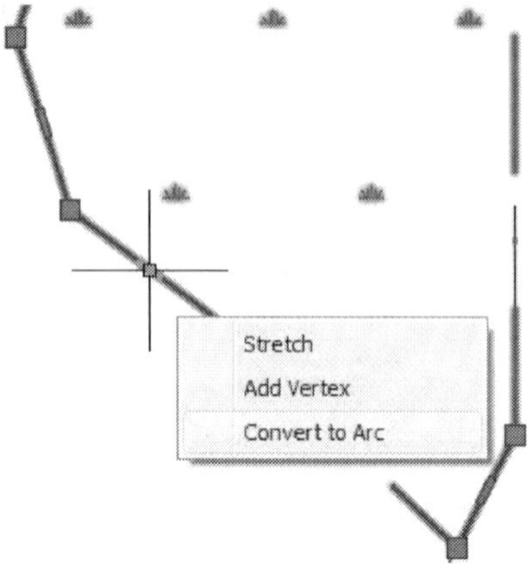

Figure 18–23

- **Arc Grip Options:** When you hover over a multifunctional arc grip, the options enable you to stretch it, add a vertex, or convert the arc to a line.
- **Remove Vertex:** To delete a vertex, hover over the multifunctional vertex grip, and select the **Remove Vertex** option.

Associative Hatch Boundaries

When you are editing associative hatches, you can use one multifunctional grip to access several options (**Stretch**, **Origin Point**, **Hatch Angle**, and **Hatch Scale**) using the dynamic list, as shown in Figure 18–24.

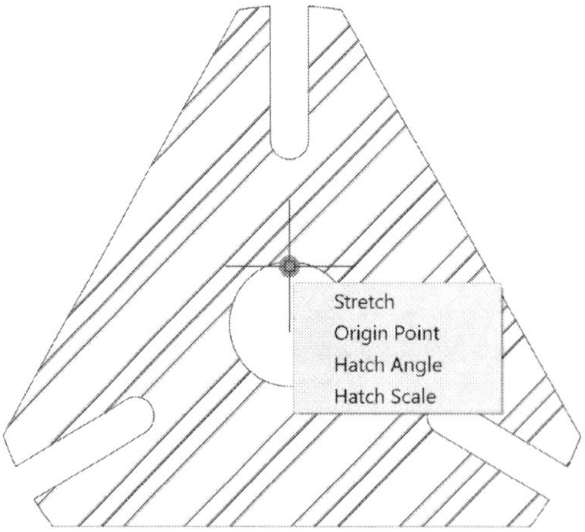

Figure 18–24

Hover the cursor over the grip and select one of the following options:

Stretch	Moves the entire hatch and makes it non-associative. This is the default when you select the grip.
Origin Point	Enables you to select a new point for the origin of the hatch.
Hatch Angle	Enables you to specify an angle at the Command Line or select a point to define the angle.
Hatch Scale	Enables you to specify a scale at the Command Line or select a point to define the scale.

Practice 18a
Add Hatching Using Tool Palettes

Practice Objective

- Add hatching to a floor plan and determine the various properties.

In this practice, you will add hatches to a floor plan using *Tool Palettes*, as shown in Figure 18–25.

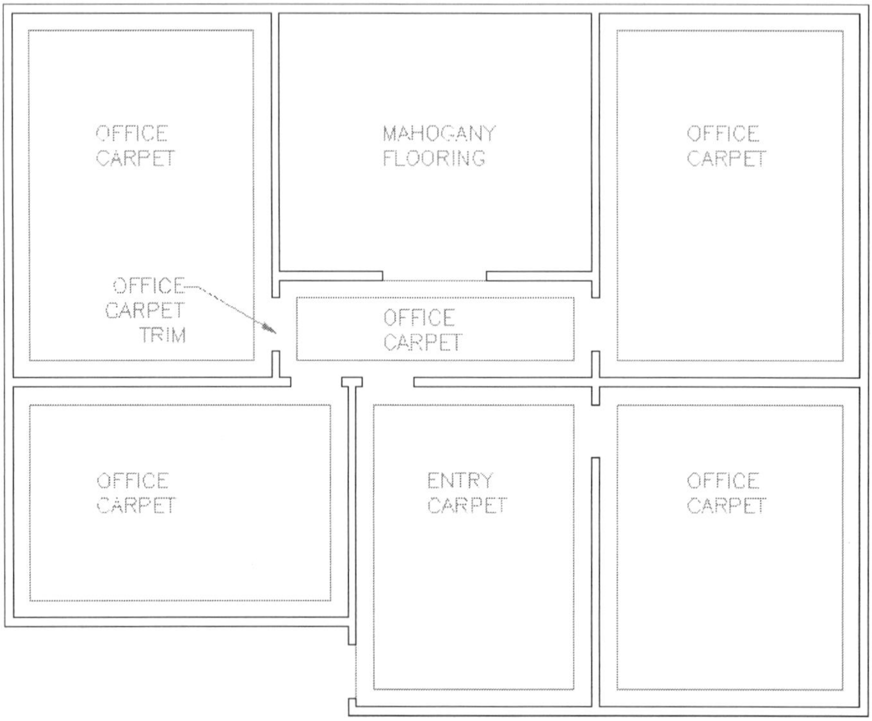

Figure 18–25

1. Open **Law Office-A.dwg** from your practice files folder.
2. Toggle off the layer **A-Door**. Toggle on the layer **A-Flor** that displays the room boundaries.
3. Open *Tool Palettes* (*View* tab>*Palettes* panel).
4. In *Tool Palettes*, in the *Hatches and Fills* tab, click on any of the solid colors. Click inside one of the **Office Carpet** areas to fill it with the solid hatch color.
5. Similarly, use the same solid color to fill all of the **Office Carpet** areas.
6. Use different solid colors for the **Office Carpet Trim**, **Entry Carpet**, and **Mahogany Flooring**.

7. Use the *Properties* palette to find the areas of the **Office Carpet Trim** and the **Mahogany Flooring**. Select the hatch and open the *Properties* palette. The *Area* displays in the *Geometry* section, as shown for **Mahogany Flooring** in Figure 18–26.

Geometry	
Elevation	0"
Area	38016.000 sq. in. (264.0...
Cumulative Area	38016.000 sq. in. (264.0...

Figure 18–26

8. Save and close the drawing.

End of practice

Practice 18b
Apply Hatching (Mechanical)

Practice Objectives

- Apply hatching to a section and modify it.
- Create a hatch with an annotative scale.

In this practice, you will apply hatching to a section and then modify it using the *Hatch Creation* contextual tab. You will also create a hatch with an annotative scale, as shown in Figure 18–27.

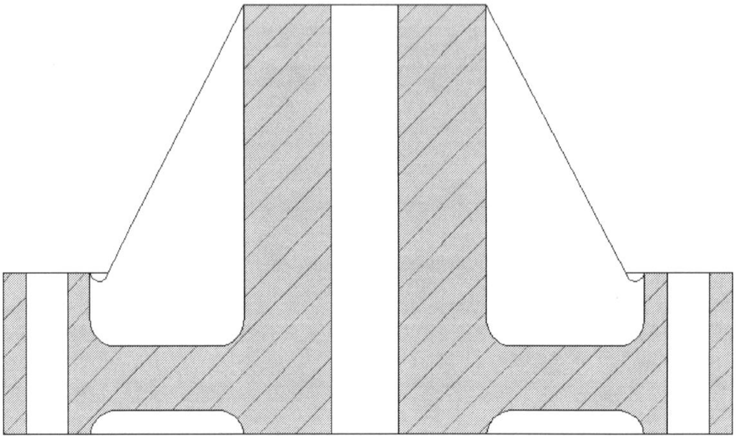

Figure 18–27

Task 1: Apply a hatch.

1. Open **Wheel-Section-I.dwg** from your practice files folder.
2. Set the current layer to **Hatching**.
3. In the *Home* tab>*Draw* panel, click  (Hatch).
4. In the *Hatch Creation* contextual tab>*Properties* panel, verify the following:
   - *Hatch Type* is set to **Pattern**.
   - *Scale* is set to **1.0000**.
   - *Angle* is set to **0**.
5. In the *Pattern* panel, verify that *Hatch Pattern* is set to **ANSI31**.
6. In the *Options* panel, select **Annotative**. In the expanded *Options* panel, verify that  (Create Separate Hatches) is NOT selected.

7. In the *Boundaries* panel, click  (Pick Points). Select points inside the four areas of the section view to display hatching, as shown in Figure 18–28.

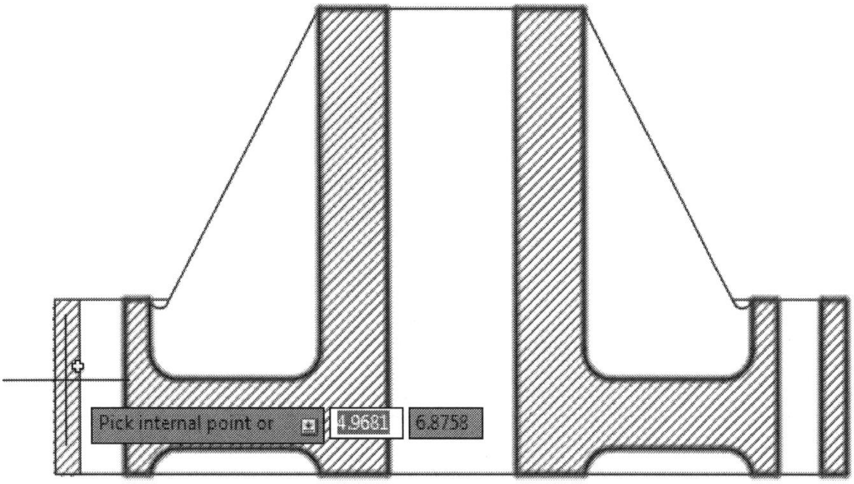

Figure 18–28

8. The hatch pattern lines are very close together. In the *Properties* panel, change the *Scale* to **2.0000**. Press <Enter> to apply the new scale to the hatching. The hatch updates in the drawing.
9. Press <Esc> to exit the hatching selection.
10. Hover the cursor over the hatch that you applied. Note that it is a single object.

Task 2: Edit a hatch pattern.

1. Select the hatch that you applied. The *Hatch Editor* contextual tab opens.
2. Set the *Scale* to **4.0** and click  (Close Hatch Editor).

3. Use the **Move** command to move each of the two vertical lines near the center of the part, **0.5** units closer to the center. (Use the **Endpoint** object snap.) The hatch pattern automatically adjusts to fill the extended area, as shown in Figure 18–29.

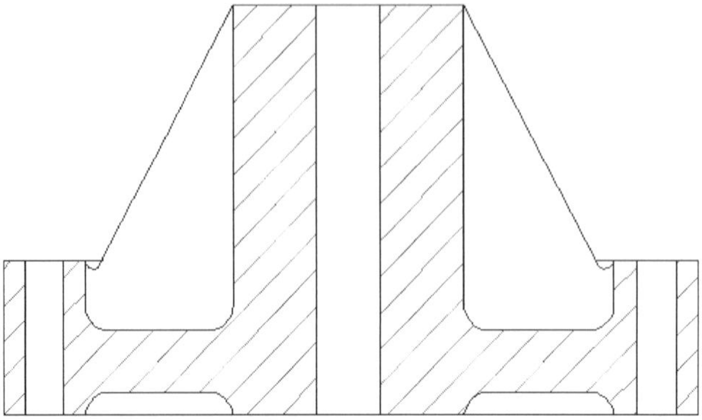

Figure 18–29

4. Save the drawing.

Task 3: Change the background color, origin, and transparency of the hatch.

1. While not in a command, select the hatch object. The grip and the *Hatch Editor* contextual tab display.
2. Change the *Background Color* to **Cyan,** as shown in Figure 18–30.
3. Set the *Hatch Angle* value to **15,** as shown in Figure 18–30.
4. Set the *Hatch Transparency* value to **6,** as shown in Figure 18–30.

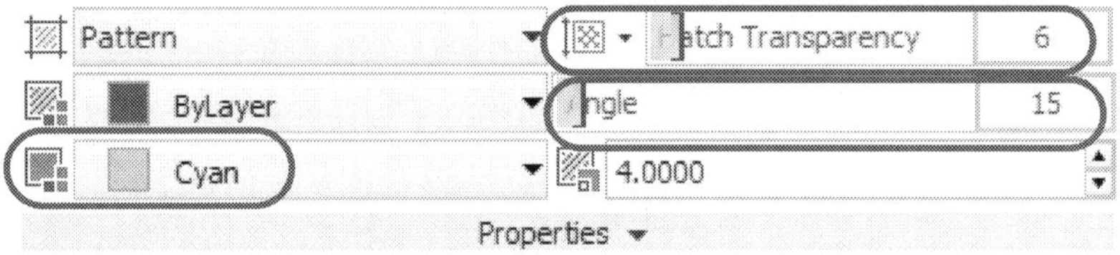

Figure 18–30

5. Note the changes to the hatch object. Click ✔ (Close Hatch Editor).

Task 4: (Optional) Hatch with the Annotative scale.

1. Switch to the **B-Sized** layout. It contains two viewports that have been set to different scales. Hatching is not displayed in either viewport because **Annotative** was selected while applying the hatch and in Model Space the hatch was set to 1:1.
2. Make the bottom viewport active by double-clicking inside it.
3. Start the **Hatch** command.
4. Use the **ANSI31** pattern and set the *Scale* to **1.**
5. In the expanded *Properties* panel, select **Relative to Paper Space**. In the *Options* pane**l,** verify that **Annotative** is selected.
6. Select the points in the four areas of the object for hatching. Click (Close Hatch Creation). The hatch displays in the bottom viewport but does not display in the top viewport.
7. With the bottom viewport still active, in the *Status Bar*, note that the scale is **1:2**.
8. Click inside the top viewport to make it active. In the *Status Bar*, note that the scale is set to **1:4**.
9. Activate the bottom viewport. Select the hatch, right-click and then select **Properties**.
10. With the hatch still selected, in the *Properties* palette>*Pattern* area, click the button to the right of *Annotative scale*, as shown in Figure 18–31.

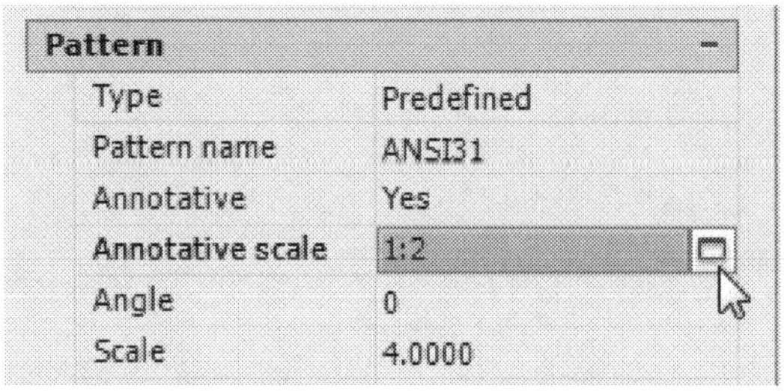

Figure 18–31

11. In the *Annotation Object Scale* dialog box, click **Add**.
12. In the *Add Scales to Object* dialog box, select the **1:4** scale from the list.

13. Click **OK** in both the dialog boxes. The hatch displays in the top viewport automatically as its viewport scale has been added, as shown in Figure 18–32.

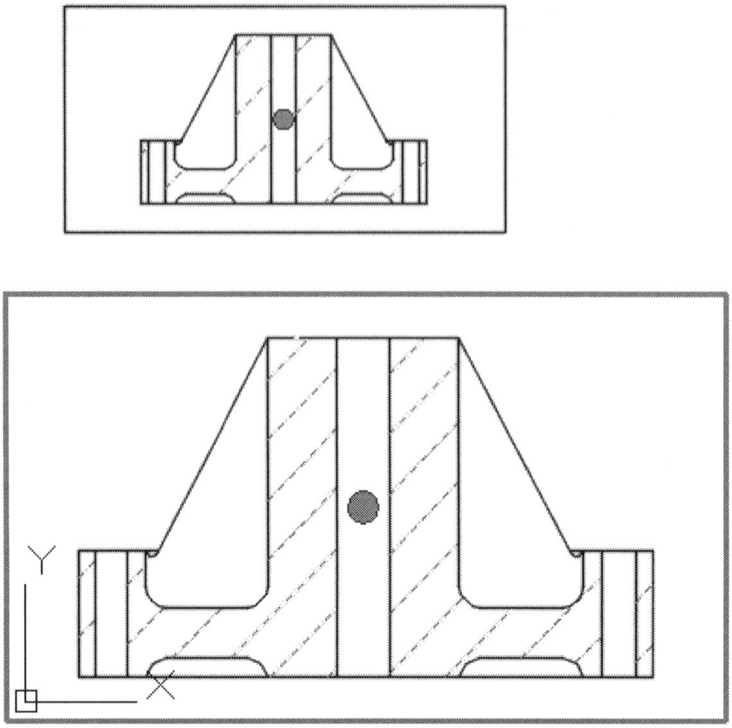

Figure 18–32

14. Press <Esc> to clear the hatch selection.
15. Save and close the drawing.

End of practice

Practice 18c
Apply Hatching (Architectural)

Practice Objective

- Apply hatching to a floor plan.

In this practice, you will apply hatching to a floor plan using the **Hatch** command, as shown in Figure 18–33.

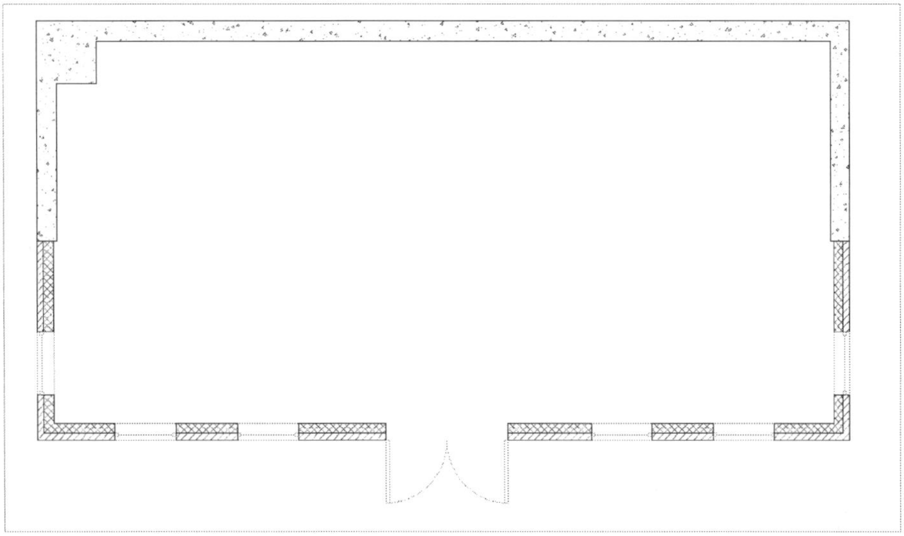

Figure 18–33

1. Open **Basement-A.dwg** from your practice files folder.
2. Set the current layer to **Hatching**.
3. Switch to the ***D-Sized*** layout tab. This layout has two viewports at different scales.
4. Double-click inside the larger viewport (lower) to make it active.
5. Start the **Hatch** command.
6. In the *Hatch Creation* contextual tab, set the *Hatch type* to **Pattern** and the *Pattern* to **AR-CONC** (used to show poured concrete). Leave the *Scale* at **1.000** and the *Angle* at **0**.
7. Click  (Pick Points). At the *Pick internal point:* prompt, select a point inside the back wall.
8. Click  (Close Hatch Creation) to close the *Hatch Creation* contextual tab.

9. Start the **Hatch** command again. Set the *Hatch Pattern* to **ANSI37** (a crosshatch that symbolizes a concrete block). Set the *Scale* to **1.000**. In the *Options* panel, select **Annotative**. Use (Pick Points) to select internal points on the inside portions of the other walls, as shown in Figure 18–34. Zoom in as required to accurately select the areas to hatch. Ensure that the *Scale* is still at **1.000**. If it is not, reset it to **1.000**. Verify that the crosshatch pattern displays properly, as shown in Figure 18–34.

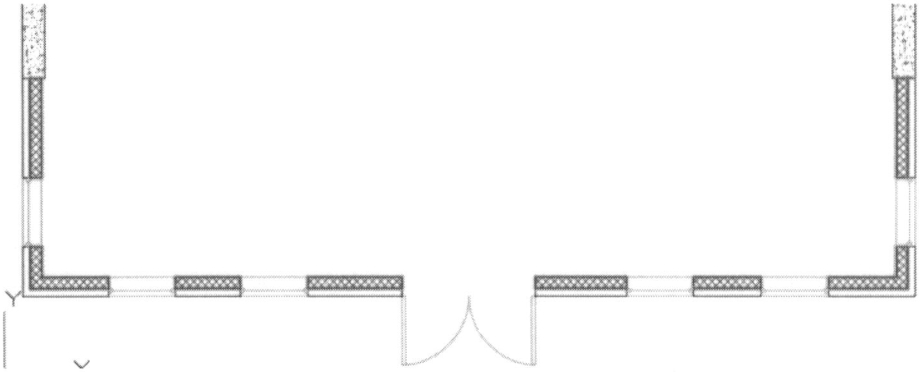

Figure 18–34

10. Click (Close Hatch Creation) to accept the hatch and close the *Hatch Creation* contextual tab.
    - If the hatch does not display correctly (i.e., as a cross hatch), you might have to select it and reset the *Scale* to **1.000** in the *Hatch Editor* contextual tab.
11. Hatch the outside portions of the walls, as shown in Figure 18–33, using the *Hatch pattern* **ANSI31**. Use a *Scale* of **1.000** and select **Annotative**.
12. Click (Close Hatch Creation) to close the *Hatch Creation* contextual tab.
13. In the larger viewport, hover the cursor over the **ANSI37** hatch. (Annotative) displays next to the cursor, indicating that it is annotative. Hover the cursor over the **AR-CONC** hatch. An icon is not displayed because it is not annotative.
14. Zoom out to display both viewports. The first hatch pattern that you applied displays in both viewports, while the other two hatch patterns (**ANSI37** and **ANSI31)** only display in the larger viewport. This is because they are annotative and only display in a viewport matching the scale **1/2"=1'0"** (scale of the lower viewport, displayed in the Status Bar).
15. Activate the upper, smaller viewport. In the Status bar, note that it is set at a scale of **1/4"=1'0"**.
16. In the lower, larger viewport, select the crosshatch (**ANSI37**), right-click, and select **Properties**. In the *Properties* palette> *Pattern* area, click the button to the right of *Annotative scale*.

17. In the *Annotation Object Scale* dialog box, click **Add**.
18. In the *Add Scales to Object* dialog box, select the 1/4"=1'0" scale from the list.
19. Click **OK** in both the dialog boxes. Press <ESC>. The hatch displays in the top viewport automatically, as shown for a portion in Figure 18–35.

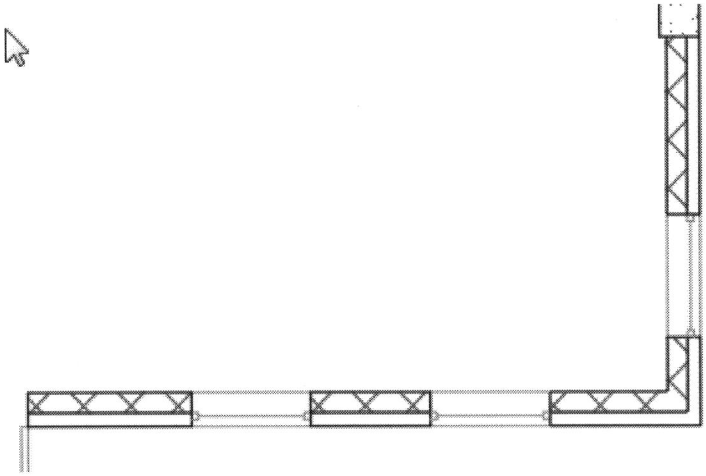

Figure 18–35

20. Similarly, add 1/4"=1'0" scale to the **ANSI31** hatch to display it in the upper viewport.
21. Save and close the drawing.

End of practice

Chapter Review Questions

1. In the *Hatch Creation* contextual tab, which tool do you use to specify an area of the drawing that you want to hatch?
   a. Inherit Properties
   b. Island Detection
   c. Remove Islands
   d. Pick Points

2. Increasing the *Hatch Angle* value creates an angled hatch pattern.
   a. True
   b. False

3. How do you find the area of a Hatch?
   a. Use the **Measure** command.
   b. Use the **Area** command.
   c. Select the hatch to display its area in the *Properties* palette.
   d. Use the **Distance** command.

4. What happens when an associative hatch is selected?
   a. Grips display at each of the boundary corners.
   b. Grips display at the midpoints of the boundary edges.
   c. Grips display at the centroid of the hatch and the midpoints of the boundary edges.
   d. A single grip displays for the hatch.

5. Which option do you use to create new vertices on non-associative hatch boundaries?
   a. Remove vertex
   b. Convert to arc
   c. Add vertex
   d. New vertex

Command Summary

Button	Command	Location
	**Edit Hatch**	• **Ribbon:** *Home* tab>expanded *Modify* panel • **Select:** (*a hatch object*) • **Shortcut Menu:** (*on a hatch object*) Hatch Edit... • **Command Prompt:** hatchedit
	**Hatch**	• **Ribbon:** *Home* tab>*Draw* panel>*Hatch* flyout • **Command Prompt:** hatch or H

Chapter 19

Adding Dimensions

In this chapter, you learn how to place linear, aligned, radial, and angular dimensions. You learn to add continuous and baseline dimensions. You also learn to edit dimensions, adjust their spacing, and add breaks in dimensions.

Learning Objectives

- Create dimensions using various commands.
- Add linear, aligned, angular, and radial dimensions to a drawing.
- Edit dimensions using grips, edit dimension text, and adjust the placement location of dimensions.

19.1 Dimensioning Concepts

The AutoCAD® dimensioning commands create dimensions based on points that you specify or by selecting the object for dimensioning. The AutoCAD software automatically draws the dimension with the appropriate extension lines, arrowheads, dimension lines, and text, as shown in Figure 19–1.

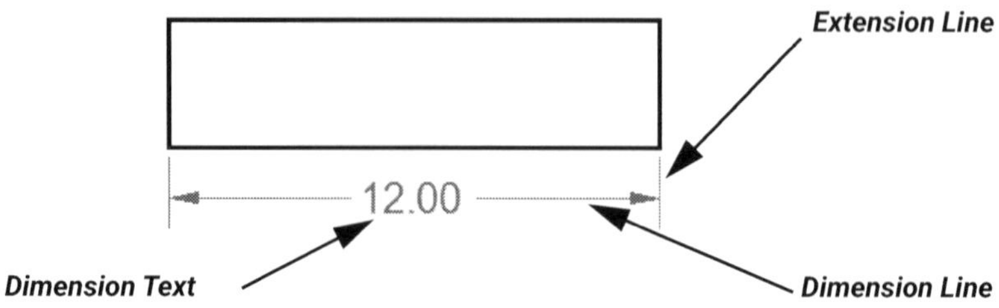

Figure 19–1

- Dimensions recalculate automatically when the objects that they refer to are modified. For example, when you stretch a wall 2'-0" to the right, the associated dimensions update.

As you prepare to dimension, you should:

- Set up a viewport in a layout that displays the part of the model that you want to dimension. You should set the Viewport Scale before you start dimensioning and lock the viewport to make it easier to zoom around the drawing without changing the scale by mistake.
- Select the layer for dimensioning.
- Select a Dimension Style to be used for dimensioning. Dimension styles can be annotative.

Use the *Annotate* tab>*Dimensions* panel, as shown in Figure 19–2, to access the dimensioning commands and set up the layer and dimension style. Some dimensioning commands can also be accessed in the *Home* tab>*Annotation* panel.

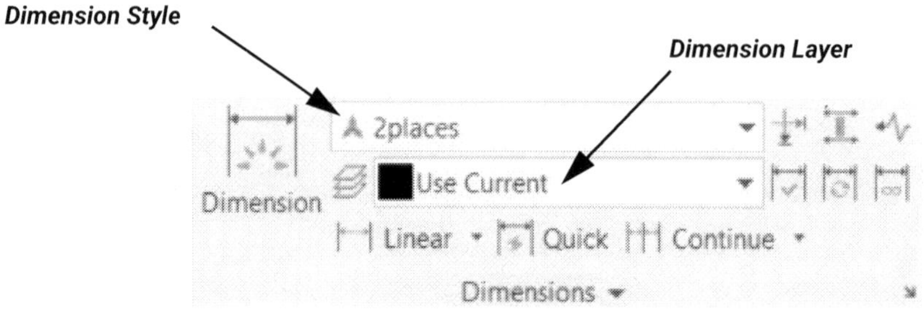

Figure 19–2

General Dimensioning

Dimensions can be added using a general dimension command or using commands specific to the type of dimension being added. The general dimension command automatically determines the type of dimension required based on the object or point selected.

- You can use a single **Dimension** command to add various dimensions, such as linear (horizontal, vertical), aligned, angular, radial etc. After placing a required dimension, the **Dimension** command remains active, enabling you to add other dimensions as required, without re-launching the command. The real-time  (Dimension) command is located in the *Annotate* tab>*Dimensions* panel or in the *Home* tab>*Annotation* panel, as shown in Figure 19–3.
- You can also use the explicit dimensioning commands such as **Linear**, **Angular**, **Aligned** and so on. These are available in the *Annotate* tab>*Dimensions* panel>*Linear* flyout or in the *Home* tab>*Annotation* panel>*Linear* flyout, as shown in Figure 19–3.

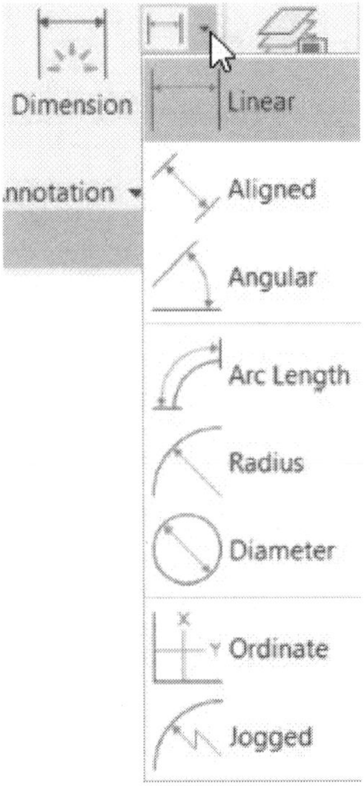

Figure 19–3

How To: Add Dimensions

1. In the *Annotate* tab>*Dimensions* panel or in the *Home* tab>*Annotation* panel, click (Dimension).
2. Hover the cursor on the object that you want to dimension. Depending on the object that touches the cursor, a preview of a relevant dimension displays, as shown in Figure 19–4.
   - Instead of selecting an object to dimension, you can use object snaps to snap to points on the objects to be dimensioned.

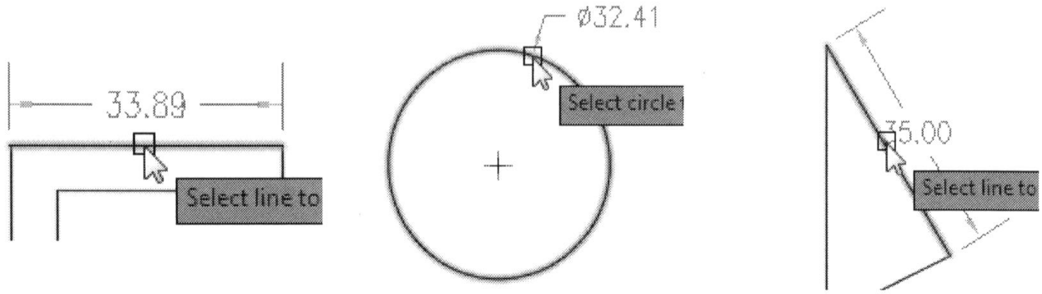

Figure 19–4

3. If the preview dimension is the correct one, click to save the dimension.
4. Drag the cursor to the location where you want the dimension to be located. Click to place the dimension or select an option from the Command Line (or use the <Down Arrow> menu).
5. Dimension another object in the drawing or press <Esc> to exit the command.

19.2 Adding Linear Dimensions

Linear dimensions measure a distance from one point to another, as shown in Figure 19–5.

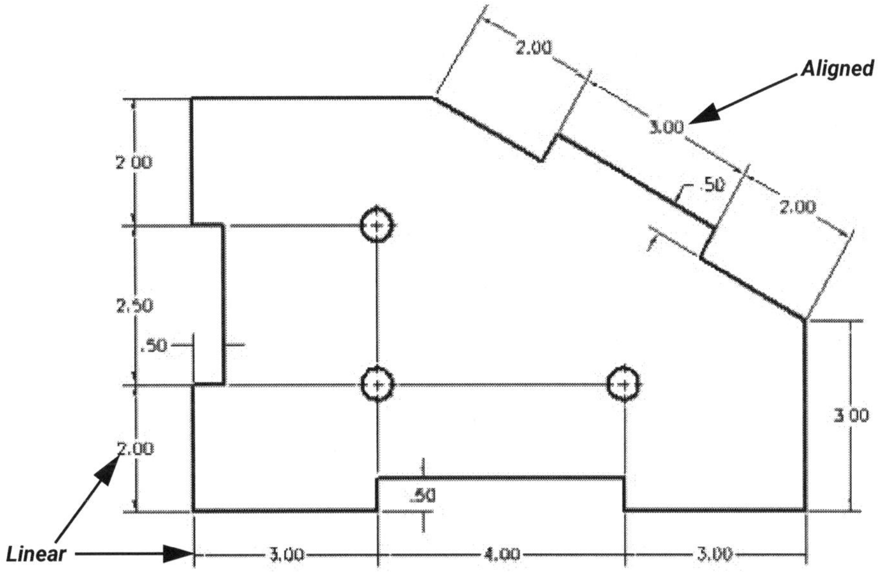

Figure 19–5

Individual Linear Dimensions

Linear dimensions can be horizontal or vertical, as shown in Figure 19–5. Aligned dimensions are also linear dimensions, however, they measure the linear distance parallel to the selected line or the selected points.The dimension line is placed parallel to the line between the points, as shown above in Figure 19–5.

- The AutoCAD software determines the linear orientation (horizontal, vertical, or aligned) based on the selected object or where you select the point for the dimension line location.

How To: Add Linear and Aligned Dimensions

1. In the *Annotate* tab>*Dimensions* panel or in the *Home* tab>*Annotation* panel, click (Dimension).
2. Select a line in the drawing.
3. Select a point to place the dimension line.

or

1. In the *Annotate* tab>*Dimensions* panel, click (Linear).

2. Select a point for the first extension line origin. Use Object Snaps to select the exact points for the extension line origins.
3. Select a point for the second extension line origin.
4. Select a point to place the dimension line.

Hint: Oblique Extension Lines

If you want the extension lines of a linear dimension to be at an angle, you can click (Oblique) in the *Annotate* tab>expanded *Dimensions* panel to angle the lines.

Adding a Break in a Linear or Aligned Dimension

In some cases, you need to have a dimension with a break because the length of the dimension is too long to display on a sheet, as shown in Figure 19–6.

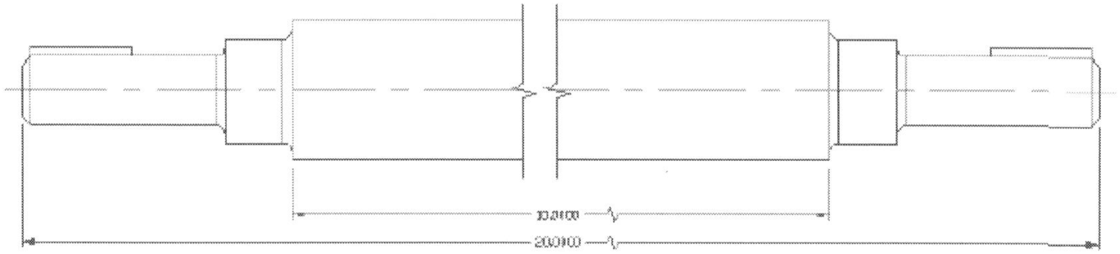

Figure 19–6

How To: Create a Jogged Linear Dimension

1. In the *Annotate* tab>*Dimensions* panel, click (Dimjogline).
2. Select the dimension to which you want to add the jog.
3. Specify the jog location along the dimension or press <Enter> to accept the default location.

- To remove a jog line, use the command's **Remove** option.

Multiple Dimensions

After you have placed a linear, aligned, or angular dimension, you can use that dimension as the beginning of a series of related dimensions by clicking (Continue) or (Baseline), as shown in Figure 19–7.

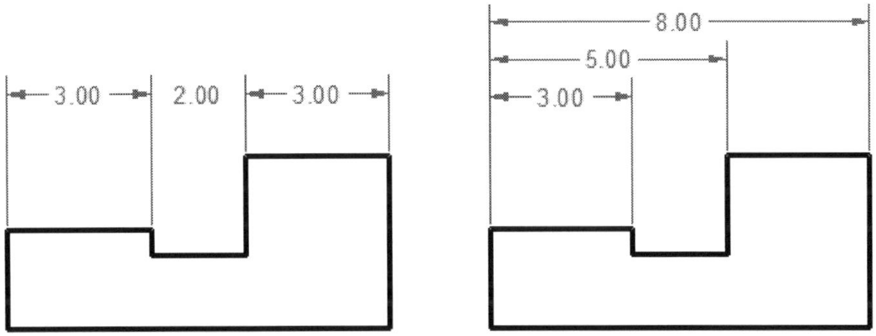

Continue Dimensions ***Baseline Dimensions***

Figure 19–7

- (Continue) dimensions use the last extension line placed as the first extension line for the next dimension. The dimension line remains at the same distance from the object.
- (Baseline) dimensions use the first extension line as the base for all other dimensions. As you select additional extension line points, the new dimension is placed over the previous one. The distance between the dimension lines is set by the dimension style.

Note: *These commands can be used with Linear, Aligned, or Angular dimensions.*

How To: Add Continue and Baseline Dimensions

1. Place a linear or aligned dimension.
2. In the *Annotate* tab>*Dimensions* panel, click (Continue) or (Baseline).
3. Select a point for the second extension line origin. The first extension line origin is automatically assumed to be from the last dimension you placed.
4. Continue selecting points for additional extension line origins.
5. Press <Enter> twice to finish the command.

- By default, the AutoCAD software uses the last dimension placed as the starting dimension. Use the **Select** option to select a different dimension to be referenced.

Quick Dimensioning

In some cases, you can place all of your dimensions along one edge of an object using one command, regardless of whether it is **Linear**, **Aligned**, **Baseline**, or **Continue**. As shown in Figure 19–8, the outside lines of the walls were selected using the **Quick Dimension** command and dimensioned at the same time.

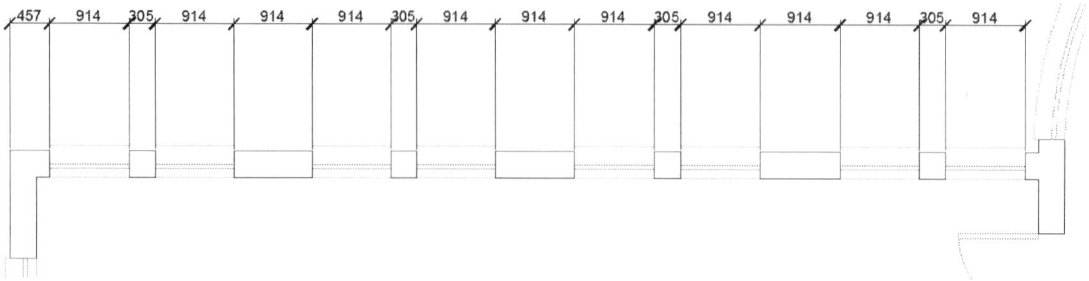

Figure 19–8

How To: Add Quick Dimensions

1. In the *Annotate* tab>*Dimensions* panel, click (Quick Dimension).
2. Select the objects that you want to dimension. When you have finished selecting objects, press <Enter>.
3. Specify the dimension line position.

- By default, the AutoCAD software creates continuous dimensions if you select linear objects or more than one object.
- You can switch between a number of other types of dimensions, including **Staggered**, **Baseline**, and **Ordinate**, in the Command Prompt, shortcut menu, or *Dynamic Input* drop-down list.
- Dimensions created using (Quick Dimension) are placed on the current layer.
- **Quick Dimension** does not enable you to place a type of dimension that is not appropriate for the selection. For example, if you select a line, you cannot place a Radius or Diameter dimension on that line.
- Baseline and Ordinate dimensions start from a common point. You can set that point using the **datumPoint** option.
- There is also an **Edit** option that enables you to add or remove points. However, it is easier to do this using other commands.

Practice 19a
Add Linear Dimensions (Architectural)

Practice Objective

- Add dimensions using various dimensioning techniques.

In this practice, you will start to add dimensions using the general **Linear** dimension command. You will then dimension different portions of the architectural drawing using **Quick**, **Baseline**, and **Continue** dimensions, as shown in Figure 19–9.

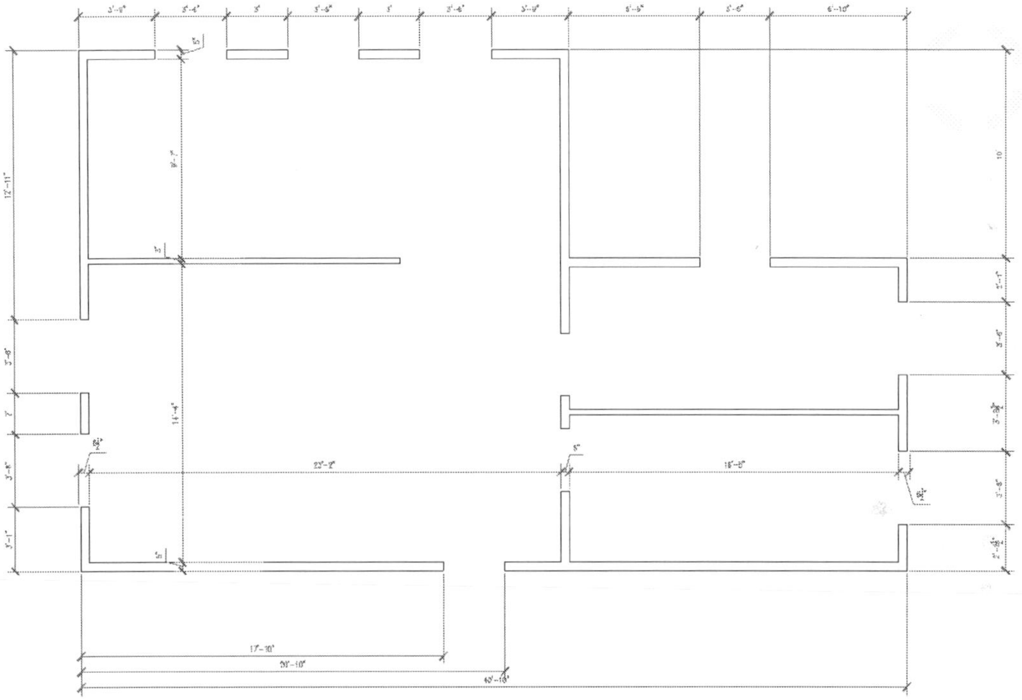

Figure 19–9

1. Open **Dimensioned Plan-A.dwg** from your practice files folder.
2. Switch to the **D-Sized** layout. Make the existing viewport active (by double-clicking inside it) and zoom to the extents.
3. In the *Status Bar*, set the *Viewport Scale* to **1/2"=1'-0"**. Pan the drawing to center it in the viewport. Ensure that the *Viewport Scale* is still set at **1/2"=1'-0"** and lock the viewport.

4. In the *Quick Access Toolbar*, in the *Layer Control* bar, set the layer to **Dimensions**, as shown in Figure 19–10. (You can also set the **Dimensions** layer current in the *Home* tab>*Layers* panel.) In the *Annotate* tab>*Dimensions* panel, note that the dimension layer is set to **Use Current**. This ensures that the dimensions are drawn on the layer **Dimensions**, which was set as the current layer. Also, ensure that the active Dimension Style is set as ***Architectural***. This is an annotative style.

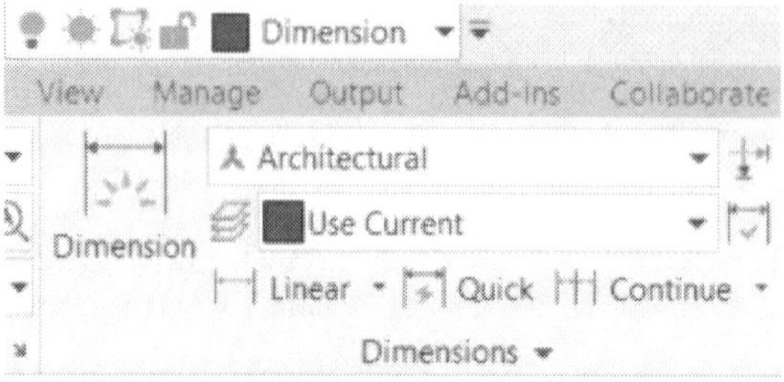

Figure 19–10

5. Freeze the layers **Doors** and **Windows** to make it easier to only select the walls to be dimensioned.
6. In the Status Bar, toggle on **Object Snap** and select the **Endpoint** object snap, if required.
7. While still active in the viewport, in the *Annotate* tab>*Dimensions* panel, click (Dimension). Hover the cursor on the top left wall (outer line), as shown in Figure 19–11.
   - You can also use the (Linear) dimension command, where you need to select the two endpoints of the wall.

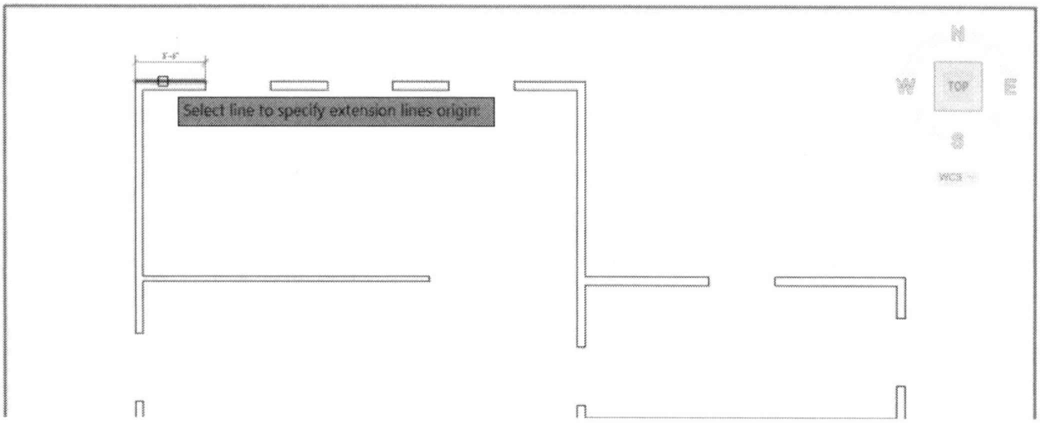

Figure 19–11

8. Select this line, drag the cursor up, and click to place the dimension outside the building.

9. In the *Annotate* tab>*Dimensions* panel, click the (Continue) dimension command. Note that the cursor is attached with the last dimension you placed. Select the left endpoint of the second wall, as shown in Figure 19–12.

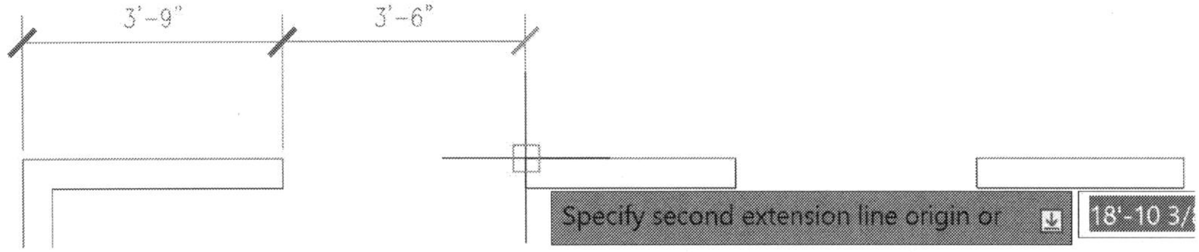

Figure 19–12

10. Select the rest of the dimension points (endpoints) along the same wall (as shown in Figure 19–9). Press <Enter> twice to complete the command.

11. Start the (Dimension) command. Select the two endpoints (first left and then right) of the bottom left wall. Place the dimension along the bottom side of the building. The order of selection of points determines the start point of the baseline.

12. Start the (Baseline) dimension command and note that the cursor dimension is attached to the left extension line of the dimension.

13. Select the left endpoint of the right side bottom wall to place the dimension.

14. Select the right endpoint of the right side bottom wall to place the third dimension. Press <Enter> twice to complete the command.

15. Start the (Quick) dimension command.

16. Add dimensions to the left side of the building (as shown in Figure 19–9) by selecting three outside wall objects (use <Shift>), pressing <Enter>, and then clicking to place the dimensions.

17. Add dimensions to the right exterior and the interior of the building, as shown in Figure 19–9.

18. Save and close the drawing.

End of practice

Practice 19b
Add Linear Dimensions (Mechanical)

Practice Objective

- Add linear dimensions to a mechanical drawing.

In this practice, you will add linear and aligned dimensions to a mechanical drawing.

Task 1: Add linear dimensions.

1. Open **Bearing Dimensions-I.dwg** from the practice files folder.
2. Switch to the **C-Sized** layout. Set the current active layer to **Viewports**.
3. There is a single viewport on the sheet. Set the *Scale* to **1:1**.
4. Using grips, resize the existing viewport around the objects. Ensure that you leave space on the left and bottom of the model such that you can add the dimensions. Using the middle square grip, move the viewport to the left side of the sheet to make room for a second viewport, as shown in Figure 19–13. Set the *Scale* to **1:1**, if it got changed, and lock the viewport. In the *Layout* tab>*Layout Viewports* panel, use (Insert View) and create a view of the right half of the model. Place this viewport to the right side of the original viewport at a scale of **2:1**. Using grips, resize the viewport so that there is space along the right, top, and bottom of the model, as shown in Figure 19–13. Set the *Scale* to **2:1**, if it got changed, and lock the viewport.

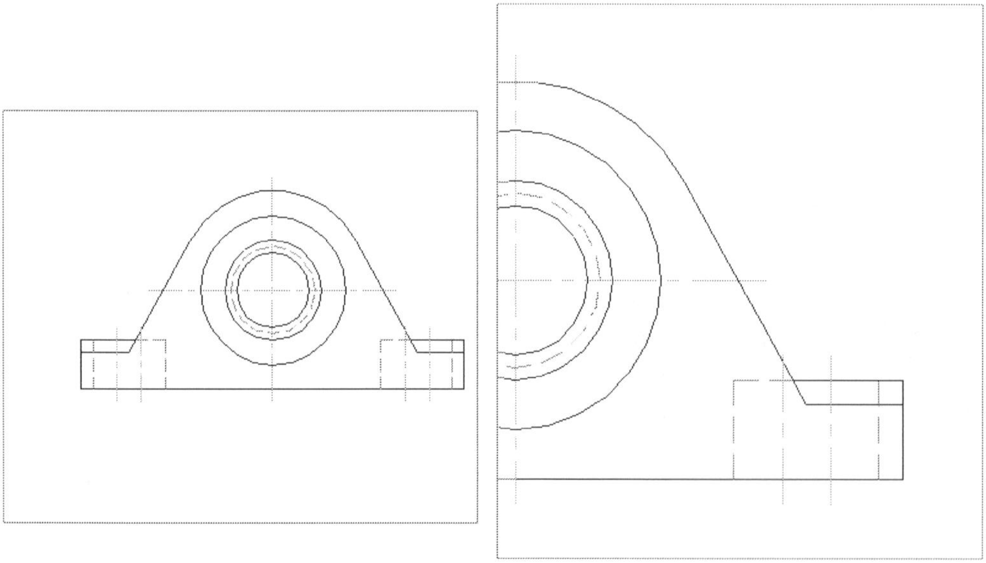

Figure 19–13

5. Make the left **1:1** viewport active.
6. Change the active dimension layer to **Dimensions** (*Annotate* tab>*Dimensions* panel, layer **Dimensions**), as shown in Figure 19–14.
7. Set the active *Dimension Style* to **2places**. This is an annotative style, as shown in Figure 19–14.

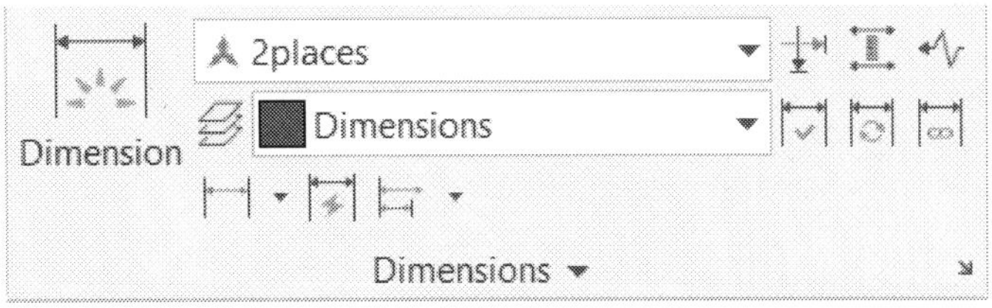

Figure 19–14

8. Start the  (Dimension) command. Select the bottom left endpoint and then select the left endpoint of the green horizontal center line. Drag the cursor left and down until a vertical dimension displays, as shown on the right in Figure 19–15. Click to place the dimension.
   - When you drag the cursor to the left, an aligned dimension might display, as shown on the left in Figure 19–15. Drag the cursor downwards to force the display of a vertical dimension instead.

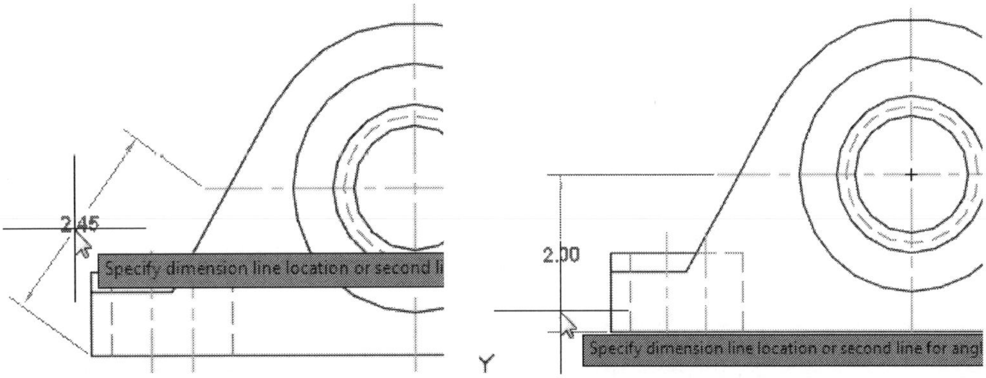

Aligned Dimension ***Vertical Dimension***

Figure 19–15

9. While remaining in the **Dimension** command, add the remaining vertical and horizontal dimensions shown in Figure 19–16. After placing all of the dimensions, exit the command.
    - Start the **Dimension** command once, select the relevant endpoints and place the dimension for each vertical and horizontal dimension using the same command. You do not have to exit or relaunch the **Dimension** command after placing each dimension.

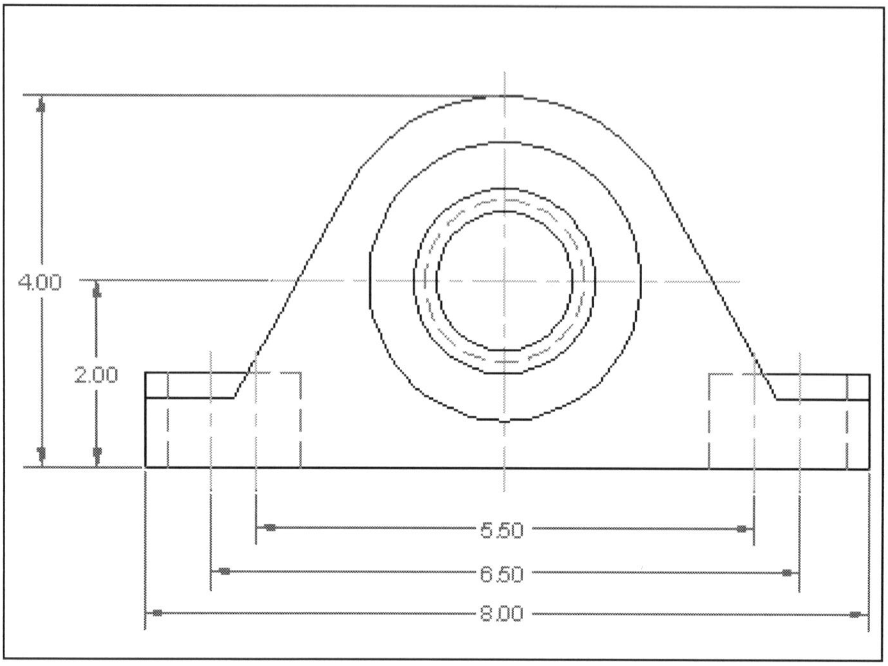

Figure 19–16

10. If required, use grips to resize the viewport to fit the dimensions into the available space.

Task 2: Add aligned dimensions.

1. Make the **2:1** viewport active.
2. Start the **Dimension** command and add the vertical dimension shown in Figure 19–17.
3. While remaining in the **Dimension** command, select the two endpoints of the aligned line on the right side and add the aligned dimension as shown in Figure 19–17. Exit the command.

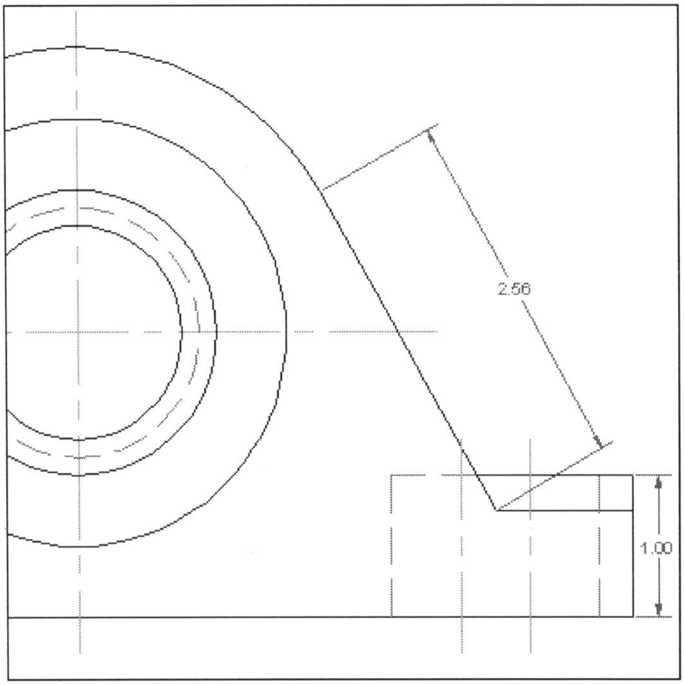

Figure 19–17

4. Save and close the drawing.

End of practice

19.3 Adding Radial and Angular Dimensions

Other types of dimensions include Radius, Diameter, and Angular dimensions. Radius/Diameter dimensions for arcs and circles are placed with a leader from the object. You can also create a Jogged Radial dimension for arcs whose center point would be outside the drawing and for dimensioning the length around the curve of an arc. Angular dimensions measure the angle of an arc or the angle between two objects.

Radius and Diameter Dimensions

Radius is typically used on arcs, while **Diameter** is normally used on full circles, as shown in Figure 19–18. You can also add a radius dimension for a circle.

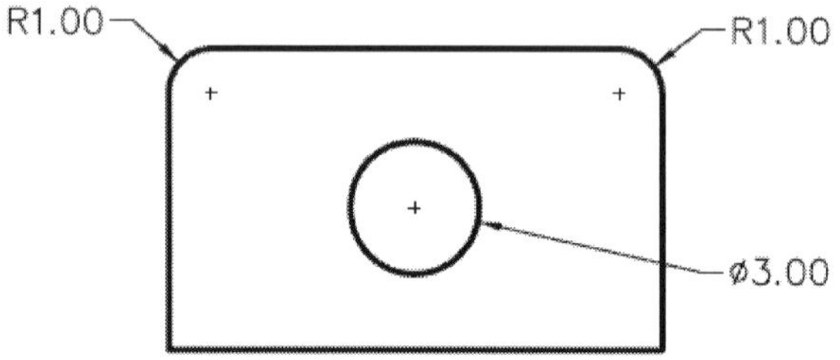

Figure 19–18

How To: Add Radius or Diameter Dimensions

1. In the *Annotate* tab>*Dimensions* panel, click (Dimension). You can also use (Radius) or (Diameter) individually.
2. Select a point on the rim of an arc or circle. (You do not need to use Object Snaps for this.)
3. Select a location along the arc or circle for the dimension line text.

- When you are dimensioning a radius, you can place the dimension beyond the arc. The AutoCAD software creates an additional arc extension line as required.
- **Quick Dimension** creates a radial dimension by default if you select an arc or circular object. However, you can select **Diameter** in the options.

Associative Center Marks and Centerlines

There are two new tools which indicate the center of an arc or circle regardless of the objects' perspective. Both tools are available in the *Annotate* tab>*Centerlines* panel.

- The  (Center Mark) tool adds an associative center mark at the center of selected circles, arcs, or polygonal arcs, as shown in Figure 19–19.

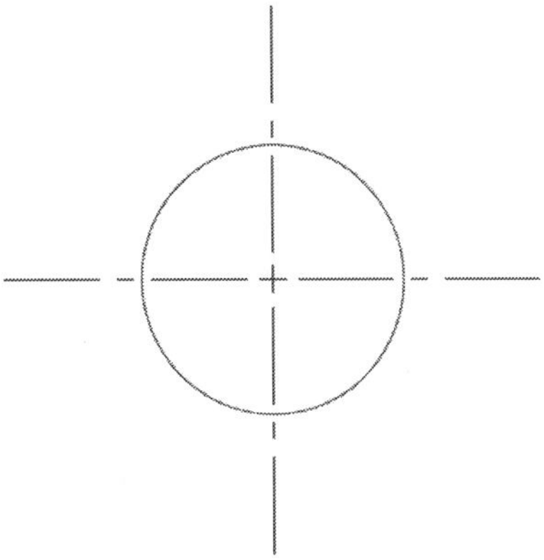

Figure 19–19

- The  (Centerline) tool creates centerline geometry that is associated with selected lines and polylines, as shown in Figure 19–20.

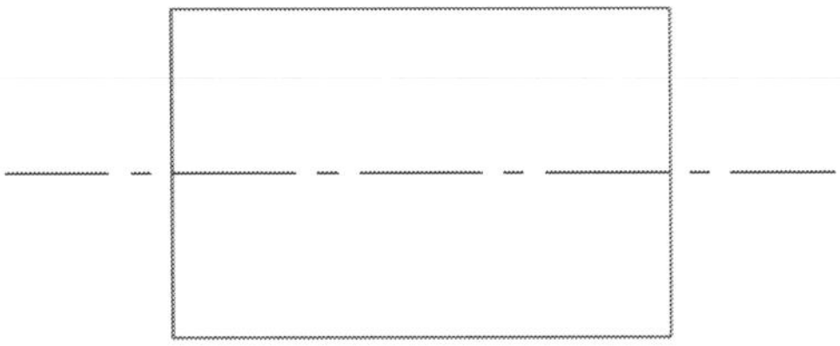

Figure 19–20

- If the associated objects move, the centerlines and center marks also update.

When a center mark or centerline is selected, grips display that enable you to control the extension line lengths, as shown in Figure 19–21. The appearance of center marks and centerlines is controlled by multiple system variables. Figure 19–21 and the table below lists the controlling variables and describes their effects.

CENTEREXE	Sets the length of the extension line overshoots for centerlines and center marks.
CENTERMARKEXE	Determines whether extension lines are created for center marks.
CENTERLAYER	Sets the layer on which the centerlines and center marks are created.
CENTERLTYPE	Sets the linetype used by centerlines and center marks.
CENTERLTSCALE	Sets the linetype scale used by centerlines and center marks.
CENTERCROSSSIZE	Sets the size of the central cross for center marks.
CENTERCROSSGAP	Sets the extension line gap between the central cross and the extension lines in center marks.

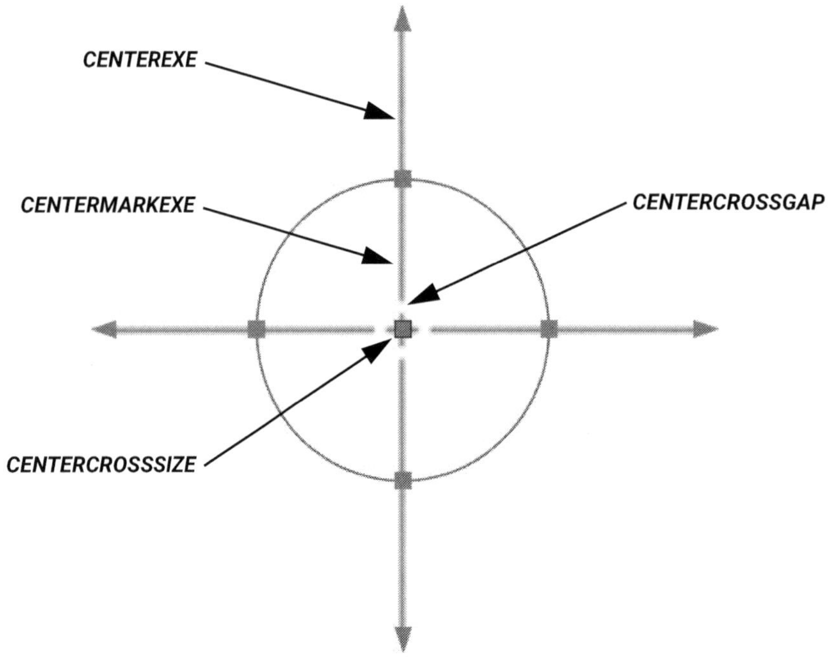

Figure 19–21

- The system variables must be set prior to creating the center mark or centerline for the variable to take effect.

- The *Properties* palette can be used to modify select attributes, as shown in Figure 19–22.

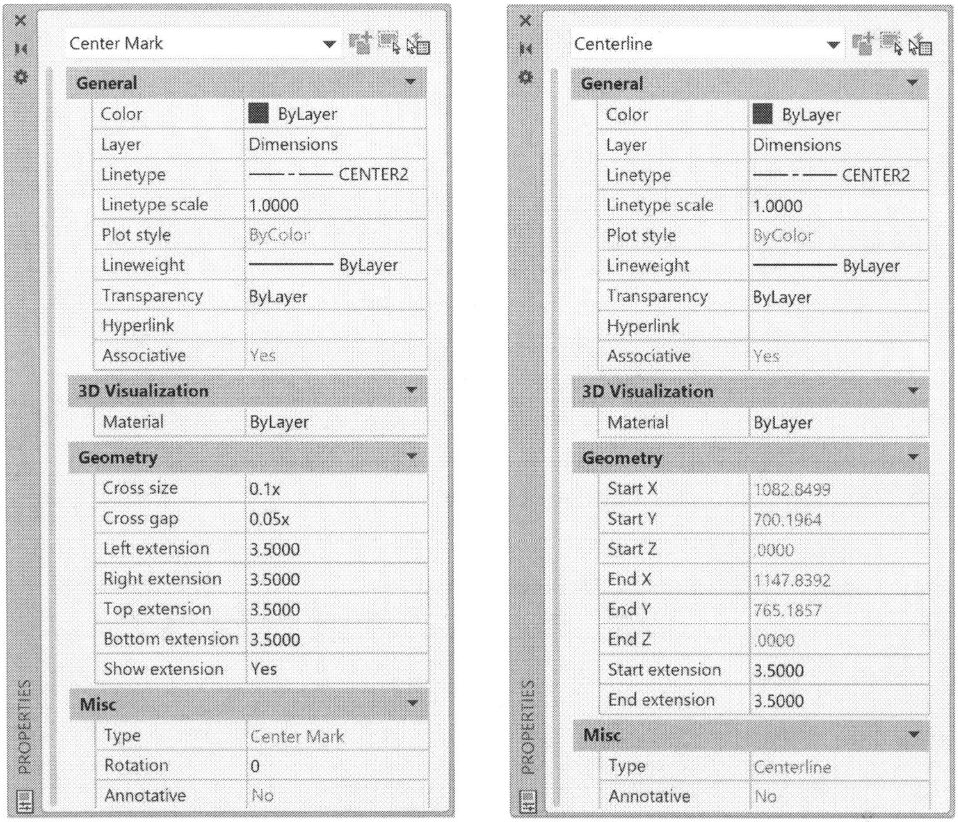

Figure 19–22

- A multi-functional grip menu offers additional controls, as shown in Figure 19–23.

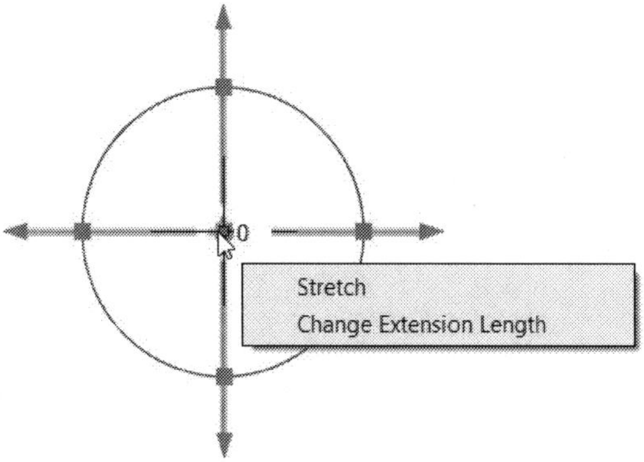

Figure 19–23

Jogged Radial Dimension

If the center mark of the circle or arc you are dimensioning does not display in the view, you can use the **Jogged** command to create an override for the center, as shown in Figure 19–24.

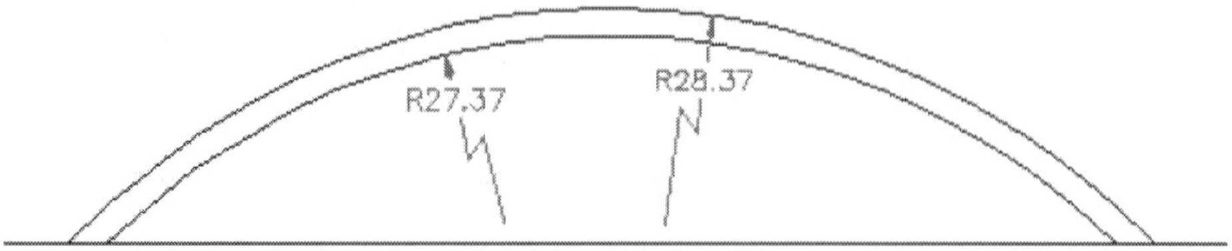

Figure 19–24

How To: Create a Jogged Radial Dimension

1. In the *Annotate* tab>*Dimensions* panel, click (Jogged). You can also find the **Jogged** option (<Down Arrow>) in the **Dimension** command.
2. Select the arc or circle that you want to dimension.
3. Specify a point for the center location override.
4. Specify the dimension line location. This also sets the location of the text.
5. Specify the jog location.

Arc Length Dimension

The arc length describes the distance from one end point of an arc to the other end point along the curve of the arc, as shown in Figure 19–25. This command can be used to dimension individual arcs or arcs that are parts of polylines.

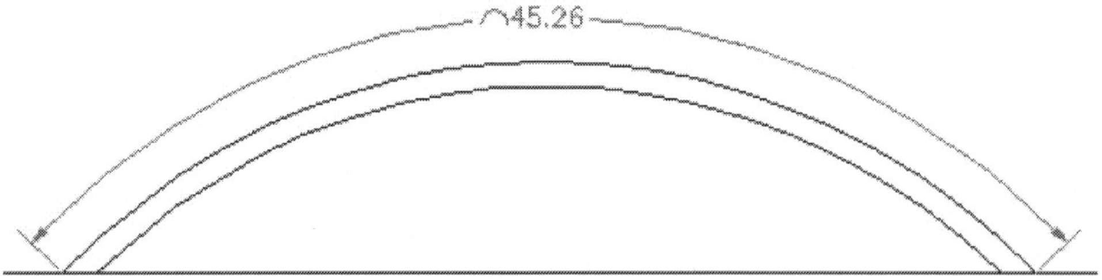

Figure 19–25

How To: Dimension the Arc Length

1. In the *Annotate* tab>*Dimensions* panel, click (Dimension) or click (Arc Length) in the *Linear* drop-down list.
2. Hover the cursor over the arc that you want to dimension.
3. Press <Down Arrow> and select **arc Length** from the list.

   Note: *The current set option is dependent on the previous DIM option used.*

4. Specify the dimension location.

Angular Dimensions

You can add angular dimensions to lines, circles, and arcs and from a vertex, as shown in Figure 19–26.

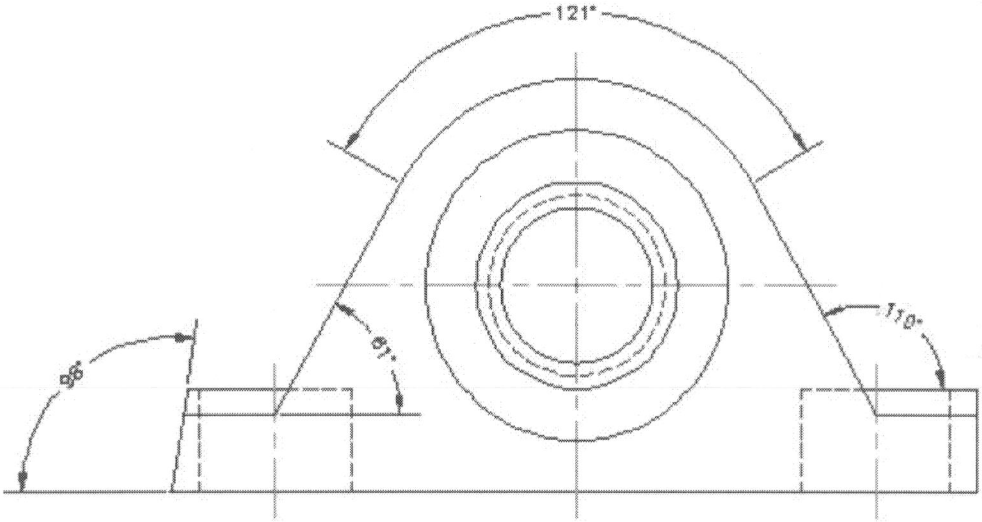

Figure 19–26

- When you are placing the Angular dimension, you can place it at any of the four quadrants of the angle.

How To: Add Angular Dimensions

1. In the *Annotate* tab>*Dimensions* panel, click (Dimension) or click (Angular) in the Linear drop-down list.
2. Select a line, arc, or circle.
3. If you select a **line**, you are prompted to place a linear dimension. As you hover the cursor over another line, the preview changes to an angle dimension, as shown in Figure 19–27. Select the second line and specify the location of the dimension line.

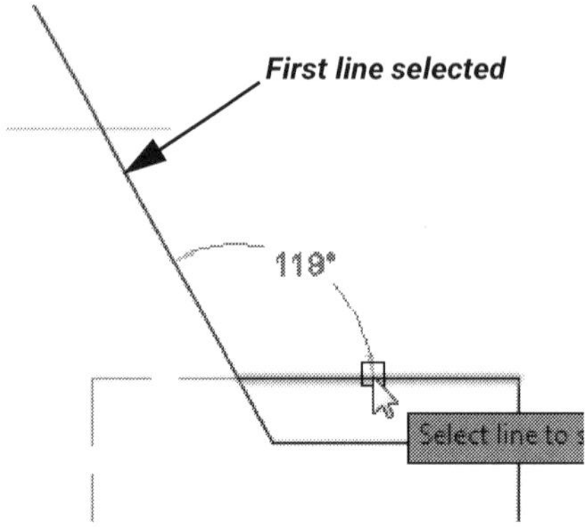

Figure 19–27

4. If you hover over an **arc**, by default you can place a radial dimension. Press <Down Arrow> and select **Angular**, then click the arc to select it. Click again to set the location of the dimension line.
5. If you hover over a **circle**, by default you can place a diameter dimension. Press <Down Arrow> and select **Angular**, then click the circle to select it. Click to specify the first side of the angle. Click again to set the second side of the angle. Click one more time to set the location of the dimension line.

- You can also dimension an angle from a vertex. Before selecting an object, press <Enter> and use Object Snaps to select an angle vertex. Specify the first and second angle end points and place the dimension line.

Practice 19c
Add Radial and Angular Dimensions (Architectural)

Practice Objective

- Add dimensions, including radial and angular dimensions, to a drawing.

In this practice, you will add angular, radial, diameter, aligned, and arc length dimensions, as shown in Figure 19–28.

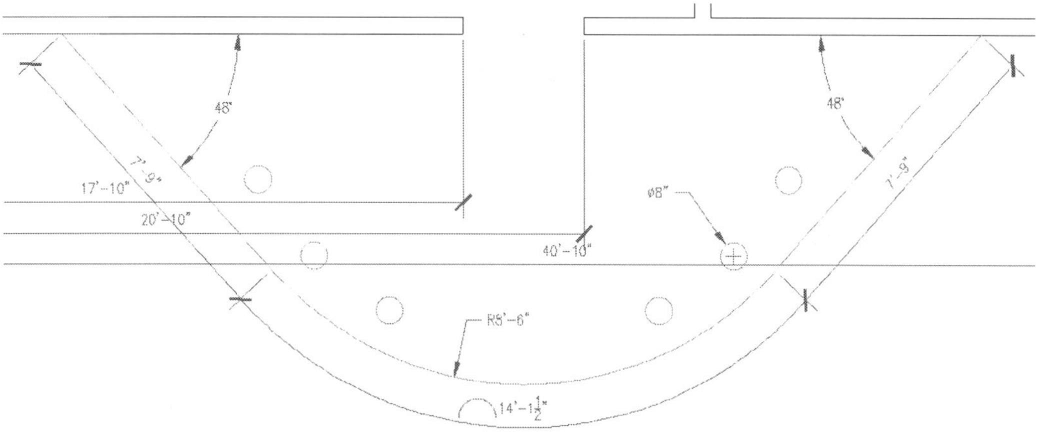

Figure 19–28

1. Open **Dimensioned Plan1-A.dwg** from your practice files folder. The drawing opens in the *D-Sized* layout tab with one viewport.
2. In *Layer Control,* toggle on the layer **Misc** to display the green entrance portico.
3. If required, use viewport grips to modify the viewport to display the entire entrance portico. Ensure that the *Viewport Scale* is set at **1/2"=1'-0"** and is locked.
4. Activate the viewport. In *Layer Control*, ensure that the layer **Dimensions** is the current layer.
5. In the *Annotate* tab>*Dimensions* panel, ensure that the dimension layer is set to **Use Current**, which is the **Dimensions** layer.
6. In the *Annotate* tab>*Dimensions* panel, click (Dimension).

7. Hover the cursor over one of the six circles (representing columns). Click on the circle to accept the diameter dimension and click again to place it at the required location, as shown in Figure 19–29.
   - If the cursor does not display the diameter dimension (while hovering over the circle), toggle off **Object Snap** in the Status Bar.
8. While remaining in the **Dimension** command, hover the cursor over the arc of the portico. The dimension that is displayed is dependent on the previously used option.
9. If the selection prompt displays an option other than arc Length, press <Down Arrow> and select **arc Length**, as shown in Figure 19–29.
   - If the prompt displays as *Select arc to specify radius*, it indicates that the **radius** option is the current one.

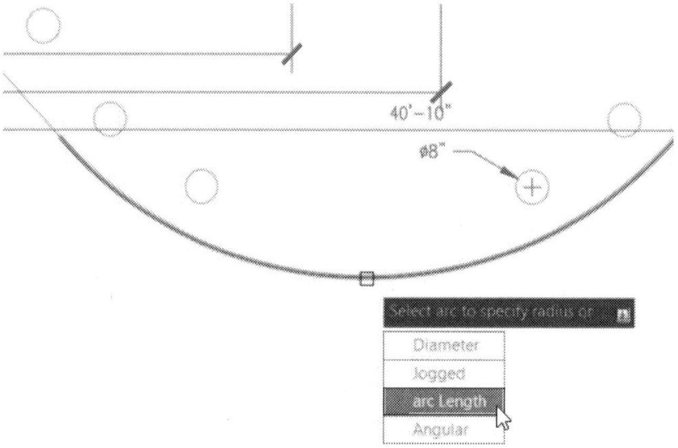

Figure 19–29

10. Select the arc and click again to place the dimension outside the arc, as shown in Figure 19–30.
11. While remaining in the **Dimension** command, hover the cursor over the arc of the portico again. Note that it displays the arc length option in the prompt, as shown in Figure 19–30. Press <Down Arrow> and select **Radius**. Select the arc and click again to place the radius dimension on the inside of the portico arc, as shown in Figure 19–28.

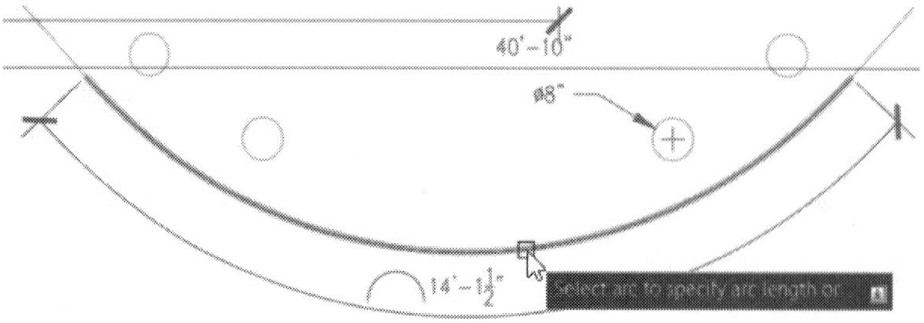

Figure 19–30

12. Toggle on **Object Snap** in the *Status Bar*, if you had toggled it off.

13. While remaining in the **Dimension** command, hover your cursor over the angled line that joins the portico arc with the building wall. Add aligned dimensions to both the angled lines, as shown in Figure 19–31. (Use the end of the arc length dimension line to keep the connected dimensions in line, as shown in Figure 19–31.)

    - You can also use the (Aligned) dimension command.

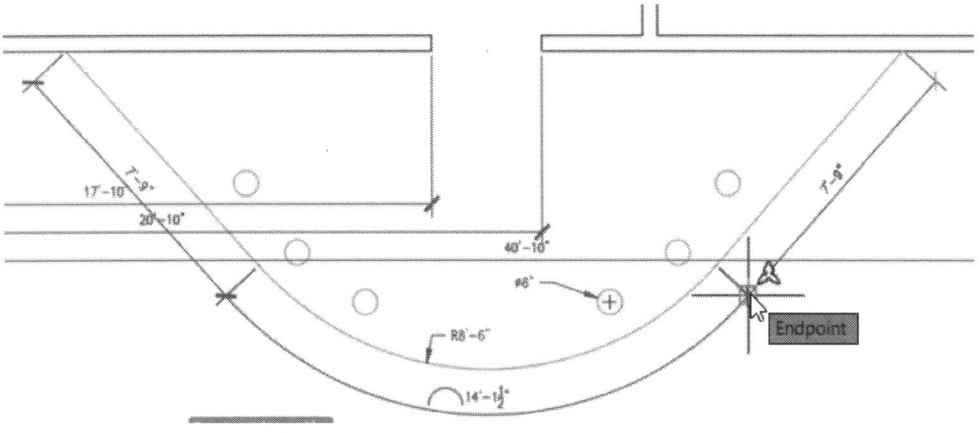

Figure 19–31

14. While remaining in the **Dimension** command, select one of the angled lines again. Hover the cursor over the wall line that touches the selected angled line to display the angled dimension, as shown in Figure 19–32.

    - You can also use the *(Angular)* dimension command.

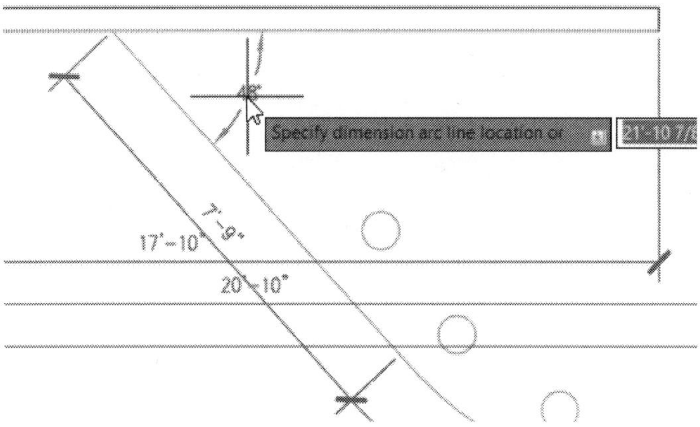

Figure 19–32

15. Select the line to accept the angled dimension and click again to place it, as shown in Figure 19–28.
16. Add **Angular** dimensions on the other side as well.
17. Save and close the drawing.

End of practice

Practice 19d
Add Center Marks and Dimensions (Mechanical)

Practice Objective

- Add a center mark and radius, diameter, and angular dimensions to a drawing.

In this practice, you will add a center mark and radius, diameter, and angular dimensions to a mechanical drawing, as shown in Figure 19–33.

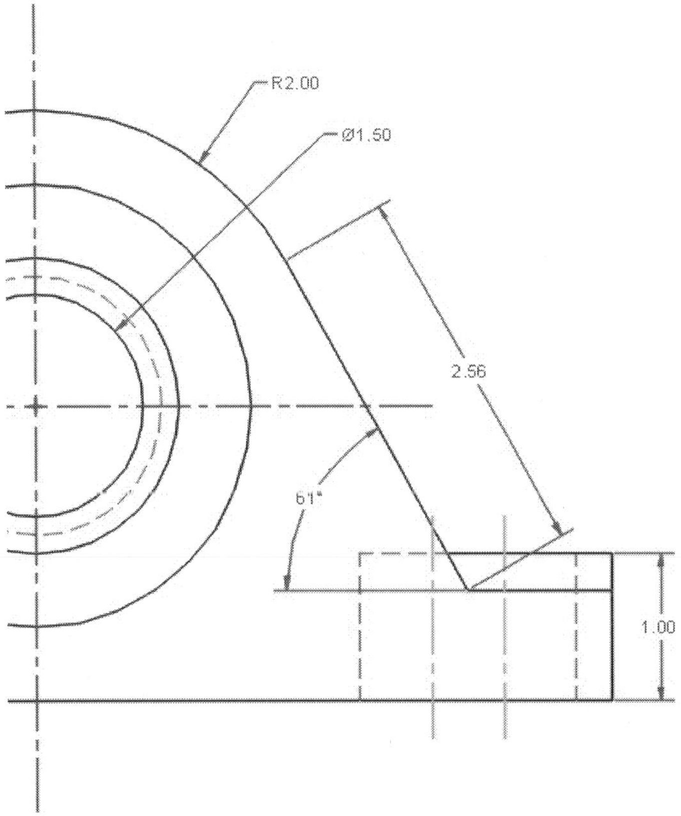

Figure 19–33

1. Open **Bearing Dimensions1-I.dwg** from your practice files folder. The drawing opens in the *C-Sized* layout tab with two viewports.
2. Activate the **2:1** (right side) viewport.
3. In the *Annotate* tab>*Dimensions* panel, set the dimension layer as **Dimensions**.

4. In the *Annotate* tab>*Centerlines* panel, click  (Center Mark). Select the innermost circle to add a center mark. Note that the extension lines of the center mark are just touching the dashed centerline circle next to the innermost circle, as shown in Figure 19–34. Press <Esc> to exit the command.

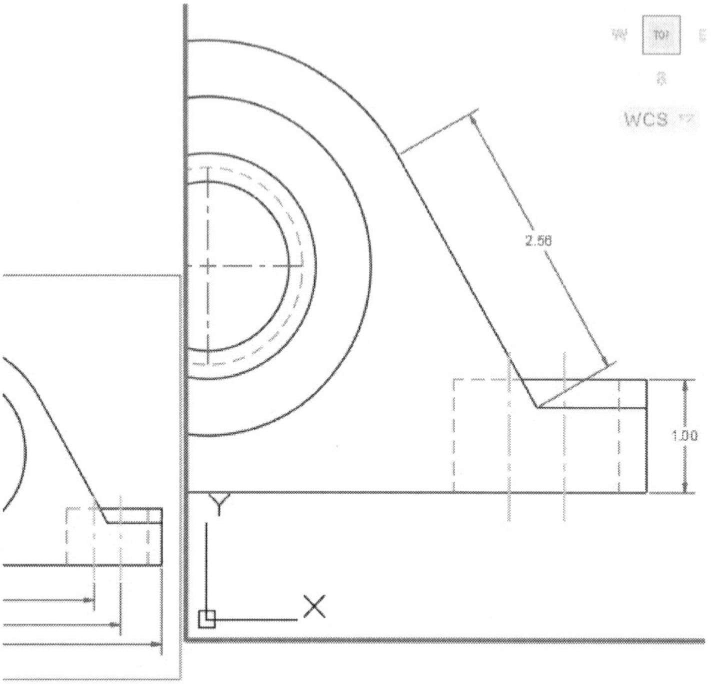

Figure 19–34

5. In the Command Line or at the Dynamic prompt, type **CENTEREXE**. Enter **2** for the value and then press <Enter>.
6. In the Command Line or at the Dynamic prompt, type **CENTERRESET**.
7. In the viewport, select the center mark and press <Enter>. The center mark extension lines extend beyond the outermost circle, as shown in Figure 19–33.
8. Add a **Radius** dimension to the arc at the top of the bearing, as shown in Figure 19–33.
9. Add a **Diameter** dimension to the innermost circle, as shown in Figure 19–33.
10. Add an **Angular** dimension to the inner angle of the sloped line, as shown in Figure 19–33.
11. Save and close the drawing.

End of practice

19.4 Editing Dimensions

If the dimensions are interfering with other parts in a drawing, as shown in Figure 19–35, you can edit and modify them using grips and special tools in the shortcut menu. You can also edit the dimension text. Additional tools available to clean up dimensions include aligning dimensions and breaking extension lines.

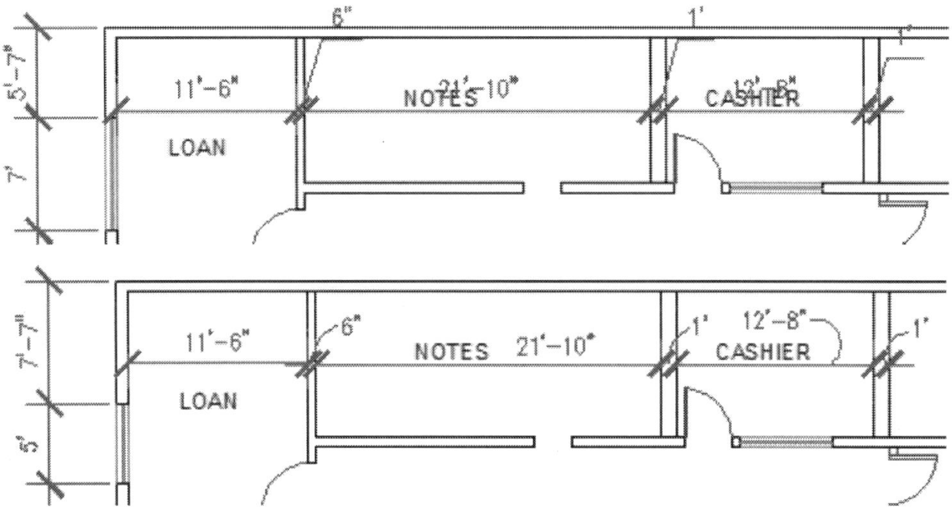

Figure 19–35

- The AutoCAD dimensions are associative. Therefore, when you change a dimensioned object, the dimensions update to reflect the change. If you move an object, the dimensions move as well. If you change the size of an object, the dimensions display the change.
- To change the dimension style of an existing dimension, select it and then set the appropriate dimension style in the *Dimension Style* drop-down list, in the *Annotate* tab> *Dimensions* panel.

Dimension Shortcut Menu

You can select a dimension or multiple dimensions, and then right-click to access additional options in the shortcut menu, as shown in Figure 19–36.

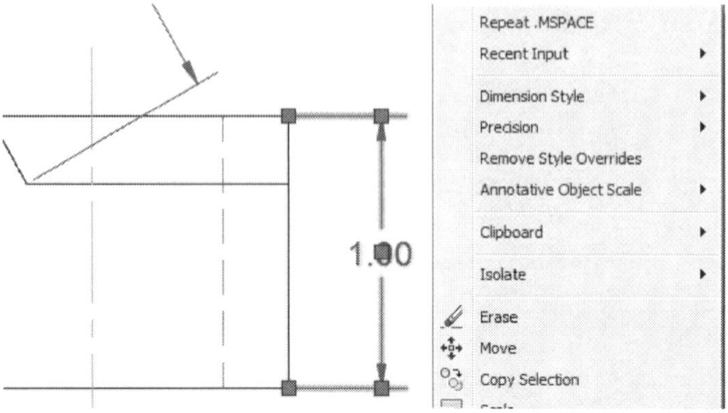

Figure 19–36

- You can change the dimension style of selected dimensions using the **Dimension Style** option. The dimension style controls the basic features of a dimension, such as the text location and number of decimal places.
- You can change the precision of selected dimensions using the **Precision** option. Precision helps you to display dimensions to a specific number of decimal places.

Editing Dimensions Using Grips

Grips can be used to relocate dimension elements. Without starting a command, select the following to display its grips at various parts of the dimension, as shown in Figure 19–37.

- Where extension lines touch the dimensioned object
- Where the extension line and dimension line meet
- On the dimension text

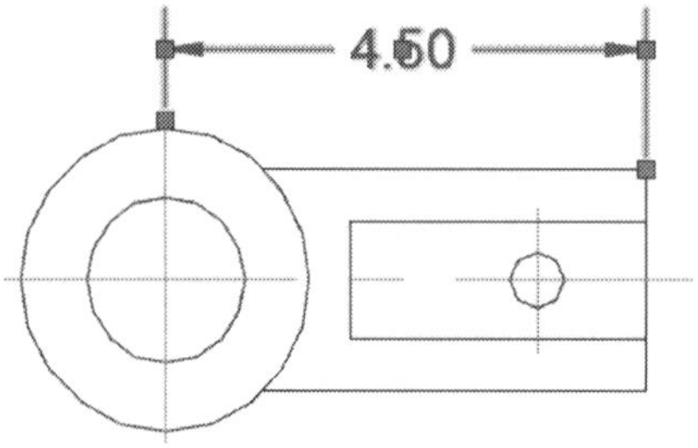

Figure 19–37

Once the dimension grips display, you can edit the dimension as follows:

- Select the grip at the dimension line and move it to change the distance from the object.
- Select the grip on the text and move it to change the location of the text (and sometimes the dimension line).
- Select the grip at the extension line origin to change the length of the dimension. (This option might disconnect the associativity to the object it is dimensioning.)
- Press <Esc> to clear the grips.

Dimension Grips Shortcut Options

Additional options are available for editing dimensions using the multifunctional grips. Hover the cursor over a grip, and select an option in the *Dynamic Input* list. Depending on the specific grip you hover over, a different list of options displays, as shown in Figure 19–38.

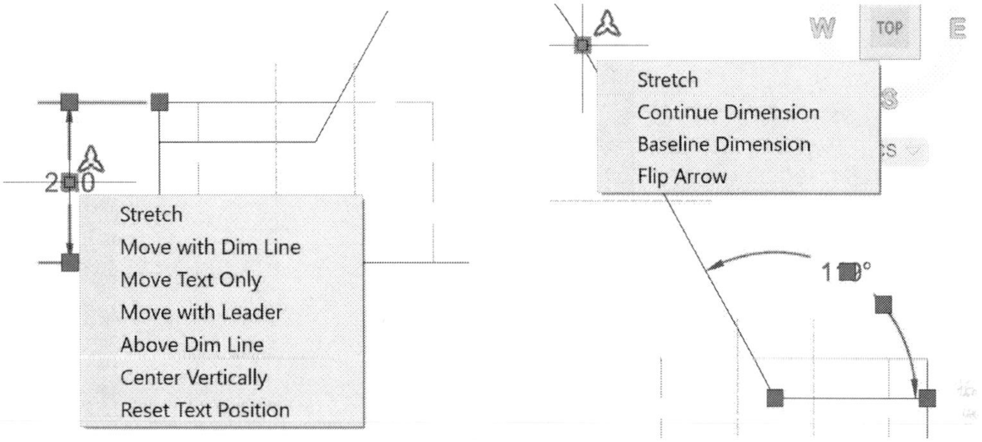

Figure 19–38

- Use the various text options, such as **Move Text Only** and **Above Dim Line**, to move the text to a different position.
- **Reset Text Position** returns the moved text to its original location.
- You can use an existing dimension as the beginning of a series of related dimensions in either **Continue** or **Baseline**.
- Use **Flip Arrow** if the arrowheads on a dimension were pushed out and you want them to be inside the extension lines or on the opposite side.

- You can also access these options by selecting a grip (making it hot), and then using <Ctrl> to cycle through the options, or right-clicking and selecting one in the shortcut menu, as shown in Figure 19–39.

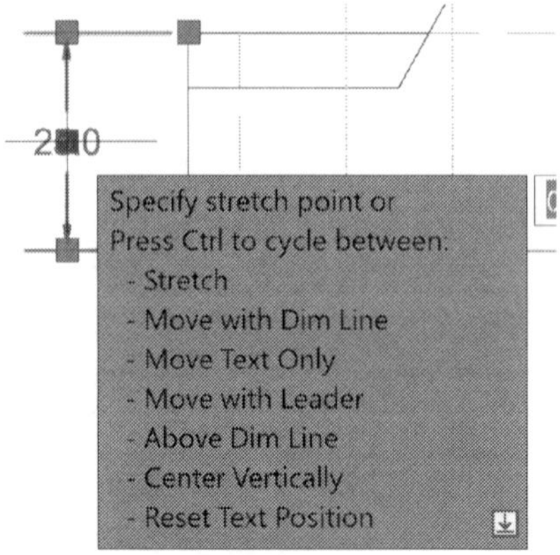

Figure 19–39

Editing the Dimension Text

Dimensions are associated with the objects they reference. However, sometimes you might need to add text to a dimension (such as +/- in renovation work), as shown in Figure 19–40.

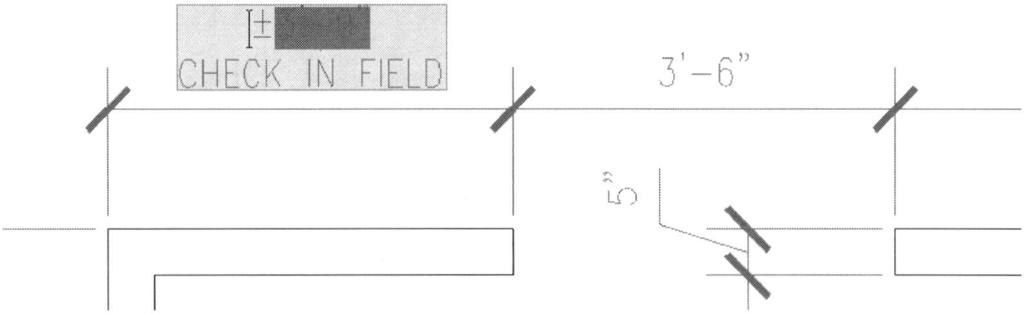

Figure 19–40

- To change the dimension text, double-click on the dimension text or type **textedit**. The default dimension text or value is inserted as a special field in the Text Editor. You can add text before or after the field, or delete the field to completely replace the default text. When editing dimension text, a width sizing control displays above the text. This enables you to adjust the text width for text wrapping, as shown in Figure 19–41.

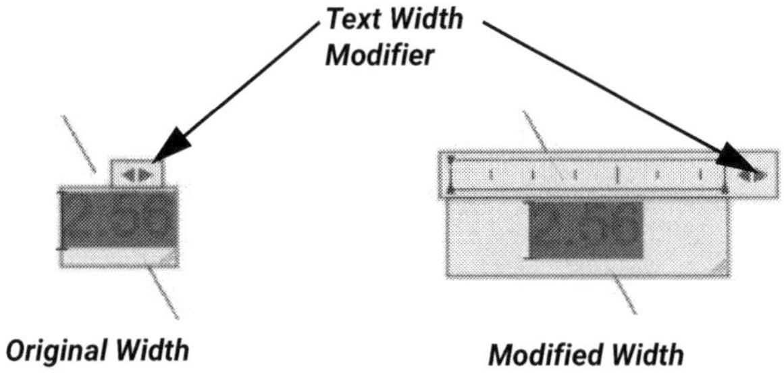

Figure 19–41

- If you remove the text associated with the dimension by mistake and want to get it back, type **<>** in the Text Editor.

Adjusting Dimension Spacing

When you create stacked angular or linear dimensions of any type, they might be too close together or unevenly spaced, as shown in Figure 19–42. Instead of moving each dimension, you can modify the space between sets of dimensions using the **Adjust Space** command.

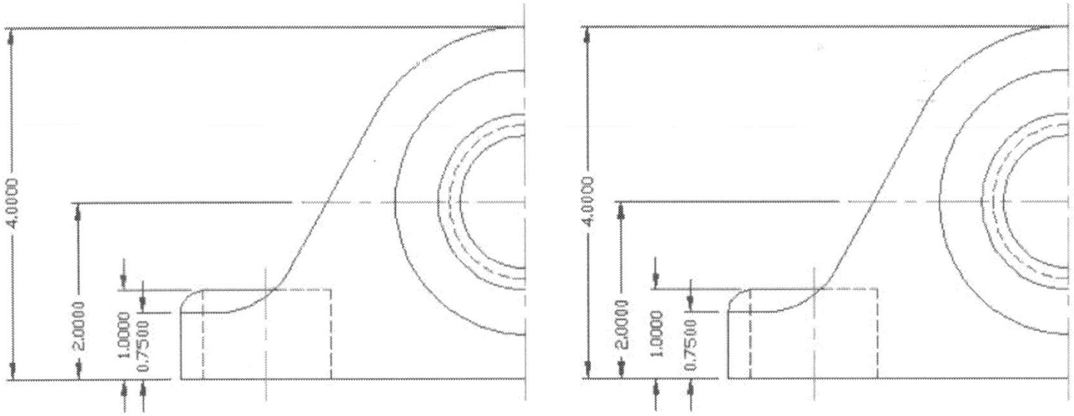

Figure 19–42

How To: Modify the Space Between Dimensions

1. In the *Annotate* tab>*Dimensions* panel, click (Adjust Space).
2. Select the base dimension (the one closest to the object) of the group you want to modify.
3. Select the rest of the dimensions in the group.
4. Enter the distance that you want to have between dimensions or press <Enter> to accept the automatic distance.

Dimension Breaks

When there are many dimensions in a drawing, the various extension lines and dimension lines can start to overlap. In that case, you can create dimension breaks without changing the associativity of the dimension object, as shown in Figure 19–43.

- When the object is stretched, the dimensions change and the breaks remain in place. This makes revising a drawing easier, as you no longer need to re-dimension a modified part.

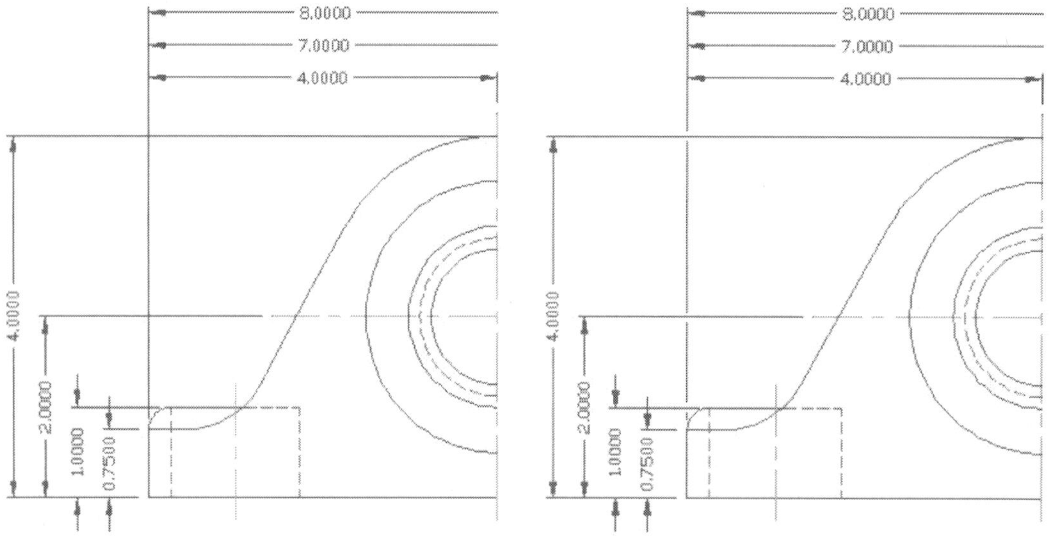

Figure 19–43

How To: Break One Dimension

1. In the *Annotate* tab>*Dimensions* panel, click  (Dimension Break).
2. Select a dimension to break.
3. Select an object to break the dimension or select one of the options.
4. Continue to select other objects to break their dimensions as required.
5. Press <Enter> to complete the command.
   - The **Multiple** option enables you to select more than one dimension to break. The selected dimensions are broken where they overlap other dimensions.
   - To remove breaks from a dimension, start the **Break** command, select the dimension, and select the **Remove** option.

Practice 19e
Edit Dimensions (Architectural)

Practice Objective

- Modify dimensions, edit dimension text, and break dimensions in a drawing.

In this practice, you will modify dimensions using grips, edit the dimension text, and break dimensions using the **Dim, Break** command, as shown in Figure 19–44.

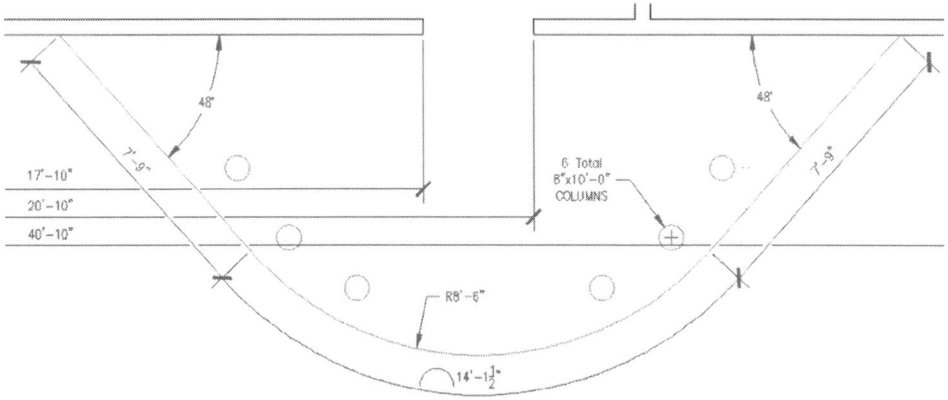

Figure 19–44

1. Open **Dimensioned Plan2-A.dwg** from your practice files folder. The drawing opens in the *D-Sized* layout tab.
2. Make the viewport active and verify that it is locked, so that you can zoom and pan as required to modify the dimensions.
3. Focusing on the portico area, use grips (as shown in Figure 19–45) to move the three horizontal dimension text to the left hand side, outside of the portico aligned dimensions.
   - If required, you might need to toggle off **Object Snap** to move the dimensions freely.

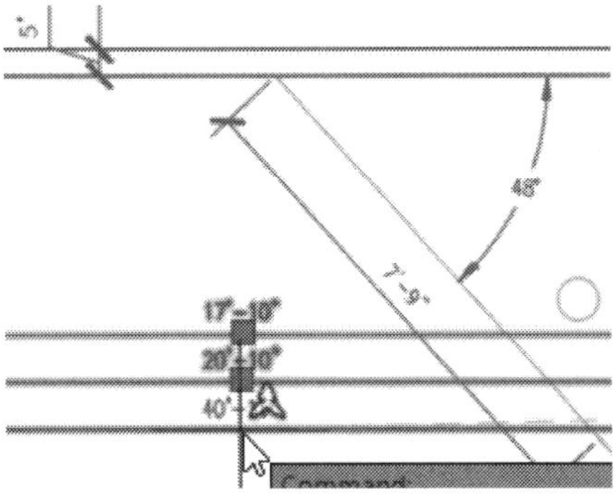

Figure 19–45

4. In the *Annotate* tab>*Dimensions* panel, click (Break) and press <Down Arrow> to open the options menu. Select **Multiple**.
5. Select the three horizontal dimension lines and press <Enter>.
6. Select the green portico line. Note that the three horizontal dimension lines break where they are passing through the portico arc object.
7. Select the aligned dimension line (red) on both sides to create a break with them as well.
8. Press <Enter> to exit the command.
9. Double-click on the diameter **Ø8"** dimension for the green circle (column). In the text editor that opens, enter **6 Total 8"x10'-0" COLUMNS ,** as shown on the left in Figure 19–46.
10. Use to change the width for text wrapping, as shown on the right in Figure 19–46. Click outside of the text editor to accept the changes.

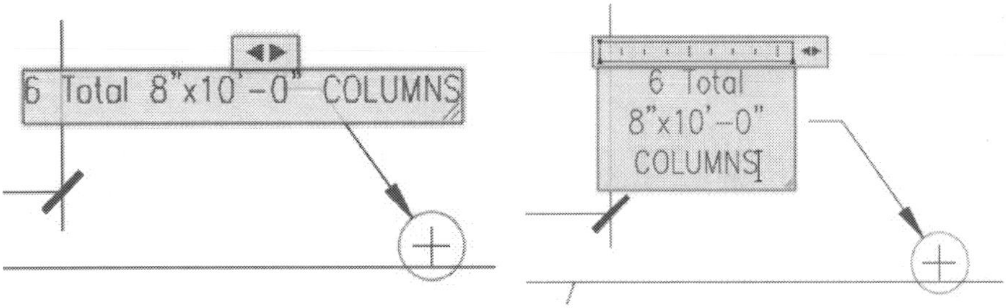

Figure 19–46

11. Press <ESC) to exit the command.
12. Save and close the drawing.

End of practice

Practice 19f
Edit Dimensions (Mechanical)

Practice Objective

- Modify the text and move dimensions.

In this practice, you will modify the text of several dimensions and move the dimensions as required using grips, as shown in Figure 19–47.

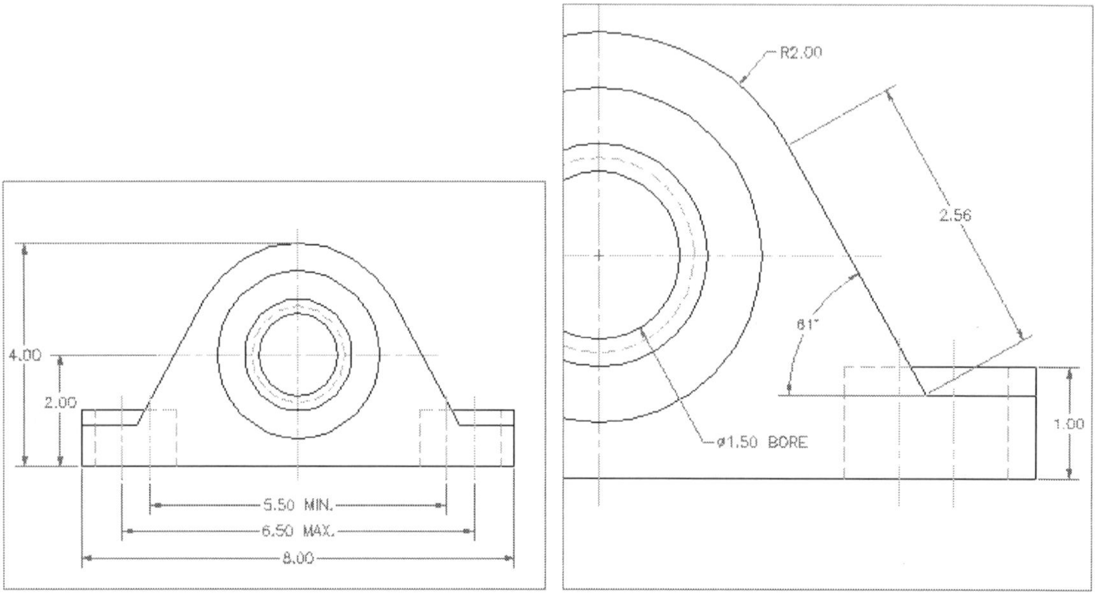

VIEWPORT SCALE: 1:1 VIEWPORT SCALE: 2:1

Figure 19–47

1. Open **Bearing Dimensions2-I.dwg** from your practice files folder. The drawing opens in the *C-Sized* layout tab with two viewports.

2. Activate the **2:1** viewport (right side). Using grips, move the diameter dimension outside of the circles (to the lower right-hand side), as shown in Figure 19–48.

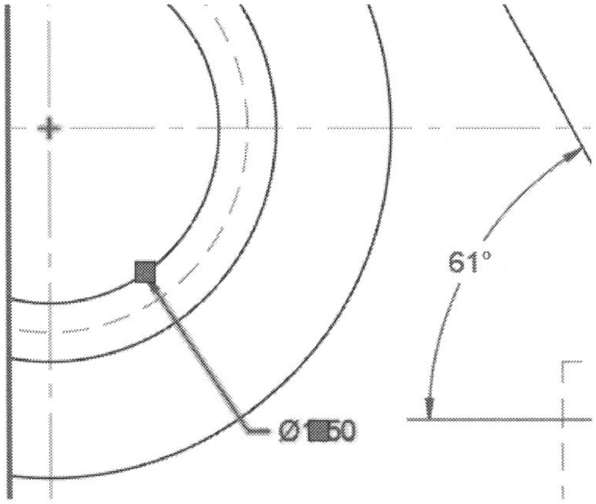

Figure 19–48

3. Double-click on the text of the diameter dimension and modify it such that it reads **Ø1.50 BORE**, as shown previously in Figure 19–47.

   • The **Ø** symbol is in the *Text Editor* contextual tab>*Insert* panel, in the @ (Symbol) flyout.

4. Activate the **1:1** viewport (left viewport) and modify the text of the two horizontal dimensions (by adding **MIN.** and **MAX.**), as shown in Figure 19–49.

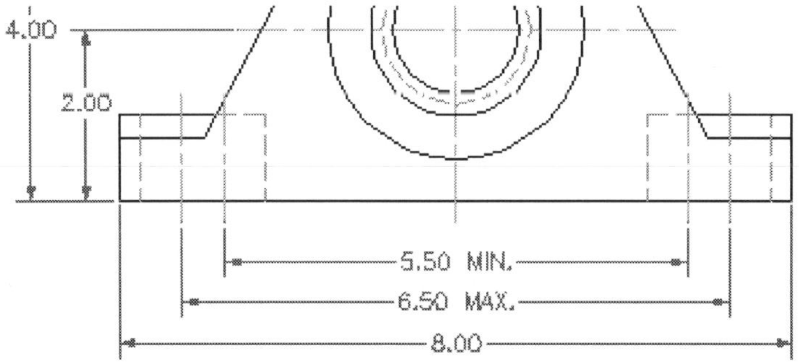

Figure 19–49

5. Use grips to move any of the other dimensions as required to a location where they are easier to read. You can also use the **Adjust Space** command to even out the bottom dimensions as required.

6. Save and close the drawing.

End of practice

Chapter Review Questions

1. Which command would you use to dimension the length of a diagonal line so that the dimension line is parallel to the diagonal line?
   a. Aligned dimension
   b. Quick dimension
   c. Baseline dimension
   d. Adjust Space

2. Dimensions recalculate automatically when the objects they refer to are modified.
   a. True
   b. False

3. The **Center Mark** tool adds an associative center mark at the center of which objects? (Select all that apply.)
   a. Lines
   b. Polylines
   c. Circles
   d. Polygonal arcs

4. Which line does the  (Continue) dimension command use as the first extension line for the next dimension?
   a. First extension line that was placed with the previous dimension.
   b. Last extension line that was placed with the previous dimension.
   c. It picks a random line.
   d. You can select the extension line to be used as the first extension line.

5. How would you move a dimension so that the dimension line is farther away from the object?
   a. Use the **Move** command.
   b. Use the **Baseline Dimension** command.
   c. Use grips to stretch the dimension.
   d. Use the **Dimension Update** command.

6. Which command do you use to clean up overlapping dimension lines?
   a. Adjust Space
   b. Dimension Cleanup
   c. Dimension Break
   d. Jogged

Command Summary

Button	Command	Location
	**Centerline**	• **Ribbon:** *Annotate* tab>*Centerlines* panel • **Command Prompt:** centerline
	**Center Mark**	• **Ribbon:** *Annotate* tab>*Centerlines* panel • **Command Prompt:** centermark
	**Dimension**	• **Ribbon:** *Annotate* tab>*Dimensions* panel or *Home* tab>*Annotation* panel • **Command Prompt:** dim
	**Dimension: Adjust Space**	• **Ribbon:** *Annotate* tab>*Dimensions* panel • **Command Prompt:** dimspace
	**Dimension: Aligned**	• **Ribbon:** *Home* tab>*Annotation* panel or *Annotate* tab>*Dimensions* panel • **Command Prompt:** dimaligned
	**Dimension: Angular**	• **Ribbon:** *Home* tab>*Annotation* panel or *Annotate* tab>*Dimensions* panel • **Command Prompt:** dimangular
	**Dimension: Arc Length**	• **Ribbon:** *Home* tab>*Annotation* panel or *Annotate* tab>*Dimensions* panel • **Command Prompt:** dimarc
	**Dimension: Baseline**	• **Ribbon:** *Annotate* tab>*Dimensions* panel • **Command Prompt:** dimbaseline
	**Dimension: Break**	• **Ribbon:** *Annotate* tab>*Dimensions* panel • **Command Prompt:** dimbreak
	**Dimension: Continue**	• **Ribbon:** *Annotate* tab>*Dimensions* panel • **Command Prompt:** dimcontinue
	**Dimension: Diameter**	• **Ribbon:** *Home* tab>*Annotation* panel or *Annotate* tab>*Dimensions* panel • **Command Prompt:** dimdiameter
	**Dimension, Dimjogline**	• **Ribbon:** *Home* tab>*Annotation* panel or *Annotate* tab>*Dimensions* panel • **Command Prompt:** dimjogline
N/A	**Dimension: Edit Text**	• **Command Prompt:** ddedit
	**Dimension: Jogged (Radial)**	• **Ribbon:** *Home* tab>*Annotation* panel or *Annotate* tab>*Dimensions* panel • **Command Prompt:** dimjogged

Button	Command	Location
	**Dimension: Linear**	• **Ribbon:** *Home* tab>*Annotation* panel or *Annotate* tab>*Dimensions* panel • **Command Prompt:** dimlinear
	**Dimension: Radius**	• **Ribbon:** *Home* tab>*Annotation* panel or *Annotate* tab>*Dimensions* panel • **Command Prompt:** dimradius
	**Oblique**	• **Ribbon:** *Annotate* tab>expanded *Dimensions* panel
	**Quick Dimension**	• **Ribbon:** *Annotate* tab>*Dimensions* panel • **Command Prompt:** qdim

Chapter 20

Projects: Annotating Your Drawing

This chapter contains practice projects that can be used to gain additional hands-on experience in the topics and commands covered so far in this guide. These projects are intended to be self-guided and do not include step-by-step information.

Learning Objectives

- *Mechanical:* Add features such as text, hatching, and dimensions to an existing mechanical part.
- *Architectural:* Add features such as text, annotative text, hatching, dimensions, layout styles, and viewports to an existing floor plan.
- *Civil:* Add features such as text, hatching, and dimensions to an existing parking layout.

20.1 Mechanical Project

In this project, you will add dimensions, hatching, and text to an existing drawing, as shown in Figure 20–1.

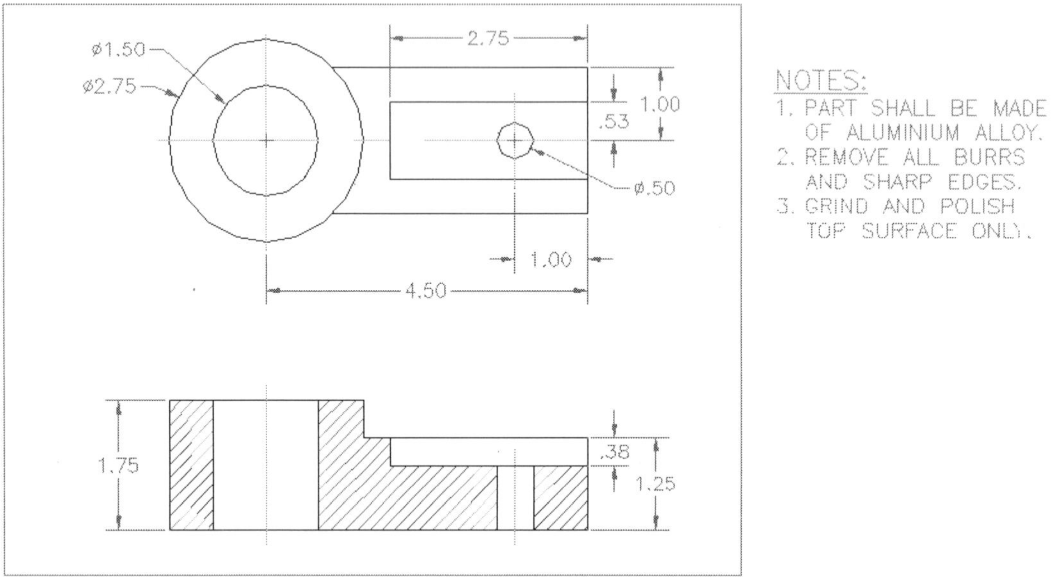

Figure 20–1

1. Open **Annotate-I.dwg** from your practice files folder.
2. Switch to the **B-Sized** layout and activate the viewport.
3. **Zoom Extents** to display the entire drawing in the viewport. Set the *Viewport Scale* to **1:1** and use viewport grips to fit it inside the sheet. Lock the viewport.
4. Make the layer **Hatching** current and hatch the lower view, as shown in Figure 20–1. Use the **ANSI 31** pattern at a *Scale* of **1** and an *Angle* of **0**. Close the *Hatch Creation* contextual tab.
5. Make the layer **Dimensions** current and add dimensions to the drawing, as shown in Figure 20–1. Use Object Snaps to place the dimensions.
6. Switch to Paper Space.
7. Make the layer **Text** current. Use multiline text to create notes on the layout to the right side of the drawing, as shown in Figure 20–1. Add numbering and format the text **NOTES** so that it is larger than the other text and underlined.
8. Save and close the drawing.

20.2 Architectural Project 1

In this project, you will add dimensions, text, and hatching to an existing drawing of a floor plan, as shown in Figure 20–2.

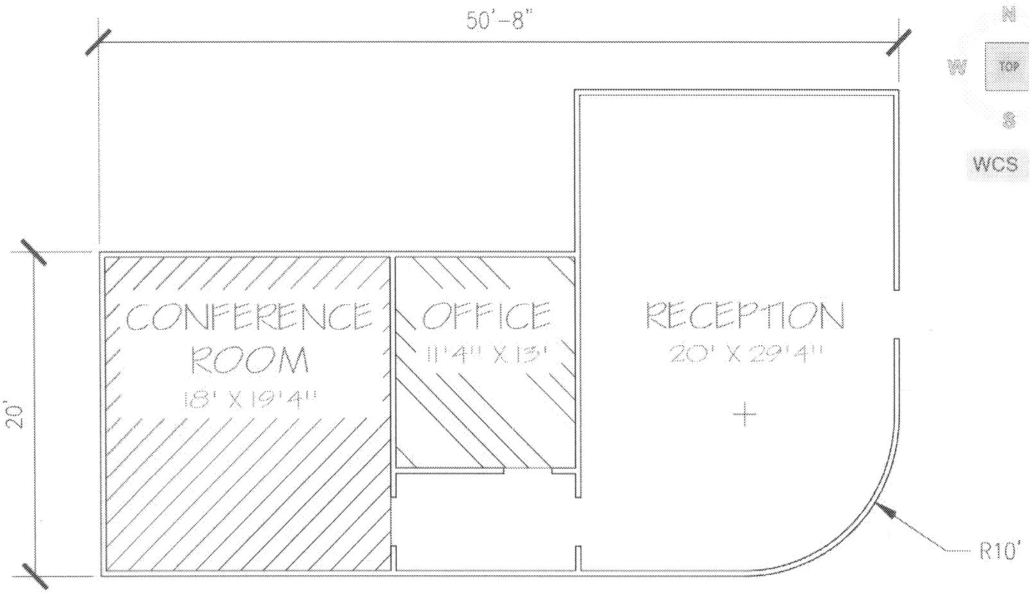

Figure 20–2

1. Open **Annotate-A.dwg** from your practice files folder.
2. Switch to the **A-Sized** layout. Activate the viewport and set an appropriate Viewport Scale. Lock the viewport. Additionally, you can use the viewport grips to resize the viewport.
3. Make the layer **Text** current. Select a text style **Hand** and add the text to label the rooms, as shown in Figure 20–2. Make the *Room Names* **1/4"** high and the *Dimension Numbers* **1/8"** high. Justify the text to **Middle Center.**

   Note: *If the text does not accommodate properly, use an appropriate text height.*

4. Toggle off the layers **Doors** and **Swing**. Make the layer **Hatching** current.
5. Draw lines across the doorways of the Office and Conference Room and hatch those rooms. Use the **ANSI31** pattern at an *Angle* of **0** for the Conference Room. Use the **ANSI34** pattern at an *Angle* of **90** for the Office. Set both hatches to **Annotative** with an appropriate scale.
6. Make the layer **Dimensions** current and add the dimensions.
7. Save and close the drawing.

20.3 Architectural Project 2

In this project, you will set up layouts with an appropriate view and Viewport Scale. You will then use annotative text, hatch, and dimensions to label a floor plan with company names and hatch each area, as shown in Figure 20–3. In a different layout, you will then add dimensions. Remember to use the correct layers and styles as you add each annotation feature.

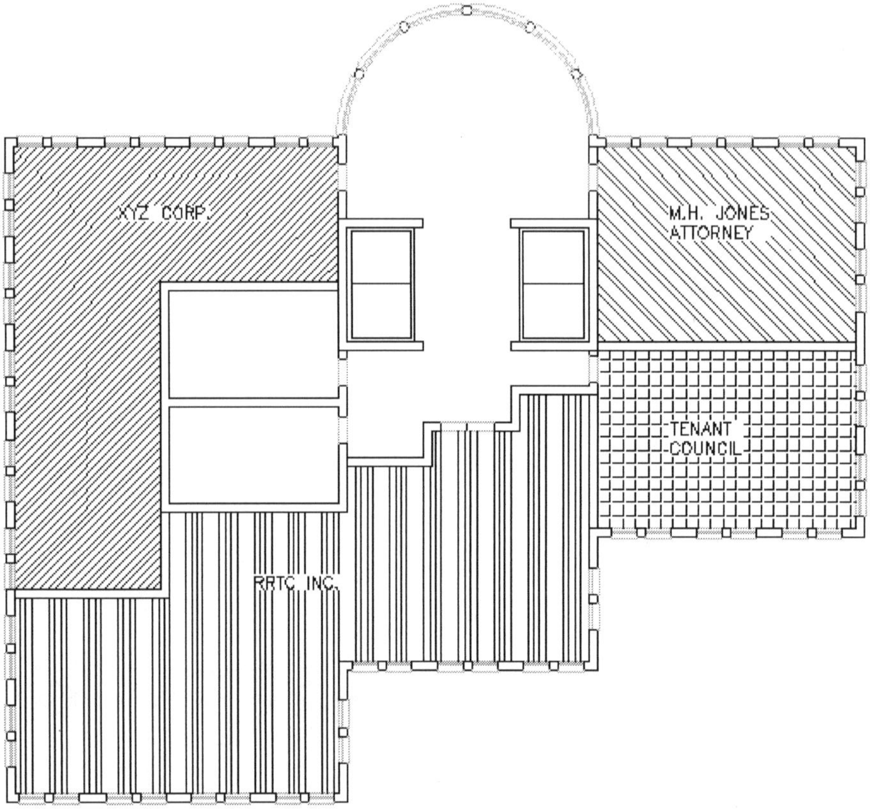

Figure 20–3

1. Open **Space-A.dwg** from your practice files folder.
2. Switch to the **D-Sized** layout. Set up the viewport so that the entire building displays with enough space around it to dimension at an appropriate scale. Set the Viewport Scale. Lock the viewport.
3. Make a copy of the **D-Sized** layout. Rename one as **Tenant Plan** and the other as **Dimension Plan**.
4. In the **Tenant Plan** layout, add the text and hatching similar to that shown in Figure 20–3.
   - Use any hatching style of your choice and set an appropriate hatching scale.

- Toggle off the layer **Doors** and toggle on the layer **Headers** to have the hatching go up to the door openings.

5. In the **Dimension Plan** layout, dimension the drawing. Add a few dimensions to identify the size of the rooms.
6. Save and close the drawing.

20.4 Civil Project

In this project, you will add hatching, text, and dimensions to a parking layout, as shown in Figure 20–4.

- Some of the colors in Figure 20–4 have been changed for printing clarity.

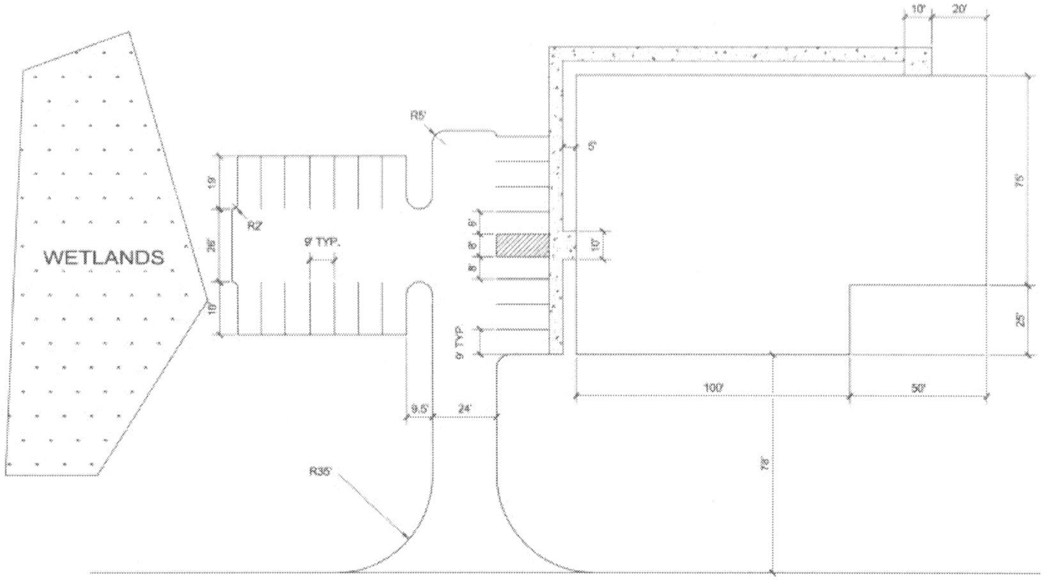

Figure 20–4

1. Open **Parking-C.dwg** from your practice files folder.
2. Switch to the **D-Sized** layout. Activate the viewport and create an appropriately scaled view of the site. (Leave a blank area around the drawing for dimensions and creating wetland.) Lock the viewport.
3. Make the layer **Pavement Edge New** current. Hatch the sidewalk with the **AR-CONC** pattern and the accessible parking space with the **ANSI31** pattern. Close the accessible parking space for hatching. Experiment with different hatch pattern scales to find the one that fits the best, as shown in Figure 20–5.

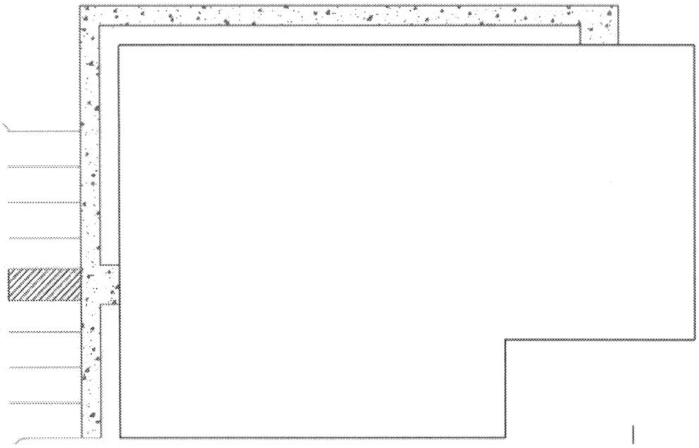

Figure 20–5

4. Make the **Wetlands** layer current. Draw an enclosed area (using the **Line** command) on the left side of the building, similar to that shown in Figure 20–4. Using an appropriate annotative text and height, add the text **Wetlands** inside the enclosed area, similar to that shown in Figure 20–4. Hatch the area with the **Swamp** pattern using an appropriate scale.
5. Make the layer **Dimensions** current. Dimension the building and parking lot. Move some of the dimensions around using grips. Edit the text to add **TYP.** with the appropriate dimensions (such as the parking spots) as shown in Figure 20–6.

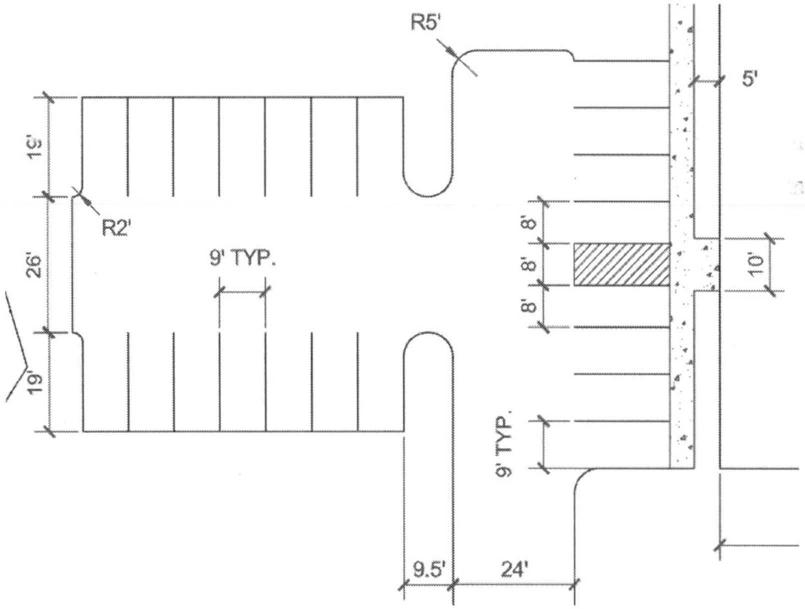

Figure 20–6

6. Save and close the drawing.

Appendix A

Skills Assessment

To test your knowledge on the course material, answer the questions that follow. Select the best answer for each question.

Part 1: General Knowledge

1. When you use the **Window** option in the **Zoom** command, everything in the window:
   a. Appears larger.
   b. Appears to shrink.
   c. Is erased.
   d. Is scaled up.

2. The **Move** and **Copy** commands both use a base point. What is a base point?
   a. The point from which you always move or copy.
   b. Always the absolute coordinate.
   c. The spacing between grid dots.
   d. A point that enables you to pick a group of objects.

3. Which phrase defines frozen layers?
   a. You see the layers and can manipulate objects on them.
   b. You see the layers but cannot manipulate objects on them.
   c. You do not see the layers but objects on them are still regenerated with the drawing.
   d. You do not see the layers and objects on them are not regenerated with the drawing.

4. A file designed to be the basis of new drawings is called a:
   a. Template
   b. Wizard
   c. Scratch File
   d. Setup File

5. How do you extend an object while you are in a **Trim** command?
   a. You cannot extend an object while in **Trim** command.
   b. Hold <Ctrl> and select the object to extend.
   c. Hold <Alt> and select the object to extend.
   d. Hold <Shift> and select the object to extend.

6. Any AutoCAD drawing can be inserted into the current drawing as a block.
   a. True
   b. False

7. The tool that controls whether you automatically snap to endpoints, midpoints, intersections, etc. is:
   a. Snap
   b. Grid
   c. Object Snap
   d. Ortho mode

8. The purpose of Polar Tracking is:
   a. To find a specific X,Y coordinate location.
   b. To copy an object in a circular pattern around a center point.
   c. To enable you to draw at angles, such as 30 or 45 degrees.
   d. To indicate the north direction.

9. To draw a series of continuous line segments that act as one unified object, you should use:

a. Tracking

b. A polyline

c. Object Snaps

d. A construction line

10. Which command creates parallel objects of the selected objects?

a. Extend

b. Fillet

c. Mirror

d. Offset

Note: *Complete either the Mechanical Drawing or Architectural Drawing sections. Answer the questions based on the provided drawings.*

Part 2: Mechanical Drawing

Start a new drawing based on **Mech-Inches.dwt**. Draw the object shown in Figure A–1, starting with the center of the **Ø3 circle** at **point 5,5**. Draw only the object, not the dimensions, and then answer the following questions.

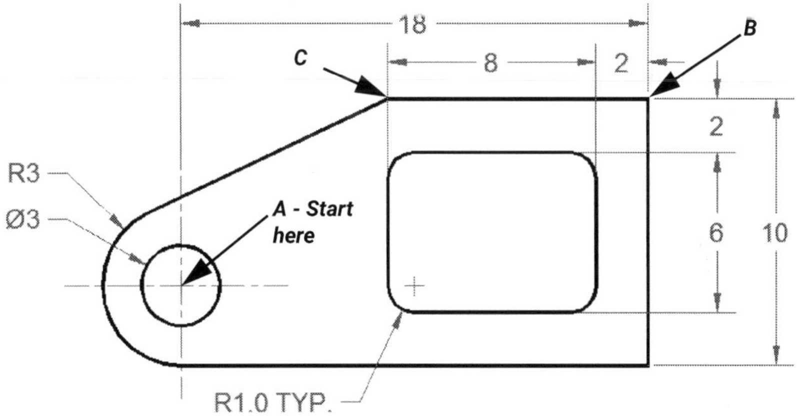

Figure A–1

1. What is the distance between the center of circle **A** and the corner at **B**?
   a. 19.8628
   b. 19.3132
   c. 17.1870
   d. 18.6794

2. What is the angle defined by the two intersecting lines at **C**? (Hint: Use an angular dimension.)
   a. 152
   b. 153
   c. 155
   d. 160

3. What is the area of the outermost shape? (Hint: Make it into a polyline.)
   a. 179.4870
   b. 179.8045
   c. 180.6243
   d. 180.5940

4. What is the area of the outermost shape minus the inner shapes?
   a. 125.7012
   b. 126.7081
   c. 125.2768
   d. 126.2891

Part 3: Architectural Drawing

Start a new drawing based on **AEC-Imperial.dwt**. Draw the floorplan shown in Figure A–2, starting with the lower left outside corner at point **5',5'**. All walls are **6" thick**. The doors are **3' wide**, and are placed **6"** from the nearest wall intersection. Draw only the walls, not the dimensions, and then answer the following questions.

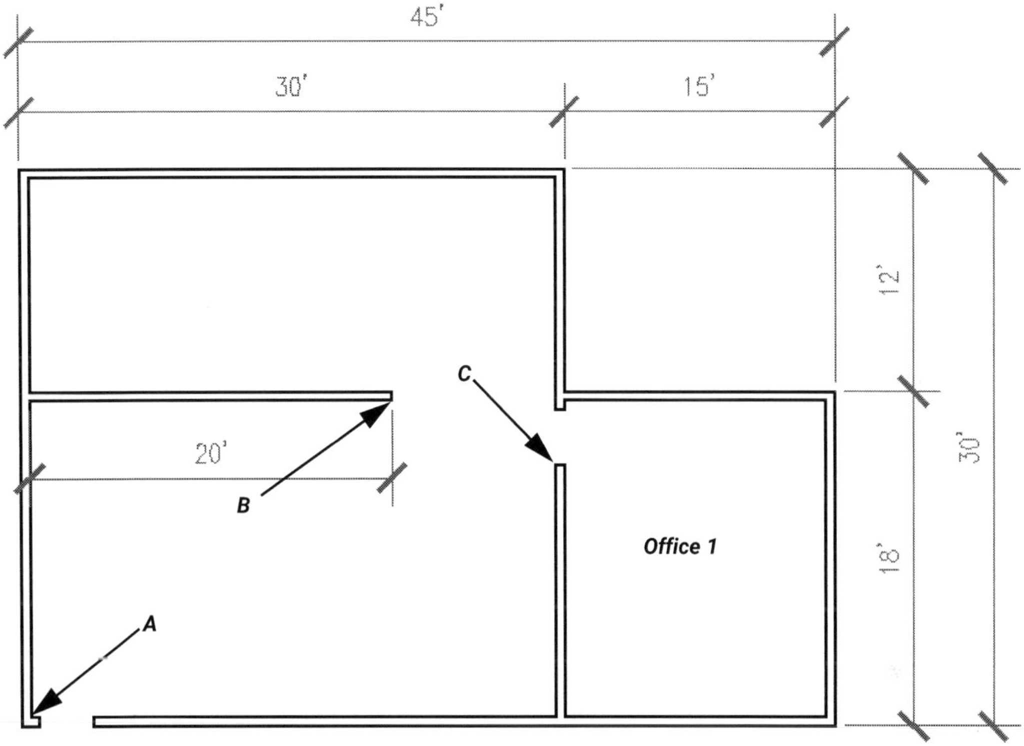

Figure A–2

1. What is the distance between the points labeled **A** and **B**?
   a. 26'
   b. 26'-3"
   c. 26'-9"
   d. 27'-3"

2. What is the distance between the points labeled **B** and **C**, rounded to the nearest inch?
   a. 8'-10"
   b. 9'-5"
   c. 9'-8"
   d. 9'-11"

3. What is the area of the room labeled **Office 1**?
   a. 242.9 square feet
   b. 246.5 square feet
   c. 248.5 square feet
   d. 252 square feet

4. What is the perimeter of the entire building around the outside? (Hint: Use the **Area** command.)
   a. 150'
   b. 151'
   c. 149'
   d. 152'

Index

M

N

O

P

Q

Made in the USA
Monee, IL
27 October 2026

66945657R00321